UNDERSTANDING
THE CONTEMPORARY
MIDDLE EAST

UNDERSTANDING

Introductions to the States and Regions of the Contemporary World
Donald L. Gordon, series editor

Understanding Contemporary Africa, 4th edition
edited by April A. Gordon and Donald L. Gordon

Understanding Contemporary Asia Pacific
edited by Katherine Palmer Kaup

Understanding the Contemporary Caribbean
edited by Richard S. Hillman and Thomas J. D'Agostino

Understanding Contemporary China, 3rd edition
edited by Robert E. Gamer

Understanding Contemporary India
edited by Sumit Ganguly and Neil DeVotta

Understanding Contemporary Latin America, 3rd edition
edited by Richard S. Hillman

Understanding the Contemporary Middle East, 3rd edition
edited by Jillian Schwedler and Deborah J. Gerner

Understanding Contemporary Russia
edited by Michael L. Bressler

THIRD EDITION

UNDERSTANDING
THE CONTEMPORARY
MIDDLE EAST

edited by
Jillian Schwedler
Deborah J. Gerner

LYNNE
RIENNER
PUBLISHERS

BOULDER
LONDON

Published in the United States of America in 2008 by
Lynne Rienner Publishers, Inc.
1800 30th Street, Boulder, Colorado 80301
www.rienner.com

and in the United Kingdom by
Lynne Rienner Publishers, Inc.
3 Henrietta Street, Covent Garden, London WC2E 8LU

Library of Congress Cataloging-in-Publication Data
Understanding the contemporary Middle East / Jillian Schwedler and
    Deborah J. Gerner, eds. — 3rd ed.
      p. cm. — (Understanding: Introductions to the states and regions of
the contemporary world)
    Includes bibliographical references and index.
    ISBN 978-1-58826-565-4 (pbk. : alk. paper)
    1. Middle East. 2. Africa, North. I. Schwedler, Jillian. II. Gerner,
Deborah J.
    DS44.U473 2008
    956—dc22

                          2008006857

British Cataloguing in Publication Data
A Cataloguing in Publication record for this book
is available from the British Library.

Printed and bound in the United States of America

    The paper used in this publication meets the requirements
    of the American National Standard for Permanence of
    Paper for Printed Library Materials Z39.48-1992.

5   4   3

For Misty
Whose patience, dedication, and smile still inspire

Contents

List of Illustrations   xi

Preface   xv

1 Introduction   *Jillian Schwedler*   1
     Organization of the Book   *4*

2 The Middle East: A Geographic Preface
     Ian R. Manners and Barbara McKean Parmenter   9
     Boundaries   *12*
     Aridity and Water   *18*
     Cityscapes   *25*
     Conclusion   *31*

3 The Historical Context   *Arthur Goldschmidt Jr.*   37
     The Ancient Middle East   *37*
     The Islamic Middle East as an Autonomous System   *41*
     The Subordination of the Middle East to the West   *50*
     The Middle East Since World War I   *60*
     Conclusion   *83*

4 Middle Eastern Politics   *Deborah J. Gerner and
     Philip A. Schrodt*   85
     The Colonial Legacy   *86*
     A Changing International Context   *88*
     Economic Development   *92*
     Informal Structures of Power   *94*
     The Myth of Political Instability   *96*

Prospects for Democratization   *97*
The Role of the Military   *100*
Political Ideologies and Institutions   *103*
Nationalist Revolutionary Republics   *107*
Traditional and Parliamentary Monarchies   *117*
Democracies and Conditional Democracies   *125*
Conclusion   *131*

5 International Relations   *Mary Ann Tétreault*   137
Sovereignty in the Middle East   *137*
Local Challenges to State Sovereignty   *141*
The Middle East and the Great Powers   *143*
Moving Toward Regional Autonomy or a New Imperialism?   *150*
The Middle East as a Foreign Policy Subsystem   *152*
The Arab-Israeli Conflict   *153*
The Kurdish Conflict   *158*
The Conflict Between Iran and Iraq   *161*
Conclusion   *167*

6 The Israeli-Palestinian Conflict   *Simona Sharoni
and Mohammed Abu-Nimer*   177
The Parties: Two Peoples—Palestinians and Israeli Jews   *178*
The History and Dynamics of the Conflict   *185*
One Land, Two Peoples: Central Issues and Points of Contention   *202*
The Rocky Road to Peace: Past and Present Attempts
   to Resolve the Conflict   *207*
Conclusion   *214*

7 The Economies of the Middle East   *Agnieszka Paczynska*   221
Middle East Economies Before World War II   *222*
Economic Development Following World War II   *224*
Labor Migration and Remittances   *228*
Economic Crisis and Structural Adjustment   *233*
Trade   *237*
The New Oil Boom   *242*
Conflict and Regional Economies   *243*
Conclusion   *251*

8 The Political Economy of Middle Eastern Oil
   Mary Ann Tétreault   255
Industry Structure   *256*
The System Unravels   *259*
Rumblings of Change   *262*

The Oil Revolution   *264*
Oil Politics in the OPEC Middle East   *266*
The Price Bust   *267*
A New Gulf War—A New Oil Regime?   *271*
Oil and Money in the Middle East   *274*
Conclusion   *276*

9 **Population Growth, Urbanization, and the Challenges of Unemployment**   *Valentine M. Moghadam*   281
Urbanization   *282*
Population Growth   *284*
Labor Force Growth and Employment Challenges   *289*
Rising Unemployment   *291*
Poverty and Inequality   *296*
Conclusion   *304*

10 **Kinship, Class, and Ethnicity**   *Laurie King-Irani*   309
Identities and Boundaries   *312*
Key Concepts   *313*
Persistent Challenges and Adaptive Strategies:
    The Environmental and Historical Context   *315*
Kinship   *318*
Ethnicity   *325*
The Historical Context of Ethnicity   *331*
Social Class   *333*
Kinship, Ethnicity, and Class in Context:
    Strategies or Straitjackets?   *335*
Conclusion   *340*

11 **The Role of Women**   *Lisa Taraki*   345
The Modern Nation-State   *346*
Economic Activity   *351*
Family and Kinship   *355*
Values and Norms   *358*
Politics   *360*
Conclusion   *369*

12 **Religion and Politics in the Middle East**   *Jillian Schwedler*   373
The Historical Role of Religion in the Middle East   *374*
The Experiences of Religious Minorities   *380*
Religious States   *382*
Religious Activism   *387*
Conclusion   *395*

13 Middle Eastern Literature   *miriam cooke*   397

European Colonialism and Its Discontents   *397*
Cultural Ferment at the Turn of the Twentieth Century   *400*
The Short Story as Literary Pioneer   *403*
Francophone Novels in North Africa   *408*
The Arabic Novel   *409*
The Iranian Novel   *412*
The Turkish Novel   *413*
The Israeli Novel   *414*
Drama: Grafting the New onto the Old   *416*
Poetry and the Hold of the Desert   *418*
Independence and Postcolonial Struggles   *420*
Emigration and Exile   *426*
The Muslim State   *429*
Translation and Recognition   *431*

14 Trends and Prospects   *Jillian Schwedler and
Deborah J. Gerner*   435

The Contemporary Middle East   *435*
Economic Development   *438*
Ethnonationalist Conflicts   *439*
Political Participation and Accountability   *440*
Conclusion   *441*

List of Acronyms   443
Basic Political Data   447
The Contributors   459
Index   461
About the Book   483

Illustrations

▓ Maps

2.1	Political Map of the Middle East	15
2.2	Extent of the Ottoman Empire	16
3.1	Extent of the Islamic Empire	46
6.1	Israel/Palestine, Showing the 1947 Partition Plan, 1948 Boundaries, and Borders After the 1967 War	188
6.2	Areas A, B, and C Within the West Bank	201

▓ Tables

4.1	Military Expenditures of Middle Eastern Countries, 2005	102
4.2	Formal Political Participation in the Middle East, 2007	108
7.1	Indicators of Development, 2005	222
7.2	Contribution of Agriculture and Industry to GDP	227
7.3	Estimated Migrant Stocks, 2000	229
7.4	Where Migrants Come From and Where They Go	230
7.5	Official Remittances in Selected Countries During the First Oil Boom	232
7.6	Official Remittances, 2006	232
7.7	GDP Growth in the Middle East, Various Years	236
7.8	Size of the Informal Economy as a Percentage of GDP, Various Years	237
7.9	Middle East Exports by Destination	240
7.10	Middle East Exports by Origin	241
9.1	Population and Urbanization in the MENA Region	283
9.2	MENA Cities with Populations Over 1 Million, 2005	285
9.3	Sociodemographic Features in MENA, 2004–2007	286

9.4   Unemployment Rates, Selected MENA Countries,
          Various Years   294
9.5   Youth Unemployment by Sex, Selected MENA Countries,
          Various Years   295
9.6   Percentage of Population Without Access to Services,
          Selected MENA Countries   299

▦ Photographs

West Bank town of Jericho/Ariha   11
Downtown Riyadh, Saudi Arabia   12
Watering troughs for camels in Oman   20
Istanbul, Turkey   26
The Cairo-Giza metropolis   30
Hajj painting in Luxor, Upper Egypt   33
The Great Sun Temple of Abu Simbel   39
Ancient Roman temple in Baalbek in Lebanon   41
Byzantine mosaics in Madaba, Jordan   42
The Blue Mosque   51
Sign on a settlement building in the West Bank   65
War-torn central Beirut, Lebanon   77
Sudanese refugees   93
Men's polling site, Sana'a, Yemen   98
Military parade in Algiers, Algeria   104
State rally in Tripoli, Libya   105
Egyptian president Hosni Mubarak   114
Kuwaiti troops prepare to liberate their country   151
Palestinians crossing a road block in the West Bank   157
Iraqi women train to fight against Iran   164
World leaders at an antiterrorism conference, Egypt   169
Palestinian woman and child in Bureij refugee camp   190
Palestinian president Yasser Arafat   199
Israeli troops confront Palestinian demonstrators   204
Israeli peace activist Uri Avnery   211
Israeli and Palestinian peace activists   213
Drip irrigation in the Egyptian Sinai   225
Construction of sa'ila, Sana'a, Yemen   245
Palestinian woman sewing embroidered cloth   250
McDonald's outlet in Tel Aviv Central Bus Station   251
Wellhead in Kuwait   256
Libyan leader Muammar Qaddafi   262
Dhow and oil tanker in Bahraini port   270

Making tea in the desert   275
Beirut cityscape   284
Graduate of Friends Boys School, Ramallah, West Bank   293
Children in a garbage dump in Cairo   298
Ethnic diversity in the Middle East   326
Cairo schoolgirls   347
Palestinian NGO worker   351
Mauritanian shopkeeper   353
Women's polling station, Baqa'a refugee camp, Amman, Jordan   361
1996 Palestinian presidential candidate Samiha Khalil   367
Qabat al-Bahr Crusader fortress, Sidon, Lebanon   376
Mosque at Job's Tomb near Salalah, Oman   377
Ommayad Mosque, Damascus, Syria   379
Orthodox Jewish youth praying in Jerusalem   383
Women protesting in Algiers, Algeria   393
Egyptian Nobel laureate Naguib Mahfouz   410
Syrian poet Nizar Kabbani and poem   419
Palestinian writer Ghassan Kanafani   428
Mourners at a funeral for Egyptian author Farag Foda   431
Satellite dishes on houses, Sana'a, Yemen   437

Preface

As this third edition of *Understanding the Contemporary Middle East* goes to press, the Middle East remains at the center of numerous cultural, political, economic, and social debates. The "war on terrorism" continues unabated, and the civil war in Iraq that has unfolded following the US-led war in 2003 shows little signs of improvement. Iran is on the defensive as the United States continues its accusations that Iran is harboring a nuclear weapons program. The Israeli-Palestinian conflict remains unresolved, despite periodic peace initiatives. Violence in Darfur continues unabated, with images of devastated Sudanese refugees again gracing the front pages of national newspapers. Scholars vie with pundits and politicians to "explain" what is happening in the Middle East, as the classrooms for courses on all aspects of the region—including language classes—remain packed.

Like the first and second editions, this updated collection draws on the expertise of more than a dozen scholars from a variety of disciplines: history, economics, politics, international relations, demography, geography, anthropology, sociology, gender studies, conflict resolution, religion, and literature. The authors have taken time from their busy schedules to undertake (sometimes extensive) revisions because they believe in the value of making their scholarship accessible to a broader readership. Like most scholars of the Middle East, they have been pulled in many directions and experienced increased demands on their time, particularly since the September 11 attacks and with the ongoing disastrous situation in Iraq. Their families, like mine, have far-too-often been pushed to the back burner out of their sense of obligation to speak with yet another student group, community organization, or stranger about the Middle East.

The authors of this volume were originally brought together under the inspiring leadership of Deborah J. (Misty) Gerner, who tirelessly saw the second edition to fruition even as she struggled with metastatic cancer. I was invited to join Misty in editing that second volume in order to enable

her to complete the project, which was always to her a labor of love, in the event her health deteriorated. She finished that work, and we were delighted that the second edition not only found its way into numerous classrooms, but was recognized by *Choice* magazine as an Outstanding Academic Title of 2004. Misty deserves credit not only for that achievement, but for keeping a group of such distinguished scholars engaged in the project and its updating.

Misty did not survive to work on the current edition, and her absence has been felt at every turn. She died on June 19, 2006, at her home in Vinland, Kansas, with her family, colleagues, and friends by her side. Nevertheless, the heart of this edition, like the two before it, captures Misty's spirit and commitment to the peaceful resolution of conflicts globally and locally.

In each of its editions, this book came together only with the tireless assistance of our friends, colleagues, and families, including dedicated educators in the Middle East who live as well as produce scholarship under conditions most of us would find impossible. The contributors to this volume deserve special thanks for agreeing to update their chapters—and in one case, write an entirely new one—while maintaining full-time teaching schedules and active research agendas.

As with earlier editions, special thanks go to Thomas Hartwell, a professional photographer based in the Middle East, for sharing his evocative images that grace many of these pages. Barbara Parmenter and Ian Manners provided financial support obtained from the University of Texas, Austin, to help cover the cost of preparing the photographs for the first edition, many of which appear again in this edition. Chris Toensing, editor of *Middle East Report,* helped locate the photos for the oil chapter and also provided detailed comments used to update the chapters for this new edition. The work of Phillip Huxtable and Rajaa Abu-Jabr in preparing the first edition remains evident even now. Two anonymous readers, as well as Donald L. Gordon, provided excellent suggestions for making the original text as student friendly as possible. The Basic Political Data and the tables in Chapters 9 and 11 were meticulously updated by Sam Fayyaz (University of Massachusetts, Amherst), who also provided tireless research assistance throughout the updating of this edition. Finally, everyone at Lynne Rienner was outstanding and a pleasure to work with. Lynne's enthusiastic interest and insightful guidance strengthened the book immeasurably, as did the always professional and accommodating assistance of Lesli Brooks Athanasoulis, Jaime Schwalb, and Sonia Smith. Lynne's support in moving forward with a third edition after Misty's death speaks to her deep friendship with Misty and their shared commitment to a text that advances understanding of an often-maligned region and the wonderful people who call the Middle East home.

Misty previously thanked her husband, Philip A. Schrodt, for joining her explorations of the Middle East in all its amazing and wonderful complexity; I know she would insist that I express this again. She also thanked

me for helping her with the second edition, though we both knew that she did the bulk of the work even on days when her health would allow her to work only a few minutes at a time.

I remain indebted to Misty for bringing me into this project, for her tireless and generous support of *Middle East Report* (she never said no to a request to read an article or attend a meeting), for the friendship and love she gave to me, and for the friendship I have since shared with Phil (and with whom I am now collaborating). To ease the heavy load of work we shared on this and other projects, we also shared laughs and drinks: beer in the garden of the Hashem Hotel in Amman, and innumerable cosmopolitans after MERIP meetings. During our shared six years with MERIP, Misty often camped at my Washington, D.C., apartment along with Shiva Balaghi; those weekends became a tradition we all cherished, even as my twin boys crawled into Misty's luggage and repeatedly "unpacked" for her.

This edition is dedicated to Misty, for the energy, love, and incredible patience she shared in every aspect of her life. She is devastatingly missed.

—*Jillian Schwedler*

1

Introduction

Jillian Schwedler

I t is an unfortunate truism that tragedy, violence, and bloodshed attract more attention than do the routine patterns and daily rhythms of peaceful human life. The classic mantra of journalism—"if it bleeds, it leads"—has meant that the Middle East remains prominent in print and broadcast media alike, and that images of bloodshed dominate the Western imagination of the region. Yet the reasons why the Middle East appears fraught with violence are not widely understood. Extraordinary events such as the attacks of September 11, 2001, by extremist Islamists reinforce these stereotypes and exacerbate existing notions of Middle East exceptionalism—the idea that there is just something *different* about the region that renders useless more conventional and familiar models of history, politics, and culture. But such events have a positive side: they inspire individuals who had little prior interest to invest their time and energy in gaining a better understanding of the Middle East. Regional specialists continue to be flooded with invitations to speak to classes, churches, community groups, and other local organizations since the September 11 attacks, and most such invitations come with an honest desire to learn about topics ranging from the Arab-Israeli conflict to political extremism to the basic tenets of Islam. Indeed, the ubiquity of rapidly written books on topics such as Islam and countries such as Saudi Arabia available near the cash registers at bookstores frustrate scholars, who know that these "quick-and-dirty" primers are full of factual errors and lazy stereotypes; however, the overall desire of ordinary citizens to learn more about the region rather than rely on conventional wisdom remains heartening. In colleges and universities, courses on topics such as "terrorism," "political Islam," "women in the Middle East," and "Middle East politics"—not to mention Arabic language classes—are choked with

1

East was largely isolated from the "outside world" prior to the spread of European colonialism, which is why it appears to remain largely traditional and to resist engagement with "the modern world." As Arthur Goldschmidt Jr. illustrates in Chapter 3, however, the peoples of the Middle East in fact have been in contact with Western peoples—indeed, with those in all geographic directions—for centuries. Ancient trade patterns persisted and changed with advents of transportation, while pilgrims from all over the globe have for centuries trekked to visit the region's many holy sites.

Intellectually, the major works of Greek philosophy were lost to Europe for centuries but survived in the Arab-Islamic world; they were only reintroduced to the West by Arab scholars. During Europe's dark Middle Ages, Muslim as well as Jewish scholars in the Middle East were substantially more advanced in many fields, including science, medicine, mathematics, architecture, literature, the visual arts, and education. The decimal number system in wide use today was developed by Arabs who later taught it to Europeans, introducing them to the concept of *zero* in the process. In terms of ordinary language, English words such as *alcohol* and *algebra* come from the Arabic.

As Deborah J. Gerner noted in the introduction to the second edition of *Understanding the Contemporary Middle East,* Middle Eastern cultural influences in the West extend well beyond science, religion, and mathematics. Since the early twentieth century, numerous Middle Eastern poets and philosophers gained sizable followings. Edward FitzGerald's nineteenth-century English translation of *The Rubayiyat of Omar Khayyam* enthralled Western readers, just as the "flower children" and peace activists of the 1960s embraced the works of Lebanese poet Khalil Gibran. In the 1990s, the poetry of Jalal al-Din al-Rumi, the eleventh-century Persian mystic, found its way onto best-seller lists in the United States. The Egyptian novelist Naguib Mahfouz was awarded the Nobel Prize in 1988, bringing the radical social critique of his writings, particularly *The Cairo Trilogy,* into millions of households (Gerner, 2004:3). The audience of Turkish novelist Orhan Pamuk has grown exponentially since he won the IMPAC Dublin Literary Award in 2003 and the 2004 translation of his novel *Snow* was named a *New York Times* Best Book of the Year; in 2006, he became the Middle East's third Nobel laureate in literature. As miriam cooke shows in Chapter 13, novels, short stories, and poetry from the region are being translated at increasing rates, introducing ever wider audiences to the diverse experiences and interventions of Middle Eastern voices.

▓ Organization of the Book

The chapters in this book explore the key themes and controversies of the Middle East in the fields of geography, history, politics, international relations, economics, sociology, demography, anthropology, gender studies, conflict resolution, religion, and literature. Each chapter stands on its own, but the authors also engage directly in the debates in the other chapters, particularly when another chapter provides an expanded discussion of a given topic. In Chapter 2, Ian R. Manners and Barbara McKean Parmenter ask a critical starting question, "What is the Middle East?" Rather than considering the region as a single, geographical entity, they argue, we should think about its multiple and shifting boundaries. Besides political boundaries, the geography of the region has been shaped (and continues to be shaped) by foreign interventions, cultural change, language, urbanization, the flow of migrant workers and refugees, and the rapid decline in water resources. In Chapter 3, Arthur Goldschmidt Jr. examines the history of the region (and its shifting geographies), from the ancient empires of Egypt and Sumer more than 5,000 years ago to the Middle East we know today. He elaborates on a central theme of the book, namely, that the Middle East has never been a closed or isolated unit—politically, economically, or culturally.

In Chapter 4, Deborah J. Gerner and Philip A. Schrodt focus on the domestic politics of Middle Eastern countries, emphasizing the ongoing effects of the colonial legacy as well as contemporary forms of political organization and the various ideologies that offer competing visions of political reform. While the chapter focuses on comparisons within the region, it draws explicit connections to global political trends. In Chapter 5, Mary Ann Tétreault develops these questions concerning international intervention, regional alliances, and various regional subsystems. From the colonial period to the Cold War to the war in Iraq, the politics of the Middle East has been intimately connected—in mostly negative ways—with the political agendas and ambitions of the Great Powers.

Chapter 6, by Simona Sharoni and Mohammed Abu-Nimer, is unique to this volume in providing a detailed analysis of a single conflict; it is also unusual in being coauthored by an Israeli Jew and a Palestinian citizen of Israel. Their careful and nuanced discussion of the Israeli-Palestinian conflict examines the history of the conflict through the lens of conflict resolution. This forward-looking perspective rejects the idea that the conflict is intractable and cannot be solved, adopting instead a framework for thinking about what a just resolution might entail.

In Chapter 7, Agnieszka Paczynska examines the economies of the Middle East, with particular attention to contemporary challenges. She builds on the themes introduced in Chapters 3, 4, and 5, examining structural adjustment, trade patterns, and economic trends in light of regional politics and the long history of foreign involvement in the region. In Chapter 8, Mary Ann Tétreault elaborates on the seminal question of oil and the profound ways in which its discovery in the early twentieth century ensured the continued and deep involvement of foreign governments even with the formal end of the colonial period. The first multinational corporations were oil companies, and their heavy-handed efforts to ensure their interests had profound effects on the shape of domestic politics in the region.

In Chapter 9, Valentine M. Moghadam explores the ways in which these economic processes affected the region's populations. She emphasizes the connections between population growth, urbanization, labor and immigration, (un)employment, poverty, and income inequality, with particular attention to the striking differences that emerge between countries of the region as well as between men and women. In Chapter 10, Laurie King-Irani explores the ways in which kinship networks, class, and ethnicity affect the daily social realities of the peoples of the region. She provides insights into the gender and family relationships that are often a source of confusion to outsiders, stressing the ways in which many aspects of kinship, class, and ethnicity are highly adaptive in their Middle Eastern contexts. Chapter 11 further develops questions of gender, as Lisa Taraki examines the effects of norms and values on women's roles, and the ways in which those are changing in the context of the region's modern nation-states. She emphasizes the diversity of experiences among women in the region, with particular attention to their changing political role.

In Chapter 12, I examine the historical role of Judaism, Christianity, and Islam in the Middle East, and the ways in which religion and politics have been interconnected historically. I then discuss the role of religion in the contemporary politics of the region, from the emergence of religious extremism, to the many and varied ways in which moderate religious activists engage peacefully in the pluralist political processes of the region's (mostly) authoritarian regimes.

In Chapter 13, miriam cooke describes beautifully the historical and cultural underpinnings of Middle Eastern literature: poetry, short stories, novels, and plays. Literature, she shows us, does not exist in a vacuum but instead reflects as well as influences its environment—the cultural ferment, the impact of colonization and struggles for independence, the experience of exile and emigration—in profound ways. As the richness of Middle Eastern literature remains unknown to most Westerners, this chapter also provides an introduction to the large and growing body of material available in English translation.

Finally, Chapter 14 outlines the challenges facing the region in the twenty-first century, as the global war on terror and the ongoing Iraq conflict color the domestic issues facing the peoples and governments of the region. Most notably, not a single state in the region is without indigenous movements demanding greater participation and accountability from their governments.

These chapters are likely to challenge some of your existing perceptions about the Middle East while confirming and fleshing out others. Like any region of the world, "reality" is a complicated notation that cannot be fully understood outside of local perspectives. While it is nonsensical to talk about a single "Middle Eastern culture," the historical experiences and daily practices of the various peoples of the region do share significant similarities in many areas (though not in others). The politics of the region dominate most of the West's common knowledge, and these chapters aim to make accessible a rich understanding of these complexities. At the same time, a primary goal of this book is to bring to life the lived experiences of Middle Eastern peoples, and many of these will feel surprisingly familiar to you. We hope you enjoy your exploration of the contemporary Middle East.

▧ Bibliography

Gerner, Deborah J. 2004. "Introduction." Pp. 1–4 in Deborah J. Gerner and Jillian Schwedler (eds.), *Understanding the Contemporary Middle East.* 2nd ed. Boulder: Lynne Rienner.

2

The Middle East:
A Geographic Preface

Ian R. Manners and
Barbara McKean Parmenter

A camel caravan crossing desert dunes, oil derricks pumping thick black crude, rows of men kneeling in prayer, bearded protesters shouting slogans—more than likely these are some of the images conjured up when the outside world thinks of the Middle East. Each of us carries our own "geography" of the world and its places in our heads, our own way of visualizing and interpreting the earth on which we live. Professional geographers attempt to correct preconceived notions and present a broader perspective. Typically, a geographical description of the Middle East, like that of any other region, would begin with an overview of the physical environment—geology, geomorphology, climate, flora, and fauna—as a backdrop for a discussion of human activities in the region, land use, resource development, population distribution, urbanization, and political organization. Yet even the best of these descriptions often fail to convey what the Middle East is "really" like.

The Middle East cannot be easily compartmentalized into book chapters or neatly divided by border lines on a map. Sharp boundaries are blurred, discontinuities appear unexpectedly, the familiarity of everyday life surprises us in our anticipation of the exotic and dangerous. Timothy Mitchell (1988) has described how European travelers to Egypt in the nineteenth century were frequently confused by what they saw when they reached Egypt: They had seen the ancient Egyptian artifacts that had been collected and displayed in Europe's capitals, even visited the Egyptian Hall at the Exposition Universelle held in Paris; some had read the *Description de l'Egypte,* the twenty-two-volume work prepared by the French artists and scholars who had accompanied Napoleon to Egypt—but nothing they saw or experienced quite matched up to what they had been expecting to see. There was often a palpable sense of disappointment. Where was the "real Egypt"? In a similar way, contemporary visitors to the Middle East are likely to find that their geographical knowledge has to be reformulated as they encounter a world that challenges many of their expectations.

The difficult path to understanding the Middle East in all its complexity is not traveled only by outsiders. In the Iranian film *Bashu*, director Bahram Bayza'i tells the story of a boy from the deserts of Khuzistan in southwestern Iran whose village is caught in a bombardment. Bashu understands little of the reasons for the conflict between his government and its neighbor, Iraq; he knows only that he is now both homeless and orphaned. Seeking refuge in the back of a truck, he falls asleep. When he awakes, he is bewildered to find himself in a quiet world of cool, deep-green forests, a paradise he never dreamed existed. The truck has brought him to Gilan province in northwestern Iran, where he is taken in by a peasant woman despite the disapproval of her neighbors. Bashu is of Arab descent and speaks a mixture of Arabic and Persian common to the borderlands of Khuzistan; the woman speaks Gilaki, a dialect of Persian. Unable to communicate with either his caregiver or her neighbors, Bashu struggles against their prejudices. But he is not alone in being different. The woman who has taken him in is struggling to manage the farm on her own while her husband is away fighting in the war. When her husband returns and demands that the boy be sent away, she refuses to comply. In a very real sense, the film is a small reflection of much larger issues in Middle Eastern society, exploring the ways in which people deal with differences and face changes related to environment, culture, government, religion, and gender.

Thus, although the term *Middle East* may appear to suggest a degree of homogeneity, the region is extraordinarily diverse in its physical, cultural, and social landscapes. For many, the desert seems the central physical metaphor for the Middle East, an image frequently repeated in films and novels. The sand seas of the Rub'al-Khali (the Empty Quarter) in Arabia perhaps best fit this image. Yet the landscapes of the Middle East also encompass the coral reefs that draw scuba divers to the Red Sea, permanent snowfields and cirque glaciers on the slopes of the great volcanic peaks of Mount Ararat (5,165 meters) in eastern Anatolia and Mount Damavand (more than 5,600 meters) in the Elburz Mountains of Iran, the salt-crusted flats and evaporation pans of the Dasht-e Kavir in central Iran, and the coastal marshes and wetlands of the Nile Delta. Most emphatically, and despite the vast expanses of desert and steppe, the Middle East is also very much an urban society, with more than half the population living in cities that face much the same environmental, infrastructural, and social problems of cities around the world.

The Middle East is likewise culturally diverse. Much of the area came under Arab Muslim influence during and after the seventh century. At various

Deborah J. Gerner

The area around the ancient West Bank town of Jericho/Ariha, located 20 feet below sea level, is a mixture of hill, desert, and lush oasis.

times, Persian and central Asian peoples and influences flowed westward into the lands around the eastern Mediterranean. Most people in the region are Muslims, but Christians and Jews constitute significant communities. The three major languages are Arabic, Turkish, and Persian, all of which are quite distinct linguistically (Arabic is a Semitic language, Persian is Indo-European, and Turkish is Ural-Altaic). Nonetheless, they have been heavily influenced by each other. Persian is written in Arabic script, as was Ottoman Turkish; only since 1928 has Turkish used a modified Latin alphabet. All three languages contain numerous words from the others, and each has a subset of distinct dialects. In addition, other peoples with their own languages are found throughout the region. There are, for example, Berber speakers in Morocco and Algeria and Baluchi speakers in southeastern Iran. Kurdish-speaking people probably constitute the fourth-largest linguistic group in the region, and the revived Hebrew language has been a central integrating force among Jews in Israel.

How, then, to describe the geography of the Middle East? In this chapter we choose to present multiple geographies of the Middle East, different ways of seeing and depicting the region. In this way, we hope to present a richer description of the area than would normally be possible in a few pages, although one that is far from comprehensive.

Full of modern concrete, steel, and glass buildings, Riyadh is the captial of Saudi Arabia and its largest city, recently surpassing Jeddah.

■ Boundaries

A geography of the Middle East must first come to grips with how to define *the Middle East.* Compared to the area portrayed in any Western atlas published in the late nineteenth century, the political landscape of the region we know today as the Middle East is virtually unrecognizable. The atlas published by the *Times of London* in 1895, for example, provides a series of maps entitled "The Balkan Peninsula," "The Caucasus," "Asia Minor and Persia," and "Palestine." Nor would these places, as depicted in the atlas, have been any more familiar to those living in the region, who would have recognized no unified geographical entity but rather a mosaic of regions. Al-Iraq referred to the area around the Shatt al-Arab waterway, and al-Jazira identified the lands between the Tigris and Euphrates rivers, including Baghdad. Sham indicated the area immediately around Damascus, and Bilad al-Sham (or country of Sham) the larger region now comprising Syria, Lebanon, Jordan, and Palestine. Egyptians still call their country *Misr,* but originally the term referred only to the Nile Delta and its narrow valley, not to the vast territory contained within its present-day boundaries. Today's map reveals a very different geography. As discussed in Chapters 3, 4 and 5, the present sovereign states are new creations almost without exception, in large measure the products of European intervention and the dismemberment of the Ottoman Empire.

The term *Middle East* is itself an unabashedly Eurocentric term. It seems to have been used first in 1902 in reference to British naval strategy in the Gulf at a time of increased Russian influence around the Caspian Sea and German plans for a Berlin-to-Baghdad railway. Largely through the columns of the *Times,* the term achieved wider circulation and came to denote an area of strategic concern to Britain lying between the Near East (another Eurocentric designation, essentially synonymous with the area remaining under the control of the Ottoman Empire), the expanding Russian empire in central Asia, and the Indian Raj (Chirol, 1903). During World War I, the British expeditionary force to Mesopotamia was generally referred to as "Middle East Forces," as distinct from Britain's "Near East Forces," which operated from bases in Egypt. After the war, these two military commands were integrated as an economy measure, but the "Middle East" designation was retained.

With the passage of time, the name became both familiar and institutionalized, first in the military commands of World War II and later in the specialist agencies of the United Nations (Smith, 1968). Yet there remain ambiguities and uncertainties in terms of its more precise delimitation. Does the Middle East include Afghanistan to the east? With the demise of the Soviet Union, should the region be reconstituted to include the new sovereign states of Armenia and Azerbaijan? Frequently, the Maghreb states of Morocco, Tunisia, and Algeria are included in discussions of the Middle East based on the fact that they share so much of its culture and history. For similar reasons, Sudan is sometimes included despite the presence of a large non-Muslim, non-Arabic-speaking population in the southern part of the country (Blake, Dewdney, and Mitchell, 1987). In this book, we have opted for a broad interpretation by including in its discussion Turkey, Iran, and Israel, together with all the states that belong to the Arab League.

What is surprising is that the term *Middle East* is also used by people within the region. The literal Arabic translation, *al-sharq al-awsat,* and the Turkish, *orta docu,* can be found in books, journals, and newspapers. Interestingly, the term is most widely used in discussions of geopolitical strategies in the region. Arab commentators, for example, might discuss "American policy in the Middle East" or "Israel's relationship to the Middle East." Thus, it is perhaps more a reference to how others, either outside the region or outside the predominant culture, view the region and less a self-describing term.

The "map view" of a region is the most skeletal of possible geographies but is both formative and informative. Looking at a contemporary political map of the Middle East, the predominance of long, straight boundary lines stretching across hundreds of miles of desert is striking (see Map 2.1). Another revealing feature of today's map, as Bernard Lewis points out, is that the names of countries are, for the most part, restorations or reconstructions of ancient names (Lewis, 1989:21–22). *Syria,* for instance, is a term that first appears in Greek histories and geographies and was subsequently adopted by the Romans as the name for an administrative province. But from the time of the Arab-Islamic conquest of the seventh century, the name virtually disappears from local use. Its reappearance dates from the nineteenth century, largely through the writing and influence of Western scholars. Similarly, although Europeans have been referring to the lands of Anatolia and Asia Minor as Turkey since the time of the Crusades, the inhabitants of this region did not use this name until the establishment of the Republic of Turkey in 1923.

To understand the changes that have occurred in the political map of the Middle East, it is helpful to recall that at the end of the sixteenth century the authority of the Ottoman Empire extended from the borders of Morocco in the west to the borders of Iran in the east, and from the Red Sea in the south to the northern and eastern shores of the Black Sea (see Map 2.2). In Europe the Ottomans twice laid siege to Vienna. But the eighteenth and nineteenth centuries saw a gradual retreat from these high-water marks. In the Tartar and Turkish principalities from the Crimea to the Caucasus, Ottoman sovereignty was replaced by Russian domination; in the Balkans, the Ottomans confronted growing nationalist aspirations and a concerted assault by Austria and its allies; in North Africa, the Ottomans had to deal with the expansion and imposition of colonial authority involving the French in Algeria (1830) and Tunisia (1881) and the Italians in Libya (1911).

In other areas, Ottoman power was greatly weakened by the emergence of strong local rulers. In the aftermath of Napoleon's unsuccessful invasion of Egypt, for example, an Ottoman military officer named Mehmet (Muhammad) Ali established a dynasty that made Egypt virtually independent of Ottoman rule. The bankruptcy of the Egyptian administration after efforts to modernize the country's economy and infrastructure in turn opened the way to more direct European intervention in the country's affairs through a French-British Debt Commission and British occupation in 1882, although the country still remained nominally under Ottoman sovereignty. In Lebanon, following a massacre of Maronite Christians by Druze in 1860 and the landing of French troops in Beirut, Britain and France forced the Ottoman sultan to establish the semiautonomous province of Mount Lebanon with a Christian governor to be appointed in consultation with European powers (Drysdale and Blake, 1985:196).

Thus, even where European powers did not control territory outright, by the end of the nineteenth century they had become deeply involved in the region's commerce and governance. The defeat of Ottoman Turkey in World War I helped create the current map of the Middle East (Fromkin, 1991). In the final dissolution of the Ottoman Empire, the remaining Arab provinces were reconstituted into the territories of Iraq, Syria, Lebanon, Transjordan, and Palestine and subjected for a brief period to direct British and French administration, albeit under the guise of a League of Nations mandate.

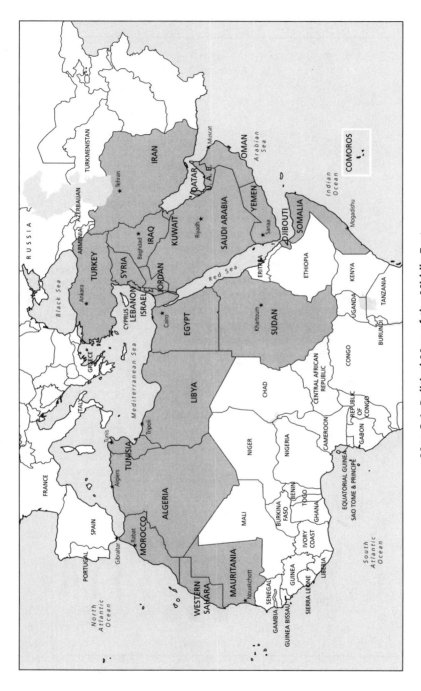

Map 2.1 Political Map of the Middle East

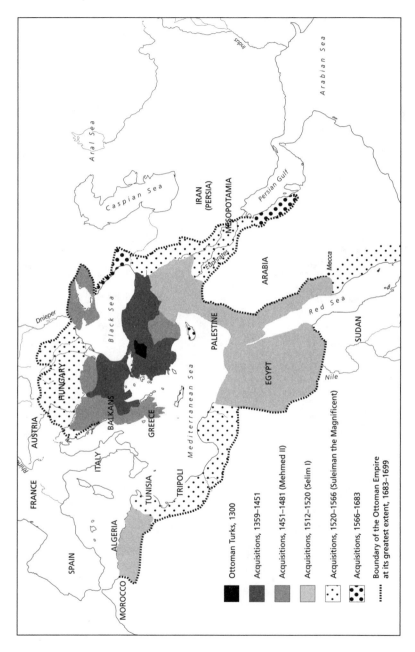

Map 2.2 Extent of the Ottoman Empire

Ottoman Turks, 1300

Acquisitions, 1359–1451

Acquisitions, 1451–1481 (Mehmed II)

Acquisitions, 1512–1520 (Selim I)

Acquisitions, 1520–1566 (Suleiman the Magnificent)

Acquisitions, 1566–1683

Boundary of the Ottoman Empire
at its greatest extent, 1683–1699

The map of the Middle East, then, is both very recent and frequently a cause of conflict. From a resource perspective, the lack of correspondence between political and hydrological boundaries has complicated the development of scarce water resources. New conflicts have arisen particularly over claims to offshore resources such as oil and natural gas. In the shallow, hydrocarbon-rich waters of the Gulf, where numerous small islands, sandbanks, and reefs with contested histories of settlement and occupation provide a basis for rival claims to sovereignty, the extension of land boundaries offshore has proven to be complicated and contentious. Such a dispute between Bahrain and Qatar, regarding sovereignty over the Huwar Islands and other coastal territories, became the subject of the longest arbitration case in international legal history, being finally resolved by the International Court of Justice in The Hague in March 2001 after nine years of litigation. In its adjudication of claims that drew from long-standing family and tribal disagreements over fishing and pearling rights dating back to the nineteenth century, the court essentially upheld a 1939 determination of boundaries by Britain, then the protectorate power in the region.

From a cultural perspective, boundaries are also problematic. The Kurds, for example, a non-Arab, predominantly Muslim people numbering several million, are spread across Turkey, Syria, Iraq, and Iran. Their quest for autonomy has at one time or another involved them in clashes with all four of these states. The distribution of Sunni and Shi'i Muslims, the two major subgroups of Islam, likewise does not adhere to national boundaries. The fault lines of this division cross the oil fields of southern Iraq and northern Arabia.

From a political perspective, the appearance, disappearance, and tentative reappearance of Palestine demonstrate that borders are still in flux. Assigned the mandate for Palestine in 1921, Britain sought to fulfill its 1917 promise to facilitate the establishment of a national home for the Jewish people while simultaneously ensuring that, as stated in the Balfour Declaration, the civil and religious rights of non-Jewish communities in Palestine were safeguarded. The establishment of Israel in 1948 realized the Zionist vision of an independent homeland in which the Jewish people could live free of persecution, a return to the land from which they had been physically separated during nearly 2,000 years of exile. A consequence of these events has been the departure, through emigration to Israel, of large numbers of Jews whose families had lived for centuries in cities and towns throughout the Middle East and the displacement of another people, the Palestinian Arabs, who fled or were forced from their homes and lands during the fighting and sought refuge in Egypt, Jordan, Syria, Lebanon, and elsewhere in the region.

In such ways have the cartographies of the region been reimagined and refashioned in the course of the twentieth century. As the century progressed, a complex body of interests grew up around the new states of the Middle

flood prevented the buildup of salts harmful to crop growth. Basin irrigation remained the dominant method of irrigation in the Nile Valley until the end of the nineteenth century, by which time the modern phase of water development had begun to take shape through the construction of barrages, annual storage reservoirs, and summer canals intended to allow for year-round irrigation and multiple cropping.

Like the basin irrigation system developed in the Nile Valley, other traditional water management devices such as the *qanats* of Iran, the *shadufs* of Egypt, and the *norias* of the Orontes River in Syria had a common purpose: to make effective use of a critical resource and thereby enable societies to survive and flourish under conditions of scarcity and uncertainty. The *qanat,* a sophisticated technique for developing, collecting, and distributing groundwater through a network of underground tunnels, may well have been in use in Iran as early as the first millennium B.C.E.: that it represented an extremely successful adaptation to a variety of local conditions is evident in the diffusion of this technique to other parts of the Middle East and North Africa, particularly during the early Arab caliphates, and from North Africa to Spain and later the "New World."

As the demand for water has grown, however, newer technologies of water development intended to make more productive use of both surface water and groundwater have frequently disrupted and displaced traditional systems. The construction of the Aswan High Dam in the 1960s, for example, enabled all of Egypt to be irrigated on a perennial basis, made possible two, and in some cases even three, crops per year, and generated power for countrywide electrification projects. These benefits came with environmental side effects, however, including serious problems of soil salinization (White, 1988).

Deborah J. Gerner

In the mountainous Dhofar region of Oman, watering troughs have been built to help the bedouin maintain strong camel herds.

Herein lies one of the major challenges facing the region today. The burgeoning demand for water to meet agricultural, industrial, transportation, and urban needs would be difficult enough to satisfy even if water supplies were more abundant. In the Middle East the problem is greatly complicated by the uneven distribution of water resources and by the lack of correspondence between political and hydrological boundaries. As a result, those countries where irrigated agriculture is of paramount importance (Egypt, Iraq, and, to a lesser extent, Israel, Jordan, and Syria) are unable to control the sources of water on which their populations and their economies depend. Roughly two-thirds of the water supply available to Arab countries has its source in non-Arab countries (Gleick, 1994). In Israel, by some estimates, between one-half and two-thirds of the water currently used for irrigation and domestic and industrial purposes actually originates outside the country's pre-1967 boundaries. In particular, the major aquifers that supply groundwater to municipalities and farms in Israel's coastal plains are actually recharged through rainfall occurring over the West Bank.

In such circumstances, it is hardly surprising that water rights and allocations became a key issue in the post-Oslo negotiations between the Israelis and the Palestinians over the future status of the West Bank. Certainly it would be quite wrong to see the conflict between Israelis and Palestinians and between Israel and neighboring Arab states as primarily a struggle over water (Libiszewski, 1995; Wolf, 2000). Nevertheless, in conjunction with other imperatives, particularly national security considerations, access to water resources is certainly a factor in strategic thinking. In 1964, for example, the Arab states made plans to divert the flow of the Hasbani and Banias headwaters of the Jordan River away from Israel (the Hasbani, which originates in Lebanon, was to be diverted into the Litani River and from there to the Mediterranean Sea, and the Banias, originating in Syria, to a storage reservoir in Jordan on the Yarmuk River via a canal along the western edge of the Golan Heights). These plans were brought to a halt by an Israeli attack on the construction works (Manners, 1974). And while water was not an overriding issue in the subsequent Six Day War of June 1967, the occupation by Israel of Syrian territory on the Golan Heights, including the Banias Springs during that war, effectively extended Israel's hydro-strategic control over this part of the Jordan drainage basin.

More recently, in October 2002, Lebanon's completion of a pumping project involving the Wazzani Springs, an important contributor to the flow of the Hasbani particularly during the dry summer months, provoked threats of retaliatory action from Israel and resurrected old arguments and animosities over rights to use the Jordan waters. That a relatively minor development project intended to provide a water supply to local villages should have necessitated the dispatch of UN and US mediators is perhaps an indication of the severity of the water crisis that confronts all states in the Jordan basin. More discouraging in the long-term is the extent to which efforts, begun in the aftermath of the Oslo Accords, to build trust and to create joint management institutions for equitable, sustainable use of the Jordan River waters have been undermined by the breakdown in the peace process since 2000 (Wolf, 1995).

The extent to which control over water resources empowers some countries at the expense of others is well illustrated in the case of the Euphrates River. The Euphrates rises in eastern Turkey, punches its way through the edge of the Anatolian Plateau in a series of dramatic gorges, then flows across the increasingly arid steppes of Syria and Iraq to a confluence with the Tigris River (which also originates in Turkey) just above Basra, Iraq. From here the two rivers flow together as the Shatt al-Arab to the Persian Gulf. Although most of the Euphrates' huge drainage basin is actually in Iraq, nearly 90 percent of the annual flow of the river is generated within Turkey. This means that the downstream users, Syria and Iraq, are vulnerable to Turkey's future development plans for the Euphrates River.

Iraq has long-established claims to the Euphrates; indeed, Mesopotamian power and culture was linked to effective control over the waters of these rivers (Jacobsen and Adams, 1958). The later Sassanian and Abbasid periods (fourth to twelfth centuries) were marked by a considerable expansion of the irrigation system. In the twentieth century, first during the British mandate and later after independence, the irrigation systems were rehabilitated and new control structures erected. In the 1970s, Iraq began planning a major storage reservoir that, like the Aswan High Dam, was intended to provide long-term storage. Despite setbacks caused by war, Iraq's long-term plans still envision greater use of Euphrates water. Syria, like Iraq, is steadily making greater use of Euphrates water for irrigation development and power generation and in 1973 completed the huge al-Thawra Dam.

But it is Turkey that holds the real key to what happens in the future, and Turkey is currently in the process of implementing a truly massive water development project in southeastern Anatolia (the Güneydocu Anadolu Projesi, or GAP) that involves both the Tigris and the Euphrates rivers. If fully implemented, the GAP would involve as many as twelve dams and storage reservoirs on the Euphrates and ten on the Tigris, plus additional power-generating facilities. This immense undertaking is intended to pump new life into Turkey's hardscrabble, semiarid southeast provinces where living standards are far below the national average, but it is clearly more than just another water development project. These provinces are home to the majority of Turkey's Kurdish population. By providing people with a more secure and comfortable livelihood, the government hopes to undercut support for the Kurdish separatist movement and bring an end to a costly and bloody conflict.

In 1990 Turkey began filling the reservoir behind the Atatürk Dam, triggering protests from both Syria and Iraq. By some estimates, the Atatürk

Dam and other proposed storage and diversion projects on the Euphrates could reduce downstream flows to Syria by 40 percent and to Iraq by as much as 80 percent, especially during the dry years. Clearly, if all the proposed water projects are carried out, the total water demand will be well in excess of the normal flow of the river. Moreover, water quality is likely to be an issue for downstream users since an increasing proportion of the available flow will consist of return irrigation flows containing high concentrations of agricultural chemicals and salts.

Some see in this situation of growing competition for limited water supplies the potential for future conflict. Unfortunately, in none of the major river basins does there exist formal agreements among all riparian states (those bordering on rivers) over water rights; there is no such agreement for the Jordan River or for the Tigris and Euphrates rivers, and legal agreements for the Nile River involve only Egypt and the Sudan, to the exclusion of the seven other upstream riparian states. Boutros Boutros-Ghali's comment when he was still Egypt's foreign minister to the effect that "the next war in our region will be over the waters of the Nile, not politics," has been widely repeated. An alternative, more hopeful view, is that water could be a vehicle for regional cooperation. Sharing of knowledge and experience with regard to using water less wastefully, for instance through drip and subsurface irrigation systems and the recycling and reuse of wastewater, or the transfer of water from water surplus to water deficit states, as in the case of the proposed peace pipeline from Turkey through Syria to Jordan, the West Bank, Israel, and Gaza, are examples of cooperation that could transform regional geographies.

As Will D. Swearingen describes in *Moroccan Mirages,* for many hydraulic engineers and government administrators, the ideal vision of water development has been "not a drop of water to the sea" (Swearingen, 1987: 39). Likewise, the region's marshes and wetlands have often been targets for major hydraulic engineering projects because they are perceived as empty spaces that "waste" potentially valuable land and water resources. But water is more than just a commodity with economic value to society, a resource to be developed, its flow regulated on a liter by liter basis: water has other values and meanings to those living in the region.

People are increasingly recognizing that water sustains a range of ecological processes, which in turn support communities of fishers, hunters, reed gatherers, salt producers, and the like. The coastal lagoons of the Nile Delta, the marshes of the Shatt al-Arab, Lake Hula in Israel and Jordan's Azraq oasis, Lake Ishkeul in Tunisia, and other wetlands scattered throughout the region were once highly productive ecosystems that provided habitat and sustenance for diverse communities of plants and animals. Those living around wetlands traditionally exploited these resources, maintaining a diverse and relatively sustainable livelihood. Other nonconventional values of wetlands include absorbing and treating human sewage and other organic wastes, recharging groundwater aquifers, and acting as vital resting and feeding sites for waterfowl and shorebirds migrating between breeding grounds in northern Eurasia and wintering grounds in Africa. In many cases, these wetlands have been drained, severely polluted, or dried out as a result of groundwater withdrawals, with devastating impacts on local communities. Fishing villages around Lake Maryut near Alexandria, Egypt, have seen livelihoods destroyed due to dumping of industrial wastes. The marshes of Azraq Oasis in Jordan have been largely drained to supplement the municipal water supply of Amman. In Iraq, the government of Saddam Hussein drained portions of the Shatt al-Arab marshes at least in part for political reasons: to exercise greater control over the Marsh Arabs, a largely Shi'i people opposed to Hussein's rule. Israelis drained the Hula marshes in the 1950s for agriculture, but later discovered that the high amount of fertilizers required to farm the drained and eroding peat was polluting the nearby Sea of Galilee. In the 1990s, the Jewish National Fund undertook a project to restore a portion of the marshes. Since the restoration was completed in 1998, the area has seen an increase in migratory waterfowl, including cranes and pelicans (Shapiro, 2002).

A framework for conserving the region's remaining wetlands is the Convention on Wetlands of International Importance (commonly known as the Ramsar Convention) signed in 1971. To date, fourteen of the countries covered in this book are contracting parties to the convention, protecting forty-two wetland areas totaling 1.8 million hectares, and are committed to following the convention's guidelines of wise use in the management of these sites (Ramsar Convention Bureau, 2003). These guidelines include setting up the legal framework for protection and participatory processes to involve local communities (Parmenter, 1996). What these initiatives will achieve in practice remains to be seen, but their very existence testifies to a growing awareness of the complexity of water issues.

There are connections here between water and life that are crucial to any understanding of environment and culture in the Middle East. The Quran holds out to all believers the promise of a paradise that is filled with fountains and cool, shaded watercourses, "gardens beneath which rivers flow" (Schimmel, 1985). Images of gardens and water, inspired by descriptions of paradise in the Quran, have had a profound influence on Islamic art and poetry (MacDougall and Ettinghausen, 1976). Nor was this promise limited to literary and artistic representations; it also found expression in a love of gardens that were imagined and conceived as a reflection of the beauty and serenity of paradise on earth.

This linking of the sacred and the secular, of water and life, is eloquently conveyed in a story Annemarie Schimmel relates about the puzzling question she was first asked in Anatolia by an old woman, *'Ankara'da rahmet var mi?'* [Is there mercy in Ankara?]. I wondered what the question might mean in a casual conversation with some unknown person. But it meant 'Is there rain in Ankara?' In Turkish, *rahmet* means both God's mercy and the blessing of rain, for it is through the blessing of rain that everything that is seemingly dead is made alive again. (Schimmel, 1985:6)

◼ Cityscapes

Closing in on our scale still further, we move from regional phenomena like water to local environments, particularly the city. In the film *Raiders of the Lost Ark,* Indiana Jones stands on a rooftop overlooking an assemblage of small white-domed houses. His Egyptian host gestures toward the scene. "Cairo," he says. "City of the living. A paradise on earth." The scene that they are looking at is more likely a small village in Tunisia. Cairo, even in the 1930s when the story takes place, was a large sprawling metropolis filled with apartment buildings, factories, government offices, theaters, museums, and all the other accoutrements of modern urban life. The film is confirming our imaginative expectations and our own assumed position vis-à-vis this Arab city. It is exotic, alluring, and inscrutable—we gaze comfortably at this fantasy place from a high vantage point and leave it to the intrepid Indy to plunge into the labyrinthine alleyways and bazaars of Cairo itself.

The Cairo of the 1930s that the film did not show might have seemed rather mundane: a vibrant, bustling city, home at that time to just over 1 million people carrying on their daily lives in ways that were far from mysterious. But vision and imagination are powerful weapons, and Middle Eastern cities have been the object of intense imaginings over the course of their history. Nowhere in the Middle East is this more evident than in Jerusalem, a city sacred to three religions. Jews, Christians, and Muslims have struggled for centuries to make Jerusalem "their" city. "The chronicles of Jerusalem," Meron Benvenisti writes, "are a gigantic quarry from which each side has mined stones for the construction of myths—and for throwing at each other"(Benvenisti, 1996:4).

Cities have always been important in the history of the region, frequently developing as nodes connecting the well-traveled routes of armies and traders. To rulers, cities were constituted as centers of power and authority. In the eyes of travelers and traders, cities were almost literally oases of security, walled and protected, centers of commerce, learning, and entertainment. Al-Hariri, in a famous twelfth-century adventure story, *al-Maqamat (The Assemblies)*, wrote admiringly of Basra in present-day Iraq: "Thy heart's desire of holy things and worldly thou findest there" (al-Hariri, 1898:164). Today the old walled cities of the region are in most cases small fractions of the larger urban fabric that changes with each passing day. As

Janet Abu-Lughod has observed, "A city at any one point in time is a still photograph of a complex system of building and destroying, of organizing and reorganizing" (Abu-Lughod, 1987:162). This system includes both the formal visions imposed by governors, conquerors, and administrators and the vernacular forces of ordinary citizens working to establish their own territories and routines.

Istanbul is a prime example of this dialectic between formal and vernacular. In the fourth century, the Emperor Constantine moved the seat of the Roman Empire from Rome to the site of a former Greek settlement, Byzantium, located on a promontory bordered on one side by the Golden Horn and on the other by the Sea of Marmara. Although the city's official name was always Konstantinoupolis Nea Rome, "the city of Constantine that is the new Rome," it quickly became known as Constantinople, a name that retained currency even among Turks, whose documents and coins frequently referred to the city as *Konstaniniye* until the end of the Ottoman Empire (Çelik, 1986:12). Christianity enjoyed a special status in this new Rome, which was seen as a sacred city, its churches and monasteries housing a unique collection of holy relics and shrines that symbolized God's special favor. Justinian's great church of Haghia Sophia, its domed basilica rising above the city, epitomized the close relationship between the Byzantine state and the Christian church. But other buildings and monuments—palaces, walls, columns, churches, and aqueducts—remain embedded within today's urban fabric to recall more than 1,000 years of Roman-Byzantine rule.

Located along the Bosporus Strait, Istanbul, Turkey, symbolically links Europe and the Middle East in a single dynamic city of 9 million people.

When the Ottomans finally captured the city in 1453 after an eight-week siege, Sultan Mehmet II inherited a prized imperial city but one in a sad state of dilapidation. The sultan initiated a massive program of repopulation and reconstruction intended to restore the city to its past grandeur and prosperity. Thousands of people were relocated to the city, since 1930 known popularly as Istanbul, from all quarters of the empire. These included skilled artisans and craftspeople to assist in the immense task of reconstruction. New palaces; great mosques with their schools, libraries, and charitable institutions; extensive bazaars and markets; and improved systems of water supply transformed the appearance of the city. These were the symbols of power and prosperity befitting the capital of a great empire.

In the twentieth century, with the final collapse of the Ottoman Empire, Turkish nationalists desiring to establish a secular republic along European lines made their own statement through urban planning and design. Turning their backs on Istanbul, they decided to construct a new capital in central Anatolia, hundreds of miles to the east of Istanbul, adjacent to the small town of Ankara. The design of the new Ankara was carefully planned to create an entirely different way of public life, one divorced from the Ottoman and Islamic past (Keleş and Payne, 1984). A German urban planner and architect, Hermann Jansen, was engaged to lay out a master plan for the city along the lines of a Garden City, a scheme popular in Europe at the time and considered to embody the "rational" approach to urban planning. The plan specified separate zones for residences, businesses, and industry, separated by wide boulevards and interspersed with parks and public squares. The government encouraged new styles of architecture that were intended to give public expression to the nation's modern image (Bozdocan, 1994). These styles applied even to the design of ordinary residences, symbolizing the desire to shape not only the structure of the city but also the fundamentals of private life.

Istanbul and Ankara are only two examples of how visions backed up by political power organize and reorganize urban landscapes. Cairo was originally laid out by the Fatimid ruler Mu'izz al-Din in the tenth century to serve as a formal, ordered imperial capital next to the bustling commercial town of Fustat. Fustat itself had grown from the encampment of the Arab army that laid siege to the fortified Byzantine settlement of Babylon during the Arab conquest of Egypt in 640 c.e.[2] In her study of Cairo, Abu-Lughod relates that by one account the conquering Fatimid general "carried with him precise plans for the construction of a new princely city which Mu'izz envisaged as the seat of a Mediterranean Empire" (Abu-Lughod, 1971:18). The new city was named "al-Qahira," the victorious city, and its monumental architecture was to become a favorite subject of European artists.

As in other cities in the Middle East, the nineteenth and twentieth centuries saw many attempts to "modernize" and "improve" Cairo. In 1867, the ruler of Egypt, Isma'il Pasha, who already had a keen interest in urban

development, attended the Exposition Universelle in Paris. There he reportedly met with Baron Georges-Eugène Haussman, the urban planner who had remade Paris into the city of broad boulevards and gardens we know today. Eager to create a modern capital before the deluge of foreign visitors who would arrive following the completion of the Suez Canal, Isma'il quickly translated Haussman's principles into a new plan for Cairo. With no time to waste, Isma'il chose to leave the medieval city essentially as it was, without gas, water, sanitation, or paved streets. Instead, he concentrated on building a new European-style city to the west, complete with Haussman-style boulevards and parks, powered by steam and lit by gaslight. This was the city foreigners would see, and their only forays into the old Cairo would be as tourists viewing the scattered monuments of a distant past (Abu-Lughod, 1971:98–111).

On the other side of this dialectic between formal and vernacular is the sheer persistence and energy of ordinary citizens. Life grows up and around, through and between, formal plans like vines on a trellis.

Abu-Lughod (1987:163) has noted how residential neighborhoods formed a crucial building block of cities in the Islamic world during medieval and even later times. These neighborhoods, which often housed people related to each other or with common ethnic or religious backgrounds, enjoyed a large measure of autonomy. The state was concerned primarily with regulating the commerce and ensuring the defense of the city. Thus meeting the needs and protecting the interests of the neighborhood was primarily a local community responsibility. This involved such things as cleaning and maintaining the streets, providing lighting, and supervising and sanctioning behavior. A wealthier neighborhood might have its own charitable institutions, organize its own water supply with public fountains, or appoint night watchmen for internal security, often paid for through endowments to religious foundations.

When Europeans tried to penetrate these neighborhoods, they were confused and threatened by what they saw as a chaotic warren of streets that frequently ended in cul-de-sacs. Yet the intent in the layout and structure of neighborhoods and even individual buildings was to minimize physical contact and protect visual separation. Thus Islamic building laws regulated the placement of windows, the heights of adjacent buildings, and the mutual responsibilities of neighbors toward one another so as to guard and protect privacy (Abu-Lughod, 1987:167). Of course, the majority of the urban population lived in modest circumstances that bore little resemblance to the luxurious lifestyles of the rich and powerful, and this reality was reflected in the shabby construction and cramped quarters of many neighborhoods.

Nor was urban life free of hazards. The common use of wood construction in Istanbul, for example, made the city particularly vulnerable to fires. Between 1633 and 1839 the city suffered as many as 109 major conflagrations, many of which wiped out entire neighborhoods; between 1853 and

1906, this number reached 229 as fires increasingly came to play a major role in reshaping and redesigning urban architecture (Çelik, 1986: 52–53). Diseases were another harsh aspect of city life, particularly bubonic plague, which until the nineteenth century periodically reappeared to carry off large numbers of the city's population.

As in many other parts of the world, the experience in Middle Eastern cities in recent years has been one of rapid urbanization, largely as a result of the influx of rural migrants in search of employment and better living conditions. These demographic shifts have dramatically transformed not only the physical appearance of cities but also the daily lives and routines of millions of people. In 1900 perhaps 10 percent of the region's population lived in urban settlements; by 1990, an estimated 57 percent resided in urban communities (UN, 1992). The dominant impression of urban life in the region today is one of incessant construction and a struggle to deal with the consequences of unrestrained growth. Everywhere one looks there are sprawling housing projects and lines of apartment blocks alongside new ring roads: in older neighborhoods, residents add more floors to buildings, squeezing space out of places where there seems to be none available.

The most explosive phase of urban growth has occurred within the last forty years as a result of migration, but many cities in the region began to experience an increase in growth in the late nineteenth century as improvements in sanitation and hygiene were reflected in declining mortality rates. By the beginning of the twentieth century, for instance, Istanbul had already begun to spread beyond the land walls that delimited the Byzantine-Ottoman city at the head of the Golden Horn. Today, the city's boundaries extend for miles along the Bosporus and along the European and Asian shores of the Sea of Marmara. Villages that in the 1950s still retained a distinctive identity now remain only as names on a map, submerged beneath a tidal wave of immigrants. The construction during the 1980s of two bridges across the Bosporus, linking Europe and Asia, symbolized the emergence of this new "greater" metropolitan Istanbul.

Cairo, which at the beginning of the nineteenth century had a population of around 250,000, had grown to a city of 1 million people by the mid-1930s. By 1960 the city's population had reached 3.5 million and by 1970 more than 5 million. Today, there are by more conservative estimates 12 million residents and by less conservative estimates 16 million residents of Greater Cairo. Put slightly differently, in the past forty years, Cairo has added to its population three cities comparable to the one that existed in 1960. The boundaries of today's city extend far into the desert, and the government has constructed new "satellite" cities in a desperate attempt to keep pace with the housing and employment needs of recent immigrants. Within the city, planners have elected to build elevated highways through neighborhoods, facilitating movement between the new, upscale residential suburbs on the city's

periphery and the banks, offices, and ministries in the center (Denis, 1997:9). Older neighborhoods near the center have been cleared away to make room for modern luxury apartments, conference centers, and five-star hotels, and the former residents relocated in public housing projects. Despite the dislocation and disruption that this entails in daily living and working arrangements, the government's efforts to transform and "improve" the appearance of the city are matched by the practices and resolve of those who have been relocated, who reconstruct the housing the state has built for them by illegally erecting partitions, adding balconies, and creating new public and private spaces to suit their needs (Ghannam, 1997:17–20).

Clearly, the pace of urbanization has overwhelmed planners. Traffic congestion, lack of services, loss of amenities and open space, air pollution, inadequate water supply, and overloaded sewage treatment systems have become an all-too-familiar experience in many cities. Perhaps only in Saudi Arabia and the Gulf states, where preexisting urban populations were smaller and where infrastructure costs and housing subsidies could be more easily absorbed, have planners been successful in imposing order on the pattern of urban growth. Elsewhere, most attempts at long-range planning have foundered as planners and politicians have tried to cope with the immediate needs of a rapidly growing population.

Even short-term government efforts to keep pace have frequently fallen short, most conspicuously in the lack of adequate low-income housing for urban migrants. Many newcomers to the cities live in "temporary" housing,

The Cairo-Giza metropolis is home to between
12 and 16 million people and continues to expand rapidly.

often referred to as squatter settlements. By one estimate there are more than 100 *ashwa'iyyat* (spontaneous communities) housing more than 6 million people in Greater Cairo (Bayat and el-Gawhary, 1997:5–6). In Turkey such spontaneous settlements are called *gecekondus*—literally, "placed there at night"—reflecting the speed with which houses are illegally erected on vacant land. By some estimates, more than 50 percent of Istanbul's population lived in such areas in the 1980s. For those of us who see such settlements only from the outside, Latife Tekin's compelling novel *Berji Kristin: Tales from the Garbage Hills* (1996) conveys some sense of what life must be like in a squatter settlement on the edge of Istanbul, the experiences, the fears, the rumors, the wind, and the dust.

Although governments have on occasion attempted to demolish illegal settlements, a more popular approach has been periodically to offer construction pardons and provide title to land. Over time, therefore, many of these squatter settlements have acquired legal status and have become functionally and administratively integrated into the urban fabric. Makeshift houses have been replaced by more permanent residences and modest apartment blocks. Thus, temporary housing has been transformed into a more permanent feature of most large Middle Eastern cities, with numerous local variations such as Cairo's City of the Dead, where families have taken over the aboveground tombs for housing. In these new neighborhoods, where public services remain inadequate, residents often organize themselves or seek assistance from nongovernmental or religious organizations to pave streets, install water lines, organize garbage collection, establish a health clinic, or start a bus service. Neighborhood self-help and improvement associations play an important, albeit often unacknowledged role in transforming neighborhoods and nurturing a sense of community and identity among recent migrants to the city. Thus, for many urban residents, the neighborhood still constitutes the most important element, both spatially and socially, in their conception of the city.

▧ Conclusion

In his essay "Geography Is Everywhere," Denis Cosgrove writes about what he sees as "the real magic of geography—the sense of wonderment at the human world, the joy of seeing and reflecting upon the richly variegated mosaic of human life and of understanding the elegance of its expression in the human landscape" (Cosgrove, 1985:120). We hope that this chapter reflects that rich mosaic and conveys a sense of interconnectedness: the ways in which water links politics, economy, and religion; the ways in which cities are shaped both by global (trading connections, colonial experiences, labor migration, flows of capital) and local practices and imaginings; and the ways in which species, water, people, goods, capital, and ideas move

across political boundaries. We would also like to emphasize the connections that places have with their pasts (Massey, 1995). By this we mean not simply the ways in which the past is present materially in the present-day landscape of the Middle East, but the ways in which the past may be present in the memories of people and in the conscious and unconscious constructions of the histories of places (Massey, 1995:187).

All of this suggests that we need to think about borderlessness as much as we do about borders in terms of understanding people's knowledge and experience of place. Connections between past and present and the absence of boundaries are brilliantly evoked in Amitav Ghosh's *In an Antique Land: History in the Guise of a Traveler's Tale* (1994), in which the writer, a Hindu researcher from India, reconstructs the journey and experience of a former Indian slave who, early in the twelfth century, had traveled to Cairo on behalf of Abraham Ben Yiju, a Jewish trader from Tunisia living in Mangalore. At one level, the writer parallels the slave's journey, traveling to Tunisia and Egypt, living with a Muslim family in a small village outside Cairo, and learning a form of spoken Arabic that later proved helpful in reading medieval documents. At another level, the research, based on the "Geniza Documents" (letters and other items found in the *geniza,* or storeroom, of a Cairo synagogue) "bears witness to a pattern of movement so fluent and far-reaching that they make the journeys of later medieval travelers, such as Marco Polo and Ibn Battuta seem unremarkable in comparison" (Ghosh, 1994:157).

As the letters between Ben Yiju and other merchants indicate, travel between Morocco, Egypt, Syria, Yemen, and India, although not free of risk (one letter describes how a merchant had been captured by pirates off the coast of Gujarat), was frequent and regular. Here is a very different construction of the geography of the region. Looking at today's political map and the divided world of the Middle East, it is very hard for us to step back and imagine the possibility of a world in which frontiers were not clearly or precisely defined, a place where Muslims and Jews and Christians traveled freely and crossed paths frequently in the course of everyday life and commerce. S. D. Goitein describes this period, roughly from the tenth through the thirteenth centuries, as the High Middle Ages when the Mediterranean area "resembled a free-trade community [in which] the treatment of foreigners, as a rule, was remarkably liberal" (Goitein, 1967:66). Goitein notes that, with few exceptions, the hundreds of documents and letters in the Geniza archive describing travels to or in foreign countries "have nothing to say about obstacles put in the way of the traveler for political reasons" (Goitein, 1967:59).

Not only merchants and traders but also artisans, scholars, and craftspeople were involved in this "continuous coming and going." Add to this the many Muslims making the hajj (pilgrimage to Mecca). Until the advent of the steamship in the nineteenth century, most hajjis traveled to Mecca with one of the great overland caravans that set out each year from Cairo,

Paintings on the outside wall of this house in
Luxor, Upper Egypt, indicate the owner has made
the hajj (pilgrimage) to Mecca, Saudi Arabia.

Damascus, or Baghdad. But even in the fifteenth and sixteenth centuries,
caravans could consist of several thousand camels, hundreds of horses, and
30,000 to 40,000 people (Peters, 1994), giving some sense of the large numbers of people involved. In earlier centuries, the round-trip journey could
take several years for people from North and West Africa, China, and Southeast Asia. From India, the seventeenth-century pilgrim Safi ibn Wali Qazvini
spent a year getting to and from Mecca (Pearson, 1994:45–46). Like other
literate pilgrims, Qazvini wrote an account of his travels that was intended at
least in part as a guide for others, providing a wealth of details about the pilgrimage route and practical information about rest stations, watering points,
and the costs of purchasing supplies.

The hajj is still an extraordinary undertaking for many Muslims in terms
of both logistics and financing. But for the two million who now make the
hajj each year, the same sort of information contained in Qazvini's narrative,
together with visa application forms, is to be found on the Internet. And
once again, through such experiences as the hajj, local places and communities are linked to and become part of the world beyond. Tourists traveling
along the Nile may be surprised to see paintings of jumbo jets adorning the

mud brick walls of humble houses. Here is a poignant and elegant reminder of the significance of the hajj in the lives of these villagers, conveyed in a tradition that has evolved over the past century whereby the experience of a lifetime—circling the Ka'bah, praying at Ararat, and making a joyful homecoming—is graphically captured and portrayed in folk art and architecture (Parker and Neal, 1995).

In contemporary atlases, the Middle East is usually divided up into a familiar mosaic of nation-states, each nation with its distinctive color like detachable pieces of a jigsaw puzzle. Benedict Anderson (1991:6–7) sees nations as "imagined political communities" in the sense that members of the nation do not know most of their fellow members yet imagine themselves part of a broader community sharing a deep sense of fraternity and comradeship. For Anderson, the "map-as-logo" contributes to this imaginative process, not least because as "this 'jig-saw' effect became normal, each 'piece' could be wholly detached from its geographic context" (Anderson, 1991:175). Our desire is that this chapter will encourage people to explore what lies beneath the surface of the map, to reconnect the map with its geographic context, to ask critical questions about how our maps and knowledge of the region have been constituted, and to imagine alternative geographies.

▥ Notes

We would like to express particular thanks to Kay Ebel and Zjaleh Hajibashi for their helpful comments on an early version of this chapter.

1. B.C.E., Before the Common Era, is viewed by non-Christians as a more neutral term for marking history than B.C., Before Christ.

2. C.E., or Common Era, is a neutral term for A.D. (Anno Domini, or Year of our Lord).

▥ Bibliography

Abou-Saif, Laila. 1990. *Middle East Journal: A Woman's Journey into the Heart of the Arab World.* New York: Charles Scribner and Sons.

Abu-Lughod, Janet. 1971. *Cairo: 1001 Years of the City Victorious.* Princeton: Princeton University Press.

———. 1987. "The Islamic City—Historic Myth, Islamic Essence, and Contemporary Relevance." *International Journal of Middle Eastern Studies* 19:155–176.

Anderson, Benedict. 1991. *Imagined Communities.* London and New York: Verso Books.

Bayat, Asef, and Karim el-Gawhary (eds.). 1997. "Cairo: Power, Poverty and Urban Sprawl." *Middle East Report* 202:2–30.

Benvenisti, Meron. 1996. *City of Stone: The Hidden History of Jerusalem.* Trans. by Maxine Kauffman Nunn. Berkeley: University of California Press.

Blake, Gerald, John Dewdney, and Jonathan Mitchell. 1987. *The Cambridge Atlas of the Middle East and North Africa.* Cambridge and New York: Cambridge University Press.

Bozdocan, Sibel. 1994. "Architecture, Modernism and Nation-Building in Kemalist Turkey." *New Perspectives on Turkey* 10:37–55.

Çelik, Zeynep. 1986. *The Remaking of Istanbul.* Seattle and New York: University of Washington Press.

Chirol, V. 1903. *The Middle East Question, or Some Political Problems of Indian Defence.* London: John Murray.

Cosgrove, Denis. 1985. "Geography Is Everywhere: Culture and Symbolism in Human Landscapes." Pp. 118–135 in Derek R. Gregory and Rex Walford (eds.), *Horizons in Human Geography.* London: Macmillan.

Denis, Eric. 1997. "Urban Planning and Growth in Cairo." *Middle East Report* 202: 8–12.

Drysdale, Alasdair, and Gerald Blake. 1985. *The Middle East and North Africa: A Political Geography.* New York and Oxford: Oxford University Press.

Fromkin, David. 1991. "How the Modern Middle East Map Came to Be Drawn." *Smithsonian* 22, no. 2:132–148.

Ghannam, Fara. 1997. "Relocation and the Use of Urban Space in Cairo." *Middle East Report* 202:17–20.

Ghosh, Amitav. 1994. *In an Antique Land: History in the Guise of a Traveler's Tale.* New York: Vintage Books.

Gleick, Peter H. 1994. "Water, War and Peace in the Middle East." *Environment* 36, no. 3:6–15, 35–42.

Goitein, S. D. 1967. *A Mediterranean Society: Economic Foundations.* Berkeley: University of California Press.

al-Hariri. 1898. *The Assemblies of al Hariri: Translated from the Arabic, with an Introduction and Notes Historical and Grammatical,* by Thomas Chenery. London: Williams and Norgate.

Jacobsen, Thorkild, and Robert M. Adams. 1958. "Salt and Silt in Ancient Mesopotamian Agriculture." *Science* 128, no. 3334:1251–1258.

Keleş, Ruşen, and Geoffrey Payne. 1984. "Turkey." Pp. 165–197 in Martin Wynn (ed.), *Planning and Urban Growth in Southern Europe.* London and New York: Mansell.

Lewis, Bernard. 1989. "The Map of the Middle East: A Guide for the Perplexed." *American Scientist* 58, no. 1:19–38.

Libiszewski, Stephan. 1995. *Water Disputes in the Jordan Basin Region and Their Role in the Resolution of the Arab-Israeli Conflict.* Zurich: Center for Security Studies and Conflict Research.

MacDougall, Elisabeth B., and Richard Ettinghausen (eds.). 1976. *The Islamic Garden.* Washington, D.C.: Dumbarton Oaks Trustees for Harvard University.

Manners, Ian R. 1974. "Problems of Water Resource Management in a Semi-Arid Environment: The Case of Irrigation Agriculture in the Central Jordan Valley." Pp. 95–114 in B. S. Hoyle (ed.), *Spatial Aspects of Development.* London: John Wiley & Sons.

———. 1990. "The Middle East." Pp. 39–66 in Gary A. Klee (ed.), *World Systems of Traditional Resource Management.* New York: Halstead Press.

Massey, Doreen. 1995. "Places and Their Pasts." *History Workshop Journal* 39: 182–192.

Massey, Doreen, and Pat Jess (eds.). 1995. *A Place in the World? Places, Cultures, and Globalization.* Oxford: Oxford University Press for the Open University.

Mitchell, Timothy. 1988. *Colonising Egypt.* Cambridge and New York: Cambridge University Press.

Parker, Ann, and Avon Neal. 1995. *Hajj Paintings: Folk Art of the Great Pilgrimage.* Washington and London: Smithsonian Institution Press.

Parmenter, Barbara. 1994. *Giving Voice to Stones: Place and Identity in Palestinian Literature.* Austin: University of Texas Press.

———. 1996. "Endangered Wetlands and Environmental Management in North Africa." Pp. 155–174 in Will D. Swearingen and Abdellatif Bencherifa (eds.), *The North African Environment at Risk.* Boulder, Colo.: Westview Press.

Pearson, M. N. 1994. *Pious Passengers: The Hajj in Earlier Times.* London: C. Hurst.

Peters, F. E. 1994. *The Hajj: The Muslim Pilgrimage to Mecca and the Holy Places.* Princeton: Princeton University Press.

Ramsar Convention Bureau. 2003. *Contracting Parties to Ramsar Convention on Wetlands, as of 20 January 2003. Key Documents of the Ramsar Convention.* www.ramsar.org/key_cp_e.htm.

Schimmel, Annemarie. 1985. "The Water of Life." *Environmental Design* 2:6–9.

Shapiro, Haim. 2002. "For the Birds." *Jerusalem Post,* November 1, Features section, p. 20.

Smith, Gordon C. 1968. "The Emergence of the Middle East." *Journal of Contemporary History* 3, no. 3:3–17.

Swearingen, Will D. 1987. *Moroccan Mirages: Agrarian Dreams and Deceptions, 1912–1986.* Princeton: Princeton University Press.

Tekin, Latife. 1996. *Berji Kristin: Tales from the Garbage Hills.* Trans. by Ruth Christie and Saliha Parker. London and New York: Marion Boyars.

UN. 1992. *Demographic Yearbook.* New York: United Nations.

White, Gilbert. 1988. "The Environmental Effects of the High Dam at Aswan." *Environment* 30, no. 7:4–11, 34–40.

Wolf, Aaron T. 1995. "International Water Dispute Resolutions: The Middle East Multilateral Working Group on Water Resources," *Water International* 20, no. 3:141–150.

———. 2000. "Hydrostrategic Territory in the Jordan Basin." Pp. 63-120 in Hussain A. Amery and Aaron T. Wolf (eds.), *Water in the Middle East: A Geography of Peace.* Austin, Texas: University of Texas Press.

3

The Historical Context

Arthur Goldschmidt Jr.

History is the study of humanity's recorded past; that of the Middle East is the world's longest. In this area, many staple crops were first cultivated, most farm animals were first domesticated, and the earliest agricultural villages were founded. Here, too, were the world's oldest cities, the first governments and law codes, and the earliest ethical monotheistic systems. A crossroads for people and ideas, the Middle East has sometimes contained one state or a single culture, but usually it has split into competing fragments. During eras of internal cohesion and power, Middle Easterners controlled remote parts of Europe, Asia, and Africa. At times of dissension and weakness, however, they were invaded and ruled by outsiders. When they could not drive out the interlopers, they adjusted to them and subtly made their rulers adapt to their own ways. The interplay between invasion and accommodation is characteristic of the region. This chapter will summarize Middle East history: the ancient empires, the rise of Islam and its civilization, the area's subordination to European control, and its struggle for political independence.

▩ The Ancient Middle East

Environment has shaped much of the region's history. As polar ice caps receded and rainfall diminished, hunters and food gatherers had to find ways to control their sources of sustenance. Hunting and gathering as a way of life died out in the Middle East some 5,000 years ago, giving way to pastoral nomadism and settled agriculture. Archaeologists have found the world's oldest farming villages in northeastern Africa and in the highlands of Asia Minor.

Many people migrated to the Nile, Euphrates, and Tigris river valleys, where they learned how to tame the annual floods to water their fields.

As grain cultivation spread, farmers improved their implements and pottery. They needed governments to organize the building of dams, dikes, and canals for large-scale irrigation, to regulate water distribution, and often to protect farmers from invading herders. Although the nomads at times served the settled people as merchants and soldiers, they also pillaged their cities and farms. Even though sedentary farmers and nomadic herders often fought against each other, they and the city dwellers built the civilizations of the Middle East.

The first states based on agriculture were the kingdoms of the Upper and Lower Nile, conjoined around 3000 B.C.E. to form Egypt, and the kingdom of Sumer, which had arisen a bit earlier in Mesopotamia, the land between the Euphrates and the Tigris rivers. Both developed strong monarchies supported by elaborate bureaucracies, codes of conduct, and religious doctrines that integrated the government system into a cosmological order. Their rulers marshaled large workforces to protect the lands from floods and invaders. A complex division of labor facilitated the development of writing, calculation, architecture, metallurgy, and hydraulic engineering.

Semitic and Indo-Iranian Invasions

The river states were disrupted and partially transformed by outside infiltrators and invaders. Sumer was conquered by peoples who spoke Semitic languages, producing Babylonia, which reached its height during the reign of the lawgiver Hammurabi (r. 1792–1750 B.C.E.). Meanwhile, Indo-European invaders from the north mixed with local peoples in Anatolia and Persia and introduced the horse into the region. The horse-drawn chariot enabled the Hyksos, another Semitic people, to occupy the Nile Delta from 1720 to 1570 B.C.E. The Babylonians absorbed their invaders, but the Egyptians expelled theirs and extended their empire into Syria.

Internal dissension and external pressures finally weakened Egypt and Babylonia, leading to a bewildering series of invasions and emerging states around 1000 B.C.E. As the Middle East's climate grew drier, Semitic peoples, including the Phoenicians and the Hebrews, migrated from the Arabian Desert into the better-watered lands of Syria and Mesopotamia. The Phoenicians of Syria's coast became the ancient world's main mariners, traders, and colonizers. They also invented the phonetic alphabet. Under King David, who ruled in the early tenth century B.C.E., the Hebrews set up a kingdom in Palestine, with its capital at Jerusalem; later this state split and fell to mighty conquerors. The Hebrews developed a faith in one God, who according to the Bible appeared to Moses on Mount Sinai and later to the prophets. Elements of this ethical monotheism had existed in earlier Middle Eastern religions,

Deborah J. Gerner

The Great Sun Temple of Abu Simbel was constructed along the banks of the Upper Nile, 50 miles north of the border with Sudan, during the reign of the Egyptian pharaoh Ramses II (thirteenth century B.C.E.).

but the Hebrews' ideas, crystallized in Judaism, profoundly shaped the intellectual history of both the Middle East and the West.

As people learned how to forge iron tools and weapons, they could form larger and longer-lasting empires. About 1350 B.C.E., Babylonia gave way to Assyria, centered in northern Mesopotamia. At its height (around 700 B.C.E.), Assyria ruled Syria and even Egypt. Its Semitic successor, Chaldea, upheld Babylon's glory for another century. Then Mesopotamia—indeed the whole Middle East—came under the rule of Persia's King Cyrus (r. 550–529).

From Cyrus's reign to modern times, the political history of the Middle East has centered on the rise and fall of successive multinational empires: Persia, Greece, Rome, the Arabs, the Seljuk Turks, the Mongols, and the Ottomans. Like Babylon, most of these empires were formed by outside invasions. External rule stirred up local resistance forces that eventually sapped the rulers' strength, causing the states to break up and fall prey to new invaders. Often the conquerors adopted the institutions and beliefs of their Middle Eastern subjects; rarely could they impose their own uniformly.

The Persian empire of Cyrus and his heirs, the Achaemenids, was the prototype of this multicultural system. Sprawling from the Indus Valley to the Nile, the empire could not make its subjects think and act alike. Instead, it accepted their beliefs and practices so long as they obeyed its laws, paid their taxes, and sent men to the Persian army. The provincial governors, or satraps, were given broad civil, judicial, and fiscal powers by the Persian emperor. A feudal landownership system kept the local aristocrats loyal, and a postal system and road network—along with a uniform coinage, calendar, and administrative language—also helped to unite the empire. Achaemenid Persia survived two centuries before it fell to Alexander the Great.

Greek and Roman Rule

Alexander's whirlwind conquest of the Middle East between 332 and 323 B.C.E. marks a critical juncture in the area's history. For the next millennium it belonged to the Hellenistic world. Alexander wanted to fuse Greek culture with that of the Middle East, taking ideas, institutions, and administrators from the Egyptians, Mesopotamians, and Persians. This fusion did not occur in his lifetime, nor was it ever complete, but from Alexander to Muhammad the Mediterranean world and the Middle East shared a common civilization. The centers of its cultural blending were the coastal cities, of which the greatest was Alexandria. Alexander's descendants in Egypt, the Ptolemies, ruled the country for three centuries. They erected monumental buildings, such as the Alexandria Lighthouse, one of the seven wonders of the ancient world, and the Alexandria Museum, or academy of scholars, which housed the largest library in antiquity.

Southern Anatolia, Syria, and Mesopotamia were ruled for two centuries by the Seleucids, who were the descendants of one of Alexander's generals. In the third century B.C.E., the Seleucids lost control of their eastern lands to another dynasty descended from some of Alexander's soldiers, and Persia regained its independence as Parthia.

Meanwhile, a new state was rising farther west: Rome. Having taken Carthage, Macedonia, and Greece by 100 B.C.E., the Roman legions marched eastward, conquering Asia Minor, Syria, and Egypt. Once again most of the Middle East was united under an ecumenical empire; only Persia and part of Mesopotamia were ruled by Parthia. Like earlier states, Rome absorbed much from its Middle Eastern subjects, including several religions, two of which, Mithraism and Christianity, vied for popular favor throughout the Roman Empire. Christianity finally won. After his conversion, the Emperor Constantine (r. 306–337 C.E.) moved the capital—and Rome's economic and cultural center—to Byzantium, renamed Constantinople. But the city gave its old name to Rome's successor state, the Byzantine Empire.

Under Roman rule, commercial cities flourished. Syrian and Egyptian merchants grew rich from the trade between Europe, Asia, and eastern Africa. Arab camel nomads, or bedouin, prospered as carriers of cloth and spices. Other Middle Easterners navigated the Red Sea, the Gulf, and the Indian Ocean. But Roman rule was enforced by a large occupying army, and grain-producing Syria and Egypt were taxed heavily. Rome's leaders

One of the most impressive Roman ruins in the
Middle East is at Baalbek, in the northern Bekaa Valley
of Lebanon. This temple was completed around 150 C.E.

did not always tolerate their subjects' beliefs. Roman soldiers destroyed the
Jewish temple in Jerusalem, and many of Jesus's early followers were mar-
tyred. Christian Rome proved even less tolerant. Many Christians in North
Africa and Egypt espoused heterodox beliefs that the emperors viewed as
treasonous. Their efforts to suppress heresy alienated many of their Middle
Eastern subjects in the fifth and sixth centuries of the common era.

Rome (and later Byzantium) had one major rival: Persia. There the Parth-
ians gave way in the third century C.E. to the Sassanid dynasty. Bolstered by a
powerful military aristocracy and the resources of many Hellenized religious
refugees from Byzantium, Sassanid Persia threatened Byzantine rule in the
Middle East. Early in the seventh century, the Sassanids briefly overran
Syria, Palestine, and Egypt. The Hellenistic era of Middle Eastern history
was coming to an end.

The Islamic Middle East as an Autonomous System

The revelation of Islam to an unlettered Meccan merchant in the early seventh
century, the unification of hitherto feuding Arab tribes under this new religion,
the rapid conquest of the Middle East and North Africa, the conversion of
millions of Asians and Africans to Islam, and the development of Islamic
civilization under a succession of empires marked a new epoch. Egyptians,

Deborah J. Gerner

Located just south of Amman, Jordan, the town of Madaba
is home to beautiful mosaics dating from the Byzantine era.

Syrians, and Persians influenced the beliefs of their Arab conquerors just as
they had transformed and absorbed earlier invaders. Yet the rise of Islam
led to new ideas and institutions, monuments and memories, which continue to affect Middle Eastern peoples profoundly.

The Arabs Before Islam

Once the camel had been domesticated around 3000 B.C.E., bands of people
began roaming the Arabian Peninsula in search of water and forage for their
flocks. These early Arabs composed poems that embodied their code of values: bravery in battle, patience in misfortune, persistence in revenge, protection of the weak, defiance of the strong, loyalty to the tribe, hospitality to the
guest, generosity to the needy, and fidelity in carrying out promises. These
were the virtues people needed to survive in the desert. Their poems, recited
from memory, expressed the joys and sorrows of nomadic life, hailed the
bravery of their heroes, lauded their own tribes, and lampooned their rivals.
Even now Arabs recite these poems and often repeat their precepts.

In Roman times the southern Arabs played a larger role in the world;
they developed Yemen, colonized Ethiopia, and crossed the Indian Ocean.
The northern Arabs were relatively isolated. Some adopted Judaism or Christianity, but most practiced animism (the belief that every object, whether

animate or inanimate, has a spirit). One of their tribes, the Quraysh, built a shrine, the Ka'ba, at a small desert city called Mecca on the main trade route between Syria and Yemen. Once a year, the pagan tribes of northwestern Arabia suspended their quarrels to make pilgrimages to the Ka'ba, which housed idols representing tribal deities.

Muhammad

In Mecca, around 570, one of the world's greatest religious leaders, Muhammad, was born to a minor branch of the Quraysh. Orphaned as a child, Muhammad was reared by an uncle as a caravan trader. Upon reaching manhood, he became the agent for a rich merchant widow, Khadija, whom he married. Until he was forty, Muhammad was simply a Meccan trader. But he was troubled by the widening gulf between the accepted Arab virtues of bravery and generosity and the blatantly acquisitive practices of Mecca's business leaders. Often he went to a hill near Mecca to meditate.

One day in the Arab month of Ramadan, Muhammad heard a voice exhorting him to recite. Despite his protest that he could not read, the voice (later identified as the Angel Gabriel) ordered him to testify to the existence of a creator-god, called Allah, to proclaim God's existence to the Arabs, and to warn them of an imminent judgment day when all people would be called to account for what they had done. As he received new revelations, he began to share them in the community. Those who accepted Muhammad's message called themselves Muslims and their religion Islam, or submission to the will of God, the creator and sustainer.

Muhammad's public recitation of his revelations disturbed the Meccan leaders. If the Arabs accepted Islam, would they stop their annual pilgrimages to the Ka'ba, so lucrative to local merchants? Why did God reveal his message to Muhammad, rather than to one of the rich and powerful Quraysh leaders? The pagan Meccans persecuted the Muslims. After Muhammad's uncle and protector died, they could no longer live in Mecca. Finally, the Arabs of Medina, a city north of Mecca, asked Muhammad to arbitrate their tribal disputes and accepted Islam as the condition for his coming there.

The *hijra* (emigration) of Muhammad and his followers from Mecca is for Muslims the crucial event in history. The Muslim calendar begins in the year it occurred, 622 C.E., for it was in Medina that Muhammad formed the Islamic *umma* (a community ruled by a divine plan). Politics and religion are united in Islam; God, speaking to humanity through Muhammad, is the supreme lawgiver. Thus the Prophet became a political leader and, when the Meccans tried to destroy the *umma,* a military commander as well. Buttressed by their faith, the Muslims of Medina defeated Meccan armies larger and stronger than their own, converted most of the pagan Arab tribes, and finally won Mecca over to Islam. In 630 Muhammad made a triumphal pilgrimage to the Ka'ba, smashed its pagan idols, and declared it a Muslim shrine. Two years later, having united much of Arabia under Islam, he died.

Islamic Beliefs and Institutions

Muslims believe in one God, all-powerful and all-knowing, who has no partner and no offspring. God has spoken to a succession of human messengers, of whom the last was Muhammad. To the Jewish prophets God imparted the Torah, and to Jesus and his disciples, the Gospels. Muslims believe that Jews and Christians corrupted their scriptures, so God sent a perfected revelation, the Quran, to Muhammad. Although Muslims regard the Quran as truer than the Bible in its present form, they do not deny any of God's prophets, honoring Abraham, Moses, and Jesus. Muslims also believe in a judgment day, when God will assess all people and consign them to Heaven or to Hell.

Muslim duties are summed up as the "five pillars of Islam": statement of belief in God and in Muhammad as his prophet; ritual prayer five times daily; fasting in the daylight hours of the month of Ramadan; payment of part of one's property or income to provide for the needy; and the pilgrimage to Mecca. Muslims also abstain from drinking alcoholic beverages, eating pork, gambling, and all licentious and dishonest acts. Standards of sexual morality are strict, limiting relations between men and women outside marriage. Muslims ascribe human misdeeds to ignorance or forgetfulness; God forgives those who repent.

Islam is a way of life. It prescribes how people relate to one another as well as their duties to God. Muhammad's *umma* aspired to serve as the ideal earthly setting in which believers could prepare for the judgment day. In the centuries after Muhammad's death, Muslim scholars *(ulama)* developed an elaborate legal code, the *sharia,* to regulate all aspects of human behavior. The *sharia* was derived from the Quran, the words and deeds of the Prophet (or those actions by his followers that he sanctioned), the consensus of the *umma,* analogical reasoning, and judicial opinion. Dynastic and doctrinal schisms soon divided the *umma;* however, the *sharia,* upheld by the *ulama,* united Muslims of diverse races, cultures, regions, and political allegiances.

The Right-Guided Caliphs and the Early Arab Conquests

When Muhammad died, his followers needed a new leader for the *umma,* although no one could succeed Muhammad as the Prophet, and Abu Bakr was chosen as the first caliph (successor). During his caliphate the Muslims won back the rebellious tribal Arabs and deflected their energies outward against Byzantium and Persia. Under Umar ibn al-Khattab, the second caliph, the Arabs routed armies mightier than their own, wresting Syria and Egypt from

Byzantine control and absorbing Sassanid Persia. The Arabs conquered most of the Middle East in a generation and much of the Old World in a century. Many Syrians, Egyptians, and Persians welcomed Arab rule as a respite from Byzantine intolerance and Sassanid exploitation. These subjects were forced neither to speak Arabic nor to become Muslims, although gradually some chose to do one or both. The new rulers, often called the right-guided caliphs, retained local administrative customs and languages and even the bureaucrats themselves; the Arabs lacked the numbers and the experience to govern their new empire unaided. Those males who did not convert were required to pay a head tax in return for exemption from military service. Jerusalem under Arab rule remained a religious center and pilgrimage site for Jews and Christians, as well as for Muslims.

Although Arab toleration of local customs promoted stability, the conquests strained the *umma* itself. The caliphs set aside some of the captured booty for charitable or communal use and put the troops on a payroll, but the sudden influx of wealth led to unrest. In 656 the third caliph, Uthman, was murdered. His friends suspected his successor, Ali (Muhammad's son-in-law), of aiding his assassination. Seeking revenge, Uthman's supporters fought Ali's backers in a battle that ended in a mediation that favored Uthman's cousin, Mu'awiya, the governor of Syria. He proceeded to name himself caliph, moved the capital to Damascus, pacified dissident Muslims, and made the caliphate hereditary in his own family, the Umayyad branch of the Quraysh tribe.

The Umayyad caliphs, who ruled in Damascus from 661 to 750, were more political than pious. They crushed their opponents and spread Arab rule to northern Africa and Spain, central Asia, and what is now Pakistan (see Map 3.1). Many Muslims resented the Umayyads. One of these dissidents was the prophet Muhammad's grandson and Ali's son, Husayn, who died during a revolt at Karbala (Iraq) in 680. Husayn's martyrdom led to a political and religious opposition movement known as Shi'ism. Even now Islam remains split between the Shi'a, who accept only Ali and his descendants as rightful leaders of the *umma,* and the Sunnis, who accept as legitimate the caliphs who actually ruled. Sunnis now outnumber Shi'a in most of the Muslim world, but Shi'ism dominates in Iran and plays a growing role in the politics of nearby Arab countries.

The First Islamic Empire

The Umayyads' power depended on their main fighting force, the Arab tribes, which the caliphs favored even after many non-Arabs converted to Islam. Some non-Arab Muslims joined revolutionary movements, often pro-Shi'a, against Umayyad rule. One such rebellion was led by the Abbasid family, who ousted the Umayyads in 750 and set up their own caliphate in Baghdad.

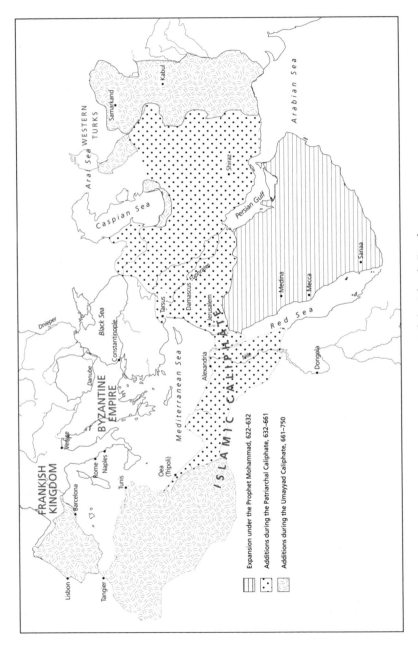

Map 3.1 Extent of the Islamic Empire

Expansion under the Prophet Mohammad, 622–632

Additions during the Patriarchal Caliphate, 632–661

Additions during the Umayyad Caliphate, 661–750

At this point, the *umma* ceased to be united, for the Umayyads kept control over Spain. The North African Berbers, tribal peoples who converted from Christianity and Judaism to Islam but did not accept Arab political dominance, soon cast off Abbasid rule. A Shi'i movement, the Fatimids, took power in Tunisia and later in Egypt. Elsewhere, ambitious governors, warlords, and religious leaders carved out their own states. Most Arabs reverted to nomadism or intermarried with their conquered peoples, many of whom had adopted the Arabic language and culture.

Despite its turbulent politics, the Abbasid era (which lasted at least nominally until 1258) was one of agricultural and commercial prosperity. As industry and trade flourished, so did science and letters. Rulers competed with one another to pay for the translation of scientific and philosophical works from Greek into Arabic, support court poets and historians, build mosques and palaces, and sponsor astronomical and medical research. Thus Muslims preserved and improved their classical patrimony, which they passed on to Europe, helping to spark the Renaissance.

Invasions from East and West

The large-scale influx of Turks from central Asia began in the tenth century. Some had already been imported as slave soldiers and bureaucrats for the Abbasid caliphs; others served the Abbasids or local Muslim rulers as frontier guards against non-Muslims farther east. Schooled in the arts of government and war, the Turkish *ghazi*s (border raiders) proved more reliable than the caliphs' other subjects and rose to positions of power.

One Turkish family serving a Persian dynasty earned an *iqta'*—land granted for military or administrative service to the state—in Ghazna (in what is now Afghanistan) around 960. This family, the Ghaznavids, built up an empire spanning eastern Persia, central Asia, and northern India. The Ghaznavids in turn gave *iqta's* to Turkish clans from central Asia. One of these, the Seljuks, proceeded to conquer lands westward across Persia and Mesopotamia and into Anatolia, where they defeated the Byzantines in 1071. The military gains of these families attracted other Turks to serve as *ghazi*s, opening the way for large-scale immigration of Turkish tribes with their horses, two-humped camels, sheep, and goats. Azerbaijan (northwestern Persia), northern Iraq, and much of Anatolia, highland areas that the Arabs had never taken, soon became mainly Turkish.

The Turks were devout Sunni Muslims who built new cities and refurbished old ones. They rescued the Abbasid caliph, who had been taken hostage by Shi'i bureaucrats, and restored his authority, although not his power. For several generations the caliph ruled in Baghdad beside a Seljuk sultan (holder of power). The Turks strengthened Sunni schools, promoted Sufism (organized Islamic mysticism), and limited reinterpretation of the *sharia.* Sufism involved Muslims more deeply in their faith but caused some to withdraw from worldly pursuits. Once Sunni Muslims could not revise the *sharia,* changing social needs led rulers and subjects to bypass it, and practices diverged ever further from Islamic precepts.

As Turkish nomads poured in from the East, a different group of invaders came from the West. In 1096 the pope proclaimed a Crusade to regain the Holy Land for Christianity. Muslims had ruled Jerusalem for more than four centuries without harming Christian interests, but the Seljuk invasion of Anatolia had weakened the Byzantine Empire and threatened the Christian pilgrimage routes to the Holy City. The Seljuks had started to disintegrate in 1092, and seven years later the Crusaders took coastal Syria and Palestine from divided and weak Muslim rulers. For almost a century, Jerusalem, purged of its Muslim and Jewish inhabitants, was the capital of a European Christian kingdom.

Outside Jerusalem, however, the Crusaders rarely uprooted the local population, and they never took the Muslim power centers: Cairo, Damascus, Aleppo, and Mosul. Once Egypt and Syria were united under a strong Sunni Muslim ruler, Saladin, the Muslims retook Jerusalem in 1187. The Crusaders held part of coastal Syria for another century and twice invaded the Nile Delta, but Saladin's descendants, the Ayyubids, kept them in check.

Far more harmful to the Middle East were the thirteenth-century invasions by the Mongols, who came from the lands north of China. Mongol armies led by Genghis Khan (r. 1206–1227) defeated weak Muslim rulers and conquered central Asia and eastern Persia. His grandson, Hülegü, pressed farther into Persia and Mesopotamia and in 1258 took Baghdad and wiped out the Abbasid caliphate. The Mongols were not Muslims. Horse nomads accustomed to grassy steppes, they saw no need for cities or the farmers who supported them. They destroyed irrigation works in Persia, Mesopotamia, and Syria, impoverishing the land and its people. Many Muslim rulers, even Anatolia's surviving Seljuks, became Mongol vassals. But in 1260 the Mongols failed to take Palestine and Egypt, where the Ayyubids had recently been overthrown by their Turkish slave soldiers, the Mamluks. The Mamluk rulers went on to build a prosperous empire in Egypt and Syria, the bulwark of Muslim power until their conquest by the Ottoman Turks in 1516–1517. Meanwhile, Persia's Mongol rulers soon adopted Islam, accepted Persian culture, and rebuilt much of what they had earlier destroyed.

The harnessing of gunpowder by Europe in the fourteenth century altered the West's relationship with the rest of the world. Firearms and long-distance sailing ships soon enabled Europeans to explore and conquer distant lands and finally to encircle the Muslim world. States using gunpowder as their main weapon require disciplined infantries rather than the feudal cavalries of the Middle Ages. The West's adoption of firearms engendered strong monarchies, a mercantile class, and eventually the Industrial Revolution. In the Middle East, some Muslim states learned how to use firearms, but others never did. The gunpowder revolution weakened the feudal landowners there, too, but failed to stimulate European-style modernization.

The Ottoman Empire

The Ottoman Empire was the archetypal Muslim state built on the use of firearms. From their humble origins in the thirteenth century as Turkish *ghazis* for the Seljuks, the Ottomans expanded their landholdings into an empire that stretched—at its height in the seventeenth century—from central Europe to the Gulf and from Algeria to Azerbaijan. Like most *ghazis*, the early Ottomans raided peasant lands on horseback. During the fourteenth and fifteen centuries, however, they developed a disciplined corps of professional foot soldiers, the famous janissaries, who used siege cannon and lighter firearms against the Europeans or their Muslim neighbors. The Ottoman state took boys as tribute from their Christian subjects. Converted to Islam, the boys were taught Turkish and Arabic and trained as soldiers or, less often, as administrators. As Ottoman sultan's slaves, the janissaries were forbidden to marry or to own land. They lived in barracks in order to be ready to fight whenever they were needed. This system of recruitment and training was called *devshirme,* as were, collectively, the Ottoman soldiers and bureaucrats it produced.

Backed by well-equipped armies and competent administrators, the Ottoman sultans, the first ten of whom were energetic and competent, conquered the Christian peoples of the Balkans and surrounded Constantinople. In 1453 they took the city and ended the 1,000-year-old Byzantine Empire. Once the world's greatest Christian city, Constantinople (now Istanbul) became a Muslim center. During the following century, the Ottomans subdued most of their Muslim neighbors, including the Mamluks of Egypt and Syria. Only the Persians, ruled after 1501 by the Safavids, remained independent, for they, too, learned to use firearms.

The first ten Ottoman sultans competed for the succession, supervised the bureaucracy, and led their troops into battle. Their rule, however, rested on two principles: (1) the ruling class's power was balanced between the landowning aristocrats and the *devshirme* soldiers and administrators; and (2) the subject peoples were organized into religious communities, called *millets,* that had autonomous control over their laws, schools, and welfare. These divisions strengthened the sultan. So long as he could play off the aristocracy against the *devshirme* class, both ruling groups performed their tasks as defenders and managers of the Ottoman Empire. The *millets* were self-sufficient but geographically scattered, unable to combine against their Ottoman overlords. These subjects looked to their communal leaders—rabbis, priests, and *ulama*—whose top members were named by and responsible to the sultan, to mediate between them and the government. For centuries, this political and social organization endured; even now, some Middle Easterners identify with their religion more than their nationality.

Of all the factors that weakened the Ottoman Empire, the most significant was the triumph of the *devshirme* bureaucrats and janissaries over the aristocracy. This happened under the greatest Ottoman sultan, Suleyman the Magnificent (r. 1520–1566), when he appointed a series of chief ministers who had risen from *devshirme* origins. Not checked by either the weaker succeeding sultans or the declining aristocracy, these former slaves used the Ottoman government to serve their own interests. Janissaries won the sultan's permission to leave the barracks, marry, buy property, and enroll their sons in the corps, which stopped training and degenerated into a hereditary, privileged caste. Military failure and corrupt government ensued. Taxes rose, especially for those unable to avoid paying them. Agrarian and commercial prosperity declined, partly because the trade routes between Asia and Europe shifted away from the Middle East. Once-loyal subjects rebelled against Ottoman misrule. By the late seventeenth century, the Ottoman Empire was no longer the scourge of Europe.

■ The Subordination of the Middle East to the West

During the eighteenth and nineteenth centuries, the West gained military, political, and economic superiority over the Middle East. Whereas Arabs and Turks had once mastered the routes between Europe and Asia, by 1800 Europe sold its manufactured goods to the Middle East in exchange for raw materials and agricultural products. Europeans in Muslim lands were exempted from local taxes and legal jurisdiction; this exemption was guaranteed by treaties called Capitulations. Whereas once the Mediterranean Sea and the Indian Ocean were controlled by Muslim navies, now European sailing ships dominated the high seas. Whereas once the Ottoman sultan could choose the time and place for an attack on Europe and could then dictate the peace terms, now his armies feared the mighty forces of Hapsburg Austria and czarist Russia. The greatest shock came when Napoleon occupied Egypt in 1798, for France had long been an Ottoman ally.

Westernizing Reforms

As early as the seventeenth century, some Ottoman sultans and their ministers saw the need for internal change. At first they regarded reform as the restoration of the institutions and practices that had made their empire strong in the past. But defeat by Western armies showed that conditions had altered, necessitating more drastic modifications. Reforms began in the military.

The Blue Mosque, built in the early seventeenth century for
Sultan Ahmet I, with its six minarets and numerous domes,
is among the finest examples of Ottoman architecture.

Sultan Selim III (r. 1789–1807) tried to set up a new army corps trained and equipped in the European fashion. The janissaries, afraid that these interlopers would take away their power, rebelled, destroyed the new corps, and deposed Selim. The conservative *ulama* and trade guilds blocked economic reforms. Even the introduction of printing was long opposed by the *ulama* and scribes, the former condemning innovation and the latter fearing the loss of their jobs.

The failure of early reform efforts taught Muslim rulers that change could not be confined to the military. Only by centering power in the state could they resist European expansion. Reform meant autocracy, not democracy. Three Middle Eastern reformers serve as examples: Muhammad Ali (r. 1805–1849) of Egypt, Sultan Mahmud II (r. 1808–1839) of the Ottoman Empire, and Nasir al-Din Shah (r. 1848–1896) of Persia. Each tried to concentrate power in his own hands; each became hamstrung by European actions serving imperialist interests.

The ablest was Muhammad Ali, an Ottoman officer commanding an Albanian regiment sent to Egypt. He took control of that Ottoman province after Napoleon's forces withdrew in 1801 and proceeded to eliminate every rival for power. He massacred the Mamluks and curbed the *ulama,* who had enjoyed special power and prestige in Egypt, by exploiting their rivalries and seizing the endowments that supported them. Advised and equipped by France, he built the region's strongest army and navy. He subordinated the rural aristocracy to the state by taking control of all farmland.

Under his rule, Egypt became the first Middle Eastern country to complete the change from subsistence to market agriculture. Tobacco, sugar, indigo, and cotton became Egypt's cash crops, earning revenues to fund his ambitious projects for industrial development and military expansion. The first non-Western ruler to recognize the Industrial Revolution, he set up textile mills and weapons factories, sent hundreds of his subjects to Europe for technical or military training, and imported European instructors to staff schools and military academies in Egypt. He even conscripted Egyptian farmers as soldiers. Officered by Turks, they became such a potent force that Muhammad Ali's son, Ibrahim, conquered Syria in 1832 and would have taken over the whole Ottoman Empire in 1839 if Britain had not intervened. Although the Ottoman Empire recognized Egypt's autonomy in 1841, Muhammad Ali felt that his ambitions had been thwarted and let his reforms lapse. However, his heirs ruled Egypt, with only nominal Ottoman control, up to the British occupation in 1882, and Egypt remained a monarchy until Farouk abdicated in 1952.

Muhammad Ali's Ottoman contemporary, Sultan Mahmud II, tried to reform his state but first had to destroy the janissary corps, the main obstacle to change. His efforts were hampered by the diversity and extent of his domains, local revolts, the lack of a loyal and trained bureaucracy, the Greek independence war (backed by Britain, France, and Russia), and the growing need of industrialized states to buy Ottoman raw materials and sell their own manufactures. Mahmud laid the groundwork for the great decree issued by his son and successor that began the Tanzimat (reorganization) era, one of intense centralization and Westernization. The Tanzimat alone could not block Russian expansion in the Balkans, so Britain and France helped the Ottomans defeat Russia in the Crimean War (1853–1856). The Europeans then made the Ottomans issue another decree that gave Christians and Jews legal equality with Muslims.

Persia was the only core Middle Eastern state never to fall under Ottoman rule. Its rulers' adherence to ancient Persian customs preserved a national identity. This was reinforced by their adherence to Shi'ism, whereas the Ottomans were Sunni Muslims. In the sixteenth and seventeenth centuries, Persia flourished under the Safavid shahs, who adorned their capital at Isfahan and formed commercial and diplomatic ties with the European countries needing allies against the Ottoman Empire.

Persia, too, declined. The Qajar dynasty (1794–1925) resisted dissolution from within and Russian and British encroachments from without. During the first three years of Nasir al-Din Shah's reign, his energetic chief minister began a series of military, financial, and educational reforms. But in 1851 the shah executed his minister, followed by new tribal and religious uprisings. Later on, Nasir al-Din began selling concessions to British investors and hiring Russian officers to train his army. Instead of reforming his government to protect Persia from foreigners, the shah let them take over. His subjects rejected his policies; a nationwide tobacco boycott made him cancel his most lucrative concession, and he was finally assassinated. Later Qajar shahs submitted to even more foreign interference.

European Imperialism in the Nineteenth Century

If Western power inspired Middle Eastern reform, European policies and actions kept it from succeeding. From 1815 to 1914, European governments preserved peace among themselves by keeping a balance of power. For the Middle East, this meant that neither Britain nor Russia could let the other become supreme. Fearing that breaking up the Ottoman Empire would give Russia control of the Balkans and of the straits linking the Black Sea to the Aegean, Britain usually tried to uphold the empire's territorial integrity. Thus the British led European opposition to Muhammad Ali's takeover of Ottoman Syria in 1839, Russia's occupation of the Romanian principalities in 1853 (which led to the Crimean War), and Russia's frequent efforts to exploit nationalism in the Balkans. Britain also backed reforms that would enable the Ottoman Empire to resist Russia, especially those during the Tanzimat era that promised equality to non-Muslims. By contrast, Russia's expansionist aims, its claim to protect the sultan's Orthodox Christian subjects, and its promotion of Balkan nationalist movements served to thwart Ottoman reform efforts.

While guarding its routes to India, Britain also vied with France for power in the eastern Mediterranean; it fought to expel Napoleon from Egypt and later to remove Muhammad Ali from Syria. Britain signed treaties with tribal leaders in the Gulf and occupied Aden in order to outflank Muhammad Ali and his French allies and to guard its sea route to India. A British company started steamship navigation on the Euphrates River in the 1830s; another built the first railroad from Alexandria to Cairo in 1851. But it was a French diplomat, Ferdinand de Lesseps, who won a concession from Egypt's viceroy to cut a canal across the Isthmus of Suez, joining the Red Sea to the Mediterranean and slashing travel time between Europe and southern Asia. Britain tried at first to block this mainly French project, but it became the Suez Canal's main user after it was opened in 1869. France expanded across North Africa, taking Algeria in a protracted war (1830–1847) and establishing protectorates over Tunisia in 1881 and Morocco in 1912. A mainly Christian part of Syria became an international protectorate as the "autonomous governorate of Mount Lebanon" from 1864 to 1914.

The Middle Eastern Reaction to the West

By the 1860s some Middle Easterners were wondering whether Westernization had gone too far. In the Ottoman Empire, a few Muslims adopted pan-
Islam, the idea that all Muslims should unite behind the sultan to counter
outside threats and the divisive nationalist movements of non-Muslim
Balkan subjects. Pan-Islam reaffirmed the tradition of Muslims uniting to
defend the *umma,* but this doctrine took on a new meaning: the Ottoman
sultan claimed for himself the caliphate, hence the allegiance of all Muslims, regardless of who actually ruled them. Because Britain, France, and
Russia all had Muslim subjects within their empires, Europeans soon saw
the fearsome potential of pan-Islam.

Westernizing reforms, especially in education and military training, led
to the growth of liberal and nationalist movements among young Egyptians,
Ottomans, Arabs, Persians, and Tunisians. These new groups challenged
their rulers' monopoly on power and called for constitutional government.
None wholly succeeded.

The Beginnings of Egyptian Nationalism

Muhammad Ali's grandson, Isma'il (r. 1863–1879), adopted new Westernizing reforms and secured Egypt's autonomy from the Ottoman Empire. He
sent explorers to find the sources of the Nile River and army expeditions to
conquer the Red Sea coast and the southern Sudan. Sections of Cairo and
Alexandria were transformed by broad boulevards, parks, gardens, and
mansions. Factories and public works built up the economy as a cotton
boom caused by a drop in US exports during the Civil War, the growing
availability of European capital, and the construction of the Suez Canal
made Egypt an attractive field for investment.

Egypt's economy skyrocketed, but so did Isma'il's problems. In 1866
he convened a representative assembly to advise his regime and impose
new taxes. Timid at first but later incited by a burgeoning press, this new
body began calling for constitutional government. Isma'il borrowed vast
sums from foreign banks to cover his expenditures. Unable to repay his
debts, he sold his government's Suez Canal shares to Britain, accepted
British and French control over Egypt's finances, and finally admitted representatives of these two creditor states into his cabinet. Egyptians resented
these changes. The assembly demanded a council of ministers responsible to
itself and purged of Europeans, control of the government's budget, and an
end to the economies that harmed many Egyptians. In 1879 Isma'il dismissed his "European cabinet" and named one that heeded the assembly's
call for constitutional government. The European powers ordered the Ottoman sultan to replace Isma'il with his son, Tawfiq.

Tawfiq obediently purged his regime of dissidents and tried to pay back some of his father's debts. But many Egyptians, harmed by European meddling, demanded independence. Their main backers were Egyptian army officers led by Colonel Urabi, who founded Egypt's first nationalist movement. In 1881, Urabi's troops surrounded the palace and called for a new cabinet responsible to an elected parliament. Tawfiq gave in, and soon Egypt had a constitution. Nationalism's triumph was brief; its leaders were split, the Europeans threatened to intervene, and Tawfiq turned against the nationalists. Landing in Alexandria, British troops invaded the Suez Canal, defeated Urabi, and occupied Cairo.

When Britain occupied Egypt in 1882, it promised to pull its troops out as soon as order was restored to the country. It was easy to defeat the nationalists and prop Tawfiq back on his throne. It was harder to remedy the causes of Egypt's disorder: huge debts, a peasantry burdened by high taxes, and a revolt in Sudan. The longer Britain stayed on to tackle Egypt's problems, the harder it was to leave. A skilled administrator, Lord Cromer, became Britain's diplomatic representative in Cairo. Backed by British troops, he reformed Egypt's finances and administration and gradually became its ruler in all but name.

Although the country prospered, British advisers sapped the authority of the Egyptian ministers. The British claimed to be preparing the Egyptians for self-rule, but in fact Egypt became a training ground for British colonial administrators. The extension of irrigation under British rule was not paralleled by expanded education or industrial development. After Tawfiq was succeeded by his son Abbas in 1892, a cabal of young Egyptians helped Abbas thwart Cromer's power. Their spokesman, a young lawyer named Mustafa Kamil, founded the National Party. The Nationalists urged Britain to withdraw its forces from Egypt and later demanded a new constitution. Cromer ignored them, but his successor promised to hasten Egypt's progress toward self-rule. Mustafa Kamil died prematurely in 1908, and his followers split between the moderate reformers and the radical pan-Islamists. A more repressive British policy forced the leaders into exile. After World War I began, Britain deposed Abbas, declared a protectorate, and severed Egypt's ties with the Ottoman Empire.

Liberalism and Nationalism Within the Ottoman Empire

As the Tanzimat era wound down, a group of Westernized Turkish intellectuals and army officers known as the New Ottomans called for a constitution that would limit the sultan's autocracy. In 1876, amid Balkan revolts, growing state indebtedness to Europe, and threats of a Russian invasion, an officers' coup placed a liberal sultan on the throne. He was soon replaced by Abdülhamid II, who proclaimed a constitution in December of that year to forestall a Russian attempt to break up his empire. For about a year, the Ottoman Empire had a popularly elected parliament. But when Russia invaded the Balkans and threatened to take Istanbul, Abdülhamid closed parliament and suspended the constitution. For thirty years the sultan further centralized state control and stifled Ottoman liberal and nationalist movements. A group of Westernized students and army officers, convinced that the empire could survive only as a constitutional monarchy, formed the Committee of Union and Progress, or the Young Turks. In 1908 they forced the sultan to restore the 1876 Constitution and hold elections; in 1909, after an abortive countercoup, they deposed him. But the Young Turk regime soon became a military junta. As Balkan revolts and Western imperialism took one Ottoman province after another, the leaders espoused Turkish nationalism, which alienated those subjects who did not regard themselves as Turkish, such as the Kurds and the Armenians.

Among the Ottoman subjects who resisted Turkish nationalism were those who spoke Arabic. Long divided by local, sectarian, or family rivalries, the people of Syria, Mesopotamia, and Arabia began to view themselves as one Arab nation. Arabic-speaking lawyers, teachers, students, and army officers formed nationalist societies in the main Ottoman cities. Some wanted internal autonomy and equal status with the Turks as Ottoman subjects; others demanded Arab independence from Turkish rule. A few hoped to restore the caliphate to an Arab ruler. Although Arab nationalism had only a few adherents at first, its ideas helped spark the Arab Revolt during World War I.

Persian Constitutionalism

Persia's Qajar shahs were autocratic and weak. They could not protect the farmers and city dwellers from nomadic tribes, nor could they stop Russian military incursions or the commercial ascendancy of the British and other Europeans. In reaction, the idea of constitutional government arose within three groups: merchants, Shi'i *ulama,* and Westernized intellectuals. The merchants resented the shahs' concessions to foreign companies, which threatened their livelihood; the *ulama* feared that Westernization would undermine Islam generally and their own influence in particular; and the intellectuals, influenced by Western liberalism and nationalism, viewed the shah, backed by foreign advisers and funds, as an obstacle to reform.

These groups wanted different things. United by nationalism, however, they engineered the 1892 tobacco boycott and a national revolution in 1906. In response to the latter event, the shah granted a constitution that provided for a popularly elected parliament *(majles),* but in 1907 his successor called in Russian troops to suppress the *majles* and its revolutionary backers. But outside the capital, the Constitutionalists continued their struggle. A prominent tribal leader helped them retake Tehran, and they replaced the shah with a more docile relative.

Once in power, though, the Constitutionalists failed to implement their reform program. Their political revolution did not change social and economic conditions, they were split into factions, and outsiders exacerbated their problems. Britain cared about protecting commerce and defending India. Russia, having earlier taken Central Asia, hoped to expand into Persia. Meanwhile, a British firm won a concession to explore southern Persia for oil. The first major discovery came in 1908, and the Anglo-Persian Oil Company was formed the next year. Soon it built a refinery at Abadan. When Britain's fleet switched from coal to oil in 1912, Persia's new role as an oil producer made it central to British imperial strategy.

Britain and Russia had agreed in 1907 to define spheres of influence within Persia. Russia's sphere covered the country's northern third, including Tehran. Britain, whose area bordered on northwestern India, allowed the Russians to tighten their grip on Persia's government before and during World War I. The 1917 Bolshevik Revolution would cause the withdrawal of Russian troops, but Britain still hoped to control Persia.

World War I, the Ottoman Jihad, and the Arab Revolt

World War I completed the ongoing subordination of Middle Eastern peoples to Western domination. Since the eighteenth century, Russia had won control over the lands north of the Black Sea, the Caucasus Mountains, most of the Caspian Sea coast, and vast stretches of Muslim Central Asia. Persia was virtually a Russian protectorate. The czarist regime hoped to gain Istanbul and the Bosporus and Dardanelles Straits in the war. France ruled North Africa. Britain held Egypt, Cyprus, and Aden; it also had treaties empowering it to protect most of the Gulf rulers. British and French capitalists had huge investments in Middle Eastern land, buildings, factories, railroads, and utilities. In 1914, Germany had become the protector of what remained of the Ottoman Empire; a German military mission was reorganizing its army, and German capital was financing construction of a rail line from Istanbul to Baghdad, raising its influence in the Ottoman interior.

Istanbul's decision to enter World War I as Germany's ally sealed the fate of the Ottoman Empire. Russian expansionism threatened its eastern provinces, and the Young Turk leaders came to fear their Armenian subjects as a fifth column, though most had remained loyal to the Ottoman Empire. The government deported most of the Armenians from their homes, causing an estimated 1.5 million deaths and much economic dislocation.

The Ottoman proclamation of jihad (struggle for Islam) failed to rally the Muslims under Allied rule to rebel. As Britain repulsed Turkish attacks against the Suez Canal and sent forces to invade Mesopotamia and Palestine, the Arabs' loyalty to the Ottoman sultan waned. Husayn ibn Ali, the emir (prince) of Mecca and sharif (leading descendant of Muhammad) of the prestigious Hashemite family, negotiated secretly with Sir Henry McMahon, Britain's high commissioner in Egypt. McMahon's letters seemed to offer British support for an independent Arab kingdom under the Hashemites if Husayn rebelled against the Turks. He reserved Baghdad and Basra for separate administration, however, and excluded Mersin, Alexandretta, and "portions of Syria lying to the west of the districts of Damascus, Homs, Hama, and Aleppo" from the areas to be ruled by Husayn. These terms fell short of the nationalists' dream of independence for all the Arabic-speaking Ottoman lands. Although Husayn was disappointed, the Ottoman government's repression of the Arabs in Syria enraged him and led him to proclaim the Arab Revolt in 1916. Together, the Arabs and the British drove the Turks from Palestine and Syria, while Anglo-Indian troops took Mesopotamia (Iraq). The Ottoman Empire surrendered in October 1918.

Because the Arabs predominated in Palestine, Syria, and Iraq, they expected to win independence in return for their support during the Arab Revolt. US president Woodrow Wilson proposed autonomy for these former Ottoman lands in the twelfth of his Fourteen Points, which Britain and France accepted as the basis for making peace. The British and French gave new assurances to the Arabs in 1918 that the Fertile Crescent and the Hejaz would be ruled by the Hashemites after the war.

But this was not to be. During the war, Britain had made conflicting commitments to other interested parties. In a series of secret pacts, the Allies had agreed that the Bosporus and Dardanelles Straits, Istanbul, and eastern Anatolia were to go to czarist Russia, portions of western Anatolia to the Greeks and the Italians, and most of the Arab lands to Britain and France. The 1916 Sykes-Picot Agreement designated part of the Syrian coast for direct French control and a larger zone of French influence in the Syrian hinterland as far east as Mosul. Britain was to rule lower Iraq and to have a sphere of influence over the rest of Iraq and Palestine, except that the Christian holy places would be under an international administration. Only in the desert were the Arabs to be free from Western rule.

Meanwhile, Jewish nationalists, or Zionists, were pressing the Western powers to recognize their claim to Palestine, or Eretz Yisrael (land of Israel). Beginning in the 1880s (partly due to anti-Jewish pogroms in Russia), some European Jews settled in Palestine, then under Ottoman rule and inhabited mainly by Arabs. During World War I, Chaim Weizmann, an eminent chemist and Zionist leader living in England, convinced members of the British cabinet, which then authorized Foreign Secretary Sir Arthur Balfour to declare his government's support for the establishment in Palestine of a national home for the Jewish people. He cautioned that this should not prejudice the civil and religious (but not political) rights of Palestine's "existing non-Jewish inhabitants," who comprised over nine-tenths of its population. The 1917 Balfour Declaration was a major victory for the nascent Zionist movement.

The Postwar Peace Settlement

All of these contradictory commitments were aired at the 1919 Paris Peace Conference. Sharif Husayn's son, Faisal, spoke for the Arab provisional government that the Hashemites had set up in Damascus. Seeking to learn what Arabs in Syria and Palestine wanted, Wilson sent out the King-Crane Commission, which found that the Arabs opposed French rule and Zionist colonization and craved independence. Its report was ignored. The British let the French troops occupy Beirut and later acceded to French control over Syria, including Mount Lebanon but not Palestine. Arab nationalists in Damascus declared Syria independent in March 1920 and vowed to resist, but the French defeated them in July and toppled the Arab provisional government.

By then, the Allies had agreed on how to rule the conquered Ottoman provinces. Owing to Wilson's self-determination policy, Britain and France did not annex these lands. Rather, under the League of Nations Covenant, Ottoman territories captured during the war were divided into small states that had developed enough to be recognized as nearly ready for independence, subject to a brief period of foreign tutelage under League supervision. Accordingly, France became the mandatory power in Syria and Britain in Iraq and Palestine. In principle, the powers were to govern these mandates to benefit the inhabitants and to prepare them for self-rule. In practice, the mandates benefited Britain and France, not their new and resentful subjects.

France split Syria into smaller administrative units to ensure its control, further embittering the nationalists. One result was the enlargement of prewar Mount Lebanon to include most of the Syrian coast, forming the Republic of Lebanon, which in 1920 had a slight Christian majority. Syria has never recognized this separation, and Lebanon's people are now predominantly Muslim.

Faisal, ousted from Damascus, was crowned in Baghdad in 1921 as the British sought to suppress a general revolt in the new kingdom of Iraq, an awkward combination of the Ottoman provinces of Mosul, Baghdad, and Basra, minus the emirate (principality) of Kuwait. For Faisal's brother Abdullah, who had been promised the Iraqi throne, the British carved from Palestine the emirate of Transjordan, a desert land inhabited by bedouin tribes. Britain helped Abdullah weld his new state into a cohesive unit by forming the Arab Legion, a camel corps made up of men from most of the tribes and led by British officers. The Zionists in Palestine protested that Abdullah's kingdom was not open to Jewish colonization, while Arab nationalists objected to the fragmentation of what they felt should have been a unified Syria. Abdullah himself hoped that, once the French left Syria, he could move from dusty Amman to historic Damascus.

■ The Middle East Since World War I

When Europe's armies laid down their weapons at the war's end, Britain seemed to dominate the Middle East. Its troops patrolled western Arabia, Palestine, Syria, Iraq, some of Persia, parts of the Caucasus long under czarist rule, and the Turkish Bosporus and Dardanelles straits. But the rise of nationalism checked Britain's control of the area. Egypt and Iraq were soon convulsed by nationwide rebellions against the British occupying forces. The Arabs rioted in Palestine against the Jewish immigrants and in Syria against the French colonists, for they viewed both groups as serving British imperial interests.

Deserted by its Young Turk leaders, the defeated Ottoman government let the British and French occupy the Turkish straits, but Ottoman attempts to demobilize the Turkish army as Greek forces invaded western Anatolia set off a mutiny led by its ablest general, Mustafa Kemal (later named Atatürk, "Father of the Turks"). Soon Kemal's followers set up in Ankara a nationalist government that replaced the Ottoman sultanate. The new Republic of Turkey rejected the 1920 Treaty of Sèvres, imposed on the Ottomans by the Allies, and drove out the Greeks.

In Persia, Britain drafted a treaty with the Qajar rulers that would have turned their country into a British protectorate, but the *majles* rejected the pact and revolts broke out in various parts of Persia. In 1921 an officer in the shah's guard, Reza Khan, took control and set up a military dictatorship, reducing Britain's role to protecting its oil fields in southwest Persia.

Western Imperialism in the Arab Lands

Despite this resistance, the British did manage to protect their communication links across the region to India. Egypt's revolutionaries did not win the independence they had sought in 1919, but the British did agree in 1922 to end the protectorate and let the Egyptians draw up a formal constitution, creating a parliament that would vie with the king for power. British troops remained to guard Cairo, Alexandria, the Suez Canal, and such vital infrastructure as airports and radio transmitters. Sudan remained under a formal Anglo-Egyptian condominium, but the British held almost all the power. London also reserved the right to defend Egypt against outside aggression and to protect foreign residents and minorities from nationalists or Muslim extremists. Under the new constitution, the Egyptians held parliamentary elections in 1923. Egypt's purported delegation (in Arabic, *wafd*) to the Paris Peace Conference turned into the Wafd Party, which could win any election not rigged by the king.

Palestine came under the direct control of Britain's Colonial Office, with a high commissioner governing in Jerusalem. The Jewish community had a Jewish Agency and an elected assembly to manage its internal affairs. The Muslim and Christian Arabs had no such organizations, and their leaders rejected a proposed legislature. Jews and Arabs spoke different languages, lived in distinct villages or separate neighborhoods, and related as little as possible to each other as communities, although some individuals or families got along well with their rivals. Jewish immigrants from war-torn revolutionary Russia or central Europe viewed local Arabs as threatening brigands, greedy landlords, or backward peasants. The Palestinian Arabs feared that the Zionist movement would take away their lands and their homes. Jews and Arabs, both having long memories of powerlessness, showed scant sympathy for each other as they began competing for Palestine.

The French accepted control over Syria but resented having to forgo Palestine and oil-rich western Iraq. France was determined to turn its League of Nations mandate over Syria into a colony. Soon after French troops had driven out the Arab nationalists, France divided the country into districts: Damascus, Aleppo, the north Mediterranean coast for the Alawis (a breakaway Shi'i sect), the highlands south of Damascus for the Druze (also a past offshoot of Shi'ism), and the special Republic of Lebanon already mentioned. French rule in Syria benefited farmers and merchants, as the mandatory regime invested in roads and other public works, but did not allay the chagrin of the nationalists who had craved Arab independence.

In North Africa, the French treated Algeria as an integral part of France. European settlers held most of the cultivatable land, dominated political life, and controlled Algiers and the other major cities. The Algerian Muslims, mainly Berber but including many Arabs, had no political rights and only belatedly formed a secular nationalist party. A Muslim bey (governor) ruled in Tunisia and had Muslim ministers, but real power was held by the French governor-general and his advisers. European settlers were less numerous than in Algeria, though. An emerging professional class formed the Destour (Constitution) Party to seek Tunisia's independence.

Morocco, which unlike the rest of North Africa had never been under Ottoman rule, was now divided between a Spanish enclave in the north, the international city of Tangier, and a French protectorate over most of the country. A French governor-general advised the sultan and his ministers, who normally obeyed. A large-scale rural rebellion was suppressed in 1925 after a fierce struggle. Although Morocco's urban nationalists formed the Istiqlal (Independence) Party, the French invested heavily in agriculture and mining, expecting to remain. Italy, which had seized Tripolitania from the Ottoman Empire in 1911, slowly took Cyrenaica and the Fezzan, creating what is now Libya. Its administration was especially brutal. Efforts to colonize Libya with Italians displaced many Arabs but attracted few settlers.

Independence in Turkey, Iran, and the Arabian Peninsula

One of the great ironies of Middle Eastern history is that most of the Arabs, who had thrown in their lot with the Allies during World War I, did not achieve their political goals after 1918, whereas the Turks, who had joined the Central Powers and shared in their defeat, managed to retain their independence once the war was over. The Turkish-speaking lands of Anatolia and Thrace could have been divided among Britain, France, Italy, Greece, and possibly even the United States. The Sèvres Treaty might have awarded lands to Armenians and Kurds. Instead, Turkish leader Kemal led a nationwide revolt that gradually won the support of the Union of Soviet Socialist Republics (USSR), France, and Italy, expelled the Greek invaders who had occupied much of western Anatolia, and persuaded the British to withdraw their troops from the straits. A new treaty signed at Lausanne in 1923 freed Thrace and Anatolia (with no enclaves for the Armenians or the Kurds) from foreign rule and accepted Turkey's abolition of the Capitulations that had exempted Europeans from Ottoman control.

Kemal also abolished the sultanate and the other political institutions of the moribund Ottoman Empire in 1923. Ankara was the new capital of Turkey, the first republic in the modern Middle East. More drastic reforms followed, as Kemal ended the Islamic caliphate and dismantled Turkey's Muslim institutions, including its *sharia* courts and schools, its dervish and Sufi orders, and even its holidays. The Arabic alphabet, in which Turkish had been written for a thousand years, was replaced by a Roman one. The Gregorian calendar and Western clocks became standard, as did the metric system of weights and measures. Kemal discouraged women from veiling their faces and ordered men to wear hats with brims in place of the fezzes that had become the customary head covering for Muslim officers and officials. The *ulama* lost most of their power as judges and educators. Kemal wanted to wrest Turkey out of the Middle East and make it a part of Europe. Because he had saved his country from a hated Allied occupation, most Turks obeyed him.

Kemal had an imitator in Persia, where Reza Khan had seized control in 1921. When civilian politicians quarreled and the Qajar shah dithered, Reza crowned himself as the new shah in 1925. He founded the Pahlavi dynasty and decreed that Persia should be called Iran ("land of the Aryans"). Like Kemal, Reza Shah weakened the *ulama* and secularized their courts, schools, and welfare institutions. He outlawed the veiling of women and required both sexes to dress like Europeans. The new shah also curbed the nomadic tribes that had dominated rural Persia by forcing them to settle down as farmers. Trying to strengthen state control over the countryside, he extended the telegraph and road networks and decreed the construction of the Trans-Iranian Railway. The presence of the Anglo-Iranian (formerly Anglo-Persian) Oil Company, owned and managed by the British, limited Iran's economic sovereignty, but Reza Shah did manage to renegotiate its concession to the host country's benefit. As oil output expanded, more and more Iranians went to work for the company. As nationalist feelings spread, Iranians began to ask why such a vital resource should be controlled by foreigners.

Petroleum exploration began in other Middle Eastern countries as well. British companies found deposits in Iraq and Kuwait, as did US companies operating in Bahrain. A coalition of US firms that became the Arabian American Oil Company (ARAMCO) prospected for oil in the deserts of Arabia. This peninsula had long been dominated by feuding Arab tribes, but in the early twentieth century, a remarkable military leader named Abdul Aziz ibn Saud took over much of Arabia. Having subdued most of the tribes in central and eastern Arabia, Ibn Saud managed to take Mecca and Medina from the Hashemites in 1925. After conquering Asir, Ibn Saud proclaimed the Kingdom of Saudi Arabia in 1932. His country remained poor until ARAMCO struck oil; only much later did Saudi Arabia evolve into an economic giant.

Yemen remained a separate state under a dynasty of Zaydi Shi'i imams (religious leaders), mountainous and colorful but lacking education, healthcare, industry, and oil. To the south of Yemen, where the Red and Arabian Seas meet, lay the British colony of Aden. The tribal shaikhs near the coasts of the Arabian Sea and the Gulf had made treaties that placed them under British protection. Oman, which in previous centuries had been an autonomous actor in regional affairs, had also become a British protectorate. Oil was found in some of these areas, too, but little was extracted or sold until the 1960s.

The Retreat of Western Imperialism

With the spread of education and communications, nationalism grew among the Arabic-speaking peoples under British and French control. This feeling was expressed either as Arab nationalism, the idea that all people who speak Arabic should be united in one nation-state, or as a more localized patriotism. As more Arabs attended schools and colleges and as a burgeoning press fueled their desire for independence and unity, they openly attacked the British and French mandates in the Fertile Crescent and the prolonged British domination over Egypt and Sudan. Indeed, the British meant to prepare Iraqis, Transjordanians and Palestinians, and Egyptians and Sudanese for self-rule and eventual independence, but as separate countries, not as a single united state (as Arab nationalists wanted).

Leading the Arabs' march to independence was the Kingdom of Iraq. Although its subjects were less advanced than the Syrians or Egyptians, the British certified that Iraq was ready for sovereign statehood. In 1932 Iraq achieved formal independence and was admitted to the League of Nations. The next year King Faisal I died suddenly and was succeeded by his minor son. A rebellion by the Assyrian Christians was suppressed by Iraqi troops, who massacred many villagers. Other ethnic minorities (mainly non-Arab Kurds and Turcomans living in the north, who made up one-fifth of Iraq's population, but also Jews in Baghdad) were barred from power. Most of Iraq's Arab Muslims were Shi'a, who also suffered from discrimination.

Iraq's parliament was dominated by landowning tribal leaders, and a few aristocratic families monopolized cabinet posts. Then several military coups brought a succession of army officers to power, culminating in an Arab nationalist government that was toppled by Britain's military intervention in 1941, leaving a legacy of anti-Western hostility that would resurface under Abd al-Karim Qasim (r. 1958–1963) and Saddam Hussein (r. 1979–2003).

The brother of Iraq's King Faisal I, Abdullah, managed to unite Transjordan, which gained its independence in 1946. Its most viable institution, the Arab Legion, had helped the British suppress riots in Palestine west of the Jordan, the area subject to the Jewish-Arab contest for the "twice-promised land."

The Zionist movement aimed to persuade enough Jews to migrate to Palestine to form a Jewish state. Few came during the 1920s, lulling the Arab majority. But in 1929 a quarrel at Jerusalem's Western Wall sparked large-scale rioting in which many Arabs and Jews were killed or injured. A British investigating commission reported that sales of Arab-owned lands to Jewish settlers were taking many Palestinian Arab farmers' tenancy rights and hence their livelihoods. The Jewish settlers blamed Arab agitation for the riots and claimed they had brought prosperity to Palestine.

The Nazi takeover in Germany speeded up Jewish immigration in the 1930s, fueling Arab fears that they would soon become a minority. In 1936 their political parties, hitherto divided on family and religious lines, united as the Arab Higher Committee, which organized a general strike against the mandate. A three-year civil war ensued. A British commission of inquiry visited Palestine in 1937 and recommended forming separate enclaves in Palestine for Jewish immigration and settlement. Neither the Palestinians (backed by newly independent Iraq and Egypt) nor the Zionists favored this partition. The British revised their proposal and then, anxious about their strategic bases in Egypt and Iraq in case war with Germany broke out, issued the May 1939 White Paper, which limited Jewish immigration and land purchases in Palestine. The Zionists felt betrayed, for Europe's Jews were in mortal peril and no other country would admit them. The Arabs doubted British promises of independence, even though they were the majority in Palestine, and argued that Zionism was another manifestation of Western imperialism.

If the British were distrusted in Palestine, the Arabs hated France's mandates in Syria and Lebanon. Only Lebanon's Maronites wanted the French presence; most other Christians and virtually all Muslims in Syria wanted Arab unity and independence. During an interval when a leftist government held power in Paris, the French offered independence, only to retract it when a more conservative cabinet took over. France's sudden defeat by Nazi Germany in 1940 enabled Britain and the United States to pressure the anti-Nazi Free French to recognize the independence of Syria and

The sign, in English and Hebrew, reads: "This market was built on Jewish property stolen by Arabs after the 1929 massacre." It hangs on the wall of a controversial Jewish settlement building in the West Bank city of Hebron/Khalil. The area was previously part of a Palestinian market.

Lebanon in 1943, but the last French troops there did not leave for another three years.

In the 1920s and 1930s, Egypt was the most populous Arab state. It had the most newspapers and magazines, the leading universities, the largest cinema and record companies, and the most influential writers. Yet Egypt lagged behind the other Arab countries in gaining independence because of competition between King Fuad and the Wafd Party and due also to Britain's continued occupation of the Nile Valley. Britain and Egypt finally signed a treaty in 1936 because both feared Italy's expansion in Libya and Ethiopia, countries that bordered on Egypt and Sudan. The British agreed to limit their forces to the Suez Canal zone, Cairo, and Alexandria, reducing them to 10,000 men in peacetime. Sudan remained under an Anglo-Egyptian condominium.

Egypt's King Fuad died in 1936 and was succeeded by his young and initially popular son, Farouk. But he lost his popularity in 1942 when the British made him appoint a cabinet that would back their wartime presence in Egypt. Egypt was occupied by even more British imperial troops during World War II than in World War I, as Fascist Italy and Nazi Germany invaded from Libya, and the Suez Canal had to be defended at all costs. Antidemocratic groups such as pro-Fascist Young Egypt, Communists, and Muslim Brothers vied for Egyptian support, while parliamentary parties seemed

outdated. Once the war ended, Egyptians demanded that British troops leave their country, including Suez and Sudan.

The Struggle Between Arab Nationalism and Zionism

The idea of Arab unification gained support in the Fertile Crescent, Egypt, and the Arabian Peninsula during World War II. Nuri al-Said, Iraq's prime minister, proposed a union of Syria, Lebanon, Transjordan, and Palestine with his own country. But King Farouk of Egypt and King Ibn Saud of Saudi Arabia also wanted to lead the Arabs. Egypt, therefore, proposed a looser organization for all sovereign Arab states. The Arabs accepted the latter alternative, and the Arab League came into being in 1945, with its headquarters in Cairo and an Egyptian as its secretary-general. The Arab countries also joined the United Nations that same year. Although Arab peoples still craved unity, their governments went their separate ways.

The issue that seemed to unite all Arabs was Palestine. Europe's Jews, decimated by the Nazi *Shoah* (Holocaust), sought a safe haven. Palestine's Arab majority feared a flood of refugees who would demand statehood at their expense. As Britain enforced its White Paper immigration restrictions even after World War II, some Jews resorted to terrorism. The British government became ever more hostile to Zionism and to Jewish settlement, and fighting intensified among Jews, Arabs, and British troops.

In 1947 Britain announced that it could no longer govern its mandate and submitted the Palestine issue to the UN. The UN General Assembly set up a special committee, which went to Palestine to look into the problem and recommended that its lands be divided into seven parts, three for the Jews and three for the Arabs, leaving Jerusalem and Bethlehem as a separate area under UN control. The Arab states opposed this plan, which would award more than half the territory (including the fertile coastal area) to the Jews, who numbered only a third of the population and owned about 7 percent of the land. Pressured by the United States, more than two-thirds of the General Assembly members voted for the partition proposal.

Despite military threats by the Arab states to block partition, British troops prepared to pull out of Palestine, and the UN debated how to restore order. On May 14, 1948, the day before Britain's mandate was to end, the Jewish Agency met in Tel Aviv to declare the independent State of Israel in the lands that they controlled. The United States and the USSR recognized the Jewish state, even as the Arab states sent their armies to destroy it.

Israel's creation was a revolutionary event for both Jews and Arabs. There had been no Jewish state for millennia; now one existed as an enclave in a predominantly Arab region. As the armies of Egypt, Iraq, Syria, Lebanon, and Transjordan failed to take Palestine, most Palestinian Arabs fled from their homes, driven by the realistic fear that the Israelis would

drive them out and consoled by the fatuous hope that the Arab armies would bring them back. More than 750,000 Arabs became refugees. They were placed in camps in those areas of Palestine—the West Bank and the Gaza Strip—not captured by the Israelis or in the neighboring countries, mainly Syria, Lebanon, and Jordan. These Palestinian refugees refused assimilation into the Arab states and demanded the right under international law to return to their homes. Israel offered to readmit a few refugees, but only as part of a general peace settlement. The Arab states signed separate armistice agreements with Israel in 1949 but did not recognize the new state. Israel declared that all Jews had the right to become citizens, took in survivors of the *Shoah,* and gave refuge to Jews from Arab lands.

Political Changes in the Arab Countries

The defeat of the Arab armies in the 1948 Palestine war was one of the causes of the army coups that afflicted many Arab states, starting in 1949 with three successive revolts in Syria. Arab monarchies were toppled in Egypt in 1952, Iraq in 1958, Yemen in 1962, and Libya in 1969. The major causes of these revolutions were the demands for greater popular participation and for a fairer distribution of each country's resources. The trend was toward government by an officer corps coming from middle-class (as opposed to landowning) backgrounds and committed to reform. The presence of Palestinian refugees also reminded Arabs in many countries of their old regimes' failure to defend them against Zionism and imperialism. The Palestinians themselves, ever more educated and politicized, often pressed the Arab governments to restore their rights by continuing the fight against Israel.

Revolutionary Arab regimes espoused socialism, a policy viewed as halfway between the communism of the USSR and the capitalism of the West, and Arab unification. The leading spokesman for these policies was Egyptian president Gamal Abdul Nasser. Nasser had led the officers' conspiracy that overthrew Farouk in 1952, negotiated a new pact with Britain in 1954 securing the latter's evacuation of the Suez Canal zone, and renounced Egypt's claims to rule Sudan, which became independent in 1956.

As the Americans tried to fill the power vacuum caused by the British retreat from the Middle East, Nasser resisted efforts to draw him into an anti-Communist alliance that was being formed by Iraq, Britain, Turkey, Iran, and Pakistan in 1955. He chose instead to buy $200 million worth of arms from the Soviet bloc, a move that aroused Western fears of Communist gains in the Arab world. The US government, working with Britain and the World Bank, offered to lend Egypt the money to build a new dam near Aswan that would control the Nile floodwaters and increase the country's farmland and hydroelectric generating capacity, but it later withdrew its offer due to Nasser's perceived pro-Communist policies. Nasser responded in July 1956 by nationalizing the Suez Canal Company. The British and French governments denounced the seizure and conspired with Israel to attack Egypt. Although the attackers retook the canal, they were opposed by nearly every UN member, including the United States. Ultimately, they had to withdraw, and Nasser emerged as an Arab hero for standing up to the West.

Early in 1958, Egypt acceded to Syria's request to form an organic union of the two countries, which they called the United Arab Republic (UAR). Many Arab nationalists hoped that other governments would join the new political entity. Instead, Jordan and Iraq formed their own federation, which soon foundered when a coup overthrew the Iraqi monarchy. A civil war broke out in Lebanon between Arab nationalists (mainly Muslim) who sought closer ties with the UAR and Lebanese particularists (mainly Christian) who wanted independence from the Arabs. US troops occupied Lebanon in July 1958 and helped restore order.

The general trend seemed to be toward pan-Arabism, as north Yemen federated with the UAR, the army seized power in Sudan, and even Saudi Arabia replaced a weak king with a brother who was thought to favor Nasser. Not only was Arab unity strong in the late 1950s, but many governments followed Nasser's lead in redistributing large estates to hitherto landless farmers, nationalizing companies owned by foreign or local capitalists, and expanding public education and welfare institutions. The watchwords of the day were "neutralism" and "Arab socialism."

Like the eastern Arab world, North Africa was also emerging from colonialism. Libya, ruled by Italy up to World War II and by Britain under a temporary trusteeship after the war, was the first to gain independence, in 1951. France gave up its protectorates over both Tunisia and Morocco in 1956, but resisted in Algeria. More than a million European settlers wanted to keep Algeria a part of France, while Algerian Muslims chafed under oppressive colonial rule. A few formed the Front de Liberation Nationale (National Liberation Front, FLN) to gain greater autonomy.

A small FLN uprising, begun in 1954, escalated into a major insurgency, which became an eight-year civil war marred by terrorism and torture by both colonists and nationalists. The French government and army grew tired of fighting rearguard colonial wars, and in 1962 President Charles de Gaulle granted independence to Algeria. The Algerian revolution, the sole instance where an Arab people successfully overthrew a colonial rule, became an inspiration to third-world liberation movements, but at a cost of eighteen thousand French and a million Algerian lives. More than two million Algerians were displaced during the fighting, and after Algeria became independent, more than a million Europeans, Jews, and Muslim supporters of French rule fled. The new leaders soon declared their support of Nasser and Arab socialism, but later, as Algeria grew rich from its oil, the FLN turned into an authoritarian, secular, ruling party. When the FLN voided an election in 1992 that would have brought a Muslim party to power, another civil war erupted that lasted for a decade and cost 150,000 Algerian lives.

The Northern Tier

Not all Middle Eastern states are Arab. Turkey and Iran, although predominantly Muslim, are proud of their distinctive cultures and heritages. Both stood up to the British and kept their independence after World War I. Both bordered on the USSR and had to come to terms with it. Ismet Inönü, who had succeeded Atatürk as president, kept Turkey out of World War II and prevented the Allies from using the Bosporus and Dardanelles straits to supply the USSR. Stalin's postwar demand to station Soviet troops on the straits led the United States to back Turkey in the 1947 Truman Doctrine, the first step toward an American policy of defending the Middle East. In 1952 Turkey joined the North Atlantic Treaty Organization (NATO), having sent troops to Korea to fight the Communists.

Turkey took the lead in moving toward democratic government. Inönü's government consented to the formation of a rival party that ousted the Kemalists from power in 1950. Gradually, other parties with strong socialist and Islamist agendas have entered the political arena, but the Turkish army remains strong. Turkey has continued to industrialize its economy and modernize its society, but its recent history has been punctuated by military coups and by challenges from militant Marxists, Muslims, and Kurdish separatists. Turkey remains a bridge between the West and the Middle East and has become a link to the former Soviet republic of Azerbaijan and to Central Asia. It has for years sought to join the European Union, so far unsuccessfully.

Iran also had to protect its independence from the USSR. Even though the two countries had signed a pact that authorized the Soviets to enter Iran whenever it was occupied by troops hostile to the USSR, Moscow had little influence as long as Reza Shah reigned. In the 1930s, his regime drew close to Nazi Germany, whose doctrines of Aryan supremacy appealed to local pride and offered a means to fight Anglo-Russian control. When the Nazis invaded the USSR in 1941, the Soviet and British governments demanded the expulsion of German advisers from Iran and seized control of the Trans-Iranian Railway to ship Western munitions to the beleaguered USSR. They also forced Reza to abdicate in favor of his son Mohammad. At the war's end, British troops left Iran, but the Soviets tried to set up puppet regimes in Kurdistan and Azerbaijan. It took a general UN condemnation, US threats, and clever Iranian diplomacy to oust the Soviet army.

But Britain still controlled Iran's oil, and in 1951 a cabinet headed by Mohammad Mosaddeq nationalized the Anglo-Iranian Oil Company. Iran's nationalists were elated, but Western countries supported Britain by refusing to buy any oil from Iran. In 1953 an army coup, engineered in part by

British and US intelligence agencies, overthrew Mosaddeq's government. The shah, who had fled from Iran during the turmoil, regained his throne. He began a policy of concentrating control in his own hands at the expense of Iran's landowners, merchants, and *ulama*. He also joined the anti-Communist alliance with Turkey, Pakistan, Britain, and Iraq. Britain and the US viewed Iran, Turkey, and Pakistan as a bulwark against a possible Soviet drive toward the oil-rich Gulf. The West sold vast quantities of weapons to these countries, but skeptics wondered whether those arms would be used just to keep their regimes in power.

The Intensification of the Arab-Israeli Conflict

In the late 1950s and early 1960s, Israel's conflict with its Arab neighbors seemed to die down as Arab states tried to unite and leaders struggled for power. The UAR lapsed when Syria broke away in 1961. A popular nationalist movement, the Baath Party, committed to Arab unification and socialism, seized power in Iraq and then Syria early in 1963. The Baath tried to form a new Arab union with Egypt, but the talks broke down. An army coup had ousted the Yemeni monarchy in 1962, but the new republican regime needed Egyptian military aid and troops to stay in power, while Saudi Arabia began backing tribes loyal to the overthrown imam. A draining civil war ensued in Yemen.

What brought the Arabs back together was Israel's completion of a development scheme that drew water from the Jordan River to irrigate new agricultural lands within the Jewish state. Early in 1964, Nasser invited the other Arab heads of state to Cairo to discuss ways of countering the Israeli scheme, which would deprive Jordan and other Arab states of fresh water needed for their irrigation projects. The Arabs agreed to prepare for future action against Israel and formed the Palestine Liberation Organization (PLO) to unite the Palestinian Arabs politically. Meanwhile, Fatah, led by Yasser Arafat, launched commando raids inside Israel. Although abetted by Syria, these attacks tended to come from the West Bank, which was controlled by Jordan. To deter future raids, Israel's army attacked West Bank villages late in 1966, though some Israelis blamed Syria.

An aerial dogfight broke out between Israel and Syria in April 1967. The USSR told Egypt that Israeli troops were massing to attack Syria. Nasser, anxious to remain the champion of Arab nationalism, ordered the UN to withdraw its peacekeeping forces, which had patrolled the Sinai and the Gaza Strip since the 1956 war. As Israel mobilized its reserves, Egypt declared a blockade in the Gulf of Aqaba against Israeli shipping. Arab governments, their press and radio stations, and their people all called for defeating Israel and restoring the Palestinians to their homes.

Although many in the United States and Western Europe favored Israel, their governments hoped to avoid war by taking the issue to the UN. Israel, fearing an Arab offensive, launched a preemptive strike. On June 5, 1967, Israeli fighter planes bombed Egypt's military airfields and wiped out most of the Egyptian air force. Before the Arabs could hit back, the Israelis annihilated the other Arab air forces. They invaded the Egyptian Sinai, Gaza, the Jordanian-ruled sector of Jerusalem and the West Bank, and finally Syria's Golan Heights. In six days, Israel used its superior technology, organization, and air power to defeat Egypt, Syria, and Jordan, tripling the area under its control.

Although the Arab states accepted UN-mediated cease-fires, they refused to make peace. At a summit held in Khartoum, Sudan, the Arab leaders agreed not to negotiate with Israel, but to rearm and regain their lost lands by force. The PLO tried but failed to mobilize the Palestinians of the Gaza Strip and the West Bank, numbering more than 1 million people, to resist Israeli military rule. After a lengthy debate, the UN Security Council unanimously passed Resolution 242, calling on Israel to withdraw from lands occupied in the recent war but ordering all countries to recognize the right of "every state in the area" to exist "within secure and recognized boundaries." Israel, Egypt, Jordan, and Syria, as UN members, were all bound under the UN Charter to accept Security Council resolutions, but each made its own interpretation of this one, to which all member states have paid lip service since 1967. Resolution 242 did not mention the Palestinians, who felt that neither the major powers nor the Arab governments really cared about their interests.

In 1969, Arafat was elected chairman of the PLO, the umbrella group for most Palestinians. Some became guerrillas and resorted to attacking not only Israel but also pro-Western Arab states, notably Jordan and Lebanon. Palestinian guerrilla groups seemed to resist Israel more effectively than had the armies of Egypt, Syria, and Jordan in 1967. While Israeli propaganda assailed "Arab terrorism," most Arabs flocked to support the PLO.

Nasser launched his War of Attrition against Israel's troops in the Sinai in 1969 partly to counter PLO claims to lead the struggle. Israel's counterattacks obliged Egypt to seek more military aid from the USSR, leading to aerial dogfights over the Suez Canal. US secretary of state William Rogers proposed a peace plan that would halt the War of Attrition and set up indirect talks to bring Egypt and Israel to a peace settlement based on Resolution 242. Nasser accepted the Rogers Peace Plan but indirectly undercut it by positioning Soviet missiles near the Suez Canal. Meanwhile, Palestinian guerrillas threatened to take over Jordan, but the Jordanian army, loyal to King Hussein, crushed them. Nasser's efforts to restore peace among the Arabs led to his fatal heart attack on September 28, 1970. His funeral in Cairo inspired demonstrations of grief throughout the Arab world because of his heroic stand against Western imperialism. Nasser's successor, Anwar Sadat, vowed to continue the fallen leader's policies of Arab nationalism, opposition to Israel, neutralism, purchases of Communist arms, and socialism. Soon, however, Sadat set his own course, liberalizing Egypt's economy and society, and expelling most Soviet advisers in 1972.

The Rogers Peace Plan had collapsed in 1971 as neither Israel nor the Arabs would make the concessions needed. Sadat threatened to renew war against Israel if it did not withdraw from Sinai and recognize Palestinian political rights. He also tried to cement a union with Syria, Libya, and Sudan. Neither his threats nor his union scheme worked. Palestinian commando groups committed terrorist actions against civilian Israelis and foreigners, hoping to convince Israel and its backers that the Arab lands captured in 1967 were not worth keeping. But Israel argued that it had to retain the territories until the Arabs agreed to negotiate for peace. As the Arabs quarreled among themselves and Egypt distanced itself from its erstwhile Soviet backers, Israel and its supporters became overconfident.

Israel's complacency was shaken on October 6, 1973, when Egypt and Syria attacked Israeli positions in the Sinai and the Golan Heights. Taken by surprise, the Israelis called up their reserve soldiers and brought them to both fronts. By the second week, Israel was driving back the Syrians and Egyptians. The USSR and United States rushed to rearm their Middle Eastern clients on a massive scale. Then the Arabs decided to unsheathe an economic weapon. In 1960, the leading nonindustrialized oil producers had created the Organization of Petroleum Exporting Countries (OPEC), which tried to limit oil production and set common prices. OPEC had begun to affect the world oil market in 1971, and the October 1973 war gave it a pretext to raise prices 400 percent. The Arab members of OPEC announced that they would sell no oil to the United States and the Netherlands and would reduce supplies to other oil importers (Spain, France, and Muslim countries were exempted) until Israel pulled out of all occupied lands and recognized the Palestinians' political rights. So vital had Arab oil become to Europe and Japan that many countries made political promises to ensure winter supplies. The UN Security Council adopted Resolutions 338 and 340, calling for a cease-fire and for immediate negotiations between Israel and the Arabs.

The Israelis had won the war, but as other governments turned against them, they felt that they had lost politically. US secretary of state Henry Kissinger worked to disentangle the Egyptian and Israeli armies and to organize a general peace conference that met briefly in Geneva in December 1973. Then Kissinger began flying between Jerusalem and Cairo, dealing with Egypt's and Israel's leaders separately. Finally they agreed to separate the two armies by creating demilitarized zones between them. After that, tensions lessened and the oil embargo ended. Kissinger engineered a similar agreement between Israel and Syria. Both agreements enabled the Arab states to regain some of the lands Israel had taken in 1967 or 1973. Both sides took steps that, it was hoped, would lead toward future peace talks.

A second agreement between Egypt and Israel in 1975, again brokered by Kissinger, led to a further Israeli pullback and to an Egyptian renunciation of force to settle the Arab-Israeli conflict. Both sides feared political deals: the Israelis might jeopardize their security by conceding too much to the Arabs; Egypt and Syria feared making concessions that might anger other Arabs, especially the Palestinians. In 1974, the Arabs agreed that only the PLO could speak for the Palestinians, but Israel refused to talk to what it viewed as a terrorist group. When a nationalist coalition, headed by Menachem Begin (who had led the underground paramilitary group Irgun Zvai Leumi up to 1948), won Israel's 1977 election, the country seemed to be on a collision course with the Arabs. US president Jimmy Carter wanted to reconvene the Geneva Conference (with the Soviet Union) and to include Palestinians in the new talks, to Israel's dismay.

Then Egyptian president Anwar Sadat surprised everyone by announcing that he would go to Jerusalem to parley with Israel's government. Although startled, Begin agreed to receive him and a new peace process began, leading to US mediation and finally to an extraordinary summit held at Camp David, with Carter as host and Sadat and Begin as chief negotiators. A tentative agreement was reached for peace between Egypt and Israel, and the three leaders signed the pact in September 1978. Diplomats ironed out the details, and the final Egyptian-Israeli peace treaty was signed in March 1979. The treaty provided for Israel's phased withdrawal from the Sinai, full diplomatic relations between Jerusalem and Cairo, and ongoing negotiations on the status of Palestinians under Israeli occupation. The other Arab states and the PLO denounced Sadat's policy, broke diplomatic ties with Egypt, and vowed to continue their opposition to Israel.

The Islamic Revolution in Iran

While the West watched the Egyptian-Israeli peace talks, a revolution was brewing against the government of Mohammad Reza Shah Pahlavi, who had ruled Iran for almost thirty-seven years. The United States and most European governments had long backed the shah as a bulwark against Soviet expansionism and pan-Arabism, selling Iran billions of dollars worth of Western arms. Iran's surging income caused by the oil price hikes in 1973 drew US and European investors to Tehran, where the shah proclaimed grandiose development schemes. These plans, run from the top down, gave little attention to what the Iranian people needed. They stressed showcase projects instead of making basic changes in the villages where most Iranians lived or in the factories or on the farms where most Iranians worked. The shah tolerated no opposition to his policies; a large intelligence bureau,

Sazman-e Ettelaat va Amniyat-e Keshvar (SAVAK), spied on dissidents and jailed or tortured his critics.

Opposition to the shah came from nationalists who had backed Mosaddeq in 1951–1953, Marxists, labor leaders, intellectuals, and students. None of these groups could withstand threats of imprisonment, torture, or even death at the hands of SAVAK agents. The best-organized and most popular opposition came from Muslim leaders, in part because Iran is a Shi'i country, and Shi'ism empowers its *ulama* to reinterpret Islamic law. One such leader was the Ayatollah Ruhollah Khomeini, who in his sermons and writings attacked the shah's tyranny and US interference in Iranian affairs. Exiled from Iran in 1964, Khomeini continued to stir up opposition from Iraq and later from Paris. His sermons were smuggled into Iran and passed from hand to hand; some were even read aloud in the mosques.

An attack on Khomeini in the Iranian press sparked popular demonstrations early in 1978, and government efforts to suppress them led instead to larger protests. Urban merchants, or Bazaari, had already launched a series of strikes in opposition to new economic policies, and by the summer the Bazaari and clerical supporters of Khomeini had united in their opposition to the regime. Growing numbers of Iranians joined the movement—including intellectuals, feminists, students, trade unionists, and many others—and demanded the liberties and human rights advocated by President Carter. Many in the United States, fearing the shah's regime would fall, called for a nationalist government that would unite all Iranians. The shah, stricken with cancer and cut off from the people, appointed a nationalist premier and left Iran in January 1979, expecting the United States to restore his regime as it had done in 1953. This did not occur.

The Iranian people, elated at the shah's departure, staged demonstrations to bring back the ayatollah. In February Khomeini returned, the shah's army defected to the ayatollah's side, and the government turned over its power to the revolutionaries. A cabinet whose members held opinions ranging from nationalist to Marxist to ultra-Islamic temporarily took charge of Iran, and revolutionary *komiteh*s (committees) rounded up SAVAK agents and the shah's supporters, trying many and jailing and executing some of them. A popular plebiscite backed Khomeini's demand that Iran become an Islamic republic.

The Iranian revolution was a turning point in modern Middle East history. A government committed to rapid Westernization was toppled by a populist regime dedicated to making Islam the basis of its policies and the guide for its economy, society, and culture. The new leaders vowed to export the revolution throughout the Muslim world. The emirates and shaikhdoms of the Gulf, with their vast oil revenues and wide disparities between rich and poor, were vulnerable. Some had Shi'i populations likely to be influenced by Iran. Iran's seizure of the US embassy and the taking of fifty-two hostages outraged Westerners, but it also encouraged Muslims to criticize Washington and other Western governments viewed as hostile to Islam.

US diplomatic and military efforts to secure the release of the hostages failed. Soviet troops, observing US weakness after the Iranian revolution, occupied Afghanistan in December 1979. Military aggression seemed to be in fashion, as Iraqi president Saddam Hussein renounced a treaty he had signed with the shah's government in 1975 letting Iran share control with Iraq over the confluence of the Euphrates and Tigris rivers, the Shatt al-Arab waterway, and proceeded to invade southwestern Iran in 1980. This dispute was a pretext for deeper antagonisms between the two countries: Iraq wanted to replace Egypt as the Arabs' leader; Iran urged all Muslims, especially Shi'a, to replace their secularized regimes with Islamic republics.

Iraq made huge inroads into Iran at first, but the Iranians fought back and eventually regained the captured lands and even seized strategic points near Iraq's second largest city, Basra. Neither the Shi'i majority in Iraq nor the Arab minority in Iran rebelled against its government, but each state spent billions on weapons and suffered heavy losses of personnel and equipment, as well as destruction of oil refineries, homes, shops, and factories. Both sides drafted what males they could find, even foreign workers and young boys, into their armies to replenish their fallen soldiers. Both, especially Iraq, fired missiles at the enemy's cities and used poison gas in combat.

Iran soon realized that it would have to release the US hostages to gain international support for its war effort. Algerian diplomats mediated the dispute and secured the release of all fifty-two hostages after 444 days in captivity. Although US president Ronald Reagan's administration may have encouraged Iraq to attack, offered its regime credits to buy American grain, and provided military intelligence, it sold US missiles and spare parts to Iran for secret funds that could later be used to finance anti-Communist rebels in Nicaragua. When Iran and Iraq attacked each other's oil tankers in the Gulf and then started firing on the ships of other countries, the US government took to reflagging Kuwaiti tankers and using its warships to escort them. In 1988, the United States and Iran almost went to war with each other when a US naval officer accidentally shot down an Iranian passenger plane over the Gulf, but Tehran found that almost no country would back it. The UN Security Council had passed a resolution calling for a cease-fire between the warring states. Iraq had already accepted the resolution, and in July 1988 Iran reluctantly followed suit.

The Iranian revolution had many repercussions beyond the war with Iraq. Between 1979 and 1987, Tehran tried to foment revolts throughout the Muslim world, using its Islamic Republican Party to export its ideology. Iranian guerrillas set up training camps for revolutionaries as remote as the Moros in the Philippines and the Polisario rebels opposing Moroccan control of the Western Sahara. Especially important, however, was Iran's aid to Lebanon's Shi'a, once poor and unheeded but emerging in the 1980s as major players in that country's civil war.

Lebanon: Cockpit of Middle Eastern Rivalry

Ever since independence, Lebanon had presented one face to the West: that of a democratic, urbane society, the "Switzerland of the Middle East." To many of its own inhabitants, and certainly to other Arabs, however, it showed another face: one of unfair privileges enjoyed by its Christians at the expense of Lebanon's Muslims (both Sunni and Shi'i) and Druze. As more Lebanese moved to the cities, where disparities of wealth and power were visible, and as the Muslim percentage of Lebanon's population rose relative to that of the Christians, discontent mounted. Economic and social conditions improved after the 1958 civil war, but Lebanese Muslims and Palestinian refugees still resented their inferior status. Skirmishes sometimes broke out between Muslims and Christians or between Palestinians and Lebanese. Usually they were settled quietly, but in 1975 Sunni Muslim and Maronite Christian militias started fighting in earnest, the PLO soon joined in, and a major civil war began. In 1976, the Lebanese government invited Syria into the country to help suppress Muslim and Palestinian militias. Syrian troops did indeed buttress the Maronite-dominated government in 1976, but they stayed in Lebanon and soon shifted to the Muslim side. Early in 1978, Israel invaded southern Lebanon, partly to keep the Syrian army away from its northern border, but withdrew after the UN stationed a buffer force in the parts of Lebanon bordering Israel.

But low-intensity conflict dragged on. Ignoring the UN buffer, Palestinian commandos sometimes raided northern Israel; Israeli troops bombed suspected PLO bases in Lebanese villages and even Beirut neighborhoods. In 1982 Israel invaded southern Lebanon, repulsed the Syrian army and PLO militias, bypassed the UN force, and besieged Beirut. Lebanon's parliament elected a Maronite president aligned with Israel against the Palestinians and their Arab backers. When he was killed in an explosion, Israel's troops invaded Beirut. While they were there, Maronite militias invaded the mainly Palestinian neighborhoods of Sabra and Shatilla, where they killed hundreds of old men, women, and children. Appalled by the massacre, which Israel's army abetted, the Western powers sent a multinational force into Lebanon.

Washington hoped to persuade Syria and Israel to leave Lebanon and the various militias to hand over their arms and their powers to a reconstituted Lebanese government. Instead, the Israelis and the multinational force angered not just the Sunni Muslims and Palestinians but also Lebanon's hitherto quiet Shi'i citizens. Some young Shi'a, trained by the Iranians, drove trucks

In 2002, a significant number of buildings in central Beirut, Lebanon, remained in a state of total disrepair, a visual reminder of the intermittent war that engulfed the country for more than two decades.

loaded with explosives into Western embassies, the barracks of the foreign armies, and Maronite strongholds, killing or injuring hundreds. These suicide squads wrought such havoc among the European, US, and Israeli forces that they withdrew, although Israel continued to occupy southern Lebanon for fifteen more years. These militant Muslims gained prestige from ousting Western foreign troops from Lebanon.

Meanwhile, Palestinians under Israeli occupation launched a general uprising, or intifada, that lasted from 1987 until 1993 and caused 160 Israeli and 1,162 Palestinian deaths. The intifada did not shrink or enlarge the lands controlled by Israel, but it raised the prestige of the Palestinians living in Gaza (where the uprising began) and the West Bank in the eyes of other Arabs. The PLO formally declared the "independence" of the State of Palestine, Chairman Arafat denounced terrorism, and US-Palestinian talks occurred briefly in 1989, but Washington's attention was soon drawn away to a crisis in the Persian Gulf.

The Iraq-Kuwait Crisis and Israeli-Arab Negotiations

Iraq has long suffered from always being the number two Arab state, whether overshadowed by Egypt as the Arabic cultural center or second to Saudi Arabia as the area's largest oil producer. Iraq's war against Iran in the 1980s left it heavily indebted to Saudi Arabia and other Gulf states. Iraqis also call Kuwait a dynastic enclave that serves the interests of Western oil importers. At times Iraq has tried to annex Kuwait, hoping to enlarge its coastline and become the leading power on the Gulf. In July 1990, Iraq accused Kuwait of "slant-drilling" for oil under Iraqi territory and of demanding repayment of loans it had made to Iraq during the war against Iran. Other Arab governments tried to mediate the dispute, but Saddam ordered Iraqi troops to occupy Kuwait on August 2, 1990.

Iraq failed to foresee that US president George H. W. Bush would oppose its annexation of Kuwait. When Arab leaders failed to make the Iraqis withdraw, the Bush administration began an intense campaign to liberate Kuwait, initially by diplomacy and later by sending troops and matériel to Saudi Arabia in what became known as Operation Desert Shield. Economic sanctions backed by increasingly strident UN Security Council resolutions warned Iraq to remove its troops from Kuwait. Kuwaitis who escaped to other Arab lands demanded military measures instead of economic sanctions. Saudi Arabia, hitherto opposed to any concentration of foreign troops in its territory, which includes Mecca and Medina, became a base for a US-led coalition of Arab and foreign forces opposed to Iraq's action.

Far from being intimidated, Saddam warned that any attempt to dislodge the Iraqis from their reclaimed province would lead to the torching of Kuwait's oil fields. Nevertheless, the coalition attacked Iraq on January 16, 1991, launching Operation Desert Storm. When six weeks of intense aerial bombing did not dislodge Iraq from Kuwait, the coalition forces began a ground war that succeeded, within 100 hours, in expelling the Iraqis. Bush then stopped the hostilities, even as the allied coalition was entering southern Iraq. Some critics argue that the troops should have occupied Baghdad and deposed Saddam, but the UN resolutions called only for the liberation of Kuwait.

Shi'a in the south and Kurds in the north revolted against Iraq's central government, but the help they needed from the US and its allies never came. Both uprisings were suppressed. Any dissident officers in the Iraqi army who sought to topple their leader were killed, jailed, or expelled. UN sanctions remained in effect, keeping Iraq from importing consumer goods for its people, but Saddam stymied the UN inspectors who could have certified that his nuclear, chemical, and biological weapons were destroyed. The allied coalition had won a hollow victory.

As Bush had promised (to gain Arab support for the war against Iraq), the Bush administration convened a conference, initially in Madrid, later in Washington and then Moscow, at which Israeli and Arab delegations met to talk peace. Although Israel refused direct talks with the PLO, representatives from the Occupied Territories were admitted into a joint Jordanian-Palestinian delegation. While public talks dragged on, Israeli and PLO representatives met secretly in Oslo and forged an agreement that surprised everyone when it was first announced in 1993. The public signing of a Declaration of Principles by

Israel and the PLO in the presence of President Bill Clinton ended the intifada and led to intense negotiations, focused initially on how to withdraw Israeli troops from Gaza and Jericho.

After many delays, Israel reached an agreement in May 1994 with Palestine's "self-governing authority," enabling Arafat to return to Gaza. Israel could still manipulate the supposedly autonomous Palestinians by retaining troops in Gaza and the West Bank and by barring Palestinian workers from entering Israel during times of crisis. Few jobs were available to them in the autonomous areas. Some frustrated Palestinians forsook the PLO for such radical movements as Hamas. Jordan and Israel signed a peace treaty in October 1994, and several North African and Gulf states entered into diplomatic or commercial relations with the Jewish state. Israel reached a further agreement with the PLO in September 1995, providing for troop withdrawals from major West Bank population centers. Jerusalem's status was left for later negotiations, though, and most Palestinian lands remained under Israel's control. Prime Minister Yitzhak Rabin was murdered by an Israeli who believed that his government had already given up too much to the Arabs. A new government, headed by Benjamin Netanyahu, was elected in 1996. It stepped up Jewish settlements in the West Bank and repressive policies against Palestinians. Only intense US pressure made Netanyahu give up part of Hebron in 1997 and a few other occupied lands in 1998. When his fragile coalition collapsed, he called for early elections.

In 1999, the Labor Party leader, Ehud Barak, won by a narrow margin. He offered to cede most of the West Bank and Gaza to Arafat during negotiations at Camp David and Sharm al-Shaikh in 2000, but the Palestinians rejected a deal that would have left Israel in control of key points of the West Bank and obliged them to give up their right of return to other lands now part of Israel. Palestinians and Israelis stepped up attacks on each other, and a new intifada broke out in September 2000. The hawkish general, Ariel Sharon, accused of fomenting the 1982 Palestinian massacre at Sabra and Shatilla, defeated Barak in a special election in 2001 and reoccupied most of the West Bank and Gaza.

In 2002, the European Union, the UN, and the Russian and US governments proposed a "road map to peace." In mid-2003, however, the plan foundered on the intransigence of the Jewish settlers in the Occupied Territories; Israel's construction of a "security fence" on the West Bank, its "targeted killings" (assassinations) of Palestinians, and its armed incursions into Palestinian-controlled areas; and the inability of the Palestinian Authority to curb ongoing attacks on Israeli civilians by Palestinian suicide bombers.

Terrorism and Democracy in the Middle East

Terrorism became the last resort of increasingly desperate Arabs, who sent suicide bombers into Israel to kill civilians, blew up US embassies in Kenya and Tanzania in 1998, damaged a US Navy warship in Yemen, and on September 11, 2001, launched a dramatic hijacking of four US civil airliners to attack New York's World Trade Center and the Pentagon in Washington, D.C. Except for the suicide bombings in Israel, the group Al-Qaida ("the Base") was behind all of these attacks. Its headquarters was in Afghanistan, from which it had expelled the Soviet forces in the late 1980s, but its members were mainly Arab and its leader, Osama bin Laden, came from Saudi Arabia. Indeed, the nineteen hijackers involved in the September 11 attacks were all Arabs, mostly citizens of Egypt and Saudi Arabia. They protested US favoritism toward Israel, Washington's preference for dictatorial regimes over Islamist ones (notably in Algeria), and the domination of US culture in much of the Muslim world. US president George W. Bush declared a "war against terrorism" and directed US forces to bombard and occupy Afghanistan to capture bin Laden and destroy Al-Qaida.

His administration identified Iraq as a major supporter of terrorism and demanded that it fulfill the UN Security Council's Gulf War resolutions to destroy its weapons of mass destruction: nuclear, chemical, and biological. If Iraq's government failed to prove that it had done so, and the UN inspectors could not verify their absence, the US armed forces, aided if possible by its allies, would invade Iraq and oust Saddam's government. On March 20, 2003, a "Coalition of the Willing" consisting of 40 nations led by the United States and Britain attacked Iraq, bombarded and occupied the country, and drove Saddam's regime from power on April 9.

Yet in the ensuing months, coalition forces failed to protect government buildings, museums, and libraries from looters. They could not ensure supplies of electricity, gasoline, food, and medicine to most Iraqis, or create a stable political system. The Bush administration ordered the dissolution of the Iraqi armed forces and the Baath party, which had been the mainstay of the old political system. Creating a new government to represent Iraq's diverse mix of Sunni and Shi'i Muslim Arabs, Kurds, Turcomans, and Christians took longer than expected; meanwhile, dissidents assaulted coalition forces, exploded bombs aimed at both local and foreign targets, and sabotaged oil installations. The US-led coalition became frayed as Iraqi insurgents captured soldiers from some of the smaller armies as hostages, and as Al-Qaida in Europe launched massive attacks on public transport in Madrid and London. Coalition forces in Iraq imprisoned thousands of civilians suspected of terrorism. Some were tortured or sexually abused by US soldiers in the Abu Ghraib prison compound near Baghdad, an abuse documented not only by press reports but also by digital photographs taken by the alleged tormenters. The dissemination of the pictures spread anger throughout the Muslim world and discredited the Iraq War among many people in the United States.

In 2005 the United States sought to prove that it had brought democracy to Iraq by arranging three elections: one in January for a transitional National

Assembly to write a constitution, one in October to ratify the document thus drafted, and one in December for representatives to parliament under the terms of the new constitution. Although most Iraqis were happy to have the chance to vote, most Sunni Iraqis boycotted the first two elections, making the new constitution seem biased in favor of Shi'a and Kurds. The new parliament, whose elected members were unaccustomed to democratic procedures, took months to choose a cabinet and has not yet passed a law that would ensure the equitable distribution of oil revenues to all parts of Iraq.

During this time, the US and other coalition troops had to battle insurgents in Falluja, Mosul, Ramadi, Samarra and Sadr City, among other places, with heavy loss of civilian life and a growing number of refugees, both internally displaced persons fleeing from one part of Iraq to another, and Iraqis who left for nearby countries, notably Syria and Jordan.

Although the Iraq War may be viewed as an attempt by Iraqi nationalists to resist the presence of US and other coalition forces within their country, there are no clear battle lines and no united resistance force. The Kurdish region of northern Iraq functions independently of Baghdad, even though Iraq's president is a Kurd and Kurds also serve in the cabinet and parliament. Sunni and Shi'i militias have arisen that oppose the Iraqi government, which most foreign countries recognize as legitimate and constitutional, but which many Iraqis claim was imposed on them by the occupying armies. Clashes between Sunni and Shi'i Iraqis have become increasingly frequent and deadly, leading some local and foreign observers to ask whether Iraq is even a nation and to propose dividing the country into Kurdish, Sunni, and Shi'i states, or at least autonomous regions.

Neighboring Iran could be said to have benefited from the Iraq War, which has empowered Iraqi Shi'a over the once dominant Sunnis, but the presence of large numbers of US troops in both Iraq and Afghanistan has also made Iranians fearful for their own security. Both Israel and the United States have expressed concern about Iran's effort to develop nuclear energy and to enrich uranium, lest these activities lead to an Iranian nuclear bomb. European Union diplomats persuaded Iran to suspend its nuclear activities in 2004–2005, but these have now resumed, due in part to elections that produced a conservative Islamist majority in the *majles* (Iran's parliament) in 2004 and the choice of Tehran mayor Mahmud Ahmadinejad to become president of Iran in 2005. His public statements advocating Israel's destruction and questioning the Holocaust have added to Israeli fears and to the urgent desire of its supporters and some members of the Bush administration to launch a preventative attack against Iran's nuclear facilities before its regime has nuclear weapons. Such an attack would probably cause Iranian counterattacks against US forces in Iraq and possibly the oil installations of pro-Western countries and would certainly incite anger in such Muslim countries as Pakistan and Egypt.

Iran and its supporters have played a growing role in both Lebanon and Palestine. Lebanon recovered economically from the protracted civil war of 1975–1991, but power within the country remained unevenly distributed among the various sects. Israel withdrew its remaining troops from southern Lebanon in 2000, but 25,000 Syrian troops still occupied the country and tended to favor Shi'i Muslim interests, while Israel and the West still supported the Maronites and other Christians. Lebanon's most prominent leader was its Sunni Muslim prime minister, Rafiq Hariri, who had spearheaded the country's economic revival. He was assassinated on February 14, 2005, an act widely ascribed to Syrian intelligence. The popular revulsion to this assassination led to a coalition of Christian and Sunni Muslim parties that demanded that Syria withdraw its troops from Lebanon. Lebanon's unrest did not abate, though, as its Shi'a, who constituted a plurality if not the majority of the population, threw their support to Hizbullah, a militant Islamist organization, which accumulated Syrian and Iranian weapons and increasingly used them against Israel, whose troops retaliated in kind. When Hizbullah captured two Israeli soldiers in July 2006, Israel attacked its Lebanese strongholds by air, land, and sea, killing, maiming, and displacing thousands of civilians as well as Hizbullah fighters. Hizbullah rockets struck northern Israel and caused damage to Haifa and some Jewish and Arab villages in Galilee. The fighting ended after thirty-four days under UN Security Council Resolution 1701, which dispatched a new peace-keeping force to southern Lebanon. Neither side really won, and tension persists on the Israeli-Lebanese border.

The Arab-Israeli conflict has gradually morphed in the past twenty years into a struggle between Israel and the Palestinians (or, more accurately, descendants of the Arabic-speaking refugees of the 1948 Arab-Israeli war). Israel and its backers had gradually come to accept the need for a Palestinian state, and the Arab governments offered to recognize Israel in return for its withdrawal from the Golan Heights, the West Bank, and the Gaza Strip, the lands Israel had taken in the 1967 war and occupied ever since. Regrettably, though, the Palestinians and Israel continued to fight against each other. The second intifada, which followed the failure of the 2000 Camp David summit, dragged on, as the Palestinians increasingly resorted to suicide bombings against civilians in Israel and the Israeli army raided and occupied large swaths of the West Bank and Gaza, destroying houses and killing or maiming Palestinians. The number of Jewish settlers in the West Bank and Gaza doubled between 1993 and 2004, further dimming hopes for peace. The Road Map led to brief peace talks in 2003, which were soon suspended.

Realizing that the Jewish state faced a demographic challenge if it occupied Palestinian lands indefinitely, Israel hoped to pull back from areas in which it had no long-term interest, starting with the Gaza Strip in 2005. It withdrew its settlers and soldiers, hoping for peace with the Palestinians but, in part because it continued to control land, water, and air access to Gaza, dissatisfied Palestinians attacked southern Israel with rockets and Israel retaliated with targeted killings and military invasions. The 2006 war in Lebanon overshadowed a concurrent deadly conflict in Gaza. As for the West Bank, Israel had begun building a security fence in 2002. Intended to keep raiders and suicide bombers out of Israel, it impeded Palestinian movement within the West Bank and cut off some of the captured lands, especially those occupied by Jewish settlers, from Palestinian areas. Not surprisingly, when Palestinians were able to elect representatives to their parliament in January 2006, most chose Islamist deputies loyal, not to Fatah, but rather to Hamas, which formed a new cabinet that openly opposed the Oslo Accords and recognition of Israel. As Israel blockaded Gaza, Hamas militias began fighting forces loyal to Fatah. In June 2007 the PLO president, Mahmud Abbas, dismissed the Hamas government. Hamas took over in Gaza, while Fatah retained control of the West Bank. The Bush administration has tried to bring Israel's prime minister and Palestine's president to Annapolis for a peace conference that might draft a settlement between Israel and the Palestinians, but neither leader enjoys much credibility among his own people.

◼ Conclusion

The peoples and the countries of the Middle East are not at peace, either with one another or, indeed, with themselves. Secular nationalism competes with Islam as the leading ideology for many Middle Eastern Arabs, Iranians, and Turks. The breakup of the Soviet Union has drawn some Middle Eastern countries into competition over the new republics of the Caucasus and Central Asia. The Cold War may have ended, but Washington articulates its Middle East policy goals not by diplomacy, but by force. Borders between countries, drawn mostly by Western imperialists for their own interests, rarely reflect natural frontiers and are often violated by the armies of strong states preying upon weaker ones. Many Middle Easterners have moved to burgeoning cities, acquired years of schooling, and been exposed to radio and television propaganda, swelling their ambitions beyond what their societies actually have to offer. Young adults feel especially frustrated, a feeling often enhanced by their migration from countries of high population and little oil (such as Egypt) to others that are poor in labor but rich in oil (such as Saudi Arabia), separating them from their parents, spouses, children, and friends. Although no other region's problems threaten world peace as often as those of the Middle East, this chapter has stressed that both internal factors and foreign meddling in its domestic affairs have created these conflicts and problems. As other chapters show, there can be no lasting resolution of these conflicts without addressing the multiple causes of the region's instability.

▨ Bibliography

Abu-Nasr, Jamil M. 1987. *A History of the Maghrib in the Islamic Period.* New York: Cambridge University Press.

Allen, Mark. 2006. *Arabs.* London: Continuum Publishers.

Cleveland, William L. 2004. *A History of the Modern Middle East.* 3rd ed. Boulder, Colo.: Westview Press.

Findley, Carter V. 2005. *The Turks in World History.* Oxford: Oxford University Press.

Gelvin, James. 2005. *The Modern Middle East: A History.* Oxford: Oxford University Press.

Goldschmidt, Arthur, Jr., and Lawrence Davidson. 2006. *A Concise History of the Middle East.* 8th ed. Boulder, Colo.: Westview Press.

Halm, Heiz. 2007. *The Arabs: A Short History.* Trans. by Allison Brown and Thomas Lampert. Princeton: Markus Wiener Publishers.

Kamrava, Mehran. 2005. *The Modern Middle East: A Political History Since the First World War.* Berkeley: University of California Press.

Keddie, Nikki. 2006. *Modern Iran: The Roots and Results of Revolution.* New Haven: Yale University Press.

Lapidus, Ira M. 2002. *A History of Islamic Societies.* 2nd ed. New York: Cambridge University Press.

Sachar, Howard M. 2007. *A History of Israel from the Rise of Zionism to Our Times.* 3rd ed. New York: Alfred A. Knopf.

4

Middle Eastern Politics

Deborah J. Gerner and Philip A. Schrodt

Hezbollah stages maneuvers near Israeli border . . . Bush looks to forestall incursion into Iraq in talks with Turkish Prime Minister . . . Syria's Assad tells French envoys Lebanon should hold elections without foreign interference . . . U.S. military deaths in Iraq at 3,850 . . . Egypt's ruling party opens possible path for Mubarak's son's succession . . . Israeli aircraft strike northern Gaza . . . Al-Qaida accuses Libya's Gadhafi of being an enemy of Islam . . . Morocco recalls ambassador in flap with Spain over enclaves . . . Oil tops $96 a barrel . . . US pushes UN Security Council for tougher sanctions on Iran over nuclear program.
—*Associated Press,* November 1–5, 2007

Viewed from the perspective of daily headlines, politics in the Middle East appear confused, chaotic, and often violent. When asked why they are interested in taking a course in Middle Eastern politics, students often say they want to be able to understand the news stories but don't know where to begin. This chapter focuses on the current political situation of the Arab world, Iran, Israel, and Turkey. It first describes several general factors that influence the contemporary Middle East, such as its colonial legacy, the evolving international context, and the level of economic development, and then reviews a variety of political institutions and ideologies that function in the region. Particular attention is given to distinguishing those characteristics of Middle Eastern domestic politics that are relatively unusual, for example, the prevalence of ruling monarchies, from those attributes that are more common, such as close relations between the state and the military establishment. The critically important issue of gender, which is only touched on here, is treated more comprehensively in Chapters 9, 10, and 11.

▓ The Colonial Legacy

Domestic politics in the Middle East are influenced by a paradox: this ancient region, with a history that dates back to the earliest years of human settlements, has only recently been organized politically into modern states, that is, centralized political units with sovereignty over a fixed territory and population. In Chapter 3, Arthur Goldschmidt Jr. describes the paths these countries took to reach the beginning of the twenty-first century. This section briefly summarizes one of the most significant aspects of that history for understanding contemporary politics: the impact of European imperialism in the region.

The term *imperialism* refers to the establishment of political and economic control by one state or empire over a foreign territory. In the context of the Middle East, the involvement of European powers, particularly Britain and France, was highly interventionist and, from the perspective of regional history, often arbitrary. At the same time, the extent and nature of European control varied considerably, both between subregions (e.g., North Africa versus the Arabian Peninsula) and also between adjacent areas within a single region (e.g., Syria versus Jordan). Decisions made during the colonial era had effects that persist today and continue to influence the Middle East's political development.

In contrast to the Americas, sub-Saharan Africa, and Asia, which were subjected to colonial exploitation after being "discovered" by Europeans, the geographical extent and the resources of the Middle East were known to the political powers of Europe since antiquity. Prior to the middle of the nineteenth century, however, widespread colonial activity by Europe was blocked by the military power of the Ottoman Empire. When Europeans did begin to assert their authority, opportunistically as Ottoman control weakened, that expansion occurred in the context of existing competing European imperial systems. The pattern of a single colonizer exercising control over a large contiguous territory—as with the British in North America and southern Asia or the Spanish in Latin America—did not occur, and so the colonial experience of states in the Middle East varied substantially across time and place.

Egypt provides an illustration of the political complexities of colonialism. As Goldschimdt shows in greater detail in Chapter 3, Egypt was occupied by Napoleonic France at the beginning of the nineteenth century. French forces were defeated by the British, who restored Ottoman control to Egypt; however, Ottoman rule was soon challenged by Muhammad Ali— a soldier originally appointed by the Ottomans to administer Egypt—who began to develop Egypt as a powerful and autonomous state. Ali's successors were unable to continue this independence and, in conjunction with construction of the Suez Canal, the country fell into deep debt to European financiers. These financial problems provided the pretext for a British invasion in 1882 and the consolidation of forty years of direct British control. In 1923, Britain granted nominal independence to Egypt but maintained the pro-British monarchy and reserved the right to station troops in the country (which it did during World War II as Germany sought to gain control of the Suez Canal). Even after the British-imposed monarchy was overthrown in 1952, Britain and France briefly invaded Egypt in 1956 in a final attempt to reassert European authority over the canal.

Although the details vary, similar intensity and intricacy of colonial involvement can be found in most of the major countries of the region. Most significantly, British and French colonial interests competed throughout the region. On occasion this caused conflict between the European states, as with the Fashoda dispute in Sudan in 1898; at other times Britain and France agreed to sweeping divisions of authority, as with the Sykes-Picot Agreement in 1916, which divided up former Ottoman districts into modern-day Syria, Lebanon, Iraq, Jordan, Israel, and the Palestinian territories. Algeria was actually made an administrative part of France and won independence only through a long and costly war; Tunisia, too, was colonized by the French but its freedom came more easily. Europe and the United States considered the Gulf region peripheral—allowing Abdul Aziz ibn Saud to assemble an independent state on the Arabian Peninsula without external interference—until the 1930s with the discovery of oil. Although Britain and France were responsible for most of the colonial activity in the region, other European states—notably Italy in Libya and Russia in Iran—also exercised substantial influence.

These diverse colonial interactions left a patchwork of widely differing political circumstances, as illustrated by comparing the experiences of Israel, Jordan, and Lebanon. The heavily populated parts of these countries occupy a small geographical area that, in the absence of borders, could be easily driven around by car in a day. But in the second half of the twentieth century, the experiences of the three countries could not be more different. Lebanon—in the French sphere of influence under the Sykes-Picot division—developed as a confessional parliamentary democracy that attempted to balance Muslim and Christian interests while maintaining the dominant position of the latter. Modern Israel developed out of a League of Nations mandate for Palestine—itself a relic of the Ottoman Empire—that under British control was promised as a "homeland" to the Zionist movement in the 1917 Balfour Declaration. Jordan was forged from another area under British control and politically constituted as an Arab monarchy ruled by a family from the Arabian Peninsula to whom Britain owed a favor. At the beginning of the twenty-first century, still another political entity—some form of Palestinian state situated between Israel and Jordan and between Egypt and Israel—struggled to emerge. Consequently three (and potentially four) very different states have been established in an area that for most of its history was intertwined economically and culturally.

As this example shows, the colonial experience has been critically important in determining the contemporary political environment. Differences between the North African states of Morocco, Algeria, Libya, and Egypt reflect in part the fact that they were, respectively, under Arab, French, Italian, and British authority during the early twentieth century. When British prestige in the Gulf waned, it was smoothly replaced with US influence, whereas the Algerian political system was strongly influenced by its bloody war for independence from France. A few countries—Morocco, Turkey, Saudi Arabia, and Oman—escaped direct European domination almost entirely (although they were still profoundly affected by the threat of this control), whereas others—Djibouti, for instance, or the Western Sahara, whose referendum on independence has been delayed repeatedly—are among the last areas in the world to achieve political sovereignty. As was true in Africa, the boundaries imposed by European powers often had little correspondence to the distribution of ethnic groups on the ground—most notably in the division of the Kurdish region between Turkey, Iraq, and Iran—or created states whose legitimacy could be called into question, as with Iraq's claims on Kuwait or Syria's claims on Lebanon. The colonial empires are gone, yet their effects not only linger but have substantial influence.

■ A Changing International Context

Following European decolonization during the 1940s, 1950s, and 1960s, the foreign affairs of the Middle East have been dominated by three major conflicts: the Cold War, the Arab-Israeli dispute, and a series of wars involving Iraq. The first of these has now disappeared, but the second and third continue to have implications for the region's domestic politics. In addition, the rising military power of Shi'i political actors in Lebanon, Iraq, and Iran has begun to play a role in the first decade of the twenty-first century.

The end of the Cold War and the dissolution of the Soviet Union had profound effects on Soviet allies such as Syria, Iraq, Libya, and particularly the former People's Democratic Republic of Yemen (PDR Yemen). Those countries can no longer count on the former superpower for military or economic assistance (although Russia will still gladly sell arms for hard cash), nor is Russia interested in providing the preferential trade arrangements that were often used by the Soviet Union to secure alliances. Allies of the United States face an equally difficult situation. In the absence of the "Communist threat" and in an environment of growing public disdain for US policies with respect to Iraq and Israel, governments that are seen as too dependent on US support find that this policy generates significant domestic opposition, as both Egypt and Saudi Arabia have learned.

Since the middle of 2002, foreign relations in the eastern half of the Middle East have been dominated by the US conflict with Iraq. This began with about a year of increasing hostilities that culminated in a relatively quick invasion of Iraq by the United States, Great Britain, and some additional allies in March and April of 2003. While a clear military victory was achieved over the regular Iraqi forces, the Bush administration had gone against the advice of its senior military officers and had sent inadequate forces to insure stability of the country following the dissolution of the regime of Saddam Hussein (Woodward, 2004). This was compounded by misguided strategies intended to rapidly transform Saddam's centralized Sunni dictatorship, which had been brutally repressing the Shi'i majority and the Kurdish minority, into a flourishing democracy. These policies instead had the effect of plunging Iraq into a state of widespread internal conflict involving both Iraqi attacks on the forces of the United States and its allies and extensive ethnic conflict between Sunni, Shi'i, and Kurdish groups within Iraq itself (Galbraith, 2006; Woodward, 2006).

US administrators in Iraq, who generally had no prior Middle East experience, became isolated in fortified compounds (Chandrasekaran, 2006; Ricks, 2006), and basic services such as electricity, water, and oil production could not be restored to their prewar levels. Although the Iraqi government achieved a few early benchmarks toward democratic government, notably two national legislative elections in 2005, the parliamentary system quickly became stalemated as it divided along ethnic lines.

While the Bush administration continued to maintain that its Iraq policy was working, and the US Congress failed to produce any alternative to that policy, criticism from within the military itself (Aylwin-Foster, 2005; Yingling, 2007) led to a major shift in policy in early 2007 under the direction of a new US commander, General David Petraeus. His strategy implemented new counterinsurgency theories developed in response to these earlier failures (Petraeus, 2006), combined with an increase—nominally temporary—in the number of US troops. As of November 2007, the level of violence in Iraq has been declining, but long-term stability remains unlikely.

Even if the military situation stabilizes, the US invasion of Iraq will leave numerous long-term consequences for the region. The war and subsequent ethnic violence has generated an estimated two million international refugees, and more than a million "internally displaced persons" (Peteet, 2007). These internal population changes may be moving Iraq toward a situation where an ethnically mixed central state is no longer possible, leading instead to either a confederation with a weak central state or possibly even outright division of the country. The northern Kurdish area—which has generally avoided the violence plaguing Sunni and Shi'i Iraq—is already essentially an autonomous state; this, in turn, however, is causing considerable tensions with Turkey, which also has a large Kurdish minority. With the escalation of attacks in Turkey by Kurdish rebels operating from northern Iraq,

Turkish troops have been amassed along the Iraqi border, and Turkey has made clear that it would engage in cross-border attacks as necessary. As of this writing, Turkey has taken its first steps in this regard, bombing suspected Kurdistan Workers' Party (PKK) positions in northern Iraq.

The Arab-Israeli conflict also continues, primarily between Palestinians and Israel. Egypt and Jordan have officially normalized relations with Israel, and visitors can now pass freely, if not easily, among these three countries. Syria, economically disadvantaged and deprived of Soviet support, can refuse negotiations on the Israeli-occupied Golan Heights, but it cannot force the issue militarily. Southern Lebanon, on the other hand, remains a source of tension. Israel withdrew from Lebanon in 2000 after nearly two decades of occupation, but the Israeli-Lebanese border remains a major flashpoint in the conflict between the Shi'i Hizbullah movement and Israel. A war ensued in the summer of 2006, with Hizbullah firing missiles that reached the Israeli northern city of Haifa and Israel bombing Lebanese territories as far north as Beirut.

With the Oslo Agreement of 1993, the election of Israeli prime minister Ehud Barak in May 1999, and the resumption of Israeli-Palestinian talks a few months later, genuine rapprochement between Palestinians and Israelis briefly appeared likely. The disastrous Camp David talks in 2000 and the subsequent outbreak of the second intifada (sparked by Ariel Sharon's provocative visit to the Haram al-Sharif/Temple Mount in September 2000) ended these hopes.

As of November 2007, the peace process of the 1990s is in complete disarray. Israel has reoccupied much of the land it ceded to the Palestinians as part of the Oslo peace process and is nearing completion of a physical "separation/security barrier"—a structure that is merely a well-patrolled fence in rural areas and a massive ten-meter-high concrete wall with guard towers and fortified gateways in major urban areas—to separate West Bank Palestinians both from Israel and in many instances from their ancestral farm lands and water resources. (Mary Ann Tétreault, in Chapter 5, and Simona Sharoni and Mohammed Abu-Nimer, in Chapter 6, explore this issue more fully.) Israel withdrew its military forces and settlements from the Gaza Strip in the summer of 2005, but the combination of rocket attacks launched from Gaza into Israel and retaliatory Israeli air strikes and economic blockades have meant that Gaza has seen nearly continuous military activity.

The prospects for a resolution of the Israeli-Palestinian situation are further hampered by the nearly complete political paralysis by all of the major actors involved, with the possible exception of the European Union. Palestinian president Yasser Arafat died in November 2004 and was weakened by illness for some years prior to that; while Mahmoud Abbas is his nominal successor, Abbas has not had the skill in balancing the multiple competing constituencies in the West Bank, Gaza, and the Palestinian diaspora. This situation was further complicated in January 2006 when the Islamic Hamas party won a majority in parliamentary elections in a free and fair democratic election—an electoral victory that was as much a vote against the corruption and ineffectiveness of the secular Fatah Party of Abbas as an endorsement of Hamas. Despite the democratic mandate of Hamas, the United States and European Union have largely refused to deal with it, leaving the political institutions of the Palestinian Authority, which were weak in the best of circumstances, in complete disarray. This culminated in June 2007 with the outbreak of civil war in Gaza and the expulsion of Fatah from that territory. At the time of this writing, Hamas and Fatah are essentially operating parallel Palestinian governments in Gaza and the West Bank.

While the security and economic situation is better on the Israeli side, the political situation is not. Having asserted strong control in the summer of 2005 with the successful evacuation of Israeli settlements in Gaza, Prime Minister Sharon suffered a severe stroke in January 2006, and has not regained consciousness since. His successor, Ehud Olmert, has neither Sharon's charisma nor effectiveness, and has seen wild swings in his political popularity: in March 2007 a poll showed only 3 percent of Israelis, a figure statistically indistinguishable from zero, willing to re-elect Olmert (Reuters, 2007), though by September 2007 his approval rating had risen to 35 percent following an air-strike on a possible Syrian nuclear facility (Associated Press, 2007). Meanwhile Israel continues to grapple with the issue of the nature of the Jewish state. Israelis face the challenge of violent Jewish fundamentalist movements, the rise of ethnically defined political parties, and heated debates on the extent to which the government should legislate religious practices (Sprinzak and Diamond, 1993; Cohen-Almagor, 2005; Yiftachel, 2006). Ironically, as Israel is being reluctantly accepted in parts of the Arab world, its political problems are also coming to resemble those of its neighbors.

Finally, the United States, bogged down in an unpopular war in Iraq, appears to have neither the time nor the political capital to invest in the Israeli-Palestinian issue. This might open up the possibility of peace negotiations facilitated by the European Union (EU), which compared to the United States has played a very limited role in mediating the conflict. Whether the EU is willing to increase its involvement and how effective it can be remains to be seen.

Another major factor that has arisen in the past decade is the emergence of the Shi'a of Iran, Iraq, and Lebanon as a significant military force in the region (Nasr, 2006; MERIP, 2007). This has resulted from the confluence of a number of events, including Hizbullah's unexpectedly effective attacks against Israel in the summer of 2006 and the creation of large Shi'i militias, most notably the "Mahdi Army" of Muqtada al-Sadr, in the ethnic conflicts of Iraq. Furthermore, the Iranian government of Mahmoud Ahmadinejad has developed advanced capabilities in long-range ballistic missiles and has been accused by the United States of developing nuclear weapons, although international agencies have found no proof of such programs.

The implications of these developments are unclear. Sunni-Shi'i divisions are not a new phenomenon in the Middle East, though for most of recent history these were always resolved in favor of Sunni-dominated political institutions except in Iran, which was culturally as well as religiously distinct from the Arab world. As the Shi'i majority gains political power in Iraq, a semiautonomous Shi'i area is established in southern Lebanon, and the large Shi'i populations in states such as Saudi Arabia and Bahrain assert claims for greater political participation, the issue moves into key areas of the Arab world itself. This is further complicated, as Jillian Schwedler argues in Chapter 12, by the fact that conservative Sunni movements such as Al-Qaida regard Shi'ism as heretical, a distinction frequently lost upon Western commentators who lump together Al-Qaida, Saudi Wahhabism, and the Shi'i Islamic Republic of Iran as "Islamic fundamentalists." This internal division, particularly with the new military effectiveness of Shi'i nonstate actors, could prove quite destabilizing in the future.

■ Economic Development

Like all decolonized areas, the states of the Middle East confront the problem of economic development. This issue will be covered in detail in Chapters 7, 8, and 9; here we point out several aspects that are most salient to domestic politics. (See Richards and Waterbury, 1996, for an extensive treatment of the Middle East's political economy through the mid-1990s; and Russell, 2006, for a more recent analysis.)

Any discussion of economics must deal separately with states that have significant oil revenues and those that do not. The oil wealth of the era of the Organization of Petroleum Exporting Countries (OPEC) made possible policies of almost unimaginable extravagance such as growing wheat in the desert using desalinated water. The subsequent instability of oil prices, however, has left a series of new problems for the petroleum-based economies. In contrast, states that have little or no oil face a fairly conventional set of development issues, similar to those of any newly industrializing country.

The 1980s and 1990s saw a continued drop in the price of oil, briefly falling below its pre-1973 levels when measured in real dollars. The drop in oil revenues in turn created several sources of domestic instability. The most obvious issue was that governments had fewer funds available to deal with potential opponents of the regime, either by co-opting them or paying for the coercive power required to suppress them. In a number of countries, economic restructuring programs mandated by the International Monetary Fund

More than 2 million people have been killed by fighting and famine during the civil war that has engulfed eastern and southern Sudan since the early 1980s. Millions more have lost their homes and must live in makeshift shelters like this one.

(IMF) in the 1980s and 1990s led to civil unrest as governments began eliminating social services and subsidy programs on which poorer citizens relied.

The oil-price decline reversed around 2000, and prices have steadily increased to the point where, by 2008, they (in constant dollars) were higher than their peak in 1981. This increase has been caused by supply disruptions and instability in Iraq and by the rapidly growing economies of Asia, notably China. While the first situation will presumably be eventually resolved, Asian demand for oil will almost certainly accelerate until such point that renewable energy resources begin to substantially replace oil, a process that will require decades.

The response of oil-rich Middle Eastern states to this most recent upward trend in oil prices is likely to be different than what it was in the 1970s. The oil price decline of 1980–2000 led to a realization that oil-derived wealth was not permanent, and a sense that, should oil revenues again become abundant, they needed to be used more prudently to develop a diversified, sustainable economy, based on professional services such as trade, banking, engineering, information technology, and education. This requires a well-educated indigenous middle class, which, if the Middle East follows the pattern of numerous other countries, will result in pressures for greater democratic openness. Alternatively, these states may be able to use these renewed revenues to follow the "Confucian capitalism" model of China and Singapore, where a world-class technological elite accommodates a nondemocratic central authority that maintains its legitimacy through the provision of political stability and economic growth, but not liberal democracy. This possibility is discussed in greater detail later in this chapter.

Outside the oil-rich states, the political problems of development differ little from those found elsewhere in the world. On average, the Middle East is neither unusually wealthy nor unusually poor, although there are extremes on either end: Turkey and Israel have achieved economic growth comparable to that of the most successful Asian industrializing countries, whereas resource-poor Djibouti, Mauritania, Sudan, and Somalia have very limited prospects for development. International war has disrupted economic expansion in Iran; civil war has had the same effect in Algeria; Lebanon and Iraq have faced the dislocations of both civil and international wars.

■ Informal Structures of Power

To fully understand the processes of Middle Eastern politics, one must look beyond the formal structures of governance—kings, emirs, parliaments, presidents, and prime ministers—which are discussed below. Of particular importance are the informal structures of family and social networks: the average citizen in the Middle East, whether Arab, Israeli, Turk, or Persian, finds these far more important in influencing political loyalties than would typically be the case for a citizen of North America or Western Europe.

The word that many Western analysts have attached to these networks is *tribes,* but this term is not particularly accurate since Middle Eastern political networks frequently do not differ in language, religion, or cultural traditions, attributes that are distinguishing characteristics of a tribe as the word is commonly used. (When such distinctions do exist—for instance, with the complex religious differences within Lebanon or the linguistically distinct Kurds—they usually translate into politically salient alignments.) Instead, as Laurie King-Irani discusses in Chapter 10, the networks are usually based on extended families and geographical connections to a region or village.

Within these networks, linkages are first and foremost social or economic and only then political. However, as politics become more local, the strength of the existing social networks increases. As a consequence, political control can change at the top of the system with relatively little change at the bottom: Egypt was under foreign political control for 2,284 years—from the defeat of the last Pharaonic dynasty by Alexander the Great in 332 B.C.E. to the overthrow of British-supported King Farouk in 1952—yet in the villages of the Nile Delta or the neighborhoods of Cairo, local politics persisted. The Ottoman Empire recognized this aspect of Middle Eastern life and guaranteed local control of local issues through its *millet* system (which placed each religious community under the jurisdiction of its own religious authorities for most legal, social, and cultural affairs). In contrast, the efforts by European colonial powers to develop centralized and uniform governance frequently caused chaos and inefficiency, as Western bureaucratic institutions created extensive systems of patronage and nepotism, much as they had done in most of Europe until the past century or so.

At the same time, the old systems of social networks are less pronounced today than a century ago. Within the Middle East, rapid urbanization has disrupted and weakened centuries-old alliances based in isolated villages. Although immigrants to major cities such as Cairo, Istanbul, and Tehran are still influenced by family and village, new loyalties and affiliations challenge the older bonds. These traditional loyalties are further eroded by the migration of many expatriate workers—often the best and brightest young people of a generation—to jobs in the Gulf, Europe, or North America, where the old ties are difficult to maintain, particularly for an immigrant's daughters and sons born in a distant land.

Consequently, the contemporary Middle East sees a mix of old and new political structures. The royal family of Saudi Arabia and King Abdullah of Jordan, for instance, still base much of their power—particularly in the military and security services—on systems of loyalty based on family and village. Desert bedouins, not the Palestinians who form the majority of the population, dominate the Jordanian monarchy's security services while tribal groupings put forth political candidates to represent their distinct interests. Most of former Iraqi leader Saddam Hussein's inner circle of advisers and administrators came from his home village of Tikrit. In contrast, the urban economic elites of Beirut and Istanbul are more likely to follow a European model of social relationships, and some may, in fact, feel more comfortable in European circles than in Arab or Turkish social groups.

However, the systems do coexist. Within Israel, the Labor Party, which tends to attract individuals whose parents or grandparents immigrated to Israel from Europe, has a European-style system of flexible loyalties based on ideology. In contrast, the Shas Party, which emerged in the 1990s as a major player in Israeli politics, attracts voters from the ethnically Arab Jewish communities who immigrated from Morocco, Yemen, and Iraq. Shas places far greater importance on traditional relationships and political guidance from conservative rabbinical leaders. This tension between various styles of political organi-zation is likely to be a pervasive factor in Middle Eastern politics for the foreseeable future.

■ The Myth of Political Instability

Early on, any discussion of the domestic politics of the Middle East that is di-rected to a Western audience must confront one of the most pervasive—but at the same time most conspicuously untrue—myths about the region: that gov-ernments in the Middle East are precarious and extremely changeable. Noth-ing could be further from the truth. In the past several decades, many have been extraordinarily stable. (This leaves open the question of whether the form this stability takes is or is not desirable, as shown, for example, in the complex contrasts between the Saddam Hussein and post–Saddam Hussein era in Iraq.) Until his death from cancer in 1999, King Hussein of Jordan was the longest-ruling leader in the region, having served as king for nearly five decades. King Hassan II, who also died in 1999, had governed Morocco since 1961. Despite predictions of a chaotic transition, power passed smoothly to their sons, as also happened following the death of Syria's Hafiz al-Assad in 2000. Djibouti has had only two leaders since gaining independence in 1977: Hassan Gouled Aptidon, president until April 1999, and his nephew Isma'il Omar Guelleh, who was elected to succeed him. Egypt's Hosni Mubarak has been in power for more than twenty-five years.

Egypt, Saudi Arabia, and Israel have handled transfers of power smoothly under the difficult conditions of assassination; Jordan, Oman, and Tunisia have replaced, more or less gracefully, leaders whose mental or physical condition had deteriorated; Jordan, Morocco, Syria, and Bahrain each dealt with the death of a longtime leader and the transition to a new generation with apparent ease. The political system established in Turkey in the 1920s has survived to the present day and has been far more stable than the gov-ernments of such European Mediterranean states as Spain, Italy, Yugoslavia, and Greece during the same seventy-year period, notwithstanding three coups by the Turkish military. Significant revolutionary transformations have oc-curred—conspicuously, in Iraq (1958), Libya (1969), and Iran (1979) with the overthrow of Western-imposed monarchies—but even these changes were arguably no more dramatic than those that occurred in Eastern Europe and the Soviet Union in the late 1980s and early 1990s.

To be sure, Middle Eastern states see their share of military interven-tions, irregular transfers of power, and internal political intrigues, but no more so than in Latin America or Southeast Asia and less so than in much of Africa. The Middle East probably did experience an unusual number of political upheavals in the years immediately following decolonization (as did almost every other newly independent region), but the norm since the mid-1960s has been continuity.

Prospects for Democratization

With the virtual demise of Marxist-Leninist governments around the world, liberal democracy, characterized by the regular, open, honest electoral competition of political parties and protection of rights to organize politically, has become the dominant ideological basis for legitimizing political power. In contrast to many areas of the world that have successfully adapted Western liberal democratic structures and norms to local conditions (Japan, India, and Latin America, for instance), democratization poses several problems in the Middle East.

Perhaps the most fundamental challenge lies in the preexistence of many democratic—but not *liberal* democratic—institutions in the region. The successful monarchies have maintained and expanded extensive consultative structures and in Bahrain, Jordan, Kuwait, and Morocco have even established liberal democratic institutions, albeit with highly constrained powers. The revolutionary regimes base their legitimacy on mass political party structures, even though these have deteriorated into mere shells. Most countries in the region also hold regular elections for a nationally elected assembly. The importance of these "representative" institutions for governance varies considerably from state to state, but in countries as diverse as Morocco, Lebanon, Turkey, Bahrain, Iran, and Yemen, citizens remain willing to stand in long lines to cast their ballots on polling day.

Consequently, much of the Middle East, although not liberal democratic, is not devoid of structures for political participation (in contrast, for instance, to the military regimes of Latin America in the 1970s). The claim of a regionally constructed "Arab democracy" has some credibility. Nevertheless, the existing Middle Eastern models for liberal democracy have significant flaws. The extreme secularism of Mustafa Kemal Atatürk's constitution for Turkey is not acceptable in the current environment of Islamic revivalism and is challenged even in Turkey itself. Lebanon's initial attempts at confessional democracy—a system that assumes religious affiliation is the primary factor in how society is organized politically and constitutionally ensures the power of various groups—led to a devastating civil war in the 1970s and strongly contributed to the current governmental paralysis. Surprisingly, public opinion polls repeatedly show that Israel's model of government is widely admired by Arabs in countries as diverse as Jordan, Kuwait, and Egypt, despite popular opposition to Israel itself.

Moreover, the major liberal democratic powers have done little to encourage democracy in the region, notwithstanding US rhetoric in the wake

In 1997, men waited in long lines in Sana'a to vote in
parliamentary elections, Yemen's second since unification.

of the 2003 military campaign against Iraq. In the mid–twentieth century, Britain left absolute monarchies in place as it retreated. The United States has consistently tolerated undemocratic policies in its allies, including the monarchies of Saudi Arabia and Oman, the police state of Reza Pahlavi (the shah of Iran), and single-party rule in Egypt. France's experiment in Lebanon failed, and it has been accused of complicity in the cancellation of elections in Algeria in 1992. Hamas's parliamentary victory in a well-supervised election in January 2006 led to retaliation, rather than acceptance, by the democratic states of North America and Western Europe. The US attempts to impose democratic institutions on Iraq by military force have thus far resulted only in increasing ethnic conflict and instability in the country.

However, at least three factors suggest that democratization will continue to be an issue in the Middle East. First, the creation of a literate, urbanized middle class has consistently, in a variety of cultures, led to prodemocratic political movements, even in the most repressive states. Second, the most dynamic economies of the region—Turkey, Israel, and pre–civil war Lebanon—have thrived under democratic regimes. Third, the conditions that legitimized nondemocratic regimes—notably post-colonial politics and the Cold War competition—are declining in importance.

Most contemporary democratic theory emphasizes the importance of the institutions of "civil society" in buttressing liberal democracy. As Egyptian sociologist Saad Eddin Ibrahim explains:

> While there are a variety of ways of defining [the concept of civil society], they all revolve around *maximizing volitional, organized, collective participation in the public space between individuals and the state.* In its institutional form, "civil society" is composed of non-state actors or nongovernmental organizations (NGOs), including political parties, trade unions, professional associations, community development associations, and other interest groups. Normatively, "civil society" implies values and behavioral codes of tolerating—if not accepting—others and a tacit or explicit commitment to the peaceful management of differences among individuals and collectivities sharing the same "public space"—that is, the polity. (1995:29)

Traditional Middle Eastern society already has a rich set of institutions and nonstate actors, including labor unions and political parties, that mediate between public and private space. These often exist in the nondemocratic context of the mosque, family, or clan but are not less valid (nor less valuable) for that reason. Informal arrangements also serve many of the same functions as formal civic institutions. A farmer does not need to form a cooperative when his village has been sharing in the task of the olive harvest for generations; a mother has less interest in forming a parent-teacher association when her child's instructor is a cousin she has known since birth. Transplanting Western institutions of civil society into the Middle East—an objective of many North American and European development projects—is like trying to pour coffee into a cup that is already full: very little new coffee will remain in the cup, and in the meantime one has created a mess.

This suggests the possibility that a distinctly Middle Eastern model of democratic accommodation could develop, much as "Confucian capitalism" (Yao, 2002) has developed in lieu of Western liberal democracy in China and parts of Southeast Asia. While the Confucian cultural element is obviously irrelevant to the Middle East, the model is applicable in the sense of a strong, oftentimes paternalistic leadership providing a path that satisfies a growing professional class through modification of existing norms and political structures rather than through the importing of Western institutions such as competitive political parties.

This experiment is most evident in the small Gulf states such as Qatar and the United Arab Emirates (UAE), which have embarked on policies seeking a high level of economic liberalization and integration into the global capitalist economy without political liberalization. It is less clear whether this approach can be sustained over the long haul or whether, as occurred in the culturally Confucian states of South Korea and the Republic of China (Taiwan), the middle class will eventually force democratic reforms. It is also unclear whether a model that works in oil-rich city-states will generalize to larger or less wealthy states, such as Egypt. Somewhat improbably, however, the Confucian capitalism model has thus far been successfully transplanted from the city-state of Singapore to the vastly larger People's Republic of China. Finally, the strong central leadership required to maintain such a policy may not be present with countries such as Saudi Arabia and Iraq.

However, the Western political models also face significant challenges. Clearly, any liberal democratic movement will need to accommodate Islam explicitly in some form. According to Arab democratic theorists, this presents few problems: many interpretations of Islamic theology are at least as sympathetic to democratic ideals as is Christianity (and are more so than the Hinduism of India, where nonetheless a thriving liberal democracy has been established). However, many of the most politically powerful trends in contemporary Islam are highly conservative (for example, regarding the role of women).

Furthermore, any democratic movement must deal with the unresolved issues of ethno-national and religious minorities in Turkey, Iran, Iraq, Lebanon, Israel, and elsewhere. In addition to indigenous groups such as the Egyptian Coptic Christians and the Kurds, many of the smaller states have very large populations of "foreign" workers, some of whom have been residents for generations. Refugee flows also create complex problems concerning political rights, as illustrated by the ongoing problems of Palestinian refugees in Jordan, Lebanon, and Syria (and elsewhere), and the two million Iraqi refugees who have made their way primarily to Jordan and Syria. Establishing the rights and roles of such groups is a problem even for established democracies, as the experiences of the United States, France, and Germany illustrate; it is more difficult still in states for which political independence is relatively new and liberal democracy is an experiment some already regard with skepticism.

■ The Role of the Military

Throughout the Middle East, the military continues to play a critical role in both the construction and the implementation of domestic policy; furthermore, the region is the most highly militarized in the world. Several factors, some specific to the area, others more generally applicable to newly independent states, explain this continuing trend.

First, neither the period of European colonization and occupation nor the political situation immediately after independence was conducive to the establishment of formal civic groups. Colonial powers, intent solely on exploiting the resources of the region, discouraged or suppressed indigenous institutions for fear that these would be used as centers of opposition to colonial rule. Many of these policies continued after independence, particularly when rulers had been installed by the departing European power or were supported through the anti-Communist agenda of the United States. When states were allied with the Soviet Union, the opposite problem occurred: most grassroots civic activity was channeled into officially recognized, state-controlled institutions, leaving little room for independent action.

Thus, the focus of social organization was on rapid modernization and the creation of a military capable of addressing internal and external threats to the fragile regimes. In both Turkey under Atatürk and Iran under the Pahlavi dynasty, the government claimed its authoritarian rule was necessary for the country's economic development. Elsewhere, civil and international conflicts—the Iran-Iraq War, the invasion of Kuwait, long-standing Arab-Israeli tensions, civil war in Sudan, Kurdish autonomy movements, and so on—provided a justification (some would argue an excuse) for a massive buildup of military forces throughout the region.

In 1999, the Middle East (including North Africa), with just over 5 percent of the world's population, accounted for more than 13 percent of the world's armed forces with 2.8 million soldiers (US Department of State, 2002:5). Through the 1980s and 1990s, the region accounted for an astonishing 40 percent of global arms imports, although most of these purchases were concentrated in a small number of countries: Saudi Arabia, Egypt, Israel, Kuwait, Iran, and the UAE. Saudi Arabia was by far the largest arms importer during this period, followed by Israel (which also has an indigenous arms industry). By the end of the 1990s, Middle East arms imports had declined somewhat but still accounted for over 26 percent of total world imports in 1999 (US Department of State, 2002:9). As the military expenditure figures for 2005 illustrate (see Table 4.1), this trend still continues. The budgetary priority granted to defense spending in the Middle East has given greater political influence to the military, even in the domestic arena, than in countries in which the military establishment accounts for a much smaller portion of central government spending.

Second, military power frequently played a key role in the origins of the ruling regimes, resulting in a significant intertwining of the political and military elites. For instance, the unification of the central Arabian territory into the state of Saudi Arabia during the first three decades of the twentieth century can be attributed almost entirely to the military prowess of Abdul Aziz ibn Saud (although Ibn Saud also deserves credit for the political consolidation of the areas he conquered). In Algeria, the eight-year war of independence left the country virtually demolished, with the National Liberation Front (FLN) the one political-military institution that was intact and able to rule. Muammar Qaddafi came to power in Libya in 1969 through a military coup, and the military remains a key source of his power.

During Israel's early years, the military was clearly associated with the Mapai (which later evolved into the Labor Party); thus the political and the

Table 4.1 Military Expenditures of Middle Eastern Countries, 2005

Country	Total Expenditures (US$ millions)	As Percentage of GDP	Per Capita (US$)	Armed Forces (per thousand people)
Algeria	2,842	2.8	86	3.9
Bahrain	5160	4.0[a]	710	15.1
Djibouti	29.10	4.1[a]	37	12.6
Egypt	2,511	2.8	34	5.7
Iran	8,541	4.50	125	6.4
Iraq	n/a	n/a	n/a	n/a
Israel	9,749	7.9	1413	26.5
Jordan	978	7.7	181	18.7
Kuwait	4,606	5.7	1842	6.4
Lebanon	1,118	5.2[a]	280	18.0
Libya	1,293	3.1[a]	219	12.2
Mauritania	18	1	6	5.2
Morocco	2,219	4.3	74	6.5
Oman	3,268	10.6	1257.12	16.2
Qatar	n/a	n/a	n/a	14.8
Saudi Arabia	25,431	8.2	1101	4.6
Sudan	1,311	4.7[a]	36	2.9
Syria	1,533	5.4[a]	807	15.9
Tunisia	430	1.5	431	3.5
Turkey	11,629	3.2	161	11.4
United Arab Emirates	2,464	1.9	548	11.3
Yemen	835	5	40	3.2
United States	508,400	4.1	17153	5.1

Sources: World Bank Group, 2007, www.worldbank.org; International Monetary Fund, 2007, www.imf.org; Stockholm International Peace Research Institute, 2007, www.sipri.org.
Notes: a. 2000 figures for military expenditures as share of GDP.
n/a indicates data not available.

military were inextricably associated. In recent years, the military has become more autonomous (especially with Labor's political decline) but remains quite powerful. The common military experience of the majority of Jewish Israeli citizens has left an indelible mark on that country's politics: high rank, preferably in a selective army unit, and combat experience in one or more of Israel's many wars are attributes for success in the political arena, and most recent prime ministers have had impressive military credentials.

Finally, in a number of countries, elite military units, combined with effective secret intelligence forces (in Arabic, *mukhabarat*), are essential in securing the regime against political opposition. This was certainly the case in Iraq under Saddam Hussein; some sixteen divisions of military intelligence, with varying degrees of power, were each responsible for a specific type of crime (Makiya, 1993:339). Admittance into the military academies required membership in the Iraqi Baath Party; once accepted, military personnel were expected to show absolute commitment to Iraq and to the dictates of the president. In the aftermath of the Gulf War, following Iraq's invasion of Kuwait in 1990, reports emerged of mutinies and high-level defections from the elite Republican Guard. However, the *mukhabarat* and other security services continued to function efficiently, which minimized organized opposition to the regime.

Often, a leader will assign relatives or long-term allies to handle critical security functions. Within the Saudi military establishment, close family members hold all the significant positions and King Abdullah has retained command of the National Guard, which he has been head of since 1962. Similarly, in Jordan an overwhelming majority of the military officers are from East Bank families with links to the royal family that can be traced back to the earliest days of the state.

The implications of extensive military involvement in the governance of Middle Eastern countries are profound. When a regime must rely on the military to protect it from opposition movements, terrorism, or civil unrest, that regime becomes vulnerable to praetorianism, a situation in which "the civil authorities face constant threats from powerful military forces who try to shape all kinds of political decisions while remaining formally out of government" (Wilson, 1996:135). The repeated ultimatums given by the Turkish military in 1997 to force the resignation of Prime Minister Necmettin Erbakan, head of the Islamic Refah Party, illustrate how these pressures operate. Furthermore, "once they begin to perform the functions typically associated with parties, legislatures, and interest groups, . . . militaries render those political institutions irrelevant" (Bill and Springborg, 1994:235), which makes political liberalization all the more difficult.

Political Ideologies and Institutions

As is true for most newly independent countries, the basic political challenge for the Middle East in the post–World War II era has been the task of state building: the creation of governments that are legitimate, stable, and capable of acting autonomously both regionally and globally (Hudson, 1977; Luciani, 1990). For a variety of reasons, this has not been easy. First, the current political structures of many Middle Eastern countries were imposed by outside powers, rather than resulting from a gradual, internally driven process. Thus the governments of these newly independent countries often lacked the political, economic, and social institutions and the widespread legitimacy that would have existed had the state-building activity

Thomas Hartwell

Female soldiers participate in a military parade in Algiers, Algeria.

begun at the grassroots level. In many countries, the presence of powerful multinational corporations (notably international petroleum companies) meant that the new states were immediately drawn into the global political economy without having the opportunity to determine the type of relationship that would be of greatest benefit to their own development. This, too, has made the tasks of governance more difficult.

A further complication has been "the blurred boundaries between [the] state and [the] collective, supra-state identity inspired by common Arab-Islamic culture, history, and vision" (Sela, 1998:4). As a result, the utopian dream of a united pan-Arab nation with a shared history, culture, and sense of common identity stretching from the Strait of Hormuz to the Atlantic is in tension with the practical dictates of more than twenty politically sovereign Arab states. In a different world, a single Arab nation-state might have emerged. The region is at least as ethnically cohesive as India, Russia, or Indonesia and is comparable in size. However, European colonial involvement and the competing interests of both indigenous and international elites prevented this outcome. Nonetheless, some Arabs view the existing political divisions as illegitimate and reject, for instance, the separation of Lebanon from Syria. In this context, they believe it is perfectly appropriate for one state to intervene in the internal affairs of another, since all are part of the greater Arab nation.

Sources of Governmental Legitimation

Throughout the 1950s and 1960s, Arab leaders attempted to gain legitimacy in a variety of ways and with considerable ideological innovation (e.g., Baathism), balancing state-based claims with the aspirations of the Arab nation as a whole. By the early 1970s, two forms of governance—conservative monarchies and military or single-party revolutionary republics—dominated the political landscape. The monarchies, such as those of the Arabian Peninsula, were strongly patriarchal, with the king or emir taking on the role of a domineering yet benevolent father doing what he believes is best for his family. Constitutional monarchies like those of Jordan, Morocco, and Iran under the shah maintained the monarch as the ultimate political authority but also established elected legislatures with modest amounts of authority and developed significant governmental bureaucracies.

In contrast, some of the revolutionary states functioned under authoritarian personalistic leadership (most notably Libya, Syria, and Iraq), whereas others (e.g., Algeria, Egypt, Mauritania, Tunisia, and PDR Yemen) relied on the strength of a dominant political ideology, as expressed through a single political party, to provide support and legitimacy for the state leadership. The distinctions between these models should not be overstated, however, as they overlap in a variety of ways (see Anderson, 1991). Lebanon stands out as the one Arab country that had neither a king nor revolutionary leadership in the twentieth century. Its creation as an explicitly Christian-dominated Arab state, codified in the 1943 National Pact, made it unique.

Guards hold back the crowds at a state rally in Tripoli, Libya. The large poster pictures Qaddafi.

Turkey and Israel also do not fit neatly into either a monarchical or a revolutionary model. Yet they reflect the same pressures of political development that have influenced the entire region. The governments of both Turkey and Israel are products of late-nineteenth-century and early-twentieth-century liberal European ideologies such as nationalism. In the creation of their political structures, both countries were inspired by Western-style political modernization approaches (in the case of Turkey, due to its proximity to Europe; in Israel, as a consequence of its initial origins as a diaspora nationalist movement) rather than by the family-oriented, personalistic style of rule present in much of the region. Consequently, the Israeli and Turkish regimes are based on secular and formally democratic norms—although without the political integration of ethnic or religious minorities—and accept the principle of public accountability for the political leadership. In the 2000s, however, both countries were dealing with substantial challenges from groups seeking to radically redefine the role of religion within these states, as well as to challenge their liberal democratic nature and treatment of minorities. Turkey's experience with the Islamic Justice and Development Party in power since 2002 has demonstrated that political Islam can be reconciled with a democratic political system, not unlike political Christianity that has been associated with the Republican Party in the United States.

Political Islam

The political patterns established in the initial years of independence continue to exist today, although with some modifications in response to pressures for increased political liberalization (Norton, 1995). At the same time, in recent decades a new model—the Islamic republic—has mounted an increasingly significant challenge to the secular, nationalist ideologies used to legitimize both existing regimes and opposition movements in the revolutionary states. (Jillian Schwedler explores this issue in greater detail in Chapter 12.) This mirrors two global patterns.

First, people who see their world changing and feel that the values they hold dear are threatened, and believe that the government is not responding to their concerns, often turn to religion as a source of tradition and stability. Religious expression thus becomes a way to articulate frustration with the existing political structures. For instance, the twentieth-century founder of the Muslim Brotherhood, Hassan al-Banna (1906–1948), argued that the colonial domination of the region in the nineteenth and twentieth centuries was a direct result of the declining importance of Islam in the lives of ordinary people; a return to Islam would allow for an improved political situation. Second, individuals often focus on the political dimensions of religion when they perceive themselves as oppressed by the existing secular government.

Both elements were present in Iran under the rule of Pahlavi leader Mohammad Reza Shah. The shah combined extreme repression of opponents and claims of a historical right to rule with strongly Western-oriented modernization policies such as the land reforms of the White Revolution. Yet a few years before the Iranian revolution, the shah held an incredibly expensive celebration linking his rule to that of the ancient Persian empire. The Iranian population viewed this spectacle with skepticism, and, in retrospect, the celebration illustrated the fragility of his position.

Although the most successful contemporary implementation of political Islam occurred at the edge of the Arab world, in Iran, Islamic models have subsequently been applied in Sudan and Mauritania, present a major challenge in Algeria, and have influenced political dynamics across the entire region, including Iraq, among Palestinians, in Egypt, and in previously Christian-dominated Lebanon. Islam's grounding in the impressive history of the region; its emphasis on the socioeconomic equity and justice promised but not achieved by the nationalist revolutionary ideologies; its comprehensive belief system, which gives guidance on virtually all aspects of life; and its extensive critique of Western goals and values are all crucial to understanding the success of groups using Islam as an instrument of political action.

A Framework for Grouping Countries

Governments in the Middle East can be roughly classified into one of four groups: nationalist revolutionary republics, monarchies, Islamic states, and conditional democracies. Nationalist revolutionary republics such as Algeria, Libya, Egypt, Syria, and Iraq are generally characterized by single-party rule with a strongly institutionalized state structure. Monarchies, whether traditional or parliamentary, include Jordan, Morocco, Saudi Arabia, and a number of small Gulf states. Turkey, Israel, and Lebanon are generally classified as democratic states, although each has elements that may call this into question, whereas Iran, Mauritania, and Sudan have labeled themselves Islamic republics (notwithstanding that Iran has significant democratic elements).

Of course, any such effort at classification is a static, imperfect reflection of reality; most countries' political institutions have elements of several different systems. For instance, the Islamic Republic of Iran holds regular and contested elections, and Islam plays a significant role in several of the revolutionary republics. This categorization does, however, provide a convenient way to discuss the diversity of forms that Middle Eastern governments take (see Table 4.2).

▧ Nationalist Revolutionary Republics

For much of the twentieth century, the nationalist revolutionary state was one of the most important political models for the Middle East. Although the region suffered from its proximity to Europe by experiencing two centuries

Table 4.2 Formal Political Participation in the Middle East, 2007

Country	Year of Independence	Executive (a, e, h, s)[a]	Legislature (a, e)	Political Parties Legal?	Date of Female Political Suffrage	Date Females First Represented in Legislature (a, e)
Algeria	1962	President (e), Prime Minister (a)	National People's Assembly (e), Council of Nations (a, e)	Yes	1962	1962 (a)
Bahrain	1971	King (h)	Council of Representatives (e), Consultative Council (a)	No	2002	2002 (a)
Comoros	1975	President (e)	Assembly of the Union (e)	Yes	1956	1993 (e)
Djibouti	1977	President (e)	Chamber of Deputies (e)	Yes	1946	2003 (e)
Egypt	1922	President (e), Prime Minister (a)	People's Assembly (a, e), Advisory Council (a, e)	Yes	1956	1957 (e)
Iran	1925	Supreme Religious Leader (a), President (e)	Islamic Consultative Assembly (e)	Yes	1963	1963 (a, e)
Iraq	1932	Presidency Council (s), Prime Minister (s)	Council of Representatives (e), Federation Council (not yet formed)	Yes	1980	1980 (e)
Israel	1948	President (e, ceremonial), Prime Minister (e)	Knesset (e)	Yes	1948	1949 (e)
Jordan	1946	King (h), Prime Minister (a)	Chamber of Deputies (e), House of Notables (a)	Yes	1974	1989 (a)
Kuwait	1961	Amir (h), Prime Minister (a)	National Assembly (e)	No	2005	2005 (a)
Lebanon	1943	President (s), Prime Minister (s)	National Assembly (e)	Yes	1952	1963 (e)
Libya	1951	Revolutionary Leader (Colonel)	General People's Congress (e)[b]	No	1964	—
Mauritania	1960	President (e), Prime Minister (a)	National Assembly (e), Senate (e)	Yes	1961	1975 (e)
Morocco	1956	King (h), Prime Minister (s)	Chamber of Representatives (e), Chamber of Counselors (e)	Yes	1963	1993 (e)
Occupied Palestinian Territories[c]	1996	President (e), Prime Minister (s)	Legislative Council (e)	Yes	1996	1996 (e)

(continues)

Table 4.2 continued

Country	Year of Independence	Executive (a, e, h, s)[a]	Legislature (a, e)	Political Parties Legal?	Date of Female Political Suffrage	Date Females First Represented in Legislature (a, e)
Oman[c]	1951	Sultan (h) Council of State (a)	Consultative Council (e)	No	2003	2000 (a)
Qatar	1971	Amir (h),[d] Prime Minister (a)	Advisory Council (a)	No	2003	—
Saudi Arabia	1932	King (h)	Consultative Council (a)	No	—	—
Somalia[e]	1960	—	—	—	—	—
Sudan	1956	President (e) Council of States (e)	National Assembly (a)[f]	Yes	1964	1964 (e)
Syria	1946	President,[g] Prime Minister (a)	People's Council (e)	Yes	1953	1973 (e)
Tunisia	1956	President (e), Prime Minister (a)	Chamber of Deputies (e), Chamber of Advisors (a, e)	Yes	1959	1959 (e)
Turkey	1923	President (s, ceremonial), Prime Minister (s)	Grand National Assembly (e)	Yes	1930	1935 (a)
United Arab Emirates	1971	President (a), Prime Minister (a)[i]	Federal National Council (a, e)[h]	No	2006	2006 (e)
Yemen	1990	President (e), Prime Minister (a)	House of Representatives (e)	Yes	1970	1990 (e)[j]

Sources: UNDP, 2006; CIA, 2007.

Notes: a. Appointed (a), directly or indirectly elected (e), hereditary (h), selected by the legislature (s) as with the prime minister in a typical parliamentary system.
b. Indirectly elected through "people's congresses."
c. Women suffrage and representation information for Palestine and Oman determined by the authors; information was not available in UNDP 2006 statistics.
d. Current amir came to power after overthrowing his father in 1995.
e. After years of civil war and breakdown of central government, Somalia is now governed through Transitional Federal Institutions (no elections, parliamentary seats divided up among clans). Women were originally granted suffrage in 1956.
f. Although the National Assembly is currently appointed based on the 2005 Peace Agreement, it is supposed to be elected in the future.
g. President is approved by referenda.
h. First elections were held for half of the council in 2006 by a body of electoral college (of 6,689 emirates) appointed by the rulers of the emirates. Women were also included in this body and were also allowed to run; one woman won representation.
i. Both the president and the prime minister are appointed, or "elected," by the Federal Supreme Council, composed of seven emirate rulers.
j. Refers to the former People's Democratic Republic of Yemen. Yemen also has a Consultative Council (a), but it is an advisory council to the president only and not part of the legislature.

of colonial intervention and interference in the development of regional politics, this proximity provided at least one possible compensating advantage: intense exposure to the intellectual currents that accompanied the consolidation of the modern industrialized state in Europe, notably nationalism, political liberalism, and socialism.

As Goldschmidt outlines in Chapter 3, the "Arab awakening" (Antonius, 1946) began in the early to middle 1800s and culminated in a series of independence and self-determination movements in the twentieth century. Due to the constraints of colonialism, few of these ideas could be implemented prior to the 1950s, but the intellectual groundwork existed, at least some of the relevant political writings were in Arabic, and the literature spoke to the region's history (Khalidi, 1991; Tibi, 1997). In this respect, the Middle East was in a quite different situation than Asia or sub-Saharan Africa, which were relatively isolated from European political developments by the constraints of physical distance in the days before telecommunications.

The first successful twentieth-century nationalist movement in the Middle East, that of Atatürk following the end of World War I, shows the effects of these influences. Atatürk's single most dramatic innovation—the secularization of Turkey—was completely consistent with liberal revolutionary movements from the US and French revolutions forward. Although Atatürk was reluctant to share power, he did support the adoption of European political forms, such as a parliamentary system with a prime minister and cabinet chosen from the unicameral Grand National Assembly. This meant that the necessary structures for participatory government were in place after Atatürk's death.

In contrast, early efforts by the intelligentsia and the middle classes in Iran to limit the power of the Qajar monarchy and give control to an elected assembly failed. By the mid-1920s, Reza Khan, who founded the Pahlavi dynasty, had replaced the Qajar ruler. Reza Khan and his son Mohammad Reza Pahlavi combined social, economic, and military modernization with repression and authoritarian rule. Little was done to nurture the nascent parliament or develop other democratic institutions (Halliday, 1979).

Another three decades passed before the process of state building commenced in the Arab Middle East, but when decolonization began in earnest in the 1950s, significant ideological movements were ready and waiting to challenge the immediate postcolonial political structures imposed by Britain, France, and the United States. Thus the 1950s and 1960s saw a proliferation of alternative political approaches, often incorporating Islamic political values and histories into a formally secular framework. Much to the distress of the former colonizers, most of these new ideologies drew as much from the theories of Karl Marx and Vladimir Lenin as from those of Thomas Jefferson and John Locke. As a consequence, they emphasized a strong, centralized, and bureaucratized state, a characteristic that persists to this day even in countries that have in other ways moved away from this approach.

When viewed in the context of the 1950s and 1960s, there are several reasons for the appeal of centralized approaches to politics, none of which have anything to do with "Arab exceptionalism" or a distinctly Middle Eastern respect for strong leadership. First, the consolidation of state power was consistent with the prevailing Western political trends in government. During the previous two decades, the liberal democracies of Western Europe and North America had increasingly centralized authority, initially to counter the effects of the Great Depression and then to mobilize their economies for World War II. Both Marxists and progressive political theorists argued that such an expansion in central governmental authority was necessary to counter the economic power of industrialized capitalism.

Second, elements of the Soviet Union's Communist model were initially quite attractive. In a mere twenty-five years, the Soviet Union had gone from a quasi-feudal society to an industrialized power capable of withstanding the military assault of one of the most advanced European economies during World War II. It had survived the Great Depression, which had devastated most of the capitalist world, and in the 1950s the toll that Stalin's brutal policies had extracted from the Soviet people was not widely known or understood. Thus, varieties of socialism were appealing not just in the Arab world but in every area undergoing decolonization (e.g., China, Vietnam, Cuba, and parts of Africa). Indeed, socialism might have been widely implemented had it not been for the efforts of the US Central Intelligence Agency (CIA) and other Cold War agents of containment.

Finally, the political left rather than the right had consistently opposed colonialism. As discussed below, the monarchies, without exception, allied themselves with the colonial powers or their successor, the United States. Even in the era of colonialism, progressive and socialist groups had provided greater assistance in the anticolonial cause than had the liberal democracies. Indeed two of the most conspicuous of the European liberal democracies—Britain and France—had been the two most conspicuous meddlers in Arab affairs. Although the United States might have been able to exploit its anticolonial policies to promote a liberal democratic agenda (as it did briefly during the 1956 Suez crisis), it generally subordinated this goal to the pursuit of a simple anti-Communist agenda. The CIA overthrow of Iran's Mohammad Mossadeq in 1953, anti-Nasserist policies following the Suez crisis, the 1958 military intervention in Lebanon, and the deepening US military activity in Indochina by the mid-1960s ended any anti-colonial credibility the United States might once have had.

A full discussion of the diverse intellectual currents in Arab political thought during this period would fill several dozen books (and has). Here we will summarize the tenets of two ideological approaches that had a significant impact in the Middle Eastern political arena, Baathism and Nasserism.

Baathism

The Baath Party is one of the only political movements truly indigenous to the Arab world. In the 1940s, the Arab Baath Party was founded by two Syrians, Greek Orthodox Michael Aflaq (the group's intellectual leader) and Sunni Muslim Salah al-Din al-Bitar (its political strategist). This group merged in 1953 with a second organization, the Arab Socialist Party, to create the Arab Socialist Resurrection Party, also known as the Baath Socialist Party. The first members of the Baath Party came primarily from the intellectual elite, but the Baath quickly gained support among disadvantaged groups and established itself as a mass movement.

The basic Baathist ideology embraced a set of principles that drew on multiple sources of legitimacy in the Arab world: history, religion, nationalism, development, freedom, and socialism. Most important, Baathism called for social reform and economic justice, to be achieved through Arab socialism. In his writings, Aflaq resisted the temptation to rely exclusively on European socialist thinkers, with their emphasis on class struggle. Instead, he emphasized that the Baathist economic model was neither capitalist nor Communist: it was a middle way that was the product of the Arab world's unique history. A second key element of Baathism was its emphasis on pan-Arab unity, which was understood to involve the unification of existing Arab states into a single political entity as a replacement for patriotism centered on a specific state. Third, Baathism was anti-imperialist and anti-Zionist; it stressed the achievement of true Arab independence from all forms of colonialism.

Finally, Baathism called for a toleration of religious minorities within an overall Arab-Islamic political framework that included representative government and civil rights. As a result, Baathism could appeal both to the majority Muslim population and to Christians who would be left out of a more explicitly Islamic formulation of nationalism. The Baath Party is the dominant political actor in Syria, remains important in post-Saddam Iraq, and plays a more minor role in Jordan, Lebanon, and elsewhere.

Nasserism

Gamal Abdul Nasser was part of the Free Officers group who engineered the 1952 coup in Egypt that overthrew King Farouk. By the end of 1954, Nasser had begun to consolidate his position as president, prime minister, and head of the Revolutionary Command Council, which controlled Egyptian political life. To maintain power, the charismatic Nasser created a strong state bureaucracy and a variety of nationalist institutions, such as the Arab Socialist Union

(ASU), that he could dominate. Nasser's pan-Arab ideals and increasing interest in leftist ideologies evolved into a political and socioeconomic doctrine that came to be known as Nasserism.

Nasser maintained that socialism had to be adapted to the specific needs of Egypt rather than following the antireligious Marxism of the European states. Responding in part to the Muslim Brotherhood, Nasser attempted to root his economic approach in the Islamic ideal of equitable economic distribution:

> The Islamic ideal meant a society without injustice, which meant freedom from hunger, want and exploitation, which in turn implied common ownership of the means of production and a planned society. Within the framework of national unity all would be encouraged to co-operate for the national good. (Hopwood, 1985:100)

Unlike Baathism, however, Nasserism did not emerge early as a single ideology, but evolved as Nasser himself responded to domestic and foreign needs and challenges. Its impact as a political movement sharply declined after his death, and many of the Nasserist parties that had been established outside of Egypt collapsed.

States Dominated by a Single Party

Very few countries in the Middle East have genuine multiparty political systems. Instead, many have a single "government" party that dominates the political landscape and a set of ineffectual, often restricted, opposition parties that have little ability to influence the political direction of the country.

In this sense, Egypt is the quintessential model of a single-party bureaucratized state. Egypt's 1971 Constitution, as amended in 1990, identifies the country as a democratic, socialist Arab republic. It calls for a strong president, supported by a National Assembly of at least 350 people (currently there are 444 elected and 10 appointed representatives). The Egyptian National Assembly nominates the president; that name is then put to the general population in a national referendum. The person is declared president if the nomination is approved by a simple majority of those voting. Originally the constitution stipulated that the president could hold only two six-year terms, but President Anwar Sadat had this article amended to state that the president could be reelected for an unspecified number of terms. In 2005, Hosni Mubarak was "elected" for a fifth six-year term.

During the period between Egypt's independence in 1922 and the Free Officers' coup in 1952, a limited multiparty system was put in place. For the next twenty-five years, the ASU was the only legal political party. It was dissolved in 1977, shortly after Sadat announced Egypt would return to a multiparty system, and was replaced by the National Democratic Party (NDP), which has continued to dominate Egyptian politics (see Korany,

1998). In 1984, multiparty elections were held for the first time, and more than ten recognized parties were fielding opposition candidates by 2000. However, the 2005 parliamentary elections were marked by a combination of government manipulation, particularly through the use of laws governing which parties could run, and a sense that despite these efforts, government control on the electoral process was weakening, with the Muslim Brotherhood emerging as a strong opposition force. Although the organization has been formally banned, its members ran as "independents" and secured 20 percent of lower house seats (El-Amrani, 2005). The subsequent two years saw increasing crackdowns on both the religious and liberal democratic opposition, and in March 2007, constitutional changes prohibited parties from using religion as the basis for political activity, thereby stifling the most likely form of opposition.

The Egyptian political system has survived two crises that might well have led to its demise: the death of the charismatic Nasser three years after Egypt's disastrous military defeat by Israel in 1967 and the assassination of Sadat in 1981. The highly bureaucratized nature of the state, the combination of co-optation and control of opposition parties, extremely limited moves toward political liberalization, and economic liberalization (the relaxation of state controls on the economy so that markets can play a greater role) have kept the governmental system established by Nasser essentially intact, even though Nasserism as an ideology has faded.

Tunisia provides another example of a formally multiparty state in which a single party completely dominates politics. As in Egypt, Tunisia's first leader after independence and the abolition of the monarchy was a strong, authoritarian figure who was able to set the direction for the country. President

Egyptian president Hosni Mubarak has been in power since 1981.

Habib Bourguiba claimed he "invented" Tunisia, and indeed his impact over three decades was enormous. According to the 1959 Constitution, Tunisia is a "presidential republic" in which the president has much more power than the elected National Assembly. Under Bourguiba, Tunisia implemented a secular, Western-style legal system and, until the 1970s, pursued socialist-style economic development. Grassroots political participation was channeled through what was for many years Tunisia's only legal political party: the Neo-Destour Party and its successor, the Destour Socialist Party, since renamed the Democratic Constitutional Rally.

In the 1980s, serious economic difficulties brought on by economic liberalization led to riots and instability in Tunisia. Advisers urged Bourguiba to open up the political process, but he refused and instead became highly repressive, directing particular attention to leaders of the opposition Islamic Tendency Movement (MTI). Eventually, the situation became so serious that on November 7, 1987, Prime Minister Zine Abidine Ben Ali overthrew Bourguiba in a bloodless coup that took advantage of a part of the Tunisian Constitution specifying that if the head of state is incapacitated, the prime minister should perform the job.

President Ben Ali, who was elected to a five-year term in 1989 and reelected in 1994, 1999, and 2004, publicly committed himself to introducing genuine political pluralism in Tunisia. However, this has not occurred. Tunisia does have a multiparty political system, with at least five opposition political parties that have been approved to compete for limited representation in the National Assembly; however, significant repression of Islamic political groups remains, and in the October 2004 elections, the Democratic Constitutional Rally won 94.5 percent of the vote. Hizb al-Nahdha (Party of the Renaissance), the successor to the MTI, is widely described as reformist rather than revolutionary and has indicated its willingness to work within the rules of a competitive, representative democracy; despite this, it continues to be excluded from the electoral process. On several occasions, opposition groups have boycotted national elections, arguing that the electoral system is heavily biased in favor of the government. Electoral results tend to support this contention. Thus Tunisia, like Egypt, remains de facto a single-party state, despite its formal multiparty label.

Personalistic Systems

The distinction between single-party and personalistic states is not sharp, as James A. Bill and Robert Springborg make clear in their description of personalism:

> The Middle Eastern leader has led by virtue of his personal relations with his followers. Formal organizations and institutions have seldom effectively

intervened. Even when institutions such as formal bureaucracies have developed, the real business of ruling and political decision making has resided in personal networks. (1994:160)

Examples of this style of rule include Syria, Libya, and Iraq under Saddam Hussein, all with strong leaders who govern as dictators despite the formal presence of legislative bodies.

Until recently, Syria's political system combined Baathism and a cult of personality around President Hafez al-Assad. Syria gained independence as a republic in 1946 after twenty-six years under a mandate granted to France by the League of Nations. With little experience as a modern autonomous entity, Syria experienced tremendous political instability: between 1949 and 1954 there were four military coups. After Syria's short-lived and disastrous merger with Egypt between 1958 and 1961, the Baathists achieved a dominant position within the Syrian government as a result of the March 1963 military coup and have remained in control ever since. Hafez al-Assad assumed power in 1970 in a bloodless coup and became president in 1971, holding that position until his death on July 17, 2000. His son Bashar succeeded him and was confirmed to a second seven-year term in 2007 in a referendum where he was the sole candidate.

According to the 1973 Constitution, Syria is a socialist and democratic republic with a strong president and legislation based on Islamic law. Presidential elections are held every seven years; however, only one candidate appears on the ballot. The 250-person People's Assembly approves the national budget and responds to laws issued by the Baath Central Committee. In recent years, several minor political parties have served as a token "loyal opposition" to the dominant Baath Party and are represented in the assembly.

Syria has been relatively stable for the past three decades, especially when compared with its early years of independence. This stability can be attributed to a number of factors, including "the fact that Syria was dominated by only one all-powerful political faction with a highly reliable and effective security apparatus" (Van Dam, 1996:137). The severe economic crisis of the 1980s, with its potential for political repercussions, was alleviated somewhat by the transition away from a statist economy and toward economic liberalism (Melhem, 1997; see also Kienle, 1994). Nevertheless, there are several serious potential challenges to the regime, particularly from the Muslim Brotherhood, which has attempted to overthrow the regime on several occasions, most dramatically in an uprising in the city of Hama in 1982. Syria's long border with Iraq has made it one of the prime destinations of Iraqi refugees, currently estimated to number about 1.5 million in a country whose own population is only 19 million (Refugees International, 2008), which could have unpredictable political consequences.

■ Traditional and Parliamentary Monarchies

The Middle East is the only area of the world where traditional monarchies (as distinct from constitutional monarchies, which exist in parts of Europe) have persisted in a number of states. At times, this has been used to label the domestic politics of the region "medieval" or even "primitive." A closer look suggests that the monarchical regimes might better be characterized as an adaptation of established forms of patrimonial leadership to the contemporary nation-state system. Drawing on a variety of traditional sources of legitimacy such as custom, a history of family governance, ancestral ties to the prophet Muhammad, a leader's personal attributes, and the royal family's role as a symbol of nationalism, the current Arab monarchies have proved remarkably resilient.

This persistence is particularly striking when we recall that in the 1950s and 1960s six monarchies were unable to survive the critical postcolonial period and were removed from power: Egypt, 1952; Tunisia, 1956; Iraq, 1958; Yemen, 1962; South Arabia (which became PDR Yemen), 1967; and Libya, 1969. Yet since 1969, only a single additional monarchy—the Pahlavis of Iran—has been overthrown, suggesting that the remaining royal rulers have found ways to repress democratic sentiment, co-opt opposition movements, or otherwise adapt their rule to address, at least minimally, popular pressures for political reform.

Thus the challenge for the Arab monarchies today is less one of validating their political control through tradition and more one of "establishing a linkage with modernity," as Michael C. Hudson argued thirty years ago (1977: 230). Sociopolitical structures such as the *diwan* (informal gatherings in the homes of elites at which there is wide-ranging discussion regarding contemporary issues), along with the Islamic concept of *shura* (consultation), have allowed for a fair amount of grassroots input without moving to a liberal-democratic model. Furthermore, significant economic resources have made it possible in some instances to buy off the opposition (Gause, 2000). In addition, all of these states have chosen to align themselves politically with the West. In the name of anticommunism (originally) or anti–Islamic revivalism (currently), the United States in particular has been willing to supply the Arab ruling elites with whatever weapons and expertise they require to maintain internal security.

In four countries—Bahrain, Kuwait, Morocco, and Oman—the same extended family has held political power for more than 200 years, albeit over units much different (and smaller) than those they control today. The current ruling family in Oman has governed the coast of the country (although not the interior) since 1749; Sultan Qaboos ibn Said al-Said became the leader in 1970 when he overthrew his father in a bloodless coup that was supported by the British. The Sabah family of Kuwait traces its rule to the early 1700s, when a group of formerly nomadic clans settled along the northeastern Arabian coast; the related al-Khalifah family established its authority in Bahrain in 1782 after defeating the Iranians who had previously controlled the islands.

The most enduring Arab regime is found in Morocco. Monarchical government in that country dates back twelve centuries. The Alawi family, which traces its roots to the prophet Muhammad, came to power in the 1660s and consolidated its control over virtually all of modern-day Morocco in the early 1700s. Unlike most of the Arab world, Morocco largely escaped both European and Ottoman colonialism. After a brief period of Spanish and French control in the early twentieth century, Morocco regained its independence in 1956 and is now governed by King Mohammed VI, who succeeded his father, King Hassan II, in July 1999. The Moroccan regime consequently fits into a small set of states in which a long-standing monarchy has been able to resist the inroads of colonialism and emerge intact in the postcolonial period. (Ethiopia, prior to the overthrow of Haile Salassie, Siam/Thailand, and Japan are three other examples of this unusual pattern.)

The other Arab monarchies are either the result of twentieth-century consolidations of power, as in the case of Saudi Arabia, or are relatively recent "dynasties" that gained their political position either in part (Qatar, the UAE) or entirely (Jordan) from the assistance of the retreating colonial powers. In the 1800s, the British signed treaties with a variety of local leaders in the Gulf, adopting a policy of indirect rule and support for the specific families with whom they negotiated agreements. This reinforced the position of the Gulf's ruling families and converted them into "royalty," who took full control of the newly independent countries when the British withdrew from the Gulf.

Some of these new dynasties failed due to incompetence, as in Iraq, where neither of the two successors to King Faisal I were able to hold the country's diverse population together. Others, such as the Idris regime in Libya, were never accepted by the population on whom they were imposed and could not survive in power once European support was withdrawn. In non-Arab Iran, the Pahlavi dynasty, which replaced the Qajar dynasty in a bloodless coup in the 1920s, maintained control only with the support of the CIA and was eventually overthrown.

Aspects of Arab Kingship

The Arab concept of kingship differs significantly from the European model in two significant ways. First, the conflict between the monarchy and the political power of the church that characterized so much of European history between the end of the Roman Empire and the Protestant Reformation has no counterpart in the Arab world. The authority of an Arab monarch still can be challenged on religious grounds, as occurred with the revolt in Arabia of the religiously fundamentalist Ikhwan (brethren) against Abdul Aziz ibn Saud in the late 1920s. But there is no Islamic "pope" (or Confucian bureaucracy) to whom a monarch can appeal for legitimacy independent of his own religious authority, or conversely, who can threaten a monarch by withholding approval.

Second, the absence of a widely recognized succession procedure limits the development of the extended family dynasties such as the Hapsburgs in Austria (r. 1282–1918) and the German-English House of Hanover. The status of sharif—a descendant of the prophet Muhammad—enhances the legitimacy of a ruler, but tens of thousands of individuals carry this designation. Consequently, being a sharif does not carry the same power as being the eldest son of a king would in Europe, and marriage into such a family does not by itself guarantee that someone can claim political control.

As a result, Arab monarchies do not generally show the pattern—common in Europe—of a weak or decadent leader being kept in power in order to preserve the traditions that also legitimize the power of organized religion and the lower nobility. An ineffective or otherwise problematic ruler can be replaced by a family member—as happened in modern times in Oman and Qatar—without threatening the legitimacy of the entire regime.

Furthermore, because the ruler must demonstrate leadership and piety, he must be accessible to the population through a wide range of traditional institutions. For instance, shortly after he became king in 1999, Abdullah II of Jordan is said to have disguised himself as a taxi driver, left behind his bodyguards, and driven around Amman listening to ordinary citizens complain about the government. This unusual action, reminiscent of Abdullah's father, King Hussein, in the early years of his reign, was widely acclaimed and echoed the legends of great Arab monarchs in classical times who would leave their palaces disguised as beggars and roam the streets and marketplaces to assess public opinion. The "absolute" power of the Bourbons of France or the Romanovs of Russia—who ruled in nearly complete isolation from the populations of their territories—has no counterpart in Arab tradition. (This is of particular note because "Orientalist" images often ascribe to the Arab monarch greater unfettered power than that found in European monarchies.)

One disadvantage of this system is that Arab monarchies are potentially more vulnerable than European monarchies to leadership crises upon the death of a ruler because the line of succession may be less well established. Furthermore, because the system is entirely patrilineal, half the population is excluded from direct power. Although the Arab system has avoided weak kings such as George III of England and Nicholas II of Russia, it has also never produced strong queens such as Elizabeth I and Victoria of England or Catherine the Great of Russia.

Saudi Arabia

Among the Gulf states, Saudi Arabia is clearly the most powerful; it is also the most inscrutable due to its tight control of access by non-Saudis and non-Muslims, rendering scholarly research highly difficult. Widespread restrictions on civil rights and political freedoms further limit knowledge about the kingdom. King Abdullah, a son of the country's founder Abdul Aziz ibn Saud, serves as monarch and rules Saudi Arabia; he succeeded his half-brother Fahd upon the latter's death in August 2005, and as crown prince he held very substantial power in the decade after Fahd suffered a stroke in 1995.

Drawing on its considerable political and economic resources, the Saudi leadership has consistently argued that it has pursued domestic policies in support of modernization with an emphasis on cooperation, negotiation, and compromise that is consistent with the Quran. Nonetheless, the royal family has not been immune to criticism and threats to its political legitimacy. Opponents of the regime—whether secular or religious—maintain that the oil wealth has been used to enrich the Saudi family more than the country as a whole, that the government is corrupt, and that the refusal of the House of Saud to share power is non-Islamic. There is also dissatisfaction among many with the close ties between Saudi Arabia and the United States.

Shortly after the 1991 Gulf War, a group of Western-educated intellectuals tried to persuade King Fahd to introduce democratic reforms in Saudi Arabia: the creation of a constitutional monarchy, greater respect for human rights, and the opportunity for political parties and universal suffrage. In response, a number of religious leaders urged Fahd instead to transform Saudi Arabia into a fully Islamic state along the lines of Iran. In an attempt to quell this nascent dissent, in February 1992 King Fahd announced the establishment of a sixty-man *majlis al-shura* (consultative council) whose appointed members were drawn from the professional, academic, religious, business, and retired military elites of the country. The *majlis* has subsequently expanded its membership from sixty to one-hundred-fifty persons representing a variety of sectors of Saudi society including academics (from both religious and secular institutions), bureaucrats and professionals, businessmen, police, diplomats, and military personnel. The council can propose legislation; however, its actions have no binding force.

States of the Arabian Peninsula

The remaining monarchies of the Arabian Peninsula have several attributes in common. They are all relatively small in terms of both land and population, with little arable land; each has a significant expatriate population that is responsible for much of the economic activity; and all rely on petroleum and natural gas for a significant portion of their export revenue. The rulers of each country face internal pressures for political liberalization; most have chosen to respond cautiously by lifting some restrictions on speech and the media, decentralizing the government and giving greater power to individual ministries, establishing elected or appointed consultative councils, and introducing constitutions.

Qatar, Oman, and the UAE. Similar to Saudi Arabia in some ways, Qatar is a religiously conservative, traditional emirate, ruled by Hamad ibn Khalifah ibn Hamad al-Thani, who ousted his father, Khalifah, in a nonviolent coup on June 27, 1995. In this wealthy emirate, the decisions of the monarch are binding, and members of the al-Thani family hold many of the significant political positions. Hamad, who is significantly younger than the other Gulf leaders (except for Bahrain's Hamad ibn Isa al-Khalifah), sees himself as a modernizing ruler. He has allowed for increased political debate in the public arena and has begun to enfranchise the population: on March 8, 1999, some 23,000 Qatari women and men voted in the first-ever elections for a twenty-nine-member advisory Municipal Council. (The number of voters was small because individuals who are in the military or police and those who have been Qatari citizens for less than fifteen years were ineligible to participate, as was the more than 75 percent of the population that is expatriate.) Six women were among the more than 200 candidates, although none were elected.

Oman, too, has begun to move slowly toward constitutional rule and limited popular political participation. In September 2000, Oman held elections for an eighty-two-person Consultative Assembly. Both men and women were granted suffrage rights, and close to two dozen women were among the more than 550 individuals who stood for office (two women were elected). Previously, membership in the council was determined by Sultan Qaboos, and he still exercises some control over who is permitted to run. The assembly advises the government, reviews legislation, and provides a formal means for community leaders to provide input to the government.

The third of the small, traditional Gulf states is the UAE, a union of seven sheikhdoms formed when Britain withdrew from the Gulf in the early 1970s. Independence was to be followed by the creation of a permanent constitution and elections, but even limited elections—for half of the council through a 6,689-member electoral college—did not occur until December 2006. Thus, although the UAE is technically a republic, in reality it is a federation of emirates with no suffrage and no political parties. Governance of the 4.4 million residents (only about 20 percent of whom are indigenous to the area) is by the Supreme Council, composed of the leader of each emirate and headed by Shaikh Khalifa ibn Zayid al-Nuhayyan of Abu Dhabi. There is also a forty-person Federal National Assembly, whose membership reflects the power distribution of the UAE: Abu Dhabi and Dubai have eight representatives each; Sharjah and Ras al-Khaimah have six each; and Umm al-Quaiwan, Fujairah, and Ajman have only four each. Periodically, tensions erupt among the emirates over the dominance of Abu Dhabi and Dubai; however, because these are the largest and wealthiest regions, the federation could not easily exist without their involvement, and criticism is constrained.

Bahrain and Kuwait. The constitutions of both Bahrain and Kuwait call for a legislative body; however, until recently in the multi-island country of Bahrain, parliamentary rule was a legal fiction. The thirty-person National Assembly, partially elected by a small number of male Bahraini citizens in 1973, was suspended in 1975 after it "balked at endorsing a broadly written decree that would enable the government to detain critics and opponents at will for 'statements' or 'activities' deemed to threaten the country's 'internal or external security'" (Stork, 1997:34). Emir Isa ibn Salmon al-Khalifah, who ruled Bahrain from independence until his death on March 6, 1999, then suspended the constitution and dismissed the parliament.

More than two-thirds of the Bahraini population is Shi'a, and over the years there have been allegations of Iranian-supported plots to overthrow the Sunni-controlled government. Demands of the opposition members include political rights for women, the restoration of the constitution and parliament, and more economic opportunities. The response of Emir Isa's government was to increase political repression: detaining dissidents without charge, using torture, and increasing restrictions on freedom of expression (Human Rights Watch, 1997).

Government policy changed significantly with the accession of Hamad ibn Isa al-Khalifah in 1999. The new emir called for a national plebiscite, and in February 2002 Bahrain became a constitutional monarchy. The first elections for the parliament were held on October 24, 2002. In parliamentary elections in 2006, Al Wifaq, the largest Shi'i "political society," won the greatest number of seats. Bahrain appointed a female cabinet minister in 2004, and when Bahrain was elected to head the UN General Assembly in 2006, it appointed a woman as president of that body, only the third woman in history to hold the position.

Of all the Gulf states, Kuwait has arguably been the most successful in preempting revolutionary pressures. This is due in large part to

> the massive and successful program of the al-Sabah dynasty . . . to preserve its power by building the region's first modern welfare state. . . . For decades, the Kuwaiti government has lavishly subsidized everything from

electricity to housing, has underwritten travel abroad for those seeking education or medical treatment, and has created comfortable, well-paying, white collar jobs for 96 percent of its working citizens. (Sadowski 1997:7)

Kuwait liberalized its laws on female suffrage in May 2005, although in the next parliamentary elections in June 2006, none of the women candidates were successful. Until 1996, suffrage was granted only to adult males who were residents of Kuwait prior to 1920 and their male descendants. The vote has since been extended to the (very few) naturalized citizens who have been citizens for at least twenty years, but the electorate is still tiny compared with the total population. The fifty-person National Assembly has a checkered history: the emir suspended the assembly and ruled by decree during 1975–1981 and 1986–1992, arguing that Kuwait could not afford the divisiveness facilitated by democracy, and he dissolved it and called for new elections in two other instances, in 1999 and in 2006.

Jordan and Morocco

The role of parliaments in Jordan and Morocco is more substantial than in the other Middle Eastern monarchies: they are popularly elected, and political parties are legal, although in Morocco the fundamentalist "Justice and Charity" movement is not recognized.

Jordan, the only royal kingdom remaining in the Levant, has been a constitutional monarchy since the 1928 Constitution established an elected legislative council (although ultimate responsibility still rested with the Hashemites). A new constitution promulgated in February 1947 called for a bicameral National Assembly, with an 80-person lower house elected by popular vote (subsequently expanded to 110 seats, including 6 seats guaranteed to women) and a smaller upper house appointed by the king, currently with 55 seats. However, internal instability and dislocations surrounding Jordan's loss of the West Bank in its 1967 war with Israel led to parliamentary institutions being suspended from 1967 to 1989. In the wake of riots through the country in April 1989, King Hussein decided to reliberalize the political system, allowing nonpartisan parliamentary elections in November 1989.

In reopening the political process slightly, Hussein was attempting to deflate dissent around poor economic conditions. Faced with a strong Islamic movement, the king chose to integrate Islamists into the government rather than banning them, as occurred in Algeria, Egypt, and Tunisia. In fact, Jordan's Islamists had long been allies of the monarchy in the conflict with leftists in the 1950s and 1960s, and the Palestinian Liberation Organization in 1970. After reliberalization in the early 1990s, Islamist ministers sought (mostly unsuccessfully) to introduce laws restricting activities such as the consumption of alcohol or requiring gender separation in public swimming pools and sports facilities. At the same time, participation in the government required the Islamists to compromise and forge alliances with other political entities.

Subsequent multiparty elections were held in 1993, 1997, 2003, and 2007. In 1993, some two dozen parties reflecting a diversity of views contended for representation. By the November 1997 elections, however, Human Rights Watch reported with dismay that there was "a clear intent to discourage Jordanians from organizing and participating in public discussion of political issues that segments of the civil society deem to be of national importance" and questioned whether, under these circumstances, any elections could be considered free and fair (cited in Andoni, 1997:19). Changes in the election law clearly strengthened the position of traditional regime loyalists at the expense of opposition groups, which led nine opposition parties, including the large Islamic Action Front, to boycott the election, leaving the field wide open for progovernment candidates to gain a substantial majority in the lower house. The 2003 elections, held more than eighteen months late, also returned a progovernment assembly. A new quota guaranteed women six seats in the assembly: if six female candidates did not win outright (none did), the six who won the largest percentage of votes in their districts were given seats. The 2007 elections also returned a strong progovernment assembly.

The Kingdom of Morocco has also attempted to address political dissent through a new, slightly more liberal constitution. However, just as in Kuwait and Jordan, the king can dissolve the parliament at will and indeed did so for more than a decade beginning in 1965. Under the 1996 Constitution, the king maintains significant political control: he must approve all members of the cabinet and can override the parliament at will.

At present, Morocco has a two-tiered legislative body: a 325-member Chamber of Representatives, which is directly elected for a five-year term, and a Chamber of Councilors, which is indirectly elected by local councils, professional organizations, and labor groups for staggered nine-year terms. Both women and men have suffrage; women are guaranteed 30 seats in the Chamber of Representatives.

In elections in September 2007, the second since Muhammed VI took the throne in 1999, the governing coalition of the Socialist Union of Popular Forces (38 seats) and the nationalist Istiqlal Party (52 seats) maintained control, but with a diminished number of seats from the previous parliament. The Islamist Justice and Development Party increased its representation slightly by winning 46 of 325 seats, making it the second largest party in parliament. The share of seats held by women decreased slightly from 37 to 34. While the election, like that in 2002, was generally regarded as orderly and fair by international observers, the turnout was only 37 percent—the lowest in Morocco's electoral history.

▦ Democracies and Conditional Democracies

As discussed above, a few states in the Middle East—Israel, Lebanon, Turkey, and perhaps Iran—can be considered at least nominally democratic as a function of their formal political institutions. Yet even these countries are not fully "liberal." Instead, due to the emphasis on religion and ethnicity that is inherent in their political structures, all four might better be labeled "conditional" democracies. To a certain extent, the first three countries used variations on the liberal democratic model—adopting European norms and appealing for European assistance—to make the best of a bad situation (Turkey to recover what it could from the remains of the Ottoman Empire, Lebanon because it was small and divided, and Israel because it was considered illegitimate by its Arab neighbors).

A comparison between Turkey and Iran is particularly interesting. Neither, we would argue, is a fully consolidated democracy. In both cases, sovereignty is divided, with an elected president and legislature constrained by either the military (in the case of Turkey) or religious authorities (in Iran). This requires an incredibly detailed constitution, which both countries have, and an active judiciary to interpret the laws while following a clear ideological position. As illustrated below, the challenges facing Israel and Lebanon have less to do with divided sovereignty and more with attempting to maintain certain positions of privilege for a portion of the population based on religion.

Turkey

In Turkey's parliamentary system, formal power rests with the 550 members of the Grand National Assembly, whose terms run for a maximum of five years. The president, who has a largely ceremonial position, has been traditionally elected by the members of the assembly, but a recent constitutional amendment requires that the position be filled via popular elections every five years. Political parties are permitted; however, the government consistently denies the right of Kurds to organize an ethnically based political party and attempts to limit their power as a distinct ethnic group through an unusually high electoral quota (10 percent) that makes it difficult for a Kurdish-oriented party to join the Assembly. The government's position is that Kurds may have full civil rights as Turks but cannot express these in the context of Kurdish self-determination. In addition, Turkey has moved to restrict political expression by Islamic movements, most recently by forcing the Refah Party out of the assembly despite its being part of the governing coalition at the time. The repeated, although short-lived, interventions by the military to preserve the Atatürk model, as well as long-term suppression of the civil liberties of the Kurds and of religious liberties in the name of "secularism," weaken Turkey's democratic credentials.

A major transformation in Turkish politics started to take place with the overwhelming victory of the Justice and Development Party (AKP), headed by Recep Tayyip Erdoğan, in the November 2002 elections. For the first time in decades, a single political party—one that was a successor to a long line of banned Islamic parties—gained a majority of seats in the parliament and was able to form a stable and functioning administration; its success was replicated in subsequent elections in July 2007. Given AKP's moderate agenda, with no attempts to implement *sharia,* and the strong public support it maintained, the military could no longer challenge the party and its administration without risking its own legitimacy.

As the AKP government came to power in 2002—just as the United States was pushing for a military intervention to change the Iraqi regime— its leaders demonstrated a moderate foreign policy stance that was not anti-Western, as many had feared. The AKP government was reaffirmed in 2007 and has continued to prioritize Turkey's gaining membership to the European Union. It has also worked closely with the United States to reach an agreement over the stationing of troops in Turkey to facilitate attacks along Iraq's northern border. While Turkey's Islamist leaders came to a tentative agreement with Washington, the Turkish parliament voted against the presence of the foreign troops. Nevertheless, the process by which that decision was taken illustrates not only the functioning of democratic institutions in Turkey, but also that leaders associated with political Islam do not always adopt anti-Western positions. However, the combination of continued instability in Iraq in general and the emergence of a quasi-independent Kurdish state in northern Iraq in particular, as well as the failures of the government to make noticeable headway toward EU membership, continue to place considerable strain on the pro-Western positions of the government.

Israel

For its Jewish citizens, Israel is the most open political system in the Middle East. However, its founding principle of maintaining the Jewish character of the state and its failures in dealing with the political rights of the Palestinians, both within Israel, where there is systematic legal and budgetary discrimination (Ghanem, 2001), and particularly in the Occupied Territories, limit the extent to which it can be called fully "liberal." Furthermore, in the 1990s a substantial challenge to democratic norms by "Jewish revivalism" emerged.

Israel's political system is based directly on democratic norms. Most of the Zionist leaders who helped found Israel were advocates of democratic socialism, and Israel has had liberal democratic institutions from the very beginning. Although military service is critical to advancing a political career, the Israeli military has never intervened to overthrow a government, and non-Jewish citizens—notably the sizable Palestinian minority within Israel—are permitted to vote and stand for election, although non-Jewish members of the Israeli parliament (Knesset) were not included in governing coalitions until quite recently.

The structure of power in Israeli politics has gone through three distinct phases. In the early years of the state, politics were dominated by a single party, Labor, whose leadership consisted almost entirely of individuals of European descent. The Labor Party exercised control not only through the legislative mechanisms of the Knesset but also through interlocking control of the labor unions and state enterprises, which provided ample opportunities for patronage.

In 1977, the Labor Party's dominance was challenged by a group of conservative parties that coalesced under the name Likud. In addition to providing alternatives to Labor policies—for example, Likud was interested in restraining the Labor-dominated state enterprises—Likud appealed to a number of Jewish voters who had emigrated from Arab countries such as Morocco, Yemen, and Iraq. Likud broke the Labor monopoly on political control of Israel and held power for a number of years, either alone or in "national unity" coalitions with Labor.

The third phase began with a change in electoral laws—effective in 1996—that provided for the direct election of a prime minister. Prior to this, the leader whose party gained a plurality of votes in an election was given the first opportunity to negotiate with other party leaders to create a ruling coalition. If successful, that person became the prime minister; if not, the president would turn to the party with the second highest number of votes and give that leader the same chance to form a government.

Although intended to make the prime minister less dependent on the unstable parliamentary coalitions within the Knesset, the direct election of the prime minister had the unexpected effect of encouraging the growth of a number of small, single-interest parties in the elections of 1996 and 1999. Both Labor and Likud lost substantial numbers of seats to new, ethnically oriented parties, notably Israeli B'Aliyah, which primarily represents recent Russian emigrants, and Shas, which appeals to religious conservatives and now has the third largest number of seats in the Knesset. Labor and Likud both supported a repeal of the Direct Election Law in February 2001 and the country returned to a more traditional parliamentary system in which the prime minister is the head of the party that is able to form a government after single-ballot general elections. The Knesset election on January 28, 2003, gave Likud a plurality of the seats and the right to form the new government.

However, in November 2005, the right wing split over the issue of partial disengagement from the occupied territories, with Ariel Sharon forming the pro-disengagement Kadima Party, while the remainder of Likud remained under the leadership of former prime minister Benjamin Netanyahu. Likud suffered a major electoral defeat in March 2006, receiving only twelve seats, whereas Kadima achieved a plurality with twenty-nine seats and formed a coalition government with Labor and Shas. Sharon's subsequent incapacitation by a stroke in January 2006, however, has left Kadima without clear leadership, and its future is uncertain.

In addition to the potential parliamentary instability caused by the proliferation of small parties, the liberal character of Israeli democracy is also openly questioned by some of the religious parties, who wish to see much more power granted to religious authorities. For example, the relative domains of secular and religious courts are being sharply contested, despite the fact that religious councils already have considerably greater power in Israel than they have in most other liberal democracies. Consequently, Israel is confronting many of the same issues of balancing secular and religious power that Muslim states in the region are facing.

Lebanon

Constitutionally, Lebanon is a parliamentary republic with an elected 128-member Chamber of Deputies reflecting confessional divisions with at least eighteen separate entities designed to create a form of sectarian proportional representation. By law and tradition, the president is a Maronite Christian, while the prime minister is a Sunni Muslim and a Shi'i Muslim is the speaker of the parliament, in which an equal representation of Christians and Muslims is guaranteed based on the 1989 Taif Accords.

The return to democracy after fifteen years of civil and international conflict has not been easy, however. Relationships with Syria, questions surrounding the legitimacy and the efficiency of the Taif system, and Hizbullah activities in southern Lebanon continue to pose serious challenges to the country's stability. This became all too apparent in September 2004, when an effort to change the constitution to extend the term of pro-Syrian president Emile Lahoud led to a parliamentary deadlock. In February 2005, former prime minister Rafik Hariri, a leader of the anti-Syrian faction, was assassinated by a car bomb. Although the perpetrators have not been identified, Syria has been widely suspected of involvement, forcing it to withdraw from Lebanon in April 2005 following massive street demonstrations.

Subsequent politics in Lebanon have become deadlocked over the issue of Syria, rather than the historical confessional divisions. An anti-Syrian coalition led by Sa'ad Hariri, Rafik Hariri's son, holds a majority—but not the two-thirds majority required to dismiss Lahoud—in parliament and has representatives of Sunni, Druze, and Christian parties. A somewhat surprising pro-Syrian opposition has also emerged under the leadership of the

Christian Maronite former prime minister Michel Aoun, drawing most of its support from the Shi'i Hizbullah, which in December 2006 led massive antigovernment demonstrations in Beirut. At the time of this writing, Lebanese domestic politics remain in disarray with no resolution in sight.

An Islamic Quasi-Democracy

In February 1979, following months of increasingly widespread civil unrest, the staunchly pro-Western, authoritarian Pahlavi regime in Iran was overthrown. Much to the surprise of Western observers—although not to many in the region—the government that eventually gained control came not from Iranian elites, nor from leftist movements that the shah had brutally suppressed, but from a conservative Islamic movement led by Ayatollah Ruhollah Khomeini, a prominent Shi'i cleric who returned from exile in Paris. With the success of the Iranian revolution, a new era of political Islam was born.

Khomeini's "Islamic Republic" was a radical departure from the earlier revolutionary movements in the Middle East. In contrast to Nasserism and Baathism, which combined a variety of anticolonial, Western, and Arab ideas, Khomeini and his followers implemented a conservative political agenda derived almost entirely from traditional Islamic thought and practice. Although the details of the nature of "Islamic" governance are complex and hotly debated (including—in fact, particularly—within the Islamic Republic itself), three characteristics distinguish it.

The first is the use of Islamic law—*sharia*—in place of various systems of civil law. This went directly against the twentieth-century tendency in the Middle East and other postcolonial regions to replace, at least in part, traditional legal systems based on religion and custom with uniform secular legal codes, often derived from the legal systems of former colonial powers. In practice, the implementation of *sharia* also involves the imposition of additional conservative social norms that are not actually addressed in the Quran, most conspicuously regarding restrictions on the behavior of women.

Second, the Islamic Republic of Iran placed the supreme authority of the state in the hands of religious councils. These councils also chose a supreme religious leader, a post held by Khomeini until his death in 1989. However, the remaining familiar structures of a modern state—a president, popularly elected parliament, court system, and so forth—remained intact and play an important role in ruling the state. The religious authorities can overturn the decisions of these secular structures, but such decisions must be made on the basis of Islamic law and tradition rather than personal whim. Candidates for election to the secular government require approval from the religious authorities, and during his lifetime Khomeini retained absolute authority on issues regarding war and other foreign policy matters, although he often chose not to exercise his power.

Finally, Khomeini followed an approach to Islam that placed a high priority on missionary efforts. Consequently, the Islamic Republic saw itself in the vanguard of an international revolution and immediately sought to export its model of conservative political Islam to other states. (In this regard, the agenda of Iranian fundamentalism appeared to the West to be similar to that of international communism, and was treated similarly.) Iran has had only limited success in its effort to promote political Islam, but the concept of a conservative Islamic state following *sharia* has had tremendous influence throughout the Middle East.

Almost thirty years after Khomeini's triumphant return to Iran, the experiment of the Islamic Republic can be regarded as a mixed success. Contrary to the predictions of many skeptics who expected an early end to a "medieval" governing structure imposed on an industrializing, urbanizing state, the Islamic Republic has survived, has been generally stable, and has thus far successfully coped with several major difficulties, including a devastating war with Iraq, the collapse of the price of oil in the 1990s, and substantial refugee inflows from Iraq and Afghanistan.

In contrast to many depictions in the West, the Iranian model is not one of a totalitarian religious state. A functioning secular government remains in place, both for theological reasons (Islam emphasizes the importance of the *umma,* the Muslim community as a whole, and not merely the *ulama,* the religious elites) and presumably because the Shi'i clerics have little interest in taking on the responsibility for filling potholes and collecting garbage. These secular political institutions provide a natural source of opposition to the power of the religious authorities, particularly in urban areas. Furthermore, the religious authorities derive their power from the approval and respect of their followers, not from any intrinsic "divine right." No leader with Khomeini's broad support has emerged since his death, and competition for leadership within the religious councils weakened their control somewhat.

For a period of time, it appeared that the hold of the religious authorities in Iran was weakening substantially. The February 2000 parliamentary elections were extremely competitive, with 6,000 candidates vying for the 270 seats, and ended with a major victory for the leftist, reform-oriented Islamic Participation Front.

However, this sixth parliament was still constrained by the Council of Guardians, which limited its ability to implement the types of changes that its supporters had hoped to see (Rezaei, 2003; Ehteshami and Zweiri, 2007). In February 2004, conservatives reasserted control of parliament in elections after thousands of reformist candidates were disqualified by the Council of Guardians prior to the vote. This control was solidified in June 2005 when Mahmoud Ahmadinejad, Tehran's ultraconservative mayor, won a run-off vote in presidential elections, defeating the more moderate cleric and former president Akbar Hashemi Rafsanjani.

At present, two international factors dominate Iran's political environment, and neither is conducive to democracy (Ehsani, 2006). A large US military is in place across Iran's long border with Iraq, and in 2007 and 2008, the Bush administration was issuing almost daily threats of potential future military action against Iran, although due to the limitation of US ground forces, these would probably be largely in the form of aerial bombardment. Ahmadinejad, meanwhile, has adopted a largely confrontational approach to the international community, particularly on the issue of Iran's nuclear programs.

At the same time, however, Iran has a young, educated population that, in the early 2000s, appeared ready to reduce the control of religious authorities on Iran's political institutions (MERIP, 2006). Were the external threat of the United States removed, these liberalizing tendencies might reassert themselves; conversely, the liberalizing momentum may have been lost for a considerable time, particularly if Iran finds itself actively engaged militarily with the United States.

■ Conclusion

At the beginning of a new millennium in the Christian calendar, the states of the Middle East are confronting several major political challenges. First, the region is undergoing a generational change in both its leaders and its political issues: the faces and agendas that dominated the last three decades of the twentieth century seem unlikely to be as critical in the first decades of the twenty-first century. Most governments in the Middle East have been remarkably stable, with individual leaders remaining in power for decades. However, many pivotal figures in the region have recently died or are likely to do so in the near future. Even when successors have been clearly designated, the new leaders do not have the experience or outlook of their predecessors. When succession is unclear—as in Egypt, Oman, Libya, or Saudi Arabia once the sons of Ibn Saud are no longer available as kings—substantial periods of instability are possible.

As the leaders of the elder generation are fading, so are many of the older issues. The Cold War, during which the superpowers both used and were used by many states in the region, ended at the beginning of the 1990s. The revolutionary secular ideologies of the postcolonial period—Nasserism and Baathism—have faded and no longer inspire serious intellectual debate. The future agenda appears unlikely to mirror the past. In place of these concerns, a new domestic issue clearly dominates: the often competing pressures for either democratic or religious governance that would provide increased popular involvement in government. This has affected the full range of states, including countries with strong parliamentary traditions such as Turkey and Israel, and the Arab Gulf states, several of which have recently established consultative councils and held elections. Such moves toward greater democratization are consistent with trends in most of the world.

The US invasion of Iraq and the resulting instability in that country has ramifications throughout the region. Iraq affects, at a minimum, the international politics of Turkey due to the possibility of an autonomous Kurdish entity in northern Iraq; Jordan and Syria due to the massive flow of refugees into these relatively small states; and Iran due to the tensions between that state and the United States. In addition, the loss of credibility that the United States has suffered due to its inability, at least to date, to provide security and stability in Iraq has implications for the policies of long-time US allies such as Saudi Arabia, Kuwait, and Egypt, who are feeling pressure to distance themselves from those policies. Few expect the US involvement in Iraq to end quickly, so these factors are likely to persist for some time.

Tensions involving Israel and its neighbors also remain a critical concern. While aspects of the Arab-Israeli conflict have been addressed successfully (most notably the Egyptian-Israeli and Jordanian-Israeli peace treaties), relations between Israelis and Palestinians are still unresolved, and the brief war with Hizbullah in June 2006 showed that Lebanon remains a flashpoint despite Israel's 2000 withdrawal from Lebanese territory. The Palestinian National Authority is now both geographically and politically split and faces the long-term ghettoization of Palestinian cities and villages due to Israeli military closures, roadblocks, the "security wall," and Jewish-only housing settlements. These and other factors have left the economy in tatters and nongovernmental organizations warning of a possible humanitarian disaster if the situation does not change. Neither Palestinians nor Israelis perceive themselves as secure, and the sense of deep despair is palpable.

With such a tense and violent situation, where mutual trust is all but nonexistent, one might be tempted to conclude that this conflict will never be resolved. However, people feared the same dire future for South Africa, which is now a vibrant pluralist society despite the horrific legacy of apartheid. The conflict between Israeli Jews and Palestinians is extremely difficult, to be sure, but there is no inevitability to its continuance.

Finally, governments throughout the region are under increasing pressure to implement policies that will improve economic performance and respond to a global economy that, due to concerns about the effects of fossil fuels on climate change and the rising price of oil, will be increasingly looking for alternative energy sources. While the short term has seen an increase in oil revenues, in the long term there will be greater pressure on Middle Eastern regimes to industrialize and diversify their economies. The professional class of accountants, engineers, and doctors who once lived as politically powerless expatriates is likely to demand a greater share of political power. The Middle East will also need to reassess its role in the global economy to decide, for instance, whether or not to pursue regional integration, link with the more-developed economies of Europe, or join with the less-developed economies of Africa and southern and central Asia. These will be difficult questions for the new generation of Arabs, Iranians, Israelis, and Turks in the twenty-first century.

▓ Note

An earlier version of this chapter benefited enormously from the comments of Donald L. Gordon and Gwenn Okrulick. Jillian Schwedler and several outside reviewers made excellent suggestions for this and earlier revisions. Ömür Yilmaz, Tyra Blew, and Sarah Stacy assisted in updating and verification of various tables and factual material. None of the above should be held responsible for whatever errors of fact or interpretation remain despite their wise counsel.

▓ Bibliography

Anderson, Lisa. 1991. "Absolutism and the Resilience of the Monarchy." *Political Science Quarterly* 106, no. 1:1–15.
Andoni, Lamis. 1997. "Jordanian Elections: Setback for Democratisation." *Middle East International,* December 5, p. 19.
Antonius, George. 1946. *The Arab Awakening: The Story of the Arab National Movement.* New York: G. P. Putnam's Sons.
Associated Press. 2007. "Mysterious Airstrike in Northern Syria Boosts Olmert's Popularity: Poll." *International Herald Tribune,* September 18.
Aylwin-Foster, Nigel R. F. 2005. "Changing the Army for Counterinsurgency Operations." *Military Review,* November-December 2005:2–15.
Bill, James A., and Robert Springborg. 1994. *Politics in the Middle East.* 4th ed. New York: HarperCollins.
Chandrasekaran, Rajiv. 2006. *Imperial Life in the Emerald City: Inside Iraq's Green Zone.* New York: Alfred A. Knopf.
CIA (Central Intelligence Agency). 2007. *CIA World Factbook.* www.cia.gov/library/publications/the-world-factbook.
Cohen-Almagor, Raphael (ed.). 2005. *Israeli Institutions at the Crossroads.* New York: Routledge.
Ehsani, Kaveh. 2006. "Iran: The Populist Threat to Democracy." *Middle East Report* 241:4–9.
Ehteshami, Anoushiravan, and Mahjoob Zweiri. 2007. *Iran and the Rise of Its Neoconservatives: The Politics of Tehran's Silent Revolution.* London: I. B. Tauris.
El-Amrani, Issandr. 2005. "Controlled Reform in Egypt: Neither Reformist nor Controlled." *Middle East Report Online,* December 15, 2005. Available from http://merip.org/mero/mero121505.html (accessed 26 October 2007).
Galbraith, Peter W. 2006. *The End of Iraq: How American Incompetence Created a War Without End.* New York: Simon & Schuster.

Gause, F. Gregory, III. 2000. "The Persistence of Monarchy in the Arabian Peninsula: A Comparative Analysis." Pp. 167–186 in Joseph Kostiner (ed.), *Middle East Monarchies: The Challenge of Modernity*. Boulder, Colo.: Lynne
Rienner.

Ghanem, As'ad. 2001. *The Palestinian-Arab Minority in Israel, 1948–2000*. Albany: State University of New York Press.

Halliday, Fred. 1979. *Iran: Dictatorship and Development*. 2nd ed. New York: Penguin Books.

Hopwood, Derek. 1985. *Egypt: Politics and Society 1945–1984*. 2nd ed. London:
Allen and Unwin.

Hudson, Michael C. 1977. *Arab Politics: The Search for Legitimacy*. New Haven,
Conn.: Yale University Press.

Human Rights Watch. 1997. *Routine Abuse, Routine Denial: Civil Rights and the
Political Crisis in Bahrain*. New York: Human Rights Watch.

Ibrahim, Saad Eddin. 1995. "Liberalization and Democratization in the Arab World:
An Overview." Pp. 29–57 in Rex Brynen, Bahgat Korany, and Paul Noble
(eds.), *Political Liberalization and Democratization in the Arab World*, Vol. 1:
Theoretical Perspectives. Boulder, Colo.: Lynne Rienner.

Khalidi, Rashid (ed.). 1991. *The Origins of Arab Nationalism*. New York: Columbia
University Press.

Kienle, Eberhard (ed.). 1994. *Contemporary Syria: Liberalization Between Cold
War and Cold Peace*. New York: St. Martin's Press.

Korany, Bahgat. 1998. "Restricted Democratization from Above: Egypt." Pp. 39–69
in Bahgat Korany, Rex Brynen, and Paul Noble (eds.), *Political Liberalization
and Democratization in the Arab World*, Vol. 2: *Comparative Experiences*.
Boulder, Colo.: Lynne Rienner.

Luciani, Giacomo (ed.). 1990. *The Arab State*. Berkeley: University of California
Press.

Makiya, Kanan. 1993. *Cruelty and Silence: War, Tyranny, Uprising, and the Arab
World*. New York: W. W. Norton.

Melhem, Hisham. 1997. "Syria Between Two Transitions." *Middle East Report* 27,
no. 2:2–7.

MERIP. 2006. *Iran: Looking Forward*. *Middle East Report*. Special Issue No. 241.

MERIP. 2007. *The Shi'a in the Arab World*. *Middle East Report*. Special Issue No.
242.

Nasr, Vali. 2006. *The Shia Revival: How Conflicts Within Islam Will Shape the Future*.
New York: W. W. Norton.

Norton, Augustus Richard (ed.). 1995. *Civil Society in the Middle East*. Vol. 1. Leiden: E. J. Brill.

Peteet, Julie. 2007. "Unsettling Categories of Displacement." *Middle East Report*
244:2–9.

Petraeus, David H. 2006. "Learning Counterinsurgency: Observations from Soldier-
ing in Iraq." *Military Review*, January-February 2006:2–12.

Refugees International. 2008. "The Iraqi Displacement Crisis." January 31. www
.refugeesinternational.org/content/article/detail/9679.

Reuters. 2007. "Rivals Thrash Israel's Olmert in TV Popularity Poll." March 7.

Rezaei, Ali. 2003. "Last Efforts of Iran's Reformists." *Middle East Report* 226
(Spring):40–46.

Richards, Alan, and John Waterbury. 1996. *A Political Economy of the Middle East*.
2nd ed. Boulder, Colo.: Westview Press.

Ricks, Thomas E. 2006. *Fiasco: The American Military Adventure in Iraq*. New
York: Penguin Press.

Russell, James A. 2006. *Critical Issues Facing the Middle East: Security, Politics, and Economics.* New York: Palgrave Macmillan.

Sadowski, Yahya. 1997. "The End of the Counterrevolution? The Politics of Economic Adjustment in Kuwait." *Middle East Report* 27, no. 3:7–11.

Sela, Avraham. 1998. *The Decline of the Arab-Israeli Conflict: Middle East Politics and the Quest for Regional Order.* Albany: State University of New York Press.

Sprinzak, Ehud, and Larry Diamond. 1993. *Israeli Democracy Under Stress.* Boulder, Colo.: Lynne Rienner.

Stork, Joe. 1997. "Bahrain's Crisis Worsens." *Middle East Report* 27, no. 3:33–35.

Tibi, Bassam. 1997. *Arab Nationalism: Between Islam and the Nation-State.* 3rd ed. New York: St. Martin's Press.

UNDP (UN Development Programme). 2006. *Human Development Report.* New York: Oxford University Press.

US Department of State, Bureau of Verification and Compliance. 2002. *World Military Expenditures and Arms Transfers 2000.* Washington, D.C.: US Government Printing Office.

Van Dam, Nikolaos. 1996. *The Struggle for Power in Syria: Politics and Society Under Asad and the Ba'th Party.* London: I. B. Taurus.

Wilson, Frank L. 1996. *Concepts and Issues in Comparative Politics: An Introduction to Comparative Analysis.* Upper Saddle River, N.J.: Prentice-Hall.

Woodward, Bob. 2004. *Plan of Attack.* New York: Simon & Schuster.

———. 2006. *State of Denial: Bush at War Part III.* New York: Simon & Schuster.

Yao, Souchou. 2002. *Confucian Capitalism: Discourse, Practice and the Myth of Chinese Enterprise.* New York: Routledge Curzon.

Yiftachel, Oren. 2006. *Ethnocracy: Land and Identity Politics in Israel/Palestine.* Philadelphia: University of Pennsylvania Press.

Yingling, Paul. 2007. "A Failure in Generalship." *Armed Forces Journal,* May 2007. www.armedforcesjournal.com/2007/05/2635198 (accessed October 26, 2007).

5

International Relations

Mary Ann Tétreault

▓ Sovereignty in the Middle East

All the bounded areas on modern world maps are called nation-states, but their qualities as political communities are not alike. Many barely qualify as nations, defined by Anthony Smith (1991:14) as a population "sharing [a] historic territory, common myths and historical memories," a common economy, and a popular culture. Some also fail the test for states, compulsory political organizations claiming a monopoly on the legitimate use of force to execute orders over a specific territory (Weber, 1978; Jackson, 1990). Whatever their failings when viewed from within, however, the post–World War II order inaugurated an era during which nation-states were seen from without as equally sovereign members of the international community. Nation-state members of international organizations as varied as the UN, the Organization of Petroleum Exporting Countries (OPEC), and the Arab League claim equal formal status. Sometimes called negative sovereignty, this status stems from the principle that every state has the same rights under international law, including the right to be free from external interference in its internal affairs.

Negative sovereignty is not always fully observed. But as compared to the status of most places in the world prior to World War II, this norm truly defined a new era in international relations. Earlier, nation-states were only one among several forms of political organization, few of which were sovereign in this sense. European governments and their agents—not only armies and navies but also privateers and for-profit corporations such as the British East India and West India Companies—freely pursued imperial ventures of various types, mostly outside Europe. By the late nineteenth century, the "state ideal"—the desire to have a state of one's own—had spread. Opposition to imperialism became more common, and nationalist movements blossomed. European imperialists countered, justifying their continued control of foreign territories as fulfilling a "civilizing mission" that required them to bear the "white man's burden," which was to rule nations "unfit" to govern themselves (Jackson, 1990:71).

This justification wore thin during World War I. The US government, led by President Woodrow Wilson, declared "self-determination," or the right of a people to choose their own government, to be an important goal of the war. Afterward, however, this principle was applied only in Central and Eastern Europe, where the imperialists formerly in charge were on the losing side and the residents of former colonies were white Europeans. Imperialist winners of World War I did not want self-determination in Asia and the Middle East, where nonwhite local populations were regarded as inferior people. Just as important, the winners themselves either were the colonial powers in those regions or others who wanted the stability that colonial rule by friendly governments could offer to safeguard direct foreign investments by their citizens.

The Middle East was a strategic and economic crossroads linking Europe to Asia. The Suez Canal and Palestine were important way-stations on the route to India, explaining some of Britain's reluctance to relinquish control over the region. The French also had imperial interests in the Middle East, including dependencies in North Africa and a long-standing patronage of the Christian community on Mount Lebanon. Both Britain and France desired privileged access to territories such as Iraq, rumored to be rich in petroleum reserves. The US government, with plenty of US investors' interests to protect, also wanted colonial domination of the Middle East to continue. In spite of its invention by Wilson, US as well as British leaders were reluctant to apply the principle of self-determination to Palestine, where both supported establishing a homeland for Jews in a land where the vast majority of the population was Arab (Christison, 2000).

Keeping the Ottoman Empire—the "sick man" of Europe—alive had been a concern of European foreign offices for decades. European leaders feared that if the Ottoman Empire were to collapse, their own countries would be drawn into a war to divide up its carcass. This picture changed after Britain and France became allies, their German rival was defeated in World War I, and revolution and the consequent preoccupation with internal consolidation that took Russia out of the "great game" (imperial competition with Britain in western Asia) altered the balance of power in Europe. The "sick man" was allowed to die because the wartime victors were confident that they could control the "successor states" without having to go to war. They never intended to give up their imperial "burdens"; meanwhile, the new "states" remained vulnerable to European insistence that some were simply too "immature" to be fully sovereign.

Europeans decided that colonial possessions like Algeria would remain colonies after the war. Protectorates and bonds, the "special relationships" that allowed Britain to control the foreign policies of the small Gulf states, also remained in effect (Anscombe, 1997). The League of Nations, forerunner of today's UN, granted "mandates" allowing Britain and France to control nominally independent states carved from the old Ottoman Empire. Leaders and populations throughout the Middle East felt cheated of their Wilsonian right to self-determination, and negative sovereignty became a cherished goal of their political regimes. Unfortunately, the persistence of "traditional ideas on the privileges and vulnerability of states and a substantial amount of confusion between the national state apparatus and those who are manipulating it [resulted in] twenty-two . . . weak Arab states in a highly integrated world system" (Salamé, 1990:31).

This untidy situation arose from the aftermath of World War I and how it shaped the foreign and domestic relations of Middle Eastern states. As we have seen in previous chapters, the formal boundaries of these states were mostly products of postwar, Great Power politics. Rather than conforming to local interests and traditions, territories and peoples were divided or combined to satisfy the interests of the major powers and to weaken potential local challengers to their imperial domination. Large parts of Syria, the heart of the Arabs' hoped-for independent state, were sheared off by European imperialists or appropriated by ambitious locals. An independent Lebanon was carved from Syria to suit the French and their Maronite Christian protégés. In consequence, Syria became smaller, less viable economically, and therefore more dependent on France. Syria lost ground also against the founder of modern Turkey, Mustafa Kemal. Known after 1933 as Atatürk (father of the Turks), Mustafa Kemal refused to accept the victorious powers as the sole arbiters of the boundaries defining the postwar Middle East. Taking to the battlefield, he extended the territory of Turkey through military conquest, adding a piece of greater Syria to the area under his new government's control.

When the European map-makers redrew the boundaries of Syria, they were oblivious to the consequences their exercise would have for Lebanon's integrity. The core of the new state, the community of Mount Lebanon, had evolved over 400 years under Ottoman rule as a politically pluralist, multicultural community. The new state of Lebanon also was multicultural, incorporating substantial populations of Sunni and Shi'i Muslims and Druze along with the French-favored Maronite Christians. Their minority status increased the dependence of the Maronites on their French protectors. With French backing, the Maronites squeezed constitutional concessions from non-Christian groups, giving Christians the lion's share of political authority in the new state. Even when their relative proportion of the Lebanese population declined, the Maronites resisted allowing others to enjoy the same political rights as themselves. This undermined the legitimacy of the state and, beginning in 1958, led to recurrent civil war (Maktabi, 2000).

The fate of the Hashemite dynasty offers another example of initiatives by postwar map-makers that sabotaged the sovereignty of Middle Eastern states. As detailed by Arthur Goldschmidt in Chapter 3, one reason why the British divided their Palestine mandate to create the kingdom of Transjordan was to reward Abdullah ibn Hussein with a land of his own to rule. Faisal ibn Hussein, Abdullah's brother and the local leader most closely identified with the Arab Revolt, was proclaimed king of Syria in 1920. Postwar Syria was far from the "Arab state" that Faisal had dreamed of leading and, as things turned out, he did not get to lead it for long. A British protégé like his brother Abdullah, Faisal was ousted from Syria by France, the new mandatory power there. In 1921 Faisal became king of Iraq, a British mandate.

Iraq presents one of the clearest examples of the perversity of boundary-drawing and state-building under the mandates described by Ian Manners and Barbara McKean Parmenter in Chapter 2. Iraq was assembled from large segments of what used to be three Ottoman districts: Baghdad, with its majority of Sunni Muslim Arabs; Basra, where the majority of the population is Shi'i Arab; and Mosul, where Iraqi oil was first discovered on the territory of primarily Sunni Muslim Kurds (Marr, 1985). Other minorities also lived in Iraq. Before the 1948 Arab-Israeli war, Baghdad was the city with the largest Jewish population in the world. Iraq's chronic problems with "state building" are rooted in its troubled history as a multicultural state governed by members of only one group (Allawi, 2007; Makiya, 1996). Some scholars argue that "positive sovereignty"—popular legitimacy plus the capacity to govern—is lacking throughout the Middle East.

The transition from an international system where only the most powerful states enjoyed negative sovereignty to one where negative sovereignty was declared a right of every state coincided with modern state formation in the Middle East. Ghassan Salamé (1990) believes that this produced not only small, weak, and externally dependent regimes, but states with a minimal capacity to mobilize the support and loyalty of their citizens to govern independently. Citizen-nationalists and governments alike tended to blame their countries' problems on Western imperialism. Leaders of Middle Eastern states constructed national ideologies—"state ideas"—incorporating strong opposition to external interference. Yet all around the world and especially in the Middle East, wherever states were too weak to prevent it, external intervention by major powers continued. In today's rapidly changing international system, the Middle East, like the Balkans, is a favored target of those seeking to extend the authority of dominant states over the internal politics of regions where they have economic and strategic interests (Havel, 1999; Rogers, 2002; Zanoyan, 2002).

External intervention did bring some advantages to states with oil and gas reserves. These were discovered and developed by foreign companies, most based in Britain or the United States. Oil incomes at first were limited to royalties and fees, but they grew at astronomical rates following the oil revolution of the early 1970s. This revolution both pushed crude oil prices upward and transferred control of oil and gas reserves from foreign companies to national governments. As I describe in Chapter 8, however, oil has been a mixed blessing to its owners. Although it gave them more choices and greater leverage in foreign policy, it also insulated state-building elites from domestic demands for political participation. Democratization was halted and even reversed, and the development of institutions that form the bedrock of state capacity to preside over a self-sufficient society and economy was retarded (e.g., Crystal, 1990; Gasiorowski, 1991; Vitalis, 2006; Zanoyan, 2002). Hydrocarbon resources allowed oil-exporting regimes to take the easy way out. They supported both a strategy of economic development that offered ample room for corruption—but little support for a vibrant private sector (see Luke, 1983, 1985)—and a strategy of political and social development based on paying off disgruntled citizens rather than accommodating their demands for autonomous participation in national life (Beblawi, 1990; Tétreault, 2000; Zanoyan, 2002).

Oil reserves are unevenly distributed among the states of the Middle East, but oil income affects nearly all of them. Especially before the collapse of world oil prices in 1986, oil-exporting states spent lavishly on foreign aid (Hallwood and Sinclair, 1982), salaries paid to guest workers (Ibrahim, 1980), and direct foreign investments in neighboring countries (Stephens, 1976; Tétreault, 1995). As oil incomes shot upward beginning in 1970, a sizable proportion of this money was spent on arms (Dawisha, 1982–1983; Nitzan and Bichler, 2002). It is no secret that having money gives governments and persons more choice and freedom. As foreign-aid donors and arms buyers, Middle Eastern states could exercise independent leverage abroad. Its assistance to Islamist groups allowed Saudi Arabia to influence populations in other Arab states, while in Central Asia, Saudi money (along with US arms) nourished the most radical Islamist factions, including the Taliban and Al-Qaida (Coll, 2004; Rashid, 2001). But the oil and arms circuit also left these states vulnerable to foreign governments able to use their strategic dependence to extort lucrative contracts for arms purchases (Clawson, 1995; Nitzan and Bichler, 2002).

▨ Local Challenges to State Sovereignty

The arbitrary nature of state boundaries in the Middle East provided a focus of activism to those who wanted political integration to match the common religious, historical, and linguistic roots that they saw as uniting this region. Movements such as Arab nationalism and Islamism that transcend ethnic divisions, along with "historic missions" that transcend state boundaries—

such as defeating imperialism, liberating Palestine, reconstructing Eretz Yisrael, achieving Arab unity, and defending religious and cultural values (Salamé, 1994:87; Dawisha, 2003)—were used to justify territorial encroachment and intervention in the domestic affairs of Middle Eastern states by their ambitious neighbors.

In addition to these grandiose claims, simple boundary disputes also plagued the region. In the Gulf, borders had been poorly defined by the colonial powers while a long history during which various empires, states, and tribes controlled oases, rivers, and ports at different times made claims that a piece of territory within the boundaries of one state "really" belonged to another plausible. In recent years, however, several disputed boundaries between Saudi Arabia and Oman, Yemen, and Qatar have been resolved. An interstate boundary was drawn to divide the former Neutral Zone, a jointly controlled territory established under the 1922 Treaty of Uqair to accommodate the migration of bedouin tribes between Saudi Arabia and Kuwait (Dickson, 1956). Oman and its other neighbors resolved most of their boundary disputes. Perhaps the most notable of these relatively peaceful resolutions of border conflicts ended a long dispute between Qatar and Bahrain. Disputes over the Hawar Islands and Fasht al-Dibel rocks, both controlled by Bahrain but claimed by Qatar, and Zubarah, controlled by Qatar but claimed by Bahrain, persisted after decades of unsuccessful mediation. In 1991, Qatar petitioned the International Court of Justice (ICJ) in The Hague to rule on this matter. The ICJ gave its decision in March 2001, using several different principles not only to allocate the disputed lands but also to construct a maritime boundary between the two states through an area thought to contain oil and gas resources (N.A., 2001). This dispute between Bahrain and Qatar had almost led to war in 1986, and both governments were relieved when what the court had called the longest case in its history was finally settled (Gerner and Yilmaz, 2004).

A long-standing boundary dispute with imperialist roots centers on the Western Sahara, a former Spanish colony located on the Atlantic coast of Africa. Parts of this territory were claimed by Morocco and Mauritania, which sent armies to occupy it in 1975 when Spanish imperial authority was waning under the pressure of a national liberation movement that had evolved into an armed insurgency. Encroachment by neighboring Morocco and Mauritania forced thousands of Saharawis into exile in Algeria. There they live in refugee camps that are "surprisingly well organized" and led by native administrators under the direction of a popular council with an elected president (Berke, 1997:3). The remaining insurgents forced Mauritania to relinquish its claims in 1979, but Morocco continues its occupation and insurgents continue to oppose it, although military activity is low-level and sporadic. UN mediation efforts continue to be unsuccessful. Morocco refuses even to meet with representatives of the government-in-exile, and a proposed referendum on the political future of the area has been delayed repeatedly.

The Western Sahara conflict aggravates relations between Morocco and its other neighbors: Algeria, which supports the government-in-exile, and Spain, which still occupies two islands off the Moroccan coast. Morocco attempted to seize one of them, Parsley Island, in the summer of 2002, but pressure from the European Union forced Morocco to withdraw its troops. The tension created by more than a quarter century of dispute over the Spanish Sahara destabilizes the whole western Mediterranean and, like the dispute between Bahrain and Qatar, shows the potential of conflicts over sovereignty to explode into war. Boundary conflicts between Iran and Iraq, and Iraq and Kuwait, along with Israel's occupation and annexation of Arab territories, have led to full-scale wars. Some of these boundary conflicts continue and will be discussed in subsequent sections of this chapter.

■ The Middle East and the Great Powers

As Deborah Gerner and Philip Schrodt discuss in Chapter 4, most areas of the Middle East began the twentieth century as clients or dependencies of one or another European power. Even modern Turkey, the core of the old Ottoman Empire, had been an economic colony of its European creditors since the establishment of the Ottoman Debt Commission in 1881. Western ideologies were powerful in Turkey, and the Turkish state incorporated elements of what Atatürk saw as the greatest strengths of the West: modernization, secularization, and state-centered nationalism. His aim was to make Turkey an equal of the Great Powers, not a dependency of them. He pursued that goal with some success, wresting control of far more territory than the victors of World War I had intended to leave for the rump Turkish state that emerged from the shambles of empire.

North African communities were among the most eager to avoid or overthrow European rule. Examples of bitter and protracted anticolonial conflict include the bloody conquest of what is now Libya by the forces of Fascist Italy, and the vicious eight-year war that ended 130 years of French control of Algeria. The Algerian war was exemplary in its brutality (Horne, 1977). It included widespread terrorist violence by both sides, and the systematic torture, execution, and assassination of thousands of Algerian women and men by the French military (Morgan, 2006; Shatz, 2002). French forces had been disgraced by their nonperformance against Germany in the "phony war" of 1940 and by having been beaten at Dien Bien Phu, the 1954 battle that ended a nine-year attempt to crush the anticolonial movement in Vietnam. Chillingly depicted in Gillo Pontecorvo's 1966 film *The Battle of Algiers,* what historian John Talbott (1980) called "the war without a name" brought France itself to the verge of civil war, while the philosopher of Algerian liberation, Franz Fanon, glorified revolutionary violence in his 1961 book *The Wretched of the Earth* as the only way to restore a culture with a degraded and degrading past.

Far from purifying, violence erupted across Algeria during the still smoldering civil war that began in 1992. The uprising was ignited when the Algerian military, representing the forces that had controlled the country since liberation in 1962, canceled parliamentary elections that they feared would mean the victory of their Islamist rivals. The ensuing civil war, with its own toll of tens of thousands of tortured, executed, and assassinated Algerians on both sides, is both legacy and echo of the long and ugly war against the French.

Although many Middle Eastern leaders fought against European intervention, others sought it out. Toward the end of the nineteenth century, Shaikh Mubarak, the emir of Kuwait (r. 1896–1915) actively angled for British protection. He hoped both to prevent his country from being attached to the Ottoman Empire by an energetic Turkish governor (Anscombe, 1997; al-Ebraheem, 1975) and to get some assistance first to consolidate his own power and then to ensure that his lineal descendants would rule Kuwait after his death (Rush, 1987). Abdul Aziz ibn Saud manipulated British officials to help him acquire more than half the territory of Kuwait in 1922 (Dickson, 1956). Until the conclusion of World War II, he relied on British and US gold to help him consolidate his conquests on the Arabian Peninsula and keep the leaders of subordinate tribes firmly in his camp (Anderson, 1981). Nearly every Middle Eastern government was ready to welcome foreign-owned companies willing to pay for the right to prospect for oil. In consequence, external intervention by the Great Powers or their agents was neither always nor uniformly condemned by Middle Eastern political leaders, although as Bob Vitalis (2006) recounts about Saudi Arabia, citizen nationalists often saw things differently.

Nationalists protested the grave burdens that imperialism imposed on their countries. Along with strategic interests such as protecting the route to India, imperial powers used their colonies and dependencies primarily to make themselves rich (Wolf, 1982). Local economies were truncated by drawing national boundaries through areas and populations that were parts of larger trading and commercial markets. Colonies and economic dependencies were bled for the benefit of settlers and overseas investors. Oil companies took the lion's share of profits from their often wasteful exploitation of the region's petroleum reserves (see, e.g., Penrose, 1968; Rand, 1975; Tétreault, 1995). Foreign occupiers violated local customs with impunity and mocked the religion, society, and culture of the populations they were exploiting (Ahmed, 1992; Lazreg, 1994; Tétreault, 1995). Zionist immigration into Palestine, which began decades before the Balfour Declaration of

1917 pledged British support for a Jewish homeland there, threatened communities and the livelihoods of the native population. All these political, economic, and psychological burdens were aggravated by the imperialists' practice not only of playing social groups within countries against one another to enhance their political control (Migdal, 1988; al-Naqeeb, 1990), but also of pitting one country against others in situations, such as negotiations for oil concessions, to increase the colonizers' economic returns.

Dependency

Dependency is a relationship of inequality between a developing and a developed country (Caporaso, 1978). Creating dependency is a conscious aim of colonization and imperialism. During the eighteenth century, when the American states were colonies of Britain, the British passed laws such as the Navigation Acts that required the colonies to sell raw materials to Britain and then buy British products. Britain benefited both from the trade itself and also from processing the raw materials purchased from the colonies. Both provided jobs for British workers and tax revenues for the government. Colonial trade was a relationship of exchange, but the exchange was unequal in the present and was intended to remain unequal in the future. The American colonies had to win a war of independence to throw off the crippling yoke of British imperialism.

During the nineteenth and twentieth centuries, imperialism enabled first Europe and then the United States to acquire preferential access to raw materials located in the Middle East. Governments signed exclusive contracts with British and US oil companies to develop local hydrocarbon industries. Oil companies purchased supplies and equipment from their home countries and imported all but the most menial workers (Vitalis, 2006). Oil development also distorted local economies. In oil-rich Hasa in Saudi Arabia, agriculture was destroyed to accommodate pipelines and pumping stations (Munif, 1989). Most of the oil was sold overseas as a raw material that was processed and consumed outside the countries where it had originated.

Foreign oil companies no longer own all of the Middle East's oil and gas reserves. However, the way these reserves were developed and the way the domestic economies of oil-exporting countries were constructed around oil production and sales tied the economies of these states to global markets and made them economically dependent even after governments nationalized these industries in the early 1970s. When oil prices fall, for example, there is little that one or even several oil exporters can do to bring them back up and keep them there. OPEC had some success stabilizing oil prices in the 1960s and raising them in the 1970s. However, that success was ephemeral, enhanced by circumstances such as the closing of the Suez Canal by the 1967 Arab-Israeli war and surging US oil demand for the Vietnam

War. Within a few years, structural changes, such as the discovery and de-velopment of new oil fields outside OPEC countries, brought world oil prices back down. They fell to historically low levels in the mid-1980s, cre-ating economic hardship and domestic conflict in many oil-exporting coun-tries (Hunter, 1986).

The domestic economies of the wealthiest oil-exporting countries were organized to spend oil revenues rather than to produce a wide range of goods and services to satisfy local needs and wants. Rivers of cash from oil sales, along with growing demand for foreign products from tanks and ma-chine guns to cars and television programs, created consumption patterns that depended on imported goods. Oil exporters expanded production capac-ity to ensure that they could continue to buy what they wanted from over-seas. As global capacity expanded, some exporters were compelled to in-crease oil production, not only to justify their investment but also to support growing populations. But producing more oil glutted markets, pushing prices down and encouraging even more production to keep income levels up. This vicious circle came around again in the late 1990s, but talk of struc-tural reform never turned into action. When oil prices went back up, incen-tives for governments of exporting countries to make fundamental changes to reduce dependency disappeared. Despite ups and downs in the oil market, the Middle East remains dependent on oil and gas sales as a primary source of government revenues.

Cliency

Cliency is a strategic relationship between a major power seeking a local base and a less powerful state whose assets are compatible with the needs of the major power (Gasiorowski, 1991; Tétreault, 1991). The client's stock in trade can include geographic location, port and basing facilities, and a regime will-ing to act on behalf of the major power. In return for one or more of these assets, the major power patron transfers arms, military training and equip-ment, and other types of military and economic assistance to the less power-ful client. Both sides gain from cliency but, unlike dependency, cliency offers the government of the smaller state proportionately more than it offers the larger partner. Indeed, as the client becomes embedded in the foreign policy strategies of its patron, the dependence of a patron on a client's strategic as-sets may grow at the same time that patron leverage against the client govern-ment declines. Meanwhile, the extranational assets it receives from its patron allows the client government to protect itself against external and internal challenges by buying off foreign and domestic enemies or using patron-supplied force against them.

The Cold War increased the importance of cliency in the relationships of Middle Eastern states with major outside powers. The superpowers were interested in economic gains, especially from their relations with oil-exporting states, but strategic concerns were primary. A large portion of foreign aid from the superpowers took the form of military assistance. Nearly all of it imposed obligations in the form of services required of Middle Eastern client states: diplomatic and military support and preferential access by the patron state and its agents to the client's domestic resources. Sometimes resources provided by patron states were used by rebellious military officers against weak and unpopular client governments. One example is the 1969 overthrow of King Idris in Libya (Bill and Springborg, 1994). Some resources were used by client governments against their own populations, which occurred in Iran (Gasiorowski, 1991).

International politics changed during the Cold War and dependency relations changed as well. Competition increased in the market for Middle Eastern oil concessions, most markedly in Libya but also in Iran and the Arabian Peninsula states (Penrose, 1968). As detailed in Chapter 8, these changes helped to shift control of oil from international oil companies (IOCs) to host governments. Another apparent benefit of the Cold War was that imperialism was replaced by at least the rhetoric of negative sovereignty. The accepted convention, that all states were autonomous and could freely choose their own allies and partners, meant that the superpowers sometimes could be brought to bid for client allies, a situation that Egypt used to great advantage in financing its Aswan Dam project in the 1950s.

Too close an alliance with either superpower risked retaliation from disgruntled nationalists against overly compliant regimes. Strong leaders were able to carve out some autonomy from their Cold War patrons. In 1955, Egypt's Gamal Abdul Nasser, along with leaders of other developing countries, held a conference in Bandung, Indonesia, whose main product was the "nonaligned movement." Nonalignment was a declaration of independence from a permanent relationship to either superpower and was seen as a guarantee of the negative sovereignty of developing states. Yet despite declarations of nonalignment and promises of mutual support from other nominally nonaligned states, very few countries in the Middle East were successful at finding a middle ground between the superpowers.

One success story was Kuwait, the role model for other small Gulf emirates seeking to orchestrate a balance of power among potential patrons. Initiated as part of the state-building strategy of Mubarak al-Sabah, Kuwait's first twentieth-century emir (Anscombe, 1997; Assiri, 1990; Tétreault, 1991), a century of persistence in courting a panoply of external partners paid off for Kuwait when it was invaded by Iraq in 1990. Influential foreign nationals associated with Kuwaiti-owned companies argued the Kuwaiti case to world leaders before their views and policies were fully formed, and European governments hosting large Kuwaiti investments moved rapidly to protect Kuwaiti assets (Tétreault, 1995). Thanks to the collapse of the Cold War's rigid alliances and a history of cordial relations with the Soviet Union that included generous Kuwaiti assistance following a major earthquake there in 1989, a multinational coalition including both the United States and the Soviet Union was rapidly assembled to roll back the Iraqi invasion. Despite strong support for Iraq among the populations of nearly every state in the Middle East, the unity of their US and Russian patrons, together with positive incentives ranging from debt forgiveness to promises of future economic assistance from Kuwait, pulled nearly all of these states into the Kuwaiti camp.

Unlike Kuwait, most Middle Eastern states found that a nonaligned strategy was difficult to sustain in practice. Saudi Arabia proclaimed itself to be nonaligned. However, religious militancy and oil interests ensured that it was almost entirely oriented toward the West even though the United States and other Western governments were strong supporters of Israel (Korany, 1991; Quandt, 1981). Similar pressures upset efforts of the so-called confrontation states (those engaged militarily against Israel) to remain nonaligned. Syria, Iraq, and Egypt drifted into the Soviet orbit to obtain military support for their wars against US-backed Israel. As the region's total oil income increased, however, the Arab confrontation states found they could get foreign military assistance from their Arab oil-exporting neighbors.

Middle East Regionalism

Regionalism was a movement that began during the latter part of World War II and attracted people who wanted to help build postwar institutions that would foster peaceful international relations. Regionalists recommended that countries joined by proximity, culture, and common interests establish international organizations for functional purposes such as economic development or military security. The League of Arab States (Arab League), founded in 1945, was among the first of these new organizations. The Great Powers of World War II refused to accept the Arab League's "strong" definition of regionalism, which insisted that security be a matter wholly internal to participating states rather than subject to intervention by the larger world community (MacDonald, 1965:9–11). Even so, the Arab League was recognized by the UN and, at its inception, was hailed as a building block of the new postwar order.

Along with regional organizations like the Arab League, functional organizations such as OPEC and the Organization of Arab Petroleum Exporting Countries (OAPEC) also were established and charged with advancing the common economic interests of their members. OPEC is a multiregional organization; OAPEC is mono-regional and mono-ethnic. An important goal of OPEC and OAPEC is consensus building, the development of joint positions based on shared interests sufficiently strong to keep members together even when they come under pressure.

Transnational movements like Arab nationalism and pan-Islamism promote group identification beyond the state. In contrast to these mass movements, regional and functional organizations are creatures of the state. Their spread supports the implementation of negative sovereignty by spinning a web of agreements and structures that are both interstate and limited in membership. Theoretically, regionalism could restrict negative sovereignty by assigning formal responsibility for particular policies to the international organization. However, many such organizations, including most in the Middle East, follow decision rules requiring consensus. This affirms the authority of the individual member to veto policies it does not like, preserving sovereignty but also discouraging compromise and inhibiting collective action.

Mobilizing a consensus on any issue gets harder as the membership or the issue slate of an organization expands. New members may have important interests that are marginal to those of the founders. The Arab League was unable to progress beyond a very low level of regional integration as it grew from a group of five closely neighboring states, four of which were strongly Arab nationalist (Egypt, Syria, Iraq, and Lebanon—the fifth founding member was Jordan), to a large organization with more than twenty members spread across two continents, many with vastly different histories, economies, and political cultures. The same problems afflict OPEC, whose five founding members (Venezuela, Iran, Iraq, Kuwait, and Saudi Arabia) had the petroleum and financial resources to exercise market power collectively through production restraint. By adding small producers such as Gabon and Ecuador and economically desperate ones such as Nigeria and Indonesia, OPEC was prevented from developing effective production-restraint strategies. New members with different economic goals aggravated already endemic political conflicts within the group (Mikdashi, 1972). OPEC's founders had conflicting interests too, and the organization's charter made consensus mandatory so each could protect itself against the others. As OPEC grew, members also devised informal conventions that freed them from being bound by collective decisions under certain conditions (Tétreault, 1981:42). Consequently, OPEC was able to pursue a limited range of common interests, but it could not prevent individual members from pursuing independent interests even when their actions visibly harmed the common good.

A decrease in common interests and purposes among the members of an international organization can be triggered by changes in member governments and regimes. OAPEC was formed in 1968 to give its three founders, Libya, Kuwait, and Saudi Arabia, a base from which to resist demands by

Arab radicals that they apply the "oil weapon" regardless of their financial situations or their ability to deliver public services to their populations. But when King Idris of Libya was overthrown in 1969 by a group of military officers led by Colonel Muammar Qaddafi, the new regime in Libya suddenly introduced into the heart of the organization the very militancy that OAPEC had been established to avoid.

Organizational cohesion depends on close similarity among the structural and ideological interests of group members. The founders of the Gulf Cooperation Council (GCC, which includes Kuwait, Saudi Arabia, Qatar, Oman, Bahrain, and the United Arab Emirates) decided to exclude Yemen because it "did not share 'identical systems, identical internal and foreign policies, identical ideologies, identical aspirations and identical human, social, and political problems' [with] the Arab gulf littoral states" (Lawson, 1997:15). The GCC was formed in 1981 to replace bilateral security arrangements with a regional security regime and also to promote economic integration among its members. Reflecting Iraq's status as a belligerent in the Iran-Iraq War, the GCC also excluded Iraq from membership (Peterson, 1988).

Despite significant economic integration, GCC collective security measures continue to fall short. Some were conceptually defective, such as Saudi suggestions to centralize police records and permit police forces of member states to cross the border into another member state in cases of hot pursuit. Sometimes members simply failed to carry out their GCC obligations. The GCC members refused to assist Kuwait following liberation when, with a conflagration in its oil fields, it asked for a loan of up to 1 million barrels of oil per day to meet the requirements of its overseas refineries. This refusal exposed the hollowness of GCC institutions; the council had adopted an oil-sharing agreement just four years earlier, precisely to deal with production shortfalls in a member state (Tétreault, 1995:147). The record of the GCC shows that even where founding members perceive themselves as virtually identical, regional organizations in the Middle East are hard-pressed to overcome the shortsighted attachment of their members to narrow definitions of negative sovereignty.

■ Moving Toward Regional Autonomy or a New Imperialism?

The end of the Cold War initiated a global realignment that also affects the international relations of the Middle East. During the era of the most intense East-West confrontation, "hot wars" in the Middle East were widely viewed as proxy conflicts between superpower clients. As Soviet power weakened in the late 1980s, Soviet capacity to intervene abroad also declined. At first, local issues became more prominent in regional conflicts. This was reflected in the realignments among regional actors during the

Kuwait War (1990–1991) and shifts in support for the principals in the Arab-Israeli conflict. In 2001, a far less accommodating international system began to move against the interests of the Arab states and Iran, but how they will respond, individually and collectively, is still uncertain.

Within a few days, the 1990 invasion of Kuwait by Iraq pushed the United States from a tacit alliance with Iraq to demanding that Iraq withdraw completely from Kuwait (Sciolino, 1991; Smith, 1992; Urquhart, 2002). Working through the UN Security Council, the United States spearheaded a series of resolutions condemning Iraq and imposing severe economic sanctions against it. The Soviet Union was a prominent part of the anti-Iraq coalition. Although it preferred a negotiated settlement, the Soviet government remained part of the coalition throughout the nearly six weeks of war (Melkumyan, 1992). Soviet cooperation was critical in the UN Security Council, the formal venue for the coordination of the coalition against Iraq. Had the Soviet Union chosen to use its Security Council veto, neither economic sanctions nor the large multinational military operation that was launched in January 1991 could have been achieved. Soviet participation also muted criticism of US policy by those sympathetic to Iraq or opposed to unilateral military activities by the United States on the Arabian Peninsula.

The Soviet Union had softened its stance toward Israel before the end of the Cold War, for example, by allowing Soviet Jews to emigrate. This allowed the United States to become the predominant extraregional power

Kuwaiti troops, operating out of Saudi Arabia, prepare to liberate Kuwait in 1991. After a month-long bombing campaign, the ground war lasted just one hundred hours.

involved in the Israeli-Palestinian conflict, but its pro-Israeli bias discouraged Palestinians, whose offers of compromise were repeatedly treated as new floors for the next round of negotiations (Ashrawi, 1995). The post–Cold War realignment opened opportunities for other external partners to alter the environment of those negotiations. The Norwegian government initiated talks that allowed Israelis and Palestinians to engage simultaneously in public negotiations in Madrid and secret negotiations in Oslo. The agreement that they hammered out was signed in September 1993 in Washington, D.C.

The end of the Cold War appeared to reduce the ability of the United States to pry support from reluctant allies for policies they believed to be unwise, unnecessary, or contrary to their own national interests. Doctrines such as "dual containment," under which the United States justified demands that other countries isolate both Iran and Iraq, did not have the widespread support among US allies that the original containment policy against the Soviet Union had enjoyed. France was the only major Western ally pursuing a notably independent foreign policy toward the Middle East during most of the Cold War (Wood, 1993), but during the 1990s the negotiations leading to the Oslo Accords were only one example of growing foreign policy autonomy among several countries that had been part of the US bloc during the Cold War. As discussed later in this chapter, the United States moved to reverse this trend after George W. Bush became president.

▓ The Middle East as a Foreign Policy Subsystem

When Iraq invaded Kuwait in August 1990, a common refrain among Arabs was that such an event had never occurred before: Arab countries did not attack one another militarily. This was not exactly true. Iraq had both threatened and invaded Kuwait several times previously. Although on a smaller scale than in 1990, Iraq had sent military forces to take, hold, and occupy part of northern Kuwait in the mid-1970s (Assiri, 1990). It also used "salami tactics" to acquire territory from Kuwait, periodically sending troops to the frontier to inch the border southward (Tétreault, 1995:123–124).

Other inter-Arab conflicts also are forgotten by those claiming to be shocked by Iraq's 1990 invasion of Kuwait. Egypt conducted extensive military operations in Yemen in the mid-1960s during its proxy war against Saudi Arabia and has engaged for years in recurrent border clashes with Libya. As I discussed earlier, Libya and Algeria oppose Morocco in the Western Sahara. The government of King Hussein mounted a strong military offensive against a semi-sovereign Palestinian enclave in Jordan during the "Black September" of 1970; Syria intervened militarily in Lebanon during the civil war and its military forces remained in Lebanon until 2005, when they were withdrawn at the request of the Lebanese government and the Arab League. Arabian Peninsula border clashes were common through most of the twentieth century, while boundary conflicts, such as the conflicting claims of non-Arab Iran and the UAE to the Tunbs Islands, remain unresolved.

Among the most persistent axes of conflict in the region are those in which non-Arabs are belligerents. Examples include confrontations between Israel and various Arab opponents, conflicts in which Kurds are active participants, and hostilities between Iraq and Iran. These three sets of conflicts intersect with and amplify one another, and frequently attract involvement by one or more outside powers. At the same time, the Middle East is the home of countless regional governmental and nongovernmental organizations (NGOs) that reflect common economic, cultural, and policy interests. Some, such as OPEC, include both non-Arab and extraregional partners. Others, like the inclusive Arab League and the exclusive OAPEC and GCC, are all-Arab.

I count myself among those who are generally pessimistic about what these various attempts to promote community among Middle Eastern states have accomplished. However, I also believe that continuing these efforts both normalizes the concept of common interests and supports the gradual growth of institutions that eventually could embody what now are mostly formulaic assertions of "brotherhood" among states in this region. As Iran and the Arab states find themselves increasingly pressed by a hostile US administration, the advantages of closer cooperation compete with their long-standing reluctance to sacrifice some cherished autonomy to protect national and regional interests.

▓ The Arab-Israeli Conflict

The Arab-Israeli conflict is discussed more fully by Simona Sharoni and Mohammed Abu-Nimer in Chapter 6, but here I want to emphasize two elements in this century-long struggle: its large external dimension and the role of the Palestinians in international relations in the Middle East generally. When Zionist leaders declared Israel to be a state in 1948, both the United States and the Soviet Union rushed to recognize it. At that time, Israeli institutions such as the army and the labor movement were more socialist than liberal (Bill and Springborg, 1994:261). Even so, as Cold War positions hardened, Israel grew closer to the United States. At first, this reflected Israeli economic dependence on support from the US Jewish community as much as or more than any strategic dependence on the US government (Nitzan and Bichler, 2002).

Israel's ties to the US government strengthened following the Six Day War in June 1967. Then France, formerly Israel's primary foreign source of armaments, shifted toward the Arab states because of French concerns about the long-term security of oil supplies (Weisberg, 1977). Although the Israelis had bombed the *Liberty,* a US intelligence vessel in the Mediterranean, to prevent outsiders from discovering that they were executing Egyptian prisoners, domestic politics pushed the United States to support Israel during the 1967 war (Bamford, 2001; Christison, 2000). US support included measures to defeat the first systematic application of the Arab "oil weapon" against Israel's allies (Sankari, 1976).

The October 1973 Arab-Israeli war was deeply embedded in Cold War politics. Following as it did the 1972 migration of Egypt out of the Soviet and into the US orbit, the war put the Nixon administration in the difficult situation of having a foreign policy victory that threatened its domestic political position. Although US officials had received a series of explicit warnings beginning in spring 1973 that war between Israel and the Arab states was imminent (Tétreault, 1985:34), Arab attacks on Israeli positions took the US government by surprise. Initial Arab victories alarmed the United States, prompting a massive airlift of supplies to Israel that reversed most of the Arab gains. The war also gave the Soviet Union a chance to recoup some diplomatic losses in the region. When Israel violated the UN-brokered cease-fire agreement of October 22, 1973, the Soviet Union announced that it would send in troops and approached the United States about forming a joint US-Soviet peacekeeping force. US president Richard Nixon, fearing domestic repercussions in the midst of the Watergate investigation, would not engage in any action in the Middle East that could be construed as aiding the Arabs. Instead, he put US military forces on alert, making any joint US-Soviet action in the Middle Eastern war impossible (Kissinger, 1979: 552–611).

The possibility of global conflict during the 1973 war was ratcheted to a high level by policymakers in different countries trying to juggle incompatible domestic, regional, and global demands. National leaders in powerful countries pursued their own interests without worrying about how their actions would affect their allies. This echoes the cavalier behavior of European powers in the Middle East during and after World War I, the history of the British mandate in Palestine, and Cold War maneuvering in the region before and after the October 1973 war. Thus the 1977 decision of Anwar Sadat to go to Jerusalem, an extraordinary gesture toward resolving the Arab-Israeli conflict, can be seen as a gamble whose potential benefits included the removal of a magnet for superpower confrontation, as well as an end to the balance of terror between Arabs and Israelis and a chance to resolve the problem of what to do about displaced Palestinians.

Following the Zionist victory in the 1948 war and the consequent expulsion of thousands of Palestinians from their homes (Christison, 2000; Morris, 1989), a Palestinian diaspora fanned out across the region. Many Palestinians lived in refugee camps and enclaves. Rising oil revenues generated job opportunities, and Palestinians also formed resident communities of workers and families in oil-rich states such as Kuwait (e.g., Ghabra, 1987). Palestinians became an essential element in the Arab nationalist amalgam. A reminder of the ineffectiveness of Arab armies against Israeli armies in the field, the Palestinians evoked shame, guilt, and a sense of obligation in other Arabs and their governments. Arab leaders such as Egypt's Nasser (Nasser, 1955), Libya's Qaddafi (Zartman and Kluge, 1991), Syrian president Hafez al-Assad (Seale, 1988), and Iraqi president Saddam Hussein (Ahmad, 1991) all conceived regional historic missions that included restoring Palestinian national territory as a primary goal.

The Arab states recognized the Palestine Liberation Organization (PLO) as the legitimate government—the "state-in-exile"—of the Palestinian nation but, for many different reasons, virtually every Arab government resisted absorbing significant numbers of Palestinian refugees into its own population. "Jordan was the only Arab country to grant them citizenship," but some Palestinians still live in camps even there (Elon, 2003:6). Instead, the Arab states supported positive sovereignty for the PLO even though the PLO's lack of territory made negative sovereignty impossible. PLO embassies operated in many Arab capitals, and Arab governments in the Gulf deducted PLO taxes from Palestinian workers' paychecks. Along with regular elections to the Palestinian National Council, these tax payments, large infusions of Arab foreign aid, and the myriad informal institutions of Palestinian society nourished the development of a distinctive Palestinian identity despite the absence of a Palestinian territorial state (Gerner, 1994; Peretz, 1990).

The separate peace agreement signed by Egypt and Israel in 1979 caused the other confrontation states to lose interest in military intervention to help the Palestinians. In 1991, the dissolution of the Soviet Union removed the Arab-Israeli conflict from its position as a cockpit of the Cold War, further reducing the political salience of the Palestinians and their plight. The first intifada (uprising), which began in December 1987, expressed the despair of Palestinians who, after twenty years of increasingly brutal Israeli occupation, were enraged at the indifference of the rest of the world (Elon, 2002). It also highlighted the main structural change arising from the Egyptian-Israeli peace agreement: the Arab-Israeli conflict had become an Israeli-Palestinian conflict (Ben-Yehuda and Sandler, 2002).

At first, the intifada was successful in crystallizing a coherent, disciplined, mostly nonviolent resistance movement. As it entered its third year, however, the intifada started to flag, a result of unrelenting Israeli opposition and the exhaustion of Palestinian resources (Gerner, 1991, 1994; Hunter, 1993). Palestinians were divided between those living under occupation in the Palestinian territories and those living in exile outside. Militant insiders associated with the Muslim Brotherhood formed the core of what later became Hamas; the outsider Yasser Arafat, the leader of the largest Palestinian political faction, had to struggle to maintain his authority as leader of all the Palestinians. Arafat's otherwise shocking support of the Iraqi invasion of Kuwait reflected desperation as much as appreciation of Saddam Hussein's proposal to coordinate efforts to liberate Palestine through an Arab National Charter, and Saddam's acceptance of PLO positions on what that liberation would entail (Ahmad, 1991; Christison, 2000).

Arafat's apparent endorsement of the Iraqi invasion also provided a rationale for other Arab governments to reorient their stance toward Palestinians. Gulf governments, short of cash thanks to a decade of shrunken oil revenues and the high cost of pushing Saddam out of Kuwait, found Arafat's gesture a convenient excuse to halt foreign aid to the PLO. Palestinians working in Gulf countries were expelled as security risks, drastically reducing their financial contributions to families living in the West Bank and Gaza. Palestinians also lost diplomatic recognition and suffered other forms of retaliation. Thus, although extremists on both sides of the Israeli-Palestinian conflict engaged in increasingly blatant terrorist tactics to retard the peace process, the loss of external support pushed Palestinians toward accommodation with Israel.

After the Oslo Agreement was signed in 1993, Israeli and Palestinian radicals stepped up their opposition while the Israeli government dragged its feet on implementing interim provisions of the Oslo Accords. Even Israeli prime ministers declaring their commitment to a permanent resolution of the confict permitted settlements on Palestinian lands to expand in number and size (Agha and Malley, 2001; Elon, 2002). Meanwhile, the new Palestinian National Authority (PNA), headed by Arafat, proved to be both antidemocratic and corrupt. The failure of US-brokered negotiations in the summer of 2000 between Arafat and then–Israeli prime minister Ehud Barak, who had staked his political career on the achievement of a settlement, prompted new threats and confrontations by both sides (Agha and Malley, 2001; Malley and Agha, 2002; Morris, 2002). A highly publicized intrusion by Israeli general Ariel Sharon, accompanied by a thousand Israeli troops, on to the precincts of the al-Aqsa Mosque in Jerusalem, became the casus belli for Palestinian radicals already determined to derail the peace agreement. They launched a second, "al-Aqsa" intifada, one that never even pretended to be nonviolent.

Despite many ups and downs, the administrations of George H. W. Bush and Bill Clinton actively tried to keep the peace process on track. This changed in 2001 with the inauguration of President George W. Bush, a man already committed to the program of the Israeli right wing. His domestic constituency base was dominated by two strongly pro-Israel/anti-Palestinian groups: radical neoconservative hard-liners and the "Christian Coalition," both committed to Israel's retention of the Occupied Territories (Goldberg,

During the second intifada, Israel blocked numerous roads, such as this one from Birzeit to Ramallah, forcing Palestinians to leave their cars and walk across a rocky path. In mid-2003, numerous towns and villages were only accessible by foot.

2006). Terrorist attacks on the United States in September 2001 moved the US president even closer to Israeli prime minister Ariel Sharon. As the situation on the ground deteriorated, the intifada and Israel's military reoccupation of land that formerly had been relinquished to the Palestinian Authority under the provisions of the Oslo Agreement generated high rates of civilian casualties, hardening the hearts of populations on each side against compromise with the other (Elon, 2002). It also widened the gap between Hamas and Fatah, the latter seen as not merely corrupt but also too incompetent to achieve any real concessions from Israel in negotiations to end the conflict.

In January 2006, Hamas won legislative elections in Palestine, widening the split between it and Fatah, the party of President Mahmoud Abbas. Rivalry between Hamas and Fatah led to a brutal conflict in Gaza that ended with Fatah's expulsion in June 2007, leaving Hamas in control of the only nominally independent Palestinian territory. Supported by Israel and the United States, however, President Abbas fired the Hamas prime minister, Ismail Haniyeh, and appointed a new prime minister without legislative approval, an action that received de facto recognition from the Israeli government. Without a functioning economy, Hamas cannot provide for the population of Gaza. It also must cope with its own insider-outsider split between Haniyeh, the senior Hamas figure in Gaza, and Khaled Meshal, Hamas's overall leader who lives in Syria. As long as acute divisions among Palestinians and between Palestinians and Israelis persist, Palestine/Israel will continue as a focal point of conflict in the Middle East.

■ The Kurdish Conflict

The Kurds, like the Palestinians, are a nation without a state (McDowell, 1996). As detailed by Goldschmidt in Chapter 3, Kurds were promised an autonomous territory by the European powers under the Treaty of Sèvres following World War I. However, a large slice of "Kurdistan," the Kirkuk area, was among the first oil-producing regions in the Middle East. Because of the oil, the British wanted Kirkuk attached to Iraq, one of their mandates (Marr, 1985). Subsequently the territory of the Kurds, a non-Arab, non-Turkic people, was divided among five adjoining states: Iran, Iraq, Turkey, Syria, and the former Soviet Union (now Azerbaijan). Kurdish ethnic enclaves persist because high mountains separate communities, tribal leaders exercise strong authority over local populations, and internal Kurdish disagreements as well as tensions between Kurds and the governments of the affected states produce repeated conflicts. These struggles are more than a set of civil wars; they also feature strife among Kurds and their host governments.

Oil and separatist politics coincide in Iraq, where one of the elements holding the Kurds together was their long insistence on local autonomy and rights to a share of Iraqi oil revenues. Iraqi Kurds engaged in repeated uprisings against the central government from the earliest years of the Iraqi state. During the 1930s and 1940s, Kurdish guerrillas led by Mullah Mustafa Barzani fought an intermittent civil war in Iraq. Iranian Kurds also refused to resign themselves to assimilation. During World War II, assisted by Soviet troops, Iranian Kurds established a short-lived independent republic called Mahabad. Despite rivalry among Kurdish tribal leaders, Kurds often assist one another in wars against the states. For example, Barzani led several thousand Iraqi Kurdish fighters into Iran to help defend Mahabad against Iranian troops.

After Mahabad fell, Barzani went into exile in the Soviet Union. Following the 1958 revolution he was permitted to return to Iraq. The postrevolutionary Iraqi regime released Kurdish political prisoners and also appointed Kurds to important government posts. The common bond between Kurds and Iraq's new leader, Abd al-Karim Qasim, was opposition to Arab nationalism. This alliance ended when the Iraqi government rejected Kurdish demands for autonomy as secessionist. The civil war in Iraq resumed in 1961.

Just as Kurds sometimes cooperate with one another against a state, they also form temporary alignments with one state against another state or against another Kurdish faction. Kurdish rebels in Iraq received periodic assistance from the Iranian government, and Iraqi and Iranian troops have fought one another in the Kurdish region during uprisings. During the early 1970s, Iraqi Kurdish rebels were aided both by Iran and, through Iran, by the United States. Negotiations between representatives of the Iraqi government and the Kurds produced compromises on many issues dividing the two sides. However, it was not until 1975, when the Iranian government and the United States agreed to halt military support of Iraqi Kurds in exchange for moving the boundary between Iraq and Iran, that this phase of the fighting ended (Ahmad, 1991).

Following the Iranian revolution in 1979, Iraqi Kurds were once again a target of Iranian political manipulation. During the Iran-Iraq War (1980–1988), Saddam Hussein saw the Kurdish region as a point of strategic vulnerability. Fighting took place not only between Iraq and Iran but also between Iraqis and Kurds in both countries. In violation of international treaties, the Iraqi military used chemical weapons against Iranian troops and Iraqi Kurdish villages, including Halabja, and razed hundreds more Kurdish villages to the ground (Galbraith 2006; Makiya, 1993). After the Kuwait War (1990–1991), Iraqi Kurds rose up against the government of Saddam Hussein, but brutal repression by Iraqi troops led to a massive outflow of refugees into Iran and Turkey. Britain, France, Holland, and the United States created "safe havens" for the Kurds, including a no-fly zone policed by British and US aircraft deployed from bases in Turkey.

Within the safe haven, a Kurdish administration located in Erbil was established by two often-warring Kurdish factions, the Kurdistan Democratic Party (KDP) under Massoud Barzani (son of KDP founder Mullah Mustafa Barzani), and the Patriotic Union of Kurdistan (PUK) under Jalal Talabani. However, the economic isolation of the safe haven and its almost complete dependence on resources from outside brought the two factions into repeated conflict (Barkey, 1997). Their competition for scarce resources aggravated differences in the assumptions and goals of their leaders, and these divisions were played up by the governments of Iran, Turkey, and Iraq. US forces continued to protect the Kurds for their opposition to Saddam, and residents of the no-fly zone became accustomed to their autonomy and what some touted as a model democracy for the region (for example, see Salih, 2002).

Kurds were strong supporters of US/UK intervention to topple Saddam's regime, and their military arm, the Pesh Merga, fought side-by-side with the invaders against Saddam's forces. The Kurds retain significant autonomy and authority in the new, Shi'i-dominated Iraqi state. Jalal Talabani is the president of Iraq. Massoud Barzani, born in Mahabad when the territory was still under his father's control, is the president of the Autonomous Kurdish Government in Iraq, the only functioning political regime in post-Saddam Iraq.

The Kurdish region is among the safest in Iraq, but as insurgency and civil wars elsewhere in the country intensify, Kurds also face terrorist attacks. Meanwhile, the Kurds are exercising control over oil resources in their lands and are negotiating with IOCs to expand production as the foundation of their economy.

Turkey is ambivalent about Iraq's Kurds because it has problems with its own. The long history of Kurdish separatism in Turkey violates the keystone of Turkish state-centered nationalism. Atatürk's image of Turkey as an integrated nation-state governed by a uniform civil law replaced the Ottoman millet system that had permitted minority communities a significant degree of self-government in matters affecting personal status. Pressure on all citizens of the new Turkey to conform to Atatürk's secular, modernist, and national norms was intense and often violent, but Atatürk also made efforts to co-opt Kurds into supporting the state idea rather than simply repressing or killing them.

As in Iraq and Iran, rebellious outbursts in Turkey's Kurdish region were entangled in national and regional political movements. During a period of severe internal conflict in Turkey in the mid-1970s, a Marxist-Leninist organization, the Kurdistan Workers Party (PKK), emerged from the leftist movement. In 1984, the PKK launched an armed insurrection that killed more than 20,000 people in about a dozen years. Efforts to suppress the rebellion were estimated to cost Turkey about 3 percent of its gross domestic product (GDP) every year and tie down about 250,000 Turkish troops and security personnel (Barkey, 1997; also McDowell, 1996).

Turkey's conflicts with its Kurdish minority also feature intervention by neighboring states. Syria and Iran have backed the PKK, which established military bases in the Kurds' safe haven in Iraq. Until fall 1998, Syria provided a safe haven to PKK rebels. Relations between Turkey and Syria deteriorated alarmingly, however, and under strong Turkish pressure, the Syrians expelled PKK exiles, including PKK leader Abdullah Öçalan. The following year, Öçalan was captured by Turkish agents and jailed. His 1999 trial, at which he was found guilty and sentenced to death, was widely covered in the press. Non-Kurdish Turks welcomed the death sentence because they believe that Öçalan masterminded terrorist acts that killed large numbers of Turkish people.

In recent years, Turkey's Kurds, along with other groups who do not quite fit the Kemalist image of what a proper Turk should be, have experienced a gradual liberation thanks to Turkey's bid for membership in the European Union (EU). Human rights concerns are the primary public reasons why Europeans have objected to Turkey's accession (privately, many Europeans dislike Turkey's Muslim culture). Turkey also has a large and growing domestic constituency supporting the expansion of human rights, and profound changes in Turkish domestic politics are opening the system to "minorities" of all sorts and sizes, including Kurds. In response to EU pressure, Turkey improved some human rights practices and brought laws into line with EU standards. In August 2002, the government abolished the death penalty and also made it legal for Kurds to broadcast and teach in their own language (Yildiz, 2005).

Improvements in the position of Kurds in Turkey were spearheaded by the Islamist Justice and Development Party (JDP), which leads the governing coalition and is a strong proponent of EU accession. Turkey's Kemalist establishment is wary of the EU, which also is pressing for civilian control of the Turkish military, an integral part of the nationalist establishment. The old guard is resentful of its displacement by the JDP, but focuses complaints on the religiosity of JDP members, such as the fact that the wives of many JDP leaders wear *hijab* (headscarves). In 2007, the Turkish parliament was scheduled to elect a new president. Afraid that the government would easily capture a majority for Abdullah Gül, a JDP member whose wife wears *hijab,* the opposition walked out of the parliament to deny the body a quorum. Prime Minister Recep Tayyip Erdoğan responded by calling new elections for July and proposing to amend the constitution so that presidents would be popularly elected.

The 2007 elections were sharply contested, with tacit threats of military intervention rumbling in the background. The old guard attempted to mobilize women against the JDP by saying that its secret plan was to create an "Islamic Republic of Turkey" just like the Islamic Republic of Iran. The outcome of the election was definitive. The JDP won in a landslide, but it was not the only winner. Several Kurds running under the JDP banner were among the winners, along with twenty-three Kurds who ran as independents and forty-nine women, the highest number ever elected to the Turkish parliament (Öktem, 2007; Posch, 2007). Just as the lure of eventual accession to the EU hastened the opening of repressive regimes in Spain and Greece, the EU-led opening in Turkey has attracted a large and diverse constituency committed to improving civil rights and liberties for all Turkish citizens, including Turkey's Kurds.

▓ The Conflict Between Iran and Iraq

Both the Israeli-Palestinian conflict and the Kurdish conflict intersect the conflict between Iran and Iraq. Iran is not an Arab country and did not participate in the Arab boycott against Israel mounted to protest its establishment and to undermine its survival (Losman, 1972). In consequence, Iran was free to sell oil to Israel and increase oil production during anti-Israel Arab oil embargoes in 1967 and 1973, undercutting the effectiveness of the Arab "oil weapon" (Tétreault, 1981). Both Iran and Israel, aspiring regional military powers, became US clients and partners during the Cold War. Their cliency relationships with the United States were enhanced under the Nixon Doctrine, which advocated greater US reliance on regional proxies to further US Cold War interests (Elon, 2002; Tétreault, 1985). Thus it is not surprising that during the Iran-Iraq War the Reagan administration would initiate illegal sales of weapons to Iran in exchange for money to aid the contras in Nicaragua through the agency of an Israeli intermediary (Draper, 1991).

Unlike Iran, Iraq was a prominent defender of the Palestinians, in part because Iraqi leaders wanted to lead the Arab nationalist movement. In 1967, Iraq led radical states in demanding an Arab oil embargo against Israel's allies in the Six Day War. The resulting income losses pushed three other Arab oil-exporting countries to establish OAPEC in January 1968 to block future Iraqi demands (Tétreault, 1981). Iraq fought beside Syria in the October 1973 war, despite the strong rivalry between these two Baathist regimes whose quarrels ranged from Euphrates River water rights to oil pipeline transit fees. Iraq's role as a champion of the Palestinian cause remained untarnished even when it refused to participate in the 1973–1974 oil embargo against Israel's allies (Tétreault, 1981). Before the Egyptian-Israeli peace treaty was signed in March 1979, Iraq led a drive at the Baghdad summit meeting of Arab states in November 1978 to retaliate against Egypt should it take that step (Ahmad, 1991).

Iraq's differences with Iran can be traced back through hundreds of years of rivalry between various Arab and Persian empires, but the modern roots of this conflict are another legacy of the cavalier attitudes of the imperialists responsible for shaping post–World War I territorial settlements. Territorial struggles also draw the Kurds into this conflict:

> The borders between the two countries, arranged for the most part by outsiders, have never been firmly accepted by either side. . . . Iraqi fear of Persian hegemony was, in their minds, based on gradual Iranian encroachment on "Arab" land, including the Arab territory of Khuzistan (formerly al-Muhammarah) in 1925, the incorporation of the waters around Khurramshahr in 1937, and the 1975 treaty that gave Iran half of the Shatt al-Arab. (Marr, 1985:291)

Successful maneuvering by Iran in the Iraqi-Kurdish dispute in the mid-1970s had moved the border between the two from the Iranian side of the Shatt al-Arab to the "thalweg," an imaginary line down the middle of the waterway. Iran's victory reduced Iraq's access to the Gulf and increased its dependence on pipelines crossing Syria and Turkey to carry its oil to markets.

Following the successful 1978–1979 Islamist revolution in Iran, the new government's leaders stirred antigovernment sentiments among Iraqi Kurds in the north and made religious appeals to Iraqi Shi'a in the south. In September 1980, Saddam Hussein invaded Iran, thinking he could take advantage of the domestic turmoil caused by internal struggles among the clergy and other supporters of the revolution over who would control the postrevolutionary regime (Keddie, 1981; Moghissi, 1994). Saddam also wanted to end Iranian propaganda campaigns and border incursions. Iraqis expected a quick victory and a postwar settlement that would reverse decades of territorial gains by Iran. They were surprised at the resistance they encountered and the lack of support from ethnic Arab citizens of Iran. The conflict bogged down into a war of attrition similar to the trench warfare that claimed so many casualties on the western front during World War I (Cordesman and Wagner, 1990; Hiro, 1991).

The Iran-Iraq War had a significant oil dimension. As it ground on, Iran's far larger population base erased the strategic advantage Iraq had seized by its surprise attack. Each side sought to devastate not simply the enemy's soldiers but the capacity of the enemy to wage war at all. Iraq persuaded wealthy Arab oil exporters to support its "Arab war" against Iran in spite of their membership in the new Gulf Cooperation Council. In consequence, when Iran bombed Iraq's pipelines to cripple Iraq's capacity to earn oil revenues to buy more arms, crude production earmarked by Kuwait and Saudi Arabia to be sold "on Iraq's account" kept oil income flowing to Iraq anyway. The oil-rich Arab Gulf states sent cash and also supplied Iraq with arms. Kuwait imported war matériel destined for Iraq and even constructed a highway from Shuwaikh port to the Iraqi border to carry it north more efficiently. When Iran retaliated by bombing Kuwaiti oil tankers, the Kuwaitis appealed to the Soviet Union, the United States, and other naval powers for protection, resulting in the reflagging of Kuwaiti ships to discourage Iranian attacks (Assiri, 1990). The United States also assisted Iraq with "intelligence, economic aid, helicopters, and licenses for exports that were crucial to [Saddam's] development of, among other things, the chemical weapons that he later used with great success to blunt Iranian counterattacks and to subdue the Kurds of northern Iraq" (Urquhart, 2002:16).

Perhaps the most important component of the oil war was the expansion of oil production by Saudi Arabia that began in 1985. This flood of oil raised money for the states financing the war, but it depressed oil prices worldwide to their lowest level (in constant dollars) since the 1960s. Arab Gulf exporters with excess production capacity could compensate to some degree for the loss of income from lower prices by increasing production. But Iran, already producing at full capacity and denied other sources of foreign exchange as the result of US sanctions, suffered a sharply reduced capacity to rearm. The oil war counterbalanced Iran's advantages in manpower and helped to prevent an Iranian victory. Even so, it was not enough to allow Iraq to win the shooting war, which ended in a stalemate in 1988.

By then, conditions in the belligerent countries were far from what they had been before the war began. Despite the largesse of its Arab neighbors,

In the 1980s, young Iraqi women were
trained to fight in the war against Iran.

Iraq was forced to borrow money from Western banks. By the end of the war, Iraq owed US$15 billion to nonconcessional lenders (Tétreault, 1993:96). Meanwhile, the Iraqi people, who had lived under miserable conditions throughout the war, expected the peace to live up to all the promises their leader had made while it was going on (al-Khafaji, 1995). But Saddam Hussein could not satisfy both the banks and his population, especially given the depression in oil prices ensured by continued overproduction.

Tim Niblock (1982) sees a link between Iraqi conflicts with Iran and Iraqi assaults on Kuwait. He notes that Iran has repeatedly challenged Iraqi sovereignty and usually with success. Iraq's inability to win against Iran led it to turn against Kuwait, which is much smaller and weaker but against which it has very weak claims. Even so, before 1990, every Iraqi challenge to Kuwait was rewarded with money, land, or leverage on the domestic and foreign policies of Kuwait (Assiri, 1990).

That things turned out so differently in 1990 reflects changes in the external environment that made intervention by a coalition of extraregional states against Iraq possible, although not inevitable. Indeed, some Kuwaiti aid and investment recipients supported Iraq. Jordan violated UN sanctions against Iraq by transporting military supplies off-loaded in the Gulf of Aqaba to the Iraqi border; Yemen supported the Iraqi position in most UN Security Council votes. Yet the majority of Arab governments lined up behind Kuwait. Whether, like the governments of other GCC states, they fought in their own interests, or like Syria, because they detested the Iraqi regime, or like Egypt, because they were lured by the prospect of debt forgiveness and a new infusion of economic aid, many defied large and vocal segments of their own populations by that choice.

In the West, the differences between Kuwait and Iraq seemed clear. In the Middle East, the choice was far less obvious. Saddam Hussein's prominence as an Arab nationalist and his loud proclamations of support for the Palestinians; vast and obvious differences in wealth between Kuwaiti tourists and the masses of impoverished citizens in Egypt, Morocco, and other far less wealthy countries; and the association of the most prominent members of the anti-Iraq coalition with past imperialism and present dependency prompted many Arab citizens to support Iraq rather than Kuwait (Long, 2004). This was true not only for the common person in the "Arab street" but also for intellectuals like Moroccan sociologist Fatima Mernissi (1992). The diplomatic and economic isolation of Iraq following the liberation of Kuwait, despite Saddam Hussein's decision to set fire to Kuwaiti oil wells, repress with exemplary brutality a Shi'i intifada in the south (al-Shahristani, 1994; al-Khafaji, 1994), and crush a Kurdish uprising in the north (Kakai, 1994), only increased widespread sympathy for Iraq throughout the Arab world.

Following the end of the Kuwait War, Saddam Hussein played cat-and-mouse games with UN inspection teams sent to monitor the dismantling of Iraq's chemical and biological weapons. He was usually cheered on by some Arab governments and most Arab populations. When the Iraqi government accused US nationals on the UN arms inspection teams of spying and then expelled them late in 1997, no Arab government, not even Kuwait, supported military retaliation against Iraq. However, when all the remaining UN inspectors were withdrawn in December 1998 by Richard Butler, the head of the UN Special Commission, six Arab governments, including Egypt and Syria, reprimanded Iraq. The return of UN arms inspectors in December 2002 also evoked mixed reactions. On the one hand, despite energetic efforts, the inspectors did not uncover a "smoking gun"; on the other hand, US insistence that weapons were there, coupled with the growing conviction that the administration would go to war whether weapons were found or not, raised concerns about the whole enterprise.

The George W. Bush administration had stated months before the resumption of inspections that it wanted to see "regime change" in Iraq, which it envisioned as the beginning of a wave of democratization that would sweep across the region. The rationale for military attacks on countries whose regimes the United States wishes to change was laid out in a redefined National Security Strategy of the United States of America, published on September 20, 2002. The inexorable march toward war with Iraq took place amid leader ambivalence and popular dissent (*Middle East Report,* 2003). Saddam's neighbors were not unhappy at the prospect of seeing him go, but they were uneasy about the ultimate aims of the United States and worried about domestic reaction to another US war on Iraq.

After President Bush declared victory in Iraq on May 1, 2003, Iran's external security, along with the delicate balance among contending domestic forces, was challenged by the intense interest of factions within the US government in taking what they viewed as a successful policy "on the road," perhaps to Tehran (Hersh, 2006). The rapid fall of Saddam Hussein's regime and the failure of the United States to plan for postconflict security arrangements led to a surge of lawlessness that soon became an armed insurgency against the occupying forces and anyone in Iraq who cooperated with them. The violent implosion of Iraq was hastened by ill-conceived policies such as excluding Baath party members from jobs, disbanding the 300,000-strong Iraqi army, and failing to sequester arms and weapons located in dumps all over the country and in the hands of the disbanded soldiers (Allawi, 2007; Chandrasekaran, 2006). Political changes were rushed to suit schedules in Washington rather than in Baghdad (Allawi, 2007). Only the Kurds had the foresight to demand some institutional insulation from the rest of the country. Shi'i victories in Iraqi elections reinforced Sunni perceptions that they were being unfairly excluded from power, and soon Sunnis and Shi'a were fighting one another in cities and villages, especially in central Iraq. Meanwhile, disorder in the country made Iraq an incubator for terrorism imported from outside. Shi'i factions also vied with one another for primacy in the new central government, which they dominated thanks to their electoral majorities. Some of these factions have ties to Iran, which hoped to make the new Iraq an ally. The United States refused to work with Iran (or Syria) to stem the violence (Allawi, 2007).

When the weapons of mass destruction that served as the justification for invading Iraq could not be found, the new democratization rationale was foregrounded, making autocratic governments across the region nervous and antagonistic (Neep, 2004; Recknagel, 2004). As US hostility toward Iran intensified, the Iranian government became more hostile to the United States and embarked on a very public effort to make enriched uranium, ostensibly for electricity generation but also as a deterrent against US military intervention in Iran. Even peaceful US programs to promote democracy in Iran have come under attack by Iranian officials who see them as attempts to foster a "velvet revolution" in Iran to overthrow the government. Growing US appropriations for "advancing human rights and freedom within Iran," including support for "civil-society groups—media, legal and human rights nongovernmental organizations—both outside and inside Iran" are seen as deliberate provocations and attempts to effect "regime change" (Azimi, 2007). In reaction, the Iranian government initiated its own crackdowns, especially against students and academics. In the spring of 2007, it arrested a number of persons who held dual citizenship in Iran and a Western country, including several Iranian Americans. In July, two of the incarcerated Iranian-Americans were shown on Iranian television "confessing" to having promoted contacts between Iranian and US citizens. Throughout, neoconservative hard-liners, led by Vice President Dick Cheney, continued to push for a US military attack on Iran.

The return of extraregional powers to the Middle East, especially those ready to wage war to change regimes they do not like, evokes the same fear and rage that met earlier Great Power interventions, which, as we have seen, also imposed and deposed regimes. The irony is that the states of the Middle East were global pioneers in regionalism and, by this time, should have been able to present a united front to these outsiders. Instead, they have been unable to progress much beyond establishing international organizations and assigning them limited tasks. In consequence, the region is still so fragmented that these states remain unable to protect their sovereignty or their common interests from the great powers of the day, as well as from terrorist assaults. The combination of external intervention and domestic insecurity and unrest have created the worst of all possible worlds for the vulnerable nation-states of the Middle East.

▧ Conclusion

The international relations of the Middle East are deeply influenced by legacies of imperialism, particularly the persistence of external intervention and its perverse effects on local regimes. The region is noted both for its authoritarian rulers, supported and sometimes installed by foreign patrons near and far, and for their ineptitude in foreign policy, domestic policy—and sometimes both. This legacy has convinced leaders and populations alike that their efforts to change things for the better are still jeopardized by the whims of manipulative neighbors and the interests of the reigning great powers. Repeated efforts to create strong intraregional and extraregional alliances have failed to enable these countries to protect themselves. One reason is the prominence of negative sovereignty as a cherished principle. National leaders are unwilling to compromise until problems turn into crises that only heroic efforts can conceivably reverse. Even organizations such as OPEC, established to protect the chief economic resource of the region, have faltered time and again over the refusal of members to compromise their individual differences in the general interest. Instead, some national leaders, like President Mahmoud Ahmadinejad of Iran, continue to distract their populations with ambitious historic missions that create excuses for intraregional intervention and often extraregional intervention as well (De Bellaigue, 2006).

The end of formal imperialism did not end outside interest in the Middle East or external intervention into its affairs. Hydrocarbon resources attract economic and strategic intervention by great powers pursuing national interests or their own global historic missions (Renner, 2003). One such historic mission, winning the Cold War, promoted contests between the United States and the Soviet Union for Middle Eastern clients. These contests, along with rising oil incomes, fueled a transfer of arms from all over the world to the Middle East and its many conflicts.

The interstate boundaries drawn by departing imperial powers left other legacies. Among these are the festering nationalist conflict in Israel-Palestine and insurgencies in imaginary Kurdistan. Other time bombs exploded in recurring outbursts, such as those between Iraq and its neighbors, Iran and Kuwait. These conflicts attracted external intervention that itself caused or aggravated intraregional, civil, and interstate wars.

The end of the Cold War inaugurated a new global strategic era initially premised on collective security and international cooperation. The revival of the UN during the Kuwait War (1990–1991) encouraged world leaders to imagine intervention differently, as an openly chosen course of action to ensure security and human rights. But the lack of military response by the UN and its most powerful members to vicious conflicts in places like Bosnia and Rwanda, where oil was not among the interests to be advanced, called the new interventionism into question (Havel, 1999; Tétreault, 1995). Deployment of peacekeepers during both of those conflicts merely showed how little could be achieved without highly focused intervention by sufficient forces to stop the violence and then keep the peace. Whether the disintegration of Iraq can be repaired through such a focused and limited multinational intervention or the situation proves to be just another example of self-interested great power politics whose outcome sets the stage for a new generation of conflict is important far beyond the Middle East.

Another agent of intervention is the multinational corporation. Often regarded as agents of their home governments, multinationals under globalization pursue foreign policies to suit their own interests, sometimes in accord with and sometimes against the stated positions of political leaders in their home or host countries. One example is pipeline politics. The rush of private investment in oil and gas development in Central Asia touched off controversy regarding the number and location of pipelines required to bring these new hydrocarbon supplies to market. For political reasons, the US government first advocated a new pipeline through Turkey and then, following the defeat of the Taliban, one through Afghanistan. For economic reasons, oil companies such as Chevron and Total preferred a plan that would put a pipeline through Iran.

Oil company executives, along with academic observers, are among the most active advocates of reintegrating Iran into the international community,

World leaders gathered in Sharm el-Sheikh, Egypt, for an antiterrorism conference. Front row, from left to right: Yasser Arafat, Boris Yeltsin, Hosni Mubarak, Bill Clinton, Shimon Peres, and King Hussein.

and their concerns are far broader than the simple issue of where to locate a pipeline. Investors have interests in the long-term stability of the region as a whole, and few believe that stability can be achieved if the war in Iraq spreads to Iran or even if the country remains marginalized and impoverished.

Extraregional intervention in the Middle East by dominant countries, international organizations, and financial and economic actors has increased in response to the defeat of Saddam Hussein and collapse of Iraq. Although such intervention does not have to be either one-sided or negative in its impact, the 2003 war in Iraq does not offer reasons for optimism. Globalization, with its promise of expanding the joint benefits of investment and economic development across many nations, appeared to offer autonomous participation by Middle Eastern states and firms in the world economy. Yet strategic problems from other kinds of globalization—weapons proliferation and terrorism— along with well-documented human rights violations, offer a steady stream of excuses for direct involvement by foreign governments and NGOs in the domestic politics and foreign policies of Middle Eastern states. The war on terrorism actually aggravates domestic and regional conflict by suppressing concerns for human rights and civil liberties, causing external constraints on abusive governments and belligerent leaders to disappear. If strategic intervention were to be "globalized" through organizations like the UN, would it be less destabilizing and more effective than military intervention by major powers?

Complicating all of these scenarios is the persistent incapacity of many Middle Eastern regimes to manage domestic conflicts peacefully. Higher oil prices have reduced conflict arising from economic distress but they have had little impact on the rise of religiously based opposition groups. During the Cold War, some of these groups were viewed as foils against secular opposition groups and enjoyed the tacit and occasionally even the open protection of conservative governments (Tétreault, 2000). Their domestic revolutionary potential was revealed in Iran and Afghanistan, but their capacity to inflict damage outside the region was not fully appreciated until the September 2001 attacks on the United States by Osama bin Laden's organization. Unfortunately, the so-called war on terrorism has become a rationale for both internal crackdowns and external intervention in the Middle East. Vahan Zanoyan (2002) notes that the ability of Middle Eastern states to retain any significant autonomy depends critically on their ability to get their domestic houses in order. This includes taking regional approaches to strengthening their private sectors as a means of reducing dependency and opening their regimes to citizen participation.

A substantial reduction in conventional forms of external intervention also would be welcome. If nothing else, it would leave some space in which the nations of the Middle East could move forward with the business of creating positive sovereignty. Successes in the Arab Gulf states are evidence that if governments increase their capacity to protect and support populations, they, in turn, would protect and support their governments.

■ Bibliography

Agha, Hussein, and Robert Malley. 2001. "Camp David: The Tragedy of Errors." *New York Review of Books,* August 9. www.nybooks.com/articles/14380 (accessed January 3, 2003).

Ahmad, Ahmad Yousef. 1991. "The Dialectics of Domestic Environment and Role Performance: The Foreign Policy of Iraq." Pp. 186–215 in Bahgat Korany and Ali E. Hillal Dessouki (eds.), *The Foreign Policies of Arab States: The Challenge of Change.* 2nd ed. Boulder, Colo.: Westview Press.

Ahmed, Leila. 1992. *Women and Gender in Islam.* New Haven, Conn.: Yale University Press.

Allawi, Ali A. 2007. *The Occupation of Iraq: Winning the War, Losing the Peace.* New Haven: Yale University Press.

Anderson, Irvine H. 1981. *Aramco, the United States, and Saudi Arabia: A Study of the Dynamics of Foreign Oil Policy, 1933–1950.* Princeton: Princeton University Press.

Anscombe, Frederick F. 1997. *The Ottoman Gulf: The Creation of Kuwait, Saudi Arabia, and Qatar.* New York: Columbia University Press.

Ashrawi, Hanan. 1995. *This Side of Peace.* New York: Simon and Schuster.

Assiri, Abdel Reda. 1990. *Kuwait's Foreign Policy: City-State in World Politics.* Boulder, Colo.: Westview Press.

Azimi, Negar. 2007. "Hard Realities of Soft Power." *NYT Magazine,* June 24. www.iri.org/newsarchive/2007/2007-06-25-News-NYTMagazine.asp (accessed August 26, 2007).

Bamford, James. 2001. *Body of Secrets: Anatomy of the Ultra-Secret National Security Agency from the Cold War Through the Dawn of a New Century.* New York: Doubleday.

Barkey, Henri J. 1997. "Kurdish Geopolitics." *Current History* 96 (January):1–5.

Beblawi, Hazem. 1990. "The Rentier State in the Arab World." Pp. 85–98 in Giacomo Luciani (ed.), *The Arab State.* Berkeley: University of California Press.

Ben-Yehuda, Hemda, and Shmuel Sandler. 2002. *The Arab-Israeli Conflict Transformed: Fifty Years of Interstate and Ethnic Crisis.* Albany: State University of New York Press.

Berke, Shari. 1997. "Sahara Dispute and Environment." Trade and Environment Database, Case no. 24. www.american.edu/ted/ice/sahara.htm (accessed May 16, 2003).

Bill, James A., and Robert Springborg. 1994. *Politics in the Middle East.* 4th ed. New York: HarperCollins.

Caporaso, James A. 1978. "Dependence, Dependency, and Power in the Global System: A Structural and Behavioral Analysis." *International Organization* 32, no. 1 (Winter):13–43.

Chandrasekaran, Rajiv. 2006. *Imperial Life in the Emerald City: Inside Iraq's Green Zone.* New York: Knopf.

Christison, Kathleen. 2000. *Perceptions of Palestine: Their Influence on US Middle East Policy.* Berkeley: University of California Press.

Clawson, Patrick. 1995. "US-GCC Security Relations II: Growing Domestic Economic and Political Problems." *Strategic Forum,* August.

Coll, Steve. 2004. *Ghost Wars: The Secret History of the CIA, Afghanistan, and Bin Laden, from the Soviet Invasion to September 10, 2001.* New York: Penguin.

Cordesman, Anthony H., and Abraham R. Wagner. 1990. *The Lessons of Modern War.* Vol. 2: *The Iran-Iraq War.* Boulder, Colo.: Westview Press.

Crystal, Jill. 1990. *Oil and Politics in the Gulf: Rulers and Merchants in Kuwait and Qatar.* Cambridge: Cambridge University Press.

Dawisha, Adeed. 2003. *Arab Nationalism in the Twentieth Century: From Triumph to Despair.* Princeton: Princeton University Press.

Dawisha, Karen. 1982–1983. "The USSR in the Middle East: Superpower in Eclipse?" *Foreign Affairs* 61, no. 4:438–452.

De Bellaigue, Christopher. 2006. "Defiant Iran." *New York Review of Books,* November 2, pp. 58–62.

Dickson, H. R. P. 1956. *Kuwait and Her Neighbours.* London: George Allen and Unwin.

Draper, Theodore. 1991. *A Very Thin Line: The Iran-Contra Affairs.* New York: Touchstone Books.

al-Ebraheem, Hassan Ali. 1975. *Kuwait: A Political Study.* Kuwait: Kuwait University.

Elon, Amos. 2002. "No Exit." *New York Review of Books,* May 23, pp. 15–16, 18, 20.

———. 2003. "An Unsentimental Education." *New York Review of Books,* May 29, pp. 4, 6–7.

Galbraith, Peter W. 2006. *The End of Iraq: How American Incompetence Created a War Without End.* New York: Simon and Schuster.

Gasiorowski, Mark J. 1991. *US Foreign Policy and the Shah: Building a Client State in Iran.* Ithaca: Cornell University Press.

Gerner, Deborah J. 1991. "Palestinians, Israelis, and the Intifada: The Third Year and Beyond." *Arab Studies Quarterly* 13, nos. 3–4:19–60.

————. 1994. *One Land, Two Peoples: The Conflict over Palestine.* 2nd ed. Boulder, Colo.: Westview Press.

Gerner, Deborah J., and Ömür Yilmaz. 2004. *A Question of Sovereignty: Bahrain, Qatar, and the International Court of Justice.* Pew Case Studies in International Affairs. Washington, D.C.: Institute for the Study of Diplomacy, Georgetown University.

Ghabra, Shafeeq N. 1987. *Palestinians in Kuwait: The Family and the Politics of Survival.* Boulder, Colo.: Westview Press.

Goldberg, Jeffrey. 2006. "The Believer." *New Yorker,* February 13. www.newyorker.com/archive/2006/02/13/060213fa_fact1 (accessed May 5, 2007).

Hallwood, Paul, and Stuart Sinclair. 1982. *Oil, Debt and Development: OPEC in the Third World.* London: George Allen and Unwin.

Havel, Václav. 1999. "Kosovo and the End of the Nation-State." Trans. Paul Wilson. *New York Review of Books,* June 10, pp. 4, 6.

Hersh, Seymour M. 2006. "The Next Act." *New Yorker,* November 27, pp. 94, 96, 98, 101–104, 106–107.

Hiro, Dilip. 1991. *The Longest War: The Iran-Iraq Military Conflict.* New York: Routledge.

Horne, Alistar. 1977. *A Savage War of Peace: Algeria 1954–1962.* New York: Viking.

Hunter, F. Robert. 1993. *The Palestinian Uprising: A War by Other Means.* Revised and updated edition. Berkeley: University of California Press.

Hunter, Shireen T. 1986. "The Gulf Economic Crisis and Its Social and Political Consequences." *Middle East Journal* 40, no. 4 (Autumn):593–613.

Ibrahim, Saad Eddin. 1980. "The Negative Effects of Difference of Income Among Arab Countries on Development in Countries with Low Per Capita Income: The Case of Egypt." In *Organization of Arab Petroleum Exporting Countries (OAPEC), Sources and Problems of Arab Development.* Kuwait: OAPEC.

Jackson, Robert H. 1990. *Quasi-States: Sovereignty, International Relations and the Third World.* Cambridge: Cambridge University Press.

Kakai, Falaz al-Din. 1994. "The Kurdish Parliament." Pp. 118–133 in Fran Hazelton (ed.), *Iraq Since the Gulf War: Prospects for Democracy.* London: Zed Books.

Keddie, Nikki R. 1981. *Roots of Revolution: An Interpretive History of Modern Iran.* New Haven, Conn.: Yale University Press.

al-Khafaji, Isam. 1994. "State Terror and the Degradation of Politics." Pp. 20–31 in Fran Hazelton (ed.), *Iraq Since the Gulf War: Prospects for Democracy.* London: Zed Books.

————. 1995. "War as a Vehicle for the Rise and Demise of a State-Controlled Society: The Case of Ba'thist Iraq." *Amsterdam Middle East Papers,* no. 4 (December).

Kissinger, Henry. 1979. *White House Years.* Boston: Little, Brown.

Korany, Bahgat. 1991. "Defending the Faith Amid Change: The Foreign Policy of Saudi Arabia." Pp. 310–353 in Bahgat Korany and Ali E. Hillal Dessouki (eds.), *The Foreign Policies of Arab States: The Challenge of Change,* 2nd ed. Boulder, Colo.: Westview Press.

Lawson, Fred H. 1997. "Dialectical Integration in the Gulf Co-Operation Council." Occasional paper no. 10. Abu Dhabi: Emirates Center for Strategic Studies and Research.

Lazreg, Marnia. 1994. *The Eloquence of Silence: Algerian Women in Question.* New York: Routledge.

Long, Jerry M. 2004. *Saddam's War of Words: Politics, Religion, and the Iraqi Invasion of Kuwait.* Austin: University of Texas Press.

Losman, Donald L. 1972. "The Arab Boycott of Israel." *International Journal of Middle East Studies* 3 (April):99–115.

Luke, Timothy W. 1983. "Dependent Development and the Arab OPEC States." *Journal of Politics* 45, no. 4:979–1003.

———. 1985. "Dependent Development and the OPEC States: State Formation in Saudi Arabia and Iran Under the International Energy Regime." *Studies in Comparative International Development* 20, no. 1:31–54.

MacDonald, Robert W. 1965. *The League of Arab States: A Study in the Dynamics of Regional Organization.* Princeton: Princeton University Press.

Makiya, Kanan. 1993. *Cruelty and Silence: War, Tyranny, Uprising, and the Arab World.* New York: Norton.

———. 1996. "The Politics of Betrayal." *New York Review of Books,* October 17, pp. 8–12.

Maktabi, Rania. 2000. "State Formation and Citizenship in Lebanon: The Politics of Inclusion and Exclusion in a Sectarian State." Pp. 146–178 in Nils A. Butenschøn, Uri Davis, and Manuel Hassassian (eds.), *Citizenship and the State in the Middle East: Approaches and Applications.* Syracuse, N.Y.: Syracuse University Press.

Malley, Robert, and Hussein Agha. 2002. "Camp David: The Tragedy of Errors," *New York Review of Books,* June 13, pp. 46–49.

Marr, Phebe. 1985. *The Modern History of Iraq.* Boulder, Colo.: Westview Press.

McDowell, David. 1996. *A Modern History of the Kurds.* London: I. B. Tauris.

Melkumyan, Yelena. 1992. "Soviet Policy and the Gulf Crisis." Pp. 76–91 in Ibrahim Ibrahim (ed.), *The Gulf Crisis: Background and Consequences.* Washington, D.C.: Center for Contemporary Arab Studies.

Mernissi, Fatima. 1992. *Islam and Democracy: Fear of the Modern World.* Trans. Mary Jo Lakeland. Reading, Mass.: Addison Wesley.

Middle East Report (MERIP). 2003. "Dissent." No. 226 (Spring).

Migdal, Joel S. 1988. *Strong Societies and Weak States: State-Society Relations and State Capabilities in the Third World.* Princeton: Princeton University Press.

Mikdashi, Zuhayr. 1972. *The Community of Oil Exporting Countries.* Ithaca: Cornell University Press.

Moghissi, Haideh. 1994. *Populism and Feminism in Iran.* New York: St. Martin's Press.

Morgan, Ted. 2006. *My Battle of Algiers: A Memoir.* New York: Collins.

Morris, Benny. 1989. *The Birth of the Palestinian Refugee Problem, 1947–1949.* Cambridge: Cambridge University Press.

———. 2002. "Camp David and After: An Exchange (1. An Interview with Ehud Barak)," *New York Review of Books,* June 13, pp. 42–45.

Munif, Abdulrahman. 1989. *Cities of Salt.* New York: Vintage International.

N.A. 2001. "The Bahrain-Qatar Border Dispute: The World Court Decision, Part 2." *The Estimate* 13, no. 7 (April 6). Available from www.theestimate.com/public/040601.html (accessed January 2, 2002).

al-Naqeeb, Khaldoun Hasan. 1990. *Society and State in the Gulf and Arab Peninsula: A Different Perspective.* Trans. L. M. Kenny. London: Routledge.

Nasser, Gamal Abdel. 1955. *Egypt's Liberation: The Philosophy of the Revolution.* Washington, D.C.: Public Affairs Press.

Neep, Daniel. 2004. "Dilemmas of Democratization in the Middle East: The 'Forward Strategy of Freedom,'" *Middle East Policy* 11, no. 3 (Fall):73–84.

Niblock, Tim. 1982. "Iraqi Policies Towards the Arab States of the Gulf, 1958–1981." Pp. 125–149 in Tim Niblock (ed.), *Iraq: The Contemporary State.* New York: St. Martin's Press.

Nitzan, Jonathan, and Shimshon Bichler. 2002. *The Global Political Economy of Israel*. London: Pluto Press.

Öktem, Kerem. 2007. "Harbingers of Turkey's Second Republic." *Middle East Report Online*, August 1. www.merip.org/mero/mero080107.html (accessed August 7, 2007).

Penrose, Edith T. 1968. *The Large International Firm in Developing Countries: The International Petroleum Industry*. Cambridge: MIT Press.

Peretz, Don. 1990. *Intifada: The Palestinian Uprising*. Boulder, Colo.: Westview Press.

Peterson, Erik. 1988. *The Gulf Cooperation Council*. Boulder, Colo.: Westview Press.

Posch, Walter. 2007. "Crisis in Turkey: Just Another Bump on the Road to Europe?" European Union Institute for Security Studies, Occasional Paper No. 67, June.

Quandt, William. 1981. *Saudi Arabia in the 1980s*. Washington, D.C.: Brookings Institution.

Rand, Christopher T. 1975. *Making Democracy Safe for Oil*. Boston: Little, Brown.

Rashid, Ahmad. 2001. *Taliban: Militant Islam, Oil, and Fundamentalism in Central Asia*. New Haven, Conn.: Yale University Press.

Recknagel, Charles. 2004. "U.S.: Washington's 'Greater Middle East Initiative' Stumbles Amid Charges It Imposes Change," Radio Free Europe, March 23, 2004. www.rferl.org/featuresarticle/2004/03/aa4668e1-6bc1-46dc-9a0d-e62d8657857d.html (accessed July 14, 2006).

Renner, Michael. 2003. "Post-Saddam Iraq: Linchpin of a New Oil Order." FPIF Policy Report, January. www.fpif.org/papers/oil_body.html (accessed January 3, 2003).

Rogers, Paul. 2002. "Iraq: Consequences of a War." Oxford Research Group Briefing Paper, October.

Rush, Alan. 1987. *Al-Sabah: History and Genealogy of Kuwait's Ruling Family, 1752–1987*. London: Ithaca Press.

Salamé, Ghassan. 1990. "'Strong' and 'Weak' States: A Qualified Return to the Muqaddimah." Pp. 29–64 in Giacomo Luciani (ed.), *The Arab State*. Austin: University of Texas Press.

——— (ed.). 1994. *Democracy Without Democrats? The Renewal of Politics in the Muslim World*. London: I. B. Tauris.

Salih, Barham. 2002. "A Kurdish Model for Iraq." *Washington Post*, December 9, p. A23.

Sankari, Farouk. 1976. "The Character and Impact of Arab Oil Embargoes." Pp. 265–278 in Naiem A. Sherbiny and Mark A. Tessler (eds.), *Arab Oil: Impact on the Arab Countries and Global Implications*. New York: Praeger.

Sciolino, Elaine. 1991. *The Outlaw State: Saddam Hussein's Quest for Power and the Gulf Crisis*. New York: John Wiley and Sons.

Seale, Patrick. 1988. *Asad: The Struggle for the Middle East*. London: I. B. Tauris.

al-Shahristani, Hussein. 1994. "Suppression and Survival of Iraqi Shi'is." Pp. 134–140 in Fran Hazelton (eds.), *Iraq Since the Gulf War: Prospects for Democracy*. London: Zed Books.

Shatz, Adam. 2002. "The Torture of Algiers." *New York Review of Books*, November 21, pp. 53–57.

Smith, Anthony D. 1991. *National Identity*. Reno: University of Nevada Press.

Smith, Jean Edward. 1992. *George Bush's War*. New York: Henry Holt.

Stephens, Robert. 1976. *The Arabs' New Frontier*. London: Temple Smith.

Talbott, John. 1980. *The War Without a Name: France in Algeria, 1954–1962*. New York: Alfred Knopf.

Tétreault, Mary Ann. 1981. *The Organization of Arab Petroleum Exporting Countries: History, Policies, and Prospects.* Westport, Conn.: Greenwood Press.

———. 1985. *Revolution in the World Petroleum Market.* Westport, Conn.: Quorum Books.

———. 1991. "Autonomy, Necessity, and the Small State: Ruling Kuwait in the Twentieth Century." *International Organization* 45, no. 4:565–591.

———. 1993. "Independence, Sovereignty, and Vested Glory: Oil and Politics in the Second Gulf War." *Orient* 34, no. 1:87–103.

———. 1995. *The Kuwait Petroleum Corporation and the Economics of the New World Order.* Westport, Conn.: Quorum Books.

———. 2000. *Stories of Democracy: Politics and Society in Contemporary Kuwait.* New York: Columbia University Press.

Urquhart, Brian. 2002. "The Prospect of War." *New York Review of Books,* December 19, pp. 16, 18, 20, 22.

Vitalis, Robert. 2006. *America's Kingdom: Mythmaking on the Saudi Oil Frontier.* Palo Alto, Calif.: Stanford University Press.

Weber, Max. 1978. *Economy and Society.* Eds. Guenther Roth and Claus Wittich. Berkeley: University of California Press.

Weisberg, Richard C. 1977. *The Politics of Crude Oil Pricing in the Middle East, 1970–1975.* Berkeley: University of California Press.

Wolf, Eric. 1982. *Europe and the People Without History.* Berkeley: University of California Press.

Wood, Pia Christina. 1993. "France and the Israeli-Palestinian Conflict: The Mitterrand Policies." *Middle East Journal* 47, no. 1:21–40.

Yildiz, Kerim. 2005. *The Kurds in Turkey: EU Accession and Human Rights.* London: Pluto Press.

Zanoyan, Vahan. 2002. *Time for Making Historic Decisions in the Middle East. Strategic and Future Series,* no. 1. Kuwait: Center for Strategic and Future Studies, November.

Zartman, I. William, and A. G. Kluge. 1991. "Heroic Politics: The Foreign Policy of Libya." Pp. 236–259 in Bahgat Korany and Ali E. Hillal Dessouki (eds.), *The Foreign Policies of Arab States: The Challenge of Change.* 2nd ed. Boulder, Colo.: Westview Press.

6

The Israeli-Palestinian Conflict

Simona Sharoni and Mohammed Abu-Nimer

The Arab-Israeli conflict, and especially its Israeli-Palestinian dimension, has been at the heart of Middle Eastern politics in the twentieth century. Indeed, the Israeli-Palestinian conflict provides a unique opportunity to examine a host of concepts important to understanding Middle Eastern politics and world politics more generally. These concepts include national identity and self-determination, security dilemmas, the role of religion, the increasing importance of nonstate actors, the relative impotence of international law and international organizations such as the UN in dealing with complicated conflicts, Great Power involvement, globalization and economic interdependence, and forms of violent and nonviolent conflict resolution. Given the theoretical and political significance of these issues, it is not surprising that the Israeli-Palestinian conflict is among the most researched topics across academic disciplines as well as in applied settings; it also receives regular and prominent coverage in the media. Yet despite the growing body of literature and media accounts of the conflict, many people still view it either in a simplistic, one-dimensional manner or as distant and too complex to be grasped by ordinary people.

This chapter is designed to provide a framework for understanding the Israeli-Palestinian conflict and the prospects for its resolution. Our analysis is interdisciplinary in scope, grounded primarily in our academic training in conflict resolution. Uniquely, this chapter is coauthored by two conflict-resolution scholars: a Jewish Israeli and a Palestinian who holds Israeli citizenship. Our academic expertise notwithstanding, we have both been actively involved for the past two decades in attempts to bring about a just and lasting solution to the conflict.

All too often, media accounts and academic scholarship on the Israeli-Palestinian conflict have fallen into a trap of false symmetry. Typically, the conflict has been presented as an intractable struggle between two national movements with competing claims over the same territory. Such an interpretation obscures the asymmetrical power relations between Israeli Jews and Palestinians, both in the past and in the present. For example, it is seldom recognized that the creation of the State of Israel in 1948, which affirmed the national aspirations of the Jews, came at the expense of Palestinians, whose desire for self-determination and territorial sovereignty remains largely unfulfilled (see Nakhleh and Zureik, 1980; Said, 1980; Abu-Lughod, 1982; Quigley, 1990; Aruri, 1995). We choose to stress this point from the start not to glorify one party or vilify the other. Rather, we do so because we believe that a successful resolution of this conflict depends to a great extent on the recognition of these structured inequalities and the ability to devise a framework to transform these power relations.

Toward this end, we draw both on conflict resolution literature and on our own experience and familiarity with the region to illustrate the complexity of this conflict and highlight possible venues for its resolution. As with any other conflict, a comprehensive analysis should begin with a careful examination of the parties involved and of the historical turning points that marked its escalation and de-escalation. Keeping in mind that history in general and histories of protracted conflicts in particular are never simple or objective and always reflect particular political positions, we choose to begin our analysis with a description of the parties to the conflict to provide a context for understanding their contending interpretations of history. After an overview of central turning points and crucial dynamics throughout the history of the conflict, we examine the core issues and points of contention. Finally, we offer a framework to examine past and present attempts to resolve the conflict and identify the conditions and processes that we deem essential to a just and lasting resolution.

■ The Parties: Two Peoples— Palestinians and Israeli Jews

The Israeli-Palestinian conflict has shaped the lives of at least three generations of Israelis and Palestinians. The Arab-Israeli conflict, particularly its Israeli-Palestinian dimension, has played a central role not only in the daily lives of people throughout the Middle East but also in the lives of Palestinians and Jews living outside Israel and the Occupied Territories, many of whom see their existence as inseparable from political developments in the region (see Kelman, 1982; Segal, 1989; Heller and Nusseibeh, 1991; Rothman, 1992; Gerner, 1994; Tessler, 1994). Many scholarly and media accounts, however, tend to overlook this fact, presupposing the existence of two cohesive and unified parties locked in a conflict. Little or no attention is devoted to the composition of the parties themselves, that is, to differences not only between but also within the Palestinian and Israeli-Jewish collectivities.

To come to terms with the Israeli-Palestinian conflict requires a more complex analysis of the parties involved. Such an analysis ought to approach the parties as diverse and often fragmented communities and must take into account how the parties define themselves and how they are viewed by others. Of course, the meanings assigned to particular notions of identity and community change over time. Thus a careful examination of Palestinian and Israeli-Jewish collectivities should underscore the changes in their composition, self-image, and perceptions of and interactions with one another (Kimmerling and Migdal, 1993; Sharoni, 1995b).

Indeed, the Palestinian-Israeli conflict has played a central role in shaping the collective identities of Palestinians and Jews, for the most part in direct opposition to one another, and until recently each reflected denial of the legitimacy of the other party's identity claims (Kelman, 1982; Moses, 1990; Volkan, 1990). The terms *Palestinians* and *Israelis,* which are presently used to describe the conflict both in media and scholarly accounts, were once in themselves a topic of contention. In fact, until the mid-1970s many Jews in Israel and elsewhere as well as numerous politicians, scholars, and media analysts worldwide did not use the term *Palestinians,* thus failing to acknowledge Palestinians' rights to self-determination and territorial sovereignty (Hajjar and Beinin, 1990). Only since the 1980s has the term *Palestinians* been integrated into the mainstream discourse on the conflict, and it has been used almost exclusively (including in Israel) in both scholarly and popular references to the conflict. A similar trend has occurred in recent years, following the signing of the Oslo Accords and the establishment of the Palestinian National Authority (PNA), with the term *Palestine* beginning to replace other formulations such as *the territories* and *the West Bank and Gaza Strip* (see Usher, 1995a; Suleiman, 1995).

The extensive use of the term *Israelis* is relatively new as well, dating to the establishment of the State of Israel on May 15, 1948, when the collective reference to *Jews* was replaced by the term *Israelis.* Although large segments of the international community immediately adopted the term, until the 1990s the Arab countries and a handful of sympathizers with the Palestinian cause, including several national liberation movements, avoided the use of the term *Israelis,* using instead such terms as *Jews* or *Zionists.*

The prevalent use of the terms *Palestinians* and *Israelis* underscores the view that the Israeli-Palestinian conflict is first and foremost an intractable conflict between two national movements that claim the same piece of land. In addition, the gradual acceptance and normalization of these terms signals more than a mere semantic shift; it points to a growing recognition of the legitimacy of both parties' identity claims and opens up space for a possible reformulation of these claims in ways that are not mutually exclusive (Fernea and Hocking, 1992).

Palestinians

The term *Palestinians* refers to the Arabs—Christian, Muslim, and Druze— who have lived in Palestine for centuries. The number of Palestinians worldwide is estimated at more than five million, and they are usually divided into three major subgroups: Palestinians who live in the West Bank and Gaza Strip, those who live inside Israel's pre-1967 borders and hold Israeli citizenship, and those who live in the diaspora. The Palestinian diaspora is a direct result of the creation of the State of Israel, which resulted in the destruction of Palestinian Arab society, dispersing hundreds of thousands of Palestinians to live in exile or as refugees. Almost 70 percent of the inhabitants of the Gaza Strip and 15 percent of the inhabitants of the West Bank have lived in refugee camps since 1948 (Said et al., 1990; Yahya, 1991).

The experience of displacement and the context of a national liberation struggle have contributed to a high level of politicization among all sectors of Palestinian society. The Palestine Liberation Organization (PLO) played a central role in the process of politicization and in the consolidation of a collective Palestinian identity (Cobban, 1984; Nassar, 1991). The PLO was established in 1964 by the Arab League but gradually gained considerable independence from the Arab regimes and came to serve as the umbrella organization for different political factions with varying ideological orientations and operative strategies. The major factions included Fatah, the largest group, headed by Yasser Arafat (1929–2004); the Popular Front for the Liberation of Palestine (PFLP); the Democratic Front for the Liberation of Palestine (DFLP); and the Palestine Communist Party (PCP). The differences between these political factions notwithstanding, most Palestinians have long regarded the PLO as their "sole legitimate representative."

A careful analysis of Palestinian collectivity ought to pay attention to the social, economic, and religious makeup of the society as well as to political differences. For Palestinians in the West Bank and Gaza Strip and in Israel, the place of residence often reflects their socioeconomic status. Working-class Palestinians in the West Bank and Gaza Strip—many of whom worked until recently in Israel—reside in refugee camps and in villages; the villages are also home to peasants, whereas the elites and the petit-bourgeois class, which includes merchants, traders, and professionals, can often be found in the urban centers (Hiltermann, 1990). Another crucial social sphere that is affected by social class is education. The educational experience of Palestinians varies, depending on the geographical location as well as on the historical and political context. For example, during the Palestinian uprising that began in 1987 known as the intifada, Palestinians' access to education in the West Bank and Gaza Strip was restricted due to the widespread closure of educational institutions by the Israeli military and the arrest, imprisonment, or expulsion of both professors and students (al-Haq, 1988:419–434). Despite these difficult circumstances, Palestinians have the highest per capita rate of university graduation in the Arab world and one of the highest worldwide (Said et al., 1990).

Another fact that is often overlooked is that not all Palestinians are Muslims; Palestinian Christians live as a minority in both the West Bank and Israel (Abu-Lughod, 1987). Nevertheless, due to specific historical and political challenges that have confronted Palestinians, religious differences within Palestinian society have by and large been set aside as Palestinians sought unity under the banner of national liberation and self-determination. In recent years, however, political Islam has come to play a more prominent role within Palestinian society and politics (Taraki, 1989; Legrain, 1990; Usher, 1995a, 1995b). The early months of the first Palestinian intifada saw the emergence of the Islamic Resistance Movement (which is better known by its acronym, Hamas) in the West Bank and Gaza Strip. By the close of the 1980s, Hamas became part of the Palestinian political scene, regularly polling second only to Arafat's Fatah movement in professional and student elections across the West Bank and especially in the Gaza Strip. Since the signing of the Oslo Accords in September 1993, Hamas has established itself as the single largest political opposition group in Palestinian society (Usher, 1995b).

The redeployment of Israeli troops in some parts of the West Bank and Gaza Strip and the establishment of the PNA inevitably brought change to Palestinian society and politics. In the middle to late 1990s, Palestinians achieved limited self-rule, held general elections, and began to establish social and political institutions such as security services, a legal system, a Palestinian supreme court, and a house of representatives called the Palestinian Council. These accomplishments, however, were merely symbolic and short lived. Most of the institutions that were established failed to bring about Palestinian self-determination or to advance the struggle to establish an autonomous Palestinian state (Usher, 1995a; Rabbani, 1996; Guyatt, 1998).

Moreover, most of the autonomous Palestinian institutions were severely undermined, if not completely destroyed, by Israel between 2001 and 2003 with the excuse of crashing the al-Aqsa intifada (Jones and Pedahzur, 2005).

The delegitimization of Palestinian leadership has reached new highs following the landslide victory of Hamas in January 2006. Within days, Israel, the United States, the European Union, and several European countries cut off their aid to the Palestinians, claiming that the Islamist political party rejects Israel's right to exist. But a careful examination of Palestinian voting patterns suggests that Hamas's victory is not a sign of the Islamization of Palestine. Rather, it is a vote of no-confidence in the political status quo and a vote of support for the one party that continues to openly resist the Israeli occupation (Haddad, 2006; Murray, 2006).

The failure of the political diplomacy to bring about a just and lasting resolution to the conflict coupled with the deterioration of living conditions in Palestine in general and in the Gaza Strip has led to an unprecedented fragmentation of Palestinian society. This fragmentation has escalated periodically into open street-fighting between Hamas and Fatah (Mishal and Sela, 2006). The majority of Palestinians have condemned the fighting and urged the political factions to set their differences aside and adhere to a platform of national unity designed to end the occupation and advance the Palestinians' struggle for self-determination (Perlman, 2003; Baroud, 2006).

Israelis

The term *Israelis,* which has been in use only since the establishment of the state in 1948, invokes biblical references to the people of Israel and to the ancient Israelites. Yet many scholars have pointed out numerous inconsistencies in the theses that suggest that the Jews who presently reside in Israel are the descendants of the ancient Israelites (see Evron, 1995; Shahak, 1995). Most scholarly and media accounts of the conflict use the term *Israelis* because they assume a natural overlap between the state and its citizens. However, this usage is highly misleading because one-sixth of Israel's population consists of Palestinians who hold Israeli citizenship (Rekass, 1989; Rouhana, 1989; Smooha, 1989, 1992). The terms *Israeli Jews* or *Jews who live in Israel,* which we use in this chapter, more accurately describe this party to the conflict.

Israeli-Jewish society identifies itself as a Zionist society, morally, politically, and technically. The moral aspect of this identification is grounded in the presupposition that Jews can never hope to achieve equality of rights as religious or cultural minorities in Gentile societies. The political aspect of this identification has been predicated upon two correlative elements: (1) the mobilization of Jews throughout the world to immigrate to Palestine; and (2) the establishment of a Jewish state in Palestine, namely the State of Israel, and the mobilization of moral and material support from Jews and non-Jews worldwide for the continued existence of Israel as a Jewish state. Finally, Israel is a Zionist society technically in that its legal structure and the routine of its everyday life are determined in every domain by the distinction between Jews and non-Jews (Davis, 1986:176–177).

Divisions do exist, however, not only between Jews and non-Jews but also within the Israeli-Jewish population, which comprises more than 80 percent of Israel's overall population (Reich, 1985). Israeli-Jewish society is quite heterogeneous, composed of immigrants from numerous countries and reflecting a variety of ethnic and linguistic groups; religious preferences; and cultural, historical, and political backgrounds. The two main ethnic groupings are the Ashkenazi Jews, who originated mostly in Europe and North America, and the Mizrachim, whose origins can be traced mainly to North Africa and the Middle East. The term *Mizrachim* (Orientals in Hebrew) is gradually replacing other terms, such as *Sephardim,* previously used to refer to this segment of Israel's population (Shohat, 1988; Swirski, 1989). Another term that has been in use recently in reference to this group is *Arab Jews,* a term that highlights the sociocultural similarities between Jews from the Middle East and North Africa and their fellow Arabs. The Israeli establishment sought to suppress these similarities, using the Arab-Israeli conflict as an excuse (Alcalay, 1993), and the same excuse was used to downplay the disparities in power and privilege between Ashkenazi and Mizrachi Jews. These disparities have remained largely unaddressed as the Israeli establishment utilized the salience of the Israeli-Palestinian conflict to establish unity in the face of the enemy and to construct a strong sense of national identity (Sharoni, 1995a). The centrality of the conflict has also shaped the Israeli political system and the leading political parties.

At present, the Israeli political map includes twelve parties (some of which comprise several smaller parties) with representation in the Israeli parliament, the Knesset. The March 2006 elections changed the Israeli political scene dramatically. As a result, a new party, Kadima ("forward" in English), is currently leading the Israeli parliament. It is the first time that a third party is the dominant force on the Israeli political landscape.

Historically, the two principal political parties in Israel have been Labor and Likud. The Labor Party, which is predominantly Ashkenazi and secular, controlled Israeli politics between 1948 and 1977. Its original ideology has undergone significant transformations in recent years as it has attempted to reconcile the tensions between Zionism, socialism, and democratic practices (Kimmerling, 1983; Shapira, 1992). Over the years, the party's positions and policies on the Israeli-Palestinian conflict have been mixed. Officially, the party supports a "land for peace" solution, and therefore it is generally perceived to be more moderate and willing to compromise than Likud. At the same time, the Labor Party encouraged the construction of settlements in the West Bank and Gaza Strip after 1967, was tough in dealing with the intifada, and for many years opposed the establishment of an independent Palestinian state alongside Israel. More recently, however, the Labor Party and especially Shimon Peres and Yitzhak Rabin were credited with making a significant step toward peace with the signing of the Oslo Accords.

The Likud Party, which came to power for the first time in 1977, is more conservative economically and religiously than Labor and enjoys more support among Mizrachi and working-class Jews. The party has traditionally taken a more hard-line stance on the Arab-Israeli conflict in general and the

Palestinian issue in particular. Its original platform claimed Jewish sovereignty over all territories occupied by Israel in 1967, with the exception of the Sinai, which was returned to Egypt following the signing of the Camp David Accords in 1979 (Lesch and Tessler, 1989; Saunders, 1985). Likud and Labor have been alternating in power since 1984, with the Likud Party headed by Benjamin Netanyahu defeating Labor in the May 1996 elections. Although Likud initially opposed the Oslo Accords and the subsequent agreements and vowed to derail their implementation, its position was somewhat modified due to both internal and international pressure. Nevertheless, the policies of the Netanyahu government led to a major stalemate in the negotiations between Israel and the Palestinians, one of many factors that resulted in early elections in May 1999, with the new Labor leader, Ehud Barak, replacing Netanyahu as prime minister.

But Barak's tenure was short lived. He lost the 2000 elections to former Israeli prime minister Ariel Sharon, the Likud's candidate after the outbreak of the second Palestinian uprising, known as the al-Aqsa intifada. The massive propaganda about the far-reaching concessions that Barak had supposedly offered, and the Palestinians rejected, contributed a great deal to Sharon's victory (Hiro, 1999; Thomas, 1999; Reinhart, 2002). Despite Sharon's failure to deliver Israelis the security he promised in his election platform and the collapse of his coalition government in late 2002, he was reelected in January 2003 by a landslide with the Labor Party suffering the most significant loss in its history. Analysts argue that Sharon's reelection did not represent an unwillingness on the part of Israelis to reach a negotiated solution with the Palestinians, but rather, it called into question the Israeli political system, which was failing to represent the majority of Israelis (Reinhart, 2002).

The establishment of Kadima and its victory in the 2006 elections further complicates the analysis of the Israeli political landscape. Kadima was formed by Sharon after he left the right-wing Likud party in November 2005. During the public relations campaign surrounding the establishment of the new party, Sharon claimed that Kadima would grant him the freedom to carry out his policy of unilateral disengagement—removing Israeli settlements from Palestinian territory and fixing Israel's borders with a prospective Palestinian state. Nevertheless, quite a different scenario unfolded in the aftermath of the elections.

First, Sharon himself was not able to stand for elections after suffering a major stroke in December 2005 and was replaced by his deputy in the new party and the acting prime minister Ehud Olmert. Second, the original promise of Kadima to remove settlements and move toward the establishment of a Palestinian state was forgotten as Kadima formed a coalition government with the explicitly racist party, Israel Beitainu (Hebrew for "Israel is our home"). This relatively new party, which pushed past Likud to become one of Israel's major political parties, has focused its campaign on one key issue: ethnically cleansing Israel of the remainder of the indigenous Palestinian population (Barghouti, 2006; Levy, 2006; Makdisi, 2006). Accordingly, far from the promise to lead Israel back to the negotiation table, the coalition government that was established as a result of the 2006 elections represents a step in the opposite direction.

▨ The History and Dynamics of the Conflict

The conventional view among conflict resolution scholars and diplomats in the West is that dwelling on the history of conflicts in general and of the Palestinian-Israeli conflict in particular is counterproductive, mainly because the parties' interpretations of history often appear irreconcilable. At the same time, history played a central role in shaping people's collective identities, perceptions of one another, and general attitudes toward the conflict and the prospects for its resolution. According to this view, if history is ignored, it would be extremely difficult to establish the framework and conditions for a just and lasting peace. Thus the question is not whether to deal with history, but rather how to approach history so that its examination contributes to both the analysis of the conflict and the exploration of new venues for its resolution. Toward this end, we review some of the history of the conflict that Arthur Goldschmidt presents in Chapter 3, identify significant turning points in that history, and examine their contributions to the escalation or de-escalation of the conflict. We give particular attention to the differences and similarities in Palestinians' and Israelis' perceptions of these events.

Modern Zionism and the Partition of Palestine

The first turning point of the conflict involves the emergence of Zionism and the beginning of Jewish immigration to and settlement in Palestine in the 1880s. The Zionist movement emerged in the late nineteenth century in Europe in response to the rise of European nationalism and anti-Semitism. During and after the Holocaust, which increased the flow of Jewish immigrants to Palestine, the Zionist movement gained significant international recognition and support.

The term *Zionism* has no single definition. As with many contested terms, the meanings and practices associated with Zionism depend on the particular standpoint of the person or group defining it. Although there are different strands of Zionism (socialist or nonsocialist, religious or secular), for most Jews, Zionism is a movement for Jewish national self-determination designed to restore their right to live in the land of their ancestors (Herzberg, 1962). Palestinians and many others, however, view Zionism as an exclusive ideology that underlies the settler-colonial movement responsible for the occupation of Palestine and the dispossession and exploitation of its indigenous population (Said, 1980; Abdo, 1992; Zunes, 1994).

The divergent interpretations of this turning point by Palestinians and Jews lie not only in their differing views of Zionism both as an ideology and as a political project but also in their distinct perspectives regarding the origins of the conflict. According to prevalent Jewish interpretations, the conflict is centuries old, and Zionism was an attempt to ensure the return of Jews to the land of Israel, Eretz Yisrael, which God promised to Abraham and his "seed" (Sachar, 1964; Parkes, 1964; Grayzel, 1968; Tessler, 1994). According to Palestinian interpretations, the Palestinian-Israeli conflict is a modern phenomenon whose origins lie not in the Bible but rather in Zionist ideology and its implementation in Palestine through policies that are reminiscent of other settler-colonial projects around the world (Khalidi, 1971; Muslih, 1992; Kimmerling and Migdal, 1993; Lustick, 1993, Finkelstein, 1995; Greenstein, 1995).

Many conventional accounts of the conflict overlook the fact that Palestine was not "a land without people for the people without a land," as the Zionist slogan proclaimed; it had an existing indigenous population who sought independence first from the Ottoman rulers and later from the British. Thus, Jewish immigration to Palestine precipitated a clash between two national movements struggling for self-determination and territorial sovereignty. From the start, Palestinians were placed in a disadvantageous position. According to Palestinian historians, the root cause of the Palestinians' disadvantage lies in two political decisions made in Europe. The first decision was made in 1897 by the World Zionist Organization, which met in Basel, Switzerland, and resolved to establish a Jewish state in Palestine. The second decision, known as the Balfour Declaration, was made by the British in 1917, undermining the rights of the indigenous Palestinian population and promising to support the establishment of a Jewish national home in Palestine (Muslih, 1992).

Given this context, the collision between Zionism and Palestinian nationalism was almost inevitable and escalated into violent confrontations in 1920 in Jerusalem, in 1921 in Tel Aviv–Jaffa and the surrounding areas, and in 1929 in Jerusalem and Hebron. One of the most dramatic escalations of the conflict occurred during the Arab Revolt, which lasted from 1936 to 1939. This revolt was the longest-running Palestinian protest against Jewish national aspirations in Palestine prior to the establishment of the State of Israel. This mostly grassroots movement involved both violent and nonviolent dimensions such as strikes, nonpayment of taxes, and other forms of civil disobedience (Khalidi, 1971; Hirst, 1984).

The first period of the revolt ended at the request of the newly formed Arab Higher Committee for Palestine (AHC), which urged Palestinians to wait for the outcome of deliberations by the Palestine Royal Commission, known as the Peel Commission, which was set up by Britain to investigate the situation. The revolt's second stage was sparked by the Peel Commission report recommending the partition of Palestine into two states in order to accommodate the competing claims of Palestinians and Jews, which resulted in further escalation of the situation, with Zionist, Palestinian, and British forces fighting for control. Given the fierce resistance to the plan among both Palestinians and Jews, Britain was eventually forced to abandon the 1937 partition plan.

Nevertheless, partition plans continued to surface; these became particularly popular and gained international legitimacy in the aftermath of World War II and the Holocaust, which resulted in the near destruction of the Jewish people in Europe, as well as Gypsies, homosexuals, disabled persons, and others deemed "undesirable" by the Nazis. The best-known is the 1947 UN partition plan, also known as UN Resolution 181, which called for the creation of a Jewish state and an Arab state in Palestine (see Map 6.1). The plan, which indicated that the British mandate over the area was to end on May 15, 1948, "gave the new Jewish state 57 percent of Palestine, including the fertile coastal region." Palestinians viewed this proposal as fundamentally flawed and unjust since "at the time Jews represented only about 33 percent of the population and owned only 7 percent of the land." Indeed, UN estimates suggest that the division of territory spelled out in the 1947 partition plan would have given the Jewish state economic revenues three times as great as those of the Palestinian state. On November 29, 1947, the UN General Assembly voted in favor of this particular plan (Gerner, 1994:43).

The Zionist response to UN Resolution 181 was to endorse it with reservations, insisting that the "Jewish homeland" be distinctively Jewish rather than religiously and ethnically pluralistic. At the same time, Zionist leaders did not abandon the conviction that eventually all of Palestine should come under Jewish control. From the Palestinian perspective, the UN partition plan was an illegal and illegitimate attempt to divide Palestine. Moreover, Palestinians feared that the establishment of two states would result in the expulsion of Palestinians who lived in areas that fell within the designated territory of the Jewish state. But contrary to common representations of this event that tend to portray Palestinians as rejectionists unwilling to compromise, the Arab leadership in and outside Palestine did not simply reject the partition plan; it endorsed the alternative proposal of the UN Special Committee on Palestine, which called for a single, unified state in Palestine that would be democratic and secular and grant equal rights to all its citizens (see Flapan, 1987; Finkelstein, 1995).

The UN vote on partition sparked an unprecedented wave of violence, which escalated into a full-fledged war following the establishment of the State of Israel on May 14, 1948. The differences in the interpretations of

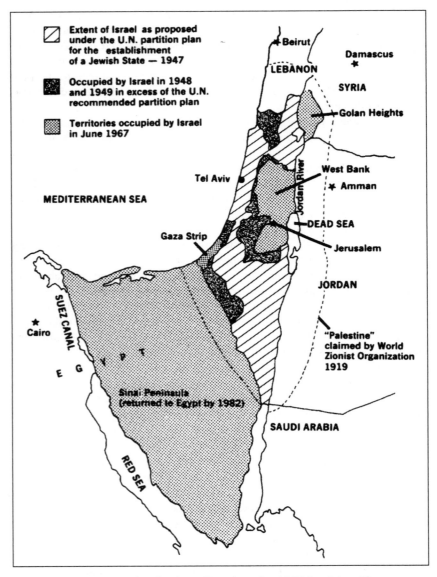

Map 6.1 Israel/Palestine, Showing the 1947 Partition Plan, 1948 Boundaries, and Borders After the 1967 War

history by Palestinians and Jews have been most evident in the ways in which they refer to this war. Jews refer to it as a war of independence, marking the fulfillment of their national aspirations with the establishment of the State of Israel. For Palestinians, however, the 1948 war (known as El-Nakbah, which means "the catastrophe") meant disaster and destruction. In the course of the war, the Palestinian community was virtually destroyed. Approximately 780,000 Palestinians became refugees as a direct result of Israel's establishment. Some Palestinians fled, others were driven out by force, and 418 Arab villages were destroyed or depopulated (Morris, 1988, 1990). The war ended with the establishment of Israel on roughly 77 percent of the total area of Palestine. The remaining 23 percent was divided between Jordan, which gained control over the West Bank (including East Jerusalem), and Egypt, which took upon itself the administration of the Gaza Strip (Muslih, 1992).

International Conflicts

In most literature on the conflict, the years since the establishment of the State of Israel are often divided into three periods: May 1948 to June 1967, June 1967 to December 1987, and December 1987 to the present. During the first period, between 1948 and 1967, Palestinians were in a state of shock and despair. The difficult circumstances and the lack of political leadership and economic resources forced them into a state of dependency on neighboring Arab states. As a result, until 1967, with the exception of the establishment of the PLO in 1964, Palestinian nationalism was for the most part muted; resistance to Israel was expressed primarily by Arab leaders residing outside Palestine. Meanwhile, on the other side of the Palestinian-Israeli divide, Israeli Jews worked to build a Western-style Jewish state in the middle of the Arab world. Consequently, the Palestinians who remained in Israel after the 1948 war were viewed as a problem for the evolving Jewish state. They were placed under military rule until 1966 and subjected to a slew of discriminatory regulations under the pretext of Israel's "national security" (Gerner, 1994:47, 57–58; Lustick, 1980; Zureik, 1979).

The June 1967 war, also referred to as the Six-Day War, is one of the most significant turning points in the history of the conflict. It dramatically changed the map of the Middle East, resulting in Israel's occupation of the West Bank and Gaza Strip, the Sinai, and the Golan Heights. Contrary to conventional Israeli interpretations, however, which have insisted that Israel occupied these territories in a war of self-defense, ample evidence illustrates that Israel initiated the war under the pretext of a "preemptive attack" (Zilka, 1992). At the conclusion of the war, Israel's conquest appeared to be just temporary. In fact, on June 19, 1967, the Israeli cabinet voted unanimously to

Deborah J. Gerner

This woman and child live in Bureij Camp, one of twenty-seven overcrowded refugee camps in the West Bank and Gaza Strip that are home to half a million displaced Palestinians.

give back the Sinai to Egypt and the Golan Heights to Syria in return for demilitarization and peace. With regard to Jordan, Israel demanded border adjustments, citing security reasons, but the status of Jerusalem was considered nonnegotiable; the city was unified and declared an indivisible part of Israel (Zilka, 1992:33). But despite UN Resolution 242, which was unanimously adopted on November 22, 1967, and called for Israeli withdrawal from the territories occupied during the war, Israel objected to a complete withdrawal and refused to withdraw from any territory before a peace treaty was signed. Syria rejected the resolution altogether, and Egypt and Jordan refused to sign a peace treaty prior to Israel's withdrawal.

Israel's victory in the Six-Day War and its conquest of the remaining 23 percent of Palestine left Egypt, Syria, and Jordan shocked and humiliated and turned Palestinians' hopes to a deep sense of despair. Those Palestinians who were not forced to flee (many for the second time) and become refugees in the surrounding Arab countries were subjected to harsh military laws imposed by Israel. In addition, large amounts of land were confiscated to build Jewish settlements in the West Bank and Gaza Strip, which Israeli officials started referring to by the biblical names of Judea and Samaria.

Jewish settlement construction in the Occupied Territories began within six months and had massive government support.

The 1973 war represents yet another significant turning point in the history of the Israeli-Palestinian conflict, marking the last war between Israel and an allied Arab force. The war began on October 6, 1973, with a coordinated attack launched by Egypt and Syria. But after a massive airlift of advanced military equipment from the United States, Israel was able to turn things around. On October 24, at the conclusion of the war, Israel recaptured most of the Sinai territory from which it had had to retreat and solidified its hold over the Golan Heights. This military victory notwithstanding, the 1973 war was politically costly for Israelis; it ended the collective sense of euphoria created in the aftermath of the 1967 war and shattered the illusion of military invincibility, clearing the way for a more realistic and critical assessment of Israeli society and politics and especially of the Arab-Israeli conflict. For Palestinians, the 1973 war marked yet another chapter in their growing disillusionment with the ability of Arab states to lead the struggle over Palestine.

As a result of the 1967 war and especially in the aftermath of the 1973 war, Palestinians sought their independent representation through the national resistance movement led by the PLO. Yasser Arafat's election as chairperson of the organization in 1969 represented an important milestone in the Palestinians' struggle for self-determination and brought international recognition of the PLO as the sole representative of the Palestinian people. By 1974, Palestinians were able to alert the international community to the plight of the Palestinian people; achieve independent representation in many international bodies, including the UN and its related organizations; and gain recognition on the world stage. Yet throughout this period, Israel refused to recognize Palestinians' existence and right of self-determination (Kimmerling and Migdal, 1993:209–239).

The civil war in Jordan in 1970, with its daily violent confrontations between Palestinians and the Jordanian regime, was a major setback in the Palestinian efforts to strengthen the national movement outside Palestine. The months of buildup escalated into eleven days of bloodshed, often referred to as Black September, which resulted in the killing of thousands of Palestinians and Jordanians, spoiled the relationship between the Palestinian leadership and the Jordanian regime, and destroyed the political and military infrastructure established by the PLO in Jordan (Tessler, 1994: 460–462). Following these events, the PLO began building its bases in Lebanon. Meanwhile, the Palestinian resistance movement in the territories was growing. Its strength and organization were reflected in the results of the first municipal elections in the West Bank in 1976. But when Likud came to power in 1977, Israel moved against these elected mayors and the newly elected municipal councils, appointing instead people who were considered more "moderate" and easy to control (Gerner, 1994:91).

Contrary to the gloomy predictions of many analysts, the unexpected victory of the right-wing Likud Party in the 1977 elections resulted in a temporary de-escalation of the Arab-Israeli conflict. A few months after Likud came to power, Egyptian president Anwar Sadat surprised the Israeli government and public, as well as the Arab world and the international community, when he became the first Arab head of state to visit Jerusalem. Another event that both reflected and contributed to the de-escalation of the conflict was the emergence of a distinct peace movement in Israel: Peace Now. The group, founded in 1978 by reserve officers and soldiers, argued that the Israeli government was not doing enough to bring about peace with Egypt (Bar-On, 1985; Wolfsfeld, 1988). Although Peace Now could not take much credit for this development, the Israeli and Egyptian governments began direct negotiations that year, and in 1979 Israel signed a formal peace treaty with Egypt, often referred to as the Camp David Accords.

The Camp David Accords have been viewed as significant in the history of the Palestinian-Israeli conflict because of the problematic manner in which they addressed the Palestinian dimension of the Arab-Israeli conflict and because they enabled the United States to establish itself as a major "peace broker" in the region and thus increase its sphere of power and influence. The accords contained two documents; the one titled "A Framework for Peace in the Middle East" attempted to address the Palestinian problem. With its vague formulation regarding the nature of Palestinian autonomy and its failure to recognize the PLO as the official representative of the Palestinian people and thus as a party to the negotiations, the document provoked strong negative reactions from the Palestinians (Lesch and Tessler, 1989).

It soon became clear that the government of Menachem Begin had no intention of allowing the Camp David Accords to lead to an Israeli withdrawal from the West Bank and Gaza Strip. To the contrary, in the 1980s Israel pursued its plan to lay the foundation for the permanent retention of the Occupied Territories. The government expanded settlement construction, applied Israeli laws to Jews residing in these areas, and took additional steps in such areas as transportation, communication, and economic activity to link the West Bank and Gaza more closely to Israel and to blur the 1967 border, often referred to as "the Green Line" (Tessler, 1994:519–521). For Palestinians, this period has been characterized by harsh economic conditions and growing dependency on Israel, a shortage of adequate housing, a crisis in education and deteriorating school facilities, and many other problems that have become more acute as a result of the Israeli occupation (Nakhleh, 1980; Tamari, 1980).

Its reservations regarding the Camp David Accords notwithstanding, during this period the PLO began to signal its readiness for a political settlement. Israel refused to acknowledge, let alone act upon, the softening in the PLO's public statements and political agenda; instead, it took actions to remove the remaining elected Palestinian leaders in the West Bank and Gaza

Strip and to set up instead the Village Leagues, whose Arab members were appointed by Israel and thus lacked credibility among Palestinians. These actions prompted fierce resistance by Palestinians, resulting in serious clashes between Palestinians and Israeli soldiers in March, April, and May 1982. Another significant event during this period was the emergence of the popular committees, including women's groups and labor unions, across the West Bank and Gaza Strip. These local committees, most of which were affiliated with the various factions of the PLO, were established to address the service needs of the Palestinian community.

The Israeli invasion of Lebanon in 1982 marked a serious escalation of the Israeli-Palestinian conflict. The Israeli government's decision to inflict damage on the PLO's political and military bases in Lebanon stemmed directly from the insistence of most members of the Israeli government at the time that the PLO was the source of unrest and troubles in the West Bank and Gaza Strip. Nevertheless, the Israeli government's previous attempt, in 1978, to destroy the PLO's headquarters and bases in Lebanon not only failed but triggered the escalation of Israeli-Palestinian hostilities across the Israeli-Lebanese border and heightened tensions between Israel and the Arab states (Gerner, 1994:124–128; Tessler, 1994:568–599). In June 1982, Israeli troops invaded Lebanon for the second time, instigating what became the most controversial war in Israel's history.

The officially stated Israeli goals were to move Palestinian fighters out of range of northern Galilee and to eliminate the PLO's political and military infrastructure in Lebanon. Yet Israeli troops proceeded into Lebanon beyond the twenty-five miles initially announced, encircling and bombing Beirut in an effort to force the evacuation of Arafat and the PLO (Schiff and Ya'ari, 1984). Israel agreed to stop the bombing only after the completion of the PLO's evacuation in late August.

The cease-fire did not last long. In mid-September 1982, following the assassination of Beshir Gemayel, the newly elected Lebanese president, Israeli troops returned to Beirut, occupying the entire city and sealing off the Sabra and Shatilla refugee camps, home to many Palestinians and poor Lebanese. These actions precipitated one of the most tragic events in the history of the conflict: the Sabra and Shatilla massacre. The massacre was carried out by Lebanese Maronite Christians, who were known for their hatred of Palestinians, with Israeli knowledge and according to some accounts even tacit approval. Forty hours later, when the camps were finally unsealed, the body count reached 700–800 people, according to Israeli estimates, the majority of whom were civilians, including many women and children. Contending accounts indicated that the number of people murdered was perhaps as high as 1,500 or 2,000 (Schiff and Ya'ari, 1984; Tessler, 1994:590–599).

The Israeli invasion of Lebanon reinvigorated existing Israeli peace groups such as Peace Now and the Committee for Solidarity with Bir Zeit University (which decided to rename itself the Committee Against the War in Lebanon). In addition, the invasion triggered the emergence of new protest groups such as Parents Against Silence, Women Against the Invasion of Lebanon, and Yesh Gvul (literally, "There is a limit") (Kaminer, 1996; Sharoni, 1995a:106–109). Questioning the legitimacy and morality of the war, Yesh Gvul called upon Israeli soldiers to refuse to serve in Lebanon. Not only did hundreds of soldiers sign petitions declaring that they were prepared to take this course of action, but also a significant number of soldiers were sent to jail for their "refusal to carry out an order" (Kaminer, 1996:36–38).

For the first time in Israel's history, Israeli citizens not only questioned their government's policies but also took to the streets to voice their discontent. From the beginning of the invasion, a flurry of protest activities included vigils and demonstrations in the streets and on university campuses, antiwar petitions, and letters to the editors. The first national demonstration against the war on June 26, 1982, drew approximately 20,000 Israelis, who demanded the immediate withdrawal of their country's army from Lebanon. A few months later, in response to the Sabra and Shatilla massacre, Israel witnessed its largest demonstration ever; according to Peace Now and media reports, about 400,000 people participated. Political protest intensified following the publication of the report by the Kahan Commission, a special inquiry commission set up to investigate Israeli involvement in the Sabra and Shatilla massacre (Kaminer, 1996:34–36). The commission's report and the public debates it triggered, coupled with the widespread antiwar demonstrations (which lasted until the partial Israeli withdrawal from Lebanon in 1985), signaled a gradual erosion of the Israeli consensus regarding issues of peace and security.

For Palestinians, the defeat of the PLO in Lebanon resulted in internal fragmentation and disputes among the different PLO factions as well as among the Arab countries that supported them. At the same time, the internal Palestinian leadership had been growing and organizing against the Israeli occupation. In fact, the destruction of the PLO infrastructure in Lebanon contributed to the emergence of a more organized grassroots, autonomous resistance movement in the West Bank and Gaza. This resistance movement gained prominence on the world's stage with the outbreak of the intifada in December 1987.

The 1987 Palestinian Uprising

The popular uprising was precipitated on December 8, 1987, "when an Israeli army tank transporter collided with a line of cars filled with Palestinian workers waiting at the military checkpoint at the north end of the Gaza Strip" (Gerner, 1994:97). The accident left four Palestinians dead and seven seriously injured, and rumors began to spread that the collision was not an accident but rather a deliberate act carried out by Israel in retaliation for the killing of an Israeli salesperson in Gaza a few days earlier. The funerals of the dead turned into a massive demonstration; Palestinians continued to protest the following day, and the demonstrations and resistance rapidly spread from the Gaza Strip to East Jerusalem and the rest of the West Bank. Although the accident is often viewed as the catalyst for the uprising, analysts agree that the conditions under which Palestinians lived resembled a pressure cooker, and thus an explosion was imminent.

The literal meaning of the Arabic word *intifada* is "shaking off." For Palestinians, this word has symbolized not only their determination to shake off the Israeli occupation but also their disillusionment with external forces—the UN, the United States, and the Arab states and Arab League—and their resolve to take matters into their own hands. Palestinian mobilization was unprecedented not only in scope and magnitude but in organization as well. People who took part in the mostly nonviolent actions that characterized the intifada—from street demonstrations, tax resistance, and commercial strikes to the establishment of agricultural cooperatives and alternative education centers—were extremely disciplined and came from various socioeconomic backgrounds, different political affiliations, and all walks of life. Within weeks, the focus of the conflict and the world's attention turned to scores of Palestinians in the West Bank and Gaza Strip, led by an indigenous leadership (the Unified National Leadership of the Uprising) who demanded the withdrawal of the Israeli military from their occupied land and a just and lasting solution to the conflict (Nassar and Heacock, 1991; Gerner, 1990; Brynen, 1991; Hunter, 1991). The grassroot led, popular uprising also caught by surprise the PLO leadership, which was based mostly in Tunisia (Aburish, 1998).

On the other side of the Palestinian-Israeli divide, the Israeli government, which the intifada had caught by surprise, was trying with great difficulty to formulate a response to the uprising and at the same time to launch a public relations campaign designed to redeem Israel's image worldwide. Indeed, the intifada marked a significant shift in power relations between Israel and the Palestinians. Although in strategic terms the advantage still lay with the Israeli side, Palestinians had the moral high ground. For the first time in the history of the conflict, the David versus Goliath analogy was used in scholarly analyses and media reports, describing Israel as Goliath, the mighty aggressor, and the Palestinians as David, the underdog who is determined to win against all odds because his cause is just (Lockman and Beinin, 1989; Schiff, 1990; Perez, 1990).

But Palestinians were well aware that in order to fulfill their aspirations for self-determination, they needed to establish their own social, political, and economic infrastructure, a project prevented by the Israeli occupation. Toward this end, Palestinians established five principal popular committees to deal with agriculture, education, food storage, health care, and security. These committees, which operated both nationally and locally, soon became the most practical mechanism for political mobilization and for the preservation of the community. For many Palestinians, the committees represented the infrastructure of the future Palestinian state, or at least transient democratic institutions designed to govern the community during the intifada. Palestinian women were actively involved in the establishment and operation of all the popular committees, which resembled the women's committees that had been active in the West Bank and Gaza Strip for more than a decade (Jad, 1990; Hiltermann, 1991; Sharoni, 1995a:72–73).

During the first two years of the intifada, the general atmosphere within the Palestinian community was extremely positive. The sense of purpose and self-reliance, coupled with the ability to forge unity within and mobilize international support for the Palestinian cause, empowered Palestinians and filled many with pride and hope that a diplomatic solution was in sight. Indeed, analysts agree that the intifada enabled Palestinians to renounce the armed struggle, recognize Israel's right to exist, and resolve to establish a Palestinian state in the West Bank and Gaza Strip alongside Israel (Tessler, 1994:717–725). This dramatic transformation became evident in November 1988, when Yasser Arafat formally and publicly endorsed the two-state solution and proclaimed the independent state of Palestine in the West Bank and Gaza Strip.

For the most part, the Israeli government ignored the significance of the 1988 declaration, and efforts to achieve a political solution foundered. Instead, the Israeli government and military continued to respond to the uprising with repression and intransigence. As happened during the 1982 invasion of Lebanon, the government's actions were met with growing public criticism and protest. Although the main currents in the Israeli peace camp had already acknowledged the destructive effects of the occupation on Israeli society long before the intifada began, the uprising was a watershed for political mobilization on the Israeli left. Women and groups who were previously involved in solidarity work with Palestinians led the struggle, which centered around one or more of the following messages: end the occupation, negotiate peace with the PLO, and create two states for two peoples (Kaminer, 1996:41–48). Although the peace movement was fairly successful in mobilizing public opinion, its efforts fell short of changing the Israeli government's policies. By late 1990 the Palestinian-Israeli conflict had settled into a grim war of attrition as the world's attention was diverted to the crisis in the Gulf (Hajjar and Beinin, 1990; Gerner, 1991).

Palestinians and Israeli Jews in the 1990s

The Gulf crisis, which began on August 2, 1990, with the Iraqi invasion of Kuwait and escalated into a war in January 1991, represents another turning point in the history of the conflict (Bennis and Moushabeck, 1991; Sifry and Cerf, 1991; Hiro, 1992). Contrary to the common view among scholars and media analysts that Palestinians made a poor political choice by siding with Saddam Hussein, the Palestinian position was far more complex (Andoni, 1991). Throughout the crisis, the official Palestinian position underscored two principles: denunciation of the Iraqi occupation and opposition to a military solution to resolve the crisis (Ashrawi, 1991:191). But like many other societies, Palestinian society is not monolithic; there were Palestinians who expressed sympathy with Saddam Hussein for standing up to the Gulf states, the United States, and the West more generally and especially to Israel. Nevertheless, regardless of their view on the Gulf crisis, Palestinians criticized the explicit double standard of the international community that utilized the UN and appeals to international law to demand Iraq's immediate withdrawal from Kuwait but failed to apply the same measures to the Israeli occupation of the West Bank and Gaza Strip (Ashrawi, 1991:192–195).

The Gulf crisis and war contributed to the escalation of tension between Israeli Jews and Palestinians. When the US-led air attacks on Iraq began, Israel imposed a twenty-four-hour curfew on Palestinians in the West Bank and Gaza Strip, which lasted a full month and a half. Iraq responded to the air attack with largely ineffective but frightening Scud missile attacks on Saudi Arabia and Israel. Although only two Israelis died directly as a result of those attacks, the country was in a state of panic, and thousands of Israelis fled from the urban areas to the countryside to avoid a possible missile attack. Israelis' sense of helplessness was compounded by the fact that they were asked not to retaliate against Iraq because the United States feared that an Israeli attack might break the already fragile coalition (Schiff, 1990). At the same time, on the other side of the Palestinian-Israeli divide, 1.5 million Palestinians were under total curfew, many on the verge of starvation, with no warning sirens against Scuds and no gas masks to protect them against the possibility of an airborne chemical attack (Strum, 1992:59–78; Sharoni, 1995a:82–83).

In addition to its effects on Israel and on Palestinian-Israeli relations, the Gulf War had grave implications for Palestinians both in the West Bank and Gaza Strip and in the Gulf. The long curfew caused great economic hardship, which intensified when Palestinians who had worked in Israel before the war discovered that their employers had replaced them with recent Jewish immigrants. Palestinians in the Occupied Territories were also affected by the fate of relatives who had been working and living in the Gulf. Close to 400,000 Palestinians living in Kuwait lost their livelihoods and were forced once again to flee and look for refuge elsewhere. Since most of these people had been supporting family members in the West Bank and Gaza Strip, their unexpected displacement translated into a direct loss of income for many families. Moreover, external contributions from the Gulf states to the PLO and to Palestinian institutions such as hospitals, schools and universities, and social welfare organizations stopped almost instantly (Andoni, 1991).

In the aftermath of the Gulf War, the Arab-Israeli conflict was back on the agenda of US Middle East policy. In October 1991, after months of intense and systematic shuttle diplomacy efforts carried out by US secretary of state James Baker, an international peace conference was convened in Madrid, Spain, under joint sponsorship of the United States and the Soviet Union (Gerner, 1992). The conference's participants included Egyptian, Syrian, Lebanese, and Israeli delegations, and a joint Jordanian-Palestinian delegation because the Israeli government refused to accept an independent Palestinian delegation led by the PLO. These peace talks continued throughout 1992 and the first half of 1993 in Washington, D.C., and elsewhere on two parallel tracks: bilateral and multilateral. Despite the fact that no agreements were reached during that period and that by mid-1993 negotiations on the Palestinian-Israeli track had reached a total stalemate, some analysts contend that the very fact that Palestinian and Israeli-Jewish officials were engaged in face-to-face negotiations was a major step forward in Palestinian-Israeli relations (Tessler, 1994:748–750).

The victory of the Labor Party in the 1992 Israeli elections triggered for many hopes for progress in the peace process. Another encouraging sign in this direction was the new government's introduction of a bill removing the ban on unauthorized meetings with members of the PLO. These developments notwithstanding, the situation in the West Bank and Gaza Strip continued to be tense, escalating into occasional violent clashes. Then in late August 1993 the world learned that secret negotiations between Israeli government officials and official representatives of the PLO had been taking place in Norway for many months. The announcement that the two parties had signed a joint Declaration of Principles (also known as the Oslo Accords) was both surprising and encouraging. Soon thereafter the world witnessed PLO president Yasser Arafat and Israeli prime minister Yitzhak Rabin shaking hands after signing the Declaration of Principles at the White House in Washington, D.C.

On July 1, 1994, after twenty-seven years in exile, Arafat set foot on Palestinian soil, greeted by hundreds of thousands of Palestinians. Soon thereafter he formed the Palestinian National Authority, and the first democratic Palestinian elections were held in January 1996. Initially, the Oslo Accords enjoyed public support on both sides of the Palestinian-Israeli divide. Ordinary people, fed up with the cycle of violence that characterized the conflict, were eager to reap the benefits of peace promised to them by their leaders. But as negotiations dragged on and living conditions failed to improve, support for the agreement, and the peace process in general, declined. Moreover, the stalemate in the process and the failure of the leadership on both sides to keep the public informed about the dynamics and

Palestinian president
Yasser Arafat served as leader
of the Palestine Liberation
Organization from 1969
until his death in 2004.

Palestinian National Authority, Central Photographic

points of contention, coupled with the lack of improvement in Palestinians' living conditions, precipitated a new wave of violence.

The atmosphere of crisis strengthened the opposition to the Oslo Accords and exposed internal divisions and conflicts within both Palestinian and Israeli societies. These divisions, which became clearer following the signing of the Oslo Accords, involve questions of identity and community and contending views not only about the boundaries between Israel and Palestine and the relationship between them but also about the social and political character of each society. The sharp political divisions within Israeli society became evident in November 1995 following the assassination of Yitzhak Rabin by a fellow Jew who opposed Rabin's notion of peace.

But contrary to common perceptions, the Oslo Accords were not a peace treaty. Rather, they constituted an agenda for negotiations covering a five-year "interim period," which was expected to lead to a permanent settlement based on UN Security Council Resolutions 242 and 338. The accords called for a transitional period during which Israel would gradually withdraw its troops from major Palestinian centers in the Occupied Territories, beginning with Gaza and Jericho (Aruri, 1995; Usher, 1995a). In May 1994, nearly five months behind schedule, following the signing of the Cairo agreement that was designed to ratify the Declaration of Principles, the Israeli military began its redeployment as the Palestinian police began to move into the newly autonomous areas.

At the end of the 1990s, the Palestinians had full autonomy in 27 percent of the Occupied Territories (Map 6.2, Area A; 6.6 percent of the territory of historical Palestine). In the West Bank, this translated into 3 percent of the total surface area, whereas in Gaza the PNA controlled 60 percent of the territory. In the West Bank villages (Area B), however, the PNA had only civil and police powers; Israel remained responsible for "internal security," the meaning of which was open to interpretation. Furthermore, because the towns and villages are mostly noncontiguous and Israel remained in command of the road network connecting them, all movement of goods and persons into and out of these enclaves as well as between them could be interdicted at will (Rabbani, 1996:4).

Further complicating the already delayed implementation of the Oslo Accords was the unexpected victory of the Likud Party, led by Benjamin Netanyahu, in Israel's May 1996 elections. Netanyahu argued, and many analysts agreed, that his policies of settlement expansion and the "judaization" of East Jerusalem merely followed those set by earlier Labor governments. Nevertheless, the blunt and uncompromising manner in which Netanyahu carried out these policies resulted in a serious escalation of Palestinian-Israeli conflicts and another major setback in, if not total collapse of, the peace process. The main disputes have revolved around two central issues: Jewish settlements and Jerusalem. Both of these issues, along with the questions of Palestinian refugees and final borders, were not addressed in the Oslo Accords but rather left to be discussed during final status negotiations, which were originally set to begin in September 1998 but had not started when the five-year Oslo transition period ended in May 1999.

The Al-Aqsa Intifada

The second Palestinian uprising started on September 28, 2000, following a provocative visit by Likud leader Ariel Sharon, accompanied by hundreds of soldiers, to the Haram al-Sharif (Dome of the Rock) in Jerusalem, one of the holiest Muslim sites. Unlike the first intifada, which was by and large an unarmed popular revolt, Palestinian armed men led the al-Aqsa intifada right from the start. The Israeli military tried to suppress the movement with massive force. More than 7,000 Palestinians were reported injured in the first five weeks of the uprising, with many suffering injuries in the head and upper body (Reinhart, 2002). In addition to further restricting the free movement of Palestinians between the West Bank and the Gaza Strip and within towns and villages in the West Bank, the Israeli military gradually but systematically invaded areas that had been handed over to the Palestinian Authority (PA) as stipulated in the Oslo Accords. Moreover, Sharon started a political assassination campaign, targeting key leaders and activists of all Palestinian factions.

Palestinian militants responded with intensified shootings directed at Israeli settlements, especially around Jerusalem, and a growing number of

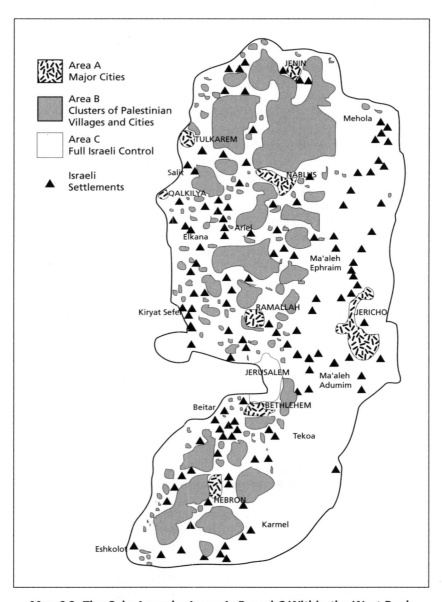

Map 6.2 The Oslo Accords: Areas A, B, and C Within the West Bank

suicide bombings targeted Israeli cities and towns. Israeli forces and policy-makers utilized these attacks as a pretext to launch massive retaliation operations into densely populated Palestinian areas in the West Bank and Gaza. The uneven nature of this violent confrontation is reflected in an ever-increasing death toll; as of September 2003, at least 2,468 Palestinians and 870 Israelis had been killed in this second intifada, a ratio of three Palestinians for each Israeli (Palestine Red Crescent Society, 2003; Israeli Foreign Ministry, 2003).

The terrorist attacks against the United States on September 11, 2001, had grave implications for the already deteriorating situation in the West Bank and Gaza Strip. Despite the fact that Palestinian leadership has continuously and unequivocally denounced the attacks and offered to help the United States in its efforts against terrorism, the coordination and cooperation between the US and Israeli governments have strengthened. Backed by the US administration, Sharon declared that Arafat was irrelevant and that there would be no negotiation until he was removed or replaced by another leader. To materialize this objective, the Israeli army twice besieged Arafat's compound and destroyed it, leaving him with a single building and isolated from the international community.

Various leaders around the world criticized Israel's systematic humiliation of Arafat. Nevertheless, by June 2002, Arafat and the Palestinian leadership more generally were isolated and in serious crisis. The PA had lost all its security forces and its ability not only to control but also to move from town to town. In addition, the economic situation reached an all-time low with unprecedented unemployment rates and the utter collapse of all economic development plans (Taraki, 2006). This crisis has contributed to the rising influence and support for Hamas and Islamic Jihad ideology in the Palestinian streets as well as for secular militant groups (Mansour, 2002; Abu-Nimer, 2003).

One Land, Two Peoples: Central Issues and Points of Contention

As the previous section illustrates, the dynamics of the conflict, the range of solutions, the role of outside actors, and the political positions of both Palestinians and Jews have dramatically changed throughout the course of the conflict. At the same time, the central issues underlying the conflict have not been dramatically transformed. One such set of issues involves the competing claims of two national movements for the same piece of land.

The Israeli-Palestinian conflict has served as both the catalyst and the touchstone for the consolidation of particular notions of national "imagined community" for Palestinians and for Israeli Jews. For Palestinians, the imagined community came to be seen as a future sovereign Palestinian state. Apart from differences concerning the territorial boundaries and the political and social character of their future state, there is a broad consensus among Palestinians that the principles of national self-determination and territorial sovereignty are inseparable and crucial to the survival of the Palestinian people. A consensus around the same principles has served as the basis for the Israeli-Jewish imagined community. Although Jews realized their dream and established a Jewish state, this has come at the expense of Palestinians, whose desire to fuse national self-determination with territorial sovereignty remains unfulfilled. This turn of events has in many ways formed the basis for the present conflict.

The principles of national self-determination and territorial sovereignty underlie the early conflicts between Zionist settlers and the indigenous Palestinian population. The dynamics and intensity of the Israeli-Palestinian conflict and its significant military component over the years have contributed to the escalation of the conflict and reinforced sharp distinctions between "us" and "them." The establishment of the State of Israel further exposed the differences between Palestinian and Israeli nationalisms: first, the difference between institutionalized state nationalism and the nationalism of a liberation movement, and second, the disparities in power relations between an occupying state and a population struggling to rid itself of that state's rule.

The emerging Jewish state has placed a special emphasis on its national security. For Palestinians, however, national liberation has emerged as the most important focus of their collective identity, especially following the Israeli occupation of the West Bank and Gaza Strip in 1967 and the emergence of the PLO as a vehicle of national aspirations. Within Israeli-Jewish society, the constant invocation of Israel's security concerns has helped reinforce an overt and covert militarization of people's lives. But for Palestinians, the centrality of the conflict has manifested itself in the privileging of national liberation not only as the primary ideology of struggle against Israeli occupation but also as the principal discourse that shapes certain ideas and ways of thinking about Palestinian identity and community.

National security and national liberation doctrines are similar in that they view the potency and unity of the nation as superior to issues raised by private citizens and various social groups within that nation. As a result of the primary emphases on national security and national liberation, different social and economic problems within both communities have been put on the back burners until the Israeli-Palestinian conflict is resolved. Nevertheless, the differences between Israeli-Jewish and Palestinian nationalisms, which are often overlooked, are far greater than the similarities. They involve fundamental differences in the history and social context of the two national movements and, most particularly, striking disparities of power and privilege between the two communities.

Israeli troops confront Palestinian demonstrators in the
highly contested West Bank city of Hebron/Khalil. The Palestinians
were protesting their lack of access to the Mosque of Ibrahim,
known to Jews as the Cave of Machpelah, where the prophet
Abraham, Sarah, and their children are believed to be buried.

In order to formulate a solution to this long-standing conflict that
would be acceptable to both Palestinians and Jews, one should first identify
the central issues for each party. During this process, it is important to pay
attention to the changes that occurred in the parties' framing of issues over
the years as well as to similarities and differences in the parties' perceptions
of central issues. Following is a preliminary list of some of the issues that
analysts view as central to a just and lasting resolution of the conflict:

- Fixed, agreed-upon borders between Israel and its neighbors
- The assurance of mutual security for all states and peoples in the
  region
- The status of Jerusalem
- Jewish settlements in the West Bank and Gaza Strip
- Compensation for Palestinians who were forced to leave their homes
  and property as a direct result of the Israeli-Palestinian conflict
- The political, civil, and national status of Palestinians who live in Is-
  rael and hold Israeli citizenship
- The economic viability of Israel, Palestine, and the other states in the
  region and the economic relations among them

- The allocation of resources such as water among the states of the region
- The role of the international community in peacekeeping, peacemaking, and peacebuilding

These points are not listed in any particular order. In fact, if Palestinians and Israeli Jews were asked to prioritize them, they would most likely come up with very different lists. Moreover, many of these issues are interrelated, and some have been addressed at least partially within the framework of the Oslo Accords. Other issues—in particular, settlements, final borders, the fate of Palestinian refugees, and the status of Jerusalem—have been identified as topics to be discussed during final status negotiations.

On these four specific issues, it is interesting to note the difference between the official Israeli and Palestinian positions. For Palestinians, these are the main issues presently underlying the Israeli-Palestinian conflict. Concerned (for good reason) that the process would break down before these issues could be discussed, Palestinians wanted to place these issues on the agenda from the start. Israel, however, preferred to defer the discussion of these four issues primarily because the resolution of any one of them would have been impossible without an Israeli concession. Although the decision to delay the discussion of these four critical issues was presented to the parties as a compromise, a careful study of the Israeli position reveals that Israel, the more powerful party in the negotiations, was able to impose its will on the Palestinians with the help of a third party who wanted to keep the peace process on track.

These same issues and power dynamics continued to haunt the Palestinian-Israeli negotiators in their last round of direct negotiation in Camp David II. With the intensive and direct intervention of President Bill Clinton, who was in his last few months in office and under pressure to deliver a major political gain to seal his presidency and long involvement in the Israeli-Palestinian peace process, Barak offered the PA control over 95 percent of Palestinians in the West Bank and Gaza Strip. Palestinians rejected the offer, arguing that the proposed settlement would prevent the creation of a viable Palestinian state due to the lack of territorial contiguity and the fact that the West Bank was to be divided into three main sections by Israeli highways designed to connect Jewish settlements. For its part, Israel did not fully accept the terms put forth in the Clinton plan, although Arafat's reservations and rejection of Barak's offer overshadowed Israel's own numerous objections.

Another bone of contention involved the question of Palestinian refugees. According to Palestinian negotiators, the number of 1948 refugees who would be allowed to return was too low; Palestinian negotiators asked for half a million, while the Israeli negotiators offered 25,000. Moreover,

Barak's proposal did not grant sovereignty on the Haram al-Sharif area. Regardless of the details of the Camp David offer, as of 2008 the same issues that had been postponed by the Oslo Accords in 1993 remained unresolved. Such an outcome is not surprising given that by the time Arafat and Barak arrived at Camp David, the level of trust among Palestinian and Israeli leaders and their faith in reaching an agreement were far lower than the euphoria of the historical breakthrough in Oslo in 1993 (Barak and Arafat did not meet face-to-face during any of the Camp David sessions).

Regardless of when the next phase of negotiation occurs, these two populations will not likely reach any sustainable and just resolution without addressing the root causes of the conflict. Among the most critical issues that must be addressed are the physical and psychological insecurity of Palestinians and Israelis, the indiscriminate killing of Israeli and Palestinian civilians, the lack of viable Palestinian statehood, the right of return for refugees, the economic deterioration (60–70 percent unemployment rate is estimated in Gaza during the second intifada), the massive collective punishment through curfews and closures, and the continued expansion of settlements.

Another point to keep in mind in examining changes that occurred in the parties' positions over time involves the question of political representation. More specifically, changes occurred in Israel's willingness to finally accept the PLO as the legitimate representative of the Palestinian people. The negotiations that led to the signing of the Camp David Accords in 1978 did not treat the Palestinians as an autonomous party, nor did they acknowledge the PLO as their sole representative. At the time, many elected officials in Israel publicly denied the existence of a Palestinian people. This situation changed dramatically with the outbreak of the 1987 intifada. Yet until summer 1993, the Israeli government refused to negotiate with the PLO. This policy was particularly evident in the period preceding the Madrid conference in 1992, when the Israeli government vetoed certain Palestinian delegates because of their suspected affiliation with the PLO. Moreover, the Israelis refused to accept an independent Palestinian delegation and insisted on a joint Jordanian-Palestinian delegation instead. According to many analysts, the Oslo Accords were signed because Israeli officials who took part in the secret meetings with PLO officials realized that if Israel were serious about peace, it would have to negotiate directly with the PLO.

Ironically, fifteen years after Oslo, Israelis and Palestinians remain embroiled in a debate over who should participate in the negotiation process. In the early stages of the second intifada, the Israeli government (backed by the United States) declared that it would not negotiate with the Palestinian leadership as long as Arafat was heading the PA. As a result, the Palestinians came under enormous international pressure to make amendments to their political system and introduce the position of a prime minister. The Palestinian leadership maintained that Sharon was not a serious partner for negotiation and had no political offer or agenda for resolution except the declaration that he would accept a Palestinian state on 42 percent of the territories. Meanwhile, his policy on the ground was contrary to any intention to reach a peaceful resolution. Nevertheless, several Palestinian leaders, such as Mahmoud Abbas (Abu Mazin) and Ahmad Qura'i (Abu Ala), met with Sharon on various occasions during 2003. At the same time, Palestinian opposition groups and nongovernmental organizations (NGOs) continued to call for political and economic reforms and refused to accept Arafat's removal, Sharon's condition for negotiation.

The "Road Map" initiative was developed by the Quartet—the United States, the European Union, Russia, and the UN—to promote a resumption of negotiations, the implementation of a cease-fire, and reformation of the Palestinian political system (including the removal of Arafat from direct day-to-day governance) in a way that would be politically palatable to both parties. Under European and US influence, Arafat appointed Mahmoud Abbas, one of the architects of Oslo, to a newly created prime minister post in early 2003. After less than a year, Abbas resigned, indicating that the unclear division of authority made his position untenable. This pressure has intensified significantly following the victory of Hamas in the 2006 elections.

In spite of completing these political revisions, the Palestinians continue to live under full Israeli reoccupation of the territories and without functioning authority. Israeli forces have now reoccupied the majority of the areas that they handed to the PA under the various terms of the Oslo Accords, including large parts of the Gaza Strip. The social welfare, health, education, and other services meeting the basic needs of large segments of Palestinian society are in a state of crisis. This crisis, which fuels resistance, must be addressed in order to de-escalate the present conflict (Taraki, 2006).

Finally, once the parties agree on a preliminary agenda and on who will be involved in the negotiations, they must address a set of very important procedural issues: when, where, and for how long negotiations will take place, whether the process requires a third party to mediate issues, and, if so, who that party should be. Before the parties meet at the negotiation tables, delegates must study the issues, prepare position papers, and review past attempts to resolve the conflict. A careful analysis of past and present conflict-resolution attempts, their successes (or failures), and the ways in which they were perceived in both communities may inspire new thinking and creative ideas for the resolution of the conflict.

■ The Rocky Road to Peace: Past and Present Attempts to Resolve the Conflict

Since the turn of the twenty-first century, numerous attempts at resolution have been carried out separately and jointly by Palestinians, Jews, and various members of the international community. Following is a partial list of some of the major scenarios that have been proposed by various actors over the years:

- Two states for two people: a Palestinian state alongside Israel, in the West Bank and Gaza Strip
- Greater Israel: a Jewish state that would annex the West Bank and Gaza Strip and "transfer" the Palestinian population to Jordan and other Arab countries
- Greater Palestine: a Palestinian state on all the territory of historical Palestine, with no Israeli Jews except those whose families lived in Palestine before 1948
- Greater Israel: a Jewish state in all the territory of historical Palestine with Palestinians as citizens
- Greater Palestine: a Palestinian state in all the territory of historical Palestine with Israeli Jews as citizens
- A partial autonomy, more or less according to the terms described in the Oslo Accords, with Palestine controlling the civic affairs and internal security in its cities and villages, and Israel administering external security and controlling the land and natural resources
- Return to the pre-Oslo situation, with Israel continuing to control the territories
- A binational state on the land of Palestine/Israel

It is important to distinguish between those attempts that have addressed primarily the needs and aspirations of one party to the conflict (Jews or Palestinians) and those that have sought to take into account the needs, aspirations, and preferred solutions of both Palestinians and Jews. According to some analysts, to come to terms with the contending resolution perspectives on the Israeli-Palestinian conflict, it may be useful to place them along a continuum bounded by the terms *exclusivist* on one end and *accommodationist* on the other (Vitalis, 1992:290). This continuum clearly reflects the dominant view, according to which the conflict stems from competing claims of two peoples to the exclusive right of national self-determination and sovereignty rights on the same piece of land. According to this view, the single-state solutions—whether Jewish or Palestinian—are exclusivist in nature since they undermine the other party's vision and claims.

Scholars writing about resolution of the conflict tend to view the transition from exclusivist scenarios to accommodationist ones as a combination of historical progression and rational choice. Thus the Zionist state-building project in Palestine, which led to the establishment of the Jewish state in 1948 by completely undermining the existence of the indigenous Arab population, is often compared with the attempts in the 1950s and 1960s of Palestinians supported by Arab leaders to liberate their homeland.

According to this interpretation, with time and the impact of particular political developments, as both Israeli Jews and Palestinians concluded that their vision of an exclusive homeland was not likely to lead to peace, they gradually began to explore accommodationist scenarios. These scenarios reflected some willingness to compromise and acknowledge, although with many reservations, the other party's national aspirations and right to the land. This acknowledgment, which is particularly evident in such proposals as the two-state solution and the binational state, is praised in the literature as a "win-win solution" and presented as the best scenario for a peaceful resolution of the conflict (Kelman, 1982; Vitalis, 1992). However, such scenarios overlook the grave power differentials between Palestinians and the State of Israel, which are crucial to the understanding of the transition from exclusivist to accommodationist visions within both communities.

Another common continuum of analysis is that between violent and nonviolent attempts to resolve the conflict. Like the exclusivist-accommodationist categorization, this continuum has been inspired by a combination of rational choice theories with some historical analysis. Accordingly, over time, most Palestinians and Israeli Jews came to the conclusion that the conflict could not be resolved through military might and that diplomacy might be a better venue. Still, most media accounts of the conflict tend to present Palestinians as more prone to violence and more reluctant to accept diplomatic solutions. This tendency also manifests itself in differential treatment of violence carried out by Palestinians, which is usually referred to as "terrorist attacks," whereas violence carried out by the State of Israel is said to be done in the name of "national security."

The debate over the use of suicide bombing campaigns carried out by Hamas and Islamic Jihad during the second intifada and the excessive use of the military and "target assassination" by Israeli security forces further illustrates the impact of such differences in power relations. Many Palestinian leaders, including Arafat, have consistently criticized the use of suicide bombing. Those Palestinians who do not denounce the use of this tactic have consistently argued that the cycle of violence stems from the occupation itself. Furthermore, systematic research on the use of suicide bombing suggests a link between the Israeli leader's policies and the suicide bombings. More specifically, some argue that Sharon's policies significantly contributed, as a matter of course and in some cases deliberately, to the persistence of suicide bombings (Sharoni, 2002; Niva, 2003).

As critical scholarship on terrorism has underscored, rather than blaming the underdog in a conflict for resorting to violent means, we must examine the conditions under which certain groups see no other alternative but violence to achieve their goal. By pursuing this line of thinking, we do not condone violence but instead look beneath the surface for its root causes in an attempt to propose a more comprehensive and long-lasting solution (see Rubenstein, 1987). Thus in the context of the Palestinian-Israeli conflict, as the PLO achieved legitimacy on the world's stage and especially after it was recognized by Israel and the United States as the official representative of the Palestinian people, it appears to have gradually and willfully moved away from military struggle to pursue diplomatic means for the resolution of the conflict.

Of course, neither Palestinian nor Israeli collectivities are homogeneous; both communities have individuals and groups who still refuse to move away from exclusivist and militant solutions to the conflict. From a conflict resolution perspective, characterizing these people as simply "enemies of peace" and therefore suppressing their activities would be a mistake. Rather, we must examine the impetus behind the behavior of these individuals and groups and their contending solutions to the conflict.

What could further complicate the dynamics of the conflict and the prospects for its resolution is the role of outside parties, with their own agendas and definitions of peace. The United States has a long and complex history of vested economic and political involvement in the Middle East. Most US administrations agree that a resolution of the Israeli-Palestinian conflict is crucial to achieving a comprehensive peace in the Middle East. Peace is viewed as synonymous with stability, which is necessary for continued US hegemony in the region. To further this end, the United States has assumed the role of referee and principal negotiator.

Yet despite its self-portrayal and peacemaking initiatives, the United States hardly fits the role of an impartial third party. In fact, many analysts have argued that in the Middle East, as in many other parts of the world, the United States has acted more as a cobelligerent than as a peacemaker. This has been the case especially after September 11, 2001 (Abu-Nimer, 2003). As Israel's chief ally and protector, the United States was simply unable to discharge its self-assigned mission as a catalyst for peace; the tensions between such roles as mediator and those of Israel's chief diplomatic backer, bankroller, and military supplier have surfaced quite often (Aruri, 1995:19–21). Moreover, due to the largely unchallenged US insistence that it is the only party that can act as a mediator between Palestinians and Israeli Jews, the services of other potential third parties have been ignored or relegated to backstage initiatives. Even in the Quartet (the UN, United States, European Union, and Russia), the United States remains the overwhelmingly dominant player. This trend has resulted in the marginalization of the UN as a potential peacemaker and in the abandonment of the once popular idea of convening a UN-sponsored international peace conference (Bennis, 1996:211–232).

When discussing past and present attempts to resolve the conflict, most media accounts, like much of scholarly literature on the conflict, tend to focus on the activities of elected officials, thus overlooking attempts by citizens on both sides of the political divide to bring about a peaceful resolution to the conflict. Some scholars have distinguished between peace-from-above and peace-from-below, or top-down and bottom-up conflict resolution attempts (Falk, 1994:189; Sharoni, 1996). In the context of the Israeli-Palestinian conflict, top-down conflict resolution takes place primarily around negotiation tables, usually outside the region, and is often characterized by attempts to apply generic, universal models of conflict resolution. Bottom-up peace initiatives, however, tend to emerge from the "inside," from within Palestinian and Israeli societies and struggles. According to those who emphasize bottom-up solutions, social movements, protest, and grassroots activism are viewed as crucial venues for peacemaking and conflict resolution (Sharoni, 1996).

Indeed, long before the much-celebrated handshake between Arafat and Rabin, Palestinians and Israelis at the grassroots level had launched both separate and collaborative initiatives designed to bring about a just and lasting solution to the conflict. Despite their absence from the negotiation table, Palestinian and Israeli-Jewish women have played a significant role in the struggle to end the Israeli occupation of the West Bank and Gaza Strip (Hiltermann, 1991; Strum, 1992; Sharoni, 1995a; Emmett, 1996). Other examples of conflict resolution initiatives at the grassroots level include such groups as Israeli-Palestinian Physicians for Human Rights, which provides medical attention and services to Palestinians in need, and joint educational projects and dialogue groups designed to counter stereotypes and fear and establish conditions for coexistence between Palestinians and Israeli Jews (Abu-Nimer, 1993; Hurwitz, 1992; Fernea and Hocking, 1992; Rosenwasser, 1992; Kaminer, 1996).

Israeli peace activists such as Uri Avnery of Gush Shalom play an important but often ignored role in promoting strategies for conflict resolution.

Deborah J. Gerner

Such activities even continued during the second intifada, although on a much smaller scale than during the first uprising. The majority of the Israeli peace groups associated with the Zionist left and center stopped their joint activities and peace protests with the intensified Israeli campaign in the West Bank and Gaza Strip and with the suicide bombings inside Israel. Besieged by Sharon's policy and the suicide bombings, only a few groups, such as Taayush, Rabbis for Human Rights, the Israeli Committee Against House Demolitions, and certain local women-led initiatives, remained active. On the Palestinian side, in response to the lack of condemnation of the Israeli military campaign against the PA, most of the NGOs responded to direct instructions from the PA in November 2000 and suspended all contacts with their Israeli counterparts. However, the PA and the NGOs resumed their cooperation and joint work in the late summer of 2001. In early 2003, the Israeli peace movement and joint Palestinian-Israeli cooperation for peace began to increase activity again. More demonstrations and protests were staged in Israeli cities and towns, and Palestinian-Israeli meetings again occurred, both inside and outside the Middle East (Abu-Nimer, 2003).

These initiatives clearly demonstrate that the expertise for resolving conflicts peacefully does not reside solely with official government personnel or procedures. Rather, citizens and groups from a variety of backgrounds and with a variety of skills can play an important role in peacemaking and conflict resolution processes. Moreover, conflict resolution experts and ordinary citizens are beginning to recognize that formal, government-to-government official interactions between instructed representatives of sovereign nations are not sufficient to secure international cooperation or resolve deep-rooted conflicts. Even if the parties to the conflict sign a peace agreement, its successful implementation depends on the support of grassroots constituencies on both sides of the political divide (Sharoni, 1996). In fact, one of the major shortcomings of the Oslo Accords was the failure of both Palestinian and Israeli-Jewish officials to draw on the experience and expertise of peace and community activists on both sides of the Palestinian-Israeli divide. This rupture in the relationship between official and unofficial peacemakers may have its roots in different definitions of peace that inform the groups' practices and affect their relations with one another.

Indeed, one more way to examine various peace and conflict resolution initiatives is by focusing on the definition of peace that informs them. One of the most popular distinctions in the field of peace and conflict resolution studies is that between negative peace and positive peace (Barash, 1991:529–590). *Negative peace* is defined merely as the absence of war or direct violence, whereas *positive peace* requires the eradication of all forms of violence, including structural violence, and a transformation of society grounded in the principles of equality, social justice, and nonviolence. In the case of the Palestinian-Israeli conflict, official representatives of the two collectivities viewed peace mostly as the absence of war and direct violence (negative peace), whereas grassroots activists within both communities envisioned peace as a transformative process grounded in the presence of justice (positive peace). The advantage of this distinction is that it enables us to come to terms with competing sets of values, experiences, and political discourses that inform various definitions of peace.

For example, peace has been defined and envisioned differently by Israeli Jews and Palestinians both before and after the signing of the Oslo Accords. Peace for Jews has primarily meant peace with security, although since the signing of the Oslo Accords this formulation has been used interchangeably with terms such as *peace and stability* or *peace and prosperity.* For Palestinians, however, references to peace have almost always been accompanied by invocation of such terms as *justice, equality, liberation,* and *self-determination* (Sharoni, 1995b:400–401). The significant differences between them notwithstanding, these definitions are not mutually exclusive but rather interdependent. Both the two-state solution and the binational-state option can accommodate these contending visions of peace.

The main challenge, however, is for each collectivity to recognize the validity of the other party's vision. Because of the asymmetrical nature of the conflict, the fulfillment of these interdependent visions appears to depend on the willingness of the stronger party to the conflict, the Israeli government, to take the first step and recognize the Palestinians' right of self-determination.

Israeli and Palestinian peace activists
often participate jointly in political demonstrations.

To win the support of its electorate for such an act, the Israeli government must introduce it not as a unilateral concession but rather as an essential step toward long-lasting peace in the region. In accepting the two-state solution and recognizing Israel's right to exist, Palestinians have demonstrated their realization that the fulfillment of their national aspirations depends on Israel's sense of security. It is imperative now that Israeli Jews understand and publicly acknowledge that their quest for security, stability, and prosperity will not materialize as long as Palestinians' quest for justice, equality, and national self-determination remains unfulfilled.

Conclusion

In the 1990s, the Palestinian leadership and Israeli government moved away from exclusivist military solutions to the conflict to more accommodationist diplomatic ones; however, this shift did not last. The two national collectivities continue to hold very different definitions of peace, informed to a great extent by the power disparities between them that the Oslo Accords failed to address. This asymmetry in power relations has been reinforced by the failure of past and present conflict-resolution attempts to successfully address the two central issues at the heart of the Palestinians' struggle—national self-determination and territorial sovereignty. Most Palestinians feel that they have already made a serious concession by giving up the dream to reclaim historical Palestine and instead accepting the two-state formula, that is, a Palestinian state in the West Bank and Gaza Strip, alongside Israel.

The implementation of the two-state solution, however, depends on a complete Israeli withdrawal from the territories it occupied in 1967 in violation of international law. So far, the Israeli government has refused to comply and return to the pre-1967 borders. The Oslo Accords offered a temporary cover-up of the situation by highlighting Israel's willingness to negotiate directly with the PLO and grant Palestinians limited autonomy to govern their internal affairs.

With the total collapse of the Oslo Accords, Israel remains in control of most of the contested land, and Jewish settlements continue to expand. As a result, Palestinians across the West Bank and Gaza Strip who have seen very little improvement in their daily lives since the signing of the Oslo Accords in 1993 are growing more and more impatient. Under the pretext of safeguarding its national security, the Israeli government has continued to engage in the assassination of Palestinian leaders and unprovoked attacks on centers of Palestinian population. The building of the omnipresent "apartheid wall" is the latest chapter in Israel's unilateral actions. Israel has continued to use its national security, which has been narrowly defined and in zero-sum terms, as a precondition for peace. In doing so, it has failed to recognize that Israelis will not be secure until Palestinians fulfill their national aspirations through a political solution they deem just (Carter, 2006).

Rather than subsume alternative visions of what peace might look like under the narrow formulations of those presently in power, we ought to treat more seriously the divergent positions of the people—Palestinians and Israeli Jews—whose lives have been entangled in the conflict. Such voices and perspectives often point out that the Israeli-Palestinian conflict is more than simply an intractable territorial dispute between two national collectivities; it also involves contending visions concerning the resolution of the conflict and the future of the Middle East that have been the subject of heated political debates and contestations within both Palestinian and Israeli-Jewish communities.

Finally, as citizens of the Middle East and as conflict resolution scholars, we would like to voice our skepticism regarding conflict resolution initiatives carried out by such interested third parties as the United States or a myriad of conflict resolution experts. Far from being neutral or impartial facilitators, these outside parties, whose intentions are sometimes noble, tend to marginalize or altogether ignore the hopes and fears of ordinary people in the region while imposing their own conflict resolution frameworks and visions of peace. In contrast, we believe that Palestinians and Israeli Jews, if not their present leaders, hold the key to a just and lasting resolution of the conflict. The role of Middle Eastern scholars and conflict resolution experts, or the international community more generally, is not to bring peace to the Middle East, but rather to empower and support those people in the region who have long been involved in the elusive search for peace.

Bibliography

Abdo, Nahla. 1992. "Racism, Zionism, and the Palestinian Working Class, 1920–1947." *Studies in Political Economy* 37, no. 2:59–93.

Abu-Lughod, Ibrahim (ed.). 1982. *Palestinian Rights: Affirmation and Denial.* Wilmette, Ill.: Medina Press.

Abu-Lughod, Janet. 1987. "The Demographic Transformation of Palestine." Pp. 139–164 in Ibrahim Abu-Lughod (ed.), *The Transformation of Palestine.* Evanston, Ill.: Northwestern University Press.

Abu-Nimer, Mohammed. 1993. "Conflict Resolution Between Arabs and Jews in Israel: A Study of Six Intervention Models." Ph.D. diss., George Mason University, Fairfax, Va.

———. 2003. "September 11 and Palestinian Reaction: No Win." In Rashied Omar (ed.), *Multiple Voices: Opportunities and Challenges for Islamic Peacebuilding After September 11.* Notre Dame: Notre Dame University Press.

Aburish, Said. 1998. *Arafat: From Defender to Dictator.* New York: Bloomsbury Publishing.

Alcalay, Ammiel. 1993. *After Jews and Arabs: Remaking Levantine Culture.* Minneapolis: University of Minnesota Press.

Andoni, Lamis. 1991. "The PLO at the Crossroads." *Journal of Palestine Studies* 81:54–65.

Aruri, Naseer. 1995. *The Obstruction of Peace: The US, Israel, and the Palestinians.* Monroe, Maine: Common Courage Press.

Ashrawi, Hanan Mikhail. 1991. "The Other Occupation: The Palestinian Response." Pp. 191–198 in Phyllis Bennis and Michel Moushabeck (eds.), *Beyond the Storm: A Gulf Crisis Reader.* Brooklyn: Olive Branch Press.

Barash, David. 1991. *Introduction to Peace Studies.* Belmont, Calif.: Wadsworth.

Barghouti, Omar. 2006. "The Israeli Elections: A Decisive Vote for Apartheid." www.zmag.org/content/showarticle.cfm?ItemID=10035 (accessed December 9, 2007).

Bar-On, Mordechi. 1985. *Peace Now: The Portrait of a Movement.* In Hebrew. Tel Aviv: Hakibbutz Hameuchad.

Baroud, Ramzy. 2006. *The Second Palestinian Intifada: A Chronicle of a People's Struggle.* London: Pluto.

Bennis, Phyllis. 1996. *Calling the Shots: How Washington Dominates Today's UN.* Brooklyn: Olive Branch Press.

Bennis, Phyllis, and Michel Moushabeck (eds.). 1991. *Beyond the Storm: A Gulf Crisis Reader.* Brooklyn: Olive Branch Press.

Brynen, Rex (ed.). 1991. *Echoes of the Intifada: Regional Repercussions of the Palestinian-Israeli Conflict.* Boulder, Colo.: Westview Press.

Carter, Jimmy. 2006. *Palestine: Peace Not Apartheid.* New York: Simon and Schuster.

Cobban, Helena. 1984. *The Palestinian Liberation Organization: People, Power, and Politics.* Cambridge: Cambridge University Press.

Davis, Ury. 1986. "Israel's Zionist Society: Consequences for Internal Opposition and the Necessity for External Intervention." Pp. 176–201 in Ejaz Eaford (ed.), *Judaism or Zionism: What Difference for the Middle East?* London: Zed Books.

Emmett, Ayala. 1996. *Our Sisters' Promised Land: Women, Politics, and Israeli-Palestinian Coexistence.* Ann Arbor: University of Michigan Press.

Evron, Boas. 1995. *Jewish State or Israeli Nation?* Bloomington: Indiana University Press.

Falk, Richard. 1994. "World Order Conceptions and the Peace Process in the Middle East." Pp. 189–196 in Elise Boulding (ed.), *Building Peace in the Middle East: Challenges for States and Civil Society.* Boulder, Colo.: Lynne Rienner.

Fernea, Elizabeth Warnock, and Mary Evelyn Hocking (eds.). 1992. *The Struggle for Peace: Israelis and Palestinians.* Austin: University of Texas Press.

Finkelstein, Norman. 1995. *Image and Reality of the Israel-Palestine Conflict.* London: Verso.

Flapan, Simha. 1987. *The Birth of Israel: Myths and Realities.* New York: Pantheon Books.

Gerner, Deborah J. 1990. "Evolution of the Palestinian Uprising." *International Journal of Group Tensions* 20, no. 3:233–265.

———. 1991. "Palestinians, Israelis, and the *Intifada:* The Third Year and Beyond." *Arab Studies Quarterly* 13, nos. 3–4:19–60.

———. 1992. "The Arab-Israeli Conflict." Pp. 361–382 in Peter J. Schraeder (ed.), *Intervention in the 1990s: US Foreign Policy in the Third World.* Boulder, Colo.: Lynne Rienner.

———. 1994. *One Land, Two Peoples: The Conflict Over Palestine.* 2nd ed. Boulder, Colo.: Westview Press.

Grayzel, Solomon. 1968. *A History of the Jews.* New York: New American Library.

Greenstein, Ran. 1995. *Genealogies of Conflict: Class, Identity, and State in Palestine/Israel and South Africa.* Hanover: Wesleyan University Press.

Guyatt, Nicholas. 1998. *The Absence of Peace: Understanding the Israeli-Palestinian Conflict.* London: Zed Books.

Haddad, Toufic. 2006. The Hamas Victory: Green Dawn, Red Dusk? *The Electronic Intifada,* January 31. http://electronicintifada.net/v2/article4434.shtml.

Hajjar, Lisa, and Joel Beinin. 1990. *Palestine and Israel: A Primer.* Washington, D.C.: Middle East Research and Information Project.

Al-Haq. 1988. "Repression of Education." Pp. 419–448 in Al-Haq, *Punishing a Nation: Human Rights Violations During the Palestinian Uprising.* Ramallah, West Bank: Al-Haq.

Heller, Mark, and Sari Nusseibeh. 1991. *No Trumpets, No Drums: A Two-State Settlement of the Israeli-Palestinian Conflict.* New York: Hill and Wang.

Herzberg, Arthur (ed.). 1962. *The Zionist Idea: A Historical Analysis and Reader.* New York: Doubleday.

Hiltermann, Joost. 1990. "Work in Action: The Role of the Working Class in the Uprising." Pp. 143–158 in Jamal Nassar and Roger Heacock (eds.), *Intifada: Palestine at the Crossroads.* New York: Praeger.

———. 1991. *Behind the Intifada: Labor and Women's Movements in the Occupied Territories.* Princeton: Princeton University Press.

Hiro, Dilip. 1992. *Desert Shield to Desert Storm: The Second Gulf War.* London: HarperCollins.

———. 1999. *Sharing the Promised Land: A Tale of Israelis and Palestinians.* Brooklyn: Olive Branch Press.

Hirst, David. 1984. *The Gun and the Olive Branch: The Roots of Violence in the Middle East.* 2nd ed. London: Faber and Faber.

Hunter, Robert. 1991. *The Palestinian Uprising.* Berkeley: University of California Press.

Hurwitz, Deena (ed.). 1992. *Walking the Red Line: Israelis in Search of Justice for Palestine.* Philadelphia: New Society.

Israeli Foreign Ministry. 2003. Information available from www.israel.org/mfa/go (accessed September 14, 2003).

Jad, Islah. 1990. "From Salons to the Popular Committees: Palestinian Women 1919–1989." Pp. 125–142 in Jamal Nassar and Roger Heacock (eds.), *Intifada: Palestine at the Crossroads.* New York: Praeger.

Jones, Clive, and Ami Pedahzur (eds.). 2005. *Between Terrorism and Civil War: The Al-Aqsa Intifada.* New York: Routledge.

Kaminer, Reuven. 1996. *The Politics of Protest: The Israeli Peace Movement and the Intifada.* Sussex, UK: Academic Press.

Kelman, Herbert C. 1982. "Creating the Conditions for Israeli-Palestinian Negotiations." *Journal of Conflict Resolution* 26:39–75.

Khalidi, Walid. 1971. *From Haven to Conquest: Readings in Zionism and the Palestine Problem Until 1948.* Beirut: Institute for Palestine Studies.

Kimmerling, Baruch. 1983. *Zionism and Territory: The Socio-Territorial Dimensions of Zionist Politics.* Berkeley: University of California Press.

Kimmerling, Baruch, and Joel Migdal. 1993. *Palestinians: The Making of a People.* New York: Macmillan.

Legrain, Jean-François. 1990. "The Islamic Movement and the Intifada." Pp. 175–189 in Jamal Nassar and Roger Heacock (eds.), *Intifada: Palestine at the Crossroads.* New York: Praeger.

Lesch, Ann M., and Mark Tessler (eds.). 1989. *Israel, Egypt, and the Palestinians: From Camp David to the Intifada.* Bloomington: Indiana University Press.

Levy, Gideon. 2006. "One Racist Nation," *Haaretz,* March 26, 2006. www.israelblog.org/1143439405 (accessed December 9, 2007).

Lockman, Zachary, and Joel Beinin (eds.). 1989. *Intifada: The Palestinian Uprising Against Israeli Occupation.* Boston: South End Press.

Lustick, Ian. 1980. *Arabs in the Jewish State: Israel's Control of a National Minority.* Austin: University of Texas Press.

———. 1993. *Unsettled States, Disputed Lands: Britain and Ireland, France and Algeria, Israel and the West Bank and Gaza.* Ithaca: Cornell University Press.

Makdisi, Saree. 2006. "3 Views of the Israeli Election: The Real Winner in Israel." *San Francisco Chronicle,* March 31, 2006. www.sfgate.com/cgi-bin/article.cgi?file=/c/a/2006/03/31/EDGORI0EFB1.DTL (accessed December 9, 2007).

Mansour, Camille. 2002. "The Impact of 11 September on the Israeli-Palestinian Conflict." *Journal of Palestine Studies* 31, no. 2:5–18.

Mishal, Sahul, and Avraham Sela. 2006. *The Palestinian Hamas: Vision, Violence, and Coexistence.* New York: Columbia University Press.

Morris, Benny. 1988. *The Birth of the Palestinian Refugee Problem, 1947–1949.* Cambridge: Cambridge University Press.

———. 1990. *1948 and After: Israel and the Palestinians.* Oxford: Oxford University Press.

Moses, Rafael. 1990. "Self, Self-View, and Identity." Pp. 47–55 in *The Psychodynamics of International Relationships.* Vol. 1. Lexington, Mass.: Lexington Books.

Murray, Eoin. 2006. "Palestinian Elections: Forcing the West To Awake to the Voices of the People," *Live from Palestine,* January 26. http://electronicintifada.net/v2/article4424.shtml (accessed December 16, 2007).

Muslih, Muhammad. 1992. "History of the Israeli-Palestinian Conflict." Pp. 62–79 in Elizabeth Warnock Fernea and Mary Evelyn Hocking (eds.), *The Struggle for Peace: Israelis and Palestinians.* Austin: University of Texas Press.

Nakhleh, Emile (ed.). 1980. *A Palestinian Agenda for the West Bank and Gaza.* Washington, D.C.: American Enterprise Institute.

Nakhleh, Khalil, and Elia Zureik (eds.). 1980. *The Sociology of the Palestinians.* New York: St. Martin's Press.

Nassar, Jamal R. 1991. *The Palestine Liberation Organization: From Armed Struggle to the Declaration of Independence.* New York: Praeger.

Nassar, Jamal, and Roger Heacock (eds.). 1991. *Intifada: Palestine at the Crossroads.* New York: Praeger.

Niva, Steve. 2003. "A Predictable Cycle of Violence." *Al-Ahram Weekly,* no. 627 (February 27–March 5, 2003). http://weekly.ahram.org.eg/2003/627/op192.htm (accessed May 28, 2003).

Palestine Red Crescent Society. 2003. Information available from www.palestinercs.org (accessed September 14, 2003).

Parkes, James. 1964. *A History of the Jewish People.* Baltimore: Penguin Books.

Perez, Don. 1990. *Intifada: The Palestinian Uprising.* Boulder, Colo.: Westview Press.

Perlman, Wendy (ed.). 2003. *Occupied Voices: Stories of Everyday Life from the Second Intifada.* New York: Thunder's Mouth Press/Nation Books.

Quigley, John. 1990. *Palestine and Israel: A Challenge to Justice.* Durham, N.C.: Duke University Press.

Rabbani, Mouin. 1996. "Palestinian Authority, Israeli Rule: From Transitional to Permanent Arrangement." *Middle East Report* (October–December):2–6.

Reich, Bernard. 1985. *Israel: Land of Tradition and Conflict.* Boulder, Colo.: Westview Press.

Reinhart, Tanya. 2002. *Israel/Palestine: How To End the War of 1948.* New York: Seven Stories Press.

Rekass, Elie. 1989. "The Israeli Arabs and the Arabs of the West Bank and Gaza: Political Affinity and National Solidarity." *Asian and African Studies* 23, nos. 2–3:119–154.

Rosenwasser, Penny. 1992. *Voices from a "Promised Land": Palestinian and Israeli Peace Activists Speak Their Hearts.* Willimantic, Conn.: Curbstone Press.

Rothman, Jay. 1992. *From Conflict to Cooperation: Resolving Ethnic Conflict and Regional Conflict.* Newbury Park, Calif.: Sage.

Rouhana, Nadim. 1989. "The Political Transformation of the Palestinians in Israel: From Acquiescence to Challenge." *Journal of Palestine Studies* 3:38–59.

Rubenstein, Richard. 1987. *Alchemists of Revolution: Terrorism in the Modern World.* New York: Basic Books.

Sachar, Abram Leon. 1964. *A History of the Jews.* New York: Knopf.

Said, Edward. 1980. *The Question of Palestine.* New York: Vintage.

Said, Edward, Ibrahim Abu-Lughod, Janet Abu-Lughod, Muhammad Hallaj, and Elia Zureik. 1990. *A Profile of the Palestinian People.* Chicago: Palestine Human Rights Campaign.

Saunders, Harold. 1985. *The Other Walls: The Politics of the Arab-Israeli Peace Process.* Washington, D.C.: American Enterprise Institute for Public Policy Research.

Schiff, Ze'ev. 1990. *Intifada: The Palestinian Uprising—Israel's Third Front.* New York: Simon and Schuster.

Schiff, Ze'ev, and Ehud Ya'ari. 1984. *Israel's Lebanon War.* New York: Simon and Schuster.

Segal, Jerome. 1989. *Creating the Palestinian State: A Strategy for Peace.* Chicago: Lawrence Hill Books.

Shahak, Israel. 1995. *Jewish History, Jewish Religion: The Weight of Three Thousand Years.* London: Pluto Press.

Shapira, Anita. 1992. *Land and Power: The Zionist Resort to Force, 1881–1948.* New York: Oxford University Press.

Sharoni, Simona. 1995a. *Gender and the Israeli-Palestinian Conflict: The Politics of Women's Resistance.* Syracuse, N.Y.: Syracuse University Press.

———. 1995b. "Peace as Identity Crisis." *Peace Review* 7, nos. 3–4:399–407.

———. 1996. "Conflict Resolution and Peacemaking from the Bottom Up: The Roles of Social Movements and People's Diplomacy." Paper prepared for the fourth seminar of the International University of People's Institutions for Peace (IUPIP), Rovereto, Italy.

———. 2002. "Sharon's War Threatens Israel's Security." www.alternet.org/story.html?storyID=12768 (accessed August 2, 2003).

Shohat, Ella. 1988. "Sephardim in Israel: Zionism from the Standpoint of Its Jewish Victims." *Social Text* 19, no. 10:1–35.

Sifry, Micah, and Christopher Cerf (eds.). 1991. *The Gulf War Reader.* New York: Times Books/Random House.

Smooha, Sammy. 1989. *Arabs and Jews in Israel.* Vol. 1: *Conflicting and Shared Attitudes in a Divided Society.* Boulder, Colo.: Westview Press.

———. 1992. *Arabs and Jews in Israel.* Vol. 2: *Change and Continuity in Mutual Tolerance.* Boulder, Colo.: Westview Press.

Strum, Philippa. 1992. *The Women Are Marching: The Second Sex and the Palestinian Revolution.* New York: Lawrence Hill Books.

Suleiman, Michael (ed.). 1995. *US Policy in Palestine: From Wilson to Clinton.* Normal, Ill.: AAUG Press.

Swirski, Shlomo. 1989. *Israel: The Oriental Majority.* London: Zed Books.

Tamari, Salim. 1980. "The Palestinians in the West Bank and Gaza Strip: The Sociology of Dependency." Pp. 84–111 in Khalil Nakhleh and Elia Zureik (eds.), *The Sociology of the Palestinians.* New York: St. Martin's Press.

Taraki, Lisa. 1989. "The Islamic Resistance Movement in the Palestinian Uprising." Pp. 171–177 in Zachary Lockman and Joel Beinin (eds.), *Intifada: The Palestinian Uprising Against Israeli Occupation.* Boston: South End Press and the Middle East Research and Information Project.

———— (ed.). 2006. *Living Palestine: Family, Survival, Resistance, and Mobility Under Occupation.* Syracuse: Syracuse University Press.

Tessler, Mark. 1994. *A History of the Israeli-Palestinian Conflict.* Bloomington: Indiana University Press.

Thomas, Baylis. 1999. *How Israel Was Won: A Concise History of the Arab-Israeli Conflict.* Lanham, Md.: Lexington Books.

Usher, Graham. 1995a. *Palestine in Crisis: The Struggle for Peace and Political Independence After Oslo.* East Haven, Conn.: Pluto Press in association with the Transnational Institute and the Middle East Research and Information Project.

————. 1995b. "What Kind of Nation? The Rise of Hamas in the Occupied Territories." *Race and Class* 37, no. 2:65–80.

Vitalis, Robert. 1992. "The Palestinian-Israeli Conflict: Options and Scenarios for Peace." Pp. 285–313 in Elizabeth Warnock Fernea and Mary Evelyn Hocking (eds.), *The Struggle for Peace: Israelis and Palestinians.* Austin: University of Texas Press.

Volkan, Vamik. 1990. "An Overview of Psychological Concepts Pertinent to Interethnic and/or International Relationships." Pp. 31–46 in Vamik D. Volkan, Demetrios A. Julius, and Joseph V. Montville (eds.), *The Psychodynamics of International Relationships.* Vol. 1. Lexington, Mass.: Lexington Books.

Wolfsfeld, Gadi. 1988. *The Politics of Provocation: Participation in Protest in Israel.* Albany: State University of New York Press.

Yahya, Adil. 1991. "The Role of the Refugee Camps." Pp. 91–106 in Jamal Nassar and Roger Heacock (eds.), *Intifada: Palestine at the Crossroads.* New York: Praeger.

Zilka, Avraham. 1992. "History of the Israeli-Palestinian Conflict." Pp. 7–61 in Elizabeth Warnock Fernea and Mary Evelyn Hocking (eds.), *The Struggle for Peace: Israelis and Palestinians.* Austin: University of Texas Press.

Zunes, Steve. 1994. "Zionism, Anti-Semitism, and Imperialism." *Peace Review* 6, no. 1:41–49.

Zureik, Elia. 1979. *The Palestinians in Israel: A Study in Internal Colonialism.* London: Routledge and Kegan Paul.

7

The Economies of the Middle East

Agnieszka Paczynska

The Middle East has been at the crossroads of international trade for centuries. As early as the second century B.C.E., the Silk Route connected Europe, the Mediterranean, Central Asia, and China and carried silk, spices, silver, textiles, and other commodities. By the eighteenth century, however, as Europe's trade grew, the Middle East became largely peripheral to the global trading system, although it continued to export silk, wools, coffee, and cereals. In the twentieth century, the Middle East and North Africa were once again geopolitically important due to having the world's largest petroleum reserves.

By the end of the twentieth century, as world trade and capital movements grew at unprecedented rates and new forms of production increased global economic interdependence, the Middle East nevertheless remained poorly integrated into these new trading, investment, and production networks. And despite the wealth generated by oil exports and a long history of foreign economic assistance, many of the regions' peoples remained impoverished.

In fact, one of the striking features of the region is the stark contrast between socioeconomic classes within and among countries. The Middle East is among the most inequitable regions of the world. It is home to societies with some of the highest per capita incomes as well as some of the world's lowest. It is home to the shiny new skyscrapers of the Gulf petro-states and to the crowded alleys of the Gaza Strip, the refugee camps around Khartoum, and the violent streets of Baghdad. This chapter will explore the evolution of the region's economies along these different trajectories and examine the particular role that conflict has played in generating such disparities.

Table 7.1 Indicators of Development, 2005 (US$ billions)

Country	Rank	GDP	GDP/Capita	% Literate (1995–2005)	HDI Score[a] (2005)
Algeria	104	102.3	3,112	69.9	0.733
Bahrain	41	12.9	17,773	86.5	0.866
Comoros	134	0.4	645	n.a.	0.561
Djibouti	149	0.7	894	n.a.	0.516
Egypt	112	89.4	1,207	71.4	0.708
Iran	94	189.8	2,781	82.4	0.759
Iraq	n.a.	n.a.	n.a.	74.1	n.a.
Israel	23	123.4	17,828	97.1	0.932
Jordan	86	12.7	2,323	91.1	0.773
Kuwait	33	80.8	31,861	93.3	0.891
Lebanon	88	21.9	6,135	n.a.	0.772
Libya	56	38.8	6,621	84.2	0.818
Mauritania	137	1.9	603	51.2	0.550
Morocco	126	51.6	1,711	52.3	0.646
Oman	58	24.3	9,584	81.4	0.814
Palestinian Authority	106	4.0	1,107	92.4	0.731
Qatar	35	42.5	52,240	89.0	0.875
Saudi Arabia	61	309.8	13,399	82.9	0.812
Somalia	n.a.	n.a.	n.a.	n.a.	n.a.
Sudan	147	27.5	760	60.9	0.526
Syria	108	26.3	1,382	80.8	0.724
Tunisia	91	28.7	2,860	74.3	0.766
Turkey	84	362.5	5,030	87.4	0.775
United Arab Emirates	39	129.7	28,612	88.7	0.868
Yemen	153	15.1	718	54.1	0.508

Source: Data from UNDP, *Human Development Report 2007/2008.*
Notes: a. Human Development Index (HDI) was created to provide a more accurate picture of development levels than was possible when using only gross domestic product (GDP) per capita. HDI includes such measures as access to education and health services, life expectancy, child mortality rates, and access to potable water, among others.
n.a. indicates data not available.

■ Middle East Economies Before World War II

Trading patterns in the Middle East and North Africa changed significantly beginning in the eighteenth century as the Ottoman Empire, which controlled these areas, weakened. In the sixteenth century, the empire exported to Europe wheat and luxury goods such as silk and carpets. By the seventeenth century, it was also exporting cattle, wool, hides, cotton, and tobacco as well as olive oil, dried fruit, and angora. In the eighteenth century, cotton, maize, and tobacco exports grew significantly, as did exports of semiprocessed goods, in particular textiles. The empire imported about three to four times more than it exported to Europe. During this time the Ottomans also actively traded with Asian countries, importing pharmaceuticals, perfumes, precious stones, spices, indigo, and cloth. They also imported dyes, sugar, and coffee from European colonies in the Americas. However, it was the internal trade within the empire that was most important to both its economic prosperity and to its political cohesion (Panzac, 1992).

The end of the Napoleonic Wars in 1815 fundamentally changed the political orientation of European powers. While during the wars they focused on continental conflicts, now their competition for domination became externalized as they sought to spread their influence internationally. Changes in manufacturing and organization of production increased Europe's need for raw materials and pushed European states, and in particular Britain and France but also Belgium, Switzerland, and Germany, to look for new export markets for their products. The technological revolution in the first part of the nineteenth century introduced railways and steamships for the first time, allowing profitable shipment of bulk goods. Trade was further facilitated by the development of international money markets (Issawi, 1995).

During this period cash crops expanded. Egypt specialized in cotton exports, Lebanon in silk, Tunisia in olive oil and phosphates, Palestine in oranges, and Algeria in wine. Europe on the other hand exported manufactured products as well as tea, coffee, and sugar to the region. As European interests in the region increased, maintaining access to these markets became vitally important. Under pressure from European powers, commercial laws were enacted by Middle Eastern states that allowed European merchants to travel and trade freely in the region and to have commercial disputes resolved in special tribunals and not in Islamic courts. In November 1869 the Suez Canal, linking the Mediterranean and Red seas, opened to commercial traffic. It inaugurated new trade routes between Europe and Asia that were especially important to the British Empire (Hourani, 1991).

In response to European penetration of the region, local rulers sought to modernize their states and gain control over imports and exports. As a consequence, the foreign debt of many Middle Eastern and North African Ottoman provinces grew, resulting in ever greater reliance on Europe and a gradual loss of independence. By 1875 the Ottoman government was no longer able to meet its debt obligations, and in 1881 foreign creditors established the Public Debt Administration. Between 1830 and 1911, Europe took over financial control of the governments of Algeria, Egypt, Tunisia, and Morocco, when these countries began struggling to repay their large foreign debts. In 1911 Italy invaded Libya. This was the era of "new imperialism," when Europe established colonies in the Middle East and North Africa and sub-Saharan Africa (Hourani, 1991). Despite this European penetration of the region, between 1820 and 1913 the share of the Middle East in global trade fell from 3 percent to 1.5 percent (Issawi, 1995).

Following World War I, as the Ottoman Empire crumbled, European powers expanded their control over the Middle East. Britain gained control over Iraq, Palestine, and Transjordan, while France took control of Syria and Lebanon. This allowed them to maintain open markets for their manufactured goods such as textiles and machinery and gave them access to important raw materials for industrial production, and increasingly oil. It also provided them with a field for investments, in particular in mining and agriculture.

In Iran, oil was discovered in 1908 and its extraction began in 1914. In the 1920s, it was discovered in Iraq and Bahrain and during the next decade in Saudi Arabia and Kuwait. As a consequence of these discoveries, colonial powers intensified their interest in the region. For the first few decades of oil extraction, British, French, Dutch, and US companies controlled the production process. As Mary Ann Tétreault discusses in Chapter 8, eventually states in oil-producing countries came to own the oil production facilities. The growing importance of oil fundamentally changed the economic profiles of some states and the trading profile of the region.

▪ Economic Development Following World War II

The presence of oil has had a profound impact on both oil producers and those lacking petroleum resources in the region. Equally important to understanding the dynamics of economic development in the Middle East have been its climate, demographic characteristics, geopolitical location, and conflict dynamics. The region's very limited rainfall and arid soils make unirrigated agriculture difficult (Richards and Waterbury, 1990:52). Its rapidly growing population puts tremendous pressure on public services and labor markets. The involvement of great powers and the funds funneled to purchase weapons has contributed to regional arms races that have drained resources from the civilian economy, and the persistence of conflicts both between and within states has undermined economic development in a number of countries.

As detailed in Chapters 3, 4, and 5, the political map of the region changed significantly following the end of World War II. As the colonial empires disintegrated, new independent states emerged in the Middle East and North Africa. With the exception of the small Persian Gulf states, which remained under British control until the 1970s, most gained independence by the 1960s. And in 1948 Israel was established as a Jewish homeland. The United States emerged as the dominant international actor in the region and

Drip irrigation makes agriculture possible even in the Egyptian Sinai.

for decades contested the Soviet Union for influence. Economic policies also changed and emphasized developing national industrial capacity and social development. In many countries large segments of the economy were brought directly under state control.

At the end of World War II, as the European colonial empires ceded direct political control of the region's states to local elites, the Middle East seemed poised to become one of the wealthier and more developed areas of the world. Egypt's level of development was no different from that of Greece; Algeria's economic prosperity was closely tied with that of France; and as part of the Truman Doctrine, Turkey was the beneficiary of a large US aid package. As Clement M. Henry and Robert Springborg note,

> Casablanca was home to big French industrial interests poised to transform the picturesque Morocco protectorate into Europe's California. At the eastern end of the Mediterranean, a newly independent polyglot Lebanon would become the Middle East's Switzerland. . . . the open Syrian economy boomed with new manufacturing and agricultural development. (Henry and Springborg, 2001:2)

The future of Iraq and Iran seemed even more promising thanks to the large oil deposits in the two countries. As we will see in the course of this chapter, these high expectations have been largely dashed. Israel can boast a technologically advanced and diversified economy. Turkey has also experienced significant improvement in its level of economic development, especially in the past ten years, making accession negotiations with the European Union possible. Other countries, however, have experienced very different patterns of development. Unexpectedly, it is the Gulf states that have seen the most spectacular economic expansion thanks to oil discoveries. Those countries that seemed to hold most promise at the end of World War II have seen their economies stumble.

In many of the region's states following independence the new political elites sought to launch economic development projects that would make their countries less dependent on former colonial empires and also ensure that the deep social inequalities that characterized the region, and which were seen by nationalists as a direct consequence of colonial exploitation, would become a thing of the past. The new political coalitions that now became dominant in many states incorporated previously excluded social strata, for instance peasants and labor. In order to maintain these groups' political support and to fulfill the object of raising income levels of the poorest segments of society, the new regimes expanded the provision of services, such as health, education, and consumer subsidies (Waldner, 1999).

At the same time, economic policies shifted significantly. The new regimes implemented land reforms aimed at both undercutting the power of the old agrarian elites as well as providing greater access to and control over land to peasants. Most states also placed a new emphasis on promoting industrialization, which was seen as the backbone of economic development. As in many other developing countries, states in the Middle East initiated import substitution industrialization (ISI) policies, which aimed at developing local industries to reduce dependence on exports and promote local development. In order to shield these infant industries from international competition and allow them time to develop, countries relied on protective tariffs. With expanding industrial employment opportunities, the previously largely agrarian societies became increasingly urban.

Regardless of the prevailing political ideology, most state elites during the 1960s were dubious about the private sector's ability to launch an economic development project. As Alan Richards and John Waterbury point out,

> throughout the region it was assumed that the private sector could not be relied upon to undertake this kind of resource mobilization and planning. The least critical saw the private sector as too weak and financially too close to a commercial and trading, rather than an industrial, past and too concerned with short term profit to be the agents of structural transformation. (Richards and Waterbury, 1990:189)

Some states that espoused a socialist ideology, like Algeria, Egypt, and Tunisia, went further in redistributing wealth and were more hostile to foreign capital and the local private sector. In these countries the state became directly involved both in economic planning as well as in production. During the 1960s, the number of state-owned enterprises expanded significantly, providing the local markets with new consumer goods and ensuring employment possibilities to the growing labor force. However, even in countries that placed more faith in market mechanisms, such as Jordan and Morocco, the state became more involved in both production and in provision of welfare services. Because state control over the economy expanded so significantly, private sector businesses also became highly dependent on state contracts and state subsidies (Bellin, 2002).

Initially, the results of this new approach to economic development were encouraging. Literacy levels improved, urbanization rates accelerated, and access to medical care expanded. In countries where the agricultural sector used to dominate, industrial production and services came to play a more significant role.

By the late 1960s to early 1970s, however, economic problems emerged. Living standards first stagnated and then began to deteriorate. Public sector enterprises were plagued by inefficiencies, production bottlenecks, and bloated employment rolls (Waterbury, 1993). State bureaucracies expanded, making interactions with public administration more cumbersome. A number of countries that had promoted socialist principles, in particular Tunisia and Egypt, began to abandon them. Egyptian president Anwar Sadat, for instance, initiated a policy of *infitah,* or economic liberalization, in 1974 which sought to reorient economic policies toward a greater reliance on domestic and foreign private investment. Nonetheless, even where private

Table 7.2 Contribution of Agriculture and Industry to GDP (percentage)

Country	1958 Agriculture	1958 Industry	1968 Agriculture	1968 Industry	1978 Agriculture	1978 Industry
Algeria	25	20	n.a.	n.a.	7	49
Egypt	33	24	25	24	24	27
Iran	32	30	22	34	9	46
Iraq	20	50	15	43	7	67
Israel	12	32	8	34	4	23
Jordan	18	14	15	21	6	21
Lebanon	n.a.	n.a.	11	21	9	21
Libya	n.a.	n.a.	4	65	2	68
Morocco	35	26	32	29	18	33
Saudi Arabia	n.a.	n.a.	6	62	1	79
Sudan	59	12	39	15	36	14
Tunisia	n.a.	n.a.	18	21	16	27
Turkey	30	28	25	27	17	37

Source: Tuma, 2004: 230.
Note: n.a. indicates data not available.

investment was encouraged, the state continued to dominate the economy, and public sector employment expanded.

In the early 1980s, much of the developing world began experiencing deep economic problems and struggled with mounting foreign debts. The crisis came to a head in 1982 when Mexico announced that it was suspending its debt repayments. Most developing countries turned to the International Monetary Fund (IMF) and the World Bank for assistance in dealing with the macroeconomic and financial crises and began implementing structural adjustment reforms to address underlying weaknesses in their economies. Although most countries in the Middle East tinkered with economic reforms during the 1980s and sought to reduce the state's role in economic planning and production, these attempts were generally half-hearted and did not result in significant transformation of the region's economies.

A number of reasons account for this lack of progress in economic reform implementation. As in other regions, the initiation of structural reforms was politically difficult. Social groups that had benefited from the prevailing economic arrangements resisted reforms. These groups included elites, who through connections to regime insiders were able to secure profitable contracts, as well as organized labor, which benefited from access to public sector jobs with higher salaries and benefits and job security than were available in the private sector. The riots that erupted in Egypt in 1977 when President Sadat attempted to cut subsidies on consumer goods were a stark reminder of the political costs reforming leaders were likely to incur.

At the same time, leaders in the Middle East faced less pressure to reform than their counterparts in other regions. Most important, the oil-producing countries provided direct aid to other states in the region, and workers from resource-poor countries migrated to the Gulf, thus relieving pressure on local labor markets and sending remittances back home. The region's strategic importance to the two superpowers, the United States and the Soviet Union, also ensured large amounts of aid and assistance to their client states.

The United States has been the most important source of economic aid, although since the Camp David Peace Accords of 1978 the overwhelming majority of this assistance has been channeled to Egypt and Israel. Before its disintegration, the Soviet Union was also an important source of foreign aid. Most of its aid went to Egypt, Syria, and Iraq. Europe and China have also provided assistance, albeit at lower levels. In other words, the availability of oil and strategic rents made reforming economies a less urgent task in the Middle East than in many other parts of the developing world.

Labor Migration and Remittances

Labor migration and workers' remittances have played a key role in economic dynamics in the region. In fact, the Middle East has the highest ratios of migrants to the total population in the world (Baldwin-Edwards, 2005). The Middle East and in particular the Gulf states are a major destination for migrant labor. The region also serves as a transit area for migrants from other areas, especially sub-Saharan Africa, who are looking to migrate to Europe. Although exact figures of migrants are hard to pin down, most analysts agree that the data collected by the UN underestimates their total numbers.

For a number of countries in the region and in particular Turkey and the Maghreb, workers' remittances have been crucial. Morocco, for instance, has encouraged migration out of the country in order to maintain unemployment at politically acceptable levels. At the beginning of the twenty-first century, approximately 2.3 million Moroccans, or about 10 percent of the total population, lived abroad, sending back $3.3 billion in remittances, which accounted for 9.7 percent of gross domestic product (GDP) (Baldwin-Edwards, 2005: 4). Although initially encouraged, emigration of skilled workers from Morocco and Algeria, sometimes referred to as "brain drain," has presented a problem for local businesses, which have often been unable to find the technical staff they need and have been forced to turn to more expensive, foreign professionals.

For decades, migrants' primary destination has been the Gulf states. However, the composition of foreign labor in the oil-producing states has

Table 7.3 Estimated Migrant Stocks, 2000 (thousands and as a proportion of total population)

Country	N	Percentage
Qatar	409	70.4
United Arab Emirates	1,922	68.2
Kuwait	1,108	49.3
Jordan	1,945	38.6
Bahrain	254	37.6
Israel	2,256	37.3
Oman	682	26.1
Saudi Arabia	5,255	23.7
Lebanon	634	18.2
Libya	570	10.9
Syria	903	5.5
Turkey	1,503	2.2
Yemen	284	1.4
Algeria	250	0.8
Tunisia	38	0.4
Egypt	169	0.2
Morocco	26	0.1

Source: UN, 2004, *World Population Policies 2003.*

Table 7.4 Where Migrants Come From and Where They Go

Country of Origin	Bahrain	Kuwait	Oman	Qatar	Saudi Arabia	United Arab Emirates
India	100,000	295,000	300,000	100,000	1,400,000	1,000,000
Pakistan	50,000	100,000	70,000	70,000	1,000,000	450,000
Egypt	275,000	15,000	35,000	1,000,000	130,000	1,455,000
Yemen	1,000,000	35,000	1,035,000			
Bangladesh	160,000	110,000	450,000	100,000	820,000	
Sri Lanka	160,000	35,000	350,000	160,000	705,000	
Philippines	60,000	50,000	500,000	120,000	730,000	
Jordan/Palestine	50,000	50,000	270,000	110,000	480,000	
Syria	95,000	170,000	265,000			
Iran	45,000	80,000	20,000	40,000	185,000	
Indonesia	250,000	250,000				
Sudan	250,000	250,000				
Kuwait	120,000	120,000				
Turkey	100,000	100,000				
Total	280,000	1,475,000	630,000	420,000	7,000,000	2,488,000

Source: International Fund for Agricultural Development, www.ifad.org/events/remittances/maps/middle.htm.

changed over time. Prior to 1974, the overwhelming majority of migrants came from other Arab countries. In the 1970s and early 1980s, during the first oil boom, the Gulf states, with huge financial windfalls but small, young and poorly educated populations, sought to attract skilled workers from the United States and Europe as well as from the Middle East in order to fulfill their ambitious development plans. Resource-poor countries in the region, on the other hand, were eager to export workers, since their own labor markets were unable to meet the demands of an expanding population. They also saw in the remittances an important source of foreign exchange. The number of Arab migrants soared. Egyptians, Yemenis, and Palestinians in particular relocated to the Gulf during this period.

For workers, migration to the Gulf was very attractive. The salaries that prevailed there were much higher than in resource-poor states. Unskilled workers could earn almost thirty times more in Saudi Arabia than they could in rural Egypt. Skilled workers as well could anticipate their incomes to triple (Richards and Waterbury, 1990:377). Citizens of Gulf states on the other hand, who were the beneficiaries of generous welfare programs set up by governments following the rise in oil prices, were often reluctant to take on many of the available jobs.

Migration to the Gulf thus reduced pressures on the labor market in the resource-poor states in the Middle East. In a number of countries with large migrant worker populations, especially Egypt, Jordan, and Yemen, the departure of large numbers of laborers created new employment opportunities for less skilled workers and new entrants in their home countries. Simultaneously, as workers moved from rural to urban areas lured by new job opportunities, agricultural wages increased at unprecedented rates. In addition, the remittances that migrant workers sent back to their home countries stimulated local consumption. They were also, although to a lesser extent, invested in real estate and land, and to set up small businesses. Remittances proved to be an important source of foreign exchange used to finance imports (Richards and Waterbury, 1990:388–389).

The exact volume of remittances is difficult to estimate. Government figures reflect only those remittances that have come through official banking channels. However, in the majority of the developing world, including the Middle East, most of the money that migrants send back home is sent through informal channels. For example, a survey conducted by the International Labor Organization in the mid-1980s estimated that official figures captured only 13 percent of remittances workers were sending back to Sudan. If correct, this meant that rather than the $249 million that was officially recorded, more than $1.9 billion was coming annually into that country.

In the Middle East like in other parts of the developing world, informal channels of transferring money are an effective mechanism for people with low incomes who "may be outside the read of the formal financial sector and who transfer relatively small sums that are often subject to prohibitively high minimum charges at conventional institutions" (Buencamino and Gorbunov, 2002:1). These informal channels operate, often very openly, parallel to the official banking sector. Today, there are two large systems in operation worldwide: the *hawala*, which originated in South Asia, and the *fe-ch'ien*, which originated in China. The *hawala* system, in which money is transferred through a network of brokers, is widely used in the Middle East as well as in parts of Africa and Asia. Money transferred through informal channels likely amounts to anywhere from $100 billion to $300 billion annually (Buencamino and Gorbunov, 2002:2). By 2006, more than $40 billion were remitted to the Middle East annually.

During the latter part of the 1970s, the number of Arab migrants in the Gulf began to decline while the number of those coming from Asia, especially India, Pakistan, and Sri Lanka, increased. Governments in the Gulf states came to prefer non-Arab migrants, whom they saw as less politically troublesome and less likely to stay permanently. Moreover, as the major construction projects funded by the oil boom were completed, demand for unskilled workers who tended to come from Arab countries eased.

After oil prices fell in 1982, workers were increasingly recruited from Asia rather than the Middle East. During this period, more women began migrating to the Gulf area, especially from the Philippines, Bangladesh, and Sri

Table 7.5 Official Remittances in Selected Countries During the First Oil Boom (US$ millions)

	1973	1976	1979	1982
Egypt	123.0	842.0	2,269.0	2,481.0
Jordan	55.4	401.8	509.0	932.9
Morocco	211.0	499.0	891.0	840.0
Sudan	6.3	36.8	115.7	107.1
Tunisia	91.0	128.0	271.0	361.0

Source: International Fund for Agricultural Development, www.ifad.org/events/remittances/maps/middle.htm.

Table 7.6 Official Remittances, 2006

	US$ (millions)	Percentage of GDP
Algeria	5,399	4.7
Egypt	3,637	3.4
Iran	2,001	0.9
Iraq	3,238	n.a.
Jordan	2,681	18.9
Lebanon	5,723	25.2
Libya	134	0.3
Morocco	6,116	10.7
Palestinian Authority	1,225	30.2
Sudan	769	2.0
Syria	699	2.0
Tunisia	1,559	5.1
Yemen	821	4.3

Source: International Fund for Agricultural Development, www.ifad.org/events/remittances/maps/middle.htm.
Note: n.a. indicates data not available.

Lanka, to work primarily as domestic workers. As we will see later on in this chapter, the rise in oil prices during the first decade of the twenty-first century once again promoted an explosion of development projects in the Gulf, generating an unprecedented construction boom that again increased the demand for foreign workers in the Gulf Cooperation Council (GCC) states.

Foreign workers have also been migrating in increasing numbers to Israel. Initially, after the 1967 war, Palestinians from the Occupied Territories began working in Israel, primarily as day laborers. By 1986 they composed about 7 percent of the labor force (Baldwin-Edwards, 2005). After the first Palestinian intifada in 1987, Israel began recruiting foreign workers. This trend accelerated in the 1990s. By 2003 foreign workers, primarily from Romania, Thailand, and the Philippines, made up more than 13 percent of the labor force. They were employed in agriculture, nursing and domestic services, as well as construction. There were also illegal immigrants, mostly from West Africa, South America, and Eastern Europe, working in housekeeping, childcare, and the food services industry (Baldwin-Edwards, 2005).

Although labor migration had a number of positive ripple effects in the sending countries, it also had a number of negative consequences. Two in particular proved significant for the sending countries' economies. The first was the brain drain that accompanied labor migration. Many skilled workers and professionals left their countries in search of better employment opportunities first in the Gulf and then toward the end of the twentieth century, increasingly in Western Europe and the United States. This meant that businesses in the sending countries faced a shortage of personnel with appropriate expertise. By the late 1990s, this problem became especially acute in a number of Maghreb countries and especially in Morocco.

The second negative consequence of labor migration was the large-scale return of migrants during economic downturns and in moments of political turmoil. In those circumstances, not only did returning workers flood local labor markets, thus contributing to the rise of unemployment rates, but also their return signaled a decrease in the value of remittances that were a critical source of sending countries' foreign exchange (Yousef, 2005). The difficulties that could be generated by the return of migrant labor to their home countries was brought to stark relief during the 1991 Gulf War when 800,000 Yemeni workers were expelled from GCC states and primarily Saudi Arabia; 700,000 Egyptians went home from Iraq, Kuwait, and Jordan; and 200,000 Jordanians and 150,000 Palestinians returned from working in the Gulf. This sudden influx of workers put tremendous strain on their home labor markets (Baldwin-Edwards, 2005:5).

Economic Crisis and Structural Adjustment

In the 1980s most countries in the Middle East and North Africa experienced deep economic crises. In response they turned to the IMF and the World Bank for financial assistance. These organizations, however, were willing to offer assistance only if far-reaching structural adjustment programs were implemented. The international financial institutions (IFIs) subscribed to the increasingly dominant neoliberal analysis that identified state involvement in the economy as the primary reason much of the developing world, including the Middle East, faced such profound economic difficulties in the 1980s.

Structural adjustment programs, therefore, emphasized limiting that involvement and allowing the unencumbered functioning of markets. Often dubbed the "Washington Consensus," structural adjustment policies had a number of common features. They emphasized reducing public expenditures, liberalizing the trade regimes, encouraging foreign direct investment (FDI), and the privatization of state-owned enterprises (Williamson, 1990).

These economic changes and the belt-tightening measures, including the slashing of consumer subsidies, meant that the relationship between the state and society had to be fundamentally renegotiated. The state would no longer provide employment or subsidies, and market forces would now determine the allocation of resources in the economy. It did not take long for those negatively affected by these changes to make their opposition to these new economic policies heard. Across the region bread riots erupted: Egypt in January 1977, Morocco in January 1984, Tunisia in January 1984, Sudan in March 1985, Algeria in October 1988, and Jordan in April 1989.

Most states in the Middle East agreed that reforming their economies was essential if growth was to resume and if the region's states were to become more competitive in the increasingly globalized world economy. However, their record of reform implementation has been decidedly mixed. Although most have succeed in stabilizing their macroeconomic situation, structural and institutional reforms have proven to be much more difficult to implement, and in many countries they remained largely on the drawing boards.

During the initial phase of structural adjustment reforms in the late 1980s and in the 1990s, the progress of institutional reforms was slow as governments concentrated their efforts primarily on privatizing public sector enterprises and cutting government expenditures (Alissa, 2007). By the beginning of the twenty-first century, both international financial institutions as well as Middle East governments came to increasingly recognize that sustained economic growth was unlikely without significant reforms of institutions indispensable to the functioning of a market economy. As issues of good governance took center stage, the region's governments increasingly began to focus on reforming the judiciary, corporate governance, and tax codes, among others.

Despite two decades of reforms, most economies in the Middle East remain dominated by the state. Furthermore, although a number of countries have achieved impressive growth rates, economic recovery has not benefited all social strata. On the contrary, one of the characteristics of this economic recovery has been the anemic job growth. The Middle East continues to have the highest unemployment rates in the world, hovering over 15 percent in 2006. However, in some countries, especially Algeria, Morocco, and Djibouti, unemployment levels are closer to 20 percent and are even higher in Iraq, the Gaza Strip, and the West Bank (World Bank, 2006:6). Unemployment has been an especially acute problem among better-educated young people.

In many countries economic growth rates have not kept up with population growth, resulting in lower GDP per capita. For instance, the per capita

GDP in Saudi Arabia fell from $22,634 in 1980 to just over $12,000 in 2000 (Alissa, 2007). With high unemployment rates, the number of people living in poverty has increased in many countries. At the same time, social inequalities have grown. Although fertility rates in the region have fallen significantly since the 1950s, from 6.9 children per woman to 3 per woman in 2007, the Middle East trails only sub-Saharan Africa in the rate of population growth, making generating sufficient employment opportunities that much more challenging. In Egypt, for instance, an estimated 500,000 people enter the workforce on an annual basis (Radwan, 2002).

As happened during the first wave of economic reforms in the late 1970s and in the 1980s, during this second phase of implementing structural adjustment policies, the growing social inequalities and high unemployment levels have contributed to rising social tensions. Although the largest demonstrations have focused on expressing solidarity with the Palestinians, protesting the US-led invasion of Iraq, and demanding political accountability and democracy, demonstrations that focused more explicitly on economic issues have also occurred—for example, in August 1996, Jordanians protested the lifting of wheat subsidies (Andoni and Schwedler, 1996). Egypt has also experienced two waves of massive labor unrest. The first in the late 1990s when over 170 workers' protests took place (Paczynska, 2006). The second, even larger wave of workers' strikes and demonstrations occurred in 2006 and 2007 (Beinin and el-Hamalawy, 2007).

Despite renewed efforts on the part of many Middle Eastern governments to attract FDI, the results have been mixed. Although capital flows to the region have grown, the Middle East continues to lag behind other developing countries. FDI flows to Egypt have been increasing, reaching $10 billion in 2006, as have inflows into Sudan. In the former, investments have primarily poured into non-oil-related projects, whereas in the latter, most of the new investments have been channeled toward developing the petroleum industry.

Additionally, a number of large-scale privatization projects in the early years of the twenty-first century, such as the telecommunications companies' sale in Jordan and Turkey, encouraged the entry of foreign investors into the region. Likewise, FDI has increased to the Gulf countries and Turkey, reaching $60 billion in 2006, a 44 percent increase over the previous year. In particular, the high oil prices have attracted FDI in the hydrocarbons industries. At the same time, efforts by the Gulf petroleum producers to begin diversifying their economies brought new foreign investments into the manufacturing sector. In response to the high oil prices, a number of Gulf countries, especially Kuwait, have begun to invest abroad.

One consequence of structural adjustment programs has been the expansion of the already large informal sector of the economy. Economic growth that does not generate sufficient employment opportunities or improved

Table 7.7 GDP Growth in the Middle East, Various Years (percentage)

	2004	2005	2006	2007
Middle East–North Africa	5.6	6.0	5.6	5.2
Resource-poor/labor abundant	4.8	4.0	5.4	5.4
Egypt	4.2	4.9	5.5	5.8
Jordan	7.7	7.2	6.0	6.0
Lebanon	6.3	1.0	—	—
Morocco	4.2	1.5	5.0	4.0
Tunisia	5.8	5.0	5.5	5.5
Resource-rich/labor-abundant	4.7	5.5	5.3	5.1
Algeria	5.2	5.5	5.7	5.4
Iran	4.8	5.9	5.5	5.3
Syria	3.6	4.0	4.0	4.0
Yemen	2.6	3.8	3.5	3.0
Resource rich/labor importing	6.5	7.2	5.8	5.3
Bahrain	5.4	6.9	7.0	6.8
Kuwait	6.2	8.5	6.2	5.0
Libya	9.3	8.5	—	—
Oman	3.1	4.1	6.0	5.5
Qatar	9.9	8.8	8.0	7.5
Saudi Arabia	5.2	6.5	5.1	4.8
United Arab Emirates	8.5	8.0	6.5	6.0

Source: World Bank, *Economic Developments and Prospects 2006: Financial Markets in a New Age of Oil* (Washington, DC: World Bank, 2006), p. 33.

income distribution does not reduce the size of the informal sector. In much of the developing world, including the Middle East, structural adjustment policies and the cutbacks in public sector employment were not accompanied by a sufficient expansion of the private sector to compensate for the job losses. Often business regulations have discouraged the formal private sector from investing in labor-intensive production, focusing instead on establishing capital-intensive manufacturing, which is unable to absorb sufficient numbers of job-seekers. Furthermore, the reduction of many consumer subsidies meant that low-income families had to find new means of supplementing their formal incomes. In the Middle East, the employment situation was further complicated by the high population growth rates and the large number of first-time workers who entered the job market annually, the increased migration from rural to urban areas, and the growing number of women entering the labor market. As one study estimated, in 2004 "non-agricultural employment share of the informal workforce" was 78 percent in Africa, 57 percent in Latin America and the Caribbean, and 45–85 percent in Asia

Table 7.8 Size of the Informal Economy as a Percentage of GDP, Various Years

Country	1990/2000	2001/2002	2002/2003
Algeria	34.1	35.0	35.6
Egypt	35.1	36.0	36.9
Iran	18.9	19.4	19.9
Israel	21.9	22.8	23.9
Jordan	19.4	20.5	21.6
Kuwait	20.1	20.7	21.6
Lebanon	34.1	35.6	36.2
Mauritania	36.1	37.2	38.0
Morocco	36.4	37.1	37.9
Oman	18.9	19.4	19.8
Saudi Arabia	18.4	19.1	19.7
Syria	19.3	20.4	21.6
Tunisia	38.4	39.1	39.9
Turkey	32.1	33.2	34.3
United Arab Emirates	26.4	27.1	27.8
Yemen	27.4	28.4	29.1

Source: Data from Friedrich Schneider, "The Size of the Shadow Economies of 145 Countries all over the World: First Results over the Period 1999 to 2003," Discussion Paper No. 1431 (Bonn, Germany: Institute for the Study of Labor, December 2004).

(Becker, 2004:8). In the Middle East, the informal sector accounts for close to 40 percent of GDP in some cases and over 20 percent in nearly all countries in the region. Most of activities performed within the informal economy are legal, although they are performed outside of the formal business, tax, and labor regulations. Informal production tends to be small-scale and labor intensive, offers lower wages than does the formal sector, and provides no social security coverage.

Trade

Although petroleum products dominate the region's exports, other goods and services are also produced and sold by the region's countries. Egypt's exports, while dominated by petroleum, are more diversified than that of the Gulf countries. It also exports textiles, clothing, and to a lesser extent steel, chemicals and fertilizers, and food products. The United States has been Egypt's main trading partner, and the volume of Egyptian exports to the United States has been growing. Thanks to the Qualifying Industrial Zone (QIZ) protocol, in which Egypt began participating in 2005, companies located in these zones have gained access to the US market free of tariffs and nontariff barriers if the products contain inputs produced in Israel. Jordanian and Moroccan exports have been highly dependent on potash. Since the late 1980s, however, both have expanded manufacturing exports. Like Egypt, Jordan has also gained duty-free access to the US market for products that contain inputs made in Israel through the QIZ protocol of 1996.

Since 1998, ten such zones have been designated in Egypt and 13 in Jordan. As a result, Jordanian and Egyptian exports to the United States have grown significantly. Jordanian exports increased from $31 million in 1999 to $1.1 billion in 2004, while Egyptian exports grew from about $1.3 billion in 2004 to over $2 billion in 2006. The existence of QIZ meant that the ending of the Multifiber Agreement in 2005 had a less dramatic impact on Egypt's textile exports. The Multifiber Agreement gave Egypt, Morocco, and Tunisia textile exports privileged access to European markets. Tunisia and especially Morocco, on the other hand, have been hit hard by the Agreement's expiration, especially since it coincided with the slow-down of European economies (World Bank, 2006:18–19).

Syria, in addition to cotton and textiles, has been exporting fruits and vegetables, meat and live animals, petroleum products, and machinery. Tunisia's exports are dominated by agricultural commodities, phosphate, and iron as well as textiles and light manufacturing. Lebanon, since the end of its devastating civil war in 1990, has concentrated on rebuilding its financial services sector and the tourist industry. It exports agricultural products, prepared foodstuffs, textiles, and machinery. In most non-oil-dependent states, imports exceed exports, leading to an adverse balance of trade. Israel has the most diversified exports. These include agricultural commodities, chemicals, telecommunications and equipment, weapons, and precious stones.

Regional trade in the Middle East and North Africa has been small. Establishing trading relationships has been difficult because most states in the region produce similar commodities in competition with one another. Since the late 1980s, however, as most countries of the region began implementing economic reforms and opened their markets to international competition, there has been a renewed effort to improve regional economic cooperation and to establish new trading relationships with countries outside the region. In addition to the GCC, the Arab Maghreb Union was created in 1989 by Algeria, Libya, Mauritania, Morocco, and Tunisia. The Aghadir trade agreement signed in 2004 by Egypt, Tunisia, Morocco, and Jordan is expected to increase the volume of trade between these four countries. Egypt is also negotiating free-trade agreements with Russia, China, and Turkey. In 2005 the Greater Arab Free Trade Area (GAFTA) was established. This project, initiated at the Arab League Summit in Amman, Jordan, in 1997, aims to create an Arab economic bloc that will allow the region to more effectively compete internationally.

The Euro-Mediterranean Free Trade Area is anticipated to be in place by 2010, although the initial bilateral agreements between Middle Eastern and European countries have not produced the anticipated increases in the volume of trade. Eventually this free-trade area will cover the European Union, the European Free Trade Association (EFTA), the EU customs unions with third states, the EU candidate states, and partners in the Barcelona process to establish the free-trade area. Finally, a new US plan proposed in 2003 is expected to expand economic ties with the region through trade and investment framework agreements, bilateral investment treaties, and free trade agreements, with the goal of establishing a US–Middle East free trade area by 2013. To date, the United States has signed free-trade agreements with Israel (1985), Jordan (2000), Morocco (2005), and Bahrain (2006). Talks between the United States and Oman concluded in 2005 and are ongoing with the United Arab Emirates (UAE). As of 2007 Israel, Jordan, Morocco, Bahrain, Egypt, Tunisia, Oman, Kuwait, the UAE, Qatar, Saudi Arabia, and Turkey are members of the World Trade Organization (WTO). Lebanon, Algeria, Yemen, Libya, Iraq, and Iran were negotiating for full membership. Syria has also expressed an interest in joining the organization.

Although the volume of trade has increased, the Arab world continues to play a minor role in global trade, accounting in 2005 for only 4 percent of the world's total. Oil accounted for 90 percent of exports from the region.

Oil producers are primarily members of the GCC: Bahrain, Kuwait, Oman, Qatar, Saudi Arabia, and United Arab Emirates, as well as Yemen, Libya, Egypt, and Algeria. Iraq, historically an important oil producer, has since the April 2003 US invasion struggled to increase production, which has been hampered by the precarious security situation. Although in recent years the oil-producing countries have sought to diversify their economies, they remain highly dependent on oil exports. In 2006 in Iran, Kuwait, and Saudi Arabia, oil accounted for 90 percent of the countries' exports, and in Algeria for 98 percent. Most oil exporters also sell natural gas on the world markets.

Since 2000, trading partners of the Gulf states have significantly changed. Most significant, the importance of the United States has declined. Most of the Gulf countries have expanded their exports to China, Japan, South Korea, Taiwan, and India. Trade between the Gulf and Asia doubled between 2000 and 2005, reaching $240 billion, and China has begun increasing its investments in the region. Since 1993 China has become a net importer of oil, most of it coming from the Middle East. It is interested in securing oil deliveries and promoting its own oil-service products. At the same time, various refineries, port development projects, and oil-tank farms in China are being funded and built by Dubai, Kuwait, and Saudi Arabia. In July 2004 China and the GCC began negotiations on a China–Gulf Cooperation Council free-trade zone. India-GCC non-oil trade reached $19.48 billion in 2005–2006, and in 2007 they were close to signing a free-trade agreement.

Table 7.9 Middle East Exports by Destination (percentage)

| Country | Year | Developed Economies | | | Developing Economies | | | | |
		Europe	United States	Japan	Africa	Latin America	East/South Asia	Western Asia	Other[a]
Algeria	1990	70.2	19.2	0.9	2.5	2.1	0.6	1.7	2.8
	2000	63.8	15.7	0.1	1.4	8.2	0.8	6.3	3.7
	2005	54.4	22.6	0.1	2.0	6.6	2.3	3.9	8.1
Egypt	1990	43.3	8.6	2.7	3.7	0.0	6.9	8.2	26.6
	2000	48.0	12.8	2.0	4.1	0.9	9.7	11.2	11.3
	2005	38.2	13.0	0.7	7.0	1.2	8.1	18.6	13.2
Iran	1990	50.0	1.5	20.7	—	4.4	10.9	3.1	9.4
	2000	26.8	0.6	18.1	6.0	0.2	30.0	4.2	14.1
	2005	23.5	0.3	16.9	5.5	0.0	28.4	8.9	16.5
Israel	1990	39.5	28.8	7.3	1.3	2.6	8.6	0.7	11.2
	2000	30.2	36.8	2.6	1.5	2.8	15.2	1.5	9.4
	2005	31.2	36.5	1.9	1.5	3.1	15.5	2.4	7.9
Jordan	1990	4.1	0.6	2.1	8.1	0.1	40.3	40.9	3.8
	2000	4.0	4.9	1.0	8.7	0.4	32.9	39.0	9.1
	2005	3.4	26.2	0.6	6.4	0.3	12.5	38.2	12.4
Kuwait	1990	23.5	6.8	18.6	1.8	1.9	29.2	6.0	12.2
	2000	13.9	14.4	24.1	1.0	0.5	42.8	2.7	0.6
	2005	10.5	11.9	19.7	0.9	0.2	52.7	3.4	0.7
Morocco	1990	62.8	1.8	3.6	6.2	1.3	7.3	4.9	12.1
	2000	73.2	3.4	3.8	3.7	1.8	6.3	2.1	5.7
	2005	70.0	2.6	1.1	4.3	3.5	7.1	2.8	8.6
Saudi Arabia	1990	18.4	24.0	19.0	4.0	3.3	19.1	9.4	2.8
	2000	17.9	17.4	17.3	5.5	1.5	31.8	6.8	1.8
	2005	16.2	16.8	16.5	3.3	1.1	35.4	8.8	1.9
Sudan	1990	39.0	2.8	6.0	7.1	0.0	24.9	10.5	9.7
	2000	10.5	0.1	17.2	2.8	0.7	58.4	9.5	0.8
	2005	2.7	0.3	12.0	3.0	0.3	73.8	6.3	1.6
Syria	1990	42.4	0.9	0.1	2.8	0.0	0.5	18.6	34.7
	2000	62.7	3.0	0.3	2.7	0.1	1.7	24.2	5.3
	2005	32.1	3.1	0.1	10.1	0.6	0.9	51.5	1.6
Tunisia	1990	77.7	0.9	0.3	9.5	0.9	4.1	3.5	3.1
	2000	79.4	0.7	0.2	8.3	1.1	3.4	2.5	4.4
	2005	80.5	0.9	0.2	9.0	0.7	2.5	2.1	4.1
Turkey	1990	59.0	7.2	1.8	5.6	0.3	7.7	8.7	9.7
	2000	55.5	11.3	0.5	4.9	1.0	3.7	4.8	18.3
	2005	53.4	6.7	0.3	4.9	0.9	3.8	9.5	20.5
United Arab Emirates	1990	9.5	4.0	37.7	2.7	0.5	25.2	5.0	15.4
	2000	5.2	2.2	33.0	3.8	0.2	32.7	7.0	15.9
	2005	11.7	1.5	24.5	3.5	0.1	35.4	7.2	16.1

Source: UNCTAD, 2006.
Note: a. Other indicates other developed economies and transitional economies.

Table 7.10 Middle East Imports by Origin (percentage)

| Country | Year | Developed Economies | | | Developing Economies | | | | |
		Europe	United States	Japan	Africa	Latin America	East/South Asia	Western Asia	Other[a]
Algeria	1990	67.6	11.6	4.6	1.8	2.6	1.4	2.5	7.9
	2000	59.8	11.6	3.0	2.1	2.9	6.3	4.5	9.8
	2005	61.4	5.4	2.5	2.2	4.8	11.2	6.3	6.2
Egypt	1990	48.7	14.0	3.7	1.4	2.9	8.6	2.9	17.8
	2000	39.3	16.9	3.7	1.6	3.1	14.6	6.9	13.9
	2005	35.6	10.6	2.6	2.7	5.1	16.5	10.6	16.3
Iran	1990	53.1	0.3	10.3	—	3.7	8.0	9.7	14.9
	2000	40.4	0.7	4.8	1.5	6.7	17.2	10.5	18.2
	2005	42.3	0.2	3.4	0.6	3.3	22.3	14.5	13.4
Israel	1990	61.3	17.8	3.6	1.8	1.1	3.3	0.2	10.9
	2000	48.0	18.1	3.2	1.0	0.9	10.8	1.7	16.3
	2005	44.3	13.4	2.8	0.7	2.2	15.1	2.9	18.6
Jordan	1990	34.5	17.5	3.2	3.0	0.5	9.1	26.9	5.3
	2000	32.8	9.9	3.9	1.9	2.7	14.5	23.9	10.4
	2005	25.5	5.6	2.8	4.6	1.8	20.2	32.1	7.4
Kuwait	1990	37.9	10.9	11.4	0.1	1.0	14.1	2.5	22.1
	2000	34.2	12.1	8.7	1.4	1.5	20.3	18.1	3.7
	2005	36.1	14.1	8.4	0.7	1.8	18.0	16.7	4.2
Morocco	1990	52.8	5.5	1.6	6.6	2.3	3.2	10.4	17.6
	2000	58.4	5.6	1.7	4.6	3.2	8.7	10.4	7.4
	2005	51.7	3.4	1.8	5.4	4.3	11.5	10.1	11.8
Saudi Arabia	1990	43.5	6.2	2.9	21.1	1.9	8.8	0.6	15
	2000	33.3	3.9	2.7	20.9	1.7	14.5	1.2	21.8
	2005	33.7	4.2	1.9	21.2	6.7	14.0	2.6	15.7
Sudan	1990	42.8	3.6	3.9	16.2	0.1	9.5	19.5	4.4
	2000	33.2	1.3	2.3	5.6	1.5	31.1	18.2	6.8
	2005	17.9	1.9	5.1	8.1	2.8	33.2	22.8	8.2
Syria	1990	48.8	10.8	3.3	2.7	2.9	4.3	11.9	15.3
	2000	36.6	4.3	2.4	2.1	2.2	17.4	8.5	26.5
	2005	24.6	1.1	1.7	8.3	3.0	19.3	32.4	9.6
Tunisia	1990	68.0	4.9	1.6	5.4	2.5	4.4	3.8	9.4
	2000	72.4	4.6	2.0	6.5	1.6	4.7	3.6	4.6
	2005	70.2	2.5	1.6	6.4	2.4	6.3	4.1	6.5
Turkey	1990	47.5	9.9	4.8	5.8	2.4	7.9	10.1	11.6
	2000	52.4	7.2	3.0	5.0	1.2	10.2	3.3	17.7
	2005	46.0	4.6	2.7	5.2	1.7	17.0	2.7	20.1
United Arab Emirates	1990	34.9	9.1	14.2	0.5	1.0	24.8	8.6	6.9
	2000	38.8	7.9	9.6	1.0	0.7	30.9	6.9	4.2
	2005	35.1	9.4	5.4	1.6	1.3	36.1	6.6	4.5

Source: UNCTAD, 2006.

Note: a. Other indicates other developed economies and transitional economies.

■ The New Oil Boom

With oil prices reaching record levels—by mid-2008 hitting $139 per bar-rel for the first time—the oil economies of the Gulf region have been expe-riencing unprecedented growth rates. Unlike in previous periods of buoyant prices, the GCC states have been more careful about how they spend the windfall and are "building up liquidity through external reserves, oil stabi-lization funds, and paying down debt" (World Bank, 2006). They are also attempting to diversify their economies to ensure continued economic growth once oil reserves are depleted.

The high price of oil has spurred an unprecedented construction boom in the Gulf states that is fundamentally transforming that region. The addi-tional oil rents have allowed these states to begin to establish themselves as the regional finance, business, and tourist hub (World Bank, 2006). In order to realize these ambitions, huge development projects have been commis-sioned by governments and are transforming the Gulf coastline through rec-lamation projects and construction of whole new cities that will eventually accommodate hundreds of thousands of permanent residents and millions of tourists annually. Among the largest of these are the King Abdullah City in Saudi Arabia priced at US$26 billion, Blue City in Oman at $15 billion, and Lusail development in Qatar priced at $5 billion (Property World Middle East, 2005). Dubai, however, is leading the construction boom with an esti-mated $200 billion worth of projects underway. The biggest among these is the $9.5 billion theme park and World Palm Islands development; these two tourist sites will increase United Arab Emirates beachfront by over 160 per-cent. Dubai is also constructing what will be the world's tallest building once completed, the Burj Dubai. This half a mile tall tower will also house what will be the world's largest shopping mall of 12 million square feet (World Bank, 2006:46). Additionally, Dubai is developing free-trade zones, located mostly in desert areas, that with

> marketing and infrastructure, attract cutting-edge companies. There is Med-ina City, Internet City, Knowledge Village and plans for Dubai Outsource Zone, Dubai Tachno Park and Dubai Biotechnology and Research Park among others. There are no taxes, no customs, no restrictions on transferring funds, little red tape. Then, there is the rare combination of highly skilled workers and cheap laborers. (Shadid, 2006)

Others in the Gulf, in particular Qatar and Saudi Arabia, are also establish-ing such free trade zones to attract high-tech companies from abroad.

The boom in the Gulf, however, has exacerbated social tensions, leading to especially serious confrontations in Dubai, where foreign workers re-belled against working conditions. Similar protests have occurred in Kuwait, Saudi Arabia, Qatar, Bahrain, and Oman. In Dubai workers destroyed cars and construction equipment and broke windows in office buildings. In Kuwait, Bangladeshi workers stormed their own embassy to protest working conditions (British Broadcasting Corporation, April 24, 2005). In most of these states, an overwhelming majority of laborers working in the private sector, sometimes as high as 98 percent, are noncitizen migrant workers, primarily from Asia. These workers enjoy few legal protections, and reports of substandard housing, lack of potable water and sanitary facilities, hazardous work sites, and nonpayment of wages are common. Consequently, labor unrest has been increasingly common although vastly underreported.

The same high oil prices that have allowed the GCC states to experience high rates of economic growth have presented severe challenges to the resource-poor states in the Middle East. During the previous era of high oil prices, these resource-poor states also experienced economic expansion thanks to a number of mechanisms that allowed wealth generated in the Gulf to trickle through the rest of the region. Most important, the GCC states funneled financial aid to their resource-poor neighbors, and workers from the resource-poor states found employment in the Gulf countries, thus allowing them to send significant remittances back home. This time, however, these sources of funding have greatly diminished, although intraregional tourism continues to be a significant source of foreign exchange for the resource-poor countries. At the same time that financial inflows from the Gulf countries have diminished, the resource-poor countries are facing higher oil import bills. Jordan in particular has been hit hard by the increase in petroleum prices, since for years it benefited from access to cheap Iraqi oil during the UN-mandated Oil for Food Program.

■ Conflict and Regional Economies

The region has been highly conflict prone. Its geopolitical location has attracted foreign powers to intervene in local political dynamics. During the Cold War, the United States and the Soviet Union funneled military aid to the region, helping to fuel arms races. The establishment of the State of Israel in 1948 was followed by a number of wars with its Arab neighbors in 1956, 1967, 1973, and 1982, as well as the most recent 2006 Israeli invasion of Lebanon during its clash with Hizbullah. Additionally, a protracted and bloody conflict has been ongoing between Israel and the Palestinians, a conflict that has continued despite the signing of the Oslo Accords in 1993. Other recent conflicts that have erupted in the region include the war between Iran and Iraq; the 1990 Iraqi invasion of Kuwait and the US-led intervention that followed; the 2003 US-led invasion of Iraq; civil wars in Sudan, Lebanon, Yemen, Somalia, and Algeria; and the conflict between Morocco, Mauritania, and the Polisario independence movement over Western Sahara.

All these conflicts have had a profound impact on the economies of the states involved in these clashes and often reverberated through the economies of states not directly engaged in them.

One of the consequences of the high levels of conflict in the region coupled with the involvement of outside powers has been an extremely high level of militarization of the Middle East. Yahya M. Sadowski estimates that in the 1980s the Middle East was the world's largest arms market, importing at least $154 billion worth of weapons (Sadowski, 1993:1), siphoning money that could have been used for economic development. The militarization of the region thus affected the development prospects of all states involved in the arms races. Conflict has had an even more profound impact on those states that experienced long-term conflict and violence—in particular Lebanon, Sudan, the Gaza Strip and West Bank, Iraq, Yemen, and Algeria.

Algeria and Yemen had to address challenges stemming from civil conflicts while implementing structural adjustment programs. In other words, the challenge in both Algeria and Yemen was not only to undertake reconciliation and reconstruction, but also to implement reforms aimed at ensuring that market mechanisms rather than state planning determined the allocation of resources and that appropriate institutions indispensable to the functioning of a market economy were established.

Yemen has experienced conflict since the unification of North and South Yemen in May 1990. Four years of negotiations over new political arrangements followed, eventually collapsing into a civil war in May 1994. Although the fighting was over within a couple of months, other conflicts have simmered since then, making launching of an economic development program difficult. In particular, clashes between the central government in Sana'a and the Houthi group in the Saada governorate in the northern part of Yemen have caused serious damage to infrastructure in that part of the country. Although by 2007 a truce appeared likely and the government pledged to finance the governorate's reconstruction, the slow pace of structural reform implementation, low growth rates, and high inflation rates contributed to social tensions and to repeated popular protests, especially in the southern part of the country (World Bank Group Sana' Office, 2007:1–2). Although the new effort to implement economic reforms in 2006 allowed Yemen to be reinstated to the Threshold Program of the Millennium Challenge Account and thus tap into additional financial assistance, it continues to face development obstacles. Among the most difficult of these is the depletion of its oil resource and water scarcity. The World Bank estimates that "at current rates of crude oil production and domestic consumption Yemen could be a net importer by 2015 and will cease production in 2018" (World Bank Group Sana'a Office, 2007:10).

Between 1992 and 1998, Algeria experienced what was essentially a civil war which killed at least 100,000 people according to official figures,

Workers lay cut stones in the
sa'ila (drainage canal) in the
old city of Sana'a, Yemen. The
channel directs water outside of
the city during the wet seasons
and is used as a thoroughfare
for cars and pedestrians during
the rest of the year.

although other sources put the figure even higher (International Crisis Group, 2001). The conflict erupted after the cancellation of parliamentary elections that the Islamic Salvation Front was poised to win. Although in 1999 it appeared that the conflict was over, violence continued to plague the country, as did popular dissatisfaction with the regime. In December 2007 two bombs exploded in Algiers, one close to the Constitutional Court, the other next to the UN headquarters, casting doubt on the ability of the Algerian government to ensure long-term stability.

Despite the violence, the hydrocarbon industry has remained attractive to foreign direct investors. The main reason why the sector has remained largely immune to the political carnage is its location far from the main urban centers in the Saharan desert. However, although the hydrocarbon industry has maintained its production levels and accounts for 97 percent of Algeria's foreign export earnings, the rest of the economy has felt the aftershocks of the civil war (International Crisis Group, 2001). Public and private investment in other sectors of the economy has remained stagnant for years and the unemployment levels have been extremely high.

As a recent IMF study concluded, although Algeria's structural reforms have focused on reducing the role of the state in the economy through privatization of the public sector and institutional reforms, the high levels of violence have had a deep and negative impact on employment generation, a challenge unique to countries experiencing violent conflict during the transition from a planned to a market economy (Kpadar, 2007). In response to the persistent economic problems and taking advantage of the high oil prices, Algeria launched a new $60 billion, five-year development program in 2005 with the goal of diversifying the economy and making it less dependent on the fluctuations on the petroleum markets. However, increasing foreign tourism has proven to be difficult in light of the persistent violence (OECD, 2007).

Before civil war erupted in 1975, Lebanon with its free-market, liberal economy was the banking center of the Middle East. In the years before the eruption of the civil war, it enjoyed steady growth rates and rising per capita incomes. Tourism, transit trade, services, and workers' remittances were all important sources of foreign exchange. However, this growth was highly uneven and socioeconomic disparities were deep. The civil war that lasted from 1975 to 1989 devastated the country. Although the exact numbers are not known, it is estimated that as a result of the initial years of civil war, 1975–1976, 600,000 to 900,000 people fled the country. Even though some began returning following the cessation of hostilities and the beginning of the postwar reconstruction program, the reoccurring violence, most recently in 2006 and 2007, have reversed this inward flow.

At least 100,000 people were killed during the sixteen years of fighting. Along with its human toll, the civil war destroyed infrastructure, especially in Beirut. Industrial production declined and the tourist sector was essentially destroyed. The conflict also sparked high inflation rates and led to massive capital flight and to persistent fiscal and monetary instability. The war also destroyed state institutions indispensable to the management of public policies. As the state disintegrated, rival militias established parallel institutions for tax collection, administration, and production and frequently operated their own ports, airports, and services (Adwan, 2004).

The Taif Agreement was signed at the end of the civil conflict and the beginning of the reconstruction effort. The top priorities were the rebuilding of the devastated city of Beirut and the reconstruction of Southern Lebanon, Mount Lebanon, and public institutions and infrastructure. The results of these efforts, however, were mixed. The process quickly became mired in accusations of corruption, nepotism, mismanagement, and waste. Furthermore, the presence of the Syrian army on Lebanese territory as well as a large number of Syrian migrant workers further complicated and politicized the reconstruction effort. Nonetheless, the government made significant progress in rebuilding the country's infrastructure. Beirut city center revitalization, spearheaded by Rafik Hariri, a billionaire businessman and later Lebanon' prime minister, was especially successful. Hariri's assassination in February 2005, however, underscored how volatile the political situation in Lebanon continued to be.

Nonetheless, by the time Syrian troops departed in April 2005, the Lebanese economy was growing at a healthy rate, and the tourist, trade, and banking sectors were again the principal agents of growth. Once again, however, conflict and violence brought the economy to a standstill when in the summer of 2006 the Israeli army clashed with Hizbullah militia in a month-long conflict. The Israeli air raids in response to Hizbullah's capture of Israeli soldiers caused widespread damage of the Lebanese infrastructure, roads, bridges, air and sea ports, and the housing stocks. The tourist sector, one of the most important sources of income, was once again devastated, as was agricultural and industrial production. The conflict also caused extensive environmental damage, and the estimates of the direct and indirect costs of this round of conflict are estimated at between $US10 billion and $US15 billion (UNEP, 2007a).

Another country whose economic development has been deeply shaped by conflict is Sudan. Since achieving independence from Britain in 1956, Sudan has experienced internal conflict almost continuously, with the exception of a fragile peace that held between 1972 and 1983. As a result of the civil war, more than five million Sudanese have been displaced and agricultural production has been brought to nearly a standstill in large parts of the country. Although a peace agreement was signed between the Sudanese government and the Sudan People's Liberation Army in January 2005, ostensibly ending the conflict between the northern and southern parts of the country, the long-simmering tensions in the Darfur region in the western areas of Sudan erupted in a new civil war in 2003.

Although the economy has been growing at a fast rate since January 2005, primarily due to the expanding oil industry and the agricultural sector, the decades of conflict have meant that the Sudanese economy still faces a number of challenges. Among these are land degradation and deforestation, which together with climate change pose a challenge to ensuring long-term food security and sustainable development (UNEP, 2007b:6). These environmental issues have also contributed to the persistence of tension and violence in Sudan through competition over land and other natural resources, such as the recently discovered oil and gas reserves, timber, and water.

Conflict has also had a devastating effect on the Palestinian and the Iraqi economies. Ironically, since the signing of the Oslo Accords between Israel and the Palestinian Authority in 1994, the economic situation in the Palestinian Territories has deteriorated significantly. The signing of the accords was followed by increasing fragmentation of the Palestinian territories as Israel constructed checkpoints, barriers, and settler roads within the Gaza Strip and the West Bank. Sara Roy estimates that since 1994, these have cost the Palestinian economy 5 percent annually (Roy, 2006). A key reason for this economic deterioration has been the Israeli policy of closure, which bars Palestinian workers from entering Israel as day laborers and stops regular trade flows across the border. Because of the economic integration of the Israeli and Palestinian economies that followed the 1967 war, the closures have caused massive disruption of the Palestinian economy, leading to extremely high unemployment and poverty rates.

Since the beginning of the second intifada in 2000, economic conditions in the Palestinian territories have deteriorated further and territorial fragmentation has intensified. In 2004 for instance, more than 700 Israeli checkpoints divided Palestinian territories and an estimated 60 percent of Palestinians were living below the poverty line (Arab Human Development Report, 2005). The extensive demolition of Palestinian houses, office buildings, and factories, and the bulldozing of cultivated farm areas by the Israeli army have significantly disrupted social and economic life in Palestinian territories.

The economic situation in the Gaza Strip deteriorated further even following the Israeli disengagement in August 2005. Gaza Strip Economic Development Strategy designed by the Palestinian Authority at that time sought to launch a sustainable economic development program in the area. However, the goals of the strategy remain unfulfilled, and Gaza is experiencing an "acute and debilitating decline marked by unprecedented levels of poverty, unemployment, loss of trade, and social deterioration especially with regard to delivery of health and educational services" (Roy, 2006).

The situation has been especially dire since the Hamas victory in Legislative Council elections in 2006. Following the formation of the Hamas-led government, aid from international donors was suspended and Israel began withholding Palestinian tax revenue (a policy suspended in June 2007), leading to a severe fiscal crisis in the Palestinian territories. Palestinian trade levels in 2006 were 30 percent below what they were in 1996 and 49 percent lower than in 1999. This was particularly devastating since trade represents about 85 to 90 percent of Palestinian GDP. As a study by the World Bank noted, since the Israeli departure from the Gaza Strip,

> with the exception of cement and gravel, Gazans have only a single entry and exit point at the Karni/Al-Mountar border crossing for the export and import of all goods needed to sustain an economy of nearly 1.5 million. Karni was closed a majority of the time in 2006. On average only some 20 trucks crossed the border on a daily basis. (World Bank Technical Team, 2007)

The uncertainty generated by the closures, furthermore, has made the private sector extremely reluctant to invest, thus adding to the economic contraction. As a result of the economic crisis, unemployment in Gaza and the West Bank has hovered around 30 percent in 2007, although among the young it is estimated to be much higher (UNRWA, 2007). In addition to the almost complete suspension of trade, the agricultural and industrial sectors have been devastated, public investment in infrastructure has nearly ceased, and large amounts of capital have fled abroad. Consequently, the economy is increasingly relying on foreign aid, borrowing, and workers' remittances (World Bank, 2007).

Iraq's economic development has also been profoundly affected by conflict. First came the war with Iran, which began in 1980, followed by the 1991

Gulf War when an international coalition led by the United States ousted Iraq from Kuwait. Next came a period of economic sanctions imposed by the United Nations, followed by the 2003 US-led invasion. The cumulative effects of these years of war and sanctions have reduced what in 1980 had been a middle-income country with abundant natural resources, well-developed infrastructure, a highly educated workforce, and a widely admired health-care system, to a poor, violence-plagued one. In 1980 the per capita income was around $3,600, with oil dominating exports, an expanding public sector, and a large agricultural sector (World Bank, 2007). After an economically draining conflict with Iran when Iraq's oil exports plummeted, Iraq's infrastructure was devastated by allied bombing in 1991, followed by years of UN sanctions that contributed to the gradual contraction of the public sector and the expansion of the private informal sector. At the same time, Iraq's foreign debt increased at a brisk rate, reaching $80 billion by 1988 and by 2003 hovering around $130 billion (Pan, 2003). Shortly before 2003, one report estimated that

> industry has ceased to exist and unemployment may be as high as 50 percent. The agricultural sector is in complete disarray, leaving more than 60 percent of the population to rely on the UN Oil for Food program [for basic needs]. About 40 percent of the nation's children are suffering from malnutrition. (Parker and Moore, 2007)

The US-led invasion of Iraq did not lead to the turnaround of the economy that was anticipated once hostilities ceased. The initial period following the invasion witnessed the large-scale looting and destruction not just of infrastructure but also of documents from various ministries. The de-Baathification of public administration ordered by the coalitional Provisional Authority further depleted experienced civil servant ranks. Following the dismantling of the old state structures, however, the US-led coalition found it difficult to create new administrative institutions and to restore basic infrastructure (Arab Human Development Report, 2004). One of the main assumptions the coalition made following the invasion was that the private sector would help jump-start the Iraqi economy. Without security, however, bringing in investors has proven to be difficult. The only part of the economy that has expanded since the invasion is the informal economy. Indeed as one recent study finds, "militias supporting or opposing the Iraqi government—not the government itself—control import supply chains and, indeed, regulate whole sectors of the Iraqi economy" (Parker and Moore, 2007).

Furthermore, the long periods of conflict and sanctions have affected the availability of skilled workers in Iraq. During the last three decades, public infrastructure and education has deteriorated; literacy levels among women, for example, have plummeted from 75 percent in 1987 to 25 percent by 2007. As a consequence of inflation, food shortages, and insecurity, people came to rely on the informal market and on smuggling of goods across

Palestinian women have found that small-scale economic
activities such as sewing and embroidery allow them to earn
much-needed money while preserving a part of their culture.

international borders for survival. One study estimates that the informal
sector accounted for 65 percent of Iraqi GDP by 2005 (Looney, 2006:999).

Additionally, because of the continuing violence, large numbers of Iraqis,
many of whom are highly educated professionals, have fled the country. The
UN estimates that the violence in Iraq has displaced more than 4.4 million
Iraqis or about 15 percent of the population. Some 2.2 million of them have
become internally displaced, while 2.2 million have fled the country to
Syria and Jordan as well as Iran, Egypt, Lebanon, Yemen, and Turkey. By
2007 the continuing violence was forcing an average of 60,000 people a
month to leave their homes. The growing number of Iraqi refugees is exporting economic problems from Iraq to neighboring countries and in particular to Jordan and Syria (UNHCR, 2008). In the early months after the
invasion, many of those fleeing the violence were members of the middle
class and skilled professionals. As the conflict has dragged on, those seeking to escape the conflict have had fewer assets they could draw on to sustain themselves in exile. Numbers of Iraqi refugees have been swelling in
urban areas of neighboring countries (Peteet, 2007). Many of these refugees,
with shrinking savings, "are now living on the margins of society in the host
countries, and their overall condition is deteriorating. Most are restricted from
obtaining gainful employment, and have limited access to services" (Mokbel,
2007). Children's education has been especially hard hit with close to 30 percent of Iraqi children in Syria unable to attend school. As the numbers of

refugees have swelled in the main destination countries, putting pressure on Syrian and Jordanian economies, straining their infrastructure, and adding to political tensions, both countries' governments have made it increasingly more difficult for refugees to enter.

Conclusion

The Middle East has entered the twenty-first century as a region that has undergone profound transformations since most states gained independence following World War II. Yet, the trajectory of these changes has been different than the one that was anticipated in the 1950s. The countries that seemed to hold the most promise in terms of achieving high levels of economic development, in particular Iraq and Lebanon, have seen their economies devastated by long-simmering conflicts. Egypt, Syria, and Algeria have struggling economies as a result of years of ineffective state economic planning. On the other hand, the countries of the Gulf, many of which were little more than sleepy fishing outposts in the middle of the last century, have turned into extremely wealthy states thanks to some of the largest oil deposits in the world.

What has not changed, however, are the deep social inequalities that continue to plague the region. Despite impressive gains in providing education and health care to their citizens, many Middle Eastern societies still

The influence of US-based multinational corporations can be seen throughout the Middle East. This McDonald's fast food outlet is in the Tel Aviv Central Bus Station in Israel.

rank low on the UN Human Development Index. Furthermore, although the arms races that were fueled by the Cold War between the United States and the Soviet Union are over, the militarization of the region has not been reduced. Continuing conflicts within the region have had a profoundly negative impact on the economic development in numerous countries. The challenges that the region's economies thus face in the twenty-first century are many. In addition to launching sustainable development programs that can address the poverty and inequality that still plague the region and resolving economically, socially, and politically ruinous conflicts and rebuilding destroyed societies, the region also faces the challenge of diversifying its economies to make them relevant and competitive in the new global economy.

▨ Bibliography

Adwan, Charles. 2004. "Corruption in Reconstruction: The Cost of National Consensus in Post-War Lebanon," December 1. Washington, D.C.: CIPE.
Andoni, Lamis, and Jillian Schwedler. 1996. "Bread Riots in Jordan," *Middle East Report,* no. 2001 (October-December):40–42.
Arab Human Development Report. 2005. *Toward Freedoms in the Arab World.* New York: UN Development Programme.
Baldwin-Edwards, Martin. 2005. "Migration in the Middle East and Mediterranean," *Mediterranean Migration Observatory.* Athens: Panteion University.
Becker, Kristina Flodman. 2004. *The Informal Sector.* Stockholm: Swedish International Development Cooperation Agency.
Beinin, Joel, and Hossam el-Hamalawy. 2007. "Strikes in Egypt Spread from Centers of Gravity," *Middle East Report On-Line,* May 9. www.merip.org/mero/mero 050907.html.
Bellin, Eva R. 2002. *Stalled Democracy: Capital, Labor, and the Paradox of State-Sponsored Development.* Ithaca: Cornell University Press.
Buencamino, Leonides, and Sergei Gorbunov. 2002. "Informal Money Transfer Systems: Opportunities and Challenges for Development Finance," *DESA Discussion Paper,* No. 26. New York: United Nations.
Henry, Clement M., and Robert Springborg. 2001. *Globalization and the Politics of Development in the Middle East.* Cambridge: Cambridge University Press.
Hourani, Albert. 1991. *History of the Arab Peoples.* Cambridge, MA: Harvard University Press.
International Crisis Group. 2001. *Algeria's Economy: The Vicious Cycle of Oil and Violence.* Africa Report, no. 36, October 26.
Issawi, Charles. 1995. *The Middle East Economy: Decline and Recovery.* Princeton, N.J.: Markus Wiener.
Kpadar, Knagni. 2007. "Why Has Unemployment in Algeria Been Higher Than in MENA and Transition Countries?" *IMF Working Paper,* August. Washington, D.C.: International Monetary Fund.
Looney, Robert. 2006. "Economic Consequences of Conflict: The Rise of Iraq's Informal Economy," *Journal of Economic Issues* 40, no. 4 (December):991–1007.
Mokbel, Madona. 2007. "Refugees in Limbo: The Plight of Iraqis in Bordering States," *Middle East Report,* no. 244 (Fall):10–17.

OECD. 2007. *Africa Economic Outlook.* Paris: Organization for Economic Cooperation and Development.

Paczynska, Agnieszka. 2006. "Globalization, Structural Adjustment, and Pressure to Conform: Contesting Labor Law Reform in Egypt," *New Political Science* 28, no. 1 (March):45–64.

Pan, Esther. 2003. "Iraq: The Regime's Debt," December 31. New York: Council on Foreign Relations.

Panzac, Daniel. 1992 "International and Domestic Maritime Trade in the Ottoman Empire During the Eighteenth Century." *International Journal of Middle East Studies* 24, no. 2 (May):189–206.

Parker, Christopher, and Pete W. Moore. 2007. "The War Economy of Iraq," *Middle East Report,* no. 243 (Summer):7–11.

Peteet, Julie. 2007. "Unsettling the Categories of Displacement," *Middle East Report,* no. 244 (Fall):2–9.

Property World Middle East. 2005. "Qatari Diar Launches Qatar's Single Biggest Development," December 21. www.propertyworldme.com/content/html/1140 .asp.

Radwan, Samir. 2002. "Employment and Unemployment in Egypt: Conventional Problems, Unconventional Remedies." *Working Paper* no. 70. Cairo: The Egyptian Center for Economic Studies, August.

Richards, Alan, and John Waterbury. 1990. *A Political Economy of the Middle East: State, Class, and Economic Development.* Boulder, Colo.: Westview Press.

Roy, Sara. 2006. "The Economy of Gaza," October 4. http://wilpf.org/pipermail/ wcusp_wilpf.org/2006-October/000332.html.

Sadowski, Yahya M. 1993. *Scuds or Butter? The Political Economy of Arms Control in the Middle East.* Washington, D.C.: The Brookings Institution.

Shadid, Anthony, "The Towering Dream of Dubai," *Washington Post,* April 30, 2006.

Sufyan, Alissa. 2007. "The Challenge of Economic Reform in the Arab World: Toward More Productive Economies," *Carnegie Papers,* no. 1, May 2007. Washington, DC: The Carnegie Endowment for International Peace.

UN. 2004. *World Population Policies 2003.* New York: United Nations.

UNCTAD. 2006. *Handbook of Statistics 2006–2007.* New York: UN Conference on Trade and Development.

UNDP. 2007. *Human Development Report 2007/2008. Fighting Climate Change: Human Solidarity in a Divided World.* New York: UN Development Programme.

UNEP. 2007a. *Lebanon: Post-Conflict Environmental Assessment.* Geneva: UN Environment Programme.

———. 2007b. *Sudan: Post-Conflict Environmental Assessment.* Geneva: UN Environment Programme.

UNHCR (UN High Commissioner for Refugees). 2008. "Iraq Situation." www.unhcr .org/iraq.html.

UNRWA. 2007. "UNRWA Emergency Appeal Progress Report, January–June 2007," UN Relief and Works Agency for the Palestinian Refugees in the Near East, June 30.

Waldner, David. 1999. *State Building and Late Development.* Ithaca: Cornell University Press.

Waterbury, John. 1993. *Exposed to Innumerable Delusions: Public Enterprise and State Power in Egypt, India, Mexico and Turkey.* New York: Cambridge University Press.

Williamson, John (ed.). 1990. *Latin American Adjustment: How Much Has Happened?* Washington, D.C.: Institute for International Economics.

World Bank. 2006. *Economic Development and Prospects 2006: Financial Markets in a New Age of Oil.* Washington, D.C.: The World Bank.

————. 2007. "Two Years After London: Restarting Palestinian Economic Recovery." Economic Monitoring Report to the Ad Hoc Liaison Committee, September 24. Washington, D.C.: The World Bank.

World Bank Group Sana'a Office. 2007. *Yemen Economic Update.* Fall. Sana'a: World Bank Group.

World Bank Technical Team. 2007. "Potential Alternatives for Palestinian Trade: Developing the Rafah Trade Corridor," March 21. Washington, D.C.: The World Bank.

Yousef, Tarik. 2005. "The Changing Role of Labor Migration in the Arab World." Georgetown University, Edmund A. Walsh School of Foreign Service, Working Paper Series, February.

8

The Political Economy of Middle Eastern Oil

Mary Ann Tétreault

The Middle East is the geographic "center of gravity" of the world oil industry. Oil is valuable. It is a convenient fuel and, if there is enough to export, it is a source of foreign exchange. To many oil-producing developing countries, however, the blessing of oil can be a curse. Oil attracts intervention by major powers and, domestically, contributes to militarization, political corruption, and, paradoxically, foreign debt. Oil wealth also distorts national economies and interferes with development strategies. This chapter examines the political economy of the Middle East's most lucrative resource.

The curse of oil may be linked to a colonial past, but its effects differ from the impact of other forms of colonial exploitation. Oil production is geographically localized; its technology and capital intensity also isolate it from the rest of a national economy. In consequence, to all but the most local life patterns, oil exploitation is less shattering socially than a shift from subsistence agriculture to cash crops (Munif, 1989; Vitalis, 2006). The relative ease with which foreigners could control oil exploitation in their own interests allowed them to rely on local officials rather than replacing them with client regimes, as they often did in places where imperial powers established plantation economies. Yet oil money did change the balance of power between state and society in oil-exporting countries. It gave local rulers effective tools for suppressing popular institutions and thwarting traditional checks on their authority (Gasiorowski, 1991; Vitalis, 2006). On the whole, oil decreased legitimate political participation in the Middle East (Crystal, 1990; Tétreault, 2000).

As in Iran, Iraq, Saudi Arabia, and most of the Gulf States, Kuwait's oil extraction and transport infrastructures are carefully maintained to enable the government to move petroleum products swiftly into the global market. This part of the installation is called a "Christmas tree."

Kuwaiti Petroleum Company/courtesy of World Oil

▓ Industry Structure

The oil industry is intrinsically global. Crude production and customers for products often are located in different countries (Penrose, 1968), which made oil an engine of globalization from the industry's earliest days (Sampson, 1975). Oil's importance in the evolution of the modern Middle East helps explain why this region is hyper-globalized, a nexus of world investment and trade. The complexity and global reach of the oil industry present many points of political and economic leverage where an actor such as a firm or a country can exert significant control. One such "choke point" is oil production (Blair, 1976). Whoever possesses rights to the land and its minerals controls access to them. As in many other countries, mineral rights belong to the state in Middle Eastern nations. When oil was first developed there, oil companies had to negotiate with local governments for exploration and production rights.

Before World War II, Middle Eastern countries competed for oil company investment in a market where the biggest companies were more afraid of a glut of oil than oil shortages. In the 1920s these companies agreed among themselves to limit production, fix prices, and reduce competition in product markets. In the Red Line Agreement of 1928, the three largest international oil companies (IOCs), Exxon, Shell, and British Petroleum (BP),[1] along with a few smaller partners, decided not to explore for oil or develop new production capacity anywhere in the old Ottoman Empire unless every partner consented. Countries inside the Red Line had difficulty attracting investment in oil exploration because the Red Line companies were so afraid of oversupply and falling prices. This problem was worst for Iraq because Red Line companies owned all the oil rights there (Anderson, 1981; Sampson, 1975).

Inexperience led most future Middle Eastern oil exporters to deal with only one company (e.g., Chisholm, 1975). Although many were joint ventures (partnerships of two or more oil companies), host countries still found themselves sitting across from a single operator on the other side of the bargaining table. When oil was first developed in Kuwait, the only operating company was the Kuwait Oil Company (KOC), a partnership between Gulf and BP. Even though both Gulf and BP invested the capital and took the profits from Kuwait's oil, all their business in Kuwait was conducted by a single entity, KOC. Meanwhile, the IOCs participated in several operating companies worldwide, enabling them to coordinate production based on what each learned about the others from their joint dealings. This structure also helped partners avoid competing for new contracts and provided a means to coordinate other global operations.

Kuwait's freedom to choose which company it would sign with was limited by the British government, whose treaties with Kuwait gave Britain the final authority to determine who would exploit any oil found there. The British would not permit the Kuwaitis to contract with a non-British company, though the emir was able to hold out for a company that had at least one non-British partner (Chisholm, 1975). After the concession was granted, Kuwait's autonomy was even more limited. The terms of its contract with KOC gave the company exclusive rights for ninety years to find and produce oil over Kuwait's entire land area. If the government were to try to seek better terms elsewhere during the period of the KOC concession, that firm would face legal challenges from BP and Gulf. An even bigger threat was the possibility of intervention by a home government—in Kuwait's case, Britain and the United States—should Kuwait try to remove KOC from its privileged position.

The powerful home governments of the IOCs also intervened in the domestic affairs of the governments of exporting countries. In 1951 the Iranian government, under Prime Minister Mohammad Mossadeq, nationalized Iran's oil. Iran's operating company was unusual in the Middle East because a single company, BP, owned it all. When BP's holdings were nationalized, the company obtained court orders enjoining other IOCs from buying oil from the Iranian government. Afraid of the example that a successful nationalization might set for other Middle Eastern oil-exporting states, the British and US governments worked to destabilize and eventually to overthrow the Mossadeq regime (Gasiorowski, 1998). The restoration of the shah of Iran in 1953 following a brief period of ouster also reinstated IOCs as managers of the nationalized Iranian oil company. However, instead of restoring BP to its former position as sole owner, the Iranian government sought a "Kuwait solution." The shah invited non-British participation in the National Iranian Oil Company (NIOC). When the NIOC was reorganized, US companies and the French National Oil Company (CFP) were given 60 percent of the shares, and BP was left with only 40 percent (Sampson, 1975).

The one company–one country pattern of concessions throughout much of the Middle East helped to make the region the marginal supplier of oil to the international market, that is, the source of however much oil was needed to balance global supply and demand. This balancing act was made possible by the participation of the largest IOCs, whose production holdings stretched across the globe, in various Middle Eastern concessions. Once they had decided what total supply should be, the companies could regulate production by increasing or decreasing offtake in countries whose governments could not easily retaliate against them. The one company–one country pattern did not hold in Libya, whose oil was discovered and developed much later than that of most of the Gulf countries (Rand, 1975). As long as most exporting countries had little leverage over their operators, however, the companies' cartel was difficult to overthrow.

The company-managed oil cartel was able to suppress production and reduce competition some of the time in some markets even during the Great Depression, when world demand for oil dropped to very low levels. The Depression also eliminated whole companies and thereby made the management task of the survivors much easier (Nitzan and Bichler, 2002). The cartel received another boost from declining production in two major oil-producing countries. Geological problems caused Mexico's production to fall from its high levels in the early 1920s; an international boycott imposed when Mexico nationalized its oil industry in 1938 caused it to drop even further. Also, after Joseph Stalin assumed leadership of the Soviet Union, he reduced oil production there because he preferred to emphasize other fuels (Tétreault, 1985).

Governments and corporations in developed countries tried to regulate oil production to protect domestic industries and foreign investments. Regulations were even applied in the United States, where the antitrust tradition was strong but not so strong as to counter either the threat of business failure in the 1930s or the Cold War politics of the period following World War II (Prindle, 1981). Indeed, oil policy during the Cold War found IOCs and their home governments continuing to cooperate for their mutual benefit. The companies developed an ethic of oil statesmanship to justify their interference in politics and markets and to explain why they were entitled to their home governments' assistance. The governments, in turn, expanded their use of oil companies as foreign policy surrogates in relations with host governments. By the end of World War II, foreign oil was widely regarded as an important ingredient of national power and one of the most lucrative businesses in the world (Penrose, 1968).

▨ The System Unravels

Economic theory tells us that when firms make huge profits, new competitors will enter the industry, eventually reducing profits for all. This is exactly what happened in the international oil industry. The success of even imperfect cartel arrangements made oil vastly profitable. The IOCs were among the world's largest and richest firms. Competition came from brand-new companies, companies that formerly operated only in their own home countries, and from state-owned firms. The new competitors offered potential oil-exporting countries more money and better terms, including attractive terms for offshore rights in countries whose onshore operators had not thought to ask for them in their original contracts. This willingness to write contracts highly favorable to host countries encouraged Middle Eastern governments to ask all their operating companies to liberalize contract terms.

Even the largest IOCs had to compete for new contracts. Some agreed to sweeten the terms of ongoing contracts to maintain good relations with their hosts. Others were asked to relinquish territory they were not developing so that the host governments could sell the rights to those lands to someone else. These adjustments increased the costs of doing business and reduced company profits. Competition in other segments of the market also squeezed profits. Shortly after the end of World War II, the Venezuelan government threatened to nationalize foreign oil operations unless the companies agreed to split their profits on Venezuelan oil 50–50 with the government. Mindful of Mexico's nationalization in 1938, companies operating in Venezuela agreed. Soon after, Middle Eastern governments began demanding the same terms. This was the trigger of the conflict between Mossadeq's Iran and BP in the early 1950s.

A requested reinterpretation of a 1926 US tax law allowing US companies to deduct taxes paid to foreign governments from their US tax liabilities helped the four partners in Saudi Arabia's Arabian American Oil Company (ARAMCO). This favorable treatment was available to every US firm operating abroad, but BP was not able to pass a similar amount of its foreign taxes along to taxpayers in Britain, causing the community of interests among the IOCs to diverge. Another unexpected source of competitive pressure on the oil companies came from the Soviet Union. US Cold War policies restricted Soviet trade with the West, forcing the USSR to rely increasingly on oil and gold sales to earn foreign exchange. Under Nikita Khrushchev, the Stalinist policy was reversed and total Soviet oil production doubled in the five years following Stalin's death in 1953.

Perhaps the last straw for the IOCs was the 1959 decision of the US government to impose a limit—a quota—on the amount of oil that they could import into the United States. The US market was the biggest in the world and doubly lucrative because the high cost of domestically produced oil gave sellers of lower-cost foreign oil the potential to reap greater than normal profits. But US oil companies that operated entirely at home were politically strong in the postwar era and sought a quota to defend against competition from companies with cheap oil supplies from abroad. These domestic producers, citing national security and the risk of becoming dependent on foreign oil imports, demanded protection against cheap imported oil and, in 1959, what had started as a voluntary program in 1954 became law (Vietor, 1984).

The IOCs could see which way the wind was blowing in their markets and shifted their strategy for propping up declining profits. In the early 1950s they had developed the "posted price" system to help host governments estimate their anticipated oil revenues more easily. The companies "posted," or published, these prices, and host governments used them to calculate the amount of taxes the companies would have to pay even though little oil actually traded at these prices. When posted prices were first introduced, company profits on foreign operations were very high and small deviations in the real prices at which crude oil traded did not worry them. Stable posted prices soon became an accepted industry norm. Host country governments also did not pay much attention to posted prices, lobbying instead for profit sharing and improved concession terms to increase their shares of oil profits (Penrose, 1968).

But as costs and competition increased, the operators began to look at posted prices as a tactic for boosting profits. In February 1959, after consulting one another (but not their hosts), the companies lowered posted prices—and thereby the taxes owed to host governments. An immediate outcry arose from the host governments, which sought to coordinate their own actions to protect their interests. Coordination was difficult. These countries were competitors for investment and production, and their industries, initiated at different times by different firms, were highly varied. The Venezuelan industry was organized into many independent segments instead of the one company–one country pattern common in the Middle East. The age of Venezuela's industry made it more expensive to produce oil there than in the Middle East. When the IOCs, still enmeshed in their own desires and conflicts, lowered posted prices again in August 1960, however, five oil-exporting governments tried once again to set aside politics to salvage their economic interests. These five, Venezuela, Saudi Arabia, Iran, Iraq, and Kuwait, formed the Organization of Petroleum Exporting Countries (OPEC) in September 1960 (Mikdashi, 1972).

OPEC's aims from the very beginning included helping host governments gain autonomy and greater control over their oil, but progress was incremental during its first ten years. As OPEC became stronger, other countries, some from Africa and East Asia, also joined. Competition among members remained a constant problem, one that was aggravated by political divisions between conservative, monarchical states like Saudi Arabia and post-revolutionary radical states like Iraq (Dawisha, 2003). There also were political differences between Arab and non-Arab states. One important political conflict centered on the "oil weapon," production cuts by Arab oil producers intended to force political concessions from countries supporting Israel.

The oil weapon was used in conjunction with the Arab-Israeli wars of 1948, 1956, and 1967, when it was ineffective in influencing importing-country policy. Arab production cuts were offset by higher production from other producers—including other members of OPEC—and by the ability of the oil companies to redistribute supplies internationally. Dependence on oil revenues limited the length of time the embargoing countries could manage financially. Until 1967, short and unevenly administered attempts to use the oil weapon had little impact on policy toward Israel. The 1967 oil embargo succeeded in moving France away from Israel toward closer relations with Arab governments because, following the loss of Algeria, it had fewer assured sources of petroleum. France also distrusted US leadership of the Western alliance, which made it wary of sacrificing good relations with Arab oil suppliers for the benefit of a US client with no oil.

Perceiving the 1967 Arab oil embargo as a nonevent, the IOCs became complacent. They continued to be more preoccupied by fears of oversupply than by the structural changes in the world oil market brought about by war and a booming world economy. The 1967 war closed the Suez Canal, creating an effective tanker shortage for oil shipments to Europe from the Gulf because tankers had to travel the far longer distance around Africa to reach the Mediterranean. In spite of this, the companies did not think it was prudent to take precautions against a possible supply cut by exporters on the Mediterranean. Indeed, most looked at the narrowing supply-demand gap as beneficial to their interests. They were skeptical that the global oil market could be disrupted by political pressure since so little disruption had resulted during attempts to apply such pressure in the past (Vernon, 1976).

The IOCs also were unconcerned by rising demand for oil worldwide, and by falling oil production in the United States. US oil production peaked in 1970 even as demand continued to rise and increasing amounts for ever-growing US consumption had to come from foreign sources. Another effect of the shift in the US energy balance was that as actual US production approached total production capacity, *excess* capacity under direct US control shrank. Should the oil weapon be used again, there would be no way to increase production from the United States, a tactic that had minimized the oil crises of 1956 and 1967.

▓ Rumblings of Change

In September 1969 a revolution in Libya replaced a pro-Western king with a militantly anti-US colonel determined to increase Libya's oil income. Muammar Qaddafi isolated two of Libya's more than forty operators, demanding that they increase payments to the Libyan government or else be shut down. One operator, Occidental, had no other sources of oil in the Eastern Hemisphere. It did have contracts with European buyers that included financial penalties should it fail to deliver, however, so it soon gave in. Qaddafi then moved to apply the same technique to other operators until they all agreed to the higher price. Qaddafi's success made the shah of Iran jealous, and in 1971 he demanded higher prices for the Gulf producers too.

The oil companies wanted to negotiate simultaneously with Libya and the Gulf producers to prevent their being picked off one at a time in Tehran as they had been in Tripoli. The cliency relationship between the United States and Iran prevented US companies from getting the government support they needed to make this happen. The United States could not apply pressure on Iran without making concessions to the shah or risking his strategic cooperation in the future. As the oil companies feared, alternating demands between Tehran and Tripoli led to a short volley of negotiations between Libya and the Gulf. The oil revolution was under way: oil-exporting countries were commanding ever higher prices for their oil in spite of the existence of long-term contracts specifying much lower prices.

Negotiations were speeded along by deterioration in the US economy. The US government devalued the dollar in 1971 and again in 1973, reducing

Libyan leader Muammar Qaddafi was the first Arab leader to successfully challenge Western oil companies by demanding they increase payments for petroleum. His actions set the stage for the 1973 OAPEC oil embargo.

Thomas Hartwell

the value of the dollars received by oil exporters, making them demand more dollars to compensate for the lost purchasing power. Negotiations after the second devaluation were still in progress in the fall of 1973, when other events snowballed the price issue into the larger question of who would control OPEC oil (Tétreault, 1985).

US companies also were in trouble at home. Domestic oil supplies in the highly regulated US market were falling behind demand, while restrictions on oil imports triggered spot shortages and price increases. These, in turn, prompted congressional hearings and widespread public criticism of the oil companies. The supply situation became so dire that oil import quotas were ended in April 1973. The energy crisis, which is remembered as the result of the use of the oil weapon in the October 1973 war, had in reality begun months—if not years—earlier.

The October 1973 decision by Arab oil exporters to try the oil weapon once again could have been predicted by an effective political "early warning" system. Throughout 1972–1973, Arab governments promised openly and repeatedly to use the oil weapon against the United States if a Middle East settlement conforming to UN Resolution 242, which required Israeli withdrawal from the Occupied Territories, was not achieved. Saudi Arabian officials went so far as to call in representatives of all four operating company partners to deliver a message. They said that another war between Israel and Arab governments was imminent and that, when it came, Arab oil would be cut off to supporters of Israel. One partner, Mobil, took the warning so seriously that it bought an ad in the *New York Times* to urge a settlement of the Arab-Israeli conflict. The other partners relied on private channels to communicate their message (Tétreault, 1985).

By the summer of 1973, the exposure of criminal behavior in what has come to be known as the "Watergate affair" had reached a critical stage in congressional hearings. But Richard Nixon's political problems were not alone in inhibiting direct US involvement in a Middle Eastern settlement. The new Nixon Doctrine had inaugurated a strategy based on US reliance on a few chosen client regimes, built up by foreign aid and arms transfers, that would pursue US interests throughout the world without requiring direct intervention by the United States. This was the philosophy behind the "Vietnamization" of the Vietnam War, and the arming of Israel and Iran in the Middle East. US dependence on its two Middle East clients meant that the United States could not force Israel to accept UN Resolution 242 in 1972 and 1973 any more than it could force the shah of Iran to accept joint negotiations with the oil companies in 1971 (Tétreault, 1985).

When war came in October 1973, Arab governments waited for some sign that the United States would respond to their concerns. Finally, on October 17, at the request of the Arab League, the Organization of Arab Petroleum-Exporting Countries (OAPEC)—a group that included the Arab members of

OPEC along with Bahrain, Egypt, and Syria—imposed an oil embargo against
Israel's allies (Tétreault, 1981). Intended to be effective rather than mostly
performative, as the embargoes of 1956 and 1967 had been, the 1973–1974
embargo was designed to be both more extensive and more discriminating.
OAPEC aimed to keep Arab oil from enemies of the Arab states while at the
same time allowing Arab oil to flow to friendly nations.

Some aspects were very successful. Total supplies of oil to the world
market were cut, creating local shortages and higher prices in most oil-importing countries. Another success was to alter the general perception of the
Arab governments as weak and ineffective. But despite the care with which
embargo provisions had been drawn up, the spirit of the embargo was systematically violated in ways that prevented the targeting plan from working.
As in previous applications of the oil weapon, oil supplies were exchanged
between and within companies. Arab oil that could not be sent to the United
States or Holland was swapped for unrestricted supplies from non-Arab
sources. All importing countries experienced about the same degree of short-
fall whether they supported the Arab states or Israel. The failure of targeting
meant that although the embargo did succeed in inflicting hardship on the
friends of Israel, it also inflicted hardship on the friends of the Arabs.

The most important effect of the embargo was to consolidate the oil
price revolution. Bids for "spot" or individual cargoes of crude oil reached
very high levels. The "price hawks" in OPEC, countries like Libya, Iraq,
and Iran, insisted that OPEC members stop negotiating with the companies
and simply set their own prices—very high. Others, like Saudi Arabia, supported setting an OPEC price but opposed the size of the price increase advocated by the price hawks. The two groups fought during OPEC's December 1973 meeting and eventually compromised on a price between the two
extremes. This price, US$11.65 per barrel, was four times higher than the
average price of OPEC crude just a year earlier.

■ The Oil Revolution

The oil revolution was not simply a price revolution, although that was an
important component of it. More important, it marked a change in the ownership of oil. Prior to 1973, IOCs controlled the oil of most OPEC members. These companies decided how much oil to produce and how much
money to invest in the host's national industry. Although companies and
host governments bargained over prices and production levels, the companies had the last word.

Several oil-exporting countries had nationalized their oil industries prior
to the oil revolution, but this did not always mean that control of nationalized oil had passed to the host government. Iran nationalized its industry in

1951, but the restoration of the shah also restored foreign control over Iran's oil. Nationalizations by Iraq and Libya were more effective in transferring control of domestic industries to host governments. As other countries nationalized their industries or took over ownership more gradually through "participation," decisionmaking power passed from the IOCs to the oil ministries of the host governments. This transfer of authority also took place in Iran.

The IOCs were criticized for being nothing more than "tax collectors for OPEC" rather than independent actors in the international oil market (Adelman, 1972–1973). Few of them cared and most probably were rooting for the host governments to succeed in keeping prices high. High prices made for vastly higher profits while the nationalizations neither cut off nor reduced the revenues of most oil companies operating in the Middle East (Nitzan and Bichler, 2002). Many IOCs made so much money that they invested in high-cost exploration and development outside of OPEC, even in the very expensive United States. They bought other oil companies and invested in companies producing coal and nuclear energy. Some bought firms in industries totally unrelated to energy. One even tried to buy a circus.

State-owned national oil companies took over the IOC operations. Some host countries already had state firms and others created them expressly to take charge of newly nationalized industries. This shift in corporate ownership led to a restructuring of the industry as a whole. Now that OPEC set crude oil prices, IOCs stopped using profits from oil production to subsidize other operations. In the past, they would set the "transfer prices" at which oil was sold between subsidiaries of the same company to show high profits on crude sales and low profits on refining and marketing. Because tax rates were lower in producing countries than in consuming countries, they could save money on taxes if it looked as though they were earning most of their profits from producing oil overseas rather than from refining and marketing oil in the United States, Europe, or Japan.

After the oil revolution, the price of crude oil became a real cost, not a fiction enabling IOCs to evade taxes. Without production from now-nationalized holdings, other IOC operations had to earn real—and not paper—profits. Obsolescent equipment was replaced and the "downstream" phases of the industry—refining and marketing—were rationalized wherever possible. Where these operations could not be made profitable for their owners, they were sold. Gasoline stations were snapped up by national oil companies of OPEC countries eager to have marketing outlets in oil-importing countries. Some had to take less attractive operations, like obsolete refineries, as part of these packages (Tétreault, 1995).

Another effect of the new OPEC price structure was that production anywhere in the world earned its owners "windfall profits," the difference between the marginal cost of what they produced and the much higher prices at which oil now was sold. Increasing production in the United States and elsewhere outside OPEC became a company priority, even though US regulations limited the windfall profits companies could reap and other governments began to charge higher royalties and fees for oil produced in their countries (Tétreault, 1985).

Higher oil prices also depressed demand. By 1978, inflation had eaten away most of the value of the 1973–1974 price increases. Some consumers still felt that they were paying more for oil because the nominal prices of products like gasoline and heating oil stayed about the same. But because real prices had actually fallen, consumption, which had dropped in 1974 and 1975, soon began to rise again. By the time of the second round of huge price increases during the Iranian revolution, consumer demand had reached about the same level that it was in January 1973, before the oil embargo.

■ Oil Politics in the OPEC Middle East

Higher oil prices and the increase in national autonomy and control over oil did not take oil out of Middle Eastern politics. On the contrary, OPEC's new power in the international industry increased its appeal as an arena for pursuing political goals. Ongoing ethnic, religious, and territorial disagreements between Iran and Arab Gulf nations aggravated conflicts over oil prices. Yet no single cause motivated any of the conflicts within OPEC. For example, Arab states, chiefly Libya, Algeria, and even Iraq, occasionally joined Iran to press for oil price increases, and Saudi Arabia and its allies among the smaller Gulf states opposed all of them. Thus the Arab-Iranian conflict often cut across other ongoing regional conflicts, such as the "Arab civil war" between traditional and revolutionary regimes (Skeet, 1988).

The Iranian revolution (1978–1979) aggravated conflicts within OPEC over oil prices and organization leadership. The new government led by Ayatollah Khomeini saw raising oil prices as a way to attack the United States while increasing Iran's national income and foreign exchange reserves. Iranian price militancy was effective in raising oil prices as long as the panic set off by Iran's revolution continued. Throughout 1979, Iran and other price hawks imposed extravagant price increases that pulled the prices of more moderate OPEC members up in defensive emulation. When prices weakened in 1980, Iran also proved to be an aggressive price cutter in the battle over shrinking markets, despite government denials.

Iran's aggressive nationalism in oil marketing was matched by its aggressive nationalism in regional politics. Iran hoped to export its revolution to other Islamic states, and OPEC meetings soon became places for revolutionary exhortation and guerrilla tactics. Iraq was a favorite Iranian target because of its large Shi'i population, its convenient location on the western border of Iran, and a history of enmity between the two countries. As detailed in

Chapter 5, rivalries over oil and oil revenues added to other axes of conflict between these two oil powers.

Iraq's oil power, long obscured by oil company limits on expansion of supply capacity in selected parts of the Middle East, promised to overtake Iran's. Iraq was more successful in its economic development policies than Iran, and its growing economic and political strength made its new leader, Saddam Hussein, confident that he could force a revision in its favor of the 1975 settlement with Iran of the long-running border dispute between the two countries. In September 1980, Iraq attacked Iran, setting off a long, brutal war marked by high casualties among civilians and soldiers on both sides (Cordesman and Wagner, 1991).

The effect on OPEC of the war also was devastating. Meetings turned into acrimonious shouting matches. With OPEC facing competition from new production in Britain and Norway, and the Soviet Union dumping large quantities of crude oil into West European markets, the Iran-Iraq War impeded efforts to coordinate production and maintain a united OPEC front. Even the day-to-day operations of OPEC were affected when neither Iran nor Iraq would accept a secretary-general from the other country, and the organization had to be run for several years by the assistant secretary-general, Fadhel al-Chalabi—an Iraqi.

▓ The Price Bust

The most serious effect of the Iran-Iraq War for oil exporters was that it prevented OPEC members from the mutual accommodation necessary to withstand outside assaults on the price structure. At that time there were three main threats to oil prices in addition to price cutting by OPEC members themselves. First, just as in 1973–1974, the new round of price increases depressed consumer demand; second, these high prices also prompted oil companies to expand supplies, especially supplies originating outside of OPEC; and third, the Soviet Union became an aggressive crude seller in dollar-denominated markets. These and related market developments marginalized OPEC as the dominant world supplier of crude oil and slashed OPEC government revenues.[2]

When the IOCs looked carefully at the supply situation, they found that oil exploration and development begun in response to the oil price increases of the early 1970s started paying off within a few years. New oil came to the market from the North Sea, non-OPEC developing countries, and even the United States. The Soviet Union was so attracted by the new high prices that it reneged on contracts to sell oil to its clients in Eastern Europe (Jentleson, 1986) so it could sell it at or close to OPEC prices in Western markets. Refiners bought crude oil first from these sources and only afterward from

OPEC. By 1979, OPEC production had recovered to about the same level it had been in 1973, 31 million barrels per day. In 1980 this dropped to 27 million barrels per day and by 1983 it had plummeted to 17.6 million barrels per day.

Extra crude supplies came from unexpected sources. One of them was inventories. After the 1973–1974 oil embargo, developed countries came together to form a kind of counter-cartel, the International Energy Agency (IEA). The IEA required each member to maintain a ninety-day supply of oil in a strategic reserve to be used in case of oil supply interruptions. If the amount of oil available to any member were to fall below 7 percent of requirements, it could apply to the IEA and draw supplies from its own and other members' strategic stocks. These stocks were too low to be useful during the 1979 crisis, while the crisis encouraged importers and companies to buy more stocks, contributing to the upward pressure on prices. Afterward, many found that the combination of falling consumer demand and the massive buildup of stocks resulting from their frantic purchases in 1979 and 1980 left them with much more oil than they needed to meet IEA requirements.

In 1983 and again in 1985, large quantities of excess stocks were dumped onto the market, pushing prices downward. In 1983, OPEC so feared the loss of customers, revenues, and control over the market that it lowered the price of its marker crude, the reference crude against which the prices of crudes of different quality were set, by US$5.00 per barrel. It also made mandatory a production regulation scheme it had adopted as a voluntary measure to restrict production the year before. The intention was to punish price cutters inside and outside OPEC by reducing their oil incomes, and to halt or reverse the drop in oil demand by reducing prices. Neither plan succeeded, in part because of the independent effect of exchange rate fluctuations.

US monetary policy from 1981 through most of 1985 affected exchange rates by keeping the value of the dollar, the currency for which virtually all crude oil was sold, very high. Dollars acquired through oil sales could be traded for pounds, yen, marks, francs, and other hard currencies, maintaining the purchasing power of oil sellers even after prices were cut. Although both price cutters and price defenders in OPEC complained about the oil price reduction, few actually suffered from it unless they also had to pay off loans or make purchases in dollars.

Consumers outside the United States experienced the reverse. Higher prices for the dollars needed to buy oil meant that oil prices in local currencies remained constant or actually rose after the OPEC price cut. These higher real prices erased any price incentive that nondollar consumers might have had to buy more oil. Although US consumers, whose dollar economy enjoyed the full effects of the price reduction, did react as OPEC had hoped, their contribution to world demand for crude oil was not enough to solve OPEC's problems because of the ineffectiveness of its production controls.

OPEC's inability to control production contributed to global oversupply. The production control regulations it adopted for its members were complicated and full of loopholes. For example, very heavy crudes and condensates—liquids precipitated from natural gas—were not counted as oil production. During the Iran-Iraq War, the cutoff of Iraq's pipelines by Iranian bombing led to extra production by Kuwait and Saudi Arabia "on Iraq's account," but the amounts produced tended to be more than Iraq's share and they were not cut back when exports from Iraq resumed. The depressed global economy encouraged barter and other countertrade arrangements outside normal oil sales channels, making it hard for OPEC accountants to find out which country was exporting how much oil and to whom. Several OPEC members cheated outright, producing oil over their allotted quotas, while non-OPEC members continued to enjoy a free ride on the OPEC price structure.

The main responsibility for holding OPEC production to the ceiling set by the group as a whole belonged to Saudi Arabia, the "swing producer." Saudi Arabia also was a primary target of Iranian political pressure, and the combination of declining oil production and continuing threats from Iran pushed the Saudis to push back. After months of warning, the Saudis "turned up the faucet" on their oil production in October 1985. A price that was wobbly but holding at about US$25.00 per barrel at the end of 1985 became US$12.00 per barrel and not holding six months later. The consequent drop in oil income was painful for all oil producers. In January 1986, officials of the Mexican government visited other oil-exporting countries in an attempt to stem the fall in oil prices, but it was as though a plug had been pulled out of a full bathtub: the whole OPEC price structure just slid down the drain.[3]

Prices rose a little over the next few years. They seldom reached OPEC's new target level of US$18.00 per barrel but continued to be exquisitely vulnerable to destabilizing events and rumors of events. Persistent depressed demand coupled with very low per-barrel prices affected every OPEC country. Budgets contracted and even "low absorbers," those countries whose populations were small compared to their incomes, had to make painful financial adjustments, including foreign borrowing. Adjustment coincided with fiscal strains on Arab Gulf exporters from war loans and payments to Iraq during the Iran-Iraq War, and further reductions in income when Gulf shipping became a target during the "tanker war" phase of that conflict (al-Assiri, 1990).

The end of the war in 1988 did not bring relief to economies and civil societies anywhere in OPEC. Oil demand and prices remained depressed while domestic populations grew restive, even in relatively wealthy Kuwait. There, citizen protests against the continued suspension of the parliament and constitutionally protected civil liberties, imposed in July 1986 in response to internal and external threats arising from the war (Boghardt, 2006), became widespread in 1989. High prices and a depressed local economy contributed to criticism of the regime's economic policies and to charges of corruption. The government felt pressed to satisfy the population's economic demands so as to mute the political demands it was even less happy to deal with. That year, Kuwait's oil production consistently exceeded its OPEC quota. And Kuwait was not alone. Other Gulf exporters, most notably the United Arab Emirates (UAE) and Saudi Arabia, also produced over their quotas.

Overproduction by OPEC members contributed to the market factors that depressed world oil prices. But Kuwait faced special risks in taking this route. Its boundary with Iraq had been contested since the 1930s, and years of diplomatic efforts and billions of dollars in loans and grants had not been enough to persuade Iraq to drop its claims to Kuwait. Continuing to produce at levels above its OPEC quota made Kuwait vulnerable to Iraqi retaliation.

Iraq's economic problems, which included huge war debts to foreign banks as well as to Kuwait and other Arab governments, also were pressing. It was convenient for Iraqi president Saddam Hussein to blame Kuwait for Iraq's problems. He clothed his invasion of Kuwait as an "oil war," a war to remove Kuwait's oil weapons, which he said were overproduction and theft of Iraqi oil produced along the disputed boundary. But just as many other conflicts in the Middle East concern much more than oil, so did this one. Saddam's problems required a quick infusion of cash. His diplomatic probes during the six months prior to the invasion convinced him that no power capable of stopping him would intervene if he were to invade Kuwait

A traditional *dhow* (boat) passes an oil tanker in the Bahraini port.

and take what he needed. He expected that victory in Kuwait would be quick and easy rather than the disaster that his attack on Iran a decade earlier had turned into. But Saddam was wrong in his assumptions; his 1990 invasion of Kuwait was reversed seven months later by a multilateral force led by the United States (Freedman and Karsh, 1993; Smith, 1992; Tétreault, 1993).

The Iraqi invasion began a new gulf war (1990–1991) and introduced new oil weapons into world politics. One was cited by US president George H. W. Bush when he said that the United States had to fight to keep Middle Eastern oil from being controlled by Saddam Hussein. From Bush's perspective, the war was intended to preserve an oil market where oil-exporting countries participate individually rather than under the hegemony of a regional military power. For Saddam, one objective of the war was to create such a hegemony under his leadership.

The other new oil weapons were ecological. Saddam promised to release Kuwaiti oil into the Gulf and to destroy Kuwait's production, processing, and export facilities if Iraq were attacked either at home or in Kuwait. These threats became real when the US-led coalition drove Iraq out of Kuwait and departing Iraqi soldiers set fire to Kuwait's oil fields. This demonstrates once again the strategic inferiority of oil weapons to deter undesired behavior when the stakes include the survival of a nation or its current regime.

▓ A New Gulf War—A New Oil Regime?

The end of the Kuwait War left world oil markets in a state of uncertainty. Officially, Iraq was kept out of the market by a boycott until 1996, when the UN's Oil for Food program finally went into effect. This gave the UN authority to sell Iraqi oil and spend the proceeds on humanitarian assistance to the Iraqi population. It also allowed the UN to sequester 30 percent of these proceeds to pay reparations to those making claims against Iraq for the war damages it had inflicted. Both before and after the Oil for Food program went into effect, however, illicit Iraqi oil flowed into neighboring countries and was smuggled by ship to buyers farther away. The money from this illegal trade sustained the Iraqi regime through the long years of economic sanctions imposed by the victors of the Gulf War. The primary burden of the sanctions fell on the Iraqi population in the form of food and medicine shortages and periodic bombing by the United States and Great Britain in retaliation for Saddam's activities.

In 2002 the United States and Britain spearheaded a new attack on Iraq, first in the UN, where the arms inspection regime imposed after the Kuwait War and suspended in 1998 was reinstated and strengthened. Although the inspectors reported frequently during the few months in which they were permitted to work that they had found no "weapons of mass destruction"

(WMDs; nuclear, biological, and chemical weapons) in Iraq (Blix, 2004), in March 2003, the United States, Britain, and Australia launched a military invasion. This third Gulf war differed from both of its predecessors. Rather than a result of Iraqi aggression, it marked the first time that a new US strategic doctrine, published in September 2002, was implemented. This doctrine asserted a US right to mount preemptive attacks against countries accused by the US government of aiding or harboring terrorists, or of amassing WMDs. It included as a goal the acquisition of "bases and stations within and beyond Western Europe and northeast Asia" for future US-force projections (US Government, 2002:6, 15, 29). The fallout from this new Gulf war is still unfolding and, for oil markets, bears close watching. Its effects on Middle East oil, in particular, have been massive.

The expectations of US policymakers were that the war would be over quickly, leading to a flood of Iraqi oil onto world markets that would pay for postwar reconstruction (Allawi, 2007; Packer, 2005). This did not happen, the result of faulty military strategy (Ricks, 2006), the George W. Bush administration's disdain for postconflict recommendations from planners (e.g., Crane and Terrill, 2003), and a shocking lack of intellectual resilience that prevented needed adjustment to realities on the ground (Chandrasekaran, 2006; Packer, 2005). Thanks to the lack of security anywhere in the country, what the US president called a victory rapidly devolved into insurgency and continued warfare. The chaotic conditions drew some foreign jihadists into Iraq (e.g., Packer, 2005), while conflicts between sects and among warlords within sects produced civil war conditions in much of the country (Institute for War and Peace Reporting [IWPR], *Iraq Crisis Report,* various issues). Iraqis endured kidnapping for money, gangland-style murders of civilians for sometimes unfathomable reasons, and systematic ethnic cleansing of neighborhoods and towns (IWPR, *Iraq Crisis Report,* various issues). With the exception of the Kurdish region, which had been protected from Saddam's army by US forces since mid-1991 and had maintained its hard-won political and social coherence even after Saddam had been deposed, much of the rest of the country was devastated (Allawi, 2007; Packer, 2005).

In spite of expectations that Iraq's domestic oil production could be restored quickly, postwar Iraq has had to import fuel (Allawi, 2007:256, 360). Even so, supplies have not been sufficient to generate electricity for more than a few hours per day (Najeeb, 2007). Pipelines are vulnerable to terrorist attacks, while the theft of crude and products along the entire domestic supply chain remains brisk and has kept supplies below demand (IWPR, 2007). The lag in investing in Iraq's oil infrastructure resulted from the efforts of Paul Bremer, the US Viceroy in Iraq, to guarantee that IOCs would have the first crack at Iraqi oil (Allawi, 2007:256–257). Yet the Iraqi government has been unable to reach agreement on an oil law that would establish ground rules for investing and protections for investors. In 2007, having received a green light from the US Department of State, US oil companies entered into contract negotiations with the local government in the Kurdish region (Holt, 2007; Lando, 2007a, 2007b).

IOC access to Iraqi oil seems to have been one of several motivations for the US invasion of Iraq, attested in the growing pile of books about the Bush administration written or "told by" Washington insiders (the earliest such revelation can be found in Suskind, 2004, and the most recent as of this writing is Greenspan, 2007). A majority of Iraqis—76 percent—polled in April 2006 said that the US desire to control Iraqi oil was the most important reason for the invasion (University of Michigan, 2006). Whether this goal is on the way to achievement is still unclear, especially since the Kurds have effectively decided to chart their own course, threatening the integrity of an already fragile state. If so, however, the effects would be profound. Industry insiders have believed since the 1920s that Iraq sits on an oil bonanza. Bringing this oil into the market would ease high prices, which could undermine popular support for moving away from carbon-based fuels. Iraq's desperate need for reconstruction revenues suggests that the IOCs would be urged to produce as much oil as possible, a potential threat to the new high-price structure that oil exporters around the world have become accustomed to. Other producers would have to exercise discipline to keep prices in their "comfort-zone" range, a project that the IOCs are likely to assist, just as they helped support the OPEC price increases of the early 1970s. Ultimately, market forces will adjust oil prices up or down, not only in response to new oil from Iraq but also to rising demand from India and China. If the "peakists" are correct and global oil production is trending downward (Leggett, 2007), Iraq stands to profit handsomely, whether IOCs or its own national oil company exploit its resources.

Even if oil supplies expand, consumers will continue to face consequences from Middle Eastern conflicts. Wars and rumors of wars tend to make consumers nervous, and military actions such as Iranian attacks on oil tankers during the 1980s, the torching of Kuwait's oil wells in 1991, and internal unrest in regions where oil is produced, a consequence of the 2003 war in Iraq, all raise costs and push prices up. The best example occurred following the Iraqi invasion of Kuwait, which touched off a rapid increase in oil prices that persisted for months. Political paralysis prevented the IEA from releasing oil stocks, so the entire burden of price stabilization fell on OPEC members. In January 1991, in conjunction with the allied counterattack, the IEA did initiate a planned release of stocks to keep the market from skyrocketing upward again. But IEA action was so heavy-handed that prices nearly collapsed. Oil prices have fluctuated wildly since the invasion of Iraq. "Real economy" events like strikes in Venezuela and Mexico, production shutdowns in Nigeria, civil war and genocide in Sudan, and the sharp decline in Iraqi oil production since 2003 all affected oil prices. Should the war in the Middle East spread beyond Iraq and Afghanistan, oil price stability is likely to be among the first casualties, with political stability not far behind.

■ Oil and Money in the Middle East

I began this chapter with the statement that oil is a blessing for countries that have it. One of the chief blessings of oil comes from its easy convertibility into foreign exchange. The higher oil prices that resulted first from the oil revolution and then from the revolution in Iran raised the earnings streaming into oil-exporting countries to flood levels. Yet as we all know, floods, whatever their other qualities, are also disasters. This flood was no exception; it too brought good news and bad news.

The good news was that a huge amount of money was suddenly available to oil-exporting countries to use for economic development and national defense, and to provide for the economic and social welfare of their people. The bad news was that the biggest increase came too fast and income over the medium and long term was neither steady nor predictable. In 1973, economists worried that rising oil prices would cause an economic depression in oil-importing countries. They also predicted that higher oil incomes would be virtually unusable by most oil-exporting countries, especially the Arab states along the Gulf with their small populations and very large revenues. Both worries were overstated. The "unusable" dollars that so concerned these economists turned out to be a chimera. Nicknamed "petrodollars," the cash balances of oil-exporting countries went into the international banking system, where they were recycled as loans and investments.

But all this money was a mixed blessing to the domestic economies of oil-exporting states. Rising imports and the flood of new money aggravated domestic inflation rates and demand for imports—the so-called Dutch disease. Oil exporters quickly learned to spend their money as fast as it came in so that, by the time of the second round of price increases in 1979–1980, many had started to amass their own foreign debt. Much of it went for investment and to pay for an explosion of arms purchases. As discussed in Chapter 4, arms purchases were an especially perverse outcome of the oil price increases of the 1970s (Nitzan and Bichler, 2002). The diversion of excessive amounts of oil revenue to buy weapons took resources from the domestic economies of states like Iran and Iraq, whose rural populations suffered extreme deprivation. Oil money aggravated the conflict in Israel/Palestine and financed all three Gulf wars. It made Saddam Hussein a greater power in his region than he would have been otherwise by allowing him to buy more weapons and build a larger army than he could have produced on his own.

Local workers at an oil production site take a break to brew Ceylon tea, which is served very sweet and sometimes with fresh mint or sage.

Courtesy of World Oil

Some states, like Kuwait, the UAE, and Bahrain, made extensive efforts to redistribute oil revenues across their populations. They did this through direct transfers and by subsidizing housing, utilities, education, and medical care. Some capital redistribution was effected through real estate transfers. In Kuwait, the state purchased land from citizens at highly inflated prices, while in Bahrain the government sold housing to citizens at very low prices. Both put wealth in the hands of lucky recipients. Oil money also supported conspicuous consumption, corruption, and gross waste. Kuwait's "underground" stock exchange, the Suq al-Manakh, was little more than a casino. Its collapse in 1982 resulted not only in a huge loss of capital but also in a loss of confidence in the government, which was slow to intervene because of involvement by high officials and members of the ruling family. Subsidized and pampered native populations in many Gulf states lost interest in low-status jobs, requiring the importation of guest workers to make local economies function. The economy and ecology of Saudi Arabia was damaged by government assistance, which included providing unlimited fossil water to support wheat production. Countries exporting labor to the rich oil exporters found their domestic economies and societies as radically altered as those of their richer neighbors by the roller-coaster economy they suddenly were subjected to, if only "second-hand" (Chaudhry, 1997).

Oil money also increased the foreign policy autonomy of oil-exporting countries. They found it less necessary than before to bind themselves as clients to an extraregional patron state in exchange for economic or military assistance. The oil-rich states of the Middle East are often criticized for "wasteful" development projects, yet most have done no worse than their oil-poor peers whose economic decisions are overseen by foreign bankers and officials of patron governments. Significantly, the influx of oil money

into the Middle East allowed countries such as Egypt to discard its client relationship to the Soviet Union in favor of more egalitarian relationships with
Arab oil-exporting countries. Oil money also enabled Saudi Arabia to loosen
its Israeli-mediated military dependency on the United States. But the relative weakness of Middle Eastern states implies a continued dependency on
external support. Although oil money hastened the breakdown of the kind of
great power primacy in the Middle East that had shaped the region's politics
for so long, new, oil-enabled external influences on the region are probably
not out of the question (Bloomberg News, 2007; Huus, 2006).

▦ Conclusion

Oil gave a number of Middle Eastern countries the economic independence
to try development strategies and form political bonds foreclosed to poorer
states. It also offered a substitute for conventional—that is, military—attributes of power, forcing other nations to reexamine their own foreign policies in the light of long-term economic interests. Thus it helped to erode the
post–World War II dominance of the superpowers by providing incentives
and resources for their Middle Eastern alliance partners, clients, and dependencies to act more autonomously.

But oil also instilled a false sense of power and economic security in
the minds of policymakers in oil-exporting states. Few used the fat years
following the two enormous oil price hikes to prepare for the lean years that
came after. In 1978, financial analyst Walter J. Levy (1978–1979) mourned
"the years that the locust hath eaten," the years when money was spent,
borrowed, and lent as though the golden faucet would never fail. Now the
ravages of rapid changes in income, both up and down, are visible everywhere in the Middle East.

Despite oil's opportunities, its exploitation has exacted high social, political, and economic costs. Uncertain as to the shape of the new regional
order that will rise out of the debris generated by the current wars, coming
as it does in the company of other rapid political and economic changes in
the Middle East, we can only speculate whether oil has been a blessing or a
curse to its nations and their peoples. A similar analysis of the energy politics of other regions is likely to reveal equally ambiguous effects and equally
uncertain prognoses for the futures of oil exporters and importers alike.

▦ Notes

1. To reduce the confusion that might arise from the frequent name changes of
the various oil companies operating in the Middle East, these companies will be

referred to by their contemporary names rather than by whatever names they might have been called at the time of the particular events discussed.

2. Except where noted, material in this section comes from Tétreault, 1985.

3. I have written elsewhere (1993) about the effect of the price collapse on the two combatants in the Gulf War (1990–1991). Low oil prices were felt disproportionately by Iran, which did not have neighbors sending it financial and military assistance. In an interesting way, the price collapse of the mid-1980s acted as another kind of oil weapon.

◼ Bibliography

Adelman, M. A. 1972–1973. "Is the Oil Shortage Real? Oil Companies as OPEC Tax Collectors." *Foreign Policy* 9 (Winter):69–107.

Allawi, Ali A. 2007. *The Occupation of Iraq: Winning the War, Losing the Peace.* New Haven: Yale University Press.

Anderson, Irvine H. 1981. *Aramco, the United States, and Saudi Arabia: A Study of the Dynamics of Foreign Oil Policy, 1933–1950.* Princeton: Princeton University Press.

al-Assiri, Abdul-Reda. 1990. *Kuwait's Foreign Policy: City-State in World Politics.* Boulder, Colo.: Westview.

Blair, John. 1976. *The Control of Oil.* New York: Pantheon.

Blix, Hans. 2004. *Disarming Iraq.* New York: Pantheon.

Bloomberg News. 2007. "China Targets 9 Countries for Oil Investment." March 1, 2007. www.iht.com/articles/2007/03/01/business/oil.php (accessed October 15, 2007).

Boghardt, Lori Plotkin. 2006. *Kuwait Amid War, Peace and Revolution.* London: Palgrave.

Chandrasekaran, Rajiv. 2006. *Imperial Life in the Emerald City: Inside Iraq's Green Zone.* New York: Knopf.

Chaudhry, Kirin Aziz. 1997. *The Price of Wealth: Economies and Institutions in the Middle East.* Ithaca: Cornell University Press.

Chisholm, Archibald H. T. 1975. *The First Kuwait Oil Concession Agreement: A Record of the Negotiations, 1911–1934.* London: Frank Cass.

Cordesman, Anthony H., and Abraham R. Wagner. 1991. *The Lessons of Modern War,* Vol. 2. *The Iran-Iraq War.* Boulder, Colo.: Westview Press.

Crane, Conrad C., and W. Andrew Terrill. 2003. "Reconstructing Iraq: Insights, Challenges, and Missions for Military Forces in a Post-Conflict Scenario." US Army War College, Strategic Studies Institute, February.

Crystal, Jill. 1990. *Oil and Politics in the Gulf: Rulers and Merchants in Kuwait and Qatar.* Cambridge: Cambridge University Press.

Dawisha, Adeed. 2003. *Arab Nationalism in the Twentieth Century: From Triumph to Despair.* Princeton: Princeton University Press.

Freedman, Lawrence, and Efraim Karsh. 1993. *The Gulf Conflict, 1990–1991: Diplomacy and War in the New World Order.* Princeton: Princeton University Press.

Gasiorowski, Mark J. 1991. *US Foreign Policy and the Shah: Building a Client State in Iran.* Ithaca: Cornell University Press.

———. 1998. "The 1953 Coup d'État in Iran." www.payk.net/politics/1953mossadeq coup/markgasiorowski_1998/main.pdf (accessed April 6, 2003).

Greenspan, Alan. 2007. *The Age of Turbulence: Adventures in a New World.* New York: Penguin.

Holt, Jim. 2007. "It's the Oil." *London Review of Books,* October 18. www.lrb.co.uk/
    v29/n20/holt01_.html (accessed October 14, 2007).
Huus, Kari. 2006. "In China's Oil Quest, No Deal Is Too Unsavory." MSNBC, May
    4. www.msnbc.msn.com/id/12501039 (accessed October 15, 2007).
Institute for War and Peace Reporting (IWPR). 2007. "Special Report: Oil and Cor-
    ruption in Iraq." *Iraq Crisis Report* no. 232, September 10. www.iwpr.net (ac-
    cessed October 13, 2007).
Jentleson, Bruce W. 1986. *Pipeline Politics: The Complex Political Economy of
    East-West Energy Trade.* Ithaca: Cornell University Press.
Lando, Ben. 2007a. "Kurds Talk Contracts with Big Oil: It's Now or Never." *Alter-
    net,* October 10. at www.alternet.org/workplace/64941 (accessed October 14,
    2007).
———. 2007b. "Analysis: Hunt, State Talked on Iraq Oil." UPI, October 12. www
    .upi.com/International_Security/Energy/Analysis/2007/10/12/analysis_hunt_state
    _talked_on_iraq_oil/3128/ (accessed October 14, 2007).
Leggett, Jeremy. 2007. "Oil on the Slide." *The Independent,* October 2. http://com-
    mentisfree.guardian.co.uk/jeremy_leggett/2007/10/oil_on_the_slide.html (ac-
    cessed October 15, 2007).
Levy, Walter J. 1978–1979. "The Years That the Locust Hath Eaten: Oil Policy and
    OPEC Development Prospects." *Foreign Affairs* 57 (Winter):287–308.
Mikdashi, Zuhayr. 1972. *The Community of Oil Exporting Countries.* Ithaca: Cor-
    nell University Press.
Munif, Abdulrahman. 1989. *Cities of Salt.* New York: Vintage International.
Najeeb, Fazil. 2007. "Energy Crisis Threatens Investment." IWPR, *Iraq Crisis Re-
    port* no. 209, January 19. www.iwpr.net (accessed October 13, 2007).
Nitzan, Jonathan, and Shimshon Bichler. 2002. *The Global Political Economy of
    Israel.* London: Pluto Press.
Packer, George. 2005. *The Assassin's Gate: America in Iraq.* New York: Farrar,
    Straus, and Giroux.
Penrose, Edith. 1968. *The Large International Firm in Developing Countries: The
    International Petroleum Industry.* Cambridge: MIT Press.
Prindle, David S. 1981. *Petroleum Politics and the Texas Railroad Commission.*
    Austin: University of Texas Press.
Rand, Christopher T. 1975. *Making Democracy Safe for Oil.* Boston: Little, Brown.
Ricks, Thomas E. 2006. *Fiasco: The American Military Adventure in Iraq.* New
    York: Penguin.
Sampson, Anthony. 1975. *The Seven Sisters: The Great Oil Companies and the
    World They Shaped.* New York: Viking.
Skeet, Ian. 1988. *OPEC: Twenty-Five Years of Prices and Politics.* New York: Cam-
    bridge University Press.
Smith, Jean Edward. 1992. *George Bush's War.* New York: Henry Holt.
Suskind, Ron. 2004. *The Price of Loyalty: George W. Bush, the White House, and
    the Education of Paul O'Neill.* New York: Simon and Schuster.
Tétreault, Mary Ann. 1981. *The Organization of Arab Petroleum Exporting Coun-
    tries: History, Policies, and Prospects.* Westport, Conn.: Greenwood Press.
———. 1985. *Revolution in the World Petroleum Market.* Westport, Conn.: Quorum
    Books.
———. 1993. "Independence, Sovereignty, and Vested Glory: Oil and Politics in the
    Second Gulf War." *Orient* 34, no. 1 (March):87–103.
———. 1995. *The Kuwait Petroleum Corporation and the Economics of the New
    World Order.* Westport, Conn.: Quorum Books.

————. 2000. *Stories of Democracy: Politics and Society in Contemporary Kuwait.* New York: Columbia University Press.

University of Michigan. 2006. "Iraqi Attitudes: Survey Documents Big Changes." www.umich.edu/news/index.html?Releases/2006/Jun06/r061406a (accessed October 15, 2007).

US Government. 2002. "The National Security Strategy of the United States of America." www.whitehouse.gov/nsc/nss.pdf (accessed March 15, 2003).

Vernon, Raymond (ed.). 1976. *The Oil Crisis.* New York: Norton.

Vietor, Richard H. K. 1984. *Energy Policy in America Since 1945: A Study of Business-Government Relations.* New York: Cambridge University Press.

Vitalis, Robert. 2006. *America's Kingdom: Mythmaking on the Saudi Oil Frontier.* Stanford: Stanford University Press.

9

Population Growth, Urbanization, and the Challenges of Unemployment

Valentine M. Moghadam

The Middle East has been experiencing rapid rates of urbanization and population growth over the past several decades. Although countries are at different levels of urbanization, the region as a whole has a majority of its population living in urban areas. At the same time, population growth rates in the Middle East–North Africa (MENA) region have been among the highest in the world, second only to those in sub-Saharan Africa, although fertility rates have been falling, especially among young, educated women in urban areas. The population is expected to swell to 576 million by 2025—more than double the current size. Given the aridity of much of the region, these growing numbers will place increasing demands on water and agricultural land, and urban services, currently strained, will need to be vastly expanded and improved.

Rapid urbanization and rapid population growth have transformed the structure of the labor force. In many countries, the population has shifted from one engaged predominantly in rural and agrarian production systems to one involved in various types of urban industrial and service-oriented economic activities. Moreover, because of previously high fertility rates, the age structure of the labor force is skewed toward the under-twenty-five group. Meanwhile, due to both economic and demographic factors, urban labor markets have been unable to absorb the growing labor force. This has resulted in the expansion of the urban informal sector, income inequalities, urban poverty, and rates of unemployment that are among the highest in the world. In particular, youth and women's unemployment rates are exceedingly high.

This chapter examines the interrelated processes of urbanization, population growth, employment challenges, and poverty in the Middle East and

North Africa. For ease of exposition, I examine each separately, even though
the issues are linked. Furthermore, to reflect differences in population and
labor force size as well as income levels, I frequently refer to the region in
terms of two sets of countries: the small, oil-rich states that belong to the
Gulf Cooperation Council (GCC), including Bahrain, Kuwait, Oman, Qatar,
Saudi Arabia, and the United Arab Emirates (UAE); and the larger and more
diversified countries (Algeria, Egypt, Iran, Iraq, Israel, Jordan, Lebanon,
Libya, Morocco, Syria, Tunisia, Turkey, and Yemen). To the extent possible,
I shall also include the West Bank and Gaza Strip in the analysis.

▓ Urbanization

The urban population of the region has been growing rapidly since 1950. Its
share of the total population grew from 24 percent in 1950 to 57 percent in
1990 (Omran and Roudi, 1993:21). The most rapid growth in urbanization
occurred in the oil-exporting countries; the population doubled between
1960 and 1980 in Saudi Arabia, Oman, Libya, and the UAE, and between
1950 and 1985 in Iran and Iraq (Assaad, 1995:21). Among countries that are
not already highly urbanized, the slowest rate of urbanization was in Egypt,
whose urban share increased from 32 percent in 1950 to 43 percent in 2001.
The three largest countries in the region—Iran, Turkey, and Egypt—also
have extensive land with relatively large rural populations that constitute a
pool of future rural-to-urban migrants. Yemen is the least-urbanized country
in the region, whereas Kuwait, Qatar, and Bahrain are virtually city-states.
Table 9.1 illustrates the varying levels of urbanization across the region. It
should be noted that after Latin America, which is about 71 percent urbanized, the MENA region has the highest level of urbanization in the developing world.

Urbanization is a key aspect of social change and of economic development. It entails the implementation of policies leading to the growth of
cities and rural-to-urban migration. The latter is typically fueled by both
push and pull factors: the push of population pressure on natural resources
and the lack of economic opportunity in the rural areas, and the pull of perceived economic opportunity and a better lifestyle in the big cities (Omran
and Roudi, 1993:21). The continuing growth of cities and of rural-to-urban
migration is often exacerbated by the "urban bias" of government policies
and development strategies, which leads to underdevelopment of rural
areas, greater investment in urban infrastructure, and income gaps between
rural and urban workers.

International migration can also play a part in urbanization. For example,
in the case of Israel, immigration by Jews from other countries has contributed to the growth of Tel Aviv and West Jerusalem, and in the case of the
small, oil-rich GCC countries, labor migration from other Arab countries

Table 9.1 Population and Urbanization in the MENA Region

Country	Population, 2005 (millions)	Projected Population, 2015 (millions)	Percent Urban in 2005	Percent Urban in 1950
Algeria	32.9	38.1	63.3	22
Bahrain	0.7	.85	96.5	64
Egypt	74.0	88.2	42.8	32
Iran	69.5	79.9	66.9	27
Iraq	28.8	36.5	66.9	34
Israel	6.7	7.8	91.6	65
Jordan	5.7	7.0	82.3	35
Kuwait	2.7	3.4	98.3	59
Lebanon	3.6	4.0	86.6	32
Libya	5.9	7.2	84.8	19
Mauritania	3.1	4.0	40.4	3
Morocco	31.5	36.2	58.7	26
Oman	2.6	3.2	71.5	8.6
Qatar	.8	1.0	95.4	79.2
Saudi Arabia	24.6	30.8	81.0	21
Syria	19	23.8	50.6	31
Tunisia	10.1	11.1	65.3	32
Turkey	73.2	82.6	67.3	25
United Arab Emirates	4.5	5.6	76.7	55
West Bank and Gaza	3.7	5.0	71.6	37.3
Yemen	21.0	28.5	27.3	6

Source: UN, 2006; World Bank, www.worldbank.org/data/wdi2002, tab. 2-1.
Notes: Djibouti has a population under 600,000; Comoros is 820,000.

contributed to the rapid rates of urbanization, especially during the 1970s and 1980s.

Between 1950 and 1980, there was tremendous growth of the large cities in the region, including Tehran, Cairo, Istanbul, and Baghdad, as a result of both high fertility rates and rural-to-urban migration. In 1950 only four cities had populations exceeding 1 million; by 1970 there were nine (Assaad, 1995:22). By 1990 the number of such cities had exceeded twenty, and ten years later, some twenty-five cities had populations of over 1 million. Megacities such as Cairo, Istanbul, and Tehran saw the growth of their populations during the 1980s, but so did a second tier of cities, such as Alexandria, Isfahan, Mashhad, Riyadh, Ankara, and Adana (see Table 9.2). Some of the megacities, and especially Cairo, have extremely high population densities, severe shortages of housing and services, and lack of regulation of construction and

More than half the population of heavily
urbanized Lebanon lives in the capital city of Beirut.

urban development. Indeed, the economies of the cities cannot absorb their
large urban populations, leading to unemployment, underemployment, and
poverty among urban populations. Other problems include a shortage of
clean drinking water, the growth of slums or shantytowns, polluted air, and
inadequate waste disposal systems (Omran and Roudi, 1993:30).

Population Growth

According to theories of epidemiological and demographic transitions, a population's fertility and mortality will decline from high to low levels as a result
of economic and social development. The decline in mortality usually pre-
cedes the decline in fertility. This transition occurred in European countries
during the nineteenth century and in the developing world during the twentieth century. Currently, the countries of the Middle East and North Africa are
differentially situated along the transition continuum and are characterized by
varying levels and combinations of mortality and fertility.

The Middle East and North Africa saw a population explosion in the
1950s, a result of high fertility and declines in the crude death rate, although
infant mortality rates were still very high. In the 1960s the region had the
world's highest fertility rate among developing regions, but since about 1970
fertility has been falling, and fertility rates in sub-Saharan Africa have now
surpassed those in the Middle East. MENA's annual population growth

Table 9.2 MENA Cities with Populations Over 1 Million, 2005

Country	City	Population (millions)
Algeria	Algiers	3.200
Egypt	Cairo	11.128
	Alexandria	3.770
Iran	Tehran	7.314
	Isfahan	1.535
	Karaj	1.223
	Mashhad	2.134
	Qom	1.035
	Shiraz	1.331
	Tabriz	1.510
Iraq	Baghdad	6.593
	Mosul	1.234
Israel	Tel Aviv	3.012
Jordan	Amman	1.292
Lebanon	Beirut	1.777
Libya	Tripoli	2.098
	Banghazi	1.114
Morocco	Casablanca	3.138
	Rabat	1.647
Saudi Arabia	Jeddah	2.860
	Mecca	1.319
	Riyadh	4.193
Syria	Aleppo	2.520
	Damascus	2.272
Tunisia	Tunis	n.a.
Turkey	Adana	1.245
	Ankara	3.573
	Bursa	1.414
	Istanbul	9.712
	Izmir	2.487

Source: UN, 2006.
Note: n.a. indicates data not available.

reached a peak of 3 percent around 1980, while the growth rate for the world as a whole reached its peak of 2 percent annually more than a decade earlier (Roudi, 2001).

For the region as a whole, the total fertility rate (average number of births per woman) went from 7 children per woman in the 1950s to 4.8 in 1990 and declined further to about 3.6 in 2001. Today, the total fertility rate is less than 3 in Bahrain, Iran, Lebanon, Tunisia, and Turkey, and is more than 5 in Iraq, Oman, Palestine, Saudi Arabia, and Yemen. There have been impressive fertility declines in Morocco and Egypt since the 1980s, but only a slight decline in Saudi Arabia and none at all in Yemen, where the average number of births per woman is more than 7. The fertility decline in the region is associated with effective family-planning campaigns and increases in women's education and employment (see Table 9.3).

Table 9.3 Sociodemographic Features in MENA, 2004–2007

Country	% Females Literate, Ages 15+, 2004	Net Female Enrollments, Secondary School (%), 2004	Gross Female Tertiary Enrollment (%), 2004	Female Singulate Age at First Marriage, mid-1990s	% Married Women Using Contraception (total), 2007	Total Fertility Rate, 2007
Algeria	60	68	20	24	57	2.4
Bahrain	84	93	45	23	65[c]	2.6
Egypt	59	77	n.a.	22	59	3.1
Iran	70	76	24[a]	21	74	2.0
Iraq	n.a.	n.a.	n.a.	22	50	4.9
Israel	96	89	65	24	n.a.	2.8
Jordan	85	82	41	25	56	3.5
Kuwait	91	80	30	25	52[c]	2.6
Lebanon	n.a.	n.a.	50	n.a.	63[c]	2.3
Libya	n.a.	n.a.	59	n.a.	49[c]	3.0
Morocco	40	32	10[b]	22	63	2.4
Oman	74	75	15	19	24[c]	3.4
Palestine	88	92	44	n.a.	50	4.6
Qatar	89	86	34	23	43[c]	2.8
Saudi Arabia	69	51	33	22	32[c]	4.1
Sudan	52	n.a.	6	26	10[c]	4.5
Syria	74	56	n.a.	n.a.	47	3.5
Tunisia	65	69	33	25	63	2.0
Turkey	80	n.a.	24	22	71	2.2
United Arab Emirates	n.a.	64	40	23	28[c]	2.7
Yemen	n.a.	21	5	n.a.	23	6.2

Sources: Population Reference Bureau, *Women of the World 2002* [poster]; Population Reference Bureau, *World Population Data Sheet 2007* for total fertility rate (7-9) and percent of married women using contraception (11–13); female share of tertiary enrollment from CAWTAR, 2001:tab. A/33, p. 229, and UN, 2000:tab. 4.A; and singulate age at marriage from UN, 2000.

Notes: a. The figure for Iran does not include private universities. In 2002 the female share of university enrollments rose to over 50 percent.

b. The CAWTAR report cites a figure of 21 percent female share of university enrollment in Morocco.

c. Indicates 2001 figures.

n.a. indicates data not available.

The infant mortality rate, which was as high as 200 per 1,000 live births in 1955, began to decline in 1960, and by 1990 it had reached about 70 per 1,000 live births (Assaad, 1995). Eight years later it was down to 45—still higher than Latin America, the Caribbean, eastern Asia, Europe, and Central Asia, but lower than southern Asia and sub-Saharan Africa (see World Bank, 2000:108, tab. 2.18). For some countries, the changes in infant, child, and maternal mortality occurred rapidly and dramatically. For example, in 1960, Tunisia had an infant mortality rate of 159, and its under-five child mortality rate was 255. In the 1980s these declined to 58 and 83, respectively. By 2000 the rate of infant mortality had dropped to just 30. Iran similarly saw impressive achievements in the health of children as well as of mothers during the 1990s. Indeed, maternal mortality rates have dropped throughout the region, though they remain highest in Yemen and Sudan, the poorest and most rural countries. Life expectancy varies; it is highest in the oil-rich Gulf states (72 years) and Israel (80 years), lowest in Sudan (55 years) and Yemen (56 years).

Following the analysis by Abdel R. Omran and Farzaneh Roudi (1993) but with some modifications, we may divide the countries of the Middle East and North Africa into four groups based on the trends in birth and death rates and their socioeconomic settings. Group 1 is characterized by persistent high fertility and declining mortality among middle-income and poor countries in an intermediate-to-low socioeconomic setting and includes Jordan, Iraq, Syria, Yemen, and the West Bank and Gaza Strip. Group 2 is characterized by declining fertility and mortality among middle-income countries in an intermediate level of socioeconomic development and includes Egypt, Lebanon, Turkey, Iran, Morocco, and Tunisia. A third group, made up of the rich GCC countries, is characterized by high fertility amid rapidly declining mortality in a high socioeconomic setting. Finally, Israel is the only country in the region that follows the European-style transition of low fertility and mortality in an upper-middle-income and above-average socioeconomic setting.

Iran and Turkey have had some volatility in their demographic transitions. Turkey began its transition earliest, in the 1950s, only to experience a kind of baby boom in the early 1970s. Iran's total fertility rate declined during the 1970s but increased during the 1980s following the Iranian revolution. The dramatic population growth rate of the 1980s is attributed to the pronatalist policies of the new Islamic regime, which banned contraceptives and encouraged marriage and family formation (Moghadam, 2003:chap. 6), but it may also be a result of rural fertility behavior, which was slow to decline during the 1970s. Since the reversal of the pronatalist policy following the results of the 1986 census and the introduction of an aggressive family planning campaign after 1988, there has been a change from the fertility and population growth trends of the 1980s. In the mid-1990s, fertility declined again.

In some countries, fertility rates are considerably higher in rural areas than urban areas, as confirmed by recent Demographic and Health Surveys (DHS).[1] For example, in Egypt, fertility rates remain very high in the rural areas of Upper Egypt, where infant and under-five mortality rates also are high. A 1992 DHS measured a total fertility rate of 2.9 children per woman in urban Egypt, compared with 4.9 children in rural areas. A 1990 DHS in Jordan found that women in the largest cities had 4.8 children on average, those in smaller urban areas had 5.6 children, and women in rural areas had 6.9 children. In Yemen a 1991–1992 DHS measured a total fertility rate of 5.6 among urban women, compared with 8.1 among rural women (Omran and Roudi, 1993:13).

Like the World Fertility Surveys of the late 1970s and early 1980s, the more recent Demographic and Health Surveys research confirmed the link between the mother's education and total fertility rate: the higher the educational attainment, the fewer number of children. In Jordan, for example, women with no formal education had an average fertility rate of 6.9, whereas the figure for those with a secondary or higher education was 4.1 per woman. Still, Jordan is unique in its relatively high fertility rate among educated women; this may be a function of the very low labor force participation of women.

In Morocco, Tunisia, and Turkey, fertility has declined faster in urban than in rural areas, suggesting the effect that urbanization and its correlates—mainly female education, employment opportunities, delayed marriage, and access to contraceptives and family planning information—have had in those countries. But in Turkey and Tunisia and to a lesser degree in Morocco and Iran, fertility declines are being registered in rural areas as well, partly due to the availability of contraception.

MENA countries have exhibited a variety of population policies and concerns. "Population policy" is understood to be an intention to improve the overall well-being of the nation's citizens. Definitions of "well-being" vary and are certainly debatable, as are prescriptions of how to reach objectives. In the 1990s, countries that were concerned about the rate of population growth (e.g., Iran and Egypt) faced the dual goal of improving health facilities on the one hand, thus reducing natal and infant mortality, and of decreasing the birthrate on the other hand. Other countries seek to reduce mortality rates and improve the population's health but do not actively seek to reduce birthrates (e.g., Israel and Saudi Arabia). At the level of state policymaking, the approach to population growth ranges from pronatalist to laissez-faire to pro–family planning. In several of the countries—notably Iran, Lebanon, Tunisia, and Turkey—the combined effects of socioeconomic development, women's educational attainment, and state-sponsored family planning programs have produced the lowest fertility rates of the region. Indeed, the average of about 2.5 children per woman in these MENA countries today is even lower than the fertility rate of many Latin American countries.

Still, decades of high birthrates have helped to keep the population of Middle Eastern countries young. More than 40 percent of the region's population is under fifteen years of age, whereas only 4 percent is over age sixty-five. These percentages are similar to the average for all developing countries but very different from the pattern in industrial countries. There are also variations across the region. In 2000 the share of the population under age fifteen ranged from 26.7 percent in Qatar to over 50 percent in Yemen and the West Bank and Gaza. The share of the population aged sixty-five or older ranged from 9.9 percent in Israel to 2 percent or less in Yemen, Kuwait, and Qatar (UNDP, 2002a:tab. 5). These differences in age structure are tied to the different birth rates across the region.

Countries with young populations exhibit a high dependency ratio and small tax base, a situation exacerbated by the low labor force participation of women in nonagricultural and modern occupations.

Labor Force Growth and Employment Challenges

Despite growing urbanization in the Middle East and North Africa, roughly one-third of the total population still depends on agriculture for its livelihood. The proportion of the labor force in agriculture varies from around 50 percent in Turkey, Yemen, and Syria to less than 5 percent in Israel and the small Gulf states. Economic modernization, however, has resulted in changes in the sectoral distribution of the labor force, with a growing proportion of workers involved in services and, to a lesser degree, in industry. The emergence of the services sector has been especially evident in Jordan, where the share of agriculture in total employment declined from 42 percent in the 1960s to less than 7 percent in the early 1990s (Shaban, Assaad, and al-Qudsi, 1995:71). Although the services sector has been expanding and thriving throughout the region, the manufacturing sector has not fared as well, partly due to the reliance on wealth generated from oil exports. Still, in a number of countries, the economic development strategy of the 1960s–1980s, which included protection and promotion of the manufacturing sector, did lead to increases in (mostly male) employment in industry. Throughout the region, the structural transformation of the regional economy was accompanied by the emergence of a female labor force, but it has remained a relatively small percentage of the total salaried workforce. Labor force statistics in the region are not always exact, and women's economic activity outside the formal and modern sector has tended to be underestimated, but the available evidence suggests that a large part of the female economically active population in many of the countries, such as Egypt, Iran, Iraq, Syria, and Turkey, remains rooted in agriculture.

In the highly urbanized GCC countries of Bahrain, Kuwait, Qatar, and the UAE, the agricultural workforce is quite small. There is greater involvement in agriculture in Oman and Saudi Arabia, but more so on the part of men than of women, which raises the question of whether women's agricultural activity is properly measured. In the GCC countries, with the exception of Oman, the vast majority of the female workforce (nationals) is engaged in service-sector work. Less prestigious or "culturally inappropriate" service work is performed by imported female labor. The involvement of women in industry is negligible, except in Oman.

Among the larger and more diversified countries of the region, Turkey remains anomalous, in that it is the most modernized of the countries and yet the one where women are most likely to be found in agriculture. In Algeria, Egypt, Jordan, Lebanon, and Libya, the majority of the measured female workforce is concentrated in the service sector. Only in Morocco and Tunisia are large percentages of the female workforce involved in the industrial (manufacturing) sector. In all countries, the male workforce is more evenly distributed across the sectors and more likely to be found in modern occupations. Moreover, the female share of the total salaried workforce is very small, under 20 percent. Clearly, salaried work is a male domain in the region (Moghadam, 2003:chap. 2).

The height of the region's oil-based economic development during the 1970s saw considerable intraregional labor migration, characterized by a massive outflow of surplus labor from countries such as Egypt, Jordan, Tunisia, Yemen, and Lebanon, as well as the West Bank, to capital-rich and labor-poor GCC countries, and to Libya and Iraq. These entities also imported non-Arab workers, including Koreans, Filipinos, Sri Lankans, and Yugoslavs, who were attracted by the high wages offered in the capital-rich Arab countries. In 1975, foreign labor constituted 47 percent of the labor force in the Gulf countries, and by 1990 the figure had increased to 68 percent. In Kuwait in 1990, fully 86 percent of the workforce was foreign (ESCWA, 1993). Remittances from nationals working abroad became especially important to the economies of Egypt, Jordan, and Yemen.

Jordan was unique among Arab countries in being a labor-exporting country that also imported labor. It exported skilled workers and educated professionals to the rich Gulf states, but it also imported unskilled and low-wage workers for construction, domestic services, and some public services that Jordanian nationals would not perform, such as waiting tables, cleaning buildings, and cleaning streets. Most of the imported Arab labor was (and remains) Egyptian. Most domestic workers are from the Philippines, with a smaller proportion from Sri Lanka. A rather peculiar result has been the underutilization of Jordanian women, who in the absence of labor force attachment tend to have nearly four children on average, as discussed above (see also Moghadam, 1998).

The labor migration patterns of North Africans and Turks have been different. Their preferred destination has been Europe, notably Germany for Turks and France for Algerians, Moroccans, and Tunisians (although Tunisians also went to Libya, as mentioned above). Furthermore, labor migration began earlier, during the 1950s and 1960s, in response to European guest worker programs. In the 1970s, European countries began to reduce the influx of guest workers, although the number of Turks in Germany has continued to grow through a combination of natural increase, family reunification, and illegal immigration (OECD, 1992; Omran and Roudi, 1993:24). North African emigrants continued to head to Europe in the 1980s, and, in a new development, the migration streams have started to include women on their own.

In Arab countries, political and economic instabilities have resulted in a reduction of intraregional labor flows, affecting mainly Jordanian, Palestinian, and Yemeni workers laboring in Kuwait and Saudi Arabia. The expulsion of the expatriate workers was a punishment for their countries' stance on the 1991 Gulf War, revealing once again the facade of Arab unity. At the same time, Kuwait and Saudi Arabia rewarded Egypt for its position against Iraq and in favor of the war by replacing expelled Jordanians, Palestinians, and Yemenis with Egyptian workers. Still, a large number of Egyptians left the Gulf and returned to Egypt as a result of the Gulf War. The UN's Economic and Social Commission for West Asia (ESCWA) estimated the total number of returnees at 2 million people. Most returnees were nationals of Yemen (732,000), Egypt (700,000), and Jordan (300,000, including Palestinians). The return of expatriates has been a mixed experience; in some cases returnees contributed to a boom in the construction industry and in small businesses (especially in Jordan), but in other cases returnees have experienced unemployment, slow absorption into the local labor market, or poverty. Poverty has been especially acute for Yemenis, who were largely unskilled workers unable to find employment at home.

▪ Rising Unemployment

Thus, by the mid-1990s, the demographic transition characterized by high fertility, rural-to-urban migration, and changes in the pattern of intraregional labor migration had led to rapid growth of the labor force. In a situation of economic stagnation, this resulted in high rates of unemployment, especially in urban areas.

The unemployment situation was a shock to the educated population in particular, who had come to expect guaranteed jobs in the public sector. During the 1960s and 1970s, state-sponsored economic development resulted in an expansion of public-sector employment. For example, Egypt had a policy of guaranteeing public-sector jobs to graduates of vocational secondary schools and universities. Morocco had a similar scheme, albeit one that provided "temporary employment" to graduates. As a result of these policies, some countries, such as Egypt, Jordan, and Algeria, employed more than 50 percent of the labor force in the public sector. A majority of the workforce in the GCC countries was also employed in the public sector.

As a result of the recessionary conditions experienced in the region since the mid-1980s and structural adjustment policy prescriptions to contract the public-sector wage bill, public sectors are no longer hiring as expansively as before, although they are not yet laying off large numbers of workers (as occurred in Latin America and sub-Saharan Africa, where structural adjustments were implemented earlier). Indeed, due to political and social concerns, MENA governments have preferred the strategy of wage deterioration or encouragement of early retirement rather than outright layoffs. Of course, economic restructuring in the private sector did result in worker layoffs in Tunisia, Morocco, and Turkey. But for the most part, the unemployed population has consisted of first-time job seekers, mainly but not exclusively secondary school graduates, male and female alike, who are seeking jobs out of economic need.

The contraction of public-sector employment and declines in government social spending led to the deterioration of real wages, which in turn made household incomes fall substantially in many countries (Karshenas, 1994). For example, the real wage rate in Jordan increased by 45 percent over the period 1975–1987, but by 1990 it had declined to roughly its value in 1975 (Shaban, Assaad, and al-Qudsi, 1995:74). The drop in real wages was not, however, accompanied by an increase in job creation or the demand for labor or by a decrease in the unemployment rates. This suggests that the problem in the labor market was not high wages (as in the past) but a lack of competitiveness and productivity and inefficient utilization of human resources. It also suggests the underdevelopment of the private sector in the region and its inability to absorb the growing labor force.

Compared to other regions in the world economy, unemployment rates are very high in the Middle East and North Africa, and they are exceptionally high for women. Even the GCC countries, which historically had very low rates of unemployment and in fact imported labor to meet demand, now came to face increasing joblessness among their native populations. Unemployment is often difficult to measure in developing countries. Most of the countries in the Middle East have only recently started to count those who are either unsuccessfully seeking jobs for the first time (as with high school and college graduates) or who have lost jobs due to enterprise restructuring (a far smaller proportion). Measured unemployment is usually urban, although countries are now increasingly including the rural areas in their enumeration; thus some countries now disaggregate unemployment by urban or rural area as well as by gender.

Urban unemployment rates began increasing in the 1980s and reached highs of 10–18 percent in Algeria, Tunisia, Egypt, Jordan, Iran, Turkey, and Yemen. According to ESCWA, the rates were as high as 30 percent in Yemen, the West Bank, and Gaza. As mentioned, unemployment is age-specific, with much of it consisting of new entrants to the workforce in the age groups fifteen to nineteen and twenty to twenty-four. Joblessness varies by educational attainment, but in some countries college graduates experience high rates of unemployment. In the early 1990s, unemployment rates among high school graduates were between 17 percent and 29 percent in Algeria, Egypt, Jordan, Morocco, and Tunisia; college graduates showed unemployment rates of 15 percent and 23 percent in Egypt and Morocco, respectively; and among workers with primary education or less, unemployment rates were 17–27 percent in Algeria, Morocco, and Tunisia (ILO, 1999).

In the 1990s, female unemployment rates soared to highs of 25 percent, indicating a growing supply of job-seeking women, in contrast to an earlier pattern of "housewife-ization." Table 9.4 shows that in almost all countries, female unemployment rates were considerably higher than male rates. In Algeria, unemployment rates were high for both women and men (still 29.7 percent and 33.9 percent, respectively, in 2000), but women's unemployment

This proud high school graduate of the Friends Boys School in Ramallah, West Bank, hopes that attending college in the United States will improve his chances for future employment.

Table 9.4 Unemployment Rates, Selected MENA Countries, Various Years

Country	Year	Male (%)	Female (%)	Total (%)
Algeria[a]	1992	24.2	20.3	23.8
	1997	26.9	24.0	26.4
	2000	33.9	29.7	30.0
Bahrain[b]	1991	5.5	13.4	6.8
Egypt	1995	7.0	22.1	10.4
	2000	5.1	22.7	11.8
	2004	6.3	23.9	9.9
Iraq	1987	4.3	7.4	5.1
	2004	30.2	16	n.a.
Jordan	1991	14.4	34.1	17.1
	1994	12.9	28.3	15.0
	1997	11.7	28.5	14.4
	2000	12.6	19.8	13.7
Lebanon	1996	8.6	7.2	7.0[c]
Morocco	1992	13.0	25.3	16.0
(urban)	1998	17.4	22.9	18.7
	2000	13.8	13	19.0
	2004	10.6	11.4	19.0
Oman	1993	4.7	8.7	5.1
Palestine				
West Bank	1997	17.2	17.7	15.5
Gaza	1997	26.5	29.8	26.2
Sudan	1993	8.6	9.6	n.a.
Syria	1981	3.2	2.0	3.0
	1991	5.2	14.0	6.8
	1995	5.1	11.6	6.5
Tunisia	1993	14.7	21.9	16.1
Yemen	1991	14.0	6.0	12.3
	1994	10.1	5.4	18.1
	2000	12.5	8.2	30.0

Sources: World Bank, 1995b:5; ERF, 1996:103, 1998:128; ESCWA, 2000:37; ILO, 1999: tab. 3A; Moghadam, 1998; Yemen Ministry of Planning and Development, 1998; Jordan Department of Statistics, *Employment and Unemployment Survey* (various issues); gender statistics for 2000s from World Bank Group GenderStats; total unemployment statistics from the *CIA World Factbook* 2000, 2004.

Notes: a. 1997 data on Algeria from Republique Algerienne, 1999, and World Bank GenderStats, http://genderstats.worldbank.org.

b. Bahrain had 24.8 percent female unemployment in 1991, compared to 12.3 percent for men (UNDP, 1998).

c. Lebanon's total unemployment rate for new entrants is 22 percent.

n.a. indicates not available.

was disproportionately high, given that they constituted a mere 10 percent of the labor force. This holds true also for Lebanon. Table 9.5 illustrates the prevalence of joblessness among young women, especially in Bahrain, Egypt, Jordan, Oman, Palestine, Syria, and Tunisia. Women's high unemployment

Table 9.5 Youth Unemployment by Sex, Selected MENA Countries, Various Years

Country	Year	Female (%)	Male (%)	Total (%)
Bahrain	1981	42.8	8.4	17.1
	1991	33.9	22.4	25.4
Egypt	1995	41.1	24.5	n.a.
	1998	15.8	42.8	23.1
	1999	13.8	36.7	20.4
	2001	19.2	51.1	27.7
	2002	21.4	40.0	27.1
Iraq	1987	18.5	6.3	7.7
Iran	2005	20.3	32.1	23.1
Jordan	1983	25.9	7.9	10.7
	1994	63.9	28.5	35.2
	2000	24.5	39.2	26.7
	2001	27.8	40.9	29.7
	2002	29.1	41.8	30.9
	2003	28.0	43.2	30.3
Kuwait	1985	6.3	6.3	6.3
Lebanon	1997	12.6	23.8	21.3
Oman	1993	25.8	16.2	17.6
Palestine	1997	31.6	27.7	n.a.
	2001	35.4	29.6	34.8
	2002	42.6	35.7	41.8
	2004	38.9	44.8	39.8
Qatar	1986	8.0	2.9	3.2
	1997	10.6	74.7	14.6
Sudan	1993	17.1	16.6	n.a.
Syria	1983	3.8	6.9	6.2
	1995	19.7	11.3	13.6
	2002	21.4	38.9	26.3
Tunisia	1984	17.2	30.5	n.a.
	1994	24.7	28.4	n.a.
	1997	33.3	29.0	31.8
	2005	31.4	29.3	30.7
United Arab Emirates	1985	3.5	3.7	3.7
	1995	6.4	5.7	6.3
Yemen	1986	1.8	8.6	6.5
	1994	9.8	20.2	17.9

Source: ESCWA, 2000:annexes 13–14; updates from UN Statistics Division, http://unstats
.un.org/unsd/cdb/cdb_series_xrxx.asp?series_code=29961.
Note: n.a. indicates data not available.

rates appear to be a function of both women's preferences for public-sector jobs, which are not available, and the private sector's discrimination against women, typically due to maternity leave requirements in labor law. Iranian women's very high rate of unemployment in 1991 was almost halved by 1996, and this may be because more women have been starting their own businesses and nongovernmental organizations (NGOs) and entering universities. Yemen seems to depart from the regional norm of very high rates of female unemployment, and this may reflect the effects of returning male migrant workers as well as very low rates of female labor force participation (Yemen Ministry of Planning and Development, 1998). Still, the available evidence suggests that the feminization of unemployment is a defining feature of the urban labor markets of the Middle East and North Africa.

How do the unemployed—those who expect jobs in the formal sector but do not find them—fare in countries where unemployment insurance is not in place or is not available to new entrants? Some of the job seekers— and especially the men—appear to have gravitated to the urban informal sector, which by all accounts has grown tremendously in the region. Informal-sector workers may include taxi drivers, construction workers, domestic workers, people who work in souks and bazaars (the traditional markets in the Middle East), hairdressers, barbers, seamstresses, tailors, workers in or owners of small industrial or artisan workshops, hawkers of sundry goods, and repairmen. Also included are home-based female pieceworkers, such as women in Turkey, Syria, and Jordan who are engaged in sewing and embroidery for a contractor or subcontractor. The nature and function of the informal sector has been much debated; although it serves to absorb the labor force and to provide goods and services at relatively low cost, it is also unregulated and untaxed, leading to poor labor standards and income (such as the wealth of many merchants) that is not redistributed. The informal sector both contributes to, and is a reflection of, income inequality in the society.

◼ Poverty and Inequality

Poverty and inequality are measured by household income and consumption and by quality-of-life indicators. Conventional studies distinguish between "absolute poverty" and "relative poverty," and they establish an income-based "poverty line" against which households are measured. In an alternative conceptualization, the definition of poverty is broadened to include measures of "capabilities" or "human development" such as literacy, life expectancy, and access to clean water. This better captures gender differences while also recognizing the multidimensionality of poverty. Studies show considerable improvement over time in standards of living in the Middle East and North Africa, as measured by such social indicators as life expectancy, infant mortality, maternal mortality, access to safe water, adequate sanitation facilities, rising age of first marriage, fertility rates, literacy, and school enrollments, as well as by wage rates and household incomes. However, gender gaps exist, and given the income levels of many countries in the region, the social indicators should be better. Moreover, although levels of absolute poverty have been decreasing in some parts of the region, poverty has actually been increasing in other parts. This is mainly a function of high population growth, but it is also due to the creation of new poverty groups in urban areas caused by economic recession, rising prices, deteriorating wages, and unemployment. This shift has been occurring since the mid-1980s, when the price of oil and hence gross domestic product (GDP) declined, the external debt rose, and government spending was reduced.

According to the World Bank and ESCWA, the number of poor people in the Middle East and North Africa increased from an estimated 60 million in 1985 to 73 million in 1990, or from 30.6 percent to 33.1 percent of the total population (World Bank, 1993:5; ESCWA, 1993:121; see also ESCWA, 1995b, 1995c). Poverty assessments prepared by the World Bank, which were derived from surveys of living standards undertaken within various countries, revealed growing poverty in Egypt and Jordan and the emergence of urban "working poor" in Tunisia and Morocco. According to official statistics, 23 percent of the population in Egypt in 1991 and 18 percent of the population in Jordan in 1993 were considered to be living under the poverty line. Most believed that the poverty incidence could be as high as 30 percent in both countries (Moghadam, 1997, 1998). In both countries poverty was largely rural, and the rural poor were small landholders and tenants, landless agricultural workers, and pastoralists (ESCWA, 1993:6). In Egypt the urban poor included the unemployed and female-headed households. In all countries, because of gender differences in literacy, educational attainment, employment, and income, women are especially vulnerable to poverty during periods of economic difficulty or in the event of divorce, abandonment, or widowhood.

Even though poverty is not as severe in the Middle East as in some other regions (UNDP, 2002b), it has been increasing, and according to some observers, income inequalities have been widening (el-Ghonemy, 1998; Richards and Waterbury, 1996). This is said to be the result of the new economic policies of structural adjustment and trade and price liberalization, as well as the old policies of high military spending and inadequate taxation.

In Lebanon, the main factors behind the alarming increase in the incidence of poverty have been the civil war and misguided economic policies, including tax write-offs for large firms engaged in the country's reconstruction and the absence of any property taxes. According to ESCWA, in 1996 about 1 million Lebanese (28 percent of the population) were living below the poverty line, and some 75 percent of the poor were urban dwellers. The country's unemployment rate reached 15 percent in 1996, compared with 8.1 percent of the workforce in 1975, before the country's long civil war

Children sift through a garbage dump in a poor part of Cairo,
looking for clothing and other salvageable items.

began. The ESCWA report singled out the absence of government social
spending and "unjust wealth distribution" as the factors behind the rise in
nutritional deficiencies, lack of sanitation in poor areas, and the lowering of
teaching and health standards (*Middle East Times,* 1996:19).

For some countries, poverty and lack of progress in human development
have resulted from very high military expenditures. In Iraq, Oman, Saudi
Arabia, Syria, and Yemen, military expenditures in 1990 far exceeded expenditures on education and health care (see UNDP, 1996:tab. 19). As recently as 2000, military expenditures in Saudi Arabia amounted to 11.6 percent of gross domestic product (GDP); in Jordan, the figure was 9.5 percent.
Even Turkey committed nearly 5 percent of GDP toward military expenditure, compared with 2.2 percent of GDP for education and 3.3 percent for
health care (UNDP, 2002a:tab. 17). In the case of Iraq, of course, war and
economic sanctions have exacerbated the situation of the poor and created
new poverty-stricken groups. The destruction of Iraq's infrastructure by US-
led coalition bombings in January 1991 (see Drèze and Gazdar, 1992) and
again in March–April 2003, the shortage of medical supplies and foodstuffs
caused by the long sanctions regime, and the collapse of public services following the 2003 invasion have completely transformed a country that was
once urbanized, mechanized, and prosperous.

The available evidence suggests that in the large and diversified econo-mies—such as Turkey, Lebanon, and Iran—inequalities or relative poverty are quite pronounced and have been growing. The persistence of destitution, or absolute poverty, mainly in rural areas, is a problem in such low-income countries as Egypt, Yemen, and Morocco, and perhaps also in the Gaza Strip. Social indicators on health, safe water, and sanitation reflect the qual-ity of life of citizens as well as urban-rural disparities. Although urbaniza-tion has brought about access to health, safe water, and sanitation for resi-dents in most of the countries, some countries—including Algeria, Syria, and Yemen—continue to have difficulties in the provision of such urban services, as noted earlier in this chapter. Other countries experience distinct rural-urban disparities. Table 9.6 shows the population without access to health care, safe water, and sanitation, most of whom would be rural dwellers. (The high rates of access to health care, water, and sanitation as reported by several of the countries should be viewed with some skepticism.) In terms of access to services, urban living is certainly superior to rural living, but popu-lation growth and reductions in government social spending are straining the quality and quantity of urban services. These pressures are not conveyed by

**Table 9.6 Percentage of Population Without Access to Services,
Selected MENA Countries**

Country	Health Care, 1981–1993	Safe Water, 2004	Sanitation, 2004
Algeria	n.a.	15	8
Egypt	1	2	30
Iran	27	6	n.a.
Iraq	2	n.a.	n.a.
Israel	n.a.	0	n.a.
Jordan	10	3	7
Kuwait	0	n.a.	n.a.
Lebanon	5	0	2
Morocco	38	19	27
Oman	11	n.a.	n.a.
Saudi Arabia	2	n.a.	n.a.
Syria	1	7	10
Tunisia	10	7	15
Turkey	0	4	12
United Arab Emirates	10	0	2
Yemen	84	33	57

Source: UNDP, 2006: 305–307, tab. 4.
Note: n.a. indicates data not available.

the statistics but are best discerned by visits to and stays in the nonelite sections of the cities of the Middle East and North Africa, where overcrowding, rundown and inadequate public transportation, streets in disrepair, polluted air, high noise levels, and lack of building codes are only some of the many problems that low-income urban dwellers endure.

I end this section with profiles of poverty and inequality in Morocco, Tunisia, Egypt, and the Palestinian Authority/Occupied Territories based on World Bank poverty assessments and other sources. The profiles show that in addition to external factors such as occupation, war, or unfair terms of trade, crucial internal factors in the creation or perpetuation of poverty and inequality are state policies, class structure, and the status of women.

Morocco

Morocco's 1991 living standards measurement survey counted 2.5 million poor, of whom 72 percent lived in rural areas and more than half were extremely poor. The highest poverty levels were (and remain) among rural wage earners, and women are the most disadvantaged. The survey found that in urban areas, the poor were mainly self-employed. The typical poor worker earned one-third the average wage or one-half the legislated minimum wage; poor women received as little as half the wage rate per hour earned by poor males (World Bank, 1994). During the 1980s, as Moroccan exports expanded, women's employment grew, especially in the most competitive sectors of clothing, food, leather, and shoes. But these sectors offered very low wages. Unemployment remains high in Morocco, especially among the poor and among women. Some 30 percent of the urban poor are unemployed, and women in the poorest households experience the highest rates of unemployment in urban areas. In the mid-1990s, Morocco did not have a system of social protection in place to address poverty or unemployment.

The new economic policies of the 1980s, although promoting growth through increased production and exports, also brought about rising prices, a deterioration of wages, and cuts in social spending by the government. Not enough of the national income was channeled into public spending on basic health care, schooling, and essential infrastructure services, which would have improved the well-being of the poor. In the 1980s, poor parents were forced to withdraw their children from school. Indeed, enrollments in primary education actually declined after 1982, recovering only in 1990. But as late as 2000, Morocco still did not have universal primary and secondary school enrollments, and the gender gaps in school enrollments continued to be very wide (see UNDP, 2002a:tab. 24). Such gender inequalities make Moroccan women especially vulnerable to poverty.

The World Bank's 1991 study found that rural women in Morocco were largely unpaid family workers, whereas men tended to work as independent, small-scale farmers or in commerce, and about 25 percent of them were wage earners. The structure of rural social relations and its gender dimension in Morocco was captured in the following observation: "While women rarely obtain a job of their own for a wage, they often share in their husband's work outside the household farm. And having command over family labor, women and often children, gives a laborer a competitive edge in the labor market" (World Bank, 1994:vol. 1, p. 48). Clearly what Morocco needs is more social investment by the government to create a skilled, educated, and better-paid labor force, to raise female literacy and educational attainments, and to reduce rural-urban gaps. In fact, these objectives were inscribed in the National Action Plan for the Integration of Women in Development, which was promoted by the Moroccan government and women's organizations in the late 1990s. The adoption of the plan, along with the replacement of the highly patriarchal Moudawana with the more egalitarian family law of 2003, may yield positive results in the years to come.

Tunisia

In Tunisia, poverty is predominantly rural, but a growing percentage of poor households are in urban areas. The 1990 Household Consumption Survey found that about 600,000 people, or 7 percent of the population, had annual expenditures below the poverty line, and another 7 percent were "near poor." Most of the urban poor were wage earners in the construction sector with little or no formal education. Others were involved in temporary, low-wage, and low-skill employment in the expanding sectors of tourism and textiles (World Bank, 1995a). Still others were unemployed. As mentioned earlier in this chapter, unemployment is high in Tunisia; as in Morocco, it is especially high among the poor, youth, and women. And because of the sluggish growth of the private sector, unemployment among skilled workers is also high.

In contrast to Morocco, however, Tunisia has demonstrated a commitment to social spending and has been expanding its social insurance program. The Tunisian government cut social expenditures less than other expenditure categories during its period of fiscal restraint. The social security system covers wage earners in both the public and private sectors, including self-employed workers and government employees. Furthermore, there are two types of social assistance programs to alleviate poverty—direct transfers and consumer subsidies. Free health care and schooling are available to all, and Tunisia spends far less on the military than do other countries. Among countries of the Middle East and North Africa, only Tunisia has established effective social programs to tackle poverty, increase employment through public works, and encourage employment among women. According to one report, Tunisian labor unions, though not large, were instrumental in maintaining food subsidies for the poor (see UNDP, 1999:90).

Egypt

In Egypt, poor households constitute 20–25 percent of the total, most of which are concentrated in Upper Egypt, where women and children are the most vulnerable. Female-headed households are poorer than male-headed households in both rural and urban areas. Labor among children under twelve years of age is very high, especially in rural areas, and anemia is prevalent among women and small children. The poor are agricultural laborers or farmers with little or no land. A World Bank study found that in urban areas, the poor were construction workers or service workers and included "a significant number of government employees" (World Bank, 1991:35), partly because of the drastic deterioration in real wages that the government has allowed in the public sector. Wages continued to fall in sectors where women predominate. Although most poor males in both the urban and rural sectors are engaged in casual labor, such is not the case for women. A higher proportion of poor women are employed as salaried workers, and more poor females are found working in community services and in trade and services than is the case for men, which indicates the very low wages that working women must accept. What is more, unemployment rates are strikingly higher for females than for males, as shown earlier. Poor women are also less literate and educated than poor men. In the late 1990s, whereas poor men averaged 5.8 years of schooling, poor women had only 3.1 years; 63 percent of poor men could read and write, compared to only 33 percent of poor women (Jolliffe, 1997). For the country as a whole in 2000, only 63 percent of young women aged 15–24 were literate, and the figure for all adult women was just 44 percent.

Unsurprisingly, given the gender gaps in Egypt, widows and members of multiple-person female-headed households constitute two of the most economically vulnerable groups of people. According to one account:

> Even the youngest widows have no realistic prospect of making anything but the most casual and intermittent earnings, and the more elderly none whatsoever. Despite the traditional custom of support for widows through transfers from family members, even if they do not live in the same household, many widows in practice are not adequately supported by members of their family. They are destitute and depend on casual charity from neighbors to survive. Field reports from charity organizations operating in Cairo reveal that elderly widows form the single most important client group. Non-governmental organizations recognize them as a group prone to poverty and in need of special assistance. (World Bank, 1991:11)

According to official statistics, about 12 percent of households in Cairo had a female head in 1988, although this figure now may be as high as 18 percent. Egyptian sociologist Iman Bibars studied this growing phenomenon, noting that it "is not exclusive to widows, divorcees and the deserted but to a new rising category of wives of 'useless' husbands" (1996:13), including men who are imprisoned, terminally ill, disabled, or unemployed. In one study of a poor urban quarter in Cairo, women headed 29 percent of the sampled households. The majority of those women were illiterate and either widowed or divorced. They tended to own half the disposable income of poor male-headed households, lived in poorer housing units, and possessed very few consumer durables (Fergany, 1994). In 2001, the Egyptian NGO Association for the Development and Enhancement of Women (ADEW) launched a highly effective campaign to make identification cards widely and easily accessible to low-income women, so they could legally work, inherit property, register assets, and apply for social security. Still, Egypt has an inadequate system of social protection, and many poor women have difficulties dealing with the bureaucracy. Thus they often turn to charitable foundations—many of which are now run by Islamist organizations.

The Occupied Territories

In the Palestinian Authority/Occupied Territories, Gaza has been the region worst off, which is closely related to its high share of economically deprived refugees. The most important type of household income—earnings from labor activity—has been rendered unstable by curfews, strikes, and restrictions on employment in Israel since the second intifada. But even accounting for the injustices and hardships suffered by all Palestinians, women's lot is particularly dire. Gender discrimination and social controls on women make them especially vulnerable to poverty. Early marriage, incomplete education, and high fertility have kept women tied to the home and have increased pressures on household budgets (Heiberg et al., 1994; Olmsted, 1999).

In 1992, a survey by the Fafo Institute for Applied Social Science in Oslo, Norway, estimated the total fertility at 6.84 births per woman (Heiberg et al., 1994:65). In Gaza, more than a third (37 percent) of the entire female population married under the age of seventeen—the legal minimum age for women. The Fafo survey found a female labor force participation ratio of only 14 percent, indicating that most Palestinian women worked in household production and in the domestic sphere rather than in paid employment outside the home. Examples of work in the family sphere done by housewives were contract/piecework, involvement in a family business or shop, and work on the family farm. Employment outside the family sphere requiring education and training or involvement in unskilled paid labor was relatively limited. Female labor force participation was especially low in Gaza and in the refugee camps, although these areas offered very weak employment possibilities for men as well. Divorced and separated women and wealthy and educated women had the highest labor force participation rates. Many women accepted low-paid piecework at home rather than participation in the Israeli labor market.

In a social context in which so few women directly participate in the labor force, individual women get access to economic resources and thus try to avoid poverty through other means. One source is the dowry. The Fafo study found that although jewelry constituted the major form of women's independent property ownership in the West Bank, Gaza Strip, and Arab Jerusalem, women did own other forms of property, such as land, although to a much lesser degree. Most women sampled claimed they had nothing to sell or mortgage in case they needed money badly. Over time, women's jewelry acquired at marriage gradually dissipated to pay for various investments for the family, husband, or children (Heiberg et al., 1994:295–300).

▪ Conclusion

This chapter has surveyed trends in population growth, urbanization, labor force growth, rising unemployment, and poverty. These social and demographic trends have implications for household well-being, individual capabilities, and political stability. Although urbanization holds many promises for people, including a wider range of options, activities, and services, unchecked population growth has created enormous pressures on urban services. At a time of reduced government spending, these demographic pressures on health care, education, and utilities are likely to increase inequalities and deprivation. High fertility rates have resulted in the emergence of a large population of young people who are seeking but not finding jobs. In a context of reduced government spending and rising unemployment, poverty increases rather than diminishes. Although poverty and inequality are social phenomena, reflecting a class structure and skewed distribution of income, wealth, and opportunities, gender inequality clearly renders women more vulnerable than men to poverty.

The countries of the Middle East and North Africa, therefore, are faced with a number of social and demographic challenges that require concerted action involving governments, nongovernmental organizations, citizen groups, and international organizations. Identifying problems and solutions will require short-term, medium-term, and long-term perspectives informed by both developmental imperatives and the social entitlements of citizens. These include policies and measures to enhance women's access to education and jobs as a way of stabilizing population growth and reducing fertility rates as well as expanding women's capabilities and raising household incomes; investments in the physical and social infrastructure to upgrade urban services as well as create employment; enhancement of the legal and regulatory framework to raise labor and environmental standards as well as to improve the system of taxation; and community development programs that involve high school and college graduates, as a way of mitigating youth unemployment, alleviating urban poverty, and instilling solidarity.

▨ Notes

1. The Demographic and Health Surveys (conducted during the 1990s) and the earlier World Fertility Surveys (conducted during the late 1970s and early 1980s) are international surveys undertaken by governments but coordinated by a central body elsewhere, which also undertakes the cross-national analyses and global assessments. The Demographic and Health Surveys are coordinated by Macro International, Inc., in Maryland, in the United States, and the World Fertility Surveys were coordinated by the International Statistical Institute in the Netherlands. The World Fertility Surveys sought to examine trends in fertility and its correlates (contraceptive use, mother's education, child health, mother's health); the Demographic and Health Surveys similarly have been designed to collect data on fertility, family planning, and maternal and child health.

▨ Bibliography

Assaad, Ragui. 1995. "Urbanization and Demographic Structure in the Middle East and North Africa with a Focus on Women and Children." New York: Population Council, Regional Papers no. 40 (January).

Bibars, Iman. 1996. "Women: Reconciling Contradictory Roles." *Civil Society* 5, no. 56 (August):13.

CAWTAR. 2001. *Globalization and Gender: Economic Participation of Arab Women.* Tunis, Tunisia: Center for Arab Women Training and Research.

Drèze, Jean, and Haris Gazdar. 1992. "Hunger and Poverty in Iraq." *World Development* 20, no. 7.

ERF (Economic Research Forum). 1996. *Economic Trends in the MENA Region.* The Economic Research Forum for the Arab Countries, Iran and Turkey. Cairo: ERF.

———. 1998. *Economic Trends in the MENA Region.* The Economic Research Forum for the Arab Countries, Iran and Turkey. Cairo: ERF.

ESCWA (Economic and Social Commission for West Asia). 1993. *A Conceptual and Methodological Framework for Poverty Alleviation in the ESCWA Region.* New York: United Nations, January 19.

———. 1995a. *Statistical Abstract of the ESCWA Region, 1984–1993.* 15th issue. New York: United Nations.

———. 1995b. *Survey of Economic and Social Developments in the ESCWA Region, 1994.* New York: United Nations.

———. 1995c. *Women and Poverty in the ESCWA Region: Issues and Concerns.* Series of Studies on Arab Women and Development no. 22. New York: United Nations.

———. 2000. *Women and Men in the Arab Region: A Statistical Portrait, 2000.* Amman, Jordan: United Nations.

Fergany, Nader. 1994. *Urban Women, Work and Poverty Alleviation in Egypt.* Pilot study sponsored by the International Labour Organization and the United Nations Development Programme. Cairo: Al-Mishkat Research Institute.

el-Ghonemy, M. Riad. 1998. *Affluence and Poverty in the Middle East.* London: Routledge.

Heiberg, Marianne, et al. 1994. *Palestinian Society in Gaza, West Bank, and Arab Jerusalem: A Survey of Living Conditions.* Oslo: Fafo Institute for Applied Social Science.

ILO (International Labour Organization). 1999. *World Labour Report, 1999.* Geneva: ILO.

Jolliffe, Dean. 1997. "What Do We Know About Poverty in Egypt? An Analysis of Household Survey Data for 1997." Paper presented at the annual meeting of the Middle East Studies Association, San Francisco, November 22–24.

Karshenas, Massoud. 1994. *Structural Adjustment, Wages, and Employment in the Middle East.* World Employment Program Working Paper. Geneva: International Labour Organization.

Middle East Times. 1996. November 3–9.

Moghadam, Valentine M. 1997. *The Feminization of Poverty? Notes on a Concept and Trends.* Occasional Paper no. 3. Normal: Illinois State University, Women's Studies Program, August.

———. 1998. *Women, Work, and Economic Reform in the Middle East and North Africa.* Boulder, Colo.: Lynne Rienner.

———. 2003. *Modernizing Women: Gender and Social Change in the Middle East.* 2nd ed. Boulder, Colo.: Lynne Rienner.

OECD. 1992. *Trends in International Migration.* Paris: Organization for Economic Cooperation and Development.

Olmsted, Jennifer. 1999. "Linking Fertility, Economic Policies and Gender in the Middle East and North Africa: A Case Study of Fertility Patterns Among Bethlehem Area Palestinians." Paper prepared for the sixth annual Economic Research Forum for the Arab Countries, Iran, and Turkey Conference, Cairo, October.

Omran, Abdel R., and Farzaneh Roudi. 1993. "The Middle East Population Puzzle." *Population Bulletin* 48, no. 1 (July).

Republique Algerienne. 1999. *Données Statistiques* [Statistical Data], no. 263. Alger: Office National des Statistiques.

Richards, Alan, and John Waterbury. 1996. *A Political Economy of the Middle East.* 2nd ed. Boulder, Colo.: Westview.

Roudi, Farzaneh. 2001. "Population Trends and Challenges in the Middle East and North Africa." Population Reference Bureau policy brief, October.

Shaban, Radwan A., Ragui Assaad, and Sulayman S. al-Qudsi. 1995. "The Challenge of Unemployment in the Arab Region." *International Labour Review* 134, no. 1:65–81.

UN. 1993a. *The Sex and Age Distribution of the World's Populations: The 1992 Revision.* New York: United Nations.

———. 1993b. *World Urbanization Prospects: The 1992 Revision.* New York: United Nations.

———. 1995. *World Urbanization Prospects: The 1994 Revision.* New York: United Nations.

———. 2000. *The World's Women, 2000: Trends and Statistics.* New York: United Nations.

———. 2006. *World Urbanization Prospects: 2005 Revision.* New York: United Nations.

UNDP (UN Development Programme). 1995, 1996, 1997, 1998, 1999, 2000, 2002a, 2006. *Human Development Report.* New York: Oxford University Press.

―――. 2002b. *Arab Human Development Report.* New York: United Nations Development Programme.

UNESCO. 1995. *World Education Report.* Paris: UN Educational, Scientific, and Cultural Organization.

World Bank. 1991. *Egypt: Alleviating Poverty During Structural Adjustment.* Washington, D.C.: World Bank.

―――. 1993. *Implementing the World Bank's Strategy to Reduce Poverty: Progress and Challenges.* Washington, D.C.: World Bank.

―――. 1994. *Morocco: Poverty, Adjustment, and Growth.* Vols. 1–2. Washington, D.C.: World Bank.

―――. 1995a. *Republic of Tunisia: Poverty Alleviation: Preserving Progress While Preparing for the Future.* Washington, D.C.: World Bank, August.

―――. 1995b. *World Development Report: Workers in an Integrating World.* New York: Oxford University Press.

―――. 2000. *World Development Indicators.* Washington, D.C.: World Bank.

Yemen Ministry of Planning and Development. 1998. *Yemen Human Development Report 1998.* Sana'a: Yemen Ministry of Planning and Development.

10

Kinship, Class, and Ethnicity

Laurie King-Irani

S carcely a day passes without dramatic news bulletins about conflict and violence in the Middle East. Over the past decade, this region has come to register in the consciousness of most Americans as an area of chronic volatility and dangerous divisiveness, all of which, it is assumed, arise from "essential" ethnic or religious antagonisms. The mainstream media's depictions of such conflicts as being rooted in ancient tribal or sectarian animosities might lead casual observers to conclude that political tensions in this large and diverse region are simply inevitable—encoded in the very genetic make-up or the cultural "programming" of various Middle Eastern populations. It is easy to assume that the sharp edges of the individual pieces of the Middle East "mosaic" are immutable, inherently antagonistic, and fated to "rub each other the wrong way" forever.

Anthropologists are frequently called upon to analyze the cultural values, ideologies, and political structures and processes that account for Middle Eastern conflicts. Recently, the US Department of Defense attempted to enlist anthropologists in the Human Terrain Systems (HTS) Program as "embedded ethnographers" in an effort to utilize anthropological knowledge to understand the sociocultural terrain of Iraq and Afghanistan and thus to aid US military officers and troops in negotiating the "tribal" structures of Iraqi and Afghan society. Although the American Anthropological Association (AAA) has officially opposed anthropologists' participation in the HTS on ethical grounds (AAA, 2007), it has not provided an assessment of the US military's deployment of anthropological concepts and theories. Is the HTS program based upon ethnographically sound conceptions of "tribes," "ethnicity," "sects," and "classes"? Have popular, as opposed to

academic, understandings of these sociocultural phenomena obscured rather
than clarified current daily realities on the ground in the Middle East?

The perceived salience of collective, as opposed to individual, bases of
political representation, legal categorization, and public participation under-
pins assumptions that conflicts in this region are tribal, deeply rooted, essential, and thus inevitable. Former US Secretary of State Madeleine Albright
once opined to the press that the Israeli-Palestinian conflict was so difficult
to resolve because its roots "went back to biblical times." Such invocations
of ancient history are common in the mainstream media's tendency to speak
of conflict in "The Holy Land," a term that resonates with compelling cultural images rather than reflecting contemporary political realities.

The perception that Iraqi, Lebanese, and Israeli-Palestinian societies
are tribal and rooted in age-old, religio-cultural precepts, identities, and
mentalities can easily give way to a dangerous essentialization not simply
of the conflicts, but of the parties to the conflicts. Middle Eastern peoples
are frequently depicted as war-like, troubled, violent, and barbaric. Former
Israeli prime minister Benjamin Netanyahu frequently reminded Cable
News Network (CNN) audiences that "this is a dangerous neighborhood of
the world; we can't deal with things here the way you would in the West!"[1]

The weight of history and entrenched collective stereotypes hang heavy
over Israel/Palestine, Lebanon, and Iraq. Yet as historian Ussama Makdisi
(2000) notes in his incisive study of the roots of Lebanon's protracted conflict, sectarianism is not an ancient and deeply rooted identity system.
Rather, it first appeared as a thoroughly modern response to jarring internal
and external changes in the mid-nineteenth-century Ottoman Empire. Sectarianism, like ethnicity, is about contests for power in uncertain settings. It
is not a genetically transmitted mentality, an ineluctable set of traits, or a
communally rooted phenomenon. This chapter will attempt to deconstruct
popular notions of the "tribal," "ethnic," and "sectarian" by using contemporary anthropological thinking about formal and informal politics and the
textures of everyday life in the Middle East.

Collective identities based on sectarian identity influence political representation, action, and social organization in Israel as well as in Arab countries. Indeed, it is no exaggeration to state that both Lebanon and Israel are
living remnants of the Ottoman millet system, discussed below. Citizenship—as juridical category, social institution, bundles of rights and duties,
and lived practice—differs in Israel and Lebanon from most Western nation-
states in that citizens' jural relationships to the state, as well as their political agency, are mediated through ascribed membership in hierarchically
ranked ethno-confessional sects. One's rights to attain particular offices,
own or sell land, or receive state benefits is contingent upon whether one is
a Jew or a non-Jew in Israel, or whether one is a Maronite, Sunni, Shi'a,
Druze, or any one of the eighteen officially recognized ethno-confessional

sects in Lebanon, a country unique in being composed solely of minorities. In both Lebanon and Israel, personal status issues, i.e., all matters related to marriage, divorce, child custody, inheritance, and burial, are overseen not by the state, but by various religious courts and the clergy. Hence, in Lebanon and Israel alike, civil marriage between individuals of different ethno-confessional communities is not permitted.

How and why has the Middle East come to be synonymous with political crises, bloodletting, and violent hatreds? How have state-making practices and processes over the past century shaped the emergence of new forms of identity and the experience of political violence and social dislocation in a region that went from empire to mandates to colonies to refugeedom to states to UN membership in less than a half century? The history and challenges of state formation as a political process in the Middle East requires closer analysis. Identities, actions, and ideologies unfold within state-administered frameworks. The state (or lack of a state) in some settings in the Middle East, and the state's assumed monopoly on the use of coercive force—no less than the way various state agencies, actors, and institutions are key to shaping and channeling agency and memory—are all crucial components to understanding kinship, ethnicity, and social class in the Middle East. Structures of governance and resource distribution and the authority to perform state functions (including the right to discipline and punish) are being fought over (often with violence), as much as definitions of origins, memories, and cultural identities.

The lack of a state structure for Palestinians and the weakness of the state in postwar Lebanon and Iraq render accountability and agency, and thus conflict resolution, problematic: How should people react to violations of rights and conflict over resources: as Palestinians, Iraqis, or Lebanese, or as Sunnis, Shi'a, Jews, or Christians? As citizens or as patrilineal members? All these questions have their institutional and procedural correlatives: Should people choose tribal reconciliation, family intervention, nongovernmental organizations, or courtroom justice? Personal vengeance or public compensation? For many Palestinians, whether refugees or those living in the West Bank and Gaza, that lack of a viable overarching administrative-legal-judicial structure (given the ongoing Israeli occupation and the deficiencies and weaknesses of the Palestinian Authority) makes it especially difficult to resolve problems at the local or regional level. Palestinians under occupation face some special problems not encountered elsewhere, but the weakness of the state, particularly its judicial branch, in providing mechanisms through which individuals or groups can attain justice and apportion resources is common to Lebanon and Iraq as well.

Anthropology, perhaps more than any other discipline, can help to formulate, investigate, and pose answers to the questions raised in this brief introduction.

▓ Identities and Boundaries

Few countries of the modern Middle East have homogeneous populations. Borders rarely coincide with geographic, riparian (river) or linguistic/religious/ethnic boundaries. Despite the newness of the nation-state as an administrative entity or ideological concept, informal institutions of great historical depth, traditional cultural practices, art forms, cuisines, languages, and social structures dominate daily life even as people live increasingly urban lives, participate in modern world markets and media, and adopt and enjoy the latest transportation, communication, and education technologies. In contrast to popular—and mistaken—notions about ethnicity and ethnic conflict in the contemporary Middle East, this chapter will examine the emergence, mobilization, consolidation, and institutionalization of the region's ethnic identities not as indices of unchanging biological predispositions or cultural "essences," but rather, as humanly shaped and strategic responses to specific environmental, geographical, historical, political, and economic realities. Changing configurations of ethnic identity and the dynamics of majority-minority relations in the various states in this region offer valuable lessons in the contingent and political—and therefore constructed and strategic—nature of ethnicity in the contemporary Middle East.

To understand the genesis, nature, and trajectory of Middle Eastern ethnic phenomena, we must first survey the region's ecological, historical, geographical, and administrative contexts. In other words, we must investigate the politics of identity. The formation of ethnic groups in the Middle East, as well as the dynamics of collaboration and competition among such groups and between these groups and the states in which they are situated, arises from ever-changing balances of power and shifting frameworks of decisionmaking and resource distribution at the local, national, regional, and international levels. Such political processes are present in every region of the world, but in the Middle East, long a crossroads between diverse cultures, languages, economies, and environments, political phenomena and processes arising from the cross-fertilization of diverse peoples have always been pronounced. Since ancient times, and indeed, up until the present moment, the region has been a key prize for various world powers, from the ancient Roman and Persian empires, to the European colonial powers of the nineteenth and early twentieth centuries, and ultimately, to the multinational corporations and high-tech Western armies of the present era.

Given its marked strategic importance, the Middle East and its people are no strangers to the intrigues and interventions of local, regional, and global politics. As we shall see in some of the following case studies, the most harrowing episodes of interethnic conflict in the Middle East have occurred when all three dimensions of competition for political power and economic resources—global, regional, and local—have coincided, as they did in Lebanon during its long and bloody civil war, which was also a regional war fought out on Lebanese soil, or more recently in Iraq, where the nation's marginalized Shi'i and Kurdish communities rose up in a bloody, but ultimately futile, challenge to the ruling Sunni Baathist regime of Saddam Hussein in 1991.

▉ Key Concepts

This chapter employs an anthropological perspective on kinship, ethnicity, and social class in the contemporary Middle East in order to illustrate the contexts and processes of daily interaction for peoples of the region. Kinship and ethnicity are examined here not as monolithic, unchanging facts, nor as independent variables, but rather, as social constructs, adaptive strategies, political resources, and emotionally charged symbolic expressions of belonging. An anthropological approach to any society views human social behavior through the twin lenses of modes of organization (social, economic, and political) and frames of meaning (values, beliefs, ideologies, affect, and worldviews). Kinship and ethnicity are simultaneously modes of organization *and* frames of meaning.

Although the concept of social class seems, at first glance, to be related to economic phenomena, ethnographic field research quickly reveals that collective political goals, the maintenance of key social relationships, and strategic invocations of identity and morality shape individuals' class status and life chances in ways that purely statistical data could never reveal. The sociocultural dimensions of class in the Middle East become particularly clear when we examine informal social networks and an associated, recurrent type of relationship of unequal interdependence found throughout the region: the patron-client tie (Denoeux, 1993; Roniger and Ayata, 1994; Singerman, 1995; Gilsenan, 1996).

Since Middle Eastern societies are hierarchically organized, culturally and ethnically plural, and rooted in highly literate and ancient urban cultures, we cannot examine kinship, ethnicity, and social class as isolated phenomena. In the simpler, smaller-scale societies that anthropologists commonly studied in the early twentieth century, kinship was often the primary mode of organization structuring the domains of politics, economics, law, morality, and religion. Kinship, like ethnicity and religion, intertwines and interacts dynamically with many other, often competing modes of organization and frames of meaning in the large-scale, centrally administered, and rapidly urbanizing societies of the region. Formal institutions and legal codes transcending family, faith, and tribe sometimes harmonize with, and sometimes contradict, the frames of meaning and modes of belonging provided by primary identity categories. New organizational and expressive forms, ranging from politicized Islam to hip-hop youth culture, are emerging in the cities of the Middle East (and among the Middle Eastern diaspora in European and North American cities) in response to globalized markets and media (McMurray, 2002).

Yet even in the rapidly changing nation-states and burgeoning cities of the contemporary Middle East, kinship as a symbolically rich and morally compelling system of meanings and values retains considerable power to galvanize ideologies, shape perceptions, and guide actions in the realm of politics, commerce, and administration. Symbols of shared blood and belonging help to structure the social and legal classifications that are so crucial for the establishment of large-scale state institutions and organizations (Herzfeld, 1997). Kinship imagery and symbolism have been instrumental in the construction of conceptions of citizenship and national identity in newly formed and externally imposed nation-states lacking broad-based legitimacy (Shryock, 1997; Wedeen, 1999; Joseph, 2000).

Symbols associated with family and blood ties are often used to express issues of rights and power on the local and global stage. In my own research in Nazareth, the largest Arab Palestinian city in Israel, I noted that the sentiments and values associated with close family relations, particularly the nurturing mother-child bond and the egalitarian brother-sister tie, served as models of proper political behavior for the city's Communist-dominated political coalition. Similarly, the community's conception of its relation to the state as a nonassimilating minority group (i.e., non-Jews in a Jewish state) frequently employed metaphors of foster-parenting and step-parent/stepchild relationships to emphasize an unnatural and stilted relationship devoid of strong affective ties of nurturance and belonging. The importance of kinship as a cultural system of meanings was also implicit in another term Communist Party members frequently used to describe Palestinian citizens in Israel: *aytaam* (orphans), particularly following the collapse of the Soviet Union (King-Irani, 2001).

One of the goals of anthropology is to make the strange familiar and the familiar strange. An anthropological approach to the prevailing modes of organization and frames of meaning structuring everyday life in the Middle East may lead us to ask critical questions about Western assumptions, rooted in liberal political traditions, concerning the dividing lines between the individual and the group, the formal and the informal, and the public and the private. Anthropologically informed inquiries go to the very heart of contentious issues of identity, rights, and power that now occupy center stage in Western political and media discussions about the Middle East, and can even illuminate the interactions and connections between the Middle East and the West in ways that may surprise us (Pitcher, 1998; Jean-Klein, 2000; Antoun, 2000; Mamdani, 2002; McMurray, 2002).

To understand the modes of organization and frames of meaning that impact most people's daily lives in the contemporary Middle East, we must first grasp some of the historical, ecological, and administrative contexts of kinship, ethnicity, and social class in the region before discussing how individuals and groups can employ kinship and ethnic identity to access networks of affiliation and assistance not only to make a living, but just as important, to make a meaning, in the face of the rapid changes, conflicting cultural values, and pervasive uncertainties characteristic of the early twenty-first century. Although economic pressures and political instability are certainly not unique to the Middle East, the strategies that the peoples of this region have developed in responding to contemporary challenges draw upon a particular constellation of historical experiences, cultural traditions, religious values, symbolic systems, and modes of socioeconomic organization, all of which distinguish the Middle East from European, Asian, or African sociocultural systems.

Persistent Challenges and Adaptive Strategies: The Environmental and Historical Context

Kinship and ethnicity are employed as adaptive strategies to environmental challenges. As modes of organization and identification, they help to define individual and collective rights and duties and allocate resources necessary for survival, whether in rural or urban contexts. For centuries, the most common modes of subsistence in the Middle East were agriculture and horticulture, pastoral nomadism, commerce, and small-scale industry and resource extraction. Although popular stereotypes of the landscapes and peoples of the region usually feature the camels, tents, and caravans distinctive of a nomadic lifestyle, it has been the region's urban settings and institutions that have played a decisive role in shaping the cultures, traditions, and values of the Middle East. After all, it was in the fertile river valleys of the Nile and the Tigris and Euphrates that some of the earliest cities and urban civilizations first emerged, thanks to irrigation and intensive agricultural practices.

Whether living in nomadic, agricultural, or urban settings, however, the peoples of the Middle East have not been strangers to harsh and uncertain environments, whether natural, economic, or political. Inhabiting an ecological zone characterized primarily by semiaridity, steep valleys, rugged mountains, widely separated riparian systems, unpredictable rainfall, and poor soils—as detailed by Ian Manners and Barbara Parmenter in Chapter 2—Middle Eastern communities were often compelled to combine a variety of modes of subsistence, such as pastoral nomadism, small-scale agriculture, commerce, hunting, and fishing in order to make a living. The resulting mixed economies linked urban, nomadic, and agricultural communities in interdependent (and at times unequal) relationships of reciprocity, redistribution, and market exchange. The lack of large-scale, widespread, and permanent agricultural modes of subsistence rendered the formation of large-scale, enduring, and clearly defined corporate institutions difficult. Social, economic, and administrative structures tended to have shifting borders and negotiable boundaries. Up until the nineteenth century, the region saw a lack of large-scale, long-term, economic integration and the corresponding lack of an enduring, centralized administrative integration of large areas into clearly bounded corporate structures. As a result, local and regional coalitions centering on cities, sects, and families were common modes of organizing political and economic life.

Groups dwelling in this arid and semiarid region elaborated distinctive cultural patterns and sociopolitical institutions that served to minimize the hardships and uncertainties arising from the conditions of their natural environment. Today, as in the past, the peoples of the Middle East remain justly famous for their loyal attachment to their families, distinctive rituals of hospitality and conflict mediation, and effective and flexible kin-based collectivities, such as the lineage and the tribe, which until quite recently performed most of the social, economic, and political functions of rural communities in the absence of centralized state governments (Khoury and Kostiner, 1990; Tapper, 1990).

Although far-flung empires and tribal confederations in the Middle East were replaced by clearly bounded nation-states in the nineteenth and twentieth centuries, and even though the vast majority of nomadic peoples have been sedentarized—settled into villages and cities where they earn a modest living as farmers, skilled and unskilled laborers, or professionals—everyday life in the modern Middle East continues to revolve around family membership to an extent that North Americans usually find surprising. The contemporary Middle East is a region of rich and ancient civilizational heritage and immense human potential. Yet it is also a region beset by political volatility, economic disparities, and ecological vulnerability. Despite the fact that the state bureaucracies of most countries in the region are well entrenched and heavily subsidized, few states have succeeded in distributing resources equitably, administering justice fairly, protecting and advancing the interests of the majority of the people, and thereby winning public support and popular participation through legitimate means. National integration remains a contentious issue throughout much of the region. Most states in the Middle East serve narrow elite interests rather than the common good (Sharabi, 1990; Tibi, 1990; Barakat, 1993; al-Khafaji, 1995).

The overwhelming majority of the region's population does not participate in the economic and political decisionmaking processes that will greatly influence their lives and their children's lives. Middle Eastern states usually rule rather than govern their populaces, employing various degrees of coercion, manipulation, and co-optation to achieve control and compliance.

Consequently, the peoples of the Middle East have learned to place their trust in those whom they know well and with whom they share similar interests, goals, and characteristics: their relatives, neighbors, friends, and members of their own ethnic, religious, and linguistic groups (Sayigh, 1981; Singerman, 1995).

The Middle Eastern nation-state, an externally imposed system of sociopolitical organization, still cannot claim the same kind or degree of support, loyalty, and legitimacy that Middle Eastern kin and patron-client networks have always claimed (Zubaida, 1994; Denoeux, 1993; Ayubi, 2001; Joseph, 2000). Even a half century after the nation-state's advent in the region, kinship relations (or relations modeled on a kinship pattern) mediate individuals' personal, economic, and political lives to an extent almost unimaginable to anyone who has grown up in Western Europe or North America.

For example, individuals' interactions with state bodies and governmental bureaucracies take place primarily through patron-client relationships (interdependent but unequal relationships based on an ideology of mutual benefit that reaffirm and reproduce institutionalized hierarchies) mediated by ties of kinship (actual or fictive), political party membership, or ethnic and sectarian affiliation (Cunningham and Sarayrah, 1993). In most Middle Eastern societies, governmental ministries primarily serve those who have connections and contacts (*wasta* in Arabic, *protektzia* in Hebrew). Those who participate in informal networks of interlocking patron-client relationships can traverse physical and social space through their links to individuals and groups on the other side of class, political, and ethnic dividing lines in order to pursue their interests and goals (Denoeux, 1993; Singerman, 1995). Citizenship, an identity category that derives its significance from the jural, formalized relationship of each individual to the nation-state, carries much less emotional, moral, legal, and political weight in the Middle East than do identity categories rooted in ideologies of mutual assistance, moral duty, and group solidarity—that is, kinship, ethnicity, and religion.

Understanding why citizens of Middle Eastern nation-states cling to subnational primary affiliations (i.e., family, ethnicity, and religion) will help us understand the causes of intrastate turmoil and interstate hostilities in an ethnographically sound manner. Discovering how Middle Eastern peoples strategically invoke and manipulate kin ties, ethnic affiliations, and patron-client relationships will give us a new appreciation of the creative and effective means through which individuals and groups survive and thrive in a challenging socioeconomic environment while preparing for future contingencies. To analyze the interrelationship of kinship, ethnicity, and social class formation in the context of the contemporary Middle East, let us first review some key anthropological viewpoints on these important modes of organization and frames of meaning.

▪ Kinship

At first glance, it would seem self-evident that kinship is a naturally occurring phenomenon rather than a cultural construct. After all, every living person has or has had kin (relatives), linked to him or her through blood and probably through marriage too. Common sense tells us that biological relationships are a human universal; even "test tube" babies have biological parents, regardless of whether or not they have ever met them. Anthropologists, however, are forever questioning the easy assumptions underlying "common sense." Instead of appraising human phenomena according to its obvious surface characteristics, anthropologists look at human social interaction holistically and relativistically—that is, from every possible angle and in every relevant context, in an effort to understand the totality of human experience and behavior.

The anthropologist's goal is interpretive rather than explanatory. He or she aims to decipher the meanings of the underlying concepts, attitudes, and values that guide people's choices and interactions. These meanings are not visible; they must be inferred from carefully observed behavior over time. Whereas a geneticist would examine DNA (deoxyribonucleic acid) to determine kinship, an anthropologist attends simultaneously to the biological as well as to the cultural, economic, moral, and political dimensions of kin ties. Indeed, one anthropological definition of kinship is that it concerns "biological relationships, culturally defined" (Keesing, 1975). Hence, an anthropologist investigating the kinship system of a particular community will be less concerned with discovering the actual, empirically verifiable genetic links between individuals than with ascertaining how individuals in this community conceive of kinship connections and the extent to which these cultural conceptions influence behaviors among individuals who consider themselves kin.

Although the act of sexual procreation and the phenomenon of birth are human universals, not all human societies interpret and value biological connections in precisely the same way. In societies characterized by bilateral kinship systems, such as found in North America, individuals recognize and value their links to relatives on both their mother's and father's sides of the family equally. In other societies, classified as matriarchies, only an individual's maternal relatives will be recognized for economic, social, and political purposes.

In North American society, individuals consider children of their mother's siblings (maternal cousins) to occupy the same social category and moral status as children of their father's siblings (paternal cousins). A particular set of cultural expectations and values guide interactions between cousins in North America (Schneider, 1968). Cousins are people you enjoy seeing; you feel a connection to them that is stronger than friendship but not as complicated or demanding as the tie between siblings. Very few people in North America would contemplate marrying a first cousin. In fact, such a marriage would be illegal in some US states.

In the Middle East, however, people can and do marry their first cousins; in some communities, the union of a man and his father's brother's daughter is still considered to be the preferred marriage choice (Murphy and Kasdan, 1959; Abu-Lughod, 1986). Maternal and paternal cousins are distinctly different categories in the Middle East. An individual will behave differently toward his female paternal cousin than he does toward his female maternal cousin, and the tone of his relationship to a male paternal cousin is likely to be more formal, reserved, and subdued, whereas mutual affection and joking usually characterize his relationship with a male maternal cousin. To understand the reasons for differential treatment of maternal and paternal kin and marriage preferences in the Middle East, we must examine the observed patterns of kinship relations as a system, in this case one that is patrilineal.

Anthropologists researching Middle Eastern societies as widely separated as Morocco and Iran have identified several key characteristics of kinship in the region. Middle Eastern kinship systems are patrilineal (determining membership, defining rights, and allocating resources based on blood ties through fathers, sons, brothers, and uncles), extended, patriarchal, hierarchical, and often endogamous (Murphy and Kasdan, 1959; Geertz, 1979; Abu-Lughod, 1986; Barakat, 1993; Joseph, 1994). The extended family plays a crucial economic, political, and socializing role in Middle Eastern societies. Within the family, authority and respect are accorded to men and elderly family members of both sexes, who, occupying the top positions in the family hierarchy, wield more power, prestige, and rights than female family members and children of either sex.

The Middle Eastern family is not an egalitarian structure. Men's and women's roles are considered to be complementary and integrative, not equal. Men are the primary decisionmakers and breadwinners, and they usually control material resources, although women have always exercised more power within the family "behind the scenes" than is immediately apparent (Abu-Lughod, 1986; Geertz, 1979; Friedl, 1991; Bahloul, 1992; Peteet, 1991; Sayigh, 1994; Mundy, 1995; Singerman, 1995; Kapchan, 1996; Jean-Klein, 2000; Joseph, 2000). Traditionally, a man's overarching responsibility has been to lead, protect, and provide for his family completely. A woman's primary role has been to make a comfortable home, oversee all aspects of the private, domestic sphere, and bear and nurture children.

As Lisa Taraki discusses in Chapter 11, however, gender roles in the Middle East, as in the rest of the world, are undergoing rapid changes as a result of increased education, rapid urbanization, new economic configurations, and the employment of women. Nonetheless, Middle Eastern men and women continue to place a high value not on their own personal achievements, but rather on their family affiliations in general and on their roles as generators of new families in particular. In other words, men's and women's roles as parents are more valued than virtually any other role they can fulfill. Young people in most Middle Eastern societies are not considered to be truly adult until they have completed the rites of passage of marriage and parenthood. Westerners visiting Middle Eastern societies are invariably asked about their marital status, and women who are still unmarried or married and not yet mothers after the age of twenty-five will find themselves repeatedly explaining their unusual single or childless state to their concerned Middle Eastern hosts (Fernea, 1969; Singerman, 1995).

An oft-noted characteristic of Middle Eastern kinship systems is the practice of endogamous marriage, or marriage between men and women belonging to the same kinship group. As previously mentioned, a preferred form of marriage in the Middle East has traditionally been that between a man and his father's brother's daughter (*bint 'amm* in Arabic), henceforth abbreviated as the "FBD marriage preference." Because Middle Eastern kinship systems are patrilineal, that is, based on ties of agnation and descent traced through paternal relatives, a man and his FBD are always members of the same lineage. In anthropological terminology, cousins in this category of relationship to each other are known as parallel cousins. The daughters of a man's mother's brother usually do not belong to his patrilineage; anthropologists refer to this category of cousins as cross cousins.

Marriages can and do take place between both categories of cousins in the Middle East, and many scholars have noted that endogamy refers more to an ideological preference than an actual practice. For instance, the Lebanese anthropologist Fuad Khuri (1970), conducting research among Muslim residents of Beirut in the late 1960s, discovered that only 11 percent of marriages in his sample were endogamous (FBD) marriages. My research among Palestinian citizens of Israel in Nazareth in 1992–1993 indicated that less than 10 percent of a sample of 341 households consisted of spouses who were parallel cousins (King-Irani, 2001).

Given the prevalence of labor migration and rapidly increasing urbanization in the region (see Chapter 9), extended families of grandparents, parents, brothers, sisters, cousins, aunts, and uncles living under the same roof and sharing the same resources are less and less common. In the major cities of the Middle East, where the bulk of the region's population now lives, anthropologists have discovered that unions between members of the same neighborhood, sect, ethnic group, and social class compose the overwhelming majority of marriages. Hence, a form of sociocultural, if not familial, endogamy still persists in the region because families prefer that their sons and daughters marry individuals whose social backgrounds and kinship networks are well known to them (al-Akhras, 1976; Singerman, 1995).

Endogamous marriage patterns, which are practiced by very few cultures outside the Middle East, stem not from exotic cultural beliefs, a peculiar mentality, or unquestioned obedience to ancient traditions, but rather from a desire to enhance and strengthen the group's internal solidarity and external boundaries. Endogamy is a strategy for retaining individuals' loyalty and commitment, as well as their wealth (whether in the form of bridewealth, productive property, or inheritances), within the family circle, widely defined. Such desires and strategies are indices of a long historical experience of economic scarcity, harsh environmental conditions, political uncertainty, and pronounced competition for limited resources in this vast, semiarid zone. The interplay of these ecological, political, and economic factors has at times engendered an atmosphere of unpredictability and mistrust in Middle Eastern societies (Schneider, 1971; Meeker, 1979).

In examining the patrilineal nature of Middle Eastern kinship systems, we must look beyond the domain of the nuclear family's domestic concerns to the public realm of the community's political and economic interests, which are greatly affected and conditioned by the natural and human environments. As one anthropologist notes, "kinship is the dominant mode of forming the larger groupings central to social and political life in pre-industrial societies. Kinship provides solutions to ecological and organizational challenges in space and time" (Keesing, 1975:8).

The choice of the patrilineage as the key sociopolitical mode of organization in the Middle East was not arbitrary, since "unilineal descent groups [whether matrilineal or patrilineal] were a crucial development in the evolution of tribal societies. They provided an adaptive solution in different ecological settings to the problem of maintaining political order and defining rights to land and other resources across the generations" (Keesing, 1975: 24). Nomadic, agricultural, and urban communities all evidenced patrilineal modes of organization and frames of meaning. Kinship was an idiom, a language, for expressing and negotiating economic and political relationships and assigning groups their roles within regional administrative arrangements. The lives of nomads, farmers, and city-dwellers were always in actual or potential contact, and their respective interests were occasionally in conflict (Ibn Khaldun, 1967; Nelson, 1973; Khoury and Kostiner, 1990).

In the absence of a strong, centralized governmental administration, well-armed, roving bedouin tribes (i.e., coalitions of patrilineages claiming descent from a common, distant ancestor) could easily sweep into poorly defended agricultural settlements mounted on their formidable camels and take goods, crops, livestock, and other forms of wealth by force. Some nomadic tribes coalesced into powerful federations capable of extracting payments of tribute (in effect, protection money) from sedentary villagers over a very wide area. In some cases, wealthy urban elites formed alliances with leaders of bedouin tribal federations in an effort to extract maximum economic resources from the land and people in the countryside, thus controlling the political dynamics of an entire region (Khoury and Kostiner, 1990; Barakat, 1993).

Pastoral nomadism as a primary mode of subsistence is now rare in the Middle East. A lifestyle that requires constant movement does not mesh with the needs and requirements of nation-states demarcated by well-defended, often impassable borders. Pastoral modes of subsistence continue, but the rapid and dramatic urbanization and proletarianization of the region's population eclipse them. Yet the traditional values and practices of tribally based groupings have left a deep imprint on Middle Eastern culture, society, and politics, as evidenced by oral and written literature, everyday morality, and the phenomenon of "fictive kinship" ties that link friends, colleagues, neighbors, and business partners through relationships that have the emotional closeness and moral implications of actual blood relations.

The patrilineal descent groups found throughout Middle Eastern society had their genesis thousands of years ago as an adaptive response to the interrelated ecological and political conditions of the region (Schneider, 1971; Meeker, 1979). Pastoral nomadism, previously a key component of the region's mixed economy, is a strenuous mode of subsistence that both demands and frustrates cooperative, interdependent social relations. Pastoral nomadism requires the careful and timely coordination of different activities by different people. If the needs of the herds and flocks are not met, they and the human community dependent upon them for its livelihood can easily perish. Members of nomadic groups are thus willing to pitch in for the common good and extend themselves magnanimously if the situation demands brave and generous behavior. But in this arid and unpredictable ecological zone, people also had to be selfish and calculating at times in order to survive. This fact "places heavy burdens on interpersonal relations, for everyone must think first of his immediate household's interests and needs and resist undue claims for assistance from kinsmen and friends" (Schneider, 1971:5). Among pastoral nomads, the immediate need for water may well outweigh compelling claims of blood ties.

The natural environment in which pastoral nomads live is clearly harsh and uncertain. The social environment is also threatening since it is highly competitive. It is thus imperative for all pastoral nomadic peoples to institute

> organizational solutions to the compelling ecological problem of regulating access of humans and animals to natural resources. . . . Migratory groups cannot establish rights to land on a permanent basis, or fence it off against incursions. Raiding and animal theft are therefore endemic. . . . The determination of boundary lines is subject to continual human intervention; the definition of the group is problematic as well: social boundaries are difficult to maintain, and internal loyalties are questionable. . . . Individuals and groups are at once . . . vulnerable and opportunistic. (Schneider, 1971:24)

The organizational solution instituted by peoples of the Middle East to the challenges presented to them by their difficult environment consisted of adopting a social, political, and moral idiom (i.e., symbol system and rhetorical discourse) of paternal blood relationship: the patrilineage. Members of a patrilineage could invoke their blood connections to other individuals and groups in order to obtain mutual support, defense, assistance, and protection in their unending struggle to eke a living out of the harsh environment. Patrilineal principles also facilitated the equitable division of wealth in inheritances, thus limiting the likelihood of contention and destructive conflict among surviving heirs, whose continuing cooperation was imperative for their own and their families' survival.

Depending on the need or the task at hand, nomadic peoples could employ patrilineal ideologies and rhetoric in order to mobilize groups ranging from a person's immediate male kin (brothers, father, grandfather, sons, uncles, and cousins) to a huge tribal federation numbering thousands of individuals representing many different patrilineages related through a distant founding (or "apical") ancestor. Yet since the natural environment could not support a large number of nomads and their animals living at the same place for any significant length of time, Middle Eastern patrilineages never developed into the sustained, enduring, clearly bounded unilineal descent groups found in more temperate and fertile ecological zones. Rather than becoming corporations, Middle Eastern kin groups were shifting coalitions that could be forged and broken, quickly and repeatedly, according to the relevant context and prevailing interests. Anthropologists term this process *segmentation,* and many social scientists characterize Middle Eastern societies as segmentary because of the prevalence of many similar yet differentiated components (e.g., families, lineages, guilds, ethnic groups, or sects) that can coalesce to cooperate or fragment to fight in the unending struggle for scarce and valuable resources.

Kinship, as an idiom of identity and social organization no less than as a basis of affiliation, protection, and cooperative action, is just as important in the Middle East today as it was hundreds of years ago. A person's identity as a member of a kin group entitles him or her to rights and services, just as it entails making considerable sacrifices for the sake of the group. In spite of the establishment of nation-states in the postcolonial period, often the primary identification of the peoples of the Middle East is not civil, religious, or even ethnic, but familial. For instance, the kingdom of Saudi Arabia is often called "the house of Saud" in recognition of its roots in a particular kinship grouping. Syria is and Iraq was run by tightly knit, patrilineal coalitions of brothers and cousins; indeed, the Iraqi government under Saddam Hussein was known, in diplomatic circles, as "the Tikriti regime" after the name of the Sunni Muslim village in north-central Iraq from which Saddam Hussein and his family hailed. It is instructive to note that Syria's Bashar al-Assad is, as was Iraq's Hussein, a member of a religious minority group in his own country. Sunni Muslims are the majority community in Syria, where al-Assad's Alawite community holds the decisive reins of power;

in Iraq, a majority population of Shi'a lived under the rule of Hussein, a Sunni, for more than two decades. These two leaders' rise to the top posts in their countries in spite of their minority status speaks volumes about the strength and efficacy of kin ties and networks in Middle Eastern societies and polities.

As a strategy for survival, the patrilineal kinship system has certainly proved flexible and effective over many centuries under a variety of social, economic, and political conditions in the Middle East. What began as an adaptive response to ecological and social limitations gradually became a valued institution embodying a rich cultural complex of expectations, attitudes, values, beliefs, rituals, and behaviors. The distinctive kinship systems and practices of the Middle East are a valued part of the region's civilizational heritage. Kinship is implicated in nearly every aspect of life and most social institutions, including religion and morality. Michael Meeker speculates that "the cultural uniformity which we now find in the arid zone does not reflect the traditions of a people bent on violence. On the contrary, it reflects . . . a moral response to the threat of political turmoil" (1979:19).

Despite the changes in urbanization, modernization, and emigration detailed by Valentine Moghadam in Chapter 9, individuals are still judged primarily by how they perform their family duties. An individual's identity, decisions, and social reputation are profoundly influenced by his or her kin group.

Not all anthropological studies of kinship in the Middle East center on the politics of patrilineal competition, however. Since the late 1970s, a growing number of ethnographies of Middle Eastern communities have taken women's lives, domesticity, reproduction, and sexuality as their point of departure (Geertz, 1979; Abu-Lughod, 1986; Inhorn, 2003; Mundy, 1995; Joseph, 1994; Peteet, 1991; Singerman, 1995; Kahn, 2000; Kanaaneh, 2002). The majority of these ethnographies have been written by women, and most are influenced by feminist and postmodern theories emphasizing the contentiousness of power relations, the mutability of identity, and the social construction of gender (i.e., sexual differences, culturally defined). By including the perspectives and voices of women in ethnographic depictions of daily life in Middle Eastern societies, these ethnographers have highlighted important questions about how power is conceptualized and deployed in the most intimate spaces of everyday life. A recurring theme in these works centers on strategies of resistance to hierarchical power arrangements and the elaboration of counternarratives that challenge and occasionally subvert dominant narratives that legitimate the patriarchal status quo (Abu-Lughod, 1986; Layoun, 1999).

Gender-oriented kinship studies have enriched our understanding of the symbolic and interactive processes that produce and reproduce the structures and categories of everyday life, while showing how and where changes and contradictions emerge by tracing these developments through the experience, choices, and negotiations of individuals' interactions. Gendered studies of kinship and family also highlight the affective and moral frames of meaning, in addition to the economic and political modes of organization, associated with kinship. As such, these studies show the interrelationship of men's and women's worlds and lives, no less than the connections and interrelationships between the intimate domain of the household and the public domain of governance and resource distribution (Singerman, 1995).

Let us now examine another adaptive strategy of contemporary Middle Eastern societies, which like kinship centers on the individual's identification and affiliation with extensive and potentially far-reaching networks. Through these connections, one can construct meaningful moral boundaries while obtaining access to power, protection, and resources in a highly competitive socioeconomic and political environment.

Ethnicity

It is easy to assume that ethnic differences are essentially racial differences and thus to conclude that ethnic groups are determined and delimited largely by biological criteria such as hair, skin and eye color, height, and physique, and only further distinguished by such characteristics as language, cultural patterns, and religious faith. Scholars examining the phenomenon of ethnicity, however, note that it is a strategic, more so than a genetic, phenomenon (Cohen, 1978; Royce, 1982; Anderson, 1993; Eller and Coughlan, 1993). Ethnic identity, whether referring to subjective criteria (an individual's awareness of and feelings about his or her membership in a particular ethnic category) or objective criteria (others' categorization of an individual on the basis of physical or cultural characteristics), cannot exist in a homogeneous society in which everyone shares the same cultural, religious, class, and linguistic background. Ethnicity and ethnic identity are oppositional and relational phenomena par excellence; they emerge only in societies comprising different types of peoples from a wide variety of backgrounds. Ethnicity is a product of plural societies characterized by cultural, economic, linguistic, or religious heterogeneity. Due to migration from rural to urban areas and the impact of enhanced communications and transportation systems, individuals and groups from a wide variety of cultural, linguistic, socioeconomic, and religious backgrounds are suddenly brought into contact.

Ethnicity, with its affective, symbolic, and political dimensions, has been a key topic of anthropological inquiry for decades. Urban anthropologists have tended to approach ethnic groups as "subcultures" (Hannerz, 1980), and the past thirty-five years have witnessed a gradual shift from primordialist theories of ethnicity, which view ethnic identity as somehow inborn, innate,

Ethnic diversity in the Middle East.

Egypt

Syria

Yemen

Jennifer A. Smith

Israel

Deborah J. Gerner

Kuwait

Deborah J. Gerner

West Bank

Deborah J. Gerner

Lebanon

and ascribed (Geertz, 1969; Fishman, 1980), to constructivist, utilitarian, and circumstantialist theories (Barth, 1969; Cohen, 1974; Royce, 1982), which view ethnicity as rooted in political processes and as constructed, strategic, and even achieved identity categories. The latter theoretical approach holds that ethnic identity is not a state of being, nor a "noun," but rather a verb (identifying with an ethnic group) that can be viewed from the bottom up or the top down. Bottom-up identification processes are evident in resistance movements and coalition building. Top-down identification processes are visible in state policies and legislation defining the boundaries between, and hierarchies among, groups characterized by particular cultural, linguistic, and religious characteristics. Both of these perspectives on identification processes depict ethnicity as a political phenomenon found in complex societies having centralized systems of political and economic administration.

In the rapidly growing cities of the Middle East, various ethnic groups interact and compete with one another in new and often alienating sociopolitical contexts characterized by economic scarcity and uneven development. The recognition of ethnic differences thus implies the recognition of economic and political differences as well. Depending on administrative frameworks of governance and the economic status of the groups involved, individuals' growing awareness of relative and absolute economic differences can easily lead to conflict, competition, and opposition organized along ethnic lines. As anthropologist Ronald Cohen notes, "Ethnicity is . . . one of the many outcomes of group interaction in which there is differential power between dominant and minority groups. From this perspective, ethnicity is an aspect of stratification, rather than a problem on its own" (1978:386).

The categorization of individuals or groups according to their ethnic identity and membership is a salient feature of most contemporary complex societies. What is crucial are not cultural, religious, or linguistic differences per se, but rather the structured arrangement of relationships between the different groups, and most notably, the administrative and economic frameworks in which these various groups are encapsulated. The vertical integration of ethnic groups in the context of new nation-states may be complementary or conflictual (Denoeux, 1993), but either way, what creates tension or harmony is not the supposedly essential cultural attributes or traditional customs of various groups, but rather the institutionalized structure of relationships between them. Are they egalitarian or hierarchical? Symmetrical or asymmetrical? Are differences codified in law such that identity becomes ineluctable and determinative of one's rights, duties, and life chances, as is the situation for many ethnic and religious minority groups in the new nation-states of the Middle East? If so, conflicts are likely to result.

One of the greatest challenges facing sociologists and anthropologists conducting research on societies of the non-Western developing world lies in determining the dividing lines (if any) between ethnic groups, kinship groups, and socioeconomic classes (Barakat, 1993). Ethnicity in the Middle East presents many definitional and methodological challenges for researchers since ethnic groups often behave like kin-based tribal groupings, especially in the way they mobilize their members by invoking a shared identity in some contexts, while segmenting into competing groups in other contexts. At the same time, ethnic differences seem to correspond closely to socioeconomic distinctions.

For instance, in Israeli society, Western-oriented Ashkenazi Jews, although numerically the minority community, are the dominant class in terms of wealth and control of the state's decisionmaking bodies in comparison with the more numerous Sephardic (or Mizrachi) Jews, who come from Arab countries and whose cultural attitudes and practices have long been looked down upon by Ashkenazi Jews. Prior to the convulsions of the Lebanese civil war (1975–1990), the wealthy power brokers and owners of factories, banks, and businesses in Lebanon were usually Maronite Christians, whereas the poorer, less powerful, agricultural communities in Lebanon tended to be populated by Shi'i Muslims.

There are, of course, exceptions to these correlations between class, ethnicity, and kinship. Only sustained and fine-grained research can elucidate the dynamic interrelationships of kinship, class, and ethnicity in the contemporary Middle East. Most social scientists consider ethnic political organizations and activities key phenomena of the modern world. Some scholars forecast the further solidification and entrenchment of ethnic and cultural identities as competition and conflict over limited goods increase throughout the world (Huntington, 1996). These recent predictions of social unrest and political violence between different cultural groups stand in stark contrast to the expectations of an earlier generation of academics and policymakers who, in the post–World War II era, expressed confidence that the universal adoption of a modernizing, liberal, secular, and technologically advanced culture and social system would facilitate homogenization and harmonization between different peoples within and between states. What these optimistic observers left out of their social equations were cultural dissonance, alienation, relative and absolute economic deprivation, the unequal distribution of resources, and differences in the types and amounts of power available to various ethnic groups in any given society. It is not the differences in cultural practices, religious beliefs, or linguistic characteristics that cause friction between members of opposing ethnic communities. Rather, "inequality, not ethnicity, is the basis of social stratification" and thus conflict (Cohen, 1978:400).

If Middle Eastern kin-based institutions like patrilineages and the tribe were the primary adaptive responses to the ecological challenges and socioeconomic problems of intense competition over scarce resources in a

harsh natural environment, then the ethnic group is the chief survival strategy of the politically marginalized individual in the harsh social and economic environments of the contemporary Middle East. Torn loose from the
familiar moorings of village, home, and family as a result of poverty or war;
struggling to make a decent living in crowded, impoverished, and poorly
serviced cities; and underrepresented by or underprovided for by a concerned
government, the average individual in the contemporary Middle East is likely
to feel lost, lonely, alienated, and powerless. If unable to find kin or people
from his or her region to provide guidance, mutual assistance, and support, an
uprooted individual will most likely turn to other individuals and groups with
whom he or she shares some common background characteristics, values, orientations, and goals. Hence we see the development of the ethnoreligious
group, which performs some of the same functions as the tribe but is neither
based entirely on blood relationships nor as clearly bounded in terms of its
membership as is the tribe. An organized and mobilized ethnic group or religious sect may serve the economic, social, and political needs of its members
far better than the state apparatus of many Middle Eastern countries.

At the beginning of the twentieth century, city-dwellers accounted for
less than 10 percent of the total population of the Middle East. As described
in Chapter 9, urbanization has increased dramatically in recent decades, and
studies by the UN predict that urban populations will reach 80 percent of
the total for the Middle East within the next decade. Thus the current trend
of relying on family and ethnoreligious ties to survive in Middle Eastern
cities is likely to continue. Cohen succinctly describes how comforting and
empowering an ethnic reference group and support network can be to such
displaced young people:

> If alienation is a malfunction of modern society, then ethnicity is an anti-
> dote. . . . Ethnicity provides a fundamental and multifaceted link to a cat-
> egory of others that very little else can do in modern society. . . . In a multi-
> ethnic society in which a plurality of groups, ethnic and non-ethnic, vie
> for scarce rewards, stressing individual human rights leads ultimately to
> unequal treatment. . . . Individuals are fated to obtain more rewards be-
> cause of their group identities. Organized ethnic groups can fight for equal
> rights. (1978: 401–402)

In other words, an ethnic group is not simply a racial unit or a cultural
unit but also a political unit. Ethnic groups are interest groups; they are
structured to serve the various needs of affiliated members while competing
with other interest groups for the limited resources to be obtained within the
framework of the modern state. The group that can mobilize the greatest
numbers of supporters and patrons, deliver the highest number of voters during elections, forge the strongest links with powerful groups within or without the society, and devise the most compelling and convincing arguments to

advance its rights to resources, political posts, or economic redress will take the lion's share of the services, governmental posts, protection, and wealth that can be extracted from the state. Indeed, in the Middle East, a well-organized and ambitious ethnic or religious group can even take complete control of the entire state apparatus, as did the Alawites of Syria and the Sunnis of Iraq in the early 1970s.

■ The Historical Context of Ethnicity

In the Middle East, ethnic groups and officially recognized ethnoreligious identity categories predate the creation of the region's nation-states. Prior to the advent of the nation-state system in the Middle East and even before the colonial era, most of the peoples of the region (with the exception of those living in Morocco and Iran) lived under Ottoman rule in the sociopolitical framework of a vast, decentralized empire. Day-to-day matters of administration and basic governance were in the hands of local political elites chosen by the Ottoman leadership, as well as the local clergy. As an empire, the Ottoman system was organized not according to ethnic or national principles and categories but according to religious distinctions. Individuals living in the Ottoman Empire did not identify themselves as Ottomans, Turks, Arabs, or Kurds, but rather as Muslims, Christians, Jews, or Druze. Within this system of organization, Muslims were in the majority, both in terms of absolute numbers and in terms of privilege, rank, status, and opportunities. Christians and Jews were formally recognized as religious minorities.

Considered "Peoples of the Book" and categorized as *dhimmi* communities (literally meaning "on the conscience" of the larger and more powerful Muslim community), Christians and Jews were supposed to be protected from harm or persecution by the majority Muslim community in return for their acceptance of a subordinate status, payment of a special tax *(jizyah),* and abstention from any public display of their religious practices such as processions and liturgical ceremonies. As long as the non-Muslim communities obeyed Ottoman laws and paid their taxes, they were supposed to be left unmolested to conduct their lives alongside the Muslim community. *Dhimmi* communities were under the jurisdiction of Islamic courts in criminal cases and some property disputes but obeyed the jurisdiction of their own communities' religious laws and precepts concerning any issues related to religious and family matters. As non-Muslims, Christians, Druze, and Jews were not subject to the rulings of *sharia* in matters of personal status such as marriage, divorce, inheritance, and other family issues. Instead, Christian sects and Druze and Jewish communities sought guidance, mediation, and rulings from their own religious hierarchy, the leaders of which had the power to make binding judicial decisions in the domain of family law and to represent their religious communities in official dealings with the Ottoman authorities. As detailed by Arthur Goldschmidt in Chapter 3, this system of legally recognized non-Muslim communal autonomy was known as the *millet* system (meaning "people" or "community" in Turkish).

As this brief historical overview indicates, the Middle East has always been culturally heterogeneous. During the Ottoman era, the rugged mountainous areas of the eastern Mediterranean became a refuge for a variety of Christian and Islamic religious sects and splinter groups seeking to escape persecution by orthodox religious authorities. Dwelling high atop these mountains, minority groups such as the Maronites, Druze, Shi'a, and Alawites could pursue their religious traditions free of interference from either Christian or Muslim authorities. The plural nature of Middle Eastern urban areas is inscribed in the very towers, walls, and gates that marked off the various named quarters of traditional urban settlements, such as the "Muslim Quarter," "Armenian Quarter," "Jewish Quarter," "Orthodox Quarter," and so on, as we find in such ancient cities as Jerusalem, Cairo, Damascus, Istanbul, and Baghdad. A division of labor among these distinct communities paralleled the spatial separation of different religious and ethnic groups in the traditional Middle Eastern city.

Christians, Muslims, and Jews occupied different professional categories in the Ottoman social and economic structure. The traditional city's division of labor was usually characterized by accommodation, complementarity, and integration rather than by competition and conflict. Muslims held positions in religious courts and schools as well as in the military and in local governmental administration, and non-Muslims served primarily as doctors, merchants, advisers, artisans, and religious and legal specialists for their own sectarian communities. The Ottoman division of labor is recorded to this day in the names of many Christian families from Lebanon, Palestine, and Syria, which designate the professional and artisan roles that their ancestors played in Ottoman society: *sabbagh* (dyer), *hakim* (doctor), *khabbaz* (baker), *banna* (builder), *sayigh* (goldsmith), *hayek* (weaver), *najjar* (carpenter), *khoury* (priest), and *shammas* (sexton).

The cultural and religious heterogeneity of the Middle East did not result from rapid urbanization or the establishment of nation-states in the twentieth century, nor is it a byproduct of colonialism (although colonial powers certainly employed tactics based on a policy of "divide and rule" to consolidate their control of local political systems). Different ethnic and religious groups have been living side by side in the great cities of the Middle East for centuries, sometimes in conflict but more often than not in harmony. What *is* new in the ethnic and religious configuration of the contemporary Middle East is the encapsulating social, political, and economic framework in which different groups live, work, and struggle. The relatively recent political processes that led to the region's incorporation into the global economy and then to the establishment of nation-states have altered the traditional balance of power and the system of accommodation that had prevailed during the Ottoman era (Makdisi, 2000). Although the Ottoman Empire was hardly a model of economic efficiency or social justice, it nonetheless encouraged a relatively stable and viable form of accommodation and cooperation among the region's diverse ethnic and religious groupings.

To understand how the various ethnic and religious communities of the Middle East became embroiled in conflicts that are still continuing, we must now examine the historical processes of social class formation, which exacerbated competition and thus engendered conflicts between the different ethnic communities of the region.

Social Class

Unlike the identity categories of kinship and ethnicity, social class is not based on biological or cultural criteria, but rather on economic and political differences. Like ethnic groups, social classes are oppositional phenomena: a social class cannot exist except in relation to other social classes, since the idea of a class entails a hierarchical arrangement of groups based on differences of wealth, power, and control over resources. A society whose members all share the same resources equally, own wealth in common, participate fully in all decisionmaking, and have equal rights and duties in relation to one another would be a classless society. The distinguishing criteria of any social class structure are inequalities of wealth and differential access to resources and means of economic production. Thus, class distinctions entail relationships of dominance and subordination between different competing groups, each of which continually strives to improve its relative position, or having attained a position of relative advantage, struggles to retain it.

According to social historian Philip Khoury, the social class structure of the Middle East was relatively simple and stable until the middle of the nineteenth century. Just 150 years ago, the Middle East began to be integrated into the capitalist world system. Consequently, new social classes gradually emerged as a result of changing modes of economic production and new forms of ownership and control of resources (Khoury, 1983). The most significant economic change during the nineteenth century was the advent of new forms of landownership. Following a series of military and economic defeats at the hands of rising European powers, the Ottoman leadership decided to institute a number of administrative reforms in an effort to improve and strengthen the Ottoman system by imitating European societies and governments.

Chief among these reforms were new land laws that encouraged private rather than communal ownership of productive property. Muslim and non-Muslim elites favored by the Ottoman rulers benefited from these reforms by taking control of formerly communal properties, on which they planted cash crops such as tobacco in place of subsistence crops. This agricultural regime served the interests of international markets rather than the needs of the local populace. At the same time, merchants (often Christians and Jews) in cities such as Beirut, Damascus, Acre, Cairo, Alexandria, and Ladhakia began to earn a considerable profit as middlemen overseeing trade between European producers of goods and newly wealthy Middle Eastern consumers of fine furnishings, clothing, household equipment, and medicines. This shift from local to foreign markets for consumer goods had a debilitating effect on local artisans and manufacturers, who, along with peasants displaced from agricultural lands by private landownership, high taxation, and wars, became members of a new social class formation: the urban proletariat. This period marked the advent of a sharply pyramidal class structure character-ized by the political and economic domination of a large mass of impover-ished people by a handful of extremely wealthy landowning families.

Although markets and modes of production have changed dramatically since the mid–nineteenth century, the social and economic class structure of the Middle East is still profoundly pyramidal. Despite the omnipresent stereotype of the super-rich Arab oil shaikh, the vast majority of people in the region live at or below the poverty line, and only a handful of people own and control considerable wealth derived from the oil industry, its sub-sidiaries, and the consumption habits of the oil-producing elite. Economic activity in the region as a whole consists of consumption more than produc-tion, and the exchange of goods and services between countries of the re-gion is limited, resulting in poor regional economic integration and height-ened dependency on Western goods and services (World Bank, 1996).

A close examination of the economies of the region quickly reveals a glaring absence of industry and manufacturing in most countries, with the ex-ception of oil-related industries in the Gulf region, computer and military in-dustries in Israel, and a variety of industrial activities in Turkey. By and large, the countries of the region consume much more than they produce. Agricul-ture is underdeveloped in Lebanon and Syria, countries that could technically produce significant amounts of agricultural goods; hence, most foodstuffs are imported and therefore too expensive for the average family to afford on a daily basis (World Bank, 1996).

Investments of oil revenues within the region have traditionally been limited. Until recently, well-to-do oil-producing countries preferred to invest their money in Europe and North America (Makdisi, 1991), thus limiting eco-nomic diversification and the expansion of bases of production in the region. Commercial revenue from tourism has been limited due to a series of wars and continuing political tensions, and particularly after the advent of the al-Aqsa intifada in 2000 and the Al-Qaida attacks on the United States in 2001. The pronounced reliance on oil revenue has increased the region's economic vulnerability to external developments and decisions. Indeed, the countries of the Middle East are very dependent on economic and political decisions em-anating from outside the region. Hence, "their economic autonomy, defined as their ability to develop independently and/or to take policy actions without regard to developments and reactions elsewhere, is greatly constrained. . . . This economic dependence implies political dependence" (Makdisi, 1991:133).

As a result of the poor performance of the oil sector in the 1980s, countries throughout the region felt the effects of falling oil prices in the form of decreasing remittance payments sent back to countries such as Syria, Lebanon, Egypt, and Jordan by migrant workers in the Gulf, particularly after the Gulf War of 1991. Even before the fall in oil prices, poverty in the region was already pronounced: in 1980, approximately 44 percent of the population in Morocco and Egypt were living below the poverty line (Barakat, 1993); the situation has improved little since then. During the past two decades, the Arab world has seen a

> progressive decline, or perhaps near elimination, of subsistence production, massive occupational shifts from agrarian to service . . . activities; a massive exodus of surplus rural labor to urban conglomerations [while at the same time witnessing] the rise of a new Arab bourgeoisie, a class of contractors, middlemen, brokers, agents of foreign corporations, and wheeler-dealers . . . typically engaged in nonproductive work. (Farsoun and Zacharia, 1995:273)

In the narrow space between the upper class (those few who possess and control great wealth) and the lower class (the millions of impoverished former peasants who are constantly streaming into the crowded urban areas of the region), we find the only productive sector of Middle Eastern society: a relatively small middle class composed primarily of small-scale commercial enterprises, self-employed merchants, repairmen, artisans, teachers, some white-collar professionals, and government employees. The members of this weak and vulnerable socioeconomic formation have discovered that remaining middle class requires a concerted family effort. Hence the patrilineal kinship group that emerged as a strategic adaptation to desert conditions so long ago is once again the basic productive unit among the urban middle classes in the modern Middle East. As Samih Farsoun notes, "rent income, small business income, and income from wages and other labor have emerged as key sources for an increasing number of multiple income families. . . . Most of these petty economic activities are traditional in style of organization and in the social relations of work, i.e., patriarchal and patronage" (1988:224).

▪ Kinship, Ethnicity, and Class in Context: Strategies or Straitjackets?

Negatively affected by social and political transformations and economic restructuring at the local, regional, and international levels, particularly in the post–Cold War era, individuals in the Middle East have turned to their nuclear and extended families for support and mutual assistance. They have reactivated and emphasized traditional family structures, kinship networks, affiliations to ethnoreligious groups, and ties of patronage even as they have embraced the latest developments of modern technology, such as cellular telephones and the Internet. Consequently, the contemporary Middle East is a world of startling contradictions and ironic juxtapositions.

Halim Barakat reflects that it is very difficult for observers to interpret socioeconomic developments in the region because "the contemporary Arab economic order is a peculiar cluster of different modes of production, all operating at once, which renders it simultaneously semi-feudal, semi-socialist, and semi-capitalist" (1993:77). The existence, side-by-side, of patrilineages and multinational corporations, rationalized bureaucracies and religious brotherhoods, modern nation-states and tribal federations, and traditional practices and cosmopolitan attitudes, which political scientist Bassam Tibi refers to as "the simultaneity of the unsimultaneous" (1990:127), illuminates the challenges of nation-state formation and national integration in the contemporary Middle East. It also reveals the degree to which the peoples of the region have compensated for nation-states' weaknesses by adapting and revitalizing traditional sociocultural modes of survival:

> Unlike the imperial and the territorial dynastic states that were familiar in Middle Eastern history, the externally imposed new pattern of the nation state is defined as a national, not as a communal, polity. Its underlying concept is sovereignty, which not only presupposes the capability of the central power to establish itself over the entire territory, but also requires established citizenship and a corresponding national identity and loyalty. In varying degrees, all states of the Middle East lack this infrastructure. . . . In most of the states of the Middle East, sovereignty is nominal. The tribal ethnic and sectarian conflicts that the colonial powers exacerbated did not end with the attainment of independence. The newly established nation states have failed to cope with the social and economic problems created by rapid development because they cannot provide the proper institutions to alleviate these problems. Because the nominal nation state has not met the challenge, society has resorted to its pre-national ties as a solution, thereby preserving the framework of the patron-client relationship. (Tibi, 1990:147–149)

Perhaps it is not too far-fetched to argue that extensive networks of overlapping kin- and ethnic-based patron-client relationships linking those in the government with those outside of it constitute the actual "glue" that holds the Middle Eastern nation-state together. Although patron-client relations "play an important role in facilitating the distribution of goods and services among the population and harnessing popular support behind leaders" (Khoury and Kostiner, 1990:18), ties of patronage are essentially asymmetrical: perpetuating these relationships also perpetuates and reinforces unequal power structures in the starkly stratified societies of the contemporary Middle East. Patron-client ties ensure that people are kept "in their place": the rich and powerful maintain their dominant positions, from which they have the advantage of becoming even more rich and powerful, and the less fortunate are kept in their subordinate position of dependency, remaining powerless over the decisionmaking processes and larger forces that shape their lives.

Taking a broader view of the Middle East in a global context, and examining the structures and processes through which the region is encapsulated at the international level, it appears that the vertical integration of society, polity, and economies through patron-client relations at the local and national levels have clear echoes and similarities in the asymmetrical patterns of integration between the Middle East and the global economy. Many countries in this region are clients of the world's current superpower: the United States. A holistic and contextualized anthropological approach demands that we view kinship, ethnicity, social class, and nation-states in the Middle East within all relevant contexts, including that of the global political economy. In so doing, we may discover that not all of the Middle East's problems are internally generated or self-inflicted. Critiquing the 2002 UN Development Programme report on the social and economic state of the Middle East and North Africa, historian Mark Levine noted the absence of a contextualized, culturally sensitive analysis in the report's findings:

> [The] report [does not] consider the strategic yet marginalized (or better, strategically marginalized) position of the Middle East and North Africa in the larger world political economy. Such lacunae allow the authors to avoid grappling with the cycle of Arab petrodollars for Western arms, the disproportionate and generally increasing military budgets of Arab governments, or the disastrous impact of US and European agricultural subsidies (which flood markets with under-priced Western products that force local farmers out of business) that are crucial to the region's perpetual economic dependence on the West. (2002)

The foreign aid policies of powerful states, no less than the decisions and dictates of the World Bank and the International Monetary Fund, serve to replicate relations of dependence between the most populous states of the Middle East and the West while consolidating mutually supportive ties between the regimes of the region and Western suppliers of military and economic aid packages (Pfeifer, 1999). This is not a recipe for national and regional integration, nor does it strengthen the institutions of civil society and civic participation at the grassroots level.

Although relying on subnational, primary identities and traditional relationships in order to survive in a challenging world can be interpreted as logical and strategic, it also entails costs and consequences that can have negative repercussions on individuals and collectivities in the region. Relying on kin rather than the state, affiliating with narrowly defined ethnoreligious groups rather than forming broad-based coalitions and solidarities, and participating in patron-client exchanges of goods and services that perpetuate socioeconomic inequalities while consolidating age-old forms of political domination, impede economic, cultural, and political integration on the national and regional levels and discourage processes of empowerment, the attainment of social justice, and the implementation of democratic reforms.

Turning inward to family, clan, or confessional sect is a valuable method of coping with a variety of daily challenges, but in so doing, the peoples of the region may lose sight of the common interests and goals that could unite them on bases of affiliation and organization that are much wider and potentially more effective than the narrow foundations provided by primary identities of blood and faith. Hence, Middle Eastern peoples may remain unaware of opportunities for large-scale cooperation and coordination to improve some of the difficult circumstances of their lives, particularly in areas such as environmental conservation and economic integration. Also, a public that has fragmented into separate, segmentary groups of kinsmen and coreligionists is facilitating its own control, exploitation, co-optation, and manipulation by repressive state governments. A divided population is much easier to rule, as the colonial powers so deftly proved.

The institutionalization—and essentialization—of ethnic and religious identities for legal and administrative purposes, seen most clearly in states such as Lebanon and Israel, is a double-edged sword. Although official recognition of cultural heritage and religious laws may provide answers to individuals' psychological needs and communal organizational problems, institutionalized identities can also trap individuals in the vise of inflexible collective categories not of their own choice or making, thus limiting their personal options and opportunities while preventing the development of a more inclusive sense of overarching national loyalty and identity. The most extreme example of the triumph of the ethnic group over both the individual citizen and the overarching state is that of Lebanon, a state composed entirely of seventeen officially recognized ethnoconfessional groups, membership in which defines Lebanese individuals' rights and duties in the context of the state. Reflecting on the tragedy of Lebanon, Lebanese sociologist Samir Khalaf notes that

> the very factors that account for much of the viability, resourcefulness, and integration of the Lebanese are also the factors that are responsible for the erosion of civic ties and national loyalties. . . . In short, the factors that enable at the micro and communal level disable at the macro and national level. This is, indeed, Lebanon's predicament. (1986:14)

Or, in the words of Ziad Rahbani, the bard of the Lebanese civil war whose captivating music and ironic lyrics allowed the Lebanese to look at themselves with jaundiced but compassionate eyes: *yaa zaman at-ta'ifiyya! ta'ifiyya, ta'ifiyya/kheli eidek 'alal-howia; shidd 'alaiha qad ma fiik!* ("Oh, these are confessional times, such confessional times!/So best keep your hand on your identity [card]; and grasp it for all that you are worth!"). The song refers both to the wartime retreat into primary identities and the horrifying practice of political murders perpetrated by militiamen who routinely killed civilians on the basis of their religious confession, which is recorded on every Lebanese citizen's identity card.

Another danger posed by the inward-looking tendencies and the resultant social and political fragmentation of Middle Eastern societies is that individuals and groups in this region may be less prepared to deal with the multifaceted challenges posed by media and market globalization and the coming ecological crises. As detailed by Agnieszka Paczynska in Chapter 7, the Middle East is already economically marginalized and dependent in the current world economic system. As a result, the region may be at risk of being even further sidelined by the coming global restructuring of economic and political relationships. To succeed in the new global markets, Middle Eastern countries should be integrated into a regional economic framework, rather than being more closely linked to the West and its markets than they are to one another. As long as asymmetrical vertical integration between the region and the West at the global level, economic inequalities and political conflicts at the regional and national levels, and mistrust, uncertainty, scarcity, and poverty at the local levels drive Middle Eastern peoples further into the traditional refuge of kinship, ethnicity, and patron-client ties, the peoples of the region will be unlikely to achieve national and regional integration and the resulting levels of cooperation and coordination needed to meet so many of their interrelated economic, ecological, and political challenges.

The problems of the contemporary Middle East are not cultural ones centered on the resilience of traditional practices and primary identity categories in a modern world. Rather, the region's political and economic problems stem primarily from the weaknesses and deficiencies of an imposed nation-state system that is not meeting people's basic needs, and from regional hostilities rooted in historical injustices and shortsighted policies initiated by Western powers during the colonial period and replicated in today's globalized, "neocolonial" era, characterized by a form of economic integration that is neither egalitarian nor sustainable.

The Middle East remains a region in which citizenship and its accompanying rights and duties have little meaning, but where

> membership in kin-based groups is the individual's chief guarantee of security and access to resources—hence the necessity for strong group maintenance mechanisms. Arab familism (or tribalism) must be viewed,

not as a cultural trait, but as a very ancient adaptive response to insecurity; group cohesion is as important for survival under state oppression as it is for survival in the absence of the state. (Sayigh, 1981:267)

▓ Conclusion

My goal in this chapter has been to analyze and interpret kinship, ethnicity, and social class in the contemporary Middle East by showing how sociocultural phenomena are related to ecological, economical, psychological, administrative, and political realities and how they interact with and shape one another. We have learned that social, political, and cultural behaviors in the Middle East have historically been greatly affected by the limitations of a harsh natural environment in which economic scarcity and pronounced political competition were constants, whereas sustained relationships of mutual trust and permanent, broad-based, sociopolitical formations were not. Furthermore, we have seen that the region underwent rapid economic and political changes in the nineteenth century, encapsulating the Middle East in a Western-dominated political and economic order that permanently altered traditional class structures and produced sharp socioeconomic inequalities, which were then exacerbated by colonialism and the imposition of arbitrarily defined nation-states. The resulting conundrums and inequalities remain unresolved to this day.

Lacking meaningful representation by or assistance from most nation-states of the region, many Middle Eastern peoples have turned to localized identity categories and traditional organizational structures in an effort to make a living—and to make a meaning—in the challenging world that confronts them. Although they have succeeded in this effort, it has not been without costs and consequences. In the long run, resorting to kinship, ethnicity, and patron-client ties could have a negative effect on societies that may soon be forced to reconcile their segmented and fragmentary nature with increasing political and economic pressures for integration, coordination, and cooperation in the globalizing economy.

There is much room for optimism, however. The scholars cited here demonstrate that the peoples of the Middle East are talented survivors possessing an exceptionally rich and resilient cultural heritage that can be adapted to serve them in all political, economic, and temporal environments.

▓ Note

1. Jerrold Kessel noted that "right-wing Prime Minister Benjamin Netanyahu has convinced at least half his countrymen that the Middle East is still 'a very bad neighborhood'—a place where suspicion and deep-rooted security concerns are

again the dominant sentiments. Peace lags far behind security in the double-barreled promise on which Netanyahu came to power two years ago" (Kessel, 1998).

▓ Bibliography

AAA (American Anthropological Association). 2007. "AAA Opposes the US Military's Human Terrain System Project." www.aaanet.org/blog/PR_110707.htm.

Abu-Lughod, Lila. 1986. *Veiled Sentiments*. Berkeley: University of California Press.

al-Akhras, Muhammad Safouh. 1976. *The Structure of the Arab Family*. Damascus: Ministry of Culture.

Anderson, Benedict. 1993. *Imagined Communities*. London: Verso.

Antoun, Richard. 2000. "Civil Society, Tribal Process, and Change in Jordan: An Anthropological View." *International Journal of Middle East Studies* 32:441–463.

Ayubi, Nazih. 2001. *Overstating the Arab State*. London: I. B. Tauris.

Bahloul, Joelle. 1992. *The Architecture of Memory: A Jewish-Muslim Household in Colonial Algeria, 1937–1962*. Cambridge: Cambridge University Press.

Barakat, Halim. 1993. *The Arab World: Society, Culture, and State*. Berkeley: University of California Press.

Barth, Frederik. 1969. *Ethnic Groups and Boundaries*. Boston: Little, Brown.

Cohen, Abner. 1974. *Two-Dimensional Man: An Essay on the Anthropology of Symbolism and Power in Complex Societies*. Berkeley: University of California Press.

Cohen, Ronald. 1978. "Ethnicity: Problem and Focus in Anthropology." *Annual Review of Anthropology* 7:379–403.

Cunningham, Robert B., and Yasin K. Sarayrah. 1993. *Wasta: The Hidden Force in Middle Eastern Society*. Westport, Conn.: Praeger.

Denoeux, Guilain. 1993. *Urban Unrest in the Middle East: A Comparative Study of Informal Networks in Egypt, Iran, and Lebanon*. Albany: State University of New York Press.

Eller, Jack, and Reed Coughlan. 1993. "The Poverty of Primordialism: The Demystification of Ethnic Attachments." *Ethnic and Racial Studies* 16, no. 2:183–202.

Farsoun, Samih K. 1988. "Class Structure and Social Change in the Arab World." Pp. 221–238 in Hisham Sharabi (ed.), *The Next Arab Decade: Alternative Futures*. Boulder, Colo.: Westview Press.

Farsoun, Samih K., and Christina Zacharia. 1995. "Class, Economic Change, and Political Liberalization in the Arab World." Pp. 261–282 in Rex Brynen, Bahgat Korany, and Paul Noble (eds.), *Political Liberalization and Democratization in the Arab World*, Vol. 1: *Theoretical Perspectives*. Boulder, Colo.: Lynne Rienner.

Fernea, Elizabeth Warnock. 1969. *Guests of the Sheikh*. New York: Doubleday.

Fishman, Joshua. 1980. "Social Theory and Ethnography." Pp. 84–97 in Peter Sugar (ed.), *Ethnic Diversity and Conflict in Eastern Europe*. Santa Barbara: ABC-Clio.

Friedl, Erik. 1991. *Women of Deh Koh*. New York: Penguin Paperback.

Geertz, Clifford. 1969 [1973]. *The Interpretation of Cultures*. New York: Basic Books.

Geertz, Hildred. 1979. "The Meaning of Family Ties." Pp. 315–391 in Clifford Geertz, Hildred Geertz, and Lawrence Rosen (eds.), *Meaning and Order in Moroccan Society*. New York: Cambridge University Press.

Gilsenan, Michael. 1996. *Lords of the Lebanese Marshes: Violence and Narrative in an Arab Society*. Berkeley: University of California Press.

Hannerz, Ulf. 1980. *Exploring the City: Inquiries Towards an Urban Anthropology.* New York: Columbia University Press.

Herzfeld, Michael. 1997. "The Dangers of Metaphor: From Troubled Waters to Boiling Blood in Europe." Pp. 74–88 in Michael Herzfeld, *Cultural Intimacy: Social Poetics in the Nation State.* London: Routledge.

Huntington, Samuel. 1996. *The Clash of Civilizations and the Remaking of World Order.* New York: Simon and Schuster.

Ibn Khaldun. 1967. *The Muqaddimah: An Introduction to History.* Trans. Franz Rosenthal. Bollingen Series. Princeton: Princeton University Press.

Inhorn, Marcia. 2003. *Local Babies, Global Science: Gender, Religion, and In Vitro Fertilization in Egypt.* London: Routledge.

Jean-Klein, Iris. 2000. "Mothercraft, Statecraft, and Subjectivity in the Palestinian Intifada." *American Ethnologist* 27:100–127.

Joseph, Su'ad. 1994. "Brother-Sister Relationships: Connectivity, Love, and Power in the Reproduction of Patriarchy in Lebanon." *American Ethnologist* 21, no. 1:31–54.

———. 2000. *Intimate Selving in Arab Families: Gender, Self, and Identity.* Syracuse, N.Y.: Syracuse University Press.

Kahn, Susan Martha. 2000. *Reproducing Jews: A Cultural Account of Assisted Conception in Israel.* Durham, N.C.: Duke University Press.

Kanaaneh, Rhoda Ann. 2002. *Birthing the Nation: Strategies of Palestinian Women in Israel.* Berkeley: University of California Press.

Kapchan, Deborah. 1996. *Gender on the Market: Moroccan Women and the Revoicing of Tradition.* Philadelphia: University of Pennsylvania Press.

Keesing, Roger. 1975. *Kin Groups and Social Structure.* New York: Holt, Rinehart, and Winston.

Kessel, Jerrold. 1998. "Stalled Peace Process Casts Pall on Celebration." www.cnn.com/SPECIALS/1998/israel/kessel.essay.

al-Khafaji, Isam. 1995. "Beyond the Ultranationalist State." *Middle East Report* 187–188:34–39.

Khalaf, Samir. 1986. *Lebanon's Predicament.* New York: Columbia University Press.

Khoury, Philip. 1983. *Urban Notables and Arab Nationalism: The Politics of Damascus, 1860–1920.* Cambridge: Cambridge University Press.

Khoury, Philip, and Joseph Kostiner (eds.). 1990. *Tribes and State Formation in the Middle East.* Berkeley: University of California Press.

Khuri, Fuad. 1970. "Parallel Cousin Marriage Reconsidered: A Middle Eastern Practice That Nullifies the Effects of Marriage on the Intensity of Family Relationships." *Man* 5:596–618.

King-Irani, Laurie. 2001. "Maneuvering in Narrow Spaces: An Analysis of Emergent Identity, Subjectivity, and Political Institutions Among Palestinian Citizens of Israel." Unpublished Ph.D. diss., Bloomington, Indiana University.

Layoun, Mary. 1999. "A Guest at the Wedding: Honor, Memory, and (National) Desire in Michel Khleife's Wedding in Galilee." Pp. 92–110 in Caren Kaplan, Normal Alarcon, and Minoo Moallem (eds.), *Between Woman and Nation: Nationalisms, Translational Feminisms, and the State.* Durham, N.C.: Duke University Press.

Levine, Mark. 2002. "The UN Arab Human Development Report: A Critique." *Middle East Report Online.* www.merip.org/mero/mero072602.html (accessed May 25, 2003).

Makdisi, Samir. 1991. "The Arab World and the World Economy: An Overview." Pp. 123–146 in Hala Esfandiari and A. L. Udovitch (eds.), *The Economic Dimensions of Middle Eastern History: Essays in Honor of Charles Issawi.* Princeton: Darwin Press.

Makdisi, Ussama. 2000. *The Culture of Sectarianism: Community, History, and Violence in Nineteenth-Century Ottoman Lebanon.* Berkeley: University of California Press.

Mamdani, Mahmood. 2002. "Good Muslim, Bad Muslim: A Political Perspective on Culture and Terrorism." *American Anthropologist* 104:766–775.

McMurray, David. 2002. *In and Out of Morocco.* Minneapolis: University of Minnesota Press.

Meeker, Michael. 1979. *Literature and Violence in North Arabia.* Cambridge: Cambridge University Press.

Mundy, Martha. 1995. *Domestic Government: Kinship, Community, and Polity in North Yemen.* London: I. B. Tauris.

Murphy, Robert, and Leonard Kasdan. 1959. "The Structure of Parallel Cousin Marriage." *American Anthropologist* 61:17–29.

Nelson, Cynthia (ed.). 1973. *The Desert and the Sown: Nomads in the Wider Society.* Berkeley: Institute for International Studies, University of California.

Peteet, Julie M. 1991. *Gender in Crisis: Women and the Palestinian Resistance Movement.* New York: Columbia University Press.

Pfeifer, Karen. 1999. "How Tunisia, Morocco, Jordan, and Even Egypt Became IMF 'Success Stories' in the 1990s." *Middle East Report* 210:24–30.

Pitcher, Linda. 1998. "'The Divine Impatience': Ritual, Narrative, and Symbolization in the Practice of Martyrdom in Palestine." *Medical Anthropology Quarterly* 12, no. 1:8–30.

Roniger, Luis, and Ayse Gunes Ayata (eds.). 1994. *Democracy, Clientelism, and Civil Society.* Boulder, Colo.: Lynne Rienner.

Royce, Anya Peterson. 1982. *Ethnicity: Strategies of Diversity.* Bloomington: Indiana University Press.

Sayigh, Rosemary. 1981. "Roles and Functions of Arab Women: A Reappraisal." *Arab Studies Quarterly* 3:258–274.

———. 1994. *Too Many Enemies: The Palestinian Experience in Lebanon.* London: Zed Books.

Schneider, David M. 1968. *American Kinship: A Cultural Account.* Englewood Cliffs, N.J.: Prentice-Hall.

Schneider, Jane. 1971. "Of Vigilance and Virgins: Honor, Shame, and Access to Resources in Mediterranean Societies." *Ethnology* 10:1–24.

Sharabi, Hisham (ed.). 1990. *Theory, Politics, and the Arab World: Critical Responses.* London: Routledge.

Shryock, Andrew. 1997. *Nationalism and the Genealogical Imagination: Oral History and Textual Authority in Jordan.* Berkeley: University of California Press.

Singerman, Diane. 1995. *Avenues of Participation: Family, Politics, and Networks in Urban Quarters of Cairo.* Princeton: Princeton University Press.

Tapper, Richard. 1990. "Anthropologists, Historians, and Tribespeople on Tribe and State Formation in the Middle East." Pp. 48–73 in Philip Khoury and Joseph Kostiner (eds.), *Tribes and State Formation in the Middle East.* Berkeley: University of California Press.

Tibi, Bassam. 1990. "The Simultaneity of the Unsimultaneous: Old Tribes and Imposed Nation-States in the Modern Middle East." Pp. 127–152 in Philip S. Khoury and Joseph Kostiner (eds.), *Tribes and State Formation in the Middle East.* Berkeley: University of California Press.

Wedeen, Lisa. 1999. *Ambiguities of Domination: Politics, Rhetoric, and Symbols in Contemporary Syria.* Chicago: University of Chicago Press.

World Bank. 1996. *Middle East and North Africa.* Washington, D.C.: World Bank.

Zubaida, Sami. 1994. "National, Communal and Global Dimensions in Middle Eastern Food Cultures." Pp. 33–48 in S. Zubaida and R. Tapper (eds.), *Culinary Cultures of the Middle East.* Berkeley: University of California Press.

11

The Role of Women

Lisa Taraki

Approaching the study of women in the contemporary Middle East is a difficult and challenging task. Decades of orientalist scholarship and popular and journalistic writing have left their indelible mark on the representation of the women of the Middle East. A priori assumptions, preconceptions, and stereotypes abound, and generalizations about women in a region as internally diverse as the Middle East continue to predominate in current discourse. Scholars and others attempting an objective study of Middle Eastern women must therefore contend with a heavy intellectual legacy, and it is not surprising that much of the energy of scholars today is directed at challenging long-standing preconceptions and stereotypes concerning Middle Eastern women.

The more intractable of the impediments to understanding the reality of women living in the Middle East are lodged at the level of culture. This culturalist bias has meant that the study of issues such as women's labor force participation, status within the family, marriage patterns, fertility behavior, educational attainment, and political participation continue to be addressed from within a broad framework of an unchanging and essential "Islamic" value system that is assumed to hold a firm grip not only in matters of belief and attitude but also in the conduct of everyday life.

This chapter is based on the premise that, as in all societies, a multiplicity of social, economic, political, and cultural forces and factors have shaped the statuses, experiences, and living conditions of Middle Eastern women. I also stress the fact that just as an ahistorical conception of Islamic values as determinants of practice does not advance our understanding of complex historical processes, so too does the use of the unitary concept of the "Middle Eastern woman" obscure the rich diversity in women's lives across the Middle East. Significant regional differences exist within the broad area covered in this book. In addition, within regions and countries, women's life chances, experiences, and statuses diverge and are shaped by a number of important factors, the most significant of which are class and place of residence (primarily urban or rural), ethnicity, refugee or non-refugee status, and religious affiliation. Attributes pertaining to women as individuals, such as age, marital status, and number of children, also influence women's differential status, power, and access to opportunities within households, kinship groups, communities, and even the labor force.

▪ The Modern Nation-State

We begin our discussion of the realities of women's lives with an examination of the relationship between women and the state in the modern Middle East. A number of authors have stressed the importance of understanding the relationship between women's status, rights, and position within society and state-building projects in the region (Joseph, 1991; Kandiyoti, 1991c; Moghadam, 1995, 2003; Molyneux, 1991). Whether states adopt positive strategies that effect changes in women's status or choose not to upset what is perceived to be the status quo has important implications for society in general and women in particular. The postcolonial state in the Middle East has had to face choices not only on the economic and political-strategic levels but also in relation to the kind of society it envisions for its citizens, both female and male.

As discussed by Arthur Goldschmidt Jr. in Chapter 3 and Deborah J. Gerner and Philip A. Schrodt in Chapter 4, the emergence of the modern nation-state in the Middle East in the twentieth century was accompanied in most instances by a modernizing agenda by which state elites attempted to transform or modify basic relations in society, including prevailing gender relations. A variety of legal-administrative measures, social policies, and a modernizing nationalist ideology were deployed to weaken the grip of primordial loyalties and affiliations, build the construct of *citizen* in the modern sense, and launch programs of social and economic development.

Education is perhaps the one domain where almost all Middle Eastern countries have achieved remarkable successes as a result of direct state policy. Although reforms in areas pertaining to personal status and political rights for women have been very uneven, the trend toward increasing educational levels for both women and men has been nearly universal. One measure of this success is that Arab states made some of the greatest gains in women's education anywhere in the world in the period from 1970 to 1990, more than doubling women's literacy rate in these two decades. They also nearly doubled female primary and secondary enrollment, from 32 percent in 1970 to 60 percent in 1992 (UNDP, 1995:29). But Arab states' commitment to expanding education may be eroding; the widely acclaimed *Arab Human Development Report 2002* notes that the overall rate of increase in enrollment in the three levels of education for both males and females slowed during the 1990s, with the rising expenditure on education tapering off after 1985. The report suggests that this slowing rate of growth in educational spending is related to economic difficulties and structural adjustment programs adopted by Arab states (UNDP, 2002:52–54). The *Arab Human Development Report 2005*—subtitled *Towards the Rise of Women in the Arab World*—demonstrates that women's enrollment in primary, secondary, and tertiary levels of education continues to lag behind that of men, while the rate of female illiteracy remains relatively high compared to men (UNDP, 2005:76–80).

Reforms of legislation and policies pertaining to women's rights within the family have been the subject of great debate and controversy all over the Middle East. Primarily because family legislation has historically been grounded in Islamic law *(sharia),* most state elites (with the exception of Turkey) have been very hesitant to introduce significant changes that would challenge prevailing gender hierarchies and the sexual division of labor that these laws took for granted.

Turkey was the first state in the Middle East to introduce legal and administrative reforms aimed at developing the economy and altering prevailing social relationships. The replacement of Islamic law with the Civil Code of 1926 and the enfranchisement of women in the early 1930s were measures undertaken by the new republic under Mustafa Kemal Atatürk

Girls of diverse social and economic backgrounds attend a range of public and private schools, as in this Cairo classroom.

(Father of the Turks) to change gender relations. Women became citizens of the republic, and the new laws banned polygamy and gave divorced women more rights. National ideologues and feminist writers and activists promoted a modernizing nationalist ideology stressing women's equality with men. This ideology has been viewed by some scholars as part of the arsenal of the new secular republic against the caliphate as an institution and as proof that Turkey was a democratic country, unlike the dictatorships in Germany and Italy with which it was allied (Kandiyoti, 1989:127).

In the decades that followed, Turkey continued on its trajectory as a modernizing and secular state, expanding civil and social liberties in the constitutions of 1961 and 1982. However, the civil code, although more progressive than those in surrounding countries, still grants privileges to men in the areas of child custody, determination of place of residence, and personal freedom (Arat, 1996:29). Turkey is often singled out as the Muslim Middle Eastern country to have achieved the greatest levels of "modernization" and "Westernization." If progress is measured by basic indicators, however, this leadership position is not warranted. Adult female illiteracy is still high (20.4 percent of women fifteen years of age and older are illiterate, compared to only 4.7 percent of men) and reflects a significant gap between urban and rural areas (UNDP, 2006:364). Women's labor force participation rates and school enrollment figures are also modest (Arat, 1996:30).

In addition, recent years have witnessed the unraveling of the secularists' historical hegemony in Turkish society. As with other confrontations between Islamist and secular forces throughout the Muslim world, women have been at the center of some of the most flammable debates and conflicts. The "headscarf" issue in 1999, for instance, brought Islamists and secularists to a confrontation, with implications beyond the Turkish parliament, where the issue initially exploded (Arat, 2000).

The case of Israel is unique in the Middle East and presents some contradictions. The secular political elites of the immediate poststate period were in a most favorable position to build a modern nation-state in line with the democratic and secular principles they claimed formed the basis of the new society and polity. In addition to being culturally and politically hegemonic in the new state, they were not saddled by the heavy weight of entrenched institutions (such as a powerful religious authority) and did not have to face traditional and conservative groups with a vested interest in maintaining the status quo. An examination of legislation affecting women, however, reveals that not all the opportunities were seized. The Women's Equal Rights Law of 1951, although abolishing blatant discrimination against women embodied in Ottoman law, was intended to protect the rights of women as mothers and wives, not as citizens; thus a whole range of rights outside the domestic domain—such as in employment—were left out of the law (Berkovitch, 1996:20–21).

In the area of family status, Israel is much more in line with its neighbors in the region. It has not adopted secular laws, and the religious establishment exercises considerable influence. For instance, marriages can be contracted and dissolved only in religious courts. Women are not allowed to become judges in the orthodox rabbinical state courts, and as a rule, their evidence is not accepted, especially if there are male witnesses (Yuval-Davis, 1989:105). The army is another institution in which women do not enjoy equal opportunities with men. At least 70 percent of women in the military are trained to occupy traditional women's roles; furthermore, despite the mandatory recruitment law, only 65 percent of Jewish Israeli women serve in the army. The rest either opt out on religious grounds or fall under various categories of women exempted from military service (Sharoni, 1995:45–47; see also Swirski and Safir, 1991; Yuval-Davis, 1982).

Iran under Mohammad Reza Shah was also among the first of the Middle Eastern states to articulate a modernizing agenda including the emancipation of women. However, unlike the Turkish republic, which was avowedly secular, the Iranian state in the early decades of the twentieth century was more mindful of powerful religious institutions, and thus the pace and nature of the changes were more modest. The major reforms and developments affecting women were introduced in the 1960s. Women were enfranchised in 1962, and significant gains in women's education were made during the 1960s and 1970s. In 1967, the new Family Protection Act gave women expanded rights within marriage and the family. In the early years of the Islamic Republic, however, several of these reforms were revoked, and an ideology stressing women's domesticity was articulated and encouraged.

Iran's situation calls into question some of the prevailing assumptions about the relationship between Islam and women's status. While remaining "Islamic," contemporary Iran has reconsidered certain postrevolutionary policies concerning women's rights within the family and the public domain. For example, although the Family Protection Act of 1967 was revoked after the revolution and replaced by legislation dating back to the 1930s, eventually the government responded to the agitation of Islamist women activists and revised the law to grant women more rights. Under legislation passed in 1992, for instance, divorced women are granted half of the wealth accumulated during the marital union, as well as wages for housework performed during the marriage (Hoodfar, 1995:124). Postrevolutionary population policy is another example. After dismantling family planning centers after the revolution, within a few years the state was actively reconsidering its pronatalist approach. In 1989 the state ratified a new birth control policy and launched a national campaign to convince the population to accept and practice family planning (Hoodfar, 1995:108–109). Policies in education provide a further illustration. After initially setting a maximum limit for female university applicants in a wide range of scientific and professional fields, most of the quotas were removed in 1989 (Mogha-dam, 2003:208).

Most of the Arab states began to articulate and implement their social agendas during the second part of the twentieth century, in the aftermath of achieving national independence and following the consolidation of a new state elite. As in Turkey and Iran, state elites introduced reforms in family law, encouraged women's education, and in some cases sought an increased female presence in the state bureaucracy and the labor force. Egypt, Iraq, Tunisia, and the People's Democratic Republic of Yemen (South Yemen) stand out as the pioneers, with the last instituting the most far-reaching re-visions. Exceptions to this trend include Saudi Arabia and some of the Gulf states, where the pace of reforms has been very slow.

Of the three countries of the Arab Maghreb Union emerging as inde-pendent states following colonial rule (Tunisia, Algeria, and Morocco), Tunisia was the leader in introducing significant changes. The Personal Sta-tus Code of 1956, amended in 1964, 1966, and 1981, is the most progressive in the Arab world, outlawing polygamy and granting expanded rights to di-vorced women; labor legislation enacted in 1966 provides some protection for working mothers (Galal, 1995:63–64). In Algeria, however, reform came much later and was more modest in its content. Although the state abolished all colonial legislation pertaining to family matters in 1975, it was not until 1984, after considerable agitation by Algerian women, that a new family code was finally enacted. This code, like those in all Arab countries, was en-acted within the framework of *sharia* and offered only limited modifications in marriage, divorce, and custody laws (Hijab, 1988:26–29; Lazreg, 1994: 150–157). Morocco has perhaps been the slowest country in the Arab Magh-reb Union to respond to pressures for change in matters of family law. New legislation was enacted in 1957–1958 that granted women some rights in the matter of divorce, but it was not far-reaching and has remained virtually un-changed during more than five decades (Mir-Hosseini, 1991).

Recent research on the integration of women into the nation-state in the Middle East through reforms at the state level recognizes the limits of state-sponsored policies and legislation in bringing about significant changes in social relations in general and gender relations in particular (Joseph and Slyomovics, 2000; Joseph and Kandiyoti, 2000). Despite the adoption of policies drawing women into the labor force and increasing women's edu-cation in several countries, wide gaps continue to exist between men and women in terms of labor force participation, educational attainment, and access to resources and opportunities.

This brings us to the crucial issue of the uneven manner in which state policies and reforms affect women. If we examine women's education and employment, we find that rising educational levels for women have gener-ally been accompanied by an increase in the participation of women in the

In depressed or weak economies, well-educated, urban women like this Palestinian often find their best opportunities for employment are with international nongovernmental organizations.

nonagricultural labor force, primarily in the service sector. Because most service jobs are concentrated in urban areas, women's increased participation in such work indicates that educational gains for women have been greater in urban areas and have prepared women to join occupations unrelated to the agrarian economy. These observations underline the fact that recent decades have witnessed a tremendous expansion of urban centers and an increasing differentiation between the city and the countryside. The consolidation of an urban middle class throughout the Middle East has had as an important component the increased visibility of women in the educational system, the labor force, and the public domain in general. It is these women who have been the main beneficiaries of state policies in education, labor, and other public services, which points to the fact that urban middle-class (and upper-class) women have been most positively affected by state policies. Women marginalized in the state modernization project, mainly peasant and poor urban women, live different realities and have not been able to benefit from state reforms on a wide scale.

■ Economic Activity

As Valentine Moghadam points out in Chapter 9, measuring the economic activity of the population in the Middle East, as in many other third world countries, is fraught with difficulties. Women's economic activity is particularly elusive, and national labor force figures and other statistics do not represent the true magnitude of women's role in the economy. The reasons for this situation are many. First, women's unpaid domestic labor is unregistered and unquantified; the long hours and hard work that women expend in raising children and in household management are not reflected in national statistics. Second, the contribution of women to the household economy in the form of provision of home-use items is also largely unrecorded. This is due both to biases in data collection systems and also to the perceptions of respondents in national surveys concerning economic activity. (For instance, a woman who produces food and sews clothing for her family as an economizing measure will not likely be perceived by herself or a male household member to be economically active.) Third, and most important, women's economic activity in the informal sector is largely unmeasured in standard labor force statistics. This sector is an important component of the economy throughout the Middle East and includes a wide array of activities, many of them carried out by women, either within the household or on the streets and in workplaces in the public sphere.

Due to the inadequacy of data on economic activity in the Middle East, it is indeed difficult to gain an accurate understanding of the magnitude of women's participation in the national economies of the region. Although small-scale studies of women's informal-sector activities in several countries have enriched our knowledge of the various strategies that households and women within them deploy to deal with economic hardship, we still have only formal labor force statistics—with all their weaknesses—as the most reliable cross-national indicators of women's economic activity.

Even though the participation of women in the formal labor force in the Middle East is still small compared to that in other world regions, it has been steadily increasing since the 1960s (Moghadam, 2003:chap. 2). Factors such as the tremendous expansion of the state bureaucracy and related services (especially in education, health, and social services), economic development, falling fertility levels, the rising age at first marriage, rapid urbanization, increased educational levels for women, and male labor migration from the poor to the oil-rich countries of the Gulf all played a part in encouraging the increase in rates of female employment. How these dimensions have come together in a given national setting has varied, however, and the outcomes in terms of participation levels have also been very different. Economic activity rates for women age fifteen and older in the Middle East in 2004 ranged from a paltry 10 percent in the Occupied Palestinian Territories; rates below 30 percent in Bahrain, Tunisia, Oman, Saudi Arabia, Egypt, Turkey, Jordan, and Sudan; and to 50 percent in Israel, 38 percent in Syria, 37 percent in Kuwait and Iran, and 36 percent in Qatar (UNDP, 2006:375–378).

In terms of the distribution of the female labor force by occupation, the highest percentages are found in the service sector (ranging from a high of 86 percent in the United Arab Emirates to 62 percent in the Occupied Palestinian Territories and 54 percent in Morocco), a pattern found the world over, with high percentages in agriculture recorded only in Yemen (88 percent),

Egypt (39 percent), and Turkey (56 percent) (UNDP, 2006:375–378). As Moghadam has pointed out (2003:45), however, in some countries women in agriculture are not counted as part of the labor force, which explains the low figures for this sector of economic activity.

What do these figures tell us about working women in the Middle East? First, the high concentration of women in public services (occupations such as teaching) reinforces stereotyping that identifies certain occupations as women's occupations. Women from well-off families are most likely to be formally employed, especially in the Gulf states. Other relevant conditions include the compatibility of some occupations (particularly teaching) with women's reproductive roles as mothers and domestic caregivers and the fact that most women in these occupations work in the public sector, where working women's rights (such as paid maternity leave) are generally better protected than in the private sector (Moghadam, 2003:48–55). At the same time, women have been underrepresented in administrative and managerial fields and "have been conspicuously absent from . . . private sales and services and in the sector of hotels, restaurants, and . . . trade" (Moghadam, 2003:51).

Deborah J. Gerner

Female shopkeepers remain uncommon in the Middle East except in African Arab countries such as Mauritania.

The concentration of younger women in the formal labor force is another reflection of the organic link between women's reproductive and productive activities. We can assume that most women in this age group are either single or newly married with few children and are therefore freer to take on employment outside the home. Furthermore, based on educational data for the region, these women also have the highest rates of educational achievement. Indeed, in the Middle East, employment in the formal nonagricultural labor force is positively linked to education (Moghadam, 2003:51).

An important determinant of women's formal labor force participation is the degree of public investment in working women with children, both in the provision of child-care services and in the enactment and enforcement of labor laws protecting these women's rights. Three demographic characteristics of the region are relevant in this regard: first, a substantial proportion of the female population is in the reproductive age group; second, the great majority of women are married; and third, fertility rates are high (Zurayk and Saadeh, 1995:38). These attributes, which Huda Zurayk and Fadia Saadeh cite with respect to the Arab world, apply to Iran and Turkey as well; however, the demographic profile is different in Israel.

The implication of these demographic attributes is that some of the impediments to women's labor force participation could be attenuated by increased public and private investment in child-care facilities for working women and, more important, by the enactment and enforcement of labor laws favorable to working women with children. As long as women's reproductive tasks are not socially supported and are considered private burdens, many women will not be encouraged to join the paid labor force. A further factor inhibiting women's employment is the relatively high cost of those child-care facilities that do exist (whether public or private) as compared with the low wages that women command in the market, thus making the option of employment outside the home unattractive to women and their families.

Another consideration that influences women's formal labor force participation is located at the level of the family and household. Seteney Shami (1990) has proposed that women's work should be viewed as part of the strategies deployed by families and households for adapting to the circumstances of their class. In this view, families of modest means diffuse economic risk by diversifying the employment of family members: men and boys enter the more remunerative activities due to their higher education levels, whereas women tend to enter the informal sector or become the mainstay of subsistence agriculture. Thus women perform activities related to family survival while men enter areas of the economy leading to family mobility. In those cases where women seem to be offered the opportunity for mobility, women do participate in the formal labor force and become a further economic asset to the family (Shami, 1990:xiv–xv).

A number of factors come together to condition and determine the extent and nature of women's economic activity in the Middle East. The lack of public support for women's employment, demographic factors such as those cited above, and issues having to do with the structure of the labor market and the household together explain to a large extent the low labor force participation of women.

What becomes of the widely held view that conservative attitudes deriving from an Islamic worldview constitute the major impediment to women's work in the public domain? Although it would be incorrect to dismiss the relevance of conservative attitudes—whether derived from a religious ethos or not—it is more reasonable to assume that a host of factors having to do with the structure of the economy, the educational system, population characteristics, and state policies are equally, if not more, influential in determining the magnitude and distribution of women in the labor force. To be sure, rationales and justifications for women's exclusion from employment are often part of popular idiom and are couched in religious terms, but it is important to recognize how widely they are overlooked or disregarded in practice in the Middle East. Any person familiar with urban life in the Middle East will be struck by the numbers of women engaged in some kind of employment outside the home, whether they are women bosses (*mu'allimat*) on Cairo's streets, or female vegetable peddlers in the markets of Arab Jerusalem, or the armies of young women coming out of sewing workshops at the end of a day's work in Istanbul. And of course, the increasing numbers of women students enrolled in postsecondary educational institutions all over the Middle East would not be making the considerable investment in education if they did not hope to join the labor force.

Family and Kinship

The preceding discussion has highlighted some features of Middle Eastern society relevant not only to the economic activity of women but also to dynamics within the family. We now examine some of the major features of familial gender relations, an issue also addressed by Laurie King-Irani in Chapter 10. It may be useful to begin our examination of the family with the concept of patriarchy, which in broad terms refers to a system that privileges males and elders and justifies this privilege in kinship terms (Joseph, 1994:2). The anthropologist Deniz Kandiyoti finds the clearest instances of "classic patriarchy" in North Africa, the Muslim Middle East, and southern and eastern Asia. Under this system, girls marry young into households headed by their husbands' fathers and are subordinate there to all men and to the more senior women, especially their mothers-in-law. Women frequently do not inherit from their fathers, although their access to resources and control over the *mahr* (bride price) and property can be highly variable (Kandiyoti, 1991b: 31–32).

Patriarchy, representing a gender and age hierarchy based on the household as a productive unit, has been seriously challenged in recent decades by social transformations sweeping the regions in which it prevails. Wage labor opportunities outside the household (mostly for young men but also for a growing segment of urban women), the breakup of the extended family, the increasing age of marriage for both women and men, the rise in educational levels, and rural-to-urban migration, among other factors, have begun to erode some of the foundations of this system.

Households headed by women due to divorce or death of the husband, those in which men are away for extended periods for work, or situations in which women earn wages outside the home all present problems for patriarchy. The economic independence of sons and their move away from the natal household after marriage also challenge gender and age hierarchies, both in the case of the sons vis-à-vis their fathers and in the case of the sons' wives in relation to their mothers-in-law.

However, certain circumstances can mitigate against the breakdown of patriarchy and in some cases may actually strengthen it. Let us take the example of the persistence in functional terms of the extended family household, despite the setting up of nuclear family households by married sons. Although this arrangement, which is an adaptation to the absence of social security and other state assistance to the elderly, may give sons authority over their fathers, it may also solidify the position of elder working sons vis-à-vis their sisters and brothers still at home, thus preserving gender and age hierarchies in another form. In the same vein, although the sons' wives may be liberated from the direct and daily control of domineering mothers-in-law, they may be dependent upon them if they go out to work. In the absence of adequate public facilities, women often rely on their mothers-in-law for child care, and may have to put up with the burdens—and interference in their children's upbringing—that this arrangement entails.

The preceding discussion has touched upon the issue of women's position within the household, and it is to this that we now turn. As with labor force participation, a number of factors help determine a woman's position—and particularly her authority—within the household. Age and marital status are two important determinants: a young wife is decidedly at a disadvantage compared to an older one, especially with a mother-in-law, and unmarried women generally have less authority than married ones. However, unmarried women with access to financial resources such as income from property or employment may wield considerable authority over members of the household, including their parents and younger siblings. Divorced women, unless they have adequate resources, are among the more vulnerable, and may be almost totally dependent on their fathers and brothers in financial terms, even if they do not live with them in the same household.

The number of children—especially sons—a woman bears is another factor influencing her status in the household. This feature of Middle Eastern family life has often been highlighted in accounts of the region and requires an explanation. Rather than understanding the preference for male children as derived from some primordial valuation of male offspring by Middle Easterners, it is more useful to view it as essential to the survival of the informal system of social security in Middle Eastern societies. In most societies in the Middle East, male children not only contribute their labor or income for the welfare of the household but also are a source of old-age security for their parents and any unmarried sisters in the absence of state-supported pensions and other compensations for the elderly and retired. For women, who are likely to be widowed earlier than men, the presence of sons is not so much a source of status—although it is expressed as such in the cultural idiom—but a form of security for which no real alternatives yet exist in the public sector.

Yet another important determinant of status is access to or control over economic resources. Literature on the Middle East often mentions that women, although entitled by law to a share of their fathers' estates (albeit unequal to that of their brothers), are routinely deprived of the right to inherit this property. Although Middle Eastern women do continue to be disinherited in this sense—often with their own "consent"—the social and cultural logic behind what appears to be a flagrant violation of basic rights is complex.

The material foundation of classic patriarchy, as discussed earlier, is the patrilocally extended household (Kandiyoti, 1991b:31). Within it, older males are regarded as having responsibility for the economic welfare of all members of the family, including women marrying into the household. Daughters marrying out become members of their husbands' households and are considered part of their responsibility. However, married women maintain a special relationship with their brothers, upon whose support they can count when facing marital problems, financial distress, or in the extreme case, divorce or abandonment. Clearly, this system rests on the assumption of female dependence on men, whether these men are husbands or brothers. Denial of inheritance to women is affirmation of this fact and is based on the widely acknowledged belief that men require the inherited property to meet the family obligations women are not expected to shoulder.

As patriarchy erodes due to the social transformations mentioned earlier, the inheritance system is facing new challenges. Working women who contribute their incomes to family welfare or self-supporting single women are realities with which this system increasingly has to deal. However, even within the sexual division of labor assumed by the inheritance system, women have not always been denied their inheritance.

Research findings from Palestine may be indicative of wider patterns. Anthropologist Annelies Moors has shown, for instance, that the crucial factors determining whether Palestinian women in the Nablus region receive or claim their share of inheritance are marital status, social class, and position in the family. Brotherless daughters and their widowed mothers show the most interest in claiming their shares; daughters from wealthy families are also in a better position to inherit some of the family property. In the case of the majority, that is, married women from families of modest means who do have brothers, the situation is different. Here, sisters refrain from claiming their share in favor of their brothers as part of an optimizing strategy: being ultimately dependent on their kin for their socioeconomic security, it makes sense for women to relinquish their inheritance in order to highlight their kin's obligations toward them (Moors, 1996:69–84).

The preceding discussion has shown that within the patriarchal family structure, denial of inheritance to women is not tantamount to a denial of all their rights to family resources. However, as Moors (1996:83) has pointed out, women's dependence on men, which is the basis of this system, may become increasingly shaky; as the conjugal (husband-wife) tie becomes more important and as the extended family becomes more fragmented, women will be left without the "protections" that the inheritance system entailed for them, and their vulnerability may increase.

▨ Values and Norms

The commonsense understanding of gender relations in the Middle East rests on the notion that traditional norms and values surrounding women and the family dictate current social practices and serve to limit women's freedom and opportunities. Scholarly and popular works by Westerners and Middle Easterners alike routinely attribute women's low labor force participation or educational achievement, for example, to the hold of traditional conceptions of family honor and conduct appropriate to women.

Two features of explanations of social practices that refer to "tradition" warrant closer examination. First, such explanations deal almost exclusively with non-Western societies. The assumption appears to be that non-Western and particularly Islamic Middle Eastern societies are still under the grip of immutable traditional value systems. Many examinations of women's current realities continue to be prefaced by a seemingly mandatory discussion of the traditional context. Yet it would be very strange to see a discussion of French, Swedish, or North American women's lives framed similarly by implying that we could not hope to understand their current realities before first setting out the *traditional* context of gender relations. Second, the reference to traditional norms and values is almost invariably produced when matters concerning gender relations, roles, and identities are at issue.

How can we understand social practices and behavioral patterns that at first glance appear to be dictated by timeless traditional values and norms?

To address this question, we must first recognize that norms and values are historical constructs above all; in no society are they "handed down" from generation to generation without undergoing redefinition and reformulation. This process of transformation is conditioned by changing realities and reflects the struggle between different social groups and collectivities in pursuit of their particular and common interests.

A prime example is the presumably timeless "honor code" believed to regulate women's conduct in Muslim Middle Eastern societies. Yet even the meaning of *honor* has changed considerably over the past decades, as has what constitutes the violation of the honor code. Practices and conduct that may have been viewed as a grave breach of honor decades ago do not produce similar reactions today. Segregation of men and women, which is often regarded as an underpinning of the system of honor, is one example of a practice that has been seriously undermined, if not swept away, by the major social transformations taking place in the region. Although segregation is still debated among contending social forces, hundreds of thousands of Middle Eastern women today work and study in mixed-sex institutions without social censure or opprobrium. Even Islamists, interestingly, have reinterpreted supposedly fixed honor codes such as those forbidding the mixing of men and women by adjusting them to the exigencies of modern life, as in women's participation in the labor force or study at universities. Such accommodation to modern society by Islamists is the norm rather than the exception today, as I have tried to show in the discussion of Iran above.[1]

As noted earlier, and as in any society, contending social and political forces as well as individuals are constantly negotiating the definition and boundaries of honor. The great diversity in women's dress in the Middle East today can be regarded as a reflection of this silent struggle. Large numbers of urban women have adopted various versions or degrees of "Islamic" dress; equal numbers dress in variations of international styles. All of these women are mindful of proper and improper ways of dressing but are by their choices defining the different—and differing—codes of modesty and decorum. We thus witness the almost daily setting of new standards and norms by which women are continually negotiating and stretching the boundaries of the supposedly immutable codes of honor.

We must also consider the possibility that certain values and norms are group- or class-specific and cannot be generalized at the level of whole societies, let alone the region. How the process of generalization takes place is itself a subject for investigation, since a host of factors come into play in the designation of values and norms as universal. For instance—and contrary to the impression given in much of the Western popular press—women's seclusion in the domestic sphere has not been the practice for the majority of women in Middle Eastern societies, whether in rural or urban areas. One of the main requirements for seclusion is the freedom from labor in the field, the neighborhood, or other public spaces; many women simply do not have this option, even if it is viewed as preferable.

Judith Tucker's historical research in Egypt and Palestine, for example, has shown that in the nineteenth century in Cairo and Nablus, adherence to the modesty code was tempered by class: among the upper class, notions of women's honor were important and women were confined to the harem, but for the poor, women were very much part of a public work life that precluded all but the most formal adherence to the ideal of female seclusion (Tucker, 1993:205). Agricultural communities could afford the seclusion of women even less. The pioneering research of Richard Antoun in a Jordanian village in the 1960s showed that peasant women's labor was crucial to the survival of dry-cereal farming in the village. This entailed women's presence in public space alongside men of their own families as well as unrelated men. Thus the agricultural regime and the sexual division of labor whereby women played an important part in agriculture were among the major factors that undermined adherence to the modesty code, even though it was upheld as an ideal in local discourse (Antoun, 1968:681–682).

■ Politics

Middle Eastern women's organized participation in the political process dates to the early years of the twentieth century and was linked from the start with two major overlapping currents sweeping the region: the drive for modernization and social reform and the nationalist struggle for independence from colonial domination.

The "woman question" has been an important component of the ideologies of reformist and nationalist currents throughout the Middle East. The first organized women's movements with a feminist agenda took shape in Turkey, Iran, and Egypt in the first decade of the twentieth century (Afary, 1989:66; Kandiyoti, 1991a:29). Their agenda included demands for education and work opportunities and for reform of legislation governing matters such as marriage, divorce, child custody, and inheritance (Graham-Brown, 1993:2). Rapid expansion of women's organizations all over the Middle East followed.

Significantly, the founders and, to a large extent, the members of the earlier women's organizations were drawn from the upper and middle classes; frequently they were wives, daughters, and sisters of men prominent in public life. Many of these women were also engaged in charitable work in their societies, a pursuit consistent with their status and privilege and part of a pattern found the world over. Despite these commonalities, women's participation in politics in the Middle East has not been restricted to activism within the framework of women's organizations agitating on women's issues.

Women campaign outside a women's polling site in 1997 in the Baqa'a refugee camp northwest of Amman, Jordan. Many Middle Eastern countries maintain separate polling sites for men and women.

A rich diversity of forms and modes of women's participation in politics can be identified in the Middle East. The first is women's participation as fighters and support staff in national liberation struggles or revolutionary movements, notably in the Algerian war of independence, the Palestinian resistance, and the Iranian revolution. The second mode of women's political activism is that of women's "arms" or "branches" of political parties and fronts. Third, women participate as members of political parties and groups. Fourth, women also have been active in women's organizations created or sponsored by ruling parties and states, such as women's federations in many Arab countries and Iran.

The fifth mode of women's political activism is in independent (but not necessarily apolitical) organizations whose agendas greatly vary in terms of the nature and content of their activism on gender issues and causes. Although organizations such as these, in the form of charitable societies and the like, have existed in the Middle East for a number of decades, we focus on the new, more gender-conscious organizations that have been proliferating since the late 1980s, many of which are funded by international governmental and nongovernmental organizations (NGOs). Finally, the sixth mode of women's participation in politics is involvement in the electoral process as voters and candidates and in responsible positions in governments.

This typology of modes of women's participation in politics must be treated with caution, however, since the categories are not exclusive, and considerable overlap between them may be found. For example, many Palestinian women participated in military and paramilitary activity within the framework of the Palestinian resistance in the 1970s, while at the same time being members of political parties *and* affiliated with the women's organizations of those parties.

National Liberation and Revolutionary Movements

The best-documented cases of women's participation in national liberation struggles and popular revolutions are those of Algeria, Iran, and Palestine.[2] Despite many similarities in these and other cases, it is very difficult to generalize about the role and status of women in such struggles. Algeria's and Iran's struggles were carried out on national soil, but Algeria's was an armed struggle, whereas the revolution in Iran—and women's participation in it—was not of a military nature. (As Hammed Shahidian [1997] points out, Iranian women *were* active in guerrilla organizations—primarily the People's Mujahidin Organization of Iran and the Organization of People's Fida'i Guerrillas—under the shah's rule in the 1970s, and also after the revolution and until the mid-1980s.)

In Palestine, most of the guerrilla activity was based outside Palestine in the 1970s, whereas inside, in the Occupied Territories, military struggle was crushed and did not have a popular mass base as in Algeria. While the Palestinian struggle in the Occupied Territories during the first uprising of the late 1980s and early 1990s was largely nonmilitary, the second uprising in late 2000 witnessed a significant increase in armed actions. Women, however, have been largely absent from the armed resistance, notwithstanding the few and highly publicized cases of women involved in bombings.

What is common to each of these examples is that women of all social classes, both urban and rural, participated in the struggles, although the balance was always in favor of women of more modest means. In addition, women did not have decisionmaking or frontline military positions in any of these revolutionary movements. Most of the tasks assigned to them were of a support nature. Even in Algeria, where women played an important and crucial role in the liberation war, including in the military arm of the National Liberation Front (FLN), paramilitary acts of destruction of civilian targets involved barely 2 percent of the women who joined the movement (Lazreg, 1994:124).

Women's Front Organizations

The creation of women's "front" organizations or branches by parties and movements in order to mobilize women for the larger national cause is a well-known pattern in the Middle East. The relationship between the Sudanese Communist Party and the Sudanese Women's Union is one example (see Hale, 1996:151–183); in the Palestinian case, the women's organizations attached to the various political parties and fronts in the Occupied Territories and the diaspora are another. From Iran comes another example of women's organizations affiliated to political movements before and during the revolution.

In general, women's organizations affiliated with political parties have had little autonomy; this has meant in the majority of cases that feminist concerns have been subordinated to larger national ones and that women's energies have not been primarily concentrated upon representing and fighting for the interests of women as women. This situation is not surprising, however, especially in the case of parties engaged in popular struggles for independence, such as in the Palestinian case.

The demise of mass nationalist politics in the Middle East as a whole could very well mean that women's front organizations are becoming a thing of the past. The decline of radical nationalist parties and movements, the increasing globalization of the women's movement, and the hegemony of discourses of democratization and "civil society" among intellectuals and other elites all point to the fact that women's front organizations are becoming anachronistic vestiges of old-style politics in the region. While women's front organizations continue to exist in authoritarian states, their ability to mobilize and capture the imagination of wide sections of women in their societies may be becoming increasingly compromised.

The Palestinian case may be instructive if not entirely representative of the Middle East as a whole. With the demise of nationalist mass politics in the Occupied Palestinian Territories and the installation of the Palestinian Authority in the early 1990s, women's front organizations underwent a dramatic transformation. Many remodeled themselves along the NGO model, eschewing direct association with the political parties and movements within whose frameworks they had incubated and grown. Partly through pressure from international donors but also in recognition of the fact that women's interests had been marginalized in the nationalist movement and its parties, these women's organizations began to articulate gender agendas and projects at odds with their previous discourse. Paradoxically, however, the expansion of Islamist politics and activism may be giving rise to new incarnations of women's front organizations. How successful these organizations may be in articulating women's agendas within the overall project of Islamization of the society and polity remains to be seen.

Political Parties

Women's participation in political parties has received little scholarly attention. A general familiarity with the major political parties in the region shows, however, that women have rarely achieved leadership positions in either ruling or opposition parties across the Middle East. The Islamic Action Front in Jordan and the Islah Party in Yemen have both seen women elected to their highest councils, but in practice they are expected to remain on the sidelines or confine their practical work to the parallel women's sections (Clark and Schwedler, 2003). The other exceptions are Israel and Turkey, where Golda Meir in the early 1970s and Tansu Çiller in the 1990s led political parties and headed their countries' governments. As is true in much of the world, political parties have thus been true bastions of male privilege and exclusivity in the Middle East, with little difference between liberal or leftist and more conservative right-wing parties.

One factor that accounts for the paucity of information on women's—or men's—participation in political parties is that the democratic process, whereby contending parties compete for constituencies, is still not the norm in many countries of the Middle East. In the Arab world in particular, political participation is weak at best (UNDP, 2002:9). Political parties are thus quite restricted in size, since they are robbed of their raison d'être, which is to represent their constituencies' interests in a political contest for power.

It is therefore difficult to speak about women's participation in political parties in a climate where the ability of those parties to mobilize large masses of people seems to be at an all-time low. Paradoxically, however, women organizing *outside* political parties and frameworks seems to be growing. An understanding of this state of affairs, which on the face of it may appear to indicate a depoliticization of women's activism, requires a careful examination of the global, regional, and local factors leading to the weakening of formal political groupings and the strengthening of NGO-style activism. This new style of politics is not restricted to women's work; it has permeated many other forms of organizing previously subsumed under parties, such as youth and labor organizing.

"Establishment" Women's Organizations

Many feminists have argued that women's organizations in the Middle East have not developed autonomously, that is, their agendas and activism have been dictated either by political parties or, more important, by the state. A review of the major women's organizations in the various countries of the Middle East bears out this observation. Historically, we have seen how the first women's organizations arose out of the nationalist and reformist movements of the early twentieth century and articulated demands and goals consistent with the agendas of the modernizing elements within these movements.

In the decades following the establishment of the first women's organizations, women's organizing energies were, with few exceptions, harnessed by the state and in some cases made part of its state-building project. In Iraq, for example, the ruling Baath Party created the General Federation of Iraqi Women in 1968 as a female arm of the party, with the aim of drawing women into the state and as part of its drive toward the resocialization and mobilization of women. The federation was funded by the state, and leadership positions were held by party members (Joseph, 1991:182). Iran is another case of a centralizing state attempting to contain and control women's organizing energies. In the 1960s, under Mohammad Reza Shah, the state began to solidify its control over women's organizations, ending in the establishment of the influential Women's Organization of Iran, with significant power and resources at its disposal (Najmabadi, 1991:60–61). Algeria is another example. After independence, the ruling National Liberation Front set up the National Union of Algerian Women to represent the country's female population.

The drive to set up national women's organizations was given a great boost by the UN Decade for Women, launched in 1975. Governments were thereafter required to send delegates to the successive world conferences on women and the growing number of international and regional conferences organized to discuss women's issues. The question, therefore, of how the country and its progress in achieving women's rights was to be represented acquired great importance. Many Middle Eastern countries were represented at the official level by their women's federations, which were by and large state-controlled. Forums for nongovernmental organizations were made available at the world conferences, however, and provided an opportunity for women in independent organizations to voice their concerns, which at times conflicted with the official line presented by the official delegations.

Independent Women's Organizations

The years since the late 1980s have witnessed the emergence of a new and diverse body of independent and semi-independent women's organizations (more commonly termed "women's NGOs") in the Middle East. Although many are not overtly political in the conventional sense of the term and most do not have a grassroots constituency, all may be viewed as engaged in gender politics of one kind or another. The growth of these organizations (particularly in Egypt, Turkey, Tunisia, Morocco, Jordan, Palestine, and Lebanon) is part of a wider development at the level of civil society in the Middle East, represented by the proliferation of nongovernmental organizations of various sorts. Human rights groups, development and social policy institutes, research centers, and legal assistance services are just some examples.

The new women's organizations can be distinguished from the more politicized women's "front" organizations, state-controlled women's federations, and traditional charitable organizations by their membership profile, their social and political agenda and discourse, and the range of their contacts within and outside the region. Founded and staffed mainly by urban middle-class professional women (such as lawyers, physicians, and academics), these organizations are engaged in formulating a feminist agenda around such issues as political and legal reform, social policy, reproductive health and population policy, domestic violence, and other issues of concern to women. They have become increasingly visible in international and regional forums, and have linked up with women's organizations around the world in networks of trainers, lobbyists, legal experts, policy analysts, and activists. Women's organizations have thus been vying with the official women's federations of their countries for attention in the national and international arenas and have been successful due to their familiarity with the global women's discourse and their considerable professional skills.[3] The social impact of these organizations at home, however, remains limited, since many do not have access to the sources of power in society and are largely removed from the mass of women in their own societies.

Women in the Electoral Process and in Government

Accurate data on women's participation in the electoral process are patchy. We do know that in most countries, women's participation as voters in national and local elections is moderate to substantial (with the exception, of course, of those countries that do not have electoral processes).

Women's representation in state structures, primarily parliaments and governments, however, is quite limited. Among parliaments in the Arab states, the highest percentages of female representation are found in Tunisia (19.3 percent), Syria (12 percent), and Sudan (13.6 percent). In Algeria, a little over 5 percent of representatives are women, but the numbers are still lower in Egypt (3.8 percent) and Yemen (0.7 percent). Turkey and Iran do not fare much better, with slightly over 4 percent. In Israel, 14.2 percent of representatives are women (UNDP, 2006:367–369). Kuwait changed its laws in May 2005 to allow women's suffrage, but none of the female candidates who ran in the June 2006 elections were successful.

Women's presence at the ministerial level is even less significant. Figures for 2005 show that women's membership as ministers in cabinets was at 3 percent in Sudan and Yemen; 6 percent in Egypt, the United Arab Emirates, and Syria; and 7 percent in Lebanon. Among Arab states, Iraq had the highest percentage (19 percent) followed by Jordan (11 percent), Oman (10 percent), and Bahrain (9 percent). Iran had 7 percent of ministerial posts headed by women, while Israel had the region's high at 17 percent (UNDP, 2006:380–383).

These figures must be viewed in context, however. In the United States, one-sixth of congressional representatives are women; in Japan, the percentage of women in parliament is just a little over 10 percent. This is in sharp contrast to world pioneers in women's representation in parliament: Sweden (45.3 percent), Denmark (36.9 percent), and Finland and Norway (38 percent) (UNDP, 2006:367).

Islamist Women's Activism

Feminist activism in the Middle East has had an uneasy relationship with Islam since the beginning of the twentieth century. The engagement with Islam could not be avoided in societies where many of the laws affecting women's personal status were based upon *sharia* and where state elites were not keen on antagonizing the religious establishment or adopting positions that might offend what were perceived to be prevailing religious sensibilities. Thus, from the very beginning, feminists—as well as state institutions—sought to show that Islam was not opposed to women's education, enfranchisement, participation in the public domain, and work outside the home. However, even though Islam may have been invoked to justify

Palestinian Samiha Khalil, head of the charitable society In'ash al-Usra, ran against Yasser Arafat in the 1996 presidential election.

women's emancipation, most feminists have been secular in their pursuits, lifestyles, and political convictions.

The growth of Islamist forces throughout the Middle East has posed a challenge to secular feminism and, more important, has led to the emergence of what may be called Islamist feminist currents. These currents receive state sanction in Iran, Sudan, and some Gulf states, and in the rest of the Middle East they are emerging as significant social and ideological forces in the political arena, competing with secular feminism for women's sympathies and support.

Islamist women do indeed attempt to create an alternative to secular feminism. Because Islamist women activists are by and large educated and professional women and not obscurantist male theologians or ideologues, they cannot be dismissed as archaic or irrelevant by secular feminists. Moreover, in countries all over the Middle East, ranging from Iran to Kuwait, they are gaining visibility and entering the public political arena. Although on the whole Islamist women have not publicly challenged the Islamist construct of the ideal Muslim woman or the prevailing sexual division of labor, they are, by their own lifestyles and professional and political pursuits, departing in many ways from the ideal (Clark and Schwedler, 2003). Some Islamist women have even won seats on party councils, an opportunity not available to women in most secular parties, where internal elections are seldom held. Now, at the beginning of the twenty-first century, a new model is being offered to young women, the model of an educated, professional, "Muslim" woman.[4]

One indicator of the serious challenge posed by Islamists to secular feminists is the increasing visibility and presence of Islamist women in magazines, in newspapers, and on airwaves and television channels directed at millions of Arab women. Once the preserve of secular middle-class women activists, these media (and particularly the satellite television channels) are providing forums where Islamist women are challenging the once-hegemonic discourses of secular feminism. Satellite television, reaching wide audiences all over the Arab world (and beyond), is a prime example; many of the channels provide platforms for debates between secular and "Islamist" (or conservative) feminists around women's issues ranging from polygamy to the rights of foreign domestic workers in the Gulf.

In Iran, the role of Islamist women in challenging postrevolutionary state policies that restricted women's rights has been unique and noteworthy. After the revolution, the state encouraged the development of an Islamic women's movement to counter the threat from secular feminism; very soon, however, Islamist women began to voice their criticism of some Islamization policies, such as Islamist dress codes, leading in the late 1980s to the emergence of an Islamist feminist opposition. Islamist feminists have campaigned for issues relating to rights within the family, dress codes, employment, political participation, and education (Paidar, 1996:59–62).[5] It must be noted here that the concept of Islamist feminism has not been unproblematic; indeed, a heated debate around the independence and emancipatory potential of Iranian Islamist feminism has been raging among Iranian feminists.[6]

▨ Conclusion

This chapter has attempted to highlight the diversity of women's status and realities in the Middle East while at the same time underlining the broad similarities in the social, economic, and political circumstances under which women live their lives. As we have seen, state-building projects have had important consequences for women's status in society and for the rights of which they are deprived or that they enjoy.

We have also seen that Middle Eastern women have been active in the political arena, a role not consistent with commonsense representations of Middle Eastern women as passive political subjects locked in the domestic arena. The massive participation of Iranian women in the revolution, for instance, flies in the face of such conceptualizations of Middle Eastern women as being outside the domain of politics. Women's lives in the Middle East, as elsewhere in the world, are shaped by a multiplicity of influences and factors. Concrete material factors related to socioeconomic realities and state policies explain social practices and institutions better than do monolithic belief systems. These belief systems, although important in the overall scheme of things, are variable, flexible, and dynamic.

▨ Notes

1. My research in Jordan (Taraki, 1996) supports these conclusions about Islamists' accommodation to the requirements of life in a rapidly changing society. For further discussion and analysis of Jordanian and other Islamists' preoccupation with women's conduct in modern society, see Taraki, 1995.

2. Useful sources for the study of women's participation in revolutionary movements are, for Palestine, Peteet, 1991; Sayigh, 1993; and Jad, 1990; for Algeria, Lazreg, 1994; and for Iran, Nashat, 1983; Ferdows, 1983; and Shahidian, 1997.

3. For an overview of Arab women organizing around feminist issues, see the special website launched by the Arab States Regional Office of the UN Development Fund for Women (UNIFEM) under the framework of the Arab Women Connect project: www.arabwomenconnect.org/english/main_links.html (accessed May 11, 2003). Of particular interest is UNIFEM, 2000.

4. An interesting volume including articles on women and Islamist movements in Sudan, Tunisia, Algeria, Egypt, Turkey, and Iran is Moghadam, 1994.

5. It is important to caution against viewing Islamist women in Iran as a monolithic group, however. See Moghissi, 1996, for a discussion that distinguishes between "conservative" and "reformist" Muslim elite women. The conservatives, apologists for the clerical state, occupy prominent public posts, are almost all related to powerful male elites, and are the main beneficiaries of financial and ideological support

from the state. The reformists represent a growing disenchantment with the legal system and government policies in education and employment, although it appears that they are of the same social class and background as the conservative group.

6. The journal *Iran Bulletin* (www.iran-bulletin.org [accessed May 28, 2003]) has published articles by Iranian feminists debating these issues. As examples, see Moghadam, 2000, and Moghissi, 2000.

Bibliography

Afary, Janet. 1989. "On the Origins of Feminism in Early Twentieth Century Iran." *Journal of Women's History* 1, no. 2:65–87.

Antoun, Richard. 1968. "On the Modesty of Women in Arab Muslim Villages: A Study in the Accommodation of Traditions." *American Anthropologist* 70:671–698.

Arat, Yesim. 1996. "On Gender and Citizenship in Turkey." *Middle East Report* 198 (January–March):28–31.

———. 2000. "Islamist Women, Their Headscarves, and Democracy in Turkey." Paper presented at Ben Gurion University. www.bgu.ac.il/humphrey/seminar/yasim.htm (accessed May 11, 2003).

Berkovitch, Nitza. 1996. "Women and the Women's Equal Rights Law in Israel." *Middle East Report* 198 (January–March):19–21.

Clark, Janine Astrid, and Jillian Schwedler. 2003. "Who Opened The Window? Women's Activism in Islamist Parties." *Comparative Politics* 35, no. 3 (April): 293–312.

Ferdows, Adele. 1983. "Women and the Islamic Revolution." *International Journal of Middle East Studies* 15:283–298.

Galal, Salma. 1995. "Women and Development in the Maghreb Countries." Pp. 49–70 in Nabil Khoury and Valentine Moghadam (eds.), *Gender and Development in the Arab World*. London: Zed Books.

Graham-Brown, Sarah. 1993. *Women and Politics in the Middle East*. Special MERIP Publication no. 2. Washington, D.C.: Middle East Research and Information Project.

Hale, Sondra. 1996. *Gender Politics in Sudan: Islamism, Socialism, and the State*. Boulder, Colo.: Westview Press.

Hijab, Nadia. 1988. *Womanpower: The Arab Debate on Women at Work*. Cambridge: Cambridge University Press.

Hoodfar, Homa. 1995. "Population Policy and Gender Equity in Post-Revolutionary Iran." Pp. 105–135 in Carla M. Obermeyer (ed.), *Family, Gender, and Population in the Middle East*. Cairo: American University in Cairo Press.

Jad, Islah. 1990. "From Salons to the Popular Committees: Palestinian Women, 1919–1989." Pp. 125–142 in Jamal Nassar and Roger Heacock (eds.), *Intifada: Palestine at the Crossroads*. New York: Praeger.

Joseph, Suad. 1991. "Elite Strategies for State-Building: Women, Family, Religion, and State in Iraq and Lebanon." Pp. 176–200 in Deniz Kandiyoti (ed.), *Women, Islam, and the State*. London: Macmillan.

———. 1994. *Gender and Family in the Arab World*. Special MERIP Publication no. 4. Washington, D.C.: Middle East Research and Information Project.

Joseph, Suad, and Deniz Kandiyoti. 2000. *Gender and Citizenship in the Middle East*. Syracuse, N.Y.: Syracuse University Press.

Joseph, Suad, and Susan Slyomovics. 2000. *Women and Power in the Middle East*. Philadelphia: University of Pennsylvania Press.

Kandiyoti, Deniz. 1989. "Women and the Turkish State: Political Actors or Symbolic Pawns?" Pp. 126–149 in Nira Yuval-Davis and Floya Anthias (eds.), *Woman-Nation-State.* London: Macmillan.

———. 1991a. "End of Empire: Islam, Nationalism, and Women in Turkey." Pp. 22–47 in Deniz Kandiyoti (ed.), *Women, Islam, and the State.* London: Macmillan.

———. 1991b. "Islam and Patriarchy: A Comparative Perspective." Pp. 23–42 in Nikki Keddie and Beth Baron (eds.), *Women in Middle Eastern History: Shifting Boundaries in Sex and Gender.* New Haven, Conn.: Yale University Press.

———. 1991c. "Women, Islam, and the State." *Middle East Report* 173 (November–December):9–14.

Lazreg, Marnia. 1994. *The Eloquence of Silence: Algerian Women in Question.* New York: Routledge.

Mir-Hosseini, Ziba. 1991. "Contrast Between Law and Practice for the Moroccan Family: Patriarchy and Matrifocality." *Moroccan Studies* 1:39–52.

Moghadam, Valentine (ed.). 1994. *Identity Politics and Women.* Boulder, Colo.: Westview Press.

———. 1995. "The Political Economy of Female Employment in the Arab Region." Pp. 6–34 in Nabil Khoury and Valentine Moghadam (eds.), *Gender and Development in the Arab World.* London: Zed Books.

———. 2000. "Islamic Feminism and Its Discontents: Notes on a Debate." *Iran Bulletin* 25–26:1–20. www.iran-bulletin.org/islamic_feminism.htm (accessed May 11, 2003).

——— (ed.). 2003. *Modernizing Women: Gender and Social Change in the Middle East.* 2nd ed. Boulder, Colo.: Lynne Rienner.

Moghissi, Haideh. 1996. "Public Life and Women's Resistance." Pp. 251–270 in Saeed Rahnema and Sohrab Behdad (eds.), *Iran After the Revolution: Crisis of an Islamic State.* New York: I. B. Tauris.

———. 2000. "Women, Modernity and Political Islam." *Iran Bulletin.* www.iran-bulletin.org/women (accessed May 11, 2003).

Molyneux, Maxine. 1991. "The Law, the State, and Socialist Policies with Regard to Women: The Case of the People's Democratic Republic of Yemen 1967–1990." Pp. 237–271 in Deniz Kandiyoti (ed.), *Women, Islam, and the State.* London: Macmillan.

Moors, Annelies. 1996. "Gender Relations and Inheritance: Person, Power, and Property in Palestine." Pp. 69–84 in Deniz Kandiyoti (ed.), *Gendering the Middle East: Emerging Perspectives.* London: I. B. Tauris.

Najmabadi, Afsaneh. 1991. "Hazards of Modernity and Morality: Women, State, and Ideology in Contemporary Iran." Pp. 48–76 in Deniz Kandiyoti (ed.), *Women, Islam, and the State.* London: Macmillan.

Nashat, Guity (ed.). 1983. *Women and Revolution in Iran.* Boulder, Colo.: Westview Press.

Paidar, Parvin. 1996. "Feminism in Islam in Iran." Pp. 51–67 in Deniz Kandiyoti (ed.), *Gendering the Middle East: Emerging Perspectives.* London: I. B. Tauris.

Peteet, Julie. 1991. *Gender in Crisis: Women and the Palestinian Resistance Movement.* New York: Columbia University Press.

Sayigh, Rosemary. 1993. "Palestinian Women and Politics in Lebanon." Pp. 175–192 in Judith Tucker (ed.), *Arab Women: Old Boundaries, New Frontiers.* Bloomington: Indiana University Press.

Shahidian, Hammed. 1997. "Women and Clandestine Politics in Iran, 1970–1985." *Feminist Studies* 23, no. 1:7–43.

Shami, Seteney. 1990. "Introduction." Pp. xiii–xix in Seteney Shami, Lucine Taminian, Soheir A. Morsy, Zeinab B. El Bakri, and El-Wathig M. Kameir, *Women in*

Arab Society: Work Patterns and Gender Relations in Egypt, Jordan, and Sudan.
Paris: Berg/UNESCO.

Sharoni, Simona. 1995. *Gender and the Israeli-Palestinian Conflict: The Politics of Women's Resistance.* Syracuse, N.Y.: Syracuse University Press.

Swirski, Barbara, and Marilyn Safir (eds.). 1991. *Calling the Equality Bluff: Women in Israel.* New York: Teachers College Press.

Taraki, Lisa. 1995. "Islam Is the Solution: Jordanian Islamists and the Dilemma of the 'Modern Woman.'" *British Journal of Sociology* 46, no. 4:643–661.

———. 1996. "Jordanian Islamists and the Agenda for Women: Between Discourse and Practice." *Middle Eastern Studies* 32, no. 1:140–158.

Tucker, Judith. 1993. "The Arab Family in History: 'Otherness' and the Study of the Family." Pp. 195–207 in Judith Tucker (ed.), *Arab Women: Old Boundaries, New Frontiers.* Bloomington: Indiana University Press.

UNDP (UN Development Programme). 1995. *Human Development Report 1995.* New York: Oxford University Press.

———. 2002. *The Arab Human Development Report 2002.* New York: UN Development Programme and Arab Fund for Economic and Social Development.

———. 2005. *The Arab Human Development Report 2005.* New York: UN Development Programme and Arab Fund for Economic and Social Development.

———. 2006. *Human Development Report 2006.* New York: UN Development Programme.

UNIFEM (UN Development Fund for Women). 2000. *Arab Regional Alternative Report: Five Years After Beijing.* www.arabwomenconnect.org/docs/asro_gov_arabregional.doc (accessed May 11, 2003).

Yuval-Davis, Nira. 1982. *Israeli Women and Men: Divisions Behind the Unity.* London: Change.

———. 1989. "National Reproduction and the 'Demographic Race' in Israel." Pp. 92–109 in Nira Yuval-Davis and Floya Anthias (eds.), *Woman-Nation-State.* London: Macmillan.

Zurayk, Huda, and Fadia Saadeh. 1995. "Women as Mobilizers of Human Resources in Arab Countries." Pp. 35–48 in Nabil Khoury and Valentine Moghadam (eds.), *Gender and Development in the Arab World.* London: Zed Books.

12

Religion and Politics in the Middle East

Jillian Schwedler

The Middle East is home to the three major monotheistic religions— Judaism, Christianity, and Islam—and several minor ones. Much of the politics of the region, from the Arab-Israeli conflict to the Iranian revolution to the emergence of extremist groups such as Al-Qaida, has been viewed by those inside and outside of the region as driven by religious conflict, but the politics of the Middle East has never been exclusively about religion, even when religious rhetoric and symbolism has been invoked. Politics at its heart is about power, and political actors of every ilk bring their own understandings of the causes of injustice and the appropriate means for political change. In the Middle East, many of these visions are explicitly religious in orientation; however, Western countries have also seen a resurgence of political debate around religion, from its appropriate place in national politics to the growing number of religious revivalist movements. In this regard, the politics of the Middle East is not necessarily any more about religion than are politics in Western countries. Furthermore, the role of religion is not only about the use of religious symbolism in political conflicts or the ways in which regimes and their challengers claim legitimacy based on religious authority. Religion is also a central part of daily life in every Middle Eastern country, informing the ways in which most ordinary citizens understand politics as well as their own place in the world.

In this chapter, I provide a brief background to the major religions in the Middle East and the resurgence of politicized religion, from the establishment of the Jewish state of Israel to the popular revolution in Iran that led to the creation of an Islamic state there. Then I focus on the two main categories of politicized religious activism, both of which believe that religious communities must conform more closely to their religious values.

The first group, moderate religious activists, make up the vast majority of politicized religious groups and engage in formal political processes to realize gradual political, social, and economic reforms; the second group, religious extremists, seek to rapidly overthrow the existing political order, through the use of violence if necessary. Though far fewer in number, extremists have left their mark on regional as well as global politics.

■ The Historical Role of Religion in the Middle East

The Middle East is the birthplace of the world's three Abrahamic religions: Judaism, Christianity, and Islam. In Chapter 3, Arthur Goldschmidt Jr. examines the emergence of these religions and the conflicts between them in greater detail. Here I provide an overview of each and then focus on contemporary issues of religion and politics, including the role and experiences of the followers of minority religious communities.

Judaism

The first of the three great monotheistic religions is Judaism, which is more than 4,000 years old. According to Hebrew tradition, Moses led the Jewish people, with God's guidance, out of their slavery in Egypt and brought them to the Holy Land to establish a kingdom of God (around 1450–1250 B.C.E.). Christians and Muslims share this vision of Judaism's origins, as each recognizes its faith as part of the same religious lineage (Judaism to Christianity to Islam) and believes in the same God. God revealed to Moses the first five books of the Hebrew Bible, called the Torah, which together with the Talmud (a secondary text that includes interpretations of Jewish law, the *halakah,* and the Torah) is the basic source of religious principles for the Jewish faith. As a people, Jews might best be described as a religious-racial community, one that carefully guards its communal identity (Cavendish, 1980:133–170) and emphasizes marriage and procreation from within the community more than conversion (although conversion is possible).

In 70 C.E., Jews were forced out of Jerusalem and Judea by the Romans, who also destroyed the Second Temple, which had been built on the site of Solomon's Temple (the First Temple). Exiled Jews settled in many directions and maintained a strong identity not only of a single community but of one that would one day reunite. In the Diaspora, they maintained their religious practices and rituals, sustaining their identity through close-knit communities. In Europe they lived under (largely) Christian persecution for the next 2,000 years, although they enjoyed some degree of tolerance in parts of the Muslim world, even flourishing as a religious community during the Islamic age in Spain (Cavendish, 1980:165).

In the late nineteenth and early twentieth century, increased violence and discrimination against Jews in Europe led to the emergence of a Jewish nationalist movement—Zionism—that aimed to establish a Jewish homeland and possibly even a Jewish state on the lands of historic Israel. Thousands of Zionists emigrated to Palestine over the next fifty years, sometimes living in peace with the indigenous Christian and Muslim Palestinians, and sometimes clashing, particularly over the control of land. Chapters 3, 4, 5, and 6 examine these events in greater detail. The Jewish state of Israel was formally established in 1948.

Many of the first Zionists were secular and even Marxist in orientation, viewing Judaism as an identity and Zionism as a means for this religious-racial community to live on the land to which they felt strong historical connections. As Simona Sharoni and Mohammed Abu-Nimer illustrate in Chapter 6, this perspective continues to characterize the political left in Israel today, which views the Israeli state more as a protector of the Jewish community rather than as a strictly religious state. On the religious right, Zionism is viewed as an effort to realize God's intention that the Jewish people should establish a kingdom of God on that specific land. For them, the state of Israel is a religious state, one whose role is not only to protect the community but also to ensure that its Jewish citizens adhere closely to the Torah and Talmud in all aspects of life.

Today Judaism has some 14 million adherents worldwide. In the contemporary Middle East, most Jews live in Israel, although small communities remain in Iran, Iraq, Syria, Yemen, Tunisia, and Morocco.

Christianity

Christianity is the largest religion in the world, with 1.9 billion followers. It finds its roots in the teachings of Jesus of Nazareth, a Jew whose later followers came to believe he was also the Messiah and the son of God. Jesus was born in Bethlehem and crucified by the Romans in Jerusalem some thirty-two years later. Christianity initially spread through the Mediterranean but today has large communities of followers on every continent.

Like Judaism, Christianity has an intimate history with politics. Jews (and thus early Christians) were exiled from Jerusalem in 70 C.E. by the Romans, migrating primarily to lands along the eastern Mediterranean, though often remaining under the repressive authority of Roman administrators. Christianity spread rapidly over the next 300 years, gradually gaining acceptance, as demonstrated by Constantine I's declaration of Christianity as an officially tolerated religion in 333 C.E.; by 380 C.E., the edict of Theodosius I declared Christianity the official religion of the Roman Empire. Christianity continued to thrive in Europe following the Islamic conquest of the Middle East beginning in the seventh century, though Christian communities remained active throughout the Muslim world. By the twelfth century, Christianity was deeply intertwined with European politics through the papacy. Under Pope Innocent III (pope from 1198 to 1216), the papacy controlled vast territories and exercised extraordinary social control—for example, over familial practices, marriage, education, and the legitimacy of political leaders. The power of the papacy declined over the next decades as kings, emperors, and the papacy struggled over power and authority. The relationship of Christian authority to European regimes changed forever with the Protestant Reformation (1500–1650), though the numbers of faithful themselves continued to grow.

The period before the Reformation also marked the concerted efforts of European leaders to shape Middle East politics in the name of religion. The Crusades were not a single campaign, but nine major European military invasions into the region from the eleventh to thirteenth centuries. In 1096, Christian armies responded to Pope Urban II's call to reestablish a kingdom of God in the holy lands. Their early successes were followed by numerous defeats. Following the 1099 capture of Jerusalem, the invading army formally pardoned those who surrendered, then continued to massacre all remaining Muslim survivors, including women and children (Runciman, 1992). They converted al-Aqsa Mosque and the Dome of the Rock, the third holiest site in Islam (both built on the Haram al-Sharif, also the historic site of the first and second Jewish temples), into churches. Jerusalem was recaptured in

Qabat al-Bahr (the Sea Castle), in Sidon, Lebanon, is a thirteenth-century Crusader fortress built on the site of an older temple dedicated to Baal.

1187 by Saladin, and a subsequent putsch by Richard the Lion-Hearted of England to recapture the city did not even reach the city walls. The last Crusader stronghold in the holy land, in Acre, fell to Muslim control in 1291.

Foreign Christian intervention in the Middle East returned in great strength during the European colonial period. In addition to direct political intervention by the governments of the predominantly Christian countries of Britain and France, colonialism brought Christian missionaries, with the strongest presence in lands closest to the Mediterranean. As detailed in Chapters 3, 4, and 5, Britain and France divided much of the region into new political units, often installing regimes sympathetic to colonial rule. Christian missionaries, enjoying the support of the colonial power and their emissaries in the region, opened schools, publishing houses, and hospitals, and proselytized Muslims at every opportunity. As John Esposito argues, given this historical connection of Christianity and colonialism, it is not surprising that many independence struggles against colonial powers in the Middle East were fought in the name of religion (Esposito, 1999). Outside of the region, Christians were among the strongest supporters of the creation of the State of Israel; revivalist Christian movements continue to support Israel today as well as advocate for the rights of Christian minorities throughout the region.

Today, Christians make up significant populations in Lebanon and the West Bank and Gaza, and have smaller communities in Iran, Iraq, Jordan, Syria, and Egypt. These include Copts, Maronites, Greek Orthodox, Greek Catholic, Armenians, and Chaldean Catholics, among others. The number of Christians (and particularly Catholics) in the Middle East has significantly

Mosque at Job's Tomb near Salalah, Oman, which serves as a memorial for a man important to Jews, Christians, and Muslims.

Deborah J. Gerner

increased in recent decades as a result of the presence of large numbers of foreign workers, including laborers and domestic workers.

Islam

The third of the Abrahamic faiths is Islam, founded in the early seventh century when Muhammad of Mecca (570–632 C.E.) received the last revelations of God (in 610 C.E.) via the Angel Gabriel. Muhammad was ordered to spread a simple message: that there is only one God (in Arabic, *Allah*), and no other god is worthy of worship. This message was the same as that revealed to Abraham, Moses, and Jesus, among other prophets, except that Muhammad was to be the final prophet, delivering God's last set of instructions to humankind. A follower of the Islamic faith is called a Muslim, meaning *one who submits* (to the will of God).

From the outset, Islam gained followers not only for the simplicity and clarity of its message, but because it declared—in contrast to centuries of Christian political domination in Europe—that individual believers (Muslims) had no intermediaries between themselves and God. Following Muhammad's emigration (*hijra*) from Mecca in 622 C.E., the first Muslims recaptured Mecca against much stronger armies, a success that facilitated the first of many large-scale conversions to Islam by demonstrating that God was on Muhammad's side. Jews and Christians were declared to be protected religious communities, or *dhimmi,* and were (at least officially) not to be targets of conversion (though voluntary conversion was welcome). In practice, of course, Jews and Christians often experienced discrimination, though at times they prospered under Muslim rule's relatively more tolerant environment (particularly for Jews) as compared to Europe. Because literacy is so central to Islam, Muslim leaders supported the creation of numerous centers of higher education—the oldest continuously operating university in the world is al-Azhar University in Cairo, still a major center of Sunni learning. Early Muslim scholars were also responsible for preserving the classic texts and histories of the Greek and Roman periods, and for reintroducing them to Europe during the Middle Ages.

There are several divisions within the larger Muslim *umma,* or global community, though Muslims view these differences with varying degrees of importance. The most significant divide came early in Islam's history when, following the death of Muhammad, there emerged a dispute over authority within the community. The majority view—what has come to be called the orthodox view by that virtue alone—was that authority should be shared and that a new leader, to the extent one is needed, should be selected from among the community. The followers of this view are called Sunni Muslims. The alternative view is that authority should have passed to a direct blood descendant of Muhammad, and to his nephew, Ali, in particular. These followers or

The Ommayad Mosque in Damascus, Syria, was originally constructed in 705 C.E. on the site of an ancient temple to the Roman goddess Jupiter.

partisans of Ali, literally *Shi'at Ali,* are the Shi'a (sometimes written as *Shi'ites*). Shi'a are today located throughout the Middle East but have significant communities (and sometimes majorities) in Iraq, Bahrain, Saudi Arabia, Lebanon, Yemen, and Iran.

For all Muslims the basic text of Islam is the Quran, or *recitation,* and unlike the Hebrew and Christian bibles, it is believed to be the literal word of God as conveyed to Muhammad through the Angel Gabriel. The Quran and the Sunna—the sayings (*hadith*) and doings of the Prophet Muhammad—together provide all the guidance a Muslim needs in life. The Quran and the Sunna together form the basis of *sharia. Sharia,* meaning *the path* or *the road,* is conventionally translated into English as *Islamic law,* but is more akin to a set of guiding principles derived from the Quran and the Sunna. Within Sunni Islam, there are four main schools of interpreting *sharia.* Individual Muslims may choose to follow any school they find most compelling, but a central tenet of Islam is that individual believers must make their own choices, drawing guidance from scholars who study *sharia* but ultimately responsible for making their own decision. Islamic scholars of *sharia,* the *ulama,* are often asked by followers to issue an opinion, or fatwa, on a particular topic. Many have personal followings, but their opinions and interpretations are never binding on either their followers or indeed Muslims anywhere. A Muslim must listen to the reasoned and educated opinions of others and then make one's own choice.

The Islamic conquest spread quickly throughout the Arab world and beyond; by the sixteenth century three great empires were Islamic: the Turkic
Ottoman (which dominated the Arab world), the Safavid in Iran, and the
Mogul on the Indian subcontinent. While Muslim rulers gradually lost control of the far reaches of these empires—Muslim Andalusia in southern
Spain was lost in 1492—the Islamic faith is today the world's fastest growing religion, with its 1.5 billion adherents rapidly approaching Christianity's
1.9 billion.

■ The Experiences of Religious Minorities

Muslims make up a majority of the population in all of the countries of the
Middle East except for Israel, so all of the Christian communities (and all
the Jewish ones outside of Israel) are minorities in a numerical sense. How
minority religious communities are treated varies considerably in practice.
Most Arab Jews emigrated from Iraq, Iran, Syria, Yemen, Morocco, and
Tunisia to Israel in the decades before and after 1948. As Simona Sharoni
and Mohammad Abu-Nimer show in Chapter 6, Jews of Arab or African
origin—called Sephardim or, more recently, Mizrachim, meaning "orientals"—have often experienced discrimination within Israel (Shohat, 1988).
The tiny Jewish communities that remain in Iran, Iraq, Yemen, Morocco,
Tunisia, and Syria are tolerated, often in manners similar to Christian
communities.

   Islam formally protects all Abrahamic communities, and Jews and
Christians are protected under *sharia:* they are permitted to practice their
faith and not subject to proselytizing. In Iran, the elected national assembly
even provides for representation of religious minorities: five seats (of 290)
include one for Jews, one for Zoroastrians, one for Chaldean and Assyrian
Catholics, and two for Armenian Christians. Jordan's parliament reserves
twelve seats (of 110) for religious minorities: nine for Christians (who
make up some 5–7 percent of the population) and three for minority Muslim communities (two for Circassians and one for Chechans). In Egypt,
Coptic Christians make up some 10 percent of the population and have won
seats in the People's Assembly (parliament), but not through the provision
of seats dedicated to ensure their representation.

   Although *sharia* clearly mandates the protection of minority Jewish
and Christian communities, in practice they are frequently the subject of
discrimination and even outright attacks. In Egypt, Islamist extremists operating illegal organizations have targeted Coptic Christians and their communities, attacking their churches and businesses.

   Lebanon presents a more unique situation, as various Christian sects
made up half of the population as recently as the mid-twentieth century.

The bloody fifteen-year civil war, which formally ended in 1989 with the signing of the Taif Agreement, saw internecine fighting as religious and ethnic communities formed their own militias under the leadership of warlords. The war was characterized by at least as much intra-Christian violence as Christian-Muslim violence (but, interestingly, no incidence of Sunni-Shi'i violence). The agreement that formally ended the fighting provided for a parliament with seats equally divided between Christians and Muslims, even though by that time Muslims were estimated to make up as much as two-thirds of the population. The 128-seat sectarian parliament provides a given number of seats dedicated to each religious sect: Sunnis (27 seats), Shi'a (27 seats), Alawites (2 seats), and Druze (8 seats) on the Muslim side, and Maronites (34 seats), Armenians (6 seats), Greek Orthodox (14 seats), Greek Catholic (6 seats), and other Christians (4 seats) (Norton and Schwedler, 1994:52). As illustrated in Chapters 4 and 10, sectarian conflict continues in Lebanon, though it is not always clear to what extent the fighting has to do with religious differences and to what extent it reflects power struggles between leaders who happen to belong to different religious and ethnic communities.

Sudan is another country marked by long and bloody conflict between religious communities, a sizable Christian community in the south and the Arab and Muslim government of the north. Since 1990, more than two million Sudanese have died in this civil war, which was formally ended by truce in 2005. As discussed below, Sudan's government seeks full application of *sharia,* although in practice it does little to respect, let alone protect, its significant Christian population. As the conflict in Darfur illustrates, the government also feels little obligation to protect the followers of other, traditional African faiths.

As illustrated above, Christians and Jews are not the only minority religions in the Middle East. Iran is ethnically diverse but predominantly Muslim, thought it provides formal protection and representation for Jews and Christians as well as Zoroastrians, a small community that believes in the sanctity of all aspects of the natural world. Followers of the Bahai faith, by comparison, have been subject to extreme persecution. The faith was founded by Baha'ullah in nineteenth-century Persia (Iran) and emphasizes the unity of mankind. Because its followers—who today number some 6 million worldwide—view Baha'ullah as the latest (but not final) messenger of the Abrahamic faiths, they are viewed as heretical by Muslims, who view Muhammad as the last of the prophets.

Indeed, many divides among Muslims effectively create minority religious communities, particularly sects that are considered heretical. Another minority Muslim community is the Druze, based primarily in Lebanon, Syria, Jordan, and Israel and numbering fewer than a million followers worldwide. Their beliefs developed as an offshoot of the Ismaili Shi'a, but theologically their beliefs draw on neo-Platonic philosophies and non-Abrahamic traditions. The Alawi are a minority Shi'i sect, numbering some 3 million, who (like the Druze) are considered heretical even by most Shi'a; in Syria, Alawites have held power for some forty years, though they frame their rule around Baathism's mix of socialism and Islam and not around their particular Alawi beliefs. In Saddam's Iraq, Shi'a constituted a clear majority but were excluded from power; since 2003 they have made steady gains in power, though they remain divided as Iraq's civil war continues. In Bahrain, the majority Shi'i population gained political representation when the state became a constitutional monarchy in 2002, though they remain subject to ongoing repression by the ruling al-Khalifah family, which is Sunni.

▓ Religious States

Most countries in the Middle East could be defined as religious in the sense of defining a formal place for religion. What this means in practice, however, varies dramatically from formal religious states (Saudi Arabia, Israel, and Iran) that prioritize the full application of religious law in all political, social, and economic matters, to the more nominally religious states, whether the ruling elite claim authority based on direct descent from the bloodline of the Prophet Muhammad (such as Jordan, Morocco, Saudi Arabia, Bahrain, and Kuwait), or whether the constitution provides a formal status for Islam as official religion and the president to be a Muslim (such as Egypt, Yemen, Syria, prewar Iraq, Libya, Algeria, Oman, and Tunisia).

Most regimes in the Middle East claim their legitimacy at least in part based on religion: We think of Saudi Arabia, postrevolutionary Iran, Mauritania, and Sudan as Islamic states, and Israel as a Jewish state, but religion is actually written into the constitution of most states in the Middle East. This is an important indicator of the centrality of religious values in the region, though it says little about the relationship of religion and politics in practice. Many of the challengers to the existing authoritarian regimes criticize the political elite for not living up to their claims to be guided by the values of their religion.

The Jewish Israeli State and the Symbolism of Jerusalem

In the late nineteenth century, Jewish activist Theodor Herzl (1860–1904) led the Zionist movement in its quest to establish a Jewish homeland. Zionism spread among Jews throughout Europe, particularly after the first Zionist conference was held in 1897. When the Ottoman Empire was dismantled after World War I, Britain gained control of most of Palestine and was convinced by European Zionists to draw up the Balfour Declaration. This 1917 document, which was accepted by the League of Nations, called for the establishment of a Jewish state in Palestine. Hundreds of thousands of Jews migrated to Palestine, largely from Europe but also from Arab countries. The UN passed a resolution in 1947 that divided Palestine and called for the creation of the State of Israel. In the months before May 15, 1948, when the British mandate over Palestine was set to expire, Zionists and Arabs in Palestine fought a bloody civil war that drove many Palestinians into exile. Israel declared independence on May 15, forming a modern nation-state with an overtly religious identity.

The question of Israel as a Jewish state cannot be divorced from struggles over the sovereignty of Jerusalem, a city not only claimed by both Israelis and Palestinians as their capital, but by all three Abrahamic religions as historically and symbolically central to their faiths. The status of the city is contested under international law, and the Israeli claim of Jerusalem as its capital is not recognized by most nations. For Jews, the Mishnah (a second-century compendium of Jewish laws) states that the Western Wall is the site of continuous divine presence (*scechina*) (Breger, 1996). This area was the site of King Solomon's Temple and the Second Temple, the latter of which was destroyed in 70 C.E. by Romans. The annual Passover ceremonies conclude each year with Jews worldwide reiterating the prophetic idea that Jewish exiles will eventually return to the ancestral land: "Next Year in Jerusalem."

With the establishment of Israel in 1948, Jerusalem was divided, with the Jewish quarters under Israeli control, and the eastern quarters (including

An Orthodox Jewish youth praying at the Western Wall in Jerusalem.

the Western Wall and the site of the Temple Mount/Haram al-Sharif) under Jordanian control. Israelis and Jews worldwide celebrated the reunification of the city when Israel recaptured the eastern quarters in the 1967 Six Day War.

For Christians, too, Jerusalem is a city of tremendous symbolic significance. Christianity originated in Jerusalem, where Jesus preached, died, and was resurrected. The central goal of the Crusades was the recovery of Jerusalem by Christian armies in order to establish a (Christian) kingdom of God there. Millions of Christians make pilgrimages to holy sites in Jerusalem each year, as well as to other holy sites in the West Bank (notably Bethlehem and Nazareth) and Jordan (notably the Baptismal Site on the East Bank of the Jordan River).

Jerusalem is the third holiest place in Islam, after Mecca and Medina (in present-day Saudi Arabia). The Prophet Muhammad is believed to have ascended to heaven, the *miraj haqq,* from the site of the rock on the Haram al-Sharif where Abraham was willing to sacrifice his son Isaac to God. (Jews built the First and Second Temples on the site for the same reason, where early Jewish priests practiced sacrifices to God.) Muslims also believe that the end of time will begin in Jerusalem. The loss of Jerusalem from Muslim control to Jewish control in the twentieth century is viewed by many Muslims as a dire warning from God to renew and deepen their faith. Indeed, many Islamic revival groups view the success of foreign powers in colonizing and dominating Muslims' lands as a result of the widespread loss of faith among Muslims. Only by returning to the fundamental teachings of their faith, they argue, can Muslim peoples ever hope to gain dignity and control over their destinies.

The establishment of a Jewish state has thus been monumental not only for being the first popularly driven attempt to create a modern religious nation-state in the region, but also because that success has come at great symbolic and material loss for the followers of other faiths, most notably Muslim and Christian Palestinians.

Strongly Islamic States

Israel was not the first religious state created in the modern Middle East. Putting aside centuries-old dynasties that claim authority to rule based on religious legitimacy, the Middle East has four states established in the twentieth century as religious: Saudi Arabia, Mauritania, Iran, and Sudan. Strongly religious states not only claim their legitimacy to rule on religious grounds, but give religious leaders high levels of power and the authority to exercise control over governance. What this means in practice, as we shall see, varies dramatically.

The Kingdom of Saudi Arabia was established by the House of Saud in 1932 as an Islamic state. Although perhaps a marriage of convenience, the

Saudi monarchy was formed through an alliance with a very conservative Islamic revival movement, Wahhabism, which called for a return to the letter of the Quran. King Abdul Aziz ibn Saud had in fact swept to power with the support of Bedouin and Islamic extremists, whose fearlessness and commitment to an Islamic vision led them to conquer village after village. Indeed, these early extremists, called the Muslim Brethen (no connection to the Muslim Brotherhood discussed below), were more zealous than Abdul Aziz in terms of religion and the desire for political conquest. In 1929 Abdul Aziz was forced to fight his own forces of Muslim Brethren in order to stop their continued conquest into lands controlled by the British. Despite Saudi Arabia's highly conservative brand of Islam, the United States has forged a close relation with the state since the 1940s (Vitalis, 2007).

The Iranian Revolution of 1978–1979 is conventionally understood as Islamic in character because of its symbolism and rhetoric. However, the Islamic Republic was not actually established for more than a year after the fall of the shah in 1979: clerics initially vied with nationalists for control of the new state, with the former only gradually gaining dominance and implementing a strict interpretation and application of Islamic principles. But for more than a millennium Iran (formerly Persia) had been under Islamic rule of one sort or another. Even in the twentieth century, the 1906 Constitutional Revolution had brought a new constitution that provided the clerical establishment a formal role in overseeing matters of state. That constitution was never fully realized in practice, but it formalized a relationship between the political elite (at that time, the Qajar Dynasty) and the religious establishment that ceded decisions and power on religious matters to the latter. Unlike the Safavid Dynasty before it, the Qajar did not claim authority to rule based on religious legitimacy, so their rule marked the separation of religious and political authority that was formalized in the 1906 Constitution. When Reza Khan seized control in 1921 and established the Pahlavi dynasty in 1926, the clerical establishment was marginalized but Islam remained the official state religion.

The 1979 revolution that brought down the regime of Muhammad Reza Pahlavi was realized only through a broad alliance of bazaar merchants, clerical elites, nationalists, intellectuals, feminists, students, and laborers (among others). But it took more than a year before the clerics, under the leadership of Ayatollah Khomeini, emerged triumphant against the nationalists and established the Islamic Republic of Iran. Clerics were given their full authority provided in the 1906 Constitution, wherein the Council of Guardians passes judgment on all political matters by declaring whether or not policies are in line with *sharia*. As Deborah J. Gerner and Philip A. Schrodt show in Chapter 4, in practice the Council of Guardians uses its power to exert extreme control over political, social, and economic matters, for example, by determining which candidates may stand for elections, what sorts of foreign investment are permissible, how citizens may dress, and even whether they may use contraceptives.

One of the stated goals of the early Islamic Republic was to export the revolution: to encourage and indeed support Muslims in other countries to rise up against their regimes and establish Islamic states in their wake. This objective was an overwhelming failure, although the impact of this policy (which was largely pushed to the backburner following the death of Khomeini in 1989) continues to be felt in terms of the support Iran provides to a few Islamist groups, notably Hizbullah in Lebanon. One country that did become Islamic in the wake of the Iranian revolution was Sudan. Then-president Jaafar Nimeiri declared Sudan to be an Islamic state in 1983 and called for the full implementation of *sharia* (Voll, 1991). While the country has experienced political instability in the form of two coups, a long civil war between the northern regime and southern Christians, and seeming endless conflagrations with its non-Muslim, non-Arab populations (most recently in Darfur), Sudan remains a Sunni Islamic state that utilizes *sharia* as the primary source for legislating all matters political, social, and economic.

Nominally Islamic States

Most states in the Middle East accord some formal status to religion, often stipulating Islam as the official religion. Turkey is the notable exception: when Mustafa Kemal (later Atatürk) established the modern state of Turkey in 1923, he advocated a program of forced secularism, dismantling religious courts, abolishing the Caliphate, and outlawing religious dress. Most states in the region, however, embrace an Islamic identity. The monarchies and emirs of Jordan, Morocco, Kuwait, Bahrain, Oman, and the United Arab Emirates, like Saudi Arabia, all claim authority to rule based in part on their direct descent from the blood line of the Prophet Muhammad. Jordan's King Hussein also called himself keeper of Islam's two holy places in Jerusalem (the Dome of the Rock and al-Aqsa Mosque, both on the Haram al-Sharif), a title that proved embarrassing when Jordan lost control of east Jerusalem to Israel in the 1967 Six Day War (Katz, 2004). In a similar reference to Islam, the king of Morocco uses the title Commander of the Faithful.

Many republics, too—such as Egypt, Yemen, Tunisia, Algeria, Syria, and prewar Iraq—have established Islam as the official state religion and *sharia* as a source of law and legislation. What this means in practice varies considerably. Certainly the president must be a Muslim, and it is not unusual on high Muslim holidays or during times of domestic or regional turmoil to see the president and other state officials prominently praying, televised for all to see. During the Gulf War of 1990–1991, Saddam Hussein even added the words "God is Great" to the Iraqi flag: although his religious credentials were thin, he perhaps thought that the phrase might give him greater legitimacy and, in particular, greater support from other Muslim countries.

In Egypt, the office of mufti is filled by a prominent cleric from al-Azhar University; his job is to provide a stamp of approval (or rejection) on state policies attesting to their adherence to *sharia*. Unlike Iran's Council of Guardians, this office (like a similar one in Jordan) is little more than symbolic; nevertheless, the regime's need to at least *appear* to conform to *sharia* underlines the power of Islamic symbolism in sustaining the state's authority to rule. The clerics, or *ulama,* from al-Azhar function as a conservative (but not extremist) force in Egypt and control the religious courts and provide the imams to each of the country's tens of thousands of mosques. Religious parties are explicitly outlawed in Egypt—the state is already Islamic, so it sees no need for Islamic political parties—a measure that aims to marginalize the popular Muslim Brotherhood by denying it legal status.

Overall, the vast majority of states in the Middle East accord some official status to religion. As discussed in the next section, oppositional Islamic groups find considerable space to utilize Islamic symbolism and rhetoric precisely because so many regimes already sanction Islam as the state religion. One issue on which various Islamist parties challenge the state is over the precise wording of the status of *sharia* in the constitution: Is it *masdar* (a source) of legislation and law, or *al-masdar* (the source)? Islamist groups in Jordan and Yemen have sought to have the wording changed to *the* source; their efforts were successful in Yemen but not in Jordan (Schwedler, 2006). These contentious events underline the close relationship between religion and politics in most Middle Eastern countries.

▒ Religious Activism

The contemporary Middle East has seen an expansion of religious revivalist groups, in part inspired by anticolonial struggles and the desire for cultural authenticity. Indigenous Jewish and Islamic revivalist movements have had the greatest impact, although Jewish and Christian movements based outside the Middle East have had their share of influence on the region. Much of the Arab world remained under Ottoman control by the late nineteenth century, although the farther reaches of the empire were gradually gaining local autonomy. For many parts of the Middle East, the spread of European colonialism meant the exchange of one foreign occupier (Ottoman Turks) for another. The lack of Arab autonomy was viewed as extremely humiliating, and it was in this context that a diverse range of independence movements emerged. As discussed in Chapter 4, two of the dominant narratives were Arab nationalism and Islamic revivalism; both offered means of imagining alternative political arrangements in which Arabs would regain dignity through control of their own destinies. Islamic revivalism took many forms, but a common theme was that Muslim peoples had diverged too far from their faith, and a return to the core values of their religion would restore the rightful dignity to the community—along with political, social, and economic control of their lives. Jewish religious revivalism took several forms but was consistently framed in relation to Zionism and the need to establish (and later defend) the State of Israel.

In the broadest terms, religious revivalist movements seek to reform or replace existing political structures and social practices with those viewed as more in line with core religious values. The means by which this envisioned change is to be realized, however, varies considerably, from the political violence of extremist groups to the reformist measures of groups and political parties who seek to enact change gradually, either by working within the existing political structures or from below, through education and socialization programs. All of these revivalist groups, whether Jewish, Christian, or Islamic, are sometimes called *fundamentalist.* The term *fundamentalist* is not very illuminating, however, as it could be appropriately applied to any individual or group that seeks to return to the fundamental teachings of one's faith. In practice, the term *fundamentalist* might be accurately applied to groups as diverse as Amish communities in the United States, the Protestant Christians of Europe from whence the term came, and Al-Qaida. In the media and in policy circles, the term is more specifically applied to religious revivalists actively engaged in efforts for political change. With regard to the Middle East, the term *Islamic fundamentalism* is not only applied to extremist groups such as Al-Qaida but also to groups like the Muslim Brotherhood that seek peaceful reform and accept the authority of the existing regimes. Thus the term *fundamentalism* is used in confusing, contradictory, and all-encompassing ways. Instead, I use two terms to describe different trends within revivalist movements in the Middle East: *moderate religious activism,* characterized by efforts to achieve gradual, nonviolent reform by working within the existing political systems; and *religious extremism,* characterized by efforts to bring rapid change, often through the use of political violence against regimes and sometimes also civilians. In practice, it should be noted that the extremist-moderate dichotomy does not imply that moderate groups do not seek profound change in the long run. Indeed, they may strive for the full implementation of religious law in all areas of life, but reject the use of violence as a means to achieve it. At the same time, moderates may hold views that others feel are extremist—for example, some proto-democratic Islamic groups hold highly conservative views concerning the appropriate role of women. In terms of understanding the diverse political roles of religious revivalist movements in the Middle East, however, the categories of religious extremism and moderate religious activism provide better means of understanding trends than does the term *fundamentalism* because they emphasize key differences in how these groups work to realize their religious agendas.

Moderate Religious Activism

Most religious political activism in the Middle East is moderate rather than extremist. In fact, the region is flush with religious revivalist groups from all the Abrahamic faiths that advocate gradual reform, organize political parties (and strive for legal status), and cooperate with groups of divergent ideological orientation. In much of the region, for example, Islamic groups routinely cooperate with communists, socialists, liberals, Christians, and nationalists—practices that were largely unimaginable even fifteen years ago. Indeed, the range of religious activism is so diverse that this chapter could not hope to mention every group and or examine every dimension of religion and politics. Instead, I will illustrate the major trends and the broad trajectories that will characterize the next decade.

All Muslims view Islam as a whole way of life. Some believe that as long as one adheres to the spirit and values of the Quran and the Hadith (the teachings and doings of the Prophet Muhammad), a wide range of political systems, from socialism to liberal democracy to monarchy, are acceptable. Others believe in more radical political change and have a strict view of the appropriate application of *sharia*.

Many Islamist revival movements emerged in the Middle East and Pakistan, but one of the most important was the Muslim Brotherhood, founded in Egypt in 1928 by Hassan al-Banna (1905–1949). Al-Banna was a school teacher who advocated a return to Islam's core values through reading and study groups and by working within existing political structures. The group was an early advocate of literacy programs for men as well as women, as it believes that truly Islamic society requires that all Muslims are able to read the Quran. Politically, the Muslim Brotherhood was alternately tolerated and targeted by the monarchies of kings Fuad and Farouk. After a decade of confrontations with King Farouk's regime, al-Banna was assassinated by the police in 1949 with the full knowledge of the prime minister. The Muslim Brotherhood supported Gamal Abdul Nasser and the Free Officers movement that overthrew the monarchy in 1952. When Nasser sought to consolidate his power, however, he viewed the Muslim Brotherhood as a primary threat and outlawed the organization in 1954, after accusing its members of attempting to assassinate him. From that period until Nasser's death in 1970, thousands of its members were jailed and many were executed (Mitchell, 1969).

The Muslim Brotherhood organization spread outside of Egypt as early as the 1930s. Branches were formed in Jordan, Syria, Yemen, Tunisia, Palestine, and Sudan, among other places; they were formally independent but retained close relations with the mother organization in Egypt, particularly during al-Banna's lifetime. The experience of the Muslim Brotherhood in Jordan contrasts starkly with that of Egypt. The Muslim Brotherhood gained its first followers in Jordan in the late 1930s, but the organization was not formalized until 1946, just after Jordan gained independence from Great Britain. From the beginning, the group had close relations with the monarchy: King Abdullah I even inaugurated the group's headquarters in downtown Amman in 1946. The Muslim Brotherhood has since had a symbiotic relationship with the regime, supporting the monarchy against the various communist and socialist groups that challenged the regime in the 1950s and 1960s.

Although all branches of the Muslim Brotherhood have since 1948 placed the full liberation of Muslim Palestine among their primary objectives, the experiences of the group in Jordan are instructive. During the period 1948–1967, when Jordan ruled (and had formally annexed) the West Bank, including a portion of Jerusalem, the Jordanian and West Bank branches of the Muslim Brotherhood functioned together (Boulby, 1999). After Jordan lost control of the West Bank in the 1967 Six-Day War, Palestinian militant groups—mostly leftists—began launching attacks and raids from bases in Jordan, on the east bank of the Jordan River. Jordan's King Abdullah sought to shut down these activities, culminating in months of bloody conflict in the summer and fall of 1970. What is significant about this period is that although the Muslim Brotherhood embraced the goal of liberating Palestine, in these events it sided with the monarchy against Palestinian militants. Muslim Brotherhood leaders in Jordan went on to hold prominent government positions, as high as the cabinet level (Schwedler, 2006).

The Muslim Brotherhood branches in Egypt and Jordan had almost opposite experiences during the 1950s and 1960s. In both countries the group advocated gradual reform by working within existing political structures: in Egypt by working with the republican regime and in Jordan with the monarchy. But while Nasser outlawed the group and imprisoned its members, King Hussein found in the Muslim Brotherhood ready allies against the threat from leftists and nationalists, who were the real radicals of the period. Perhaps not surprisingly, many Jordanian leftists sought refuge in Egypt during this period while many Egyptian Muslim Brotherhood members fled to Jordan. As discussed below, an extremist movement first emerged from within the Muslim Brotherhood during the period of extreme repression and imprisonment under Nasser's rule.

Following Nasser's death in 1970—and following his ignominious defeat during the 1967 Six-Day War—new Egyptian president Anwar Sadat sought a changed relationship with the Muslim Brotherhood. Sadat had forged a friendship with al-Banna in the late 1930s, and he believed that the repression of the group was neither politically expedient nor morally defensible.

While he undertook a period of economic opening, discussed in detail by Agnieszka Paczynska in Chapter 7, he also sought to improve relations with the Muslim Brotherhood and released hundreds of their numbers from prison. Since then, the group has sought to realize their reform agenda by working within the system: fielding candidates for the People's Assembly, opening healthcare clinics and schools, and participating actively in professional associations and labor unions (Wickham, 2002). After Sadat's assassination by Islamic extremists in 1980, President Hosni Mubarak repeatedly refused to grant the Muslim Brotherhood formal legal status, despite the group's condemnation of Islamic militants in Egypt. Nevertheless, the Muslim Brotherhood regularly fields candidates for the People's Assembly as well as in local elections, and they have seen significant victories on numerous occasions, most recently during the 2005 elections.

In Jordan, the Muslim Brotherhood has had legal status as a social organization since 1946, but this renders it ineligible to also register as a political party. With the reliberalization of the parliament with full elections in 1989—the assembly had been suspended under martial law enacted in 1967—the group fielded candidates and, together with a handful of independent Islamists, won twenty-seven seats (of eighty), or 40 percent of the assembly. In the early 1990s, it held five cabinet posts, though it was largely unsuccessful (and unpopular) for its efforts to implement reforms such as a ban on alcohol and a prohibition against fathers watching their daughters (and thus viewing other young girls) compete in athletic events. Nevertheless, the group remained committed to working within the political system, and when political parties were legalized in 1992, many of its prominent members joined forces with independent Islamists to form the Islamic Action Front (IAF) party. The IAF, now dominated by the Muslim Brotherhood, competes regularly in local and national elections and has forged strong relations with other opposition parties, including nationalists, communists, socialists, and liberals.

The experiences of the Muslim Brotherhood in Jordan and Egypt are in many ways typical of many Islamist groups—and not only branches of the Muslim Brotherhood—that seek to realize their reforms gradually and by working within the existing political systems. Some of these parties are outlawed (e.g., al-Nahda in Tunisia), some function but do not have legal status (e.g., the Muslim Brotherood in Egypt), and some are legal political parties (e.g., the Islah party in Yemen, Hizbullah in Lebanon, and the IAF in Jordan). Kuwait has multiple Islamist groups that hold seats in its parliament, and Islamist groups are active in parliamentary politics in Iraq, Turkey, Algeria, Sudan, and Morocco.

In addition to formal participation in elected national assemblies and local elections, moderate Islamic activist groups are also known for their provision of social services, particularly where state services are nowhere to be found. Hizbullah provided significant services in South Lebanon during the civil war and after; most moderate Islamist groups are engaged in literacy programs and schools, although the curriculum is carefully controlled. Some scholars have questioned the depth and effectiveness of these social programs, arguing that they are championed for public relations purposes but in practice are far less effective. One seminal study shows that Muslim Brotherhood–run health clinics in Cairo, for example, are seldom staffed by a medical doctor (Clark, 2003). Nevertheless, these moderate Islamic activists—those who have sought to participate peacefully and legally in economic, political, and social realms—constitute the vast majority of Islamic revivalist movements. Their popularity largely stems from providing an alternative—ideologically and substantively—to the corruption, ineffectiveness, and repression of incumbent regimes.

Religious Extremism

Extremist religious groups garner the most headlines, even though they make up a tiny proportion of Islamic revivalist groups, and the impact of their activities can be profound. Extremists tend to emerge out of the most repressive contexts and aim to achieve political change not through gradual reform, but by directly attacking those in power. Their targets include foreign agents—including troops and diplomats, but also foreign-owned businesses and tourists—as well as local regimes they believe to be illegitimate. Of the latter, this includes those imposed by colonial and imperial powers (such as Israel) as well as those regimes deemed to have abandoned Islamic values and teachings.

Of the thousands of Muslim Brotherhood members imprisoned in Egypt during the 1950s and 1960s, one was Sayyid Qutb (d.1965), whose experiences of repression led him to abandon al-Banna's commitment to working with existing Muslim governments to realize change. In his *Signposts Along the Road,* he argues that Muslims are not, in fact, obligated to accept the legitimacy of the leadership of Muslim rulers—a common interpretation of *sharia*—if those leaders are not ruling in accord with Islam. Emancipation of Muslim communities must come through movement, he argues, rather than through works (teaching) alone. This position was radical because it justified, on Islamic grounds, attacking and overthrowing Muslim regimes. Qutb was executed in 1965 along with two others for allegedly plotting against Nasser's regime; many view these charges as a setup, but, regardless, the impact of his teachings and his death have been profound.

Indeed, Qutb inspired the emergence of extremist groups in Egypt and later throughout the Muslim world. Among the Muslim Brotherhood members that Sadat released from prison were a number of followers of Qutb, who formed small groups that advocated the violent overthrow of the regime.

These included the Islamic Group (Gama'a Islamiyyah) and Islamic Jihad (Jihad al-Islami). In 1981, Jihad member Khalid Islambuli assassinated Sadat, hoping that his death would spark an Islamic revolution in Egypt and the Arab world, following the one in Iran just two years earlier. No popular uprising emerged, however, and Islambuli and his co-conspirators were arrested. Islambuli was executed, but a number of others were exiled, including several who found refuge in Afghanistan and later joined Al-Qaida. In Egypt, the Islamic Group and Jihad regrouped and mounted a series of violent acts throughout the country, culminating in the 1997 massacre in the Valley of the Kings, which claimed the lives of four Egyptians and fifty-eight foreign tourists (along with six responsible for the attack). Jihad leaders already imprisoned at the time dissociated themselves from that attack, condemning it and formally disbanding their organization. Egypt has experienced little extremism since then, though the potential for a revival of religious extremism remains considerable as long as Egypt remains a repressive, nondemocratic state.

Egypt is not the only country to suffer from domestic Islamic extremism. Algeria experienced a virtual civil war by and among Islamist groups in the 1990s, but notably that bloodshed began after the Islamic Salvation Front (FIS) won parliamentary elections that the military quickly annulled. Yemen has seen violence by extremists against tourists and missionaries, as well as against the holy shrines of minority Muslim groups and a former

In Algiers, Algeria, women march to protest the
policies of Islamic militants.

brewery in the south. Beginning in the 1970s, extremists from North Yemen assassinated hundreds of socialists from South Yemen; even after unification in the 1990s, attacks against socialists continued, particularly as the 1993 elections approached. Although these attacks subsided somewhat during the remainder of the 1990s, in 2002 the prominent socialist leader Jar Allah Umar was assassinated: he was shot point-blank as he left the stage after addressing an assembly of the Islamist Islah party's general membership.

Islamic extremism is not confined to domestic attacks; indeed, the acts of violence that have gained the most attention internationally are those that target Israel, US troops in the Middle East, and, of course, the attacks of September 11, 2001, on the Pentagon and World Trade Center in the United States. Palestinian militants have launched attacks on Israel since the 1960s, but it was not until the formation of Hamas in 1987 during the first intifada that Palestinian Islamic groups began using political violence. Hizbullah has also launched numerous attacks on Israeli troops and Israeli soil. Hamas and Hizbullah differ from many other militant Islamist groups, however, in that their attacks are aimed at ousting what they view as foreign troops illegally occupying their land. Both groups have participated in their own governments peacefully, campaigning in elections and winning free and fair elections.

Islamic extremists justify their use of violence as jihad, a legitimate use of force necessary to defend one's faith against threats. Conventional wisdom in the West holds that holy war is specific to Islam in the contemporary period, although it was famously waged by Christians during the Crusades. However, the idea of holy war also emerged early in Judaism and continues to have a strong influence in political affairs. All three Abrahamic religions view struggles to defend their religion as not only legitimate but required; in the Hebrew Bible, God (Yahweh) was always on the side of those who fought the enemies of Zion (Esposito, 1998); Muslims view the success of the Prophet Muhammad's early political campaigns in a similar light. Jews waged war against the Canaanites to gain control of the land they believe God had intended for them. Zionists view the capture of land from Arabs in 1947 and 1948 as akin to these early holy wars (Armstrong, 1991:7–12).

Many Islamist groups do invoke the concept of jihad as a justification for their political projects, particularly the use of overt force or political violence. Al-Qaida is the most famous and active transnational extremist group, one that justifies attacking foreigners and civilians as responsible for the conditions that oppress Muslim peoples worldwide. While the activities of Al-Qaida represent an escalation of Islamic extremism in the scale of its tactics and the boundlessness of its targets, the movement has never enjoyed popular support within the Arab or Muslim world. Indeed, following the September 11 attacks, dozens of Muslim countries immediately expressed condolences to the citizens of the United States, and many Muslim communities organized candlelight vigils in neighborhoods and mosques in remembrance of the victims. While the extremism of groups like Al-Qaida is abhorrent in its targeting of innocents, it is crucial to remember that such fringe organizations are not the norm.

Conclusion

Religion plays a central role in Middle East politics, in part because political struggles have for centuries been understood as religious conflicts (e.g., the Crusades; colonialism's connection to Christian proselytizing; Western support for Israel; targeting of Muslims in the "war on terror") and in part because of the intimate ties of the three Abrahamic faiths to the region. This chapter has sought to outline the major religions in the Middle East and the diverse ways in which states as well as opposition movements invoke religion in their political activities and view regional and global developments through religious lenses. The great diversity of religious experiences and practices are a core feature of the region, from whether minority religious communities enjoy inclusion or repression, to the ways in which states accept or reject religious political parties, to the diverse means of invoking religious symbols and rhetoric in expressions of dissent. Religion will undoubtedly continue to be a central component of politics in the Middle East for decades to come. But as some recent trends of inclusion and tolerance illustrate, that situation need not necessarily entail violence and contention.

Note

This chapter, new to the third edition of *Understanding the Contemporary Middle East,* replaces the chapter on religion in the first edition that was co-authored by John L. Esposito and Mohammed A. Muqtedar Khan and updated for the second edition by Jillian Schwedler. The current chapter, while entirely new, draws on sections of the earlier chapter(s), particularly in the historical sections on Judaism and Christianity.

Bibliography

Armstrong, Karen. 1991. *Holy War: The Crusades and the Impact on Today's World.* New York: Doubleday.
Boulby, Marion. 1999. *The Muslim Brotherhood and the Kings of Jordan, 1945–1993.* Atlanta: Scholar's Press.
Breger, Marshall. 1996. "Religion and Politics in Jerusalem." *Journal of International Affairs* 50, no. 1:91–118.
Cavendish, Richard. 1980. *The Great Religions.* New York: Arco Press.

Clark, Janine Astrid. 2003. *Faith Networks, Charity, and the Middle Class: Islamist Services in Egypt, Jordan, and Yemen.* Bloomington: Indiana University Press.

Esposito, John L. 1998. *Islam and Politics.* 4th ed. Syracuse, N.Y.: Syracuse University Press.

———. 1999. *The Islamic Threat: Myth or Reality?* 3rd ed. New York: Oxford University Press.

Esposito, John L., Mohammed A. Muqtedar Khan, and Jillian Schwedler. 2004. "Religion and Politics in the Middle East." Pp. 363–386 in Deborah J. Gerner and Jillian Schwedler (eds.), *Understanding the Contemporary Middle East.* 2nd ed. Boulder, Colo.: Lynne Rienner.

Katz, Kimberly. 2004. *Holy Places and National Spaces: Jerusalem Under Jordanian Control.* Austin: University of Texas Press.

Mitchell, Richard P. 1969. *The Society of the Muslim Brothers.* Oxford: Oxford University Press.

Norton, Augustus Richard, and Jillian Schwedler. 1994. "Swiss Soldiers, Ta'if Clocks, and Early Elections: Toward a Happy Ending?" Pp. 45–65 in Deirdre Collins (ed.), *Peace for Lebanon? From War to Reconstruction.* Boulder, Colo.: Lynne Rienner.

Runciman, Steven. 1992. *The First Crusade.* Abridged ed. New York: Cambridge University Press.

Schwedler, Jillian. 2006. *Faith in Moderation: Islamist Parties in Jordan and Yemen.* New York: Cambridge University Press.

Shohat, Ella. 1988. "Sephardim in Israel: Zionism from the Standpoint of Its Jewish Victims." *Social Text* 19, no. 10:1–35.

Vitalis, Robert. 2007. *America's Kingdom: Mythmaking on the Saudi Oil Frontier.* Stanford, Calif.: Stanford University Press.

Voll, John (ed.). 1991. *Sudan: State and Society in Crisis.* Bloomington: Indiana University Press.

Wickham, Carrie Rosefsky. 2002. *Mobilizing Islam: Religion, Activism, and Political Change in Egypt.* New York: Columbia University Press.

13

Middle Eastern Literature

miriam cooke

In this chapter I discuss the emergence of literature in the Middle East as a new art form. European modernity hit the countries of the Middle East hard. Everything formerly accepted as normative came under question, nothing more so than literature. Traditional notions of what literature was and what function it should fulfill in the life of the individual and society changed. No longer the repository for all knowledge, *adab* (literature) branched out into the various genres of drama, short story, novel, and a radically new conception of poetry.

It is not possible to understand the role of literature in the Middle East without first glancing at its history and, above all, its evolution during the first half of the twentieth century. Although Middle Eastern literatures have become privileged sites for recording and engaging with sociopolitical tensions and conflicts, this was not always the case. In the medieval and early modern periods, Middle Eastern literatures had been the preserve of the elite, providing them with literary frames in which they might elaborate an already familiar tradition and demonstrate formal skills and erudition. Popular literature such as *A Thousand and One Nights* also relied on the already known. The imagination and social commentary were generally downplayed in the Middle Eastern context.

▨ European Colonialism and Its Discontents

The arrival in the late eighteenth and nineteenth centuries of the French and British colonial expeditions, with their technological, cultural, and intellectual institutions, forced a new look at society and culture. Contact with

European modernity cast Islamic cultures in a poor contrastive light. Egyptians in particular, because they were the first to experience French colonialism, became concerned to learn about Western culture and science.

Under such Ottoman governors as Muhammad Ali Pasha and his son Ibrahim Pasha, groups of male scholars traveled to Western Europe, and particularly to France, to study scientific texts and to translate them into Arabic. Because of the enormity of the task, these scientific missions might stay in Europe for months on end. When they were not squirreled away in the libraries or archives, they were in the theaters watching plays by French playwrights like Jean-Baptiste Poquelin (aka Molière) or in their rooms reading short stories in French by such writers as Guy de Maupassant or the Russian Anton Chekhov in French translation. The genre that was the newest and the most intriguing was the novel, and these men returned with translations of European masterpieces by Honoré de Balzac, Gustave Flaubert, Leo Tolstoy, and Ivan Turgenev, to mention only a few.

Some of these intellectuals believed that the writing and function of literature in the Middle East had to change to accommodate the new realities in their lives. They knew, however, that those who were unfamiliar with the new genres of short story, novel, play, and modern poetry might resist their introduction. The apparent focus of European fiction writers on entertainment at the expense of traditional education, or on sociopolitical critique rather than literariness, was greeted by some with the skepticism reserved for the introduction of anything new anywhere. Like the reactionary defenders of the Western canon, who in the 1980s announced the end of civilization as we know it if subaltern, marginalized literatures were to replace some of the time-tested writings of dead white Western men, the conservative elites of the region warned of civilizational decline, even extinction. Some feared that the great classical literatures of the Arabs, Persians, and Turks might not survive the invasion into literature of the trivia of the modern world. Literary practitioners would surely lose their storehouse of classical knowledge if they did not continually tap into it and thus renew it. They would lose their verbal agility if they turned from the eloquent description of great events in history to the banality of the world around them. Others saw in the dialogue between their own cultural traditions and those of the Europeans the possibility of reimagining national identity within a common modernity.

Whether they were closed or open to the outside world, Middle Eastern intellectuals considered the question of language to be vital in the process of modernization. Some interrogated the boundary between the high-culture languages and the vernaculars, while others considered the implications of importing foreign words. In Iran, historian Mohamad Tavakoli-Targhi explains, the key was to "disassociate from the Islamic past and to project a 'pure' national origin." Arabic words that had been part of the language for half a millennium were purged, and "authentic" Persian terms were forged, and neologisms and lexicography were constituted as endeavors for "national reawakening." . . . The invention of an idealized past was contemporaneous with the restyling of language, which was achieved in a dialogic relationship with Iran's Arab-, European-, and (the often ignored) Indian-Other. . . . The Persian language was reconstituted as the essential component of Iranian national identity. (Tavakoli-Targhi, 1990:77, 86)

Language reform "was not an aftereffect of the constitutional revolutions in Iran and the Ottoman Empire but a prelude to them. Purists constituted language as the essential component of the national identity" (Tavakoli-Targhi, 1990:91). History could not be reconceived without a radical transformation of the language and its grammar.

In the case of Turkish and Arabic, the linguistic situation was more extreme because of the distance between the written and the spoken languages. Indeed, a kind of bilingualism had emerged in both cases. The written language of the Turks was so different from the spoken that it was even named differently: it was called Ottoman Turkish. Written in the Arabic script and filled with Persian and Arabic vocabulary—as much as 75 percent—this Ottoman Turkish had to be learned as an entirely distinct language with its own rules of grammar (Halman, 1982:36). Paradoxically, the poetry of the mystic Yunus Emre (d. ca. 1321), written before the Turks' importation of a foreign lexicon (partly as a result of their embracing Islam), is more accessible to Turks schooled in the post-Atatürk era than the literature they learned from their grandparents. Mustafa Kemal Atatürk's Westernization campaign, which attempted to erase Islamic elements in the language, put an end to the "bilingual" situation that had pertained in Turkey for centuries.

There has been no comparable revolution in the Arab world, and so the split between the classical and colloquial Arabic languages persists until today. The codification of the spoken language is still tentative because the Arabic of the Quran retains its place of honor as the literary medium of expression. Conservative Arab intellectuals feared that the use of colloquial expressions in literature, particularly since there was no consensus over the codification of the colloquial, might herald the demise of the scriptural language; it might put an end to a pan-Arab literature, because these vulgar languages would create a tower of Babel in which multiple, mutually incomprehensible local literatures would vie for a small spot on the grand stage of what had once been a unified literary tradition. The answer has been to create a modern standard Arabic used by the media and understood from the Atlantic Ocean to the Arabian Gulf.

Anxieties about language were compounded by the forcible introduction of colonial languages. Indeed, French had become the lingua franca among Middle Eastern intellectuals, even in countries like Turkey that had not experienced the European *mission civilisatrice* (civilizing mission). The

positive aspect of linguistic colonialism was the opening up of European literature to the Middle Eastern reader. French, English, and Russian writers of
the day, including Gustave Flaubert and Guy de Maupassant, Charles Dick-
ens and Percy Bysshe Shelley, as well as Anton Pavlovich Chekhov, Ivan
Sergeyevich Turgenev, and Leo Tolstoy in French translation, all provided
models of how to represent current crises and concerns. Translations of nineteenth-century European literature into the languages of the Middle East
were followed by literary experimentation. The Syrian-Lebanese Jurji Zaydan (1861–1914), for instance, wrote a series of historical novels and even a
short autobiographical piece. Despite the general disapproval of writing
one's own life, Zaydan published the story of his education during a time of
major upheaval, having recognized in his experiences those of others.

■ Cultural Ferment at the
Turn of the Twentieth Century

The literary hub of the Arab Middle East in the early twentieth-century was
Egypt. Intellectuals censored at home moved to Cairo. Literary salons convened men and sometimes even women to discuss the latest developments in
politics and literature. At a time when most middle- and upper-class women
were confined to their homes, these gatherings of intellectuals were almost
the only places where women could appear with men. Literary schools in
Egypt, such as the Diwan School, the New School, and the Apollo School
(none of which included women), encouraged the production of new kinds
of writing that were then often published in their own journals and newspapers. These debates and their publication produced a new space, that of the
public sphere. Discussions about national identity and the new roles women
and men were expected to play in the future nation became matters concerning everyone and were no longer restricted to a small community of scholars, often religious scholars. In the process, new conceptions of literary criticism appeared.

The new critics' insistence on the centrality of the imagination in works
of art and the need for the work to interact with and hopefully to change society influenced a new generation of critics and writers. The notion that criticism should be neither descriptive nor evaluative but rather investigative led
to some radical critical writing. Taha Husayn (1889–1973), the Egyptian author of dozens of books, including novels, works of philosophy, and his own
autobiography, titled *The Days* (1929), led the charge. In 1926 he published
On Pre-Islamic Poetry, which calls into question the dating of some of this
poetry. The book provoked a scandal because this poetry said to have been
composed before the time of the prophet Muhammad was considered to be
the paragon of literary expression, and with the Quran, it was cherished as

the perfect classical Arabic language that the prophet spoke. To cast doubt on its dating was to unsettle other certainties connected to the founding moment of Islam. New literary critical tools were opening up new ways of approaching old texts, and above all they were revolutionizing literary production.

Simultaneous with this literary activity in Egypt, two revolutions broke out in Turkey and Iran. Young Turks and Iranians brought up on Enlightenment ideals rebelled against autocratic, self-indulgent rule by the last rulers of the Ottoman and the Qajar Empires. Between 1919 and 1922, Mustafa Kemal (1881–1938, known as Atatürk after 1933), waged his war of independence against the British, French, Italians, and Greeks. The expulsion of these foreigners was followed by a series of revolutions that continued beyond the 1923 founding of the Turkish republic. Upon assuming national leadership, Atatürk abolished the Ottoman caliphate in 1924 and then implemented his secularization program. He introduced a new Europeanized dress code and declared illegal the wearing of Islamic dress, such as the veil. Most traumatic for traditional litterateurs, in 1929 he replaced the Arabic-based Ottoman script with the Latin alphabet. Yakup Kadri Karaosmanoglu (1889–1974) is the writer who best encapsulates the mood of the times, which Talat Halman describes as being marked by "the disintegration of Ottoman society, ferocious political enmities, and the immoral lives of religious sects, as well as the conflicts between urban intellectuals and poverty-stricken peasants" (1982:29). Karaosmanoglu presented the challenges facing cultural revolutionaries in his book *The Outsider.* It tells the paradigmatic story of an alienated bureaucrat in a rural outpost where the farmers remain indifferent to the cultural and nationalist revolution.

In 1905, Iran was rocked by its constitutional revolution. Nationalists confronted the British and the local feudal landlords, demanded a constitution that would vouchsafe them democracy and justice, and eventually agreed on a compromise. The period was rich with new kinds of writing, most of it referred to as *pishru* (progressive). These liberal and often socialist writings depict the turmoil of the period and react against the social irrelevance of the Qajar writers. After his coup in 1921, Mohammad Reza Shah became absolute monarch of Iran. He introduced strict censorship and centralized control, but he also concerned himself with the position of women. In 1936, perhaps in response to Atatürk's recent prohibition on the wearing of the veil, the shah enforced unveiling. While some see this measure as helpful to women, others recognize in it yet another violence done to women in the name of progress. To force a woman to unveil who is not ready to reveal her face is tantamount to asking her to strip publicly. Many writers have dealt with the topic.

Such legislation against veiling should be seen against the background of late-nineteenth-century debates about feminism that were going on throughout the Middle East and beyond. Claims on behalf of women's education were entering the public sphere. Research by feminist scholars both in the Middle East and elsewhere has revealed that it was women themselves who were the first to raise the issue of women's absence in decisionmaking positions at the national or local levels. Yet it was not until the men took up the "woman question" that it became a matter for common concern.

In 1899, the Egyptian reformer Qasim Amin (1865–1908) had published his controversial book *The Liberation of Women,* in which he called for the education of women, as the mothers of the next generation, as well as for their unveiling and greater participation in the life of the nation. Along with other modernist reformers of the period who emphasized companionate marriage and nuclear families in a world where all individuals had the right to freedom and equality, Amin was drawing attention to the fact that when half a people are absent from the activities of the other half, then the whole suffers. This emphasis on women as the gauge of a society's progress seems to reflect James Mill's reference in 1817 to India's barbarity being demonstrated by the fact that "women were in a state of abject slavery." As employee of the East India Company, Mill clearly felt himself authorized to make such pronouncements. The Western, colonial origin of these ideas was not lost on the Middle Eastern intelligentsia.

Amin's treatise was influential not only in his native Egypt but also throughout the Middle East. In 1900, *The Liberation of Women* was partially translated into Persian. Its publication in Iran did not launch the kind of debate about the rights and roles of women that it had in Egypt because it fell on fallow ground (Najmabadi, 1998:100–104). In 1921, Mohammed Ali Jamalzadeh (b. 1892) brought out his first collection of stories, titled *Once upon a Time.* The collection is as famous for its introduction, which explains the new function of literature as a mirror for the times, as it is for its satirical descriptions of Shi'i scholars and its sympathetic portrayals of the lives of ordinary women and men (Daragahi, 1984:104–123). The following year, Morteza Moshfeq Kazemi published his two-volume work *Horrible Teheran,* which takes up the cause of women by describing the numerous abuses they routinely suffer.

Atatürk may not have been directly influenced by the Middle Eastern debates surrounding the "woman question," but his fascination with the West, where feminists were beginning to attract attention, had predisposed him to advocate women's rights. After coming to power, he gave them the vote and placed some women in parliament. One of the women whom he supported was Halide Edip Adivar (1884–1964), an ardent revolutionary who was pictured during the occupation of Istanbul preceding the war of independence lecturing crowds of men even while veiled. Journalist, feminist activist, literary critic, and novelist, her 1926 autobiography describes her adventures with the nationalists, which included the experience of cross-dressing so as to be able to fight in the army with the Young Turks. Her best known work is *The Clown and His Daughter,* which appeared first in English in 1935 and a year later in Turkish. Novels during this early Republican period became a tool in the fashioning of the new nation-state.

During this same period, the European Zionist movement was becoming active and some Jews emigrated from Europe to settle the land of Palestine. Zionism at that time was primarily a socialist ideology owing more to Russian-inspired communism than to Judaism. As such it looked much like the *missions civilisatrices* that the French and the British had been dispatching to the Middle East since the eighteenth century. These alarming developments in the region gave rise to fledgling Islam-inspired reform movements. Their members warned against unthinking mimicry of the West and urged the virtues and relevance of Islam as nations strove to become part of the modern world.

▧ The Short Story as Literary Pioneer

First the short story and later the novel provided frames within which intellectuals could address the problems of their age. The short story, with its Middle Eastern precedents in folk literature such as *A Thousand and One Nights,* developed most rapidly as a local genre. It was well suited to the needs of writers who had urgent sociopolitical messages they wanted to convey in a succinct and persuasive manner. Quickly written and published often in literary magazines and newspapers, the short story became an important vehicle for socially engaged intellectuals to communicate with people beyond their immediate circle of friends and colleagues.

Egyptian Stories

The Arabic short story first took hold in Egypt, and therefore its history there can be considered to be exemplary. Lawyers like Yahya Haqqi (1905–1991) and Tawfiq al-Hakim (1898–1987), who is better known for his drama, turned some of their cases into stories that became part of a general debate about modernization. Haqqi's "The First Lesson," published in 1926, is a powerful example of naturalist criticism of the new that was often symbolized by the train. Preparing for his first day in school, the son of the station master of a remote milk-train stop watches the Nubian station guard, a deeply spiritual man and his only friend, slip off the platform and roll under the wheels of the train. The tragedy does not disrupt the day's program. The son goes to school, sits at his new desk, and tries to fulfill the teacher's first assignment to the pupils: write an essay on the advantages of the train.

Twenty-seven years later, Haqqi returned to the theme of the destructiveness of the railway in his indictment of the 1952 Free Officers' Revolution. *Good Morning!* is a novel, the only one Haqqi wrote, that contrasts the fullness of the lives of a few villagers before the introduction of the train into their lives with the pain and the suffering they experience after the station is built in their village.

Engineers and doctors also turned their professional experiences into the stuff of fiction. Whether they felt real sympathy or not is less crucial than the fact that they made the lives of the urban and rural poor available and sometimes even important for their mostly middle-class readers. Engineer Mahmud Tahir Lashin (1894–1954) wrote several stories about his professional visits to government offices, popular cafes, and also the countryside. His 1929 story "Talk of the Village," which has been described as marking the maturation of the Arabic short story (Hafez, 1992:274), confronts an urban intellectual with the reality of the romanticized village. This is no utopia but rather a place of primitive passions and traditions.

Mahmud Taymur (1894–1973), from an upper-class family of litterateurs, was drawn to the simplicity of the life of the poor but also to the injustices to which they were exposed. To write about them convincingly, he had to use their language. He is considered to be one of the pioneers in the literary usage of the colloquial. He told stories about women's abuse at the hands of unscrupulous men. He described young girls condemned to marry men older than their fathers and women paying food bills with their bodies so as to keep their families alive. The most prolific and best known of these early short story writers, Taymur kept his readers informed about the terrible lives women were leading and how the tragedy of such lives was not restricted to the individual but had implications for society as a whole.

The most diverse and complex of early Arabic short story writers was Yusuf Idris (1927–1991). He was a medical doctor who had spent years practicing medicine before he turned to story writing, and he brought his experience in the clinic to his creative work. His first collection of short stories, *The Cheapest Nights* (1954), deals not only with the customs and traditions but also with the diseases of the *fellahin* (peasants). The title story is almost a manifesto on behalf of family planning. A villager comes home one night after searching in vain for affordable entertainment, and he produces another mouth to feed! In "The Dregs of the City," Idris turns to the city to present a middle-class man preying on his servant, her theft of his watch, his humiliating recovery of the watch, and her consequent ejection to walk the streets as a prostitute. The storyline is not new; what is different and moving is the narration of inevitable destruction. In his many other collections of stories, as in his novels and plays, Idris examines the lives of his compatriots, dissecting those elements that lead people to destroy each other.

Iranian Stories

At the end of the nineteenth century, encyclopedist Ali Akbar Dehkhoda introduced the short story to Iranian readers with the publication of some satirical articles. However, it was Jamalzadeh who turned this journalistic precedent into a local literary genre with his 1921 introduction to *Once upon a Time,* described as "a manifesto for modernist Persian prose writing" (Moayyad, 1991:31). The stories in the collection provided Iranian intellectuals with a model of how to integrate this new genre into the repertoire of a transformed national literature.

The first Iranian to succeed in writing a fully developed short story in an accessible language was Sadeq Hedayat (1903–1951). Born into the Iranian nobility, he was educated in Paris, where he was attracted to surrealism. His early work described Iran's great past, whereas his later writings, which were influenced by European writers and particularly by Franz Kafka, were as dark and despairing as his life. He committed suicide in 1951. Hedayat wrote novels, critical essays, and plays, but above all short stories that portrayed with sympathy the life of the destitute in Iran's cities. He, too, used colloquial expressions, but his goal was more political than artistic: literature needed to participate in the fight against tradition and particularly religious customs as the nation strove to become part of the modern world. During the 1930s and 1940s, he published three collections, including *The Stray Dog* (1942). Through the eyes of a dog, Hedayat told a story of rejection and alienation. The use of an animal as a protagonist goes back to a strong tradition of animal fables.

Sadiq Chubak (1916–1998), a friend of Hedayat who is best known for his novels, and social critic Jalal Al-e Ahmad (1923–1969) elaborated what Hedayat began. It was Chubak who first experimented artistically with the use of the colloquial in formal writing. In *The Puppet Show* (1945), he strove to render the rhythm of the spoken language and not merely to include dissonant vernacular vocabulary for political effect. Like others, he was committed to describing and hoping to change the situation of women.

The son of a Muslim Shi'i cleric, Al-e Ahmad focused on political oppression and, in the early stages of his writing career, on religious hypocrisy. The title story of his first collection, *Exchange of Visits* (1946), cynically depicts a pilgrimage to a saint's tomb in Iraq. He has, however, been most closely associated with the notion of "Westoxification," the title of a book he wrote in 1962, which was used as a slogan against the shah in the 1960s. For Al-e Ahmad, as for many of his contemporaries, the greatest danger was the cultural, economic, and political subordination of countries like Iran to the West. As Tavakoli-Targhi says in an interview, Al-e Ahmad "envisaged an alternative modernity informed by Islam. This work became important for

Ayatollah Khomeini and other Iranian religious scholars who viewed Islam as the foundation of Iranian cultural independence" (1999). This book may be seen as an early warning of the growing conservatism and anti-West sentiments that led to the Islamic revolution of 1978.

During the 1960s, many new short fiction writers appeared, most notably Gholam Hosayn Saedi (1935–1985). Trained as a psychiatrist and practicing in Tehran, he applied his clinical experience to his thirty volumes of stories, plays, essays, and ethnographies. Like Al-e Ahmad, he was severe in his criticism of the Westernization of Iranian society. Yet once the Islamic government was in power, he did not hesitate to criticize it in drama. His 1984 play *Othello in the Wonderland* was performed in Paris, where Saedi ran less immediate risk for his mocking portrayal of the system's obsession with covering women's bodies.

The Islamic revolution produced a new generation of writers, many of whom are women. Critics like Heshmat Moayyad praise these writers, whether they called for the overthrow of the monarchy or not, for their brave stand against a corruption that had seemed endemic and unassailable for centuries. However, for some the fight became too difficult during the 1980s, and many chose exile.

Turkey's Master Storyteller

One of the earliest Turkish writers of short stories was Sait Faik Aziz Abasiyanik (1906–1954). Like his counterparts in the rest of the Middle East, Abasiyanik was interested in daily life both within and outside the cities. The most prolific and admired short story writer in Turkey, as well as in Iran, where many of his works were translated into Persian, was Aziz Nesin (1915–1995), who has been called the twentieth-century Nasreddin Hoca, a witty, eloquent folk hero. Nesin wrote dozens of books, including *Elephant Hamdi* and *Madmen on the Loose*. In "House on the Border," a Kafkaesque story about a tenant, the six thieves who prey on him, and their final forced collaboration to fight injustice, he takes on the repressive government apparatus. Nesin follows the bumbling attempts of an alienated hero to find protection and justice from institutions that were established to protect the people but then refuse accountability.

Nesin's involvement in the translation and publication of the controversial novel *The Satanic Verses* by Salman Rushdie (b. 1947) almost cost him his life. He is one of the few Middle Eastern writers who made a living from his writings; most others have had to rely on income from other professions such as journalism to allow them to write fiction. After his death, his family established the Nesin Foundation, which supports literary activity as well as social projects.

Women's Stories

Several women writers chose the short story as their frame for literary expression. In 1929, Egyptian Suhayr Qalamawi published a collection of short stories titled *Grandmother's Tales*. The figure of the "grandmother" became popular as women sought models of feminine strength and stability in a patriarchal past. The piety of the grandmother was ambivalently presented: it could be a sign of blind faith and superstition or a trace of a time when there was safety and security from outside forces threatening one's belief system. Many women have followed in Qalamawi's steps, claiming that the short story is perfectly suited to a life in which domestic preoccupations prevent concentration on a protracted plot.

Three Syrian women are exemplary. Ulfa Idilbi (b. 1917) did not start publishing until the early 1950s, but she, too, dwelt on the problems women confront in a conservative society poised on the edge of change. Ghada al-Samman (b. 1940) wrote a collection of stories under the title *Your Eyes Are My Destiny* (1961), in which she explored the possibilities for women in a male-dominated world. Colette Khoury (b. 1937), more romantic but no less revolutionary, published *Days with Him* (1959), in which the heroine rebels against men's automatic reduction of women to mothers and hostesses and insists on her dignity and worth as an individual.

One of the most famous—and notorious—short stories of the Arab world is "Spaceship of Tenderness to the Moon" (1964) by Lebanese writer Layla Baalbaki (b. 1936). The story of an early morning moment in the life of a couple, it reveals their erotic love for each other and their conflict over the desire for a baby. A trial was held to assess whether or not the story was pornographic. Baalbaki was finally acquitted, but the controversy has entered the history of twentieth-century Middle Eastern literature.

In most of these women's writings, the heroine is defeated by the struggle against patriarchy. Whether she gives in to a man or abandons him, the final decision brings no satisfaction. A single woman cannot successfully rebel when the society is not yet ready to incorporate her into its fabric.

In 1947, with the appearance of *Fire Quenched,* Simin Daneshvar (b. 1921) became the first woman in Iran to publish a collection of short stories. Farzaneh Milani has praised her for creating women who are not simply victims of an overbearing patriarchy, but rather active human beings struggling to give meaning to their lives. In the later work of women like Shahrnush Parsipur (b. 1946) and Goli Taraqqi (b. 1939), Milani recognizes Daneshvar's focus on the disappointments inherent in mostly middle-class relationships in transitional societies, where individualism is in tension with traditional values (Milani, 1992:199).

Women have not only written about domesticity, they have also written about wars. Emily Nasrallah (b. 1938) wrote prolifically on the devastating effects of the Lebanese civil war, particularly as it affected women's lives. Her three collections of war stories capture moments of horror and loss that other genres could not quite encompass. In Iraq during the war with Iran from 1980 to 1988, Aliya Talib and Daisy al-Amir published their daring criticisms of an autocratic regime in the succinctness of quirky tales.

■ Francophone Novels in North Africa

In the countries of North Africa that the French colonized in the nineteenth century (Algeria in 1830 and Tunisia in 1881), the first novelistic attempts appeared in French at the beginning of the twentieth century. In Tunisia, Jewish intellectuals like Jacques Victor Levi first used the novel to chronicle their daily lives. They described a multicultural society in which Arabs, Berbers, Italians, Maltese, Africans, Muslims, and Jews had lived together easily until the arrival of the colonizers. It was then that racial and religious differences began to matter. Novelists evoked the two worlds of the medina (old Arab city) and the *ville nouvelle* (new city) that accommodated the French and the constant border crossings between them. The hammam (Turkish bath) became the emblematic site of local authenticity and segregation.

In 1953, three years before Tunisia was to gain its independence, Albert Memmi (b. 1920) published his semiautobiographical novel. Written two years before *The Colonizer and the Colonized,* his classical study of colonial relations, *Pillar of Salt,* provides a case study of the dehumanizing effects of colonial desire both on the subject as well as on the object of domination. The colonizer wants the colonized to forget who he is and to want to become like him. He fosters that desire until it nears fulfillment and then he reveals the hope to have been always empty. Benillouche, the intelligent son of a working-class family granted permission to study at a lycèe, swings between his multiple and overlapping identities, at once loving and hating who he is but also the person he is becoming. This is more than self-criticism; it is refusal of self. The hero's highly conflicted relations with his father anticipate the novels of the Moroccans Driss Chraïbi (b. 1926) and Tahar Benjelloun (b. 1944) in the 1960s and 1970s, which dwell on the despotic rule of the father, transparent symbol for the patriarchal past, and the need to end it.

During the 1980s, Benjelloun wrote the two-volume novel *Sand Child* and *Sacred Night* that won him the Prix Goncourt, the prestigious French literary prize that until then had been awarded almost exclusively to French writers from France. The novel tells the story of a father's refusal to accept the fact that his eighth child is yet another girl. He must have a son, will have a son. So he turns infant Fatima into Ahmed and produces a freak. This postmodern novel about gender construction in an Islamic patriarchy caused a scandal in Morocco. Benjelloun was accused of pandering to French voyeuristic desire for the exotic and the perverted. Some dismissed the Prix Goncourt as Benjelloun's reward for cultural betrayal.

In Algeria and Egypt, women were the pioneers of the francophone novel.[1] In the 1940s, Assia Débèche wrote about middle-class women's experiences of biculturalism: they were educated to expect opportunities for choice in love and life, but their realities often turned out to be quite different. Francophone Lebanese-Egyptian Andrée Chedid (b. 1921) explored the same problem two years after the success of the Free Officers' Revolution. Her book *From Sleep Unbound* (1954) was praised, if not warmly, for its bleak depiction of the fate of a woman in a rural Coptic setting where any attempt, however slight, to improve a black destiny was greeted with shock and redoubled rejection. In the story, Samya's murder of her foul husband is as much activism as such a woman in such a context could be expected to exercise.

The Arabic Novel

The novel in Arabic developed a little later than the francophone novel. It was too long, too epic a form to suit the purposes of the early arabophone social and cultural reformers. More than the short story, the novel seemed an unfamiliar genre, developed as it had been for the needs and interests of the European bourgeoisie of the eighteenth and nineteenth centuries. Above all, publication was an issue. The new Arabic printing presses were given over primarily to newspapers and journals, which became the most effective outlets for works of fiction. Even today some writers continue to serialize their novels and autobiographies in these publications, which often retain the services of creative writers as though they were journalists.[2] This form of publication lends itself to the cliffhanger style familiar to European readers of nineteenth-century sociorealist fiction.

In Egypt, 1988 Nobel laureate Naguib Mahfouz (1911–2006) first brought this longer genre to maturity. After publishing a few short stories in the 1930s, he turned to the longer literary format. His novels from the 1940s onward provide a window on the evolving sociopolitical situation of Egypt and Egyptians in the world system.

In the 1940s, Mahfouz published two novels that revolve around events supposed to have happened during the times of the Pharaohs, focusing on the expulsion of invaders by ancient Egyptians. The allegorical nature of these works is transparent. This was a period of self-searching in Egypt, when local failure to act effectively in an international context was compensated for by

The late Egyptian Nobel laureate Naguib Mahfouz is best known for the sociorealist style of his novels, many of which have been translated into English.

recourse to past greatness. This turn to a past antedating the arrival of the Peninsula Arabs became a reflex in other Middle Eastern countries whose intellectuals were struggling with a crisis of identity. In Turkey, for example, just after Atatürk's death in 1938, as his successor was trying to consolidate his power in an atmosphere of uncertainty and growing repression, novelist Kemal Tahir (1910–1973) wrote *Mother State,* about the Ottoman Empire in the thirteenth and fourteenth centuries, when it was at the height of its power and glory.

Along with Turkish short-story writer Sabhattin Ali (1907–1948) and Turkish novelist Orhan Kemal (1914–1970), Mahfouz pioneered sociorealism. *Midaq Alley* (1947), the first of Mahfouz's novels to be translated into English, reflects the concerns of other Middle Eastern writers who turned city neighborhoods into rich microcosms of their countries. The setting here is World War II Cairo, and British global dominion is quickly fading. This intricate novel was followed by Mahfouz's trilogy *Palace Walk, Palace of Desire,* and *Sugar Street* (1956–1957), which many claim won him the Nobel Prize. Although he wrote the trilogy during the Free Officers' Revolution in 1952, he did not publish it until several years later. The saga of the 'Abd al-Jawads, an upper-middle-class family, parallels the key events of the first half of the twentieth century. The lives of three generations mirror the crises through which Egyptians were passing from World War I through independence. But once again history provides a disguise for current concerns. Mahfouz draws the reader into the inner sanctum of a traditional home, where women and men interact in a way invisible to the outsider. The reader is privileged to share the first moment of disobedience by a usually submissive wife. There is a penalty to be paid, but the die has been cast. Her children, who witnessed their mother's unwonted daring, become politically engaged. Their different avenues of activism, Muslim Brother as opposed to Communist, often produce internal clashes, but kinship ties do finally survive the stresses.

In 1959, Mahfouz published *Children of Gebelawi,* a novel that tells the story of the Abrahamic faiths and their adherents through the lives of individual members of the Gebelawi family. This book has been banned in several Muslim countries for its negative portrayal of the Prophet of Islam. But Muhammad is not the only one subjected to moral scrutiny; all the great prophets of monotheism, culminating with Arafa, the prophet of science, spiritual skepticism, and alienation, are presented as far from perfect. It was this book that earned Mahfouz the 1994 knife attack by a zealous Muslim fundamentalist. Mahfouz pursued this existentialist theme throughout the 1960s, depicting hopeless characters in search of some little meaning to give to their lives.

The Six-Day War of 1967 produced an intellectual crisis in the Arab world to which Mahfouz reacted very strongly in terms of both content and form. Many readers and critics regretted the loss of the linear narrative line of his first novels, as his writing of the 1970s fragmented into the staccato of alarm and surreal confusion. In the 1980s, Mahfouz changed his style and themes again. This time he turned to the classics and wrote modern versions. He produced his own take on *A Thousand and One Nights* and also a travel narrative written in response to the famous travelogue of fourteenth-century Moroccan traveler Ibn Battutah, which Mahfouz titled *The Journey of Ibn Fattouma* (1983) in recognition of the influence.

The novel has provided many writers with the frame appropriate to contain nostalgic reflections on a world that has passed. *Fragments of Memory,* by Syrian writer Hanna Mina (b. 1924), tells the tale of a village before the onslaught of foreign values. This village is like the one Muna abandons in *September Birds* (1962), by Lebanese writer Emily Nasrallah. Like many Middle Eastern heroes, Muna is faced with the challenge of modernity, namely that the village cannot provide a sustainable future. After Muna leaves her home for Beirut, she no longer knows who she is.

Unlike most Arab novelists who place their stories in the city or in the village, Saudi exile Abd al-Rahman Munif (1933–2004) situated his novels in the desert. His magnum opus is a five-volume novel titled *Cities of Salt,* which he published throughout the 1980s. Having begun his career as a petroleum economist, he was intimately familiar with the impact of oil on the economies and lives of people living in oil-rich states. The quintet traces the transformation in the environment as well as in the consciousness of the local, mostly bedouin inhabitants after the discovery of black gold. The reader witnesses the growing brutalization of the bedouin as they recognize that in this brave new world of competition and profit, there is more to be gained by individual enterprise than in tribal solidarity. This book earned its author the displeasure of his Saudi government, which deprived him of citizenship.

■ The Iranian Novel

The Iranian novel, of which the three-volume collection *Travel Diary of Ebrahim Beg* (1890s) is said to be the first, appeared before the Arabic novel. Iranian writers, more than the Arabs, tended to work in both short story and novel genres. This was true for Hedayat, Chubak, Al-e Ahmad, and Daneshvar.

One of the best-known Iranian novels is Hedayat's *Blind Owl,* which was written by 1930 but not published until 1937 in India and until 1941 in Iran, after Reza Shah abdicated and censorship was lifted. It is a book of highly introspective notes that Hedayat wrote "for my shadow." He describes a husband tortured by his relations with a wife who gives herself easily to her many lovers but not at all to him. He becomes an opium addict, a misfit, a murderer, and a madman. The despair in this novel foreshadowed Hedayat's suicide in 1951.

Chubak wrote several novels that have been praised for their keen attention to detail. In 1963 he published his first novel, *Tongsir,* to great acclaim. It tells the story of an exploited man who takes revenge on those who try to defraud him. At about the same time, both Al-e Ahmad and his wife, Daneshvar, were actively and publicly engaged in the literary scene, where left-wing intellectuals struggled to resist the shah's attempts to organize and co-opt cultural, but particularly literary, production. Al-e Ahmad's novel *The School Principal* (1958), written five years after the end of the Mosaddeq regime, criticizes the Iranian system of education in place at the time. Written at a time when political commitment was more important than art, its publication was a politico-literary event. As had been the case with the short story, Daneshvar was the first woman in Iran to publish a novel. *A Persian Requiem* (1969) takes place in British-occupied Shiraz toward the end of World War II. Neighbors and kin are at each other's throats, tribal leaders have revolted against the government, and Zari is at home trying to maintain order. She is contrasted to a woman who writes, despite the prohibition on women's literary voices, and who struggles to hold on to her autonomy but is consequently committed to a psychiatric hospital. As can be read in women's writings everywhere, this madness is not a clinical disorder but rather represents a woman's rebellion and society's disciplining of such transgressions. The novel was a bestseller and was translated into several languages (Milani, 1992:59–61, 183).

▧ The Turkish Novel

In 1922 Yakup Kadri Karaosmanolu published *Nur Baba* (*Sufi Sheikh of Light,* 1922). Advocating a Turkist idealism, the novel ridicules Sufi brotherhoods. Erdag Goknar (forthcoming) explains that

> within a few years of its publication, the Kemalist government would outlaw all dervish lodges, forcing sufism in the Turkish context underground. The novel is significant in that it anticipates some of the transformations of the Turkist cultural revolution (1922–1938), and it targets Islam as being inimical to modernization. The politicization of Islamic symbols and everyday ritual practice marks this period of literary production. In the novel, the main character Nur Baba is portrayed as a charlatan interested in his own pleasures. The mostly wealthy women who come to him end up losing their wealth and themselves to his power. . . . The novel implies that such characters will persist in exploiting members of society unless they are stopped. In short, the novel argues for the drastic measures witnessed in the Republican cultural revolution. Here, as with previous novels, women, their freedom and contribution to social life, are the gauges of modernity. (15–16)

Almost three decades later, Ahmet Hamdi Tanıpnar examined the transition between Ottoman and Turkist states (1908–1938) in *A Mind at Peace* (1949). Goknar (forthcoming) writes,

> Rather than providing an indictment of traditional Islamic practices as many Turkist writers do, Tanıpnar bears witness to the loss of lifestyles and articulates a web of narrative memory threatened with oblivion through cultural revolution (locally) and war (externally). Both [*Nur Baba* and *A Mind at Peace*] bookend this period of reform and social engineering; the former through ideological zeal and the later by dramatizing the great socio-political and psychological burden of those who have experienced a loss of empire and a marginalization of Istanbul cosmopolitanism. (16)

Two novelists in Turkey have earned international acclaim: Yashar Kemal (b. 1922) and Orhan Pamuk (b. 1948). Kemal pioneered the "village novel." Best known is his quartet titled *Memed, My Hawk,* translated into almost thirty languages, it revolves around the ultimately unsuccessful resistance of peasants against their landlords. Halman has described his work as "one of the truly stirring achievements in the history of Turkish literature" (1982:30).

Nobel laureate Orhan Pamuk's first work was a family saga titled *Jevdet Bey and His Sons* (1979), and much like Mahfouz's trilogy, it follows the fortunes of three generations. His 1985 *The White Castle*

> criticized authoritarian nationalism while reintroducing the Ottomans to a sophisticated, literary readership. . . . The Ottoman theme in his work was

picked up again with *My Name is Red* (1998), a complex and fragmented
work that redefined the flat, two-dimensionality of the Ottoman miniature
painting as a living, vital, aesthetic model pertinent to the present-day. . . .
The novel furthermore exhibits visual expressions of sixteenth century Ottoman history, autobiographical self-reflexivity, fragmented points of
view, the use of a miniaturist's aesthetic as a model of form, scholarly and
philosophical treatises, intertextual use of "Eastern" forms of the Koranic
parable, mystic romance, and fable, the revelation of the plot through
detective-work, the focus on the everyday, and frequent allegorical references to self and nation. (Goknar, forthcoming:28)

Pamuk's *Black Book* (1990) is another murder mystery, this one about
a lawyer in Istanbul whose wife and journalist brother-in-law disappear one
day. Jealous of the journalist's acclaim and writing skill, the narrator moves
into his abandoned apartment, wears his clothes, reads his personal writings, answers his telephone, converses with eager fans, imitates his style,
and eventually publishes articles in his name. His obsession costs him his
life. Critics, first in Turkey and later abroad after the book was translated
into several languages, were absolutely divided in their reactions.

Snow (2002) revolves around the hijab controversy that has pitted secular nationalists against Islamists during the past decade. The novel explores
the implications of the prohibition for Turkish girls to cover, their brave insistence on its moral and religious necessity, and their consequent suicides in
remote Kars. About Pamuk's oeuvre as a whole, Goknar writes that it "questions the very notion of a national identity based on a single ethnic, religious
or cultural characteristic. Culture and politics are implicitly conjoined in his
work. His novels reveal a narrative process that reflects transformation and
change in Turkish identity" (Goknar, forthcoming:35).

■ The Israeli Novel

Unlike all other Middle Eastern literatures, which draw on deep historical
pasts, Israeli literature is just sixty years old. The first Israeli novel, Moshe
Shamir's (1921–2004) story *Beneath the Sun,* appeared two years after the
establishment of the state in 1948. This highly political work draws the profile of the new Israeli, the *sabra,* a term used to refer to those who are born
on the land of Israel. The *sabra*s are entirely enmeshed in the new nation's
history and environment but can fall prey to unfriendly neighbors (Yudkin,
1984:42–47). A frequently translated Israeli novelist is Amos Oz (b. 1939).
After beginning his writing career with short stories, he turned to the novel.
His work has been described as heavy with threat, particularly in his best-
known novel, *My Michael* (1968). The heroine is obsessed by her conflicted
feelings of fear and desire for the Arab twins she has known since childhood.

Oz's body of work plays on borders, both real and symbolic. This is significant in a country that has from the start been uncertain about its geographical limits. Oz has situated many of his writings in the experience of the kibbutz, the communes in which many Israeli socialists lived (Yudkin, 1984: 135–143, 168).

Particularly in the post-1967 period, some Palestinians within Israel wrote in Hebrew. Anton Shammas (b. 1941) wrote *Arabesques,* an autobiographical novel that has been hailed by some as a masterpiece of Hebrew prose. Yet despite the critical acclaim, the novel has not been fully accepted as part of the canon of Hebrew literature. Shammas has retrospectively described this work as his challenge to the Israeli claim that the Palestinians living under Israeli rule could be integrated as Israeli citizens. No matter how assimilated they tried to become in Israeli society, no matter how excellent the Palestinians' command of Hebrew, they could never become Israeli citizens in the full sense of the word.

Shammas was long in conversation with A. B. Yehoshua (b. 1936), considered to be one of Israel's most important fiction writers and social critics. His fiction unveils the Arab in the Jew. From "Facing the Forest" (1962) to his first novel *The Lover* (1977), he points to the dreaded other that is always there, lying in wait for the opportunity to reveal itself. The derelict intellectual of the short story, keeping watch lest a fire destroy the forest planted to hide the traces of a Palestinian village destroyed in 1948, foreshadows the hero of the novel who recognizes his dead son in a Palestinian boy who comes to his garage in search of work. The figure of the Arab lies at the core of Israeli identity. Whether Palestinian or Mizrahi Jew, the Arab disturbs the unmarked Europeanness of Israeli identity. The more it is repressed, the more violent its ultimate eruption into consciousness.

The presence of Palestinians and Arab Jews in Israel has become an increasingly important political issue. Two popular uprisings by Palestinians living in the Occupied Territories have hardened official Israeli resolve against accommodation and thus rendered peace a distant prospect. In 2004, the Iraqi-Israeli Sasson Somekh (b. 1933) published his autobiography *Baghdad Yesterday.* Without sentimentality, he recalls his childhood and youth in one of the world's most ancient cities that is currently ravaged by war, sectarian violence, and foreign occupation. At the age of seventeen, Somekh moved to Israel where he later became professor of Arabic literature in Tel Aviv University. The reader is taken back to a time when Jews lived side by side with Muslims and Christians, and although they were aware of some cultural difference, they were not stigmatized by it. Like the Tunisian Albert Memmi, Somekh narrates the challenges faced by Jews in Arab countries who lived in the interstices between local and colonial systems that both privileged them as Jews and emphasized their outsider status.

▨ Drama: Grafting the New onto the Old

As with the other genres coming in from Europe, Middle Eastern intellectuals sought to find indigenous precedents for the theater. Some Arabs invoked the *maqama,* a tenth-century lyrical art form that told the story of an eloquent rascal who manages to deceive all, particularly a wealthy patron. Others cited the shadow play, which had its origin in the Turkish *karagoz* of the fourteenth century. Like the *maqama,* the *karagoz* is a comedy that revolves around the adventures of the uneducated but smart *karagoz.* Although the *karagoz* does deal with daily life and the struggles of the oppressed, its inherent frivolity and unchanging characters and plots resisted the serious intent of early Middle Eastern dramaturges. According to Halman, other popular performances common in Turkey include "peasant plays, pageants, rites, processions, mock fights, festival acts . . . and *Ortaoyunu* (Turkish *commedia dell'arte*)" (1976:14).

Like the novel and the short story, modern drama was introduced into the Middle East through translations. Major plays by William Shakespeare, Molière, and Chekhov were adapted for the Arab stage. Particularly in the torn, nostalgic works of Chekhov that described the passing of an age and the uncertainty of the future, Middle Easterners could recognize their own dilemmas. The theater appealed to a much wider section of the public because it did not rely on literacy. It provided a context within which writers could experiment with the introduction of colloquialisms, which were anathema to the writers of prose and poetry who feared the loss of the purity of their languages. With time, successful implementation of the colloquial in conversations between illiterate characters that were often offset by the high classical language of the educated provided models for fiction writers.

In 1873, the Turk Namik Kemal (ca. 1840–1888) staged his play *Fatherland,* which was enthusiastically greeted by audiences and censured by the government of Sultan Abdulaziz. Halman claims that this play marked the beginning of "the political significance of literature in Turkish life." Atatürk saw in drama an important aspect of Westernization that he exploited by establishing the City Theater of Istanbul in 1927. Writers in other genres like Yashar Kemal, Nazim Hikmet Ran, Orhan Kemal, and Aziz Nesin experimented in theatrical writing. Much of the dramatic writings of the 1960s are "village dramas," which marked the first significant move away from Western influence (Halman, 1976:13, 37, 41–47).

The name that stands out above all others in the field of Arab drama is that of the Egyptian Tawfiq al-Hakim (1898–1987), who wrote his first plays in the early 1920s. Unlike many of his contemporaries, al-Hakim was not supportive of the burgeoning feminist movement. While others were writing of the injustices women were facing, he criticized the "new woman" who heralded moral chaos. After three years spent studying law in Paris, al-Hakim returned to Cairo in 1928. At this point, he turned to philosophical playwriting and his treatment of women mellowed, as in *Shahrazad* (1934). This change may be due to his experiences with women in Paris, about which he wrote in his autobiography.

In 1960, al-Hakim joined other writers who were criticizing the new regime, brought into power by the Free Officers' Revolution, when he published *The Sultan's Dilemma.* The sultan is a slave whose owner, the previous sultan, had died before manumitting him. He must gain his freedom and can only do so by being bought and then freed by his next owner. He is bought in auction by a woman who has heard of his dictatorial ways but discovers that he is gentle. She gives him his freedom once he has learned its real meaning. In 1964, Yusuf Idris published *Farfoors,* a play that relied on the *karagoz* genre as well as on Sufi rituals. He wanted to prove that drama was not new to Arabic literature and that traditional forms could hold the new politically charged content.

In the late 1960s, students throughout the Arab world turned to the theater as a sanctioned space in which to stage their sociopolitical grievances. In Syria, a group of students founded the Thorn Theater Company, which produced skits and plays of surprising daring. The screen of comedy and fiction allowed actors to convey political messages that would elsewhere be deemed sedition. Government officials and censors allowed this dangerous practice to continue, recognizing that the people needed an outlet for their frustration and anger with a repressive regime. Along with other forms of cultural production but more visibly, the theater also helped to fashion a facade of democracy for the Baathist state.

Writers schooled in the Thorn Theater have continued to write on the razor's edge between dissidence and martyrdom. Some, like Sa'dallah Wannus (1941–1997) and Mamduh 'Adwan (1941–2004), stayed with the stage. Wannus's first play, *An Evening's Entertainment for the Fifth of June,* came out in 1968, just a year after the Six-Day War, and it has been described as the richest literary reaction to the terrible defeat. In it Wannus criticized, even if allegorically, the current Baathist regime. First in 1977 with *The King Is the King* and then fifteen years later with *Historical Miniatures,* he revealed the oppressive strategies of dictatorial rule. In the more recent play, he used the relationship between fourteenth-century Mongol tyrant Tamerlane and North African historian Ibn Khaldun to criticize intellectuals for their complicity with a corrupt system. 'Adwan's play *The Ghoul* (1996) focuses on the cruelty of the last Ottoman governor to be sent to Syria. The nightmares that torment his sleep might be those of any dictator.

Other graduates of the Thorn Theater, like Durayd Lahham, have moved from the stage to television or the cinema. Paradoxically, the film industry has become the most radical of all cultural producers: it is exclusively controlled by the Ministry of Culture, yet it is engaged in stringent criticism of the government. What are the political position and ultimate fate of film-makers like Muhammad Mallas, who are in the pay of the government but whose films, on the rare occasions when they are shown, leave their audiences breathless at their critical audacity? This is what I call commissioned criticism, because it serves to make the government look open-minded and democratic when it so wishes (cooke, 2007).

■ Poetry and the Hold of the Desert

Of all genres, the most resistant to change was poetry. The new emphasis on personal expression and free style was regarded almost as heresy. Throughout the Middle East, poetry has been and continues to be the most highly prized literary art. In the pre-Islamic period, politics and poetry had been intermeshed, and tribal leaders were expected to be accomplished poets. Islamic rulers generally continued to value the art of poetry and patronized it generously. Wherever it was composed, whether in Arabic, Turkish, or Persian, classical poetry retained elements of its origins in the desert. There were familiar tropes, images, meters, and form. Any changes had to be carefully introduced lest the innovation be considered a sign of incompetence. More formulaic even than prose literature, classical poetry did not allow for the expression of individual emotion.

The first attempts to make poetry more responsive to contemporary concerns began modestly in the mid–nineteenth century. Neoclassical poets like Turkish writer Yahya Kemal Beyatli (1884–1958) and the aristocratic Egyptians Mahmud Sami al-Barudi (1839–1904) and Ahmad Shawqi (1868–1932) were to give new life to classical motifs and language, with only slight modification in content. In general, they were formal conservatives (Somekh, 1992:40–41). The first substantive reform of poetry came from such poets as the Turk Ahmet Hasim (1885–1933), the Syrian Khalil Mutran (1872–1949), the Tunisian Abu al-Qasim al-Shabbi (1909–1934), and the Iranian Nima Yushij (1895–1959), who had been inspired by such French and English Symbolists and Romantics as Charles-Pierre Baudelaire and Alphonse-Marie-Louis de Prat de Lamartine, William Wordsworth, and Shelley. Their experiments with meter, form, and language transformed poetry in the Middle East.

A revolution was in the making, but opposition to free verse remained strong. In Turkey, the Marxist Nazim Hikmet Ran (1902–1963) was the first to be recognized for his free verse. Halman relates how in 1921 Atatürk had urged the already famous poet to "write poems with a purpose" (1982:25). He did, but he had to pay for his "obedience." His outright condemnations of social and political injustices as well as his poetic calls for revolution gained such a wide following that he was made to bear responsibility for political

43

When you visit me,
Wearing a new dress,
I feel what a gardener feels
When a tree blooms in his garden.

عِنْدَمَا تَزُورِينِي
بِثَوْبٍ جَدِيدٍ ..
أَشْعُرُ بِمَا يَشْعُرُ بِهِ الْبُسْتَانِي
حِينَ تُزْهِرُ لَدَيْهِ شَجَرَةٌ ..

Syrian poet Nizar Kabbani
(1923–1998). This poem is "No.
43" from *One Hundred Love
Letters.*

Lynne Rienner Publishers

unrest. During the late 1930s, just before Atatürk's death, he was imprisoned on the trumped-up charge of conspiracy to overthrow the regime, and
his writings were banned. Upon his release, Ran fled to Moscow, where he
is buried alongside such great Russian writers as Fyodor Dostoevsky. He is
the most widely translated Turkish poet. His poems "Some Advice to Those
Who Will Serve Time in Prison" and "Awakening" were written for those
who had to undergo what he did but who were not as strong:

> I mean it's not that you can't pass
> 10 or 15 years inside,
> and more even—
> you can,
> as long as the jewel
> in the left side of your chest doesn't lose its luster.

In the Arab world and in Iran, it was women who brought to fruition
what male poets had long been trying to achieve. The Iraqi Nazik al-
Mala'ika (b. 1923) finally succeeded in introducing free verse into modern
Arabic poetry. In 1949 she published her anthology of free verse, *Ashes and
Shrapnel.* Although others before her had experimented with this new poetic
form, they had had little success; critics accused them of incompetence

rather than welcoming the innovation. Her work paved the way for others like Syrian Nobel nominee Adonis (Ali Ahmad Said, b. 1930) and Iraqi poet Badr Shakir al-Sayyab (1926–1964). Both of these writers gained prominence through their adoption of mythic themes of resurrection, particularly in connection with the plight of the Palestinians. In 1968, Adonis published his pathbreaking work *The Stage and the Mirrors,* which introduces a new poetic lexicon, rhythm, structure, and sensibility. His work is highly philosophical, filled with symbols, allegories, and mythical allusions. He claims that poetry should appeal to the mind, not to the emotions, and because this new poetry is a political weapon, it must be subtly wielded.

The political nature of Arab poetry and the repressiveness of several of the regimes within which these poets function has compelled some to write indirectly, obliquely, surreally, and anonymously. Arab women, particularly in more traditional countries like those of the Arabian Peninsula, have often chosen abstract symbolism to articulate emotions otherwise considered taboo. This new poetry by women like Kuwaiti princess Su'ad Mubarak al-Sabah was at first censured, even when not quite understood, because it came from the pen of a woman. In the late 1990s, however, this kind of poetry began to find a new, international audience. In March 1997 and in places as far-flung from the United Arab Emirates as Vietnam and North Carolina, newspapers carried the story of the publication of a new anthology titled *The Female Poets of the Emirates.*

In Iran, two women poets rose to prominence. Forugh Farrokhzad (1935–1967) and Simin Behbahani (b. 1927) both rebelled against poetic norms. Behbahani's first collection of poetry, *Broken String,* came out in 1951. Whereas Behbahani's rebellion took the form of neotraditionalism (Milani, 1992:235–239), Farrokhzad's method involved rejection. In 1955 she published an anthology titled *Captive* that some considered to be "scandalously frank." But she is best known for her collection *Another Birth,* which was published in 1964. Like al-Mala'ika, she breaks with formal convention as she describes the oppressive life of a Middle Eastern woman. The personal and the political fuse in a single poetic vision.

■ Independence and Postcolonial Struggles

As previous chapters have illustrated, the second half of the twentieth century witnessed cycles of violence throughout the Middle East. There were liberation struggles followed by socialist activism followed by breakdown of law and order and widespread depression and disappointment. After independence, many wanted to reconstruct their countries and to fashion a local, "authentic" identity. Conflict and violence are so much a part of the history of the Middle East that no consideration of its literature can afford to ignore them.

Writers wanted to play a role in the new societies that came with independence from colonial rule. Acting as conscience of the people, they set out to "revolutionize the revolution." In 1946 the Iran-Soviet Society sponsored the first congress of Iranian writers, during which the centrality of ideology to literature was announced. Seven years later, in Lebanon, the first editorial of the influential monthly periodical *Al-Shi'r* declared that all forms of writing must henceforth be politically engaged. The time of art for art's sake had passed, to be replaced by a revolutionary ethic in all creative activities.

Paying the Price

This emphasis on political commitment in literature appeared at a time when the Middle East was in the throes of revolutions and wars of liberation. Literature was to make an intervention in the political realm, to praise and promote the social good, and to criticize the retrograde. Wars of liberation from colonial rule were clearly good, but some conflicts were not so easily judged as good or bad. This was the case with the Egyptian Free Officers' Revolution of 1952. It was clearly good in that it brought back Egyptian rule after what some argued was a hiatus of millennia, namely since the Pharaohs. Others soon felt misgivings about the autocratic nature of the *nouveau regime* (new regime).

As mentioned above, Haqqi's 1954 novel *Good Morning!* openly criticized Gamal Abdul Nasser and his new regime. In the same year, another lawyer, 'Abd al-Rahman al-Sharqawi (1920–1987), published *Egyptian Earth,* which filmmaker Yusuf Shahin turned into a film titled *The Land.* It examines the impact of the revolution on the lives of the fellahin and shows the oppressiveness of the centralized authority structure that the Free Officers put in place. Again, the plot revolves around the introduction of a symbol of modernization, in this case a road, into a village that has managed to keep itself aloof from the corruption of city life. The fact that the revolution, in which so many had invested great hopes, had brought only misery to the people was difficult for many to accept.

In the Middle East, writers have a moral authority that is almost unimaginable in the West. They are expected to stand up for their convictions and to lead public opinion. Their boldness may earn them prison sentences, but that is as it should be. The prisoner of conscience, the intellectual who has done time, wears this experience as a badge of honor. Many prisoners of conscience in the Middle East, particularly the Communists, have written of their incarceration.

Iranian writer Buzurg Alavi (b. 1908), who had become involved in the Marxist Tudeh Party, was imprisoned in 1937. During his four years "inside," he wrote two books: *Scrap Papers from Prison* and *Fifty Three Men.* These stories about his experiences reveal the intense emotions of the prisoners but also their determination: "I gained in spirits in the prison and became better equipped for the struggle" (quoted in Alvi, 1984:283). Along the same lines, Egyptian writer Sherif Hetata (b. 1923) wrote *The Eye with an Iron Lid* (1982), an intricately told tale of its author's thirteen years behind bars first under the British and then under Nasser. His partner, Nawal El Saadawi (b. 1931), also recorded her months spent in prison under Anwar Sadat in *Memoirs from the Women's Prison* (1983). As mentioned above, Turkey's premier poet, Nazim Hikmet Ran, wrote extensively about his years "inside." The fact that these intellectuals have had such experiences and that they then publish them gives them a moral authority that others, whose writings may be just as "good," may never achieve.

The Algerian War of Independence (1954–1962)

Tunisia and Morocco gained their independence from the French in 1956, but the Algerians, who had begun their anticolonial war in 1954, did not succeed until 1962. The war produced libraries of novels, short stories, and poetry, and even today it haunts the imagination of cultural producers, including filmmakers. Most recently, *Joseph and the Legend of the Seventh Sleeper* (1995) made the rounds of the Arab film festivals. The story tells of a prisoner of war who escapes to find his companions. He discovers that they, like the quranic sleepers in the cave, perished in a cave with their dog. He buries his erstwhile companions and then is himself killed by traitors. The theme of the betrayal of the revolution was common in the 1990s as intellectuals found themselves under attack by religious extremists.

But in the 1950s and early 1960s, hope was high, and everyone was expected to write about the war. Women like Assia Djebar (b. 1936), who wrote *The Thirst* in 1957, about women's doomed thirst for independence, were criticized by the male literary establishment for obsession with individual problems at a time when the nation was in need of all of its citizens to be as united as possible. Later novels by Djebar, including *Children of the New World* (1962) and *Naive Larks* (1967), describe women's mobilization without any sense of its significance for them in a postbellum society.

In contrast, male writers were writing with dread about women's growing power and influence in a society that was spinning out of control. One of the best-known novels of the war is *Nedjma* (1956) by Kateb Yacine (1929–1996). The critics have generally interpreted this story of a mysterious beauty, the four suitors to whom she is related, her legendary father, and her French mother, to be an allegory for Algeria. I argue that instead it narrates men's growing anxieties as they watch the emergence of the new Algerian woman out of the ashes of the war (cooke, 1997:chap. 3). This thesis is more forcefully brought out in Mohamed Dib's surreal novel *Who Remembers the Sea* (1962), where the narrator loses his mind as he loses control over his wife, a guerrilla fighter. For those writers like Malek Haddad (1927–1987) who left Algeria during the war, the dread of the woman soldier is intense. It is not so surprising, then, that when the war was over, the women were quickly returned to their homes.

The story of women's disempowerment in the aftermath of the war is well known; in fact, Arab women elsewhere refer to it as the "Algerian lesson." This lesson taught others that they must not allow society to forget women's contributions during a time of crisis and need. In the 1980s, Djebar started to bring out her quartet, which she has described as autobiographical. Each volume presents a radical revision of Algerian colonial history as seen through the eyes of women. In the second volume, *Fantasia: An Algerian Cavalcade* (1985), she links the stories of unknown nineteenth-century women resisters, omitted in the official histories and chronicles, with those of living women who had been active and then silenced during the war, and with her own story.

Djebar's quartet forms part of a national critique on the part of revolutionary women who have recognized, perhaps too late, the dangers of silence. The war of liberation was not a revolution, they claim, because its outcome did not change the material and social conditions for half the population. As long as discrimination against women continues, the expulsion of the French cannot be considered to have been a national success. During the 1990s and 2000s, the Islamic fundamentalist attacks on intellectuals, and particularly women, may be seen as the next phase of a war that was not resolved in the early 1960s.

The Question of Palestine

Immediately after the departure of the British in 1948, Palestinians wrestled with their new loss of independence. Although most Palestinian intellectuals left in 1948, a few, like poet Mahmud Darwish (b. 1942), did stay behind what came to be called the Green Line. Darwish's family left in the first exodus and then soon stole back in. They returned after the period for registering Palestinians had passed, and so the poet's writings dwell on the lack of identity papers. His poem "Identity Card" (1965) became emblematic of the Palestinian condition.

After 1967, the Palestinians who found themselves under Israeli rule in the Gaza Strip and the West Bank began to understand why it was that those who had stayed on their land inside the Israeli borders in 1948 were not necessarily complicit, but rather might be regarded as nationalists. The importance of staying, whatever the cost, became a nationalist virtue. Emile Habibi (1921–1996) was an important figure writing inside Israel. Founder of the binational Israeli Communist Party, he won both the Jerusalem Prize for Literature awarded by the Palestinian Liberation Organization and the Israel Prize. In 1974, he published *The Secret Life of Saeed, the Ill-fated Pessoptimist: A*

Palestinian Who Became a Citizen of Israel. The picaresque tale tells of a hapless Palestinian as he stumbles through life and people in Israel.

Two years later, from Nablus inside the Occupied Territories, Sahar Khalifa (b. 1941) published the first of her three novels on the experience of occupation by Israeli forces. From *Wild Thorns* (1976) to *Bab al-Saha* (1990), Khalifa paints the canvas of resistance. Her heroines demonstrate how women's ways of fighting are more effective than those of the men. Mothers who give their sons and daughters stones to throw at soldiers confuse the rules of war. Are these women and their offspring civilians or militants? Can they be shot? Or must they be tolerated, their stones deflected? This ambiguity disappeared in the later stage when the women's individual acts of resistance—like the mythical hydra, when one of its heads is cut off, two will appear in its stead—were turned into a unified strategy for revolutionary action. The militarization of local oppositions was named the intifada (uprising). It is arguable that this transformation of individual Palestinian actions into a single movement empowered the Israelis (cooke, 1997:chap. 4).

The War in Lebanon (1975–1990)

Even before civil war broke out in Lebanon in the spring of 1975, some were sensing its inevitability. This was again true before the Israeli invasion in June 1982. Both al-Samman and Etel Adnan (b. 1925) wrote works that were filled with the dread of anticipation. *Beirut 75* (1974), by al-Samman, uncannily predicts the civil war as the novel collapses into a series of nightmares. Five years later at the height of the war, she returned to the nightmare format. *Beirut Nightmares* (1979) takes the reader into the maelstrom of the fall 1976 hotels battle, which pitted opposing militias against each other for weeks. Many have read in Adnan's novel *Arab Apocalypse* (1980) a premonition of the Israeli invasion of 1982. The staccato poetry interrupted with symbols and figures lies splattered on the page like shrapnel exploding out of a bomb, like blood spurting out of a wound.

As happened in Iran after the Islamic revolution, chaos in Lebanon produced literature, much of it by women (Lewis and Yazdanfar, 1996:xix–xxi). The Beirut Decentrists, a school of women writing in Beirut during the war, wrote into the space of violence a script for a transformed society that would include all its members and treat them with justice (cooke, 1988). But during the civil war, they did more than that. These women writers showed how the men were responsible for creating the terrible conditions that threatened to destroy the postindependence country that was so fragile. Hanan al-Shaykh's (b. 1945) novel *The Story of Zahra* (1980) traces the growth in consciousness of a woman who had been a social misfit. As the war rages, she comes to see a role for herself, and she fights in her own limited but intense way to do something to end at least part of the madness.

The Iran-Iraq War and Its Aftermath

While the war in Lebanon was at its height, farther to the east the 1979 Islamic revolution ousted the shah of Iran from the Peacock Throne. Saddam Hussein, the new leader of Iraq, tried to take advantage of what he had mistakenly assumed to be total disarray in neighboring Iran. The war that he launched in late 1980 as a blitzkrieg persisted for eight bloody years. Like many dictators, Hussein had an ambivalent relationship with the intellectual elite of his country. He needed them, and therefore he feared them. Throughout the war, he coerced the writers and artists who could not or did not choose to leave to glorify the war in ink and paint. The Ministry of Culture established literary series and organized festivals designed to serve the purposes of the war. Many did as they were told. Some did not. Under the watchful eye of the censor, some writers even managed to articulate criticism of a war they were being paid to praise. Using allegory and a surreal style, they published writings that evoked the harrowing experiences through which Iraqis were forced to pass (cooke, 1997). Ironically, the Iranian government was doing exactly the same as its enemy, namely, sponsoring books of stories and autobiographies to praise the war.

The Iraqi invasion of Kuwait on August 2, 1990, and the war that several Western and Arab countries under the leadership of US president George H. W. Bush launched against Iraq on January 17, 1991, produced Kuwaiti and Iraqi journals, novels, and short stories. In *Black Barricades* (1994), Kuwait's leading woman writer, Layla al-'Uthman (b. 1951), collects stories she had written during the eight-month occupation of the capital city. The tone is one of confusion, which aptly reflects the mood of the Kuwaitis as well as of the Iraqis. The destitute, illiterate men wreaking havoc in the palaces of the Kuwaiti oil magnates may not know why they are there beyond the looting, but they do know that they do not wish to return to their home country.

Inside Iraq itself, several wrote against the brutality of the allied forces and particularly the US pilots, who seemed to consider their Iraqi targets as figures no more human than characters in a Nintendo game. The Ministry of Culture continued its publication of war stories. One of Iraq's leading women poets, Dunya Mikha'il (b. 1965), brought out her *Journal of a Wave Outside the Sea* in 1995. Far from glorifying the war as might be expected from such a government-sponsored text, this poem depicts extreme alienation in a continuing reign of terror.

In March 2003, a year and a half after the 9/11 attacks on the World Trade Center in New York and the Pentagon in Washington, D.C., the US military invaded Iraq. The pretext was Saddam Hussein's alleged complicity in 9/11 and also the determination to eliminate weapons of mass destruction the Iraqi leader was accused of manufacturing (and that as of today have not been found). After toppling Saddam Hussein, the US forces stayed with the excuse that they were trying to turn Iraq into a model democracy. At the time of writing, sectarian violence has spun out of control. Young bloggers were the first to inform the world about life in Iraq under US occupation. Two have achieved renown: Salampax and Riverbend. Both of them have published "blooks"—in other words, books of their blogs. Riverbend's *Girl Blog from Baghdad* (2005) can be read as a chronicle of the coming to literary awareness of a woman whom war imprisoned in her home and gave her time to reflect on her circumstances. The early, hurried jottings of moments of panic give way to careful crafting of her emotions and reflections.

◼ Emigration and Exile

There are many reasons for leaving the country of one's birth. Some, such as education and work opportunities, are voluntary; some, such as political oppression and intolerable violence, are involuntary. The travel of a young man, his head filled with dreams, to Europe; his apprenticeship for a period; and his disappointed return to his native land for education and the shock of return is a topos shaping many Middle Eastern works of fiction during the first part of the twentieth century. Egyptian writer Yahya Haqqi wrote the emblematic text of this "travel and return transformed" genre. *The Lamp of Umm Hashim* (1946) follows Isma'il from Cairo to London and then back to Cairo after seven years of training as an eye doctor. Only after experiencing a religious epiphany is he able to resolve the tension between traditional and Western medicine. The novella was hailed as an Islamic model of how to become a Western-style scientist while nonetheless remaining a righteous Muslim.

Twenty years later, the Sudanese al-Tayyib Salih (b. 1929) developed this theme, although without the religious angle, in *Season of Migration to the North* (1966). This novel reverses the nineteenth-century colonialist's move from the metropole to the colony; Mustafa Sa'id goes north (to England) to learn but also to wreak revenge on behalf of his oppressed people. The story of Mustafa Sa'id has often been compared to that of Othello; it has also been called the answer to Joseph Conrad's novel *Heart of Darkness* as well as to Frantz Fanon's depiction of the impotence and potential castration of the black man facing the white woman (Fanon, 1967).

Many Middle Eastern intellectuals have chosen to leave their native lands because they can no longer live there. Sometimes the reasons are economic, sometimes political. For over a century, the Lebanese and Egyptians have left for Europe and the Americas, and more recently the Turks for Germany, in search of a prosperity seemingly unavailable in the eastern and southern Mediterranean. Citizens of repressive regimes, like the former

Iraqi regime of Saddam Hussein, the Syrian Baathist government, and the Islamic Republic of Iran, have fled so as to find a place where they might breathe and speak freely. Many Middle Eastern intellectuals have congregated in Paris, London, and New York, where they have founded publishing houses and launched newspapers and magazines.

Emily Nasrallah has examined the question of emigration from a Lebanese perspective. *September Birds* (1962), a novel about a village whose vitality was being drained as the young people were lured away to the capital and to the glittering West, was supposed to have a sequel about the return of the migratory birds. The war in Lebanon forced her and others like her to understand that there was to be no return, either because they were too comfortable in their new homes or because they had failed and they were not returning because they were ashamed not to have realized the dream. In 1994 she published *Sleeping Embers,* a novel that seemed to bring closure to the question of emigration. Those who left should not come back because when they do, they disturb people's tranquillity by dredging up stories and pains that had been appropriately shelved.

The twentieth century was the century of mass migration, and so the story of the stateless person has come to symbolize the dilemma of globalization: it is often impossible to live at home, impossible to survive outside. The various political upheavals in the Middle East have caused many to leave their homes without hope of return. Ghassan Kanafani (1936–1972) was one such refugee who went to Beirut. His 1963 novel *Men in the Sun,* which was adapted into a film titled *The Dupes,* explores the possible outcome of the choice to leave one's home and to seek asylum in Arab countries. Three men entrust themselves to a Palestinian guide who has promised to drive them across the desert separating Iraq and Kuwait for an exorbitant fee. When they have almost made it, the driver is delayed at a border post. The men, hidden in the truck's empty water tank, suffocate in the heat.

Jabra Ibrahim Jabra (1919–1995), who left Palestine for Iraq and later lived throughout the region, has written several novels, all of which delve into the lives of dispersed Palestinians. *In Search of Walid Mas'ud* (1978) brings together those who have chosen to write about their situation with others who have decided to fight to change it. They debate the most appropriate means to defend a cause.

After the Islamic revolution and then during the punishing war with Iraq (1980–1988), many Iranians fled the country. They are now scattered all over Europe and North America, where some are writing in the languages of their new countries, but many continue to write in Persian. The latter include Mahshid Amirshahy (b. 1937), with her books *At Home* (1986) and *Away from Home* (1998), and Goli Taraqqi, who lives in Paris. In 1992, Taraqqi published *Scattered Memories,* a collection of stories about the pains of exile. Like Nasrallah, she reveals the impoverished lives of those who had

Palestinian writer Ghassan Kanafani, who was murdered
in a car-bomb explosion in Beirut in 1972.

emigrated. Taraqqi reminds the reader that exile means leaving the physical
home where there is privacy and autonomy, but it also entails humiliation
from being forced to depend on others. Shahrnush Parsipur, a highly acclaimed feminist writer whose 1989 book *Women Without Men* was banned
by the Islamic Republic, is now in California, where she wrote *Tea Cere-
mony in the Presence of the Wolf* (1993). This collection of short stories
elaborates on the sense of terrible loss and the condemnation to perpetual
wandering that mark the experience of exile.

Those who write in exile often feel farther from home than the miles
that mark that distance. Like the Algerians who left during the war of independence, they feel, perhaps, that they should be fighting side-by-side with
those intellectuals who have chosen to stay regardless of the cost. Yet in a
world whose borders are increasingly porous, where migration is a necessary part of many people's lives, a new kind of cultural nationalism is
emerging that allows those who are living far from their land of birth or an-
cestry to retain very real ties of identity. Literary associations in the Middle
East are slowly recognizing that their writers may not live in the country
that they claim as their nation. Turkish novelist Habib Bektas (b. 1951) is a
good example. Since 1972 he has been living and writing in Germany. In
1997, his book *The Smell of the Shadow* won the Turkish Inkilab Kitabevi
Press annual prize; it was the first time this coveted prize had been awarded

to a nonresident Turk. Bektas explained that his Turkishness did not consist in residence in Turkey but in language: he lives in Turkish. This adoption of the language as the nation is a strategy many writers in exile invoke.

■ The Muslim State

The Islamic revolution had been simmering in Iran long before it boiled over. Mention has already been made of Al-e Ahmad and Daneshvar, whose writings during the late 1960s seemed to be calling for reform of a society that was too much given over to the delights of the West. There is a pronounced Islamic tone in what they write. Two years before the revolution, Parsipur wrote *The Heat of the Year Zero*. The heroine's description of suffocation in the overwhelming heat of the summer and her stolen and then censured glances at men anticipated what the new regime had in store for its women.

In the early days of the revolution, the Islamic government of Iran, much like its royal predecessor, concerned itself with cultural production. Whatever was seen to be oppositional to its specifically Islamic interests was carefully censured. The case of Salman Rushdie has entered the annals of world history. Some writers complied with the government's will and wrote piously about the virtues of the revolution. Others, many of them women, protested the new restrictions; for example, A. Rahmani's "Short Hike" acts out a tense moment of defiance between an Islamic guard and the woman he has just reprimanded for revealing a strand of hair. Milani has noted that in the short two-year period between 1983, when compulsory veiling was generally enforced, and 1985, "126 books by or about women were published in Iran." Restrictions had forced women to speak out (Milani, 1992:231).

As previous chapters have explored, it is not only in Iran that Muslims have called for the establishment of an Islamic state. After the abolition of the Ottoman caliphate in 1924 and the consequent secularization of Turkey, Muslims elsewhere in the Middle East became nervous. This was particularly true in Egypt, where the first formal association of Muslim revolutionaries was established in 1929. Other such groups formed, and many remain active today in many countries of the Middle East. Their increasing prominence in public life became a theme in literature from the 1970s on. In 1977, during a period spent in exile in Germany, the Egyptian 'Abd al-Hakim Qasim (1935–1990) wrote a story about the attempted conversion to Islam of a poor Coptic umbrella maker. "The Mahdi" explores the new animosities arising between Christians and Muslims who had always lived together peacefully. The story also reveals the growing chasm between young Islamists and more traditional Muslims in rural Egypt.

The Islamists have played contradictory roles in the history and politics of their countries. In Egypt, for instance, they helped leaders like Nasser come to power, but they have also sought to remove such leaders. During the mid-1960s, Nasser arrested several Islamist leaders. Their years in prison produced several memoirs, of which arguably the most interesting is that of the leader of the Muslim Ladies Association, Zaynab al-Ghazali (1912–2004). In 1965, she was incarcerated for a year in the War Prison with her male colleagues. That experience inspired her book *Days from My Life* (1977). Less memoir than inspirational literature, this text recounts the tortures and miracles that mark their subject as especially blessed. It can be read as a model for young women seeking guidance as they try to combine political ambitions with their scripturally defined roles as wives and mothers.

In 1981, a group of Islamists assassinated Egyptian president Anwar Sadat. They charged him with making an unpardonable compromise in promoting the Camp David Accords with Israel. Islamists do not confine their targets to political leaders, however. As seen in Algeria in the 1990s, Islamists are increasingly focusing their attention on intellectuals who are charged with secularism and perversion of the people's morals. In 1992, Egyptian fundamentalists assassinated journalist Farag Foda for his critique of their discourse. Most annoying to them had been his book *Before the Fall* (1992). That summer, they published in paperback format the proceedings of a trial they had conducted, titled *Nawal El Saadawi in the Witness Stand*. With its cover picture of a wild, white-haired woman staring out from behind bars, the book was so widely distributed that it could be found in the streets of Cairo on the blankets of sidewalk book vendors, selling for a few piasters. These echoes of the fatwa (religious opinion) the Ayatollah Ruhollah Khomeini had pronounced on February 14, 1989, calling for Rushdie's death for his novel *The Satanic Verses,* were too loud to be ignored. Moral censure of literature had escalated to the sanction of deadly assaults on authors. El Saadawi, who is accustomed to threats from governments and Islamists, did not shake this threat off as idle. When the Egyptian government, which had imprisoned her for a few months during Sadat's regime, sent guards to keep watch on her apartment, she realized that she had to leave. She went to Duke University in North Carolina, where she spent most of the following four years writing her autobiography, *Daughter of Isis*.

Nawal El Saadawi was condemned to death because of two books. *The Fall of the Imam* (1987) is the lyrically told tale of the assassination of the highest authority in the land, a transparent reference to Sadat's assassination, and of the pursuit and execution of his assassin, who is also his illegitimate daughter, Bint Allah. *Innocence of the Devil* (1992) takes place in a psychiatric hospital, where one of the patients thinks he is God and another that he is Satan. The collapse of the God-Satan tension reveals the vanity of trying to know God through his opposite. The God who is paired with the devil is the God of organized monotheistic religions, a tyrant who must be resisted. These two novels are open attacks on the hypocrisy and emptiness

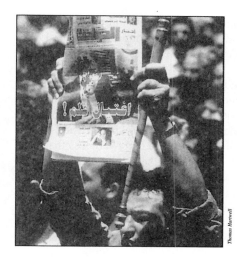

Mourners at the funeral for Egyptian author Farag Foda, who was assassinated in 1992.

of religions. Unlike El Saadawi's earlier fiction, in which women are confined to the role of victim, these novels explore the ways in which women resist the tyranny of men who use scripture to justify violence against women. Fearing them, these men link women with the devil and then justify their actions in religious terms.

Translation and Recognition

Middle Eastern writers have attracted world attention over the past forty years. Three writers have won the Nobel Prize in literature: in 1966, the Israeli Shmuel Yosef Agnon (1888–1970); in 1988, the Egyptian Najib Mahfouz; in 2006, the Turkish Orhan Pamuk. In 1989, Moroccan Tahar Benjelloun won the Prix Goncourt, the first Arab to be awarded this coveted French prize. In 1997, Turk Yashar Kemal was recognized with Italy's most prestigious prize, the Nonino Literary Award.

At the same time, more and more Arabic, Hebrew, Persian, and Turkish fiction and poetry are being translated into European languages. Previously the translation process had been idiosyncratic; random works appeared according to individual tastes of translators. By the mid-1980s, however, the translation process became more systematic. For example, in 1981, Palestinian poet and literary critic Salma al-Khadra' al-Jayyusi founded the Project for Translation from Arabic (PROTA) in the United States. At first, these translations found homes in marginal presses dedicated to publishing works by writers from the global South. By the late 1980s, however, major

European, US, and even Japanese publishing houses, including some university presses that came to consider Middle Eastern literature as potential textbooks, started adopting Middle Eastern literary series as well as the works of individual authors.

The growth of the translation industry provides readers unprecedented access to the cultural imagery of people they had previously known only through the stories of journalists, scholars, and travelers. This is important, above all, for the writers and particularly for those who have already gained a share of recognition abroad. They are writing with the awareness that their works will be translated, that what they say about their culture is being consumed far from the local readership they had originally targeted. Writing thus entails consequences that must be anticipated. Self-criticism must become what Moroccan cultural critic 'Abdelkebir Khatibi has called "double critique." The eye turned in on the injustices of a society must simultaneously look out to discern the contours of the external enemy. Local tyrannies must be held in balance with the dangers of global hegemony, with the understanding that the one interacts with the other. This double critique changes the way people think and write, and this changed writing is cultivating new tastes and creating new markets. Middle Eastern writers of the twenty-first century are seeing their work become part of a global project in which they will play an increasingly visible role.

▓ Notes

I am indebted to Guven Guzeldere and Erdag Goknar for information, invaluable advice, and stimulating conversations about Turkish culture. Warm thanks to Mohamad Tavakoli-Targhi for a careful reading of the penultimate version of this chapter and for wonderful suggestions.

1. Albert Memmi notes that between 1947 and 1986, Algerian women published thirty-seven novels and short story collections (1987:6).

2. For example, Nawal El Saadawi first published her autobiography, *My Papers My Life,* in 1995 in *Al-Musawwar,* a magazine that is distributed throughout the Arab world.

▓ Bibliography

Alvi, Sajida. 1984. "Buzurg Alavi's Writings from Prison (1940s)." Pp. 274–291 in Thomas M. Ricks (ed.), *Critical Perspectives on Modern Persian Literature.* Washington, D.C.: Three Continents Press.

cooke, miriam. 1988. *War's Other Voices: Women Writers on the Lebanese Civil War.* Cambridge: Cambridge University Press.

———. 1997. *Women and the War Story.* Berkeley: University of California Press.

———. 2007. *Dissident Syria. Making Oppositional Arts Official.* Durham, N.C.: Duke University Press.

Daragahi, Haideh. 1984. "The Shaping of the Modern Persian Short Story." Pp. 104–123 in Thomas M. Ricks (ed.), *Critical Perspectives on Modern Persian Literature.* Washington, D.C.: Three Continents Press.

Fanon, Frantz. 1967. *Black Skin, White Masks.* New York: Grove Press.

Goknar, Erdag. (forthcoming). "The Novel in Turkish: Narrative Tradition to Nobel Prize." Cambridge History of Turkish Literature.

Hafez, Sabry. 1992. "The Modern Arabic Short Story." Pp. 270–328 in Mustafa M. Badawi (ed.), *Modern Arabic Literature.* Cambridge: Cambridge University Press.

Halman, Talat Sait (ed.). 1976. *Modern Turkish Drama. An Anthology of Plays in Translation.* Minneapolis: Bibliotheca Islamica.

———. 1982. *Contemporary Turkish Literature.* Rutherford, N.J.: Fairleigh Dickinson University Press.

Jayyusi, Salma Khadra. 1992. "Modernist Poetry in Arabic." Pp. 132–179 in Mustafa M. Badawi (ed.), *Modern Arabic Literature.* Cambridge: Cambridge University Press.

Lewis, Franklin, and Farzin Yazdanfar. 1996. *In a Voice of Their Own: A Collection of Stories by Iranian Women Written Since the Revolution of 1979.* Costa Mesa, Calif.: Mazda.

Memmi, Albert. 1987. Introduction to *Anthologie du Roman Maghrebin.* Paris: Nathan.

Milani, Farzaneh. 1992. *Veils and Words: The Emerging Voices of Iranian Women Writers.* Syracuse, N.Y.: Syracuse University Press.

Moayyad, Heshmat (ed.). 1991. *Stories from Iran: A Chicago Anthology, 1921–1991.* Washington, D.C.: Mage.

Najmabadi, Afsaneh. 1998. "Crafting an Educated Housewife in Iran." Pp. 91–125 in Lila Abu-Lughod (ed.), *Remaking Women: Feminism and Modernity in the Middle East.* Princeton, N.J.: Princeton University Press.

Somekh, Sasson. 1992. "The Neo-Classical Arabic Poets." Pp. 36–81 in Mustafa M. Badawi (ed.), *Modern Arabic Literature.* Cambridge: Cambridge University Press.

Tavakoli-Targhi, Mohamad. 1990. "Refashioning Iran: Language and Culture During the Constitutional Revolution." *Iranian Studies* 23:77–101.

———. 1999. Interview by author, South Bend, Ind., February.

Yudkin, Leon I. 1984. *1948 and After: Aspects of Israeli Literature.* Manchester: University of Manchester Press.

14

Trends and Prospects

Jillian Schwedler and Deborah J. Gerner

The Middle East is a diverse and complex region whose history is as rich as its current challenges are difficult. Its long history as the crossroads for numerous ethnic and linguistic groups, the presence of oil under its desert sands, the significance of the land for the three major monotheistic religions, the diverse forms of political structure, and the complicated foreign policy relationships within the Middle East and between the region and the rest of the international community are among the factors that make the Middle East endlessly fascinating to students and scholars in a variety of disciplines.

Much of what we have discussed in this volume has looked backward, as we traced the imprint of the Middle East upon the world and of the world on these twenty-plus countries. In this final chapter, we look to the future and consider several acute challenges facing Israel, Iran, Turkey, and the Arab world. Among the most notable issues are those related to the role of religion in shaping society, the need for economic development that alleviates (rather than increases) inequality, continued foreign intervention in political as well as economic realms, and the steadily increasing demand for more accountable and participatory—even democratic—governments.

▓ The Contemporary Middle East

The Middle East is not defined only by state boundaries but by history, economic interactions, cultural patterns, and natural resources, among other attributes. All are important if we want to understand this region.

In contrast to the rich description that has been presented by authors in this book, many Europeans and North Americans still view the Middle East as "the exotic Orient" referred to in Edward Said's famous 1979 book, *Orientalism:* culturally undeveloped and unsophisticated when compared to Europe, with anachronistic and undemocratic political institutions that are inferior to those of "the West" and dominated by an extremist religion—Islam. This unfortunate attitude is shaped not only by ignorance and the fear of peoples and ideas that are different from our own, but also by the distorted images of the region that are used to justify continued Western political intervention (such as the 2003 war on Iraq) while portraying Western culture as superior.

These biases run deep, and events such as the September 11 attacks go far to perpetuate the fear and hatred many Westerners feel toward a region they hardly know, let alone understand. Yet even for those with no Arabic, Persian, Turkish, Hebrew, or Berber language skills, the region is not difficult to get to know. One place to start is with the extraordinarily rich cultural heritage, from being the birthplace of three major religions to its long literary tradition. In Chapter 12, miriam cooke illustrates the myriad of ways that "Middle Eastern literatures have become privileged sites for recording and engaging with sociopolitical tensions and conflicts," particularly those related to independence and postcolonial struggles.

Until relatively recently, most Middle Eastern intellectuals—and most of the sons of political leaders—were educated in Europe or North America. Even within the region, Western-oriented institutions such as the American University in Cairo and the American University in Beirut educated a disproportionate number of professionals and government officials. For individuals who were not part of this privileged class, education was predominantly focused on Quranic learning.

In the last decades of the twentieth century, this situation began to change. Modern communication systems were installed in all but the most remote villages, modernizing governments instituted comprehensive literacy programs, and, aided by the availability of revenues from petroleum, distinctly Middle Eastern secular universities, with large student bodies drawn from both the middle and working classes, began to thrive. As seemingly mundane items such as transistor radios, cassette players, videocassette recorders, and photocopiers became more common, Middle Easterners had increased access to information within their own countries, with other countries in the regions, and with the rest of the world. This is not to suggest that they were ever cut off, or unaware of global economic, social, and political trends.

But along with the rise of satellite television stations such as al-Jazeera, these new means of information exchange meant that governments could no longer dominate the information that reached their populations. The availability of cell phones meant that one no longer had to wait sometimes years for telephone service to be connected, nor did one have to have the wealth to bribe the necessary people. Cell phone technology has also changed the face

Satellite dishes like these in the old city in Sana'a, Yemen,
began to appear atop houses in many parts of the Middle East
years before the government legalized them.

of refugee flows, as the two-million-plus Iraqi refugees who fled to Syria, Jordan, and elsewhere often arranged for a place to stay with friends and relatives well before they arrived. Indeed, for families that left a male relative behind—often to maintain and protect family property—cell phones have proven to be a lifeline that keeps families connected as well as facilitates the flow of detailed information in both directions. Even the Internet, which remains limited in its reach as governments struggle to control content, has led to new forms of exchange, with blogs connecting diaspora communities with their home countries and voices of dissent finding wider and more diverse audiences. Upon this closer inspection, the "clash of civilizations" that is supposed to characterize the yawning divide between the West and the Middle East (among other regions) is less about religion and culture than it is about inequality and dispossession of the vast majority of the people from their wealthy, privileged political and economic elite. Incumbent leaders use the language and symbolism of Islam to justify their (mostly) authoritarian regimes as much as opposition groups appeal to Islam in their challenges to the status quo inequality. Religious revival movements mobilize and spend vast sums trying to affect the shape of government policies domestically and abroad, just as they do in the United States. Teenage bloggers in Iran complain that their parents won't let them date whomever they want, just as teenagers do in the West. This is not to suggest that there are no differences between the Middle East and the West, as there certainly are, but there are also similarities, familiar situations, and shared concerns of parents wanting children to have better lives. Thus the real challenge of understanding the contemporary Middle East is not one of learning the particularities of a different culture (although those challenges exist), but of recognizing why political, social, and economic patterns differ from elsewhere in certain ways, and why they are similar in others.

▨ Economic Development

Extremes of poverty and wealth exist in the region—Mauritania is one of the poorest countries in the world, Kuwait one of the wealthiest—but neither extreme is typical of the area as a whole. The great majority of the population live in countries such as Egypt, Turkey, and Iran that have a level of development similar to that found in much of Asia and Latin America. As Agnieszka Paczynska illustrates in Chapter 7, these countries struggle to create a basic industrialized infrastructure (roads, bridges, airports, electrical and communications grids) while simultaneously wondering how to position themselves within a global system that has, at least for the world's wealthiest states, become postindustrial.

As in most of the developing world, such efforts are frequently complicated by accumulated debt from prior failed projects, outmoded governmental institutions, and entrenched elite intent on increasing their personal wealth at the expense of the country as a whole. The economic and political legacies of European imperialism in the Middle East have also hindered the creation of autonomous industrial programs independent of foreign assistance, external borrowing, or intervention by international organizations, a pattern that is characteristic of historically colonized states throughout the world.

In addition, as Valentine Moghadam discusses in Chapter 9, domestic obstacles such as burgeoning urbanization and the environmental problems that this often creates, rapid population growth relative to available resources, rising unemployment, and restrictions on economic opportunities for women have also contributed to economic stagnation and have made autonomous development an elusive goal. Finally, since independence, numerous Middle Eastern countries have had their economic development disrupted by internal civil war (e.g., Algeria, Lebanon, Somalia, Sudan, Turkey, Yemen), international war (e.g., Kuwait), or both (e.g., Egypt, Iran, Iraq, Israel, Syria).

As Mary Ann Tétreault illustrates in Chapter 8, one characteristic of some Middle Eastern economies makes them different from most other countries: the role of oil extraction. From Algeria to Yemen, petroleum has paid for many development projects. Indeed, during the 1970s and early 1980s oil wealth was a major distinguishing feature of the region. Yet by the end of the 1990s, the price of oil had fallen to levels more or less comparable to those prior to the price increases of the 1970s. When oil prices are low, oil-based economies are forced to terminate extravagant showcase projects and curtail massive weapons acquisition programs. During these periods, countries without large oil reserves—such as Egypt, Turkey, and Morocco—benefit from lower energy costs. With oil prices exceeding $100 a barrel in mid-2008, however, these trends are likely to be reversed for the near future.

Furthermore, the "oil decade" of 1973 to 1983 left two positive legacies. First, it led to the establishment of a large, indigenous professional class of engineers, bankers, doctors, and educators. (Ironically, because of the wide use of expatriates, these professionals are often from countries without oil wealth, notably Egypt, Jordan, and Palestine.) Second, even after taking into account failed and inappropriate projects, worthless boondoggles, and greed and corruption, oil revenues did pay for considerable basic infrastructure in much of the region. Both of these factors should facilitate further economic growth and development.

■ Ethnonationalist Conflicts

In large part as a result of the historical legacy of colonialism, ethnic, religious, and territorial conflicts have emerged as Middle Eastern peoples struggle to overcome situations created nearly one hundred years ago. At the core of each such conflict is the straightforward desire to gain increased control over their political lives. In Chapter 3, historian Arthur Goldschmidt Jr. analyzes the interaction of foreign and indigenous political entities that led to the creation of states whose boundaries rarely reflect the distribution of the region's nationalities. The results have been problematic for decades.

The current circumstances of the Kurds is a key example both of this lack of correspondence between state boundaries and national groups and of the role that outside powers have played in the region. British interest in the petroleum resources of Kurdistan led to the division of the Kurdish nation among Iran, Iraq, Turkey, and Syria rather than its unification into an independent Kurdish state. The continuing tension between Palestinians and Israeli Jews over what was once the British mandate of Palestine is another example of this phenomenon. In Chapter 6, Simona Sharoni and Mohammed Abu-Nimer provide a framework for understanding this long-standing conflict and reflect on the prospects for its resolution on terms that are both just and enduring. Unfortunately, ethnonationalist conflicts defy easy solutions, but they are never intractable. Even as the civil war in Iraq increasingly looks like ethnic conflict, similar ethnically based conflicts in Iraq have been solved with the right leadership, political institutions, and inclusive national narrative (Davis, 2005).

■ Political Participation and Accountability

The peoples of the Middle East have been seeking, without exception, increased participation and political accountability from their governments. Numerous countries have undertaken political reforms that increase participation and representation, primarily through introduction or reinvigoration of elected national assemblies. In many cases, these bodies play little direct role in governance, or their power is undercut by appointed upper assemblies and executive power. However, the diversity of groups demanding increased participation and accountability—along with the fact that many regimes have introduced limited reforms—bodes well for the region's long-term democratic prospects. In the short term, entrenched authoritarian regimes, many of them handily supported by Western countries including the United States, remain the greatest obstacle to reform. But the fact that regimes feel compelled to introduce even cosmetic reforms indicates a sea change from the politics of the mid-twentieth century.

Substantive political reforms face many challenges. First, like governments everywhere, Middle Eastern states must find a way to accommodate the demands of the expanding professional and middle classes for increased influence and control over material and symbolic resources. One of the likely demands raised by these groups will be a substantial reduction in military expenditures. Military spending is an attractive target: the sheer amount of money involved is very large and there is widespread sentiment that those funds could perhaps be better spent on socioeconomic programs that provide greater good for society. Furthermore, because military spending occurs secretly under the guise of "national security," it is prone to both waste and corruption, neither of which has wide acceptability in the eyes of the new professional and middle classes.

At the same time, as Deborah J. Gerner and Philip A. Schrodt discuss in Chapter 4, the military remains a formidable force in Middle Eastern politics. Many governments have used military perks to co-opt potential opponents and secure the loyalty of ethnic minorities. The military also tends to be closely associated with internal security services, which can enable it to be tremendously disruptive in an unstable situation (as Algeria has demonstrated in the 1990s). The close association of the military with an established regime—as found in Jordan, Libya, Syria, and Yemen, among others—further complicates any serious attempt to reduce military influence.

Yet the Middle East is already in the midst of a tremendous transformation as the aging post–World War II generation of leaders is replaced by significantly younger rulers. This, too, has implications for how the issues of leadership and political accountability might play out. In some instances, particularly simple dynastic progressions, the transitions may well be routine; thus far, the new monarchs have shown significantly more interest in—even enthusiasm for—political reform than their predecessors. In contrast, replacing personalistic leaders who have governed for decades, such as Egypt's Hosni Mubarak and Libya's Muammar Qaddafi, is likely to be messy, notwithstanding the existence of formal institutions intended to address this situation. We may even see what some jokingly call the Middle East's "emerging monarchies": Syria's Hafez al-Assad was succeeded by his son, Bashar; Egypt's Gamal Mubarak appears a likely successor to his father Hosni; Yemen's Ahmad Salih to his father Ali Abdullah.

A third aspect of political accountability has already been alluded to: the need for governments to determine how best to deal with the challenges posed by both extremist and moderate Islamist groups. Options include co-optation, combat, cooperation, and coping. One of the unknown variables is whether Islam is appealing to a given population on its own merits or if its current popularity rests primarily on its status as the most effective source of opposition to the state (given that other alternatives have been cut off). Many argue that the resounding success of Hamas in the Palestinian elections of February 2006 was more a reflection of dissatisfaction with the status quo of Fatah than it was of support for Hamas's Islamist orientation.

Similarly, scholars largely agree that during the Iranian revolution, the desire to replace the corrupt and pro-Western regime of the shah was the glue that brought intellectuals, workers, feminists, students, and merchants into alliance with conservative clerics who followed Khomeini. Turkey, in contrast, had ample opportunities for secular (and military) opposition; nevertheless, a strong traditionalist Islamic movement has arisen there. In this case, the impetus may be similar to what is driving Christian fundamentalism in the United States or the Orthodox Jewish political parties in Israel: the willingness of the Islamic movement to advocate on behalf of a social agenda that the established political parties are not eager to embrace.

Even more, it is important to keep in mind that the emergence of reform movements grounded in religion is a common response to modernization, and not a characteristic unique to Islam or to the Middle East. Hindu fundamentalism is a similarly powerful force in contemporary India, for instance, and Christian revivalists in the United States saw their influence increase dramatically under the two terms of George W. Bush. While religious movements have at times totally transformed their societies—the Protestant Reformation in Europe is a prime example—the far more common pattern is for a religious movement to induce a series of changes, then fade in influence.

Conclusion

The Middle East is far from the mysterious, exotic, impenetrable region it is often portrayed to be. As the chapters in this volume have illustrated, it is a region in which diverse peoples struggle—and have struggled for centuries—to improve their lives, gain the dignity of self-governance, and live by the moral frameworks that inspire them. Every region of the world faces particular sets of challenges, obstacles that inhibit political, economic, and social reforms. The Middle East is no different, and we hope that this collection of writings has provided you with the conceptual frameworks and historical detail necessary to help you understand these challenges. We also hope that you do not dwell on what is least familiar and instead recognize and explore those issues that you share with the region's peoples and their aspirations. Whether you find that connection through literature, a strong sense of religious identity, or elsewhere, recognizing and building on those connections provides the most tangible and effective means of bridging the artificial "cultural" divides on which all conflict and violence is founded.

▓ Bibliography

Davis, Eric. 2005. *Memories of State: Politics, History, and Collective Identity in Modern Iraq.* Berkeley: University of California Press.
Said, Edward W. 1979. *Orientalism.* New York: Vintage.

Acronyms

AAA	American Anthropological Association
ADEW	Association for the Development and Enhancement of Women
AHC	Arab Higher Committee for Palestine
AKP	Justice and Development Party (Turkey)
ANAP	Anavatan Partisi (Motherland Party, Turkey)
ARAMCO	Arabian American Oil Company
ASU	Arab Socialist Union
B.C.E.	before the common era
BP	British Petroleum
C.E.	common era
CFP	French National Oil Company
CIA	Central Intelligence Agency (United States)
CNN	Cable News Network
DFLP	Democratic Front for the Liberation of Palestine
DHS	Demographic and Health Surveys
DNA	deoxyribonucleic acid
EFTA	European Free Trade Association
ESCWA	Economic and Social Commission for West Asia (UN)
EU	European Union
FDI	foreign direct investment
FIS	Islamic Salvation Front (Algeria)
FLN	National Liberation Front (Algeria)
GAFTA	Greater Arab Free Trade Area
GAP	Güneydocu Anadolu Projesi (Turkey)
GCC	Gulf Cooperation Council

GDP	gross domestic product
GNP	gross national product
Hamas	Islamic Resistance Movement (Palestine)
HDI	Human Development Index
HTS	Human Terrain Systems
IAF	Islamic Action Front (Jordan)
ICJ	International Court of Justice
IEA	International Energy Agency
IFI	international financial institution
ILO	International Labour Organization
IMF	International Monetary Fund
IOC	international oil company
IPC	Iraq Petroleum Company
ISI	import substitution industrialization
IWPR	Institute for War and Peace Reporting
JDP	Justice and Development Party (Turkey)
KDP	Kurdistan Democratic Party (Iraq)
KOC	Kuwait Oil Company
MENA	Middle East–North Africa
MNP	Milli Nizam Partisi (National Order Party, Turkey)
MSP	Milli Selemet Partisi (National Salvation Party, Turkey)
MTI	Islamic Tendency Movement (Tunisia)
NATO	North Atlantic Treaty Organization
NDP	National Democratic Party (Egypt)
NGO	nongovernmental organization
NIOC	National Iranian Oil Company
OAPEC	Organization of Arab Petroleum Exporting Countries
OECD	Organization for Economic Cooperation and Development
OPEC	Organization of Petroleum Exporting Countries
PA	Palestinian Authority
PCP	Palestine Communist Party
PDR Yemen	People's Democratic Republic of Yemen (South Yemen)
PFLP	Popular Front for the Liberation of Palestine
PKK	Kurdistan Workers Party (Turkey)
PLO	Palestine Liberation Organization
PNA	Palestinian National Authority
PPP	purchasing power parity
PROTA	Project for Translation from Arabic
PUK	Patriotic Union of Kurdistan (Iraq)
QIZ	Qualifying Industrial Zone
RP	Refah Partisi (Welfare Party, Turkey)
SAVAK	Sazman-e Ettelaat va Amniyat-e Keshvar (Iran)
UAE	United Arab Emirates

UAR	United Arab Republic
UN	United Nations
UNDP	United Nations Development Programme
UNESCO	United Nations Educational, Scientific, and Cultural Organization
UNIFEM	United Nations Development Fund for Women
UNRWA	United Nations Relief and Works Agency for the Palestinian Refugees in the Near East
USAID	US Agency for International Development
USFP	Socialist Union of Popular Forces (Morocco)
USSR	Union of Soviet Socialist Republics, the Soviet Union
WMD	weapon of mass destruction
WTO	World Trade Organization
YAR	Yemen Arab Republic (North Yemen)

Basic Political Data

The Basic Political Data was updated by Sam Fayyaz from material originally compiled by David Dolson and Deborah J. Gerner and previously updated by Waseem El-Rayes and Deborah J. Gerner. While the data are based on information from a variety of sources, accurate data on Middle Eastern political events are often difficult to obtain and conflicting accounts and dates are common. Although we have generally used at least three different sources to corroborate each item, readers may nonetheless find discrepancies in other sources, including some material presented in the chapters. All population figures are estimates from the 2006 UN Department of Economic and Social Affairs Population Division except for the West Bank and Gaza Strip, which are from the CIA World Factbook. The UN Development Programme's Human Development Index (HDI) is a composite measure based on life expectancy; adult literacy; combined primary, secondary, and tertiary enrollment in school; and adjusted per capita income in each country. The HDI score can range from 0.0 to 1.0, with higher numbers reflecting greater development in terms of longevity, knowledge, and a decent standard of living; n/a indicates the data is not available.

Democratic and Popular Republic of Algeria
Capital City   Algiers
Date of Independence from France   July 3, 1962
Population   33,858,000
HDI Score   0.733
Rulers Since Independence
1. President Ahmed Ben Bella, 1962–June 1965
2. President Houari Boumedienne, June 1965–December 1978

3. President Benjedid Chadli, February 1979–1992
4. Five-member High Council of State, headed by Muhammed Boudiaf, fulfilled the function of the head of state until January 1994
5. President Liamine Zeroual, appointed January 30, 1994
6. President Liamine Zeroual, November 16, 1995–April 25, 1999
7. President Abdelaziz Bouteflika, elected on April 15, 1999, after all six rivals withdrew, charging electoral fraud

Kingdom of Bahrain
Capital City   Manama
Date of Independence from Great Britain   August 15, 1971
Population   753,000
HDI Score   0.866
Rulers Since Independence
1. Emir Isa ibn Salmon al-Khalifah, 1961–March 6, 1999
2. Emir Hamad ibn Isa al-Khalifah, March 6, 1999. In February 2002, Bahrain became a constitutional monarchy and Hamad took the title of king

Federal Islamic Republic of the Comoros
Capital City   Moroni
Date of Independence from France   July 6, 1975
Population   839,000
HDI Score   0.561
Rulers Since Independence
1. President Ahmed Abdallah, July 1975–August 1975
2. Coup led by Ali Soilih, August 1975; president, 1976–1978 (assassinated)
3. President Ahmed Abdallah, reinstated in coup by mercenaries under Robert Denard, 1978–November 27, 1989 (assassinated)
4. Robert Denard, November 27, 1989–December 15, 1989 (removed by French government)
5. Said Djohar, December 16, 1989–March 1996
6. President Mohammad Taki Abdoulkarim, March 1996–April 30, 1999
7. Coup led by Col. Assoumani Azali, April 30, 1999–2002
8. Col. Azali temporarily stepped down, only to be elected president in April 2002–2006
9. President Ahmed Abdallah Sambi, May 15, 2006–

Republic of Djibouti
Capital City   Djibouti
Date of Independence from France   June 27, 1977
Population   833,000
HDI Score   0.516

Rulers Since Independence
1. President Hassan Gouled Aptidon, June 24, 1977; reelected June 1981, April 1987, May 1993
2. President Isma'il Omar Guelleh, elected May 8, 1999; reelected April 2005

Arab Republic of Egypt
Capital City   Cairo
Date of Independence from Great Britain   February 28, 1922
Population   75,498,000
HDI Score   0.708
Rulers Since Independence
1. King Fu'ad I, 1917–1936
2. King Farouk, 1936–1952 (overthrown in coup led by Col. Gamal Abdul Nasser and Abdul al-Hakim)
3. President Mohammed Neguib, June 1953–November 1954
4. Prime Minister Gamal Abdul Nasser, 1954–1956; president, 1956–1970
5. President Anwar Sadat, 1970–October 1981 (assassinated)
6. President Hosni Mubarak, October 14, 1981–   ; reelected 1987, 1993, 1999, 2005

Islamic Republic of Iran
Capital City   Tehran
Date of Independence   Not colonized
Population   71,208,000
HDI Score   0.759
Rulers During Twentieth and Twenty-First Centuries
1. Qajar dynasty: Muzaffar al-Din, 1896–1907; Muhammad Ali, 1907–1909; Ahmad, 1909–1924
2. Pahlavi dynasty: Reza Shah, 1926–1941; Mohammad Reza Shah, 1941–1979
3. Religious leaders: Ayatollah Ruhollah Khomeini, 1979–1989; Ayatollah Sayyed Ali Khamenei, 1989–
Presidents: Mehdi Bazargan, 1979–1980; Abolhassan Bani-Sadr, 1980–1981; Muhammad Ali Raja'i, 1981; Sayyed Ali Khamenei, October 1981–July 1989; Hojatolislam Ali Akbar Hashemi Rafsanjani, July 1989–1997; Mohammad Khatami, 1997–2005; Mahmood Ahmadinejad, 2005–

Republic of Iraq
Capital City   Baghdad
Date of Independence from Great Britain   October 3, 1932
Population   28,993,000
HDI Score   n/a

Rulers Since Independence
1. King Faisal I, 1921–1933
2. King Ghazi ibn Faisal, 1933–1939
3. King Faisal II, 1939–July 14, 1958 (overthrown)
4. Brig. Gen. Abd al-Karim Qasim, July 14, 1958–February 1963 (overthrown)
5. National Council of Revolutionary Command led by Prime Minister Ahmad Hasan al-Bakr and President Abd al-Salaam Arif, February 1963–November 18, 1963 (overthrown)
6. President Abd al-Salaam Arif, November 1963–April 1966 (died in accident)
7. President Abd al-Rahman Arif, April 1966–July 17, 1968 (overthrown)
8. Revolutionary Command Council led by President Ahmad Hasan al-Bakr, July 17, 1968–July 16, 1979
9. President Saddam Hussein, July 16, 1979–2003 (overthrown by US-led invasion)
10. Interim authority (Coalition Provisional Authority and the Iraqi Governing Council), April 21, 2003–June 28, 2004
11. Iraqi Interim Government headed by Prime Minister Iyad Allawi, June 28, 2004–May 3, 2005
12. Iraqi Transitional Government headed by President Jalal Talabani and Prime Minister Ibrahim al Jaafari, May 3, 2005–May 20, 2006
13. Prime Minister Nouri al-Maliki, May 20, 2006–

State of Israel

Capital City   Tel Aviv or Jerusalem; contested internationally
Date of Independence from Great Britain   May 15, 1948
Population   6,928,000
HDI Score   0.932
Rulers Since Independence
1. Prime Minister David Ben-Gurion, 1948–1953
2. Prime Minister Moshe Sharett, 1953–1955
3. Prime Minister David Ben-Gurion, 1955–1963
4. Prime Minister Levi Eshkol, 1963–1969
5. Prime Minister Yigal Allon (acting), 1969
6. Prime Minister Golda Meir, 1969–1974
7. Prime Minister Yitzhak Rabin, 1974–1977
8. Prime Minister Shimon Peres (acting), 1977
9. Prime Minister Menachem Begin, 1977–1983
10. Prime Minister Yitzhak Shamir, 1983–1984
11. Prime Minister Shimon Peres, 1984–1986

12. Prime Minister Yitzhak Shamir, 1986–1992
13. Prime Minister Yitzhak Rabin, 1992–1995 (assassinated)
14. Prime Minister Shimon Peres, 1995–1996
15. Prime Minister Benjamin Netanyahu, 1996–1999
16. Prime Minister Ehud Barak, 1999–2001
17. Prime Minister Ariel Sharon, 2001–2006
18. Prime Minister Ehud Olmert, January 2006–

Hashemite Kingdom of Jordan
Capital City   Amman
Date of Independence from Great Britain   May 25, 1946
Population   5,924,000
HDI Score   0.773
Rulers Since Independence
1. Emir then King Abdullah I, 1921–July 1951 (assassinated)
2. King Talal, 1951–1953 (abdicated)
3. King Hussein I, 1953–February 7, 1999
4. King Abdullah II, February 7, 1999–

State of Kuwait
Capital City   Kuwait City
Date of Independence from Great Britain   June 19, 1961
Population   2,851,000
HDI Score   0.891
Rulers Since Independence
1. Shaikh Abdullah III al-Sabah, 1950–1965
2. Shaikh Sabah al-Salim al-Sabah, 1965–1977
3. Shaikh Jabir al-Ahmad al-Jabir al-Sabah, December 31, 1977–2006
4. Shaikh Saad al-Abdullah al-Sabah, January 15, 2006–January 24, 2006 (forced to step down because of ill health)
5. Shaikh Sabah al-Ahmed al-Jabir al-Sabah, January 29, 2006–

Republic of Lebanon
Capital City   Beirut
Date of Independence from France   November 22, 1943
Population   4,099,000
HDI Score   0.772
Rulers Since Independence
1. President Bisharaal-Khuri, 1943–1952 (prime ministers: Riyad al-Solh, Sami al-Solh)
2. President Camille Chamoun, 1952–1958 (prime ministers: Abdallah al-Yafi, Sami al-Solh, Rashid Karami)

3. President Fu'ad Chehab, 1958–1964 (prime minister: Rashid Karami)
4. President Charles Hilu, 1964–1970 (prime minister: Rashid Karami)
5. President Sulayman Franjiyya, 1970–1976 (prime ministers: Rachid Anis al-Solh, Rashid Karami, Saeb Salaam)
6. President Elias Sarkis, 1976–1982 (prime minister: Salim al-Hoss)
7. President Beshir Gemayel, 1982 (assassinated)
8. President Amin Gemayel, 1982–1988 (prime ministers: Shafiq al-Wazzan, Rashid Karami, Salim al-Hoss)
9. Gen. Michel Aoun, 1988–1990 (prime minister: Salim al-Hoss)
10. President Elias Hrawi, 1990–1998 (prime ministers: Salim al-Hoss, Umar Karami, Rafiq al-Hariri)
11. President Emile Lahoud, 1998–2007 (prime ministers: Salim al-Hoss [December 2, 1998–October 23, 2000], Rafiq al-Hariri [October 23 2000–October 21, 2004], Omar Karami [October 21, 2004–April 15, 2005], Najib Mikati [April 15, 2005–June 30, 2005], Fouad Siniora July 19, 2005–   )
12. Presidency Vacant from November 23, 2007 (prime ministers Fouad Siniora July 19, 2005–)

Socialist People's Libyan Arab Jamahiriyah (Republic)
Capital City   Tripoli
Date of Independence from Italy   December 24, 1951
Population   6,160,000
HDI Score   0.818
Rulers Since Independence
1. King Idris, 1951–1969
2. Col. Muammar Mohammed Qaddafi, leader of the revolution, September 1969–

Islamic Republic of Mauritania
Capital City   Nouakchott
Date of Independence from France   November 28, 1960
Population   3,124,000
HDI Score   0.550
Rulers Since Independence
1. President Mokhtar Ould Daddah, 1961–July 10, 1978 (overthrown)
2. Lt. Col. Mustapha Ould Mohammed Salek, July 10, 1978–June 1979 (forced to resign)
3. Lt. Col. Mohammed Mahmoud Ould Louly, June 1979–January 4, 1980 (overthrown)
4. Lt. Col. Mohamed Khouna Ould Haidalla, January 4, 1980–December 1984 (overthrown)

5. Col. Maaouya Ould Sidi Ahmed Taya, 1984–2005 (overthrown); elected president in first multiparty elections, January 24, 1992; reelected December 12, 1997
6. Col. Ely Ould Mohamed Vall, August 3, 2005–2007
7. President Sidi Ould Cheikh Abdallahi, March 11, 2007–

Kingdom of Morocco
Capital City   Rabat
Date of Independence from France   March 2, 1956
Population   31,224,000
HDI Score   0.646
Rulers Since Independence
1. King Mohammed V, March 2, 1956–1961
2. King Hassan II, March 3, 1961–July 23, 1999
3. King Mohammed VI, July 23, 1999–

Sultanate of Oman
Capital City   Muscat
Date of Independence   Never officially a colony, but strong British influence
Population   2,595,000
HDI Score   0.814
Rulers During Twentieth and Twenty-First Centuries
1. Sultan Faisal ibn Turki al-Said, 1888–1913
2. Sultan Tamir ibn Faisal al-Said, 1913–1932
3. Sultan Said ibn Tamir al-Said, 1932–1970
4. Sultan Qaboos ibn Said al-Said, 1970–

Palestinian Territories: West Bank and Gaza Strip
Capital City   Contested internationally
Date of Independence   The Palestinian Authority gained control from Israel of most of the Gaza Strip and Jericho areas in May 1994. Subsequent agreements increased the land under Palestinian or joint Israeli-Palestinian jurisdiction. Since 2001, however, Israel has retaken control of many of these areas.
Population   West Bank: 2,535,927; Gaza Strip: 1,482,405
HDI Score   0.731
Rulers Since Gaza-Jericho Agreement
1. President Yasser Arafat, January 1996–2003
2. President Yasser Arafat and Prime Minister Mahmoud Abbas, 2003; President Yasser Arafat and Prime Minister Ahmad Qura'i, 2003–2004
3. President Rauhi Fattouh and Prime Minister Ahmad Qura'i, 2004–2005

4. President Mahmoud Abbas and Prime Minister Ahmad Qura'i, January 15, 2005–December 15, 2005; President Mahmoud Abbas and Prime Minister Nabil Shaath, December 15, 2005–December 24, 2005; President Mamoud Abbas and Prime Minister Ahmad Qura'i, December 24, 2005–February 19, 2006; President Mahmoud Abbas and Prime Minister Ismail Haniya, February 19, 2006–June 14, 2007; President Mahmoud Abbas and Prime Minister Salam Fayyad, June 15, 2007–

State of Qatar
Capital City   Doha
Date of Independence from Great Britain   September 3, 1971
Population   841,000
HDI Score   0.875
Rulers Since Independence
1. Emir Ahmad ibn Ali, 1971–1972
2. Emir Khalifah ibn Hamad al-Thani, 1972–June 27, 1995
3. Emir Hamad ibn Khalifah ibn Hamad al-Thani, June 27, 1995–

Kingdom of Saudi Arabia
Capital City   Riyadh
Declaration of State   September 23, 1932
Population   24,735,000
HDI Score   0.812
Rulers Since Independence
1. King Abdul Aziz ibn Saud, 1932–1953
2. King Saud ibn Saud, 1953–1964
3. King Faisal ibn Saud, 1964–1975 (assassinated)
4. King Khalid ibn Saud, 1975–1982
5. King Fahd ibn Saud, 1982–2005
6. King Abdullah ibn Saud, 2005–

Somali Democratic Republic
Capital City   Mogadishu
Date of Independence from Italy and Great Britain   July 1, 1960
Population   8,699,000
HDI Score   n/a
Rulers Since Independence
1. President Aden Abdulla Osman, 1960–1967
2. President Abdirashid Ali Shirmarke, 1967–1969 (assassinated)
3. Maj. Gen. Mohammed Siad Barre, 1969–January 27, 1991
4. No functional government, 1991–2000
5. President Abdikassim Salad Hassan, August 26, 2000–2004 (prime minister: Hassan Abshir Farah [2001–2003], Muhammad Abdi Yusuf [2003–2004])

6. President Abdullahi Yusuf Ahmed, October 14, 2004– (prime minister: Ali Muhammad Ghedi [2004–2007], Salim Aliyow Ibrow [2007], Nur Hassan Hussein [November 24, 2007–])

Democratic Republic of Sudan
Capital City   Khartoum
Date of Independence from Great Britain   January 1, 1956
Population   38,560,000
HDI Score   0.526
Rulers Since Independence
1. Prime Minister Ismail al-Azhari, 1956
2. Prime Minister Abdulla Khalil, 1956–1958
3. Prime Minister Ibrahim Abboud, 1958–1964
4. Prime Minister Sir el-Khatim el-Khalifah, 1964–1965
5. Prime Minister Muhammed Ahmad Mahgoub, 1965–1966
6. Prime Minister Sayed Sadiq el-Mahdi, 1966–1967
7. Prime Minister Muhammed Ahmad Mahgoub, 1967–1969
8. Prime Minister Abubakr Awadallah, 1969
9. President Jaafar Mohammed Nimeiri, May 1969–April 1985 (overthrown)
10. Lt. Gen. Abdel Rahman Swareddahab, chairman, Transitional Military Council, April 6, 1985–1986
11. President Ahmed Ali al-Mirghani and Prime Minister Sadiq al-Mahdi, 1986–June 30, 1989 (overthrown)
12. Prime Minister Omar Hassan Ahmed al-Bashir, June 30, 1989; appointed president October 16, 1993; reelected 1996, 2000

Syrian Arab Republic
Capital City   Damascus
Date of Independence from France   April 17, 1946
Population   19,929,000
HDI Score   0.724
Rulers Since Independence
1. President Shukri al-Quwatly, 1946–1949 (overthrown)
2. Gen. Husni al-Zaim, March 1949–August 1949
3. Gen. Sami al-Hinnawi, August 1949–December 1949
4. Col. Adib Shishakli, December 1949–February 1954 (overthrown)
5. President Sabri al-Asali, 1956–1958
6. Gamal Abdul Nasser, president of United Arab Republic (Egypt and Syria), 1958–1961 (Abdul-Hakim was the Syrian supervisor during this time)
7. President Nazim al-Qudsi, 1961–1963
8. Gen. Amin al Hafiz, 1963–1966
9. President Salah al-Jadid, 1966–1970 (overthrown)

10. President Hafez al-Assad, 1970–July 17, 2000
11. President Bashar al-Assad, July 17, 2000–

Republic of Tunisia
Capital City   Tunis
Date of Independence from France   March 20, 1956
Population   10,327,000
HDI Score   0.766
Rulers Since Independence
1. Prime Minister Habib Bourguiba, 1956–July 1957 (becomes republic)
2. President Habib Bourguiba, July 1957–November 1987 (overthrown)
3. President Zine Abidine Ben Ali accedes to the presidency, November 1987; elected October 1999; reelected October 2004

Republic of Turkey
Capital City   Ankara
Date of Independence from Ottoman Empire   October 29, 1923
Population   74,877,000
HDI Score   0.775
Rulers Since Independence
1. President Mustafa Kemal (Kemal Atatürk after 1933), 1923–1938
2. President Ismet Inönü, 1938–1950
3. President Mahmud Celal Bayar, 1950–May 27, 1960 (overthrown)
4. General Cemal Gürsel, May 27, 1960–October 1961
5. President Cemal Gürsel, October 1961–1966
6. President Cevdet Sunay, 1966–1973
7. President Fahri Korutürk, 1973–September 12, 1980 (overthrown)
8. General Kenan Evren, September 12, 1980–1982
9. President Kenan Evren, 1982–October 1989
10. President Turgut Ozal, October 1989–April 1993
11. President Suleyman Demirel, April 1993–May 2000
12. President Ahmet Necdet Sezer, May 2000–August 2007
13. President Abdullah Gul, August 2007–

United Arab Emirates
Capital City   Abu Dhabi
Date of Independence from Great Britain   December 2, 1971
Population   4,380,000
HDI Score   0.868
Rulers Since Independence
1. Shaikh Zayid ibn Sultan al-Nuhayyan, 1971–2004
2. Shaikh Khalifa ibn Zayid al-Nuhayyan, 2004–

Yemen Arab Republic (North Yemen)

Date of Independence from Ottoman Empire 1918
Rulers Since Independence
1. Imam Yahya, 1918–1948 (murdered in an attempted coup)
2. Imam Ahmad ibn Yahya, 1948–1962
3. Muhammad al-Badr, 1962 (overthrown after one week)
4. Brig. Gen. Abdullah Sallal, 1962–1967
5. President Abdul Rahman al-Iryani, 1967–1974
6. President Ibrahim Hamdi, 1974–1977
7. President Ahmad Hussein Ghashmi, 1977–1978 (overthrown)
8. President Ali Abdullah Salih, 1978–1990

People's Democratic Republic of Yemen (South Yemen)

Date of Independent from Great Britain 1967
Rulers Since Independence
1. President Qahtan al-Sha'bi, 1967–1969 (overthrown)
2. President Salim Rubayyi'ali, 1969–1978 (executed)
3. President Abd al-Fattah Isma'il, 1978–1980 (resigned)
4. President Ali Nasser Muhammad, 1980–1986
5. President Haider Abu Bakr al-Attas, 1986–1990

Republic of Yemen

Capital City Sana'a
Date of Unification May 22, 1990
Population 22,389,000
HDI Score 0.508
Rulers Since Independence
1. Interim President Ali Abdallah Salih, 1990– ; elected president 1999; reelected 2006

▣ Bibliography

Anderson, Ray R., Robert F. Siebert, and John G. Wagner. 2000. *Politics and Change in the Middle East.* 6th. ed. Englewood Cliffs, N.J.: Prentice-Hall.

Bosworth, C. E., E. Van Donzel, B. Lewis, and Ch. Pellat (eds.). 1983. *Encyclopedia of Islam.* Vol. 5. Leiden, Netherlands: E. J. Brill.

Burr, J. Millard, and Robert O. Collins. 1995. *Requiem for the Sudan War, Drought, and Disaster Relief on the Nile.* Boulder, Colo.: Westview Press.

Central Intelligence Agency. 2007. *CIA World Factbook.* Available from www.cia .gov/library/publications/the-world-factbook.

Collelo, Thomas (ed.). 1988. *Syria: A Country Study.* Area Handbook Series. Washington, D.C.: Government Printing Office.

———. 1989. *Lebanon: A Country Study.* Area Handbook Series. Washington, D.C.: Government Printing Office.

Congressional Quarterly. 2000. *The Middle East.* 9th ed. Washington, D.C.: Congressional Quarterly.

Europa Publications. 2003. *The Middle East and North Africa.* 49th ed. Rochester, Kent, UK: Staples Printers Rochester Limited.

Gordon, April A., and Donald L. Gordon (eds.). 2001. *Understanding Contemporary Africa.* 3rd ed. Boulder, Colo.: Lynne Rienner.

Handloff, Robert E. (ed.). 1990. *Mauritania: A Country Study.* Area Handbook Series. Washington, D.C.: Government Printing Office.

Hiro, Dilip. 2003. *The Middle East at Your Fingertips: A Dictionary of the Middle East.* New York: Carroll & Graf.

Korbani, Agnes. 1995. *The Political Dictionary of Modern Middle East.* Lanham, Md.: University Press of America.

Legum, Colin (ed.). 1976–1998. *Middle East Contemporary Survey.* The Shiloah Center for Middle Eastern and African Studies, Tel Aviv University. Vols. 1–22. New York: Holmes and Meir.

Metz, Helen Chapin (ed.). 1989. *Libya: A Country Study.* Area Handbook Series. Washington, D.C.: Government Printing Office.

———. 1990. *Iraq: A Country Study.* Area Handbook Series. Washington, D.C.: Government Printing Office.

———. 1991. *Egypt: A Country Study.* Area Handbook Series. Washington, D.C.: Government Printing Office.

———. 1991. *Jordan: A Country Study.* Area Handbook Series. Washington, D.C.: Government Printing Office.

———. 1992. *Sudan: A Country Study.* Area Handbook Series. Washington, D.C.: Government Printing Office.

———. 1993. *Saudi Arabia: A Country Study.* Area Handbook Series. Washington, D.C.: Government Printing Office.

———. 1993. *Somalia: A Country Study.* Area Handbook Series. Washington, D.C.: Government Printing Office.

———. 1994. *Algeria: A Country Study.* Area Handbook Series. Washington, D.C.: Government Printing Office.

———. 1994. *Persian Gulf States: Country Studies.* Area Handbook Series. Washington, D.C.: Government Printing Office.

Nelson, Harold D. (ed.). 1985. *Morocco: A Country Study.* Area Handbook Series. Washington, D.C.: Government Printing Office.

———. 1986. *Tunisia: A Country Study.* Area Handbook Series. Washington, D.C.: Government Printing Office.

Simon, Reeva S., Philip Mattar, and Richard W. Bulliet (eds.). 1996. *Encyclopedia of the Modern Middle East.* 5 Vols. New York: Simon and Schuster.

Sluglett, Peter, and Marion Farouk-Sluglett (eds.). 1996. *The Times Guide to the Middle East.* London: Times Books.

United Nations Department of Economic and Social Affairs Population Division (2006). "World Population Prospects, Table A.1" (electronic file). 2006 revision. United Nations.

United Nations Development Programme. 2007–2008. *Human Development Report 2007–2008.* New York: Oxford University Press.

Wright, John W. (ed.). 2003. *The New York Times 2003 Almanac.* New York: Penguin Books.

The Contributors

Mohammed Abu-Nimer is associate professor of international peace and conflict resolution in the School of International Service at American University in Washington, D.C.

miriam cooke is professor of Arab cultures at Duke University in North Carolina.

Deborah J. Gerner was professor of political science at the University of Kansas in Lawrence.

Arthur Goldschmidt Jr. is professor emeritus of Middle East history at Pennsylvania State University in University Park.

Laurie King-Irani is a social anthropologist and cofounder of Electronic Intifada.

Ian R. Manners is professor of geography at the University of Texas at Austin.

Valentine M. Moghadam is professor of sociology at Purdue University.

Agnieszka Paczynska is associate professor at the Institute for Conflict Analysis and Resolution at George Mason University in Virginia.

Barbara McKean Parmenter is GIS research specialist and lecturer in urban and environmental policy and planning at Tufts University in Massachusetts.

Philip A. Schrodt is professor of political science at the University of Kansas in Lawrence.

Jillian Schwedler is associate professor of political science at the University of Massachusetts, Amherst.

Simona Sharoni is associate professor of women's studies at State University of New York, Plattsburgh.

Lisa Taraki is associate professor of sociology at Birzeit University in Palestine.

Mary Ann Tétreault is the Cox distinguished professor of international affairs at Trinity University in San Antonio.

Index

Abasiyanik, Sait Faik Aziz, 406
Abbas, Mahmoud, 82, 90, 91, 157, 207
Abbas, Muhammad (Egyptian ruler), 55
Abbasid tribe, 45
Abdülhamid II (Ottoman ruler), 55, 56
Abdullah II (King of Jordan), 119
Abdullah (King of Jordan), 95
Abdullah (King of Saudi Arabia), 120
Abou-Saif, Laila, 18
Abu Bakr, 44
Abu Dhabi: governance in, 121, 122
Abu-Nimer, Mohammed, 5, 177–215
Achaemenids, 39, 40
Aden: British occupation, 53, 57, 63
Adivar, Halide Edip, 402, 403
Adnan, Etel, 424
Adonis, 420
'Adwan, Mamduh, 417
Afghanistan, 13; occupation by United
    States, 80; sociocultural terrain of, 309;
    Soviet occupation of, 75
Aflaq, Michael, 111
Aghadir Trade Agreement (2004), 238
Agnon, Shmuel Yosef, 431
Agriculture: ancient, 37, 38; aridity and
    water, 19–23; dryland, 19; grain
    cultivation, 37, 38; market, 52;
    permanent, 316; rain-fed, 19; small-
    scale, 315, 316; subsistence, 315
Ahmadinejad, Mahmoud, 81, 91, 130
Ajman: governance in, 122
Alavi, Buzurg, 421

Albright, Madeleine, 310
Alexander the Great, 40, 95
Algeria: agriculture in, 227*tab;* in Arab
    Mahgreb Union, 238; bread riots in,
    234; cancellation of elections in, 98;
    civil war in, 68, 143–144, 244, 245;
    economic development in, 222*tab,* 225,
    226, 236*tab;* elections in, 69, 144;
    exports, 240; female workforce in, 290;
    fertility rates in, 286; five-year
    development program in, 245; French
    control of, 53, 61, 87; Front de
    Liberation Nationale (FLN) in, 68, 69,
    101; in Gulf Cooperation Council, 239;
    industrial contribution in, 227*tab;*
    informal economy in, 237*tab;* interest in
    World Trade Organization, 239;
    investment in, 245; Islamic Salvation
    Front in, 245; labor migration and,
    229*tab;* military expenditures, 102;
    political participation in, 108*tab;* public-
    sector employment, 292; remittances in,
    232; single-party rule in, 105; socialist
    ideology in, 226; state involvement in
    economic planning/production, 226;
    structural adjustment programs in, 244,
    245; unemployment in, 234, 245, 293,
    294*tab;* urbanization in, 283*tab;* war of
    independence in, 101, 143, 144;
    Western Sahara refugees in, 142;
    women's literacy in, 286; women's
    rights in, 350

Ali, Muhammad (Egyptian ruler), 51, 52, 53, 86
Ali, Sabhattin, 410
ibn Ali, Husayn, 58
Al-Qaida, 80, 85, 92, 141, 334, 393, 395
Al Wifaq (Bahrain), 122
Amin, Qasim, 402
al-Amir, Daisy, 408
Amirhsahy, Mahshid, 427
Anatolia, 47, 48, 62
Anglo-Iranian Oil Company, 62, 69
Anglo-Persian Oil Company, 57, 62
Animism, 42
Anti-Semitism, 185
Aoun, Michel, 129
Aptidon, Hassan Gouled, 96
"Arab awakening," 110
Arab Higher Committee for Palestine (AHC), 186
Arabian American Oil Company (ARAMCO), 63, 259
Arab League, 13, 148, 149, 263; creation of, 66
Arab League Summit (1997), 238
Arab Legion, 59
Arab Mahgreb Union, 238
Arab National Charter, 156
Arab Revolt (1916), 58, 140, 186
Arab Socialist Resurrection Party, 111
Arab Socialist Union (ASU), 111
Arab states: demands for greater participation in, 67; early conquests by, 44–45; early scholarship in, 4; "exceptionalism" of, 111; before Islam, 42–43; nationalism and, 56; nationalization of foreign companies in, 68; political changes in, 67–69; political situation in, 85–133; socialism in, 67
Arafat, Yasir, 70, 71, 76, 79, 90, 156, 180, 181, 191, 193, 198, 202, 206, 207, 211
Armenia, 13, 57
al-Assad, Bashar, 116, 323
al-Assad, Hafez, 96, 116, 155
Assyria, 39
Aswan High Dam, 20, 67, 147
Atatürk, Mustafa Kemal, 60, 62, 101, 110, 139, 347, 401, 402, 416, 418
Atatürk Dam, 22
Ayyubids, 48
Azerbaijan, 13, 47, 49, 69

Baalbaki, Layla, 407
Baathism, 103, 112
Babylonia, 38, 39

Bahrain: agriculture in, 290; Al Wifaq in, 122; conflict with Qatar, 17, 142; economic development in, 222*tab,* 236*tab;* female employment in, 352; fertility rates in, 285, 286; in Gulf Cooperation Council, 150, 239; labor migration and, 229*tab;* large Shi'i population in, 92; military expenditures, 102; monarchy in, 117, 118, 122; political modernization in, 121; political participation in, 108*tab,* 122; political stability in, 96; prospect for democratization in, 97; trade with United States, 239; unemployment in, 294*tab,* 295*tab;* urbanization in, 282, 283*tab;* women's literacy in, 286; worker protests in, 242; in World Trade Organization, 239
Baker, James, 198
Balfour, Sir Arthur, 58
Balfour Declaration (1917), 17, 59, 87, 144, 186
al-Banna, Hassan, 106, 389
Barak, Ehud, 79, 90, 184, 205, 206
al-Barudi, Mahmud Sami, 418
Barzani, Massoud, 159, 160
Barzani, Mullah Mustafa, 158, 159
Bashu (film), 10
Bayza'i, Bahram, 10
Begin, Menachem, 73, 192
Behbahani, Simin, 420
Bektas, Habib, 428
Ben Ali, Zine Abidine, 115
Benjelloun, Tahar, 408, 409, 431
Beyatli, Yahya Kemal, 418
Bilad al-Sham, 12
Bilateral Investment Treaties, 239
bin Laden, Osama, 80, 170
Bolshevik Revolution (1917), 57
Boundaries: arbitrary nature of, 141, 312; broad interpretation of, 13; conflicts, 17, 153; cultural perspectives, 17, 18; disputes over, 142; geographical, 12–18; identity issues and, 18, 312–313; long, straight (noninclusive), 13; major changes in, 12–18; nonconformance to traditional interests, 139–141; offshore extensions, 17; political, 15; political-hydrological noncorrespondence in, 17; as products of European intervention, 12; as products of postwar politics, 139–141; urban, 29, 30
Bourguiba, Habib, 115

Boutros-Ghali, Boutros, 23
Britain: in anti-Communist alliance, 67;
attempts to prepare Middle Easterners
for eventual self-rule, 63; conflicting
commitments by, 58; domination of
Middle East by, 60; hostility to Zionism
by, 66; intervention in Syria, 52;
interventionist history of, 86, 111;
investments in Middle East, 57; Near
East and Middle East Forces of, 13;
occupation of Aden by, 53, 57, 63; in
Persia, 57; postcolonial structures
imposed by, 110; recommends partition
for Palestine, 187; reluctance to
relinquish control in Middle East, 138,
139; sphere of influence in Middle East,
57, 58
Bureaucracies, ancient, 37, 38
Bush, George H. W., 78, 156
Bush, George W., 80, 85, 89, 131, 156,
165, 166
Byzantine Empire, 40, 45, 47, 48, 49
Byzantium, 26

Caliphs: Abbasid, 45, 47, 48; right-guided,
44–45; Umayyad, 45, 47
Camp David II, 205, 206
Camp David Peace Accords (1979), 73, 79,
184; "A Framework for Peace in the
Middle East," 192
Capital: availability of, 54; European, 54;
flight, 246; foreign, 226; movement,
221; political, 91
Capitalism: Confucian, 99; economic
power of, 111; global, 99; industrialized,
111
Capitulations (treaties), 50, 62
Carter, Jimmy, 73
Chaldea, 39
Chedid, Andrée, 409
Cheney, Dick, 167
China–Gulf Cooperation Council free trade
zone, 239
Chraïbi, Driss, 408
Christianity, 26, 27, 40, 375–378; Coptic,
100, 377; Crusades and, 48; early
martyred followers, 41; Gospels in, 44;
Greek Orthodox, 377; growth of,
377–378; historical role of, 6; Maronite,
14, 64, 76, 81, 128, 377; Protestant
Reformation, 376; significant
communities of, 11; spread of,
375, 376
Chubak, Sadiq, 405, 412

Civil society: components of, 99;
institutions of, 99; and liberal
democracy, 99; nongovernmental
organizations in, 99; transplanting
Western institutions in, 99
Class, 309–341; administrative contexts of,
315; control over resources and, 333;
distinctions, 333; economic integration
and, 334; economic phenomena and,
313; education and, 180; formation, 334;
inequalities of wealth and, 333; modes
of economic production and, 333;
pyramidal structure of, 334; social, 180,
313, 333–335; social realities and, 6;
socioeconomic, 221; status, 313; urban
proletariat, 334
Cliency, 146–148
Clinton, Bill, 79, 156, 169, 205
Colonialism, 3, 4, 85; British-French
competition in, 87; cultural influences,
397–400; dependency and, 145–146;
efforts to develop centralized, uniform
governance through, 95; emergence of
Arab states from, 68; exploitation of
resources and, 100; French, 14; legacy
of, 5, 86–88; linguistic, 399–400;
opposition to from political left, 111;
suppression of indigenous institutions
and, 100; violation of local customs in,
63, 119, 144
Committee Against the War in Lebanon
(Israel), 193–194
Committee for Solidarity with Bir Zeit
University (Israel), 193
Conflict: boundary, 12–18, 142, 153;
ethnic, 89, 98, 309; ethnonationalist,
439; fishing/pearling rights, 17; inter-
Arab, 151, 152, 153; interethnic, 312;
international, 189–194; Iran-Iraq,
161–167; Israeli-Palestinian, 5; Kurdish,
158–161; mediation, 316; over water,
23; reactions to, 311; regional economies
and, 243–251; religious, 380–382;
resolution, 5, 177; tribal, 310
Constantine I (Roman Emperor), 26, 40,
375
Constitutionalism, 56–57
Convention on Wetlands of International
Importance (1971), 24
cooke, miriam, 4, 6
Crimean War, 52
Cromer, Lord, 55
Crusades, 48, 376, 377
Cultural: change, 5; diversity, 10, 312;

ferment, 6, 400–403; heterogeneity, 332; identity, 329; influences, 4; minorities, 182; similarity, 3; traditions, 94; uniformity, 324
Culture: Arab-Islamic, 104; Greek, 40; youth, 314
Cyprus: British occupation of, 57
Cyrenaica, 61
Cyrus (King of Persia), 39

Daneshvar, Simin, 407, 412
Darwish, Mahmud, 423
David (King), 38
Débèche, Assia, 409
Decolonization: socialism and, 111
Dehkhoda, Ali Akbar, 405
de Lesseps, Ferdinand, 53
Democracy: conditional, 125–131; and institutions of civil society, 99; liberal, 2, 97, 99, 111
Democratic Constitutional Rally (Tunisia), 115
Democratic Front for the Liberation of Palestine (DFLP), 180
Democratization, 79–83; decline in conditions supporting nondemocratic regimes and, 98; economic stability and, 98; ethno-national minorities and, 100; lack of support for from democratic powers, 97; and need for urbanized middle class, 98; unresolved issues in, 100
Dependency, 145–146
Destour Socialist Party (Tunisia), 115
Development: claims for need for authoritarian rule for, 101; economic, 92–94, 101, 115, 141, 282, 438–439; import substitution industrialization and, 226; industrial, 52, 226; sustainable, 247; uneven, 328
Dhimmi communities, 331, 378
Dib, Mohamed, 422
al-Din, Mu'izz, 27
al-Din al-bitar, Salah, 111
al-Din Shah, Nasir, 51, 52, 53
Djebar, Assia, 422, 423
Djibouti: economic development in, 222*tab;* military expenditures, 102; political participation in, 108*tab;* political stability in, 96; unemployment in, 234
Dubai: governance in, 122; worker protests in, 24

Al-e Ahmad, Jalal, 405

Economic: assistance, 221; control, 86; cooperation, 238; crises, 233–237; development, 92–94, 101, 115, 141, 282, 438–439; dislocation, 57; disparities, 316; distribution, 112; diversification, 334; growth, 54; institutions, 103; integration, 316, 334; interdependence, 221; justice, 111; liberalization, 99, 114, 116, 227; marginalization, 339; modernization, 289; production, 333; reform, 51, 228, 234; restructuring, 92, 292; scarcity, 328; sovereignty, 62; stagnation, 291; vulnerability, 334
Economy: diversified, 94; global, 332; market, 234, 245; mixed, 315; plantation, 255; political, 104
Education: changing gender roles and, 319, 320; erosion of Arab states' commitment to, 347; social class and, 180; women and, 346, 347
Egypt: in Aghadir Trade Agreement, 238; agriculture in, 21, 37, 38, 52, 227*tab,* 290; aid from United States, 67, 228; ancient history, 38; Arab conquest of, 44; arms imports in, 101; Aswan High Dam, 20, 67, 147; boundaries, 12; bread riots in, 234; British control of finances of, 54; British occupation of, 14, 55, 57, 65, 87; bureaucratized state in, 114; and Camp David Peace Accords (1979), 73; Christianity in, 377; colonialism and, 86; conflict with Yemen, 152; constitution in, 55, 60, 113; Debt Commission in, 14; demands for independence in, 55; economic development in, 54, 222*tab,* 225, 226, 236*tab;* elections in, 60, 114; European intervention in, 14; exports, 237, 238, 240; Fatimids in, 47; female employment in, 290, 352, 353; fertility rates in, 285, 286, 288; Free Officers group in, 111; free trade agreements, 238; French occupation of, 86; in Gulf Cooperation Council, 239; historical views, 5; importance of cities to, 25, 27, 28, 29, 30, 31; independence, 65; industrial contribution in, 227*tab;* informal economy in, 237*tab;* invasion by Napoleon, 14, 50; investment in, 54, 235; Iraqi refugees in, 250; labor migration and, 229*tab;* labor unrest in, 235; living standards in, 302–303; Mamluks in, 48, 49; military expenditures, 102; Muslim Brotherhood

in, 389, 390; National Democratic Party in, 113; nationalism in, 54–55, 60; National Party in, 55; normalization of relations with Israel, 73, 192; opposition in, 114; Ottoman rule restored in, 86; overthrow of monarchy in, 87, 111, 117; Palestinians in, 17; political participation in, 108*tab;* political stability in, 96; public-sector employment, 292; remittances in, 232; return of Sinai to, 189–190; Revolutionary Command Council in, 111; Roman conquest of, 40; single-party rule in, 98, 105, 113–114; socialist ideology in, 226; state bureaucracy in, 111; state involvement in economic planning/production, 226; toppling of monarchy in, 67; unemployment in, 293, 294*tab,* 295*tab;* in United Arab Republic, 68; urbanization in, 282, 283*tab;* use of Soviet weapons by, 71; Wafd Party in, 60, 65; in War of Attrition (1979), 71; war with Israel, 70, 71, 72; water management in, 20, 24; women's literacy in, 286; in World Trade Organization, 239; Young Egypt Group in, 65
El Saadawi, Nawal, 422, 430, 431
Emigration, 6
Environmental issues: air pollution, 30; history and, 37, 38; sanitation systems, 30; soil salinization, 20; in urbanization, 29, 30; water pollution, 24
Erbakan, Necmettin, 103
Erdoğan, Recep Tayyip, 126, 161
Eretz Yisrael (land of Israel), 58, 186
Ethiopia: colonization of, 42; Italian control of, 65
Ethnic: conflict, 89, 98, 309; identity, 312, 325, 329, 338; violence, 89
Ethnicity, 309–341, 325–331; as adaptive strategy to environmental challenges, 315–317; administrative contexts of, 315; as frame of meaning, 313; historical context of, 331–333; as mode of organization, 313; political marginalization and, 330; priority over citizenship, 317; rooted in political process, 328; social realities and, 6; stereotypes of, 312; and survival strategies, 330; theories of, 325, 328
Euphrates River: control of water flow from, 22; migrations to, 38
Eurocentrism, 13
Euro-Mediterranean Free Trade Area, 238, 239

European Free Trade Association (EFTA), 239

Faisal I (King of Iraq), 59, 63
Family: extended, 319; gender roles in, 319; importance in power structure, 94; networks, 94; women and, 355–358. *See also* Kinship
Fanon, Franz, 144
Farouk (King of Egypt), 65, 66, 67, 95, 111
Farrokhzad, Forugh, 420
Fasht al-Dibel rocks, 142
Fatah, 70, 82, 91, 157, 180, 181; conflict with Hamas, 182
Fatimids, 47
Fezzan, 61
Foda, Farag, 430, 431
France: control of Algeria, 61, 87; distrust of United States in leadership of Western alliance, 261; establishes protectorate in Tunisia and Morocco, 53, 61; expansion of colonial authority in Algeria and Tunisia, 14; imperial interests in Middle East, 138, 139; interventionist history of, 86, 111; investments in Middle East, 57; postcolonial structures imposed by, 110; relinquishes protectorates in Tunisia and Morocco, 68; sphere of influence in Africa, 57; takeover of Algeria by, 53, 61
French National Oil Company, 258
Front de Liberation Nationale (FLN), 68, 69
Fuad (King of Egypt), 65
Fujairah: governance in, 122

Gama'a Islamiyyah, 393
Gaza Strip: Christianity in, 377; civil war in, 91; deteriorating conditions in, 248; economic development in, 248; Palestinian refugees in, 67; takeover by Hamas, 82; unemployment in, 234; urbanization in, 283*tab*
Gemayel, Beshir, 193
Gender, 85; changing roles, 319, 320; family and, 319; kinship and, 324, 325; politics and, 6; poverty and, 297; social construction of, 324; values/norms and, 358–360. *See also* Women
Genghis Khan, 48
"Geniza Documents," 32
Geography, 9–34; aridity and, 18–25; boundaries, 9, 12–18; diversity in, 10; hydrological boundaries, 17;

multiple presentations of, 11; urban, 25–31
Germany: influence in Middle East, 13; Nazism in, 65, 66; as protector of Ottoman Empire, 57
Gerner, Deborah, 4, 5, 85–133, 143
al-Ghazai, Zaynab, 430
Ghaznavids, 47
Gibran, Khalil, 4
Golan Heights, 82; water control and, 21
Goldschmidt, Arthur Jr., 4, 5, 37–83, 86, 110, 185, 332, 374
Governance: aspects of Arab kingship, 118–119; authoritarian personalistic rule, 105–106, 115–116; centralized, 111; conservative monarchies, 105–106; constitutional monarchies, 105–106; democratic, 125–131; Islamic republic challenge to secular ideology, 106, 107; patriarchal, 105; self-determination and, 138; single-party revolutionary republic, 105, 113–115; sources of legitimation of, 105–106
Greater Arab Free Trade Area (GAFTA), 238
Great Powers: cliency and, 146–148; dependency and, 145–146; political agendas of, 5; relations with Middle East, 143–150
Greece: war of independence in, 52
Guelleh, Isma'il Omar, 96
Gül, Abdullah, 161
Gulf Cooperation Council (GCC), 150, 163, 239; expanded trade with Asia, 239
Gulf of Aqaba, 70, 165
Gulf States: agriculture in, 289; construction boom in, 242; diversification of interests in, 242; interest in high-tech industry, 242; labor force migration in, 18; migrant labor in, 242–243; recent social tensions in, 242, 243; uses of oil money in, 274–276
Gulf War, 271–272
Gunpowder, 48

Habibi, Emile, 423
Haddad, Malek, 422
Haghia Sophia (church), 26
Hajj, 32, 33, 34
al-Hakim, Tawfiq, 403, 416, 417
Hamas, 79, 91, 156, 157, 181, 248; conflict with Fatah, 182; election by Palestinians, 82; electoral victory of, 181, 182, 248; takeover of Gaza Strip,

82; Western world's refusal to accept electoral victory, 98
Hammurabi, 38
Haniyeh, Ismail, 157
Haqqi, Yahya, 403, 404, 426
Hariri, Rafik, 82, 128, 246
Hariri, Sa'ad, 128
Hashemites, 58, 59, 63
Hasim, Ahmet, 418
Hassan II (King of Morocco), 96, 118
Haussman, Georges-Eugène, 28
Hawar Islands, 142
Hedayat, Sadeq, 405, 412
Hetata, Sherif, 422
Hezbollah, 85
Historical issues: ancient, 37–41; environment and, 37, 38; Indo-Iranian invasions, 38–40; pastoral nomadism, 37, 38; Semitic invasions, 38–40
Hizb al-Nahdha Party (Tunisia), 115
Hizbullah, 81, 129, 246; activities in south Lebanon, 128; attacks against Israel by, 90, 91
Hoca, Nasreddin, 406
Holocaust, 185, 187
Human Terrain Systems Program, 309
Husayn, Taha, 400
Hussein (King of Jordan), 71, 96, 119, 123, 169
Huwar Islands, 17

Ibrahim Ali, 52
Identity: balances of power and, 312; boundaries and, 312–313; changing configurations of, 312; claims, 179; collective, 185, 203, 310; cultural, 329; essentialization of, 338; ethnic, 312, 325, 329, 338; ethnoreligious, 331; group, 149; humanly shaped, 312; institutionalization of, 312, 338; kinship systems in construction of, 314; mutability of, 324; national, 177, 314; Palestinian, 180–182; religious, 338; sectarian, 310; supra-state (Arab-Islamic), 104; systems, 310
Idilbi, Ulfa, 407
Idris, Yusuf, 404, 417
Idris (King of Libya), 147, 150
Imperialism: dependency and, 145–146; European, 86, 138; as method of enrichment of occupiers, 63, 119, 144; opposition to, 138; and preferential access to resources, 145; Western, 140; "white man's burden" and, 138

Import substitution industrialization, 226
Industrial Revolution, 52
Infrastructure: investment in, 282;
  urbanization and, 30
Innocent III (Pope), 376
Inönü, Ismet, 69
Institutions: bureaucratic, 95; charitable,
  28; civic, 99; corporate, 316;
  democratic, 98, 110; economic, 103;
  indigenous, 100; informal, 312; Muslim,
  62; nationalist, 111; political, 85, 91,
  103, 125–131; political-military, 101;
  public, 128, 246; sociopolitical, 316;
  state-controlled, 101; welfare, 62, 68;
  Western, 99
International Court of Justice (The Hague),
  17
International Monetary Fund: economic
  restructuring programs in, 92–93
International relations, 137–170
Intervention: by Britain, 52, 86, 111; in
  Egypt, 14; extraregional, 169; foreign, 5;
  by France, 86, 111; international, 5
Intifada, 76, 79, 156, 157, 158, 181, 183,
  184, 194–196, 200–202, 247, 334
Investment: efforts to attract, 235; in
  Egypt, 54; foreign direct, 141, 234; in
  infrastructure, 282
Iran: aggressive nationalism in oil
  marketing, 266; agriculture in, 227*tab,*
  290; Anglo-Iranian Oil Company in, 69;
  Anglo-Persian Oil Company in, 62; in
  anti-Communist alliance, 67; arms
  imports in, 101; authoritarian rule in,
  110; Ayatollah Khomeini in, 69, 70, 74;
  boundary conflicts with Iraq, 143;
  British sphere of influence in, 62;
  capabilities in long-range missile
  development, 91–92; Christianity in,
  377; conflicts with Iraq, 161–167;
  Council of Guardians in, 130; economic
  development in, 222*tab,* 225, 236*tab;*
  elections in, 130; exports, 240;
  expulsion of Germany from, 69; female
  employment in, 352; fertility rates in,
  285, 286, 287; increase in Shi'i power
  in, 88, 91; independence in, 61–63;
  industrial contribution in, 227*tab;*
  informal economy in, 237*tab;* interest in
  World Trade Organization, 239;
  investment in, 73; Iraqi refugees in, 250;
  Islamic Participation Front in, 130;
  Islamic Republican Party in, 76; Islamic
  revolution in, 73–76; Islamic rule in,

129; as Islamic state, 385–386; Judaism
  in, 375; land reform in, 107; military
  expenditures, 102; modernization
  policies in, 107, 110; monarchy in, 60,
  62, 101, 110; nationalism in, 62;
  nationalization of oil in, 257, 258;
  nuclear weapons in, 131; oil industry in,
  63; opposition to Shah in, 74; Pahlavi
  dynasty in, 62, 69, 98, 106, 107, 110,
  118; police state in, 98; political
  participation in, 108*tab;* prospect for
  democratization in, 99, 131; Qajar
  dynasty in, 118; remittances in, 232;
  repercussions of revolution in, 75, 76;
  restoration of Shah, 257; revolutionary
  transformation in, 96; SAVAK in, 74;
  secularization of, 62; seizure of United
  States embassy in, 74, 75; *sharia,*
  129; Soviet influence in, 69; support for
  Kurds from, 160; threat of nuclear
  weapons in, 92; unemployment in, 293,
  295*tab;* urbanization in, 282, 283*tab;*
  war with Iraq, 75; water management in,
  20; White Revolution in, 107; women's
  literacy in, 286; women's rights in, 349,
  350
Iran-Contra issues, 75, 162
Iraq: admission to League of Nations, 63;
  agriculture in, 21, 227*tab,* 290; in anti-
  Communist alliance, 67; anti-Western
  hostility in, 64; attack by United States
  on, 80; authoritarian personalistic rule
  in, 105, 116; Autonomous Kurdish
  Government in, 160; Baath Party in, 70,
  111; boundary conflicts with Iran, 143;
  British military intervention in, 64;
  British sphere of influence in, 58, 59;
  Christianity in, 377; claims on Kuwait,
  87; conflicts with Iran, 161–167;
  creation of, 87; economic development
  in, 222*tab,* 225, 248, 249; effect of
  ending of Cold War on, 88; federation
  with Jordan, 68; fertility rates in, 285,
  286; importance of cities to, 25, 26;
  increase in Shi'i power in, 88, 91, 92;
  independence in, 63; industrial
  contribution in, 227*tab;* informal sector
  in, 249, 250; infrastructure destruction,
  249; interest in World Trade
  Organization, 239; internal conflict in,
  89; invasion by United States, 132, 249,
  272–274; invasion of Kuwait by, 77–79,
  151, 152, 153, 270–271; Judaism in,
  375; literacy levels in, 249; long-term

stability issues, 89; Marsh Arabs in, 24; military coups in, 64; military expenditures, 102; nationalism in, 60; nationalization of oil industry, 265; "no-fly" zone in, 159; oil supply disruptions due to instability in, 93; overthrow of monarchy in, 117; political opposition in, 102, 103; political participation in, 108*tab;* prospect for democratization in, 98, 99; reconstitution of, 14; refugees from, 89, 90; remittances in, 232; Republican Guard in, 103; revolutionary transformation in, 96; ruling by patrilineal coalitions, 323; sanctions on, 249; separatist (Kurd) politics in, 158, 159; Shi'i Islam in, 63; sociocultural terrain of, 309; toppling of monarchy in, 67; unemployment in, 234, 249, 294*tab,* 295*tab;* US invasion of, 89, 90; urbanization in, 282, 283*tab;* use of chemical weapons, 75; war with Iran, 75; war with United States, 80–83; water management by, 22, 23; weakness of state in, 311; weapons of mass destruction in, 78

Iraq-Kuwait crisis, 77–79

Irgun Zvai Leumi, 73

Irrigation, 19; basin, 19, 20; drip, 23; large-scale, 37, 38; subsurface, 23; water control and, 21; year-round, 20

Islam, 378–380; beliefs and institutions, 44; building laws, 28; conversions to, 41, 47; Fatimids in, 47; first empire in, 45, 47; five pillars of, 44; fundamentalist, 388; hajj in, 32, 33, 34; hijra in, 43; historical role of, 6; jihad, 57; Mecca and, 43; moral issues in, 44; Muhammad and, 43–44; patrimony in, 47; political values in, 110; politicized, 314; Quran in, 19, 24, 44; residential neighborhood planning and, 28; right-guided caliphs and, 44–45; rise of, 41–50; *sharia,* 44, 48, 129, 331, 350, 379, 389; Shi'a, 17, 44–45, 47, 52, 75, 91, 92, 379; Sufi, 47; Sunni, 17, 45, 48, 52, 76, 82, 378–379; *ulama,* 62; *umma* in, 43, 44, 45, 378; unification of Arab tribes under, 41, 42; women's activism in, 367–369

Islambuli, Khalid, 393

Islamic Action Front (Jordan), 124, 391

Islamic Jihad, 209, 393

Islamic Participation Front (Iran), 130

Islamic Republican Party, 76

Islamic Resistance Movement, 181

Islamic Salvation Front (Algeria), 245, 393

Islamic Tendency Movement (Tunisia), 115

Isma'il, Muhammad (Egyptian ruler), 27, 28, 54

Israel: agriculture in, 21, 227*tab,* 289; aid from United States to, 228; arms imports in, 101; Ashkenazi Jews in, 183; attacks by Hizbullah, 82; bombs Syrian nuclear facility, 91; building of security fence on West Bank, 82; and Camp David Peace Accords (1979), 73; collective identity of, 179, 180, 182–185; Committee Against the War in Lebanon in, 193–194; Committee for Solidarity with Bir Zeit University in, 193; conflict over disengagement from Occupied Territories, 127–128; control in Occupied Territories, 199, 200; creation at expense of Palestinians, 178; creation of state of, 66, 87; democratic governance in, 126–128; economic development in, 222*tab,* 225; economic growth in, 94; elections in, 127; ethnically-defined political parties in, 91; ethnic cleansing of Palestinians in, 185; exports, 240; failure to deal with rights of Palestinians by, 126; female employment in, 352; fertility rates in, 286; fundamentalist movements in, 91; identification as Zionist society, 182; immigration into, 17; importance of religion in politics in, 91; industrial contribution in, 227*tab;* informal economy in, 237*tab;* invasion of Lebanon by, 76, 193, 246–247; Israel Beitainu Party in, 184; Israeli B'Aliyah Party in, 127; Israeli-Palestinian conflict and, 70–73; Kadima Party in, 128, 183, 184; labor migration and, 229*tab;* Labor Party in, 79, 95, 101, 127, 183, 198; Likud Party in, 127, 183; Mapai Party in, 101; military autonomy in, 102; military expenditures, 102; negotiations for withdrawal from Occupied Territories, 79; normalization of relations with Egypt, 192; occupation of West Bank and Gaza Strip, 189; Palestinians in, 182; Parents Against Silence in, 194; parliamentary instability in, 128; partial pullback from lands taken in wars, 73; Peace Now movement in, 192, 193, 212; peace treaty with Jordan, 79; personal status issues

overseen by religious courts in, 311;
plans for permanent retention of
Occupied Territories, 192; political
participation in, 108*tab*, 126–128;
political parties in, 183; political protest
activities in, 194; political stability in,
96; proliferation of small political
parties in, 128; reaches peace with
Egypt, 73; refusal to negotiate with
Palestine Liberation Organization, 73; as
religious state, 382–384; Sephardic Jews
in, 183; Shas Party in, 95; in Six-Day
War, 189; social diversity in, 182–183;
statehood, 17; support for construction
of settlements in Occupied Territories,
190, 191; trade with United States, 239;
urbanization in, 283*tab*; use of Israeli-
Palestinian conflict to establish unity in,
183; in War of Attrition (1979), 71; war
with Arab states, 70, 71, 72; water
management in, 24; Women Against the
Invasion of Lebanon in, 194; women's
literacy in, 286; women's rights in, 348,
349; in World Trade Organization, 239;
Yesh Gvul in, 194
Israel Beitainu Party (Israel), 184
Israeli B'Aliyah Party (Israel), 127
Israeli-Palestinian conflict, 5, 82, 153–158,
177–215; Arab Higher Committee for
Palestine in, 186; attempts at peace in,
183; defining "peace" and, 212, 213;
denial of legitimacy of each party's
claims in, 179; disarray of peace process
in, 90; dynamics of, 185–202;
exclusivist/ accommodationist
continuum for solutions to, 208–209;
history of, 185–202; identification of
central issues in need of resolution,
204–205, 206; intensification of, 70–73;
international recognition of Palestine
Liberation Organization during, 191;
intervention by Norway in, 152;
intifadas in, 200–202; Israeli perceptions
of, 185, 186; "land for peace" solution
to, 183; need for both parties to
recognize validity of other party's needs,
213–214; notion of national "imagined
community" as central issue in,
202–207; Oslo Agreement and, 90, 156,
157, 179, 181, 183, 198, 200, 201, 205,
206; Palestinian perceptions of, 185,
186; resolution attempts, 207–214;
"Road Map" initiative, 207; role of
outside parties in resolution, 210; role of

women in solutions to, 211; suicide
bombings and, 209; top-down or
bottom-up conflict resolution in, 211;
violent/nonviolent solution continuum,
209–210; weak prospects for resolution
of, 90–91
Istiqlal Party (Morocco), 61
Italy: colonial authority in Libya, 14;
control of Libya, 65, 143; in Ethiopia,
65; Fascism in, 65, 143

Jabra, Jabra Ibrahim, 427
Jamalzadeh, Mohammed Ali, 402
Janissaries, 49, 50, 51, 52
al-Jayyusi, Salma al-Khadra', 431
Jerusalem, 38; under Arab rule, 45;
Christian rule in, 48; destruction of
temple in, 41; Muslim rule in, 48; status
after Six-Day War, 190
Jewish Agency, 66
Jihad: justification for, 394; Ottoman, 57
Jihad al-Islami, 393
Jordan: in Aghadir Trade Agreement, 238;
agriculture in, 21, 227*tab*; Baath Party
in, 111; "Black September" in, 191;
boundaries, 12; bread riots in, 234;
Christianity in, 377; civil war in, 191;
clashes with Palestinian guerrillas, 71;
creation of, 87; economic development
in, 222*tab*, 236*tab*; elections in, 124;
exports, 238, 240; federation with Iraq,
68; female employment in, 290, 352;
fertility rates in, 286, 288; governmental
stability in, 96; industrial contribution
in, 227*tab*; informal economy in,
237*tab*; integration of Islamists into
governance, 123; investment in, 235;
Iraqi refugees in, 250; Islamic Action
Front in, 124; labor migration and,
229*tab*; military expenditures, 102;
monarchy in, 87, 96, 105, 118, 123–124;
Muslim Brotherhood in, 389, 390, 391;
normalization of relations with Israel,
79, 90; Palestinian refugees in, 17, 67,
100, 155; political participation in,
108*tab*, 123; political stability in, 96;
prospect for democratization in, 97, 99;
protests in, 235; public-sector
employment, 292; remittances in, 232;
service sector in, 289; state intervention
in, 227; trade with United States, 239;
unemployment in, 293, 294*tab*, 295*tab*;
urbanization in, 283*tab*; war with Israel,
71; water management in, 24; women's

literacy in, 286; in World Trade Organization, 239

Judaism, 38, 374–375; destruction of temple in Jerusalem, 41; historical role of, 6; intellectual history and, 39; Russian pogroms against, 58; significance of Jerusalem in, 382–384; significant communities of, 11; Torah and, 44. *See also* Zionism

Justice and Development Party (Turkey), 126

Justinian (Roman Emperor), 26

Kabbani, Nizar, 419
Kadima Party (Israel), 128, 183, 184
Kamil, Mustafa, 55
Kanafani, Ghassan, 427
Karaosmano, Yakup Kadri, 401, 413
al-Karim Qasim, Abd, 64, 158
Kazemi, Morteza Moshfeq, 402
Kemal, Namik, 416
Kemal, Orhan, 410, 416
Kemal, Yashar, 413, 416, 431
Khalifa, Sahar, 424
al-Khalifah, Hamad ibn Isa (emir of Bahrain), 121, 122
al-Khalifah, Isa ibn Salmon (emir of Bahrain), 122
Khomeini, Ayatollah Ruhollah, 69, 70, 74, 129, 130, 266, 406
Khoury, Colette, 407
Khrushchev, Nikita, 259
King-Crane Commission, 59
King-Irani, Laurie, 6, 94, 309–341
Kinship, 309–341; as adaptive strategy to environmental challenges, 315–317; administrative contexts of, 315; bilateral systems, 318; conflict mediation and, 316; construction of identity and, 314; cultural uniformity and, 324; defining, 318; as dominant mode of larger group formation, 321; effect on every aspect of life, 324; fictive, 322; as frame of meaning, 313; gender and, 324, 325; importance of parental roles, 320; loyalty and, 316; marriage preferences and, 318, 319, 320, 321; matriarchal, 318; as mode of organization, 313; networks, 6; patrilineal, 319, 321, 322, 323; patron-client relationships and, 317; power of, 314; priority over citizenship, 317; segmentation and, 323; as social construct, 313; social realities and, 6; symbolism, 314; as system of meanings

and values, 314; unilineal, 323; women and, 355–358

Kissinger, Henry, 72, 73
Kurdistan Democratic Party (KDP), 159
Kurdistan Workers' Party (PKK), 90, 160
Kurds: aided by Iran, 159; assistance from United States, 159; Autonomous Kurdish Government in Iraq, 89, 160; in Pesh Merga, 159; quasi-independence in Iraq for, 126; quest for autonomy by, 17, 158–161; refugees from Iraq, 159; rights in Turkey, 125; separatist movements by, 22; support for US intervention in Iraq, 159, 160; uprising against Saddam Hussein, 159

Kuwait: ability to benefit from multinational coalition, 148; agriculture in, 290; arms imports in, 101; economic development in, 222*tab,* 236*tab;* exports, 240; female employment in, 352; fertility rates in, 286; in Gulf Cooperation Council, 150, 239; informal economy in, 237*tab;* invasion by Iraq, 77–79, 151, 152, 153, 270–271; Iraqi claims on, 87; labor migration and, 229*tab;* military expenditures, 102; monarchy in, 117, 118, 122–123; political participation in, 108*tab,* 122; prospect for democratization in, 97; state-building strategy in, 20, 147; unemployment in, 295*tab;* urbanization in, 282, 283*tab;* women's literacy in, 286; worker protests in, 242; in World Trade Organization, 239

Kuwait Oil Company, 257

Labor: division of, 37, 38, 332; expulsion from Gulf Cooperation Council states, 233; flows, 291; market, 236; migration, 18, 228–233, 290, 291, 320; remittances, 18, 141, 228–233; sectoral distribution of, 289; unions, 99; women's, 231–232, 289

Labor Party (Israel), 79, 95, 101, 127, 183, 198

Lahoud, Emile, 128
Lanham, Durayd, 417
Lashin, Mahmud Tahir, 404
League of Arab States, 2
League of Nations, 14, 63, 116; granting of mandates allowing continued European control, 139; mandate for Palestine, 87; mandate over Syria, 61

League of Nations Covenant, 59

Lebanon: agriculture in, 227*tab,* 334; aid from Iran to, 76; Baath Party in, 111; banking sector in, 246; boundaries, 12; Christian population in, 76, 377; civil war in, 68, 76–77, 82, 246, 313; confessional parliamentary democracy in, 87; creation of, 87; democratic governance in, 128–129; disintegration of state in, 128, 246; disparity of wealth and power in, 76; economic development in, 222*tab,* 236*tab;* economic recovery in, 82; ethno-confessional sects in, 311; exports, 238; female workforce in, 290; fertility rates in, 285, 286; French occupation of, 59; French sphere of influence in, 14, 87; increase in Shi'i power in, 88, 91; industrial contribution in, 227*tab;* informal economy in, 237*tab;* infrastructure destruction in, 246; interest in World Trade Organization, 239; invasion by Israel, 246–247; Iraqi refugees in, 250; Israeli invasion of, 76, 193; labor migration and, 229*tab;* Maronites in, 64; military expenditures, 102; National Pact of 1943, 105; Palestine Liberation Organization in, 76; Palestinian refugees in, 17, 67, 100; personal status issues overseen by religious courts in, 311; political participation in, 108*tab,* 128–129; prospect for democratization in, 98, 99; reconstitution of, 14; religious conflict in, 380–382; remittances in, 232; Sabra and Shatilla massacres in, 193; Syrian claims on, 81, 87, 152, 246; unemployment in, 294*tab,* 295*tab;* US intervention in, 69, 70, 74, 111; urbanization in, 283*tab;* weakness of state in, 311

Levi, Jacques Victor, 408

Libya: agriculture in, 227*tab;* in Arab Mahgreb Union, 238; authoritarian personalistic rule in, 105, 116; creation of, 61; economic development in, 222*tab,* 236*tab;* effect of ending of Cold War on, 88; female workforce in, 290; fertility rates in, 286; in Gulf Cooperation Council, 239; industrial contribution in, 227*tab;* interest in World Trade Organization, 239; Italian control of, 65, 143; labor migration and, 229*tab;* military expenditures, 102; nationalization of oil industry, 265;

overthrow of monarchy in, 67, 117, 150; political participation in, 108*tab;* remittances in, 232; revolutionary transformation in, 96, 262; urbanization in, 282, 283*tab*

Likud Party (Israel), 127, 183

Literacy, 227, 249, 286; relation to economic difficulties, 347; women's, 346, 347

Literature, 397–432; and Algerian war of independence, 422–423; Arabic fiction, 409–412; drama, 416–418; folk, 403; francophone fiction, 408–409; Iranian fiction, 412; and Iran-Iraq War, 425–426; Islamic revolution and, 429–431; Israeli fiction, 414–415; Palestine and, 423–424; poetry, 418–420; professional recognition for, 431–432; short stories, 403–408; Turkish fiction, 413–414; and war in Lebanon, 424; women's, 407–408

Mahabad, 158, 160

Mahfouz, Naguib, 4, 409, 410, 411, 431

Mahmud II (Sultan), 51, 52

al-Mala'ika, Nazik, 419

Mallas, Muhammad, 418

Mamluks, 48, 49, 51

Manners, Ian, 5, 9–34

Mapai Party (Israel), 101

Marxism, 111, 112, 160

Mauritania: in Arab Mahgreb Union, 238; boundary dispute with Morocco, 142–143; economic development in, 222*tab;* female employment in, 353; informal economy in, 237*tab;* Islamic political model in, 107; military expenditures, 102; political participation in, 108*tab;* prospects for economic development, 94; single-party rule in, 105; urbanization in, 283*tab*

McMahon, Sir Henry, 58

Mehmet II (Ottoman Sultan), 27

Memmi, Albert, 408, 415

Meshal, Khaled, 157

Mesopotamia, 37, 38, 47

Middle East: aridity and water in, 18–25; boundary issues, 12–18; as center of world oil industry, 255; cityscapes in, 25–31; contemporary, 435–438; cultural ferment in, 400–403; defining, 2, 3; democracy in, 79–83; desire for independence from Western powers in, 63–66; diversity in, 10; early Western interest in, 3, 4; economic issues, 221–252; employment challenges in, 289–291; ethnicity and, 325–331; Eurocentrism in, 12, 13; Fertile Crescent countries in, 2; fertility/mortality rates, 284–289; as foreign policy subsystem, 152–153; geography of, 9–34; holy sites in, 4; identification with religion more than nationality, 50; infant/maternal mortality in, 287; international relations and, 137–170; interventions in, 2, 5; kinship and, 318–325; labor force growth in, 289–291; lack of homogeneous populations in states of, 312; Mediterranean countries in, 3; multinational empires in, 39; multiple boundaries in, 5; North African countries in, 2; oil-producing region of, 2; patron-client relationships in, 317; political issues, 85–133; political participation in, 440–441; population growth in, 284–289; poverty in, 296–304; reaction to Western world, 54; Red Sea countries, 3; regionalism in, 148–150; role of military in, 100–103; role of women in, 345–369; shared experiences in, 3; social class structure, 333–335; terrorism in, 79–83; trade in, 237–241; unemployment in, 291–296; uneven distribution of oil revenues in, 141; urbanization in, 282–284; used for balance of power by Europeans, 53; Westernizing reforms in, 50–53

Middle East, economic issues, 221–252; crises in, 233–237; dependence on decisions emanating from outside the region, 334–335; economic development in, 438–439; emergence of problems in, 227–228; emphasis on development of national industrial capacity, 225; labor migration, 228–233; new oil boom, 242–243; post–World War II, 224–228; poverty, 296–304; pre–World War II, 222–224; regional economies, 243–251; reversal of high expectations in, 225–226; state control of economies in, 225; structural adjustment programs in, 233–237; trade, 237–241

Middle East, historical context of, 37–83; ancient, 37–41; Byzantine Empire, 40; Crusades and, 48; East/West invasions, 47–49; European imperialism in, 53; feudal landownership system, 40; Greek and Roman rule, 40–41; Mongols and,

48; multinational empires in, 39; Ottoman Empire and, 49–50; outside invasions of, 39; political changes, 67–69; post–World War I, 59–83; pre-Islamic Arab world, 42–43; retreat of Western imperialism in, 63–66; rise of Islam in, 41–50; subordination to Western world, 50–59

Middle East, international relations, 137–170; cliency and, 146–148; dependency and, 145–146; foreign aid and, 146, 147; with Great Powers, 143–150; military assistance and, 147; regional autonomy and, 150–152; regionalism in, 148–150; sovereignty issues, 137–141

Middle East, literary tradition, 397–432

Middle East, oil economy, 255–277; change in ownership of oil, 264–266; industry structure, 256–258; oil revolution and, 262–264; politics of, 266–267

Middle East, politics, 85–133; Baathism in, 112; changing international contexts, 88–92; Cold War, 88; conditional democratic governance, 125–131; consequences of US invasion of Iraq in, 89, 90; domestic opposition to United States in, 88; economic development and, 92–94; government legitimation in, 105–106; grouping countries in, 107; ideologies and institutions, 103–107; informal power structures and, 94–96; Iraqi conflicts, 88, 89; Israeli-Palestinian conflict, 88, 90–92; major conflicts in, 88–92; membership in ethno-confessional sects and, 310–311; military interventions and, 96–97; military role in, 100–103; monarchies, 117–124; myth of instability, 96–97; Nasserism in, 112–113; nationalist revolutionary republics, 107, 110–116; new coalitions in, 226; notions of citizenship in, 310; perceptions of tribal bases to, 310; personalistic governance in, 115–116; political Islam and, 106–107; prospects for democratization, 97–100; religion and, 373–395; single-party rule in, 113–115; sources of government legitimation, 105–106; structures imposed by external powers, 103

Migration: extended family and, 320; international, 282; labor, 5, 18, 228–233,

290, 291, 320; rural-to-urban, 29, 283; urbanization and, 320
Mikha'il, Dunya, 425
Milani, Farzaneh, 407
Military: expansion, 52; part played in origins of ruling regimes, 101; rapid modernization of, 101; reform, 53; role in Middle East politics, 100–103
Mina, Hanna, 411
Mithraism, 40
Moghadam, Valentine, 6, 281–305, 351
Mohammed VI (King of Morocco), 118
Monarchy: alliances with colonial powers by, 111; Arab concepts of, 118–119; conservative, 104; constitutional, 67, 87; in Egypt, 67, 87; in Iraq, 67, 87; in Jordan, 87, 96, 105; in Libya, 67; in Oman, 98; overthrow of, 67, 87; parliamentary, 117–124; patriarchal nature of, 104; patrimonialism and, 117; in Saudi Arabia, 98; traditional, 117–124; in Yemen, 67
Morocco: in Aghadir Trade Agreement, 238; agriculture in, 227*tab;* in Arab Mahgreb Union, 238; boundary dispute with Mauritania, 142–143; bread riots in, 234; constitution in, 124; economic development in, 222*tab,* 236*tab;* exports, 238, 240; female employment in, 290, 352; fertility rates in, 285, 286, 288; French control of, 61, 68; as French protectorate, 53; industrial contribution in, 227*tab;* informal economy in, 237*tab;* Istiqlal Party in, 61; Judaism in, 375; "Justice and Charity" movement, 123; labor migration and, 229, 229*tab;* living standards in, 300–301; military expenditures, 102; monarchy in, 117, 118, 123–124; political participation in, 108*tab,* 124; political stability in, 96; prospect for democratization in, 97; public-sector employment, 292; remittances in, 232; Socialist Union of Popular Forces in, 124; state intervention in, 227; trade with United States, 239; unemployment in, 234, 294*tab;* urbanization in, 283*tab;* women's literacy in, 286; women's rights in, 350; in World Trade Organization, 239
Mosaddeq, Mohammad, 69, 70, 74, 111, 257
Moses, 38
Mount Lebanon, 53, 59, 128, 138, 246

Mount Sinai, 38
Movements: capital, 221; conservative, 100; ideological, 110; independence, 110; indigenous, 6; Jewish fundamentalist, 91; Kurdish separatist, 22; liberal, 54; liberal democratic, 100; nationalist, 54, 55, 110, 138; prodemocratic, 98; regional, 148–150; religious revivalist, 388; resistance, 191; revolutionary, 60, 62, 101, 110; self-determination, 110; social, 211; transnational, 149; women's, 362
Mu'awiya (governor of Syria), 45
Mubarak, Hosni, 96, 113, 169
Muhammad, 40, 43–44, 378
Muhammed VI (King of Morocco), 124
Multifiber Agreement, 238
Multinational corporations, 5, 6, 104, 168
Munif, Abd al-Rahman, 411
Muslim Brotherhood, 106, 112, 114, 116, 155, 385, 389–390, 392
Muslim Brothers, 65
Mutran, Khalil, 418

Napoleon: invasion of Egypt by, 14, 50; withdrawal from Egypt, 51
Nasrallah, Emily, 408, 411, 427
Nasser, Gamal Abdul, 67, 68, 70, 71, 111–113, 155, 421
Nasserism, 111–113
National Democratic Party (Egypt), 113
National Iranian Oil Company, 258
Nationalism, 54, 110; Arab, 56, 63, 66–67, 72, 141, 149, 158, 162; Balkan, 53; differences between Palestinian and Israeli-Jewish, 203, 204; Egyptian, 54–55, 60; European, 185; growth of, 63; institutionalized, 203; in Iran, 62; in Iraq, 60; Israeli, 203; in Ottoman Empire, 55–56; Palestinian, 189, 203; rise of, 60; secular, 82; state, 203; Turkish, 56; Zionism and, 66–67
National Party (Egypt), 55
Neocolonialism, 339
Neo-Destour Party (Tunisia), 115
Nesin, Aziz, 406, 416
Netanyahu, Benjamin, 79, 128, 184, 310, 340*n1*
Networks: conservative, 95, 96; effect of urbanization on, 95; family, 94; ideology-based, 95; migration effects on, 95; social, 94, 95, 313
New Ottomans, 55
Nile River: migrations to, 38

Nixon, Richard, 154, 263
Nixon Doctrine, 162, 263
Nomadism: formation of federations in, 321; horse, 48; pastoral, 37, 38, 315, 322; patrilineal organization of, 321
Nongovernmental organizations (NGOs): in civil society, 99; in Palestine, 207, 212; regional, 153; urbanization and, 30, 31; women's, 365–366
North Atlantic Treaty Organization (NATO), 69

Oçalan, Abdullah, 160
Occupied Territories, 79; confiscation of land in, 190; conflict over disengagement from, 127–128; construction of settlements in, 190, 191; deteriorating economic condition in, 247, 248; discrimination against by Israel, 126; female employment in, 352; Israeli control in, 199, 200; Israeli plans for permanent retention of, 192; Israeli reoccupation of, 157; living standards in, 303–304; Palestinian autonomy in, 199; political participation in, 108*tab;* US support for retention of by Israel, 156, 157
Oil: changes in ownership of, 264–266; competition in market for, 147; and decrease in legitimate political participation in Middle East, 255; dependence on, 2; early limitations on production, 256; economic development and, 92, 141, 226; effect on labor migration and remittances, 231, 232, 233; embargo, 72, 162, 261, 263, 264; expansion of supplies, 267–268; foreign involvement and, 5; impact on economic development, 224; import quotas, 263; increasing prices for, 262, 263; industry structure, 256–258; localized production of, 255; nationalization of companies, 69, 141, 257; new boom in prices of, 242–243; in Persia, 57; political economy of, 255–277; preferential access to, 145; prices, 93, 170; production, 163, 256–258; Red Line companies, 256, 257; revenues, 274–276; shortages, 263, 264; threats to prices, 267–271; unraveling of production system, 259–261; used as "weapon" in Arab-Israeli wars, 261, 263; "windfall profits" and, 265, 266
Oil companies, international: access to

Iraqi oil, 272, 273; competition for, 259–261; control taken from by nationalization, 147; coordination of production by, 257; failure to be concerned about falling production and rising demand, 261; and formation of Organization of Petroleum Exporting Countries (OPEC), 260; increases in costs, 260; intervention by home governments of in domestic affairs of exporting countries, 257; loss of ownership of oil, 264–266; negotiations with Kurds in Iraq, 160; "posted price" system, 260
Olmert, Ehud, 91, 184
Oman: agriculture in, 290; boundary disputes with Saudi Arabia, 142; British sphere of influence in, 63; economic development in, 222*tab,* 236*tab;* female employment in, 352; fertility rates in, 285, 286; in Gulf Cooperation Council, 150, 239; informal economy in, 237*tab;* labor migration and, 229*tab;* military expenditures, 102; monarchy in, 98, 117, 121; political participation in, 109*tab,* 121; political stability in, 96; prospect for democratization in, 98; unemployment in, 294*tab,* 295*tab;* urbanization in, 282, 283*tab;* women's literacy in, 286; worker protests in, 242; in World Trade Organization, 239
Operation Desert Shield, 78
Operation Desert Storm, 78
Organization of Petroleum Exporting Countries (OPEC), 72; economic development and, 92; formation of, 260; goals of, 260, 261; imposition of oil embargo by, 263–264; inability to control production, 269, 270; multiregional aspect of, 148–149; stabilization of oil prices by, 145; used as economic weapon, 72
Organizations: "establishment" women's, 364–365; functional, 149; international, 149, 177; member conflicts, 149; mobilization of consensus within, 149; regional, 148, 149, 150; social welfare, 198; women's "front," 363
Orientalism, 2
Oslo Agreement (1993), 22, 90, 156, 157, 179, 181, 183, 198, 200, 201, 205, 206
Ottoman Debt Commission (1881), 143
Ottoman Empire, 49–50; blocking of colonial activity by, 86; collapse of, 27;

confrontation of nationalist aspirations by, 14; conquering of Christian Balkans, 49; *devshirme* system of military recruitment and training, 49, 50; dismemberment of, 12, 59; European interest in continuance of, 138; liberalism in, 55–56; *millet* system in, 49, 95, 160, 310, 332; nationalism within, 55–56; use of firearms in, 49
Oz, Amos, 414, 415

Paczynska, Agnieszka, 5, 221–252
Pahlavi, Mohammad Reza Shah, 73, 98, 110
Pakistan: in anti-Communist alliance, 67
Palestine: beginning of intifada, 194–196; boundary issues, 12, 17; British recommendations for partition of, 187; British sphere of influence in, 58, 59, 60, 61; competition for, 61; conflict between Arabs and Jews in, 58, 59, 64, 66, 153–158, 177–215; Crusades and, 48; delegitimization of leadership in, 181; existing indigenous population in, 186; fertility rates in, 285, 286; flight of Arabs from, 66, 67; fragmentation of society in, 182; inability to address service needs of community, 193; Israeli-Palestinian conflict and, 70–73, 153–158; issue submitted to United Nations, 66; Jewish Agency in, 60, 61; lack of state structure for, 311; Muslim Brotherhood in, 389; nongovernmental organizations in, 207, 212; Palestinian National Council in, 155; partition of, 64, 185–189; reconstitution of, 14; reluctance of Britain and United States to apply principle of self-determination in, 138; support for as home for Jewish people, 58, 59; undermined institutions in, 181; unemployment in, 294*tab*, 295*tab;* Unified National Leadership of the Uprising in, 195; UN plan for partition of, 187; women's literacy in, 286; Zionism and, 185–189
Palestine Communist Party (PCP), 180
Palestine Liberation Organization, 70, 79, 180, 192, 193; Arab support for, 71; attempt to mobilize Palestinians to resist Israeli rule, 71; international recognition of, 191; in Lebanon, 76; loss of recognition from Gulf War stance, 156; pursuit of diplomatic resolution by, 210;

recognition of, 155; refusal of Israel to negotiate with, 73
Palestine Royal Commission, 187
Palestinian National Authority, 91, 156, 179, 181
Palestinians: access to education, 181; autonomy in Occupied Territories, 199; collective identity of, 179, 180–182; dependency on Arab neighbors, 189; desire for self-determination and territorial sovereignty, 178, 179, 186, 202–207; discrimination against in Israel, 189; displacement of, 17; election of Islamist Hamas by, 82; high degree of politicization among, 180; impedance of movement by Israel, 82; in Israel, 182; national liberation struggle of, 180; non-Muslim, 181; refugee status of, 67, 100, 155, 180, 205; residence and socioeconomic status, 180; siding with Saddam Hussein in Gulf War, 197; subgroups of, 180; undermining of rights of, 186
Pamuk, Orhan, 4, 413, 414, 431
Pan-Arabism, 68, 73, 111
Pan-Islamism, 54, 55, 149
Paris Peace Conference (1919), 59, 60
Parmenter, Barbara McKean, 5, 9–34
Parsipur, Shahrnush, 407, 428
Parsley Island, 143
Patriarchy, 355–358
Patrimonialism, 117
Patriotic Union of Kurdistan (PUK), 159
Patronage, 95
Peel Commission, 187
Peres, Shimon, 169, 183
Persia, 39, 40; British sphere of influence in, 57; constitutionalism in, 56–57; Qajar dynasty in, 52, 56; relations with Europe, 52; rivalry with Rome, 41; Russian sphere of influence in, 57; Safavid dynasty in, 49, 52; Sassanid dynasty, 41, 45; Shi'ism in, 52; tobacco boycott in, 56
Pesh Merga, 159
Petraeus, David, 89
Petrodollars, 274
Phoenicians, 38
Policy: domestic, 100; import substitution industrialization, 226; pronatalist, 287, 288; social, 346; urban bias of, 282
Political: accountability, 235; capital, 91; control, 86, 94–95; diplomacy, 182; economy, 104; fragmentation, 339;

instability, 96–97; institutions, 85, 91, 103; integration, 141; liberalism, 110; liberalization, 99, 106, 114; marginalization, 330; opposition, 102; organization, 5, 137; parties, 99; pluralism, 6, 115; power, 27; reform, 5; representation, 310; revolution, 57; violence, 311

Politics: centralized approach to, 111; domestic, 5, 6, 85, 86, 88, 92, 154; formal/informal, 310; gender and, 6; local, 94, 95; oil, 255–277; patronage, 95; regional, 5, 266; religion and, 6, 373–395; women and, 360–369

Popular Front for the Liberation of Palestine (PFLP), 180

Poverty, 296–304

Power: balance of, 333; consolidation of, 111; state, 111

Privatization, 234, 235

Ptolemies, 40

Qaddafi, Muammar, 101, 150, 262

Qalamawi, Suhayr, 407

Qasim, 'Abd a-Hakim, 429

Qatar: agriculture in, 290; conflict with Bahrain, 17, 142; economic development in, 222*tab,* 236*tab;* economic liberalization in, 99; female employment in, 352; fertility rates in, 286; in Gulf Cooperation Council, 150, 239; labor migration and, 229*tab;* military expenditures, 102; monarchy in, 121; political participation in, 109*tab;* prospect for democratization in, 99; religious conservatism in, 121; unemployment in, 295*tab;* urbanization in, 282, 283*tab;* women's literacy in, 286; worker protests in, 242; in World Trade Organization, 239

Qazvini, Safi ibn Wali, 33

Qualifying Industrial Zone protocol, 237

Qura'i, Ahmad, 207

Quran, 44, 379; *sharia* in, 44; on water, 19, 24

Quraysh tribe, 43, 45

Qutb, Sayyid, 392

Rabin, Yitzhak, 79, 183, 198, 211

Rafsanjani, Akbar Hashemi, 131

Ramsar Convention (1971), 24

Ran, Nazim Hikmet, 416, 418, 419, 422

Ras al-Khaimah: governance in, 122

Reagan, Ronald, 75, 162

Red Line Agreement (1928), 256

Refah Party (Turkey), 125

Reform: autocracy and, 51; economic, 51, 228, 234; educational, 53; institutional, 234; judicial, 234; land, 107, 226; language, 399; military, 50, 53; political, 5; social, 111; tax, 234; Westernizing, 50–53, 54

Refugees, 5, 89; cause of economic problems in host countries, 250; as central issue in Israeli-Palestinian conflict, 204, 205, 206; limited access to services, 250

Regional: alliances, 5; autonomy, 150–152; coalitions, 316; cooperation, 23; economic cooperation, 238; economies, 243–251; integration, 149, 337; nongovernmental organizations, 153; politics, 5, 266; realignments, 150, 151; security, 150; subsystems, 5; trade, 238

Religion: activism and, 387–395; *dhimmi* communities and, 331, 378; extremist, 6, 392–395; historical role in region, 374–380; minority experiences, 331–333; monotheistic, 38, 44; politics and, 6, 106, 373–395; priority over citizenship, 317; revivalist movements, 388; as source of tradition and stability in changing environment, 106

Remittances, 18, 141, 228–233; decreasing, 335; *fe-ch'ien* system, 231; *hawala* system, 231

Resources: class and control over, 333; decline in, 5; differential access to, 333; distribution of, 21, 312, 316; extraction of, 315; offshore, 17; preferential access to, 145; water, 5, 17, 18–25

Reza Khan, 60, 62

Reza Shah, Mohammad, 69, 106, 107

Rogers, William, 71

Rogers Peace Plan, 71, 72

al-Rumi, Jalal al-Din, 4

Rushdie, Salman, 406, 429, 430

Russia: Bolshevik Revolution (1917), 57; expansionism of, 13, 57; influence in Middle East, 13; in Persia, 57; regional domination by, 14; sphere of influence in Middle East, 57; takeover of Romania by, 53

al-Sabah, Mubarak (Emir of Kuwait), 20, 147

al-Sabah, Su'ad Mubarak, 420

Sabra and Shatilla massacres, 193

Sadat, Anwar, 72, 73, 113, 154, 192, 227, 228, 390–391, 393, 430

Saddam Hussein, 24, 64, 75, 78, 89, 102, 116, 155, 156, 159, 163, 165, 267, 269, 270, 323

Saedi, Gholam Hosayn, 406

Safavids, 49

Said, Ali Ahmad, 420

al-Said, Nuri, 66

Saladin, 48, 377

al-Samman, Ghada, 407, 424

ibn Saud, Abdul Aziz (King of Saudi Arabia), 63, 66, 101, 119, 144

Saudi Arabia: agriculture in, 227*tab,* 290; arms imports in, 101; base for US led coalition in Iraq-Kuwait war, 78; boundary disputes with Oman, 142; economic development in, 222*tab,* 235, 236*tab;* expansion of oil production by, 163; exports, 240; female employment in, 352; fertility rates in, 285, 286; in Gulf Cooperation Council, 150, 239; industrial contribution in, 227*tab;* informal economy in, 237*tab;* as Islamic state, 384, 385; labor force migration in, 18, 229*tab;* large Shi'i population in, 92; military expenditures, 102; monarchy in, 98, 120; political participation in, 109*tab;* political stability in, 96; proclamation of kingdom of, 63; prospect for democratization in, 98; ruling by patrilineal coalitions, 323; urbanization in, 282, 283*tab;* Western-orientation of, 148; women's literacy in, 286; worker protests in, 242; in World Trade Organization, 239

al-Sayyab, Badr Shakir, 420

Schrodt, Philip, 5, 85–133, 143

Schwedler, Jillian, 1–7, 92, 106, 107, 373–395

Sectarianism, 310

Sector, informal, 235, 236

Sector, private, 227; economic restructuring in, 292; inability to absorb workers from public-sector privatizations, 236

Sector, public, 227; cuttbacks in employment in, 236; privatization and, 234; unemployment in, 291, 292

Seleucids, 40

Selim III (Sultan), 51

Seljuks, 47

al-Shabbi, Abu Al-Qasim, 418

Shahin, Yusuf, 421

Sham, 12

Shamir, Moshe, 414

Shammas, Anton, 415

Sharia, 44, 48, 126, 129, 331, 350, 379, 389

Sharjah: governance in, 122

Sharon, Ariel, 79, 90, 91, 127, 128, 156, 157, 184, 200, 202, 206, 207

Sharoni, Simona, 5, 177–215

al-Sharqawi, 'Abd al-Rahman, 421

Shas Party (Israel), 95

Shatt al-Arab waterway, 12, 22, 24, 162

Shawqi, Ahmad, 418

al-Shaykh, Hanan, 424

Shoah (Holocaust), 66, 67

Six-Day War (1967), 71, 153, 154, 162, 189

Social: change, 282; class, 313, 333–335; development, 225; dislocation, 311; fragmentation, 339; institutions, 103; interaction, 318; movements, 211; networks, 94, 95, 313; norms, 129; organization, 101, 310; policies, 346; realities, 6; reform, 111; relationships, 313; services, 93; spending, 292; stratification, 329; structures, 312; tensions, 235

Socialism, 67, 72, 110; Arab, 68, 111, 112; decolonization and, 111; democratic, 126; US Central Intelligence Agency and, 111

Socialist Union of Popular Forces (Morocco), 124

Society: cultural/ethnic plurality in, 313; hierarchical organization of, 313; planned, 112; sociopolitical fragmentation of, 339; urban, 10; vertically integrated, 337

Somalia: economic development in, 222*tab;* political participation in, 109*tab;* prospects for economic development, 94

Somekh, Sasson, 415

Sovereignty: issues in Middle East, 137–141; local challenges to, 141–143; negative, 137, 139, 140, 147, 149; preservation of, 149; self-determination and, 138; territorial, 178, 179, 186, 203

Soviet Union: in anti-Iraq coalition, 151; stance on Israel, 151. *See also* Russia

Stalin, Josef, 111

State(s): boundaries, 139–141; building, 103, 110; bureaucratized, 111;

centralization of, 110, 111; challenges to sovereignty of, 141–143; claims for need for authoritarian rule, 101; confrontation, 148; domination of economy by, 234; as external imposition of organization, 316–317; formation, 311; ideal, 138; Islamic, 384–387; modern, 346–351; nationalism, 203; national security issues, 203; as new creations, 12; nonaligned, 148; organization, 86; religious, 382–387; service of elite interests of, 316; sovereignty issues, 137–141; structure, 311; subsidies, 227; women's relation to, 346–351

Structural adjustment programs, 5, 228, 233–237, 292; effect on literacy rates, 347

Sudan: agriculture in, 227*tab*, 247; Anglo-Egyptian condominium in, 60, 65; army seizure of power in, 68; bread riots in, 234; civil war in, 247; economic development in, 222*tab*, 247; exports, 240; Fashoda dispute in, 87; female employment in, 352; fertility rates in, 286; independence, 247; industrial contribution in, 227*tab*; investment in, 235; Islamic political model in, 107; military expenditures, 102; Muslim Brotherhood in, 390; non-Muslim population in, 13; oil industry in, 247; political participation in, 109*tab*; prospects for economic development, 94; religious conflict in, 381; remittances in, 232; unemployment in, 294*tab*, 295*tab*; women's literacy in, 286

Sudan People's Liberation Army, 247

Suez Canal, 53, 54, 65, 69, 70, 74, 86, 111; British invasion of, 55; British withdrawal from, 67; closure of, 261; nationalization of, 68

Sufism, 47

Suleyman the Magnificent, 50

Sumer, 5, 37, 38

Sykes-Picot Agreement (1916), 58, 87

Syria: agriculture in, 21, 289, 290, 334; ancient history, 38; Arab conquest of, 44; authoritarian personalistic rule in, 105, 116; Baath Party in, 111, 116; bombing of nuclear facility by Israel, 91; British intervention in, 52; challenges from Muslim Brotherhood, 116; choice of country name, 13, 14; Christianity in,

377; claims on Lebanon, 87; conquest by Ibrahim Ali, 52; creation of, 87; Crusades and, 48; economic development in, 222*tab*, 236*tab*; economic liberalization in, 116; effect of ending of Cold War on, 88; European opposition to takeover by Muhammad Ali, 53; exports, 238, 240; female employment in, 352; fertility rates in, 286; French control of, 59, 61, 116; governorate of Mount Lebanon in, 53; independence, 116; informal economy in, 237*tab*; interest in World Trade Organization, 239; intervention in Lebanon, 152, 246; Iraqi refugees in, 116, 250; Judaism in, 375; labor migration and, 229*tab*; in Lebanon, 81; Mamluks in, 48, 49; military expenditures, 102; Muslim Brotherhood in, 389; Palestinian refugees in, 17, 67, 100; political participation in, 109*tab*; political stability in, 96, 116; prospect for democratization in, 99; reconstitution of, 14; remittances in, 232; return of Golan Heights to, 190; Roman conquest of, 40; ruling by patrilineal coalitions, 323; support for Kurds from, 160; suspected of terror activities in Lebanon, 128; unemployment in, 294*tab*; in United Arab Republic, 68; urbanization in, 283*tab*; war with Israel, 71, 72; water management by, 22, 23; women's literacy in, 286

Tahir, Kemal, 410

Taif Accords (1989), 128, 246, 381

Talabani, Jalal, 159, 160

Talib, Aliya, 408

Taliban, 141, 168

Tanıpnar, Ahmet Hamde, 413

Tanzimat era, 52, 55

Taraki, Lisa, 6, 345–369

Taraqqi, Goli, 407, 427, 428

Tawfiq, Muhammad (Egyptian ruler), 54, 55

Taxation, 40, 50; reform of, 234

Taymur, Mahmud, 404

Tekin, Latife, 30, 31

Terrorism, 1, 79–83; differential definitions of, 209; war on, 6, 80

Tétreault, Mary Ann, 5, 137–170, 255–277

al-Thani, Hamad ibn Khalifah ibn Hamad (King of Qatar), 121

al-Thawra Dam, 22

Thorn Theater Company, 417
Threshold Program of the Millennium
Challenge Account, 244
Tigris River: control of water flow from,
22; migrations to, 38
Trade, 237–241; ancient, 4, 40, 221; Barce-
lona process, 239; colonial, 145; guilds,
51; international, 221; liberalization,
234; in oil, 237; patterns, 5; Qualifying
Industrial Zone protocol in, 237;
regional, 238; routes, 4, 25, 50; transit,
246; with United States, 239; volume,
239
Trade and Investment Framework
Agreements, 239
Trans-Iranian Railway, 69
Transjordan, 59; reconstitution of, 14
Treaty of Sèvres (1920), 60, 62
Treaty of Uqair (1922), 142
Truman Doctrine (1947), 69, 225
Tunisia: in Aghadir Trade Agreement,
238; agriculture in, 227*tab;* in Arab
Mahgreb Union, 238; bread riots in,
234; Democratic Constitutional Rally in,
115; Destour Socialist Party, 115;
economic development in, 115, 222*tab,*
226, 236*tab;* exports, 238, 240; Fatimids
in, 47; female employment in, 290, 352;
fertility rates in, 285, 286, 288; French
control of, 61, 68, 87; as French
protectorate, 53; Hizb al-Nahdha Party
in, 115; industrial contribution in,
227*tab;* informal economy in, 237*tab;*
Islamic Tendency Movement in, 115;
Judaism in, 375; labor migration and,
229*tab;* living standards in, 301–
302; military expenditures, 102; Muslim
Brotherhood in, 389; Neo-Destour Party,
115; 1959 Constitution, 115; overthrow
of monarchy in, 117; political
participation in, 109*tab;* political
pluralism in, 115; political stability in,
96; remittances in, 232; repression of
Islamic political groups in, 115; secular
legal system in, 115; single-party rule in,
105, 114–115; socialist ideology in, 226;
state involvement in economic
planning/production, 226;
unemployment in, 293, 294*tab,* 295*tab;*
urbanization in, 283*tab;* women's
literacy in, 286; women's rights in, 350;
in World Trade Organization, 239
Turkey: agriculture in, 227*tab,* 289, 290;
ambivalence over Kurds in Iraq, 160; in

anti-Communist alliance, 67; choice of
country name, 14; claims for need for
authoritarian rule in, 101; conflict with
Kurds in, 160; defeat in World War I,
14; democratic governance in, 125–126;
desire for European Union membership,
126, 160, 161; driven from Palestine and
Syria by Britain, 58; economic
development in, 94, 222*tab,* 225;
elections in, 161; establishment of
republic in, 14, 27, 60, 62; exports, 240;
female employment in, 290, 352, 353;
fertility rates in, 285, 286, 288;
importance of cities to, 26, 27, 28, 29;
independence in, 61–63; industrial
contribution in, 227*tab;* industrialization
in, 69; informal economy in, 237*tab;*
investment in, 235; Iraqi refugees in,
250; Islamic Refah Party in, 103; Justice
and Development Party in, 126, 161;
Kurds in, 125; labor migration and,
229*tab;* military expenditures, 102;
modernization of, 69; in North Atlantic
Treaty Organization, 69; political participation in, 109*tab,* 125–126; political
stability in, 96; prospect for
democratization in, 97, 98, 99; Refah
Party in, 125; restriction of Islamic
movements in, 125; secularization of,
60, 62, 101, 110; tensions with Iraq over
Kurds, 89, 90; unemployment in, 293;
urbanization in, 282, 283*tab;* water
management by, 22, 23; Westernization
of, 62; women's literacy in, 286;
women's rights in, 347, 348; in World
Trade Organization, 239

Ulama, 51
Umar ibn al-Khat*tab,* 44
Umm al-Quaiwan: governance in, 122
Unemployment, 234, 235; age and, 293;
growth in number of working women
and, 236; population growth and, 236;
rise in, 291–296; structural adjustment
programs and, 292; urban, 292, 293;
women and, 292, 293
United Arab Emirates: agriculture in, 290;
arms imports in, 101; economic development in, 222*tab,* 236*tab;* economic
liberalization in, 99; exports, 240;
female employment in, 352; fertility
rates in, 286; governance by Supreme
Council, 121; in Gulf Cooperation
Council, 150, 239; informal economy in,

237*tab;* labor migration and, 229*tab;* military expenditures, 102; monarchy in, 121; political participation in, 109*tab;* prospect for democratization in, 99; unemployment in, 295*tab;* urbanization in, 282, 283*tab;* in World Trade Organization, 239

United Arab Republic, 68; breakup of, 70

United Nations: Arab states' membership in, 66; calls on Israel to withdraw from territories taken, 71, 190; committee for resolution of Palestine problem, 66; inability to deal with complicated conflicts, 177; Israeli-Palestinian conflict and, 71, 82; mediates cease-fire in Six-Day War, 71; Oil for Food program, 249, 271; partition plan for Palestine, 187; resolutions on invasion of Kuwait by Iraq, 78, 151

United Nations Development Programme, 337

United Nations Economic and Social Commission for West Asia, 291

United Nations Special Commission, 165

United Nations Special Committee on Palestine, 187

United States: access to markets in, 237, 238; aid to Egypt, 67; anti-Communist agenda in Middle East, 111; anti-Nasserist policies of, 69, 70, 74, 111; assistance to Kurds, 159; decrease in importance of trade with, 239; dominance in Middle East in postwar era, 224–225; economic aid to Middle East, 228; failure to plan for postwar rebuilding of Iraq, 166; interest in continuation of colonial domination in Middle East, 138; intervention in Lebanon, 69, 70, 74, 111; invasion of Iraq, 132, 249, 272–274; Middle East aid packages, 225; National Security Strategy of, 166; as "peace broker," 192; postcolonial structures imposed by, 110; pressures United Nations for solution to Palestine problem, 66; support for Israel, 154; terrorist attacks on, 157, 202; trade with Middle East, 239; war with Iraq, 80–83

Urban III (Pope), 376

Urbanization, 5, 6, 25–31; architectural redesign and, 29; changing gender roles and, 319, 320; demographics of, 282–284; economic development and, 282; effect on traditional networks, 95;

environmental issues, 29, 30; hazards of, 28, 29; health issues in, 29; housing issues, 30, 31; infrastructure costs in, 30; international migration and, 282; modernization and, 27, 28; nongovernmental organizations and, 30, 31; overwhelming pace of, 29, 30; planning for, 27, 28; population growth and, 284–289; rapid, 95, 320; rural migration and, 29; social change and, 282; spontaneous communities and, 30, 31

US–Middle East free trade area, 239

al-'Uthman, Layla, 425

Uthman (caliph), 45

Wafd Party (Egypt), 60, 65

Wannus, Sa'dallah, 417

War of Attrition (1979), 71

Washington Consensus, 234

Water: access to, 21; agriculture and, 19–23; aridity and, 18–25; control, 19, 21, 22, 37, 38; development, 20, 22; distribution, 37, 38; diversion, 21; ecological processes and, 23, 24; management, 20; nonagricultural needs, 21, 22, 23; pollution, 24; power generation and, 22; quality issues, 23; recycling of, 23; regional cooperation and, 23; scarcity, 19; vulnerability, 22

Weapons: early adoption of firearms, 48–49; imports of, 101; of mass destruction, 165, 166, 271–272; sales of large quantities in Middle East, 70

Weizmann, Chaim, 58

West Bank, 234; Christianity in, 377; economic restructuring programs in, 92–93; Israeli security fence on, 82; Palestinian refugees in, 67; urbanization in, 283*tab*

White Paper (1939): limitations on Jewish immigration to Palestine, 64, 66

Wilson, Woodrow, 58, 59, 138

Women: considerations in entrance into labor force, 351–355; culturalist bias on, 345; economic activity of, 351–355; effect of norms and values on, 6; enfranchisement of, 347; in "establishment" organizations, 364–365; in "front" organizations, 363; in government, 366–367; increase in number working, 236; increasing educational levels of, 346; Islamist activism, 367–369; in labor force, 289;

literacy rates, 286, 346, 347; nongovernmental organizations for, 365–366; policies pertaining to rights of, 347; and politics, 360–369; regional differences in lives of, 346; relation to modern nation-state, 346–351; in revolutionary and national liberation movements, 362; role of, 345–369; in service sector, 290; stereotypes of, 345; traditional values/norms and, 358–360; unemployment and, 292, 293, 295*tab,* 296

World Trade Organization, 239

World War I: defeat of Turkey in, 14; postwar peace settlement, 59; subordination of Middle East to Western domination after, 57–59

World War II: British influence during, 65; institutionalization of name "Middle East" after, 13

World Zionist Organization, 186

Yacine, Kateb, 422

Yemen: agriculture in, 289; civil war in, 244; conflict with Egypt, 152; development of, 42; economic development in, 222*tab,* 236*tab;* effect of ending of Cold War on, 88; female employment in, 352; fertility rates in, 285, 286, 288; in Gulf Cooperation Council, 239; informal economy in, 237*tab;* interest in World Trade Organization, 239; Iraqi refugees in, 250; Islamic rule in, 63; Judaism in, 375; labor migration and, 229*tab;* military expenditures, 102; Muslim Brotherhood in, 389; overthrow of monarchy in, 117; political participation in, 109*tab;* reinstatement into Threshold Program of the Millennium Challenge Account, 244; remittances in, 232; single-party rule in, 105; structural adjustment programs in, 244; toppling of monarchy in, 67; unemployment in, 294*tab,* 295*tab;* in United Arab Republic, 68; urbanization in, 282, 283

Yesh Gvul (Israel), 194

Young Egypt Group, 65

Young Turks, 57

Yushij, Nima, 418

Zionism, 17, 58, 59, 375; and Arab nationalism, 66–67; British hostility toward, 66; differing definitions of, 185, 186; felt by Arabs to be imperialistic, 64; history of, 185–189; as ideology and as political project, 186; and Palestine, 64, 144, 145; and partition of Palestine, 185–189; political aspect of identification in, 182; and precipitation of clash between national movements in Palestine, 186

Zubarah, 142

About the Book

The third edition of *Understanding the Contemporary Middle East* includes two entirely new chapters, one on religion and politics and one on the economies of the Middle East, as well as a greatly expanded discussion of the 2003 invasion of Iraq. In addition, all of the chapters have been fully updated. Maps, photographs, and tables of basic political data enhance the text, which has already made its place as the best available introduction to the region.

Jillian Schwedler is associate professor of political science at the University of Massachusetts Amherst. Her publications include *Faith in Moderation: Islamist Parties in Jordan and Yemen,* winner of the 2007 Best Book Award of the American Political Science Association Democratization Section. The late **Deborah J. Gerner** was professor of political science at the University of Kansas. She was author of *One Land, Two Peoples: The Conflict Over Palestine,* as well as numerous articles dealing with the international relations and domestic politics of the Middle East.